REFERENCE ONLY   **1**

The Heraldic journal; recording the armorial
   bearings and genealogies of American
   families.   Genealogical Pub., 1972
4 v in 1   illus

   Reprint of the 1865-1868 ed.
   Vols. 1,2,4, ed. by W.H. Whitmore;
v.3, by W.S. Appleton

   1. Heraldry- U.S. 2. U.S.- Genealogy
I. Whitmore, William Henry

                              7/73 1850

THE
HERALDIC JOURNAL

Recording The
ARMORIAL BEARINGS AND GENEALOGIES
of
AMERICAN FAMILIES

Four Volumes In One

GENEALOGICAL PUBLISHING CO., INC.
BALTIMORE   **1972**

Originally Published
Boston
January, 1865-October, 1868

Reprinted
Four Volumes In One
Genealogical Publishing Company
Baltimore, 1972

Library of Congress Cataloging in Publication Data
Main entry under title:

The Heraldic journal.

Reprint of the 1865-1868 ed.

Vols. 1, 2, 4, edited by W. H. Whitmore; v. 3, by W. S. Appleton.

1. Heraldry—U. S.—Periodicals. 2. U. S.—Genealogy—Periodicals. I. Whitmore, William Henry, 1836-1900, ed. II. Appleton, William Sumner, 1840-1903, ed.
CS42.H422   929.1'0973   77-39169
ISBN 0-8063-0493-6

Made in the United States of America

THE

HERALDIC JOURNAL;

RECORDING THE

𝔄rmorial 𝔅earings and 𝔊enealogies

OF

AMERICAN FAMILIES.

VOLUME I.

BOSTON:

J. K. WIGGIN, PUBLISHER,

13 SCHOOL STREET.

1865.

PREFACE.

It is hoped that the first volume of the Heraldic Magazine has realized the moderate expectations of its projectors. The past year has been so full of important events, that it has been rather an unfortunate period to solicit attention to a new branch of historical study; yet a sufficient response has been made by the public to warrant a continuance of the Journal for another year.

We may be allowed to call attention to a few points wherein this Journal has possibly been of substantial service. In the first place, the Monumental Inscriptions here copied have been for the first time printed entire, that is, with those armorial insignia which are as important as any date or other fact inscribed upon the stones. The Official Seals are portions of our records hitherto neglected, but yet most worthy of preservation. The examples of seals taken from Wills, and other documents, are now preserved from that destruction to which their fragile nature renders them liable. On all these points the permanence secured by the publication seems valuable, both for the present and future genealogists.

It will also be noticed that some attention has been paid to genealogy, and several pedigrees have been printed, from original documents, which might not have appeared but for the special plan of this book.

It is believed that additional information on these points will be received during the ensuing year.

We may further add, that, by the kindness of John Gough Nichols, Esq., editor of the Herald and Genealogist, we have been enabled to place the more important articles, contributed to this Journal, before the English genealogists, who can give so much assistance. We hope that the present volume has fully demonstrated that our field of labor is purely antiquarian, and that the importance of the work is not slight. It has been shown that the founders of New England were not derived from the lowest classes in England; and that they participated in whatever advantages accrued from birth or culture to the more prosperous classes there. Hereafter it may be an important question to discuss, to what extent the prosperity of New England, and even the whole country, has depended upon the stock here first established. At present we are collecting the facts which must furnish the groundwork for future discussions.

Thus far the preliminary investigations made have assured us of abundant material for volumes to come. Not only do private collections contain much, but the public offices, like the Probate and State Paper Offices, promise a great reward. One of our associates, Mr. Perkins, has carefully examined the original Wills recorded in the Suffolk Office, and in our January number we shall commence the publication of the seals, with the necessary illustrations and notes. Arrangements have been made to have the records of the other counties searched with equal care and completeness.

It must be said, however, that we still rely much upon the assistance of our readers, in obtaining information as to detached facts. It is impossible to surmise the condition of our grave-yards, or to determine in advance in what localities armorial decorations are to be found. We therefore especially solicit information on this point, as well as on the subject of paintings, engravings, or seals, preserved in private hands. It is hardly necessary to repeat that the greatest expense attending this publication is that of the necessary wood cuts illustrating the articles, and that in this matter the parties most interested may well contribute.

It has been found that the form hitherto adopted, of a monthly publication, has many defects. It has been thought best, in order to prevent an appearance of undue partiality, to present as much variety as possible in each number. This plan has entailed the condensing of articles, and possibly has given them a fragmentary character. It is now proposed to issue the Journal as a quarterly, preserving the same number of pages in the volume, and thus allowing a more complete examination of the topics discussed.

Finally, the Committee of Publication assures the readers of this Journal that all possible dilligence will be used to obtain information on the subject of Heraldry, applicable to this country, and that the greatest care will be exercised to avoid errors. No statement will be made except upon authority, and communications will be inserted under the signatures or initials of the writers.

GENERAL INDEX.

Arms, engraved :

Appleton, 97, 107 ; Bellingham, 67 ; Bellomont (Earl of), 166 ; Bowes, 109 ; Bradstreet, 102 ; Bright, 83 ; Bulkley, 76–78 ; Cary, 74 ; Chambers, 57 ; Chauncy, 187 ; Chandler, 73 , Chetwode, 78 ; Cheever, 46 ; Colman, 58 ; Cradock, 5 ; Curwen, 143 ; Davenport, 37 ; Davie, 184 ; Denison, 91 ; Downing, 164–5 ; Dowse, 45 ; Dudley, 35, 185 ; Ellery, 182 ; Emerson, 90 ; Endecott, 68 ; Foster, 27, 55 ; Fowle, 75 ; Gilman, 150 ; Greaves, 47 ; Haynes, 50 ; Humfrey, 192 ; Jacobsen, 33 ; Jenner, 56 ; Leverett, 29, 84 ; Legg, 106 ; Lemmon, 48 ; Lowell, 26 ; Mather, 22 ; Miner, 173 ; Miller, 42 ; Palmes, 159 ; Pepperrell, 183 ; Peter, 190 ; Phips, 47, 152 ; Poole, 9 ; Prince, 8 ; Richards, 156 ; Royall, 12 ; Saltonstall, 161 ; Sewall, 70 ; Scott, 106 ; Stoughton, 10 ; Symonds, 44 ; Temple, 92 ; Thorndike, 54 ; Van Rensselaer, 33 ; Wainwright, 89 ; Wendell, 49 ; Whiting, 61, 160 ; Winthrop, 18 ; Wilkinson, 85 ; Anonymous, 112.

Baronets of New England, 163, 183.

Editorial :

Introductory, 1 ; Self-styled Colleges of Arms, 30 ; Authenticity of American Arms, 65 ; Fabrication of Arms, 100.

Esquires, List of, in New England in 1736, 14.

Genealogies :

Appleton, 97 ; Bowes, 109 ; Bright, 81 ; Bulkeley, 77 ; Chauncey, 187 ; Chandler, 82 ; Chute, 142 ; Coote, 166 ; Curwen, 143 ; Davenport, 36 ; Dudley, 185 ; Ellery, 177 ; Emmett, 95 ; Gilman, 150 ; Lowell, 25 ; Miner, 168 ; Miller, 39 ; Nelson, 94 ; Peter, 190 ; Saltonstall, 161 ; Scott, 103 ; Sewall, 68 ; Symonds, 42 ; Temple, 92 ; Thorndike, 52 ; Van Rensselaer, 33 ; Wendell, 49 ; Whiting, 59 ; Wilkinson, 85.

Gore's Roll of Arms, 1702–1720, 113–140.

Herald Painters :

Thomas Johnson, 6 ; Nathaniel Hurd, 19 ; John Coles, 95, 108.

Monumental Inscriptions :

Cambridge, 28–30 ; Charlestown, 45–48, 55–57, 74, 75 ; Dorchester, 9–13, 27–28 ; Hartford, 155 ; Ipswich, 89, 107 ; Marblehead, 106 ; Wethersfield, 76.

Notes and Queries :

Prince family, 7 ; Osgood family, 8 ; Mather arms, 21 ; Rawson arms, 22 ; armigeri in 1683, 23 ; Randolph arms, 23 ; Pemberton arms, 24 ; Colman arms, 24 ; Hopkins arms, 38 ; Carroll arms, 39 ; Colman arms, 58 ; Church plate, 59 ; Mather arms, 70 ; Bangs arms, 71 ; arms untraced,

71, 88; Hopkins crest, 72; Emerson arms, 87; mourning flag, 88; Pepperrell arms, 88; Keayne and Dixwell, 110; Wainwright crest, 110; Alex. H. Stephens' ancestry, 111; Dorchester seal on wills, 112; title of gentleman in 1761, 157; Life of Hugh Peters, 158; Hugh Peters' seal, 190; John Humfrey's seal, 192.

Origin of the Colonists of New England :
Extracts from Mather's Magnalia, 31, 61, 79.

Seals of the Governors of Massachusetts :
Andros, 141; Bellingham, 67; Bellomont, 166; Bradstreet, 102; Cradock, 5; Dudley, Thos., 35; Dudley, Joseph, 185; Endecott, 67; Haynes, 50; Leverett, 83; Phips, 152; Winthrop, 18.

Seals of Connecticut gentlemen :
Palmes, 159; Whiting, 160.

INDEX OF NAMES.

Abbe, 14.
Adams, 15.
Addington, 38, 124.
Adlard, 35.
Alford, 14.
Almy, 15.
Androsse, 141.
Appleton, 21, 23, 58, 67, 97–99, 107.
Apthorp, 120.
Arnold, 15.
Auchmuty, 5.
Avis, 88.

Bailey, 80.
Ballentine, 15.
Bangs, 71.
Barker, 127, 144.
Batter, 24.
Batting, 176.
Beach, 139.
Belcher, 15, 125.
Bell, 139.
Bellingham, 67.
Bellomont, 166.
Berkeley, 130, 144.
Berry, 15.
Blake, 73.
Bollan, 15.
Borden, 135.
Borland, 15, 137.
Bourne, 15.
Bowes, 109.
Boydell, 15.
Bradstreet, 23, 102.
Brattle, 15, 117, 122.
Bright, 81.
Brinley, 5, 15, 131, 135.
Brittan, 128, 144.
Browne, 15, 23, 127, 130.
Bulkeley, 15, 23, 62, 76, 77.
Burke, 100–101.
Burn, 135.
Burrill, 15.

Caldwell, 125.
Carroll, 39.
Cary, 15, 74.
Chambers, 57.

Chamberlain, 119.
Chandler, 15.
Chauncey, 187.
Cheever, 15, 46, 72.
Chetwode, 78.
Cheytor, 72.
Chickley, 119.
Chichester, 128, 144.
Church, 15.
Chute, 128, 132, 142.
Clarke, 140.
Coles, 3, 96, 108.
Colman, 24, 58.
Cooke, 24, 124.
Coote, 166.
Cotton, 32.
Cradock, 4, 5, 15.
Crafts, 115.
Culpepper, 131, 144.
Curwen, 145.
Cushing, 15, 138.
Cutting, 122.

Danforth, 15, 23.
Davenport, 36, 61.
Davie, 23, 164, 184.
Davis, 117.
Denison, 91.
Dixwell, 110.
Downing, 164.
Dowse, 45.
Dudley, 15, 24, 35, 36, 131, 135, 185.
Dummer, 15, 136.
Dwight, 15.
Dyer, 122, 176.
Dykewoode, 191.

Eastwicke, 15.
Eaton, 80.
Ellery, 177.
Emerson, 86, 90.
Emmett, 95.
Endicott, 67.
Epes, 45.
Evance, 122.

Fayerweather, 15, 24.
Fisher, 23.
Flint, 15, 16.

Foster, 16, 27, 28, 54, 120.
Fowle, 75.
Foxcroft, 16.
Foye, 16.
Freeman, 71.
Frizell, 58, 137.
Frost, 117.
Furnass, 21.

Gedney, 23.
Gee, 129, 144.
Gerrish, 5, 16.
Gibbs, 16.
Gilman, 150.
Goddard, 16.
Goodrich, 59.
Gookin, 23.
Gore, 3, 113, 114.
Graves, 16, 47.
Greenwood, 16.
Gressley, 176.
Grindall, 32.
Guillim, 20.

Hale, 16, 20.
Hall, 16.
Hammond, 24.
Harcop, 176.
Harvie, 119.
Hawkins, 121.
Haynes, 50.
Heath, 16.
Hervey, 176.
Hicks, 176.
Hobart, 62.
Hobbs, 176.
Hooker, 62.
Hopkins, 38, 72.
Hubbard, 16.
Hull, 23.
Humfrey, 192.
Hunt, 16.
Hurd, 19, 69, 70.
Huse, 127.
Hutchinson, 16, 24, 59, 126, 127, 133.

Jacobsen, 34.
Jay, 116.

Jeffries, 16, 71.
Jekyll, 135.
Jenkins, 48.
Jenner, 16, 56.
Johnson, 6, 24.
Jones, 16, 176.

Keayne, 110.
Kilby, 139.
Kimball, 105.
Kneeland, 139.

Latimer, 118.
Lathrop, 138.
Lee, 16.
Leete, 31.
Legg, 106, 116, 117.
Lemmon, 16, 48, 125.
Leonard, 16.
Leverett, 29, 82, 116.
Lewis, 16.
Lincoln, 16.
Loring, 16.
Lowell, 25, 26.
Lovejoy, 157.
Lucas, 128, 144.
Lyde, 16.
Lynde, 6, 16.

McAdams, 168.
Maine, 125.
Mansel, 132.
Marshfield, 16.
Mason, 19.
Mather, 21, 22, 62, 70.
Mawson, 8.
Metcalfe, 16.
Middlecott, 115.
Miller, 39, 40, 41.
Miner, 168.
Mottram, 40.
Moulton, 16.
Mountfort, 134.

Neal, 85.
Nelson, 94.
Newman, 31, 62.
Nicols, 186.
Norden, 117.
Norton, 32.
Nowell, 23.
Noyes, 63.

Oliver, 6.
Osborne, 17.
Osgood, 8.
Owen, 116.
Oxenbridge, 81.

Paddock, 138.
Paige, 126.
Palmer, 17.
Palmes, 159.
Peagrum, 17.
Pelham, 20.
Pell, 133.
Pepperrell, 14, 17, 88, 139, 164, 183.
Pemberton, 24.
Peters, 158, 190.
Phillips, 17, 21, 132.
Phips, 17, 47, 118, 120, 152.
Pickman, 135.
Poole, 9, 10, 119.
Pope, 176.
Prescott, 17.
Prince, 7.
Purefoy, 186.
Pyke, 23.
Pynchon, 17, 23.

Quincy, 17, 24, 71.

Randolph, 23.
Rawson, 22.
Rayner, 105.
Reade, 45.
Remington, 17.
Richards, 24, 117, 123, 156.
Roberts, 123.
Robbins, 7.
Rosewell, 137.
Royall, 12, 13, 17.
Ruck, 17.
Russell, 17, 23, 57.

Saltonstall, 23, 121, 161.
Salter, 71.
Sargent, 116, 118, 123.
Sartle, 17.
Savage, 133.
Savile, 14.
Sayward, 138.
Sausmarez, 140.
Scolly, 139.
Scott, 103.
Sedgewick, 116.
Sewall, 17, 20, 68.
Sherman, 64.
Shirley, 17.
Shrimpton, 116, 133.
Skinner, 119.
Smith, 19, 22, 72.
Sparhawk, 183.
Spencer, 118.
Sprague, 138.

Stanton, 73.
Stevens, 18, 111.
Stoddard, 24, 122, 123, 134.
Storrow, 99.
Sturton, 128, 144.
Swayne, 45.
Sweetzer, 130.
Symonds, 43.

Taylor, 122.
Temple, 92.
Thatcher, 63, 129.
Thaxter, 18.
Thorndike, 52, 53.
Tileston, 18, 137.
Tilton, 23.
Tolderbury, 7.
Torrey, 24.
Tothill, 134.
Trumbull, 155, 159, 168.
Turell, 24.
Tyng, 135, 136.

Vane, 51.
Van Rensselaer, 33.
Vassall, 14, 28.
Vinton, 18.

Wade, 134.
Waite, 24.
Wainwright, 18, 89, 110.
Waldron, 137.
Walley, 18, 21.
Ward, 79.
Ware, 18.
Warre, 136.
Warren, 18.
Watts, 18.
Wells, 18.
Welshed, 59.
Wendell, 18, 49.
White, 121.
Whitehorn, 130.
Whitfield, 80.
Whiting, 18, 59, 63, 160.
Whittingham, 121.
Whitwell, 139.
Wibond, 127.
Wilder, 18.
Willard, 18.
Wilson, 32.
Wilkinson, 85.
Winslow, 18, 46, 138.
Winthrop, 18, 19, 59, 115, 117, 126.
Woodbridge, 80.
Woods, 18, 47, 128, 144.

Yeomans, 133.

THE

HERALDIC JOURNAL;

RECORDING THE ARMORIAL BEARINGS AND GENEALOGIES OF
AMERICAN FAMILIES.

NO. I.   JANUARY, 1865.

INTRODUCTORY.

On commencing such an enterprise as the establishment of a journal devoted chiefly to Heraldry, we feel
bound to explain the reasons which justify it.   The terms
of this science are in general use, but so greatly has its
study been neglected that comparatively few persons
appreciate the value of its results.   Heraldry is most
intimately connected with genealogy, and to neglect
any examination of the former is to deprive us of most
valuable evidences in constructing a pedigree.

Since the time that coats-of-arms became hereditary
they have been concise and intelligible assertions of the
pedigree of their bearers.   Notwithstanding the common error, coats-of-arms do not belong to all the bearers
of a name, but are a species of personal property
inherited by the lineal descendants of the first owner,
and belonging solely to them.   These insignia were originally granted to individuals who occupied a certain
position, and their use is a distinct claim to a descent
from the grantees.

Regarded in this light we see how valuable such emblems become to the genealogist. Should he find a person in New England at an early date using a coat of arms belonging to an English family, it is the most positive mode of showing that the person claimed to be a member of that family. The attention of the student is at once directed to the point indicated, and he is spared the necessity of a protracted search through the various probate offices of Great Britain.

Could we be assured of the authenticity of all the coats-of-arms in use here, our task would be light. We should simply have to record all the documents presented, and leave it to the persons interested to follow the clue abroad. Unfortunately we have no reason to presume that any such authority attaches to all remaining examples; we have on the contrary great reason for condemning whole classes as worthless.

We see almost daily in this country, seals engraved, arms emblazoned, and engravings published, which we know are assumed without proof or inquiry. In this matter our English relatives are our rivals—but there they have facilities for making an official, if not very dignified, apology for their acts.

Discarding therefore, as entirely worthless to the genealogist, all recent assumptions of coats-of-arms, we find that the entire list of those used in New England prior to 1800 requires a careful scrutiny. At the one extreme we have the acts of the first colonists, Englishmen born; at the other end we have the fabrications of herald-painters still remembered by a few now living. Between these dates we have a century during which the Colonies were rapidly increasing in wealth and luxury, and we must discover who used armorial bearings before we can judge of their right.

It will be readily seen that the first colonists brought their seals with them—this class of evidence is most valuable and important. Later we shall find such seals used by the children and grand-children of the first settlers, and this class may be accepted with little hesitation. The doubt we feel commences with the time when seal-engraving and painting of arms was practised in New England by resident artists,—a date which we *now* consider to have been about A. D. 1730–1735.

The object of this Journal will therefore be first to collect and preserve these statements of the early colonists as to their ancestry ; secondly to collect all the examples of the use of arms after the first generation here, in order that by an extensive comparison it may be possible to discriminate between the authentic and the false. To do this it is requisite that every one who possesses a coat of arms of any antiquity whether painted, engraved, or sculptured, should send us a full and exact account of it. It is especially to be desired that the names of the early engravers and painters here should be ascertained, in order that we may judge of their opportunities to furnish authentic coats. We may safely discredit the handiwork of Cole who painted here in 1800, but what shall we think of Gore who flourished in 1710 ? It is only by an examination of many examples that we shall be able to identify the style of each artist. We propose to publish not only such facts as are furnished by individuals from private collections, but we hope to give the result of systematic searches in our probate offices, and files of official papers. We shall use every effort to obtain correct copies of inscriptions in our churches and grave-yards, and we shall attempt to bring together such heraldic and genealogical facts as are now scattered throughout our numerous family histories.

We desire to call the attention of contributors to one fact: engravings of coats-of-arms are preferable to any description. Especially is this the case where we wish to identify the artist and thus fix the date when the work was executed. The cost of these engravings, though individually small, would be more than the managers of this Journal can at present assume.

OFFICIAL SEALS.

It will be found that in Massachusetts, besides the Colonial Seal, several of the Governors used their own coats-of-arms as the seal of official documents. It is our present belief that the distinction was made between documents where the Governor represented the Crown, and where he acted as an individual. Thus civil commissions were sealed with the Colonial Seal, but commissions in the military force, signed by the Governor as Commander-in-chief, were sealed with his personal seal.

We think, therefore, a collection of these seals will prove interesting, and we propose such a series.

We commence with the coat-of-arms of Mathew Cradock, Governor of the Company, though we are not aware that he used a seal in this mode. His arms are argent, on a chevron azure, three garbs *or.*

A pedigree printed in the New England Historic-Genealogical Register, x.-122, shows that he was the son of Mathew, and grandson of Mathew Cradock of Carmarthen. The family had been settled in Staffordshire for several generations, and one branch was established at Hartforth, co. York. Mathew Cradock, cousin to Gov. C., was Mayor of Stafford, and the arms are engraved on his tomb at Caverswall Castle, co. Stafford.

Gov. Mathew Cradock married twice, but his will mentions only one child, Damaris. HUTCHINSON writes (i.-18) that "His son or grandson was a dissenting minister at Wickambrook in 1690. George Cradock Esq., now in public posts in the colony, is descended from him." This is no doubt an error, but the minister mentioned was the descendant of a brother of the Governor, and hence George Cradock of Boston was entitled to the same arms. A sketch of this George C. in the Register, viii.-27, states that he married Mary, daughter of Byfield Lyde and had daughters who married respectively Hon. Joseph Gerrish, Robert Auchmuty, Thomas Brinley, and Nathaniel Brinley.

The Cradock coat-of-arms is as follows:

HERALD PAINTERS. No. 1.

THOMAS JOHNSON.

Inasmuch as many trickings of arms are preserved here it is desirable that we should know more about the artists and their sources of information. Very few of these paintings are signed or dated, but the style of each artist may perhaps be recognized by a comparison of examples. A very interesting painting now owned by Dr. F. E. Oliver, is signed T. Johnson, and is endorsed " The arms on the other side belong to Benj. Lynde Jr. of Salem, 1740." There can be no doubt that the artist was Thomas Johnson of Boston, born in 1708, who died 8th May, 1767, aged 59, and was buried in the King's Chapel burying-ground. He was termed a " japanner," and the inventory shows he was an engraver and artist. Among the items there enumerated are the following:

" 10 small pictures, 30s.; glass arms, 4s.; 2 pictures, 62s.; Dr. Mayhew and Mr. Gee's picture, 36s.; 6 pictures, 9s.; large piece of painting, 24s.; 4 pictures, 2s.; *Book of Heraldry*, 48s.; sundry pictures, £2 16s. 4d.; 3 paint stones and brushes, 15 copper plates, 40s.; easel, burnishers &c.; one organ unfinished."

By his nuncupative will he left to his wife Bathsheba, " all my psalm-tune plates together with the press."

These plates, twelve pages in all, will be found at the end of an edition of Tate and Brady's Psalms, published by D. & J. Kneeland at Boston in 1760. They are neatly engraved, and are signed " Engraved, Painted and sold by Thomas Johnson, Brattle Street, Boston, 1755." It is highly probable that he also engraved a little portrait of Increase Mather, of which a copy is in the library of the Massachusetts Historical Society.

We trust soon to be able to give an engraving of one of his paintings; we must remind our readers, however, that his possession of a " Book on Heraldry" renders his pictures liable to the suspicion of a want of authority. Without some other proof of the arms, we should be disinclined to regard such a painting by him, as a sufficient authority.

W. H. W.

HERALDIC NOTES AND QUERIES.

I.

THE PRINCE FAMILY.

In the Register, v. 378–9, will be found an obituary by the Rev. Thomas Prince on the death of his father, Samuel Prince. It seems that he was the son of John Prince, ruling elder of the church of Hull, Mass., whose father was Rev. John Prince, Rector of East Shefford in Berkshire, Eng., by his wife Elizabeth, daughter of Dr. Tolderbury, D. D. of Oxford. It is presumable therefore, that the family ranked among the gentry, and this is confirmed by the following note in the diary of Rev. Thomas Prince, now owned by Rev. Chandler Robbins of Boston.

It was written in London, Nov. 29, 1710. " I e—* cousin Franklin Prince who presented me with ye arms of our family. ' He beareth *gules*, a saltire *or*, surmounted with a cross engrailed *ermine*. Ye crest, a

---

* Abbreviated for encountered or entertained.

dexter arm issuing out of a ducal coronet *or*, ye cuff *gules*, turned up *ermine*, holding in ye hand a Branch of a Pine Tree, *proper*, fructed *or*. By ye name of Prince, as they are entered in a book belonging to the library of ye college of Arms, marked C. 35, fo. 706· Charles Mawson, Chester, 16 Sept. 1712.'"

In the Ms. there follows a pen-and-ink tricking of the arms. We annex an engraving of this coat.

II.

In Notes & Queries, 3rd S. xi.-67 (July 26th, 1862), is a note upon John Osgood of Andover, Mass. It is there said that he brought with him from England the family arms worked in tapestry or worsted, viz: gold, three garbs; crest a demi-lion rampant supporting a garb. Can any of our readers tell us of the present possessor of this piece of embroidery?

III.

A very good article upon the terms used in Heraldry will be found in the New-England Historical and Genealogical Register, i.-225. We hope soon to reprint a portion of it with illustrations.

MONUMENTAL INSCRIPTIONS.

One very interesting class of heraldic facts will be found in the old grave-yards of the cities and larger towns. Though time and neglect have dealt hardly with these pious memorials, still not a few tomb stones remain, decorated with the shields of distinguished families here. We propose to publish all the inscriptions remaining, provided our local antiquaries will supply us with exact transcripts. As a commencement we copy four inscriptions now remaining in the old burying ground in Dorchester, Mass.

The first is that of William Pole or Poole, who died in 1674. His sister, Elizabeth Poole, was the chief promoter of the settlement at Taunton, Mass., and in 1771 a monument erected to her memory says she was " of good family, friends, and prospects." (Winthrop, i.–303.) We shall hereafter revert to the pedigree of the family; at present it is suffieient to say that the tomb has been rebuilt and besides the large slab on top containing the long epitaph, there is a slab of red stone set in two of the sides, the one bearing the following inscription :—

HERE LIETH BURIED YE BODY OF
MR. WILLIAM POOLE, AGED 81 YEARS
WHO DIED YE 25TH OF FEBRUARY IN
YE YEARE 1674.

The other contains the following coat-of-arms.

Ye epitaph of William Pole which hee himself
Made while he was yet liuing in remembrance of
his own death & left it to be engraven on his
Tomb yt so being dead he might warn posterity
Or a resemblance of a dead man bespeaking ye reader
Ho passenger tis worth thy paines too stay
& take a dead mans lesson by ye way
I was what now thou art & thou shalt be
What I am now what odds twixt me & thee
Now go thy way bvt stay take on word more
Thy staff for ought thou knowest stands next ye dore
Death is ye dore yea dore of Heaven or Hell
Be warned be armed belicue repent farewell

II.

The next is on the Stoughton tomb. The coat-of-arms, cut on the side of the lower portion, is here given from a careful sketch made on the spot by the engraver.

The inscription reads :
Gulielmus Stoughtonus, Armiger
Provinciæ Massachusettensis in Nova Anglia Legatus
deinde Gubernator

Nec non Curiæ in eadem Provincia Superioris,
Justiciarius Capitalis
Hic Jacet
Vir conjugij Nescius
Religione Sanctus
Virtute Clarus
Doctrina Celebris
Ingenio Acutus
Sanguine & Animo pariter illustris
Æquitatis Amator
Legum Propugnator
Collegij STOUGHTONIANI Fundator
Literarum & Literatorum Fautor Celeberrimus
Impietatis & vitij Hostis Acerrimus
Hunc Rhetores amant Facundum
Hunc Scriptores norunt Elegantem
Hunc Philosophi qærunt Sapientem
Hunc Doctores laudunt Theologum
Hunc Pij venerantur Austerum
Hunc omnes mirantur ; Omnibus ignotum
Omnibus licet Notum
Quid plura Viator. Quem perdidimus
Stoughtonum !
Heu !
Satis dixi Urgent Lachrymæ
Sileo
Vixit Annos Septuaginta
Septimo die Julij, Anno Salutis 1701
Cecidit
Heu ! Heu ! Qualis Luctus !
[Note. It may be added that his will in the Suffolk
Registry has a seal with the same arms.]

III.

The Royall tomb has the following coat-of-arms at the top of the slab:

The inscription is as follows:—

Here lyeth ye Body of WILLm ROYALL
of North Yarmouth, in the PROVINCE
of MAIN, who departed this Life
NOVbre 7th, 1724, in ye 85th year of his Age
this Stone is Erected to ye Pious Memory
of his Father, by his Eldest Son, Isaac,
as a last Act of a dutifull remembrance.

Here lyes the Body
of the Honble ISAAC ROYALL, Esq
Who departed this Life at his Seat in Charlestown
June ye 7th Anno Domni 1739 Ætatis 67.
He was a Gentn of Superiour natural powers and great
acquired knowledge
Civil, affable, courteous & Just to all Men
Dutifull to his Parents Kind to his Relations & Char-
itable to ye Poor
He was a faithfull Husband, a tender Father, a kind
Master, and a true Friend

Delighted in doing good

He was highly esteemed & respected during his residence at Antigua which was

near 40 years

And advanced to ye most Honourable & important
Public employments Civil &

Military

Which He discharged with ye highest reputation &
fidelity

He returned with His Family to New-England His
Native Country

July 27th 1737

where His death which soon followed was greatly
lamented by all who knew Him

But as he Lived a Virtuous Life So He was removed
by a peeceful Death

Leaving a Son & Daughter

To inherit a plentifull Fortune which He was Bles'd
with

And an Exemplary Pattern for Their imitation

At His Desire His Remains were here

Interred with His Parents

For whom He Erected This

MONUMENT

[The ancestor of these Royalls was William of
Casco, 1636, who purchased land at Wescustogo, now
Royall's river, in North Yarmouth. Williamson (Hist.
of Maine, i.–692) says "he was an Assistant in 1636
under William Gorges' short administration of New-
Somersetshire; and again in 1648, under that of Mr.
Cleaves in Lygonia." His son William and grandson
Isaac, are mentioned in the preceding inscription.

Isaac had only one son, Isaac, who lived in Medford and was a member of the Council for twenty-six years; he founded the first law-professorship of Harvard University, but being a Royalist, fled to England, and died there in 1781. His sister m. Henry Vassall, and his daughters m. respectively Thomas Savel and Sir William (Sparhawk) Pepperrell. Other members of the family, as Jacob Royall of Boston, were very prominent in the Colonial period.   w. h. w.]

A LIST OF ESQUIRES IN 1736.

The first volume of Prince's Chronological History of New England, printed in Boston in 1736, contains a list of 735 subscribers, embracing undoubtedly the most prominent patrons of literature of the day. The titles are given with punctilious care, and at the end the author writes " seeing some Gentlemen's names in the List happen to be printed without their proper additions and fearing it may be so with others, we crave pardon for such omissions." We may safely assume then that, the title Esquire annexed to 104 names on this list, was intended to designate those who were in the habit of using coats-of-arms; unless indeed an exception may be made in the case of those holding high official positions. At all events the list is well worth publishing as we shall thereby call attention to certain families whose pedigrees deserve investigation. The list is as follows:

Hon. John Alford.

Richard Abbe, of Windham.

Samuel Adams.

Job Almy, of Tiverton.

Edward Arnold, of Duxbury.

John Ballentine.

Gov. Jonathan Belcher.

Andrew Belcher.

Hon. Thomas Berry, of Ipswich.

William Bollan.

Francis Borland.

John Boydell.

Hon. Melatiah Bourne, of Sandwich.

William Brattle, of Cambridge.

Francis Brinley.

Benjamin Browne, of Salem.

John Bulkely, of Colchester.

Hon. Theophilus Burrill, of Lynn.

Samuel Cary, of Charlestown.

Hon John Chandler of Woodstock.

Hon. John Chandler, of Worcester.

Ezekiel Cheever, of Charlestown.

Charles Church, of Bristol.

George Cradock.

Hon. John Cushing, of Scituate.

Hon. Thomas Cushing, of Scituate.

Samuel Danforth, of Cambridge.

Hon. Paul Dudley, of Roxbury.

Hon. William Dummer.

Samuel Dummer, of Wilmington.

Joseph Dwight, of Brookfield.

John Eastwicke.

John Fayerweather.

John Flint, of Concord.

Henry Flynt

Richard Foster, Sheriff of Middlesex.

Hon. Francis Foxcroft.

William Foye, Treasurer of the Prov. of the Mass. Bay.

Joseph Gerrish, of Newbury.

Robert Gibbs, of Providence.

Hon. Edward Goddard, of Framingham.

Thomas Graves, of Charlestown.

Samuel Greenwood.

Robert Hale, of Beverly.

Hugh Hall.

Stephen Hall, of Charlestown.

Joseph Heath, of Roxbury.

Nathaniel Hubbard, of Bristol.

Hon. Thomas Hutchinson.

Hon. Edward Hutchinson.

John Hunt.

Hon. John Jeffries.

Thomas Jenner, of Charlestown.

John Jones, of Hopkinton.

Henry Lee, of Worcester.

Joseph Lemmon, of Charlestown.

Elkanah Leonard, of Middleboro.

Hon. Hezekiah Lewis.

Benjamin Lincoln, of Hingham.

Caleb Loring, of Hull.

Byfield Lyde.

Benjamin Lynde jr., of Salem

Israel Marshfield, of Springfield.

John Metcalfe, of Dedham,

Hon. Jeremiah Moulton, of York.

[To be continued.]

THE

HERALDIC JOURNAL;

RECORDING THE ARMORIAL BEARINGS AND GENEALOGIES OF
AMERICAN FAMILIES.

NO. II.   FEBRUARY, 1865.

A LIST OF ESQUIRES IN 1736.   (Concluded.)

Hon. John Osborne.

Hon. Thomas Palmer.

Hon. William Pepperrell.

Hon. John Peagrum.

Benjamin Pemberton.

Henry Phillips, of Charlestown.

Hon. Spencer Phipps.

Benjamin Prescott, of Groton.

William Pynchon jr., of Springfield.

Hon. Edmund Quincy.

Hon. John Quincy.

Hon. Jonathan Remington.

Jacob Royall.

John Ruck.

Daniel Russell, of Charlestown.

Nathaniel Sartle, of Groton.

William Shirley.

Samuel Sewall.

Ebenezer Stevens, of Kingston.

Hon. Anthony Stoddard.

Hon. Samuel Thaxter, of Hingham.

Thomas Tilestone, of Dorchester.

John Vinton, of Stoneham.

John Walley.

Jonathan Ware, of Wrentham.

Peter Warren, Commander of H. M. ship Squirrel.

Samuel Watts.

John Wainwright, of Ipswich.

Hon. Samuel Welles.

Francis Wells, of Cambridge.

Hon. Jacob Wendell.

Oliver Whiting, of Billerica.

Hon. Joseph Wilder, of Lancaster.

Hon. Josiah Willard.

Hon. Isaac Winslow, of Marshfield.

Edward Winslow.

Joshua Winslow.

Hon. Adam Winthrop.

Benjamin Woods, of Marlboro'.

OFFICIAL SEALS.

Our second example will be the seal of Gov. John Winthrop, of Mass., taken from a letter in the Winthrop Papers, which is as follows :

In the " Life of John Winthrop," p. 21, will be found a confirmation or grant of arms, made in 1592, to John Wynethrop Esquire, son of Adam Wynethrop, of Groton, in the county of Suffolk, gentleman; viz.: argent, three chevrons crenélé gules, over all a lion rampant sable, armed and langued azure. Crest, a hare proper running on a mount vert.

This John was son of Adam and Agnes (Sharpe) Winthrop who was born in 1498 and was grandson of Adam Winthrop, of Lavenham, co. Suffolk. Though we cannot trace the family or arms further, it is clear that from the time of this grant or confirmation, at least, the family has habitually used them. It is possible that Smith's Ms. Promptuarium Armorum, elsewhere cited in this number, gives a clue to the origin of the family. He gives " Hegineth of Wales," and " Winthrop," both as bearing this coat; and this entry may mean that when the confirmation was made, John Winthrop proved his descent from a Welsh family.

Several specimens of Winthrop seals will be found in the two volumes of Winthrop Papers published by the Massachusetts Historical Society, current series, volumes vi. and vii.   W. H. W.

HERALD PAINTERS. NO. 2.

NATHANIEL HURD.

One of the best of our Colonial engravers was Nathaniel Hurd of Boston, born in 1729, and son of Jacob Hurd and Elizabeth Mason. The family had

been goldsmiths for one or two generations, and the
advertisements of stolen or lost silver in the Boston
papers of the last century often specify that the maker's
stamp, " Hurd," was on it. I have seen a beautiful
little salver thus stamped, bearing the Oliver arms.

In the third volume of Buckingham's New England
Magazine (Boston, 1832) will be found a memoir and
portrait of Hurd. Although the writer errs in calling
Hurd our first colonial engraver on copper, an honor
probably due to Peter Pelham, it is no doubt true that
he was one of the earliest seal-cutters and die-engravers.
The only portrait which he is known to have engraved
was that of Rev. Joseph Sewall, and under that he
engraved the Sewall arms. I have also seen a Tracy
coat of arms, engraved as a book-plate by him, and
one of that of Robert Hale, of Beverly. His style of
engraving was very delicate and graceful. The shield,
in the examples seen, is of an ear-shape or shell pattern ;
in the border especially a series of scollops or folds are
noticeable. Another peculiarity is the addition on all, of
wreaths of flowers about the shield instead of the
conventional mantling.

At present it is not safe to trust too implicitly to
Hurd's authority. I think that there is strong reason to
suspect that he owned and used a copy of Guillim's
Heraldry ; and it would therefore be unwise to accept
a book-plate engraved by him as sufficient proof in
itself. Still we must be guided by the circumstances
under which he worked. A book-plate, rarely seen, is
not so public a mode of claiming arms as a seal or an
engraving on silver. I am not prepared to concede

that in Hurd's time any man would have dared to make a public claim to arms falsely, whilst I would reserve the more private use in his library for farther investigation.

Hurd died Dec. 18th, 1777, aged 48, and probably had been the most prominent engraver in the years 1750–1777. In his will he left his tools to his nephew, John Mason Furnass, on account of the genius which he displayed for engraving. One of his sisters married Mr. Walley, and was the grandmother of our distinguished fellow-citizens, Wendell Phillips and Samuel H. Walley.

HERALDIC NOTES & QUERIES.

IV.

The following extract from the Lie of Rev. Cotton Mather by his son Samuel (Boston, 1729) has long been a puzzle to the reader. "I have no great Disposition to enquire into the *remote Antiquities* of his Family; nor indeed is it matter of much consequence that in our *Coat-of-arms*, we bear *Ermine* Or, *A Fess,* Wavy, Azure, three Lions rampant; or, for a Crest, on a wreath of our Colours, a Lion Sedant, or on a Trunk of a Tree *vert.*"

Besides the manifest error of this description, no coat resembling this is in Burke or Edmondson. Mr. Appleton, however, has pointed out the printer's mistake, and corrects it to " Ermine, *on* a fesse wavy azure, three lions rampant. Crest a lion sedant *or*, on a trunk of a tree

vert." This coat of arms is found in a Ms. " Promptuarium Armorum" made in 1602–15, by William
Smith, Rouge-Dragon. It is there recorded as the coat
of William Mather of——— co. Salop; and as this is
adjoining Lancashire, undoubtedly Samuel Mather had
good grounds for claiming the arms. As to the family,
the Life of Richard Mather (Cambridge, 1670) says,
" There is in the Parish of Winwick, in the County of
Lancaster, a small Country Town or Village called
Lowton: In which Village, Richard Mather was born,
Anno 1596. His Parents, Thomas and Margaret
Mather, were of Ancient families in Lowton aforesaid,
but by reason of some Unhappy Mortgage, they were
reduced unto a low condition as to the World."

We give an engraving of these Arms.

v.

The N. E. Historical & Genealogical Register, for
January, 1865, contains a document concerning Braintree, printed from the original in my possession. It is
dated in 1683, and was written by Edward Rawson,
Secretary of the Colony, whose armorial seal it bears.

The wax is broken, but the arms are a chevron between three towers, with a crest of an animal's head erased. Among the Hutchinson papers, belonging to the Mass. Historical Society, is a letter of Ed. Rawson, dated in 1659, which has the impression of a larger seal. The arms are nearly the same, but the chevron is embattled, which is probably correct. An account of the family is in print.   W. S. A.

VI.

I have an original letter of Edward Randolph, dated 1683, and sealed with the arms of Randolph or Randall, viz.: on a cross five mullets. Randolph founded no family in this country, but if the propriety of placing him in this work be questioned, I can quote as authority Mr. Savage, who finds room for him in the Genealogical Dictionary of N. E., and declare myself quite content to err, if it be so, in such company.

W. S. A.

VII.

In the fifth volume of the Mass. Colony Records is a document from King Charles II., which shows the extremest care in the exact and proper use of titles. It in the order of " quo warranto," in 1683, summoning before his majesty, Symon Bradstreet, Ar,* Thomas Danforth, Ar, Daniel Gookin, Ar, John Pinchen, Ar, William Stoughton, Ar, Peter Bulkley, Ar, Nathaniel Saltenstall, Ar, Humphry Davy, Ar, William Brown, Ar, Samuel Nowell, Ar, John Hull, Ar, James Russell, Ar, Peter Tylton, Ar, Bartholemew Gidney, Ar, Samuel Apleton, Ar, Robert Pyke, Ar, Daniel Fisher, yeom,

* i. e. armiger.

John Waite, yeom, William Johnson, yeom, Edmund Quinsey, yeom, Elisha Cooke, Gen,* Elisha Hutchinson, mercator, Edmund Batter, yeom, Lawrence Hamond, yeom, Joseph Dudley, Ar, John Richards, Ar, William Torrey, yeom, John Faireweather, yeom, Anthony Stodder, yeom, and Daniel Turell, Sen, nigr fferrar.

VIII.

In 1727 a volume of Sermons by the Rev. Ebenezer Pemberton, Pastor of the South Church in Boston, was published in London. Prefixed was a portrait, and underneath this appeared a coat of arms, argent, a chevron between three buckets, sable. No crest. I am not sure that any other example of this use of arms can be found here, and this authority is of course of no great weight.

A similar instance is to be found in a volume of Sermons by Rev. Benjamin Colman, of Boston, published in 1728 at London. The portrait is accompanied by the following arms : Azure, on a pale radiant rayonée or, a lion rampant gules. Crest, a demi-lion. This coat is attributed in Kent's Grammar of Heraldry to the Colmans of Suffolk or Essex. In Turell's Life of Colman, it is said he was born "of reputable parents, being second son of William and Elizabeth Colman, who came from London and settled here" not long before 1673. William was son of Matthew and Grace Colman, of Satterly, near Beckles, co. Suffolk, and was baptized there August 31, 1643. This is all I can find concerning his Family."

W. H. W.

* i. e. generosus.

THE LOWELL FAMILY.

Through the courtesy of a member of the family, we are enabled to present the following sketch of the English ancestry of Percival Lowell, one of the early settlers at Newbury. This account is copied from Harl. Ms. No. 1559, in the British Museum, and is compiled from the Herald's Visitations of Somersetshire in 1573, 1591, and 1623. The essential point is the assertion that Percival Lowell, a member of this family, was in New England in 1639.

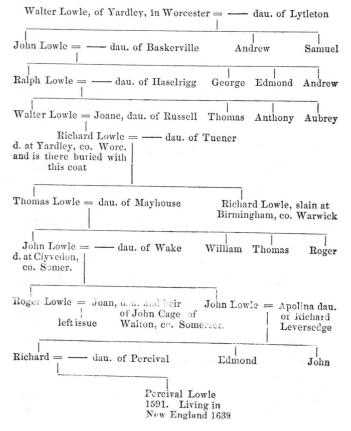

Walter Lowle, of Yardley, in Worcester = —— dau. of Lytleton

John Lowle = —— dau. of Baskerville   Andrew   Samuel

Ralph Lowle = —— dau. of Haselrigg   George   Edmond   Andrew

Walter Lowle = Joane, dau. of Russell   Thomas   Anthony   Aubrey

Richard Lowle = —— dau. of Tuener
d. at Yardley, co. Worc. and is there buried with this coat

Thomas Lowle = dau. of Mayhouse   Richard Lowle, slain at Birmingham, co. Warwick

John Lowle = —— dau. of Wake   William   Thomas   Roger
d. at Clyvedon, co. Somer.

Roger Lowle = Joan, dau. and heir   John Lowle = Apolina dau.
left issue   of John Cage of   of Richard
   Walton, co. Somerset.   Leversedge

Richard = —— dau. of Percival   Edmond   John

Percival Lowle
1591. Living in
New England 1639

The arms here emblazoned are sable, a hand couped at the wrist, grasping three darts, one in pale and two in saltire, argent. No crest.

Mr. Somerby adds that in 1591 no name was given to the father of Apolina, wife of John Lowle—but that he discovered the will of Richard Leversedge, gentleman, proved 28 July, 1547, and as he mentions a dau. Apolyn, it is hardly possible that there were two persons bearing this very strange name in the same neighborhood.

The will of this John Lowle, of Portberye, proved 8 Mar., 1552, mentions wife Appolyn, son Richard, sister Mary Collins.

In 1571 Richard Lowle was assessed at Portbury, and in 1597 Percival Lowle was assessor at Kingston-Seymour.

Richard Lowle m. a daughter of Edmund Percival, of Weston-in-Gordano, co. Somerset. The Percivals were a famous family, said to be descended from Robert, younger brother of Eudes, duke of Bretagne. In England one branch acquired the title of Lord Lovel and Holland, as will be seen in Collins' Peerage, Brydge's edition, 1812, viii.–39. They also held the title of Earls of Egmont in [the peerage of Ireland. Edmund

Percival, whose place in the family pedigree is perfectly established, m. 1st, Isabella, dau. of John Marsh, by whom he had one son and two daughters; and secondly, Elizabeth Panthuit, by whom he had three sons and four daughters. One of the children by the second marriage was the grandmother of Percival Lowell, of New England.

MONUMENTAL INSCRIPTIONS.

IV.

The other monument at Dorchester is that of the Fosters. It is an upright stone bearing the following coat of arms

and the inscriptions in two heart-shaped enclosures:

Here Lyes Buried the
Body of Mr. James Foster
who Departed this Life, Oct the
4th 1732; in the 82d
Year of his Age.
He was member in full Commu
nion with the Church of Christ
In Dorchester About 60
years

Here Lyes Buried the
Body of Mrs Anna Foster
The Consort of Mr James Fos
ter; She Departed this Life the
29th Sept. 1732 in
the 68th year of Her
age.

This James Foster was the son of Hopestill Foster,
who d. 1676, and brother of John Foster, of whom
Blake writes that he was " Schoolmaster of Dorchester, and he that made the then seal or Arms of ye
Colony, namely an Indian with a Bow and Arrow &c."
He was the grandson of Hopestill Foster, who may not
have come hither, though his family did in 1635 with
their relative, Rachel Bigg, of Kent.

It will be noticed that there were two other families of the name bearing arms here, totally different
from this; viz.: those of William Foster of Charlestown, and John Foster of Boston. The latter was from
Aylesbury, co. Bucks, grand-father of Gov. Hutchinson.

CAMBRIDGE.

The old burial-ground at Cambridge is very weak in
heraldic interest. One or two grave-stones, in which
armorial slabs were probably inserted, have been at
some time deprived of them, perhaps for the sake of
the metal in the Revolution. The well-known symbols
of the Vassall family, the goblet and sun, are carved on
a large tomb near the road-side, but no inscription
accompanies them. Our remarks, therefore, will be
confined to the large tomb, which covers the bones

and celebrates the virtues of President Leverett.

Hic jacent Reliquiæ Honoratiss, et Rev. admodum Dom.
JOHANNIS LEVERETT, Armig. qui Majoribus oriundus
illustribus, illustrius nomen reddidit quam accepit.
Virtus et pietas, Sapientia et Gravitas juventuti fuere
Laurea, nec non Senectuti Corona. Majestas et Authoritas
in oculo, voce, vultu; Benignitas et Humanitas in corde re
sederunt; in Secundis moderatus, in adversis constanti et in-
fracto fuit animo. Maritus et Pater amantissimus, amicus
dulcis et fidus, prudens Consiliarius, fortis Auxiliarius.
Linguarum et Artium Academicarum inter peri-
tissimos nec minus in Jurisprudentia et Theo-
logia quam in Philosophia Conspicuus
Omnes fere Honoris gradus conscendit et ornavit. Juvenem
admodum mirata est et plausit Academia Tutorem primari-
um et Socium : ut et postea Communinm Domus Pro-
locutorem De Probatione Testamentorum judicem et in
Superiori Tribunali Justitiarium ; Regi a consiliis assistentem
et in variis Legationibus honorificis et momentosis sagaci-
ter et integre versantem, contemplata est universa Patria.
Tandem Collegii Principalis et Societatis Regiæ soci-
us cooptatus, Scholæ Prophetarum ad annos sedecim
pari Authoritate et Lenitate præsidebat : donec morte in-
stantanea Deo visum sit a Filiis Prophetarum Dominum e
Lecto et Somno in cœlum assumere, Maii 3 MDCCXXIV. Æt. LXII.

Above the inscription is inserted a circular* slab of slate, on which are engraved the family arms, viz.: A chevron between three hares or leverets courant: crest, a leveret courant. The inscription is printed in Harris' Cambridge Epitaphs; by a comparison with the original, one or two slight errors were found and corrected. An account of the family will find a more appropriate place in the series of Governors, among whom was the grandfather of President Leverett.

W. S. A.

SELF CONSTITUTED COLLEGES OF ARMS.

In the Herald and Genealogist for March, 1864, the editor called attention to one of these deceitful institutions now doing apparently a thriving business in London, and says that this "proves the fabrication of spurious arms is by no means confined to Paris or New York."

Without attempting to defend the advertisements and pretensions of certain persons in any American city, we desire to show that the deception was practised in London some seventy years ago.

We have seen in the N. E. Historical and Genealogical Register, a certificate of arms which was undoubtedly procured in good faith. It is said to be "extracted from Ancient Records, Vol. II., folio 327, No. 109 and transferred to Modern Records, Vol. II., folio 65, No. 97. Signed Robert N. Andrews, Assist. Sec'y.

*The style of the mantlings and decorations is similar to that of the Foster coat, which is engraved above.

Examined B. Gerard, Armorer. Fees, £2. 2. 0. Heraldry office, London, Cheapside, Oct. 23, 1791."

It is a matter of current tradition, that after the Revolutionary War, many of the ship-masters of Boston and vicinity, obtained coats-of-arms in England. Not content with Cole's sketches at a guinea each, they applied for them at the "College of Heraldry" in London, and undoubtedly acted in good faith.

We beg our English friends to remember, therefore, that though we have sinned in modern times, still our greatest mistakes were when we relied upon English authorities. After crossing the ocean, our captains no doubt thought they were acquiring a sound title by purchasing their arms in London.

THE ORIGIN OF THE COLONISTS.

We propose to give a few citations from Cotton Mather's Magnalia, in which he asserts, or seemingly implies, that certain of the prominent colonists of New England were of good family. We quote from the Hartford edition of 1855.

It will be hereafter shown that most of these gentlemen used arms here, thus corroborating Mather's testimony in the strongest manner.

i.–156. "After Mr. Eaton's death they chose Mr. Francis Newman who had been for many years the secretary of the colony."

i.–157. " Upon the setting of Mr. Francis Newman, there arose Mr. William Leet, of whom let not the reader be displeased at this brief account. This gentle-

man was by his education a lawyer, and by his employment a register in the Bishop's Court."

i.–253. " There was a good heraldry in that speech of
the noble Romanus, ' It is not the blood of my progenitors, but my Christian profession, that makes me noble.'
But our John Cotton, besides the advantage of his
Christian profession, had a descent from honourable
progenitors to render him *doubly* honourable. His immediate progenitors being, by some injustice, deprived of
great revenues, his father, Mr. Roland Cotton had the
education of a lawyer bestowed by his friends upon
him, in hopes of his being the better capacitated thereby
to recover the estate whereof his family had been
wronged; and so the profession of a lawyer was that
unto which this gentleman applied himself all his days."
"Of such parents was Mr. John Cotton born, at the
town of Derby on the 4th December 1585."

i.–286. Mr. John Norton. "He was born the sixth of
May, 1606, at Starford in Hartfordshire ; descended of
honorable ancestors."

i.–303. " Mr. John Wilson, descending from eminent
ancestors, was born at Windsor in the *wonderful year*
1588, the third son of Dr. William Wilson, a prebend of
St. Paul's of Rochester and of Windsor, having for his
mother a niece of Dr. Edmund Grindle the most wor-
thily renowned Arch Bishop of Canterbury."

[To be continued.]

Copied from Windows of the Old Church built in 1656. now in possession of the Van.Rensselaer & Dudley Families.

THE

HERALDIC JOURNAL;

RECORDING THE ARMORIAL BEARINGS AND GENEALOGIES OF
AMERICAN FAMILIES.

NO. III.   MARCH, 1865.

THE VAN RENSSELAER FAMILY.

" The first ancestor of this family in America," says Holgate in his " American Genealogy," " was De Heer Kiliaen Van Rensselaer, who was born in the dorp, or village of Nieukirk, province of Gelderland, Netherlands. He was originally a pearl and diamond merchant, but had, at the period referred to, become a Director of the Dutch West India Company, and one of the nine commissioners appointed to take charge of that part of the business of the association which referred to New Netherlands, at Amsterdam."

He came hither in 1637, having previously obtained a grant of an immense territory in Albany and Rensselaer counties. He died in 1645, and his son Jeremias inherited Rensselaerwyck. The son of the latter was Kiliaen, who m. Maria Van Cortlandt, and d. 1701, leaving sons Jeremias and Stephen, successively proprietors of the Manor. Stephen, who d. 1747, was father of Stephen who m. Catharine Livingston and died 1769.

The son of this last was Gen. Stephen Van Rensselaer, b. 1 Nov. 1764, Lieut. Governor in 1795 and
1798. He was a Major General in the war of 1812.
By his first wife, Margaret Schuyler, he had a son
Stephen, the present Patroon; by a second wife, Cornelia Patterson, he had William P., Philip, Catherine,
Rev. Cortlandt, Henry, Cornelia P., Alexander, Euphe-
mia W., and Westerlo. His brother, Philip S. Van
Rensselaer, resided at Albany.

Another branch of the family commenced with
Hendrick, b. 1667; his sons were Johannes, Henry and
Kiliaen. Kiliaen was the father of Major-Gen. Henry
Van Rensselaer, whose son Solomon was also Major-
General and Adjutant-General of New York. Henry,
son of Hendrick, was father of Lieut. Gov. Jeremias
Van Rensselaer.

Mr. Holgate traces the family four generations in
Holland, viz.: from Hendrick Wolters Van Rensselaer,
whose son Johannes had Kiliaen. The son of this last
was Hendrick whose son Kiliaen emigrated hither.

He further says " The coat of arms of the family is
remarkable for a cross bearing the motto *Niemand
zonder*, ' No one without' (a cross)." The example from
which our engraving was taken was in the window of
the old Dutch church in Albany, built in 1712. We
do not know the quarterings on this shield.

The shield on the same plate is doubtless that of
Rutger Jacobsen, who was one of the magistrates at
Fort Orange in 1655 and 1660 (O'Callaghan's Register
of New Netherland, 68 & 70). He was the ancestor
of Mrs. Blandina Dudley, in whose possession the glass
now is.

OFFICIAL SEALS.

The third seal in the series of our Governors is that
of Thomas Dudley, copied from the one used on his
will in 1654.

Of his pedigree little is known, although Mr. Adlard,
in a book on the subject published in 1862, expresses
the belief that the Governor was grandson of John
Dudley of London, a presumed nephew of the third
Baron Dudley. In the Herald and Genealogist, for September 1864, will be found a very clear and courteous
criticism of this pedigree, which renders it certain that
this derivation of the family is not proven.

All that we really know about the matter is that
Thomas Dudley was born in 1577, and that his father,
Capt. Roger Dudley, " was slain in the wars when this,
his son, and one only daughter was very young." Mr.
Adlard makes the following assumptions: 1st, that
a certain Thomas Dudley, draper, who died in 1549
and was buried at St. Michael's, Cornhill, London, was
the brother of John, third Baron Dudley. Of this there
is no proof or even reasonable ground for surmise. 2d,
he makes Roger Dudley, grandson of this Thomas,
to be our Governor's father, and records two other
children, Richard, who d. 20 Aug. 1603, and Dorothy,
bapt. 31 Mar. 1603, as the children of this Roger.

Now it is clear that the Governor's father must have
died before 1590,—" when Thomas was very young"—
and could not be the father of Dorothy, baptized in 1603.

In short there seems to be no reason why this Roger was selected as the probable ancestor of the family here, especially as there was another Roger, son of Edward of St. Margaret's in Westminster, who might present equal claims.

The editor of the Herald and Genealogist makes a very good suggestion, that the name Paul, being a favorite one with the Dudleys here, may lead to the discovery of the pedigree. It had been a name in the family of Dudley of Hackney in Middlesex, as early as 1555.

As to the seal we can only say that Gov. Thomas Dudley used it as his own, and that his son used the double tailed lion on his official privy seal. It is not in itself a proof of his pedigree, but it does show that Thomas Dudley, a man in high position, meant to have it believed that he belonged to the gentle family of the Dudleys. Whether he was mistaken can only be proved by ascertaining his pedigree; and it seems certainly unfair to accuse him of intentional fraud.

THE DAVENPORT FAMILY.

Rev. John Davenport, one of the most distinguished of our early divines, was born at Coventry, co. Warwick, in 1597. His father, John Davenport, was an eminent merchant of that city, of which his grandfather had been at one time Mayor. The connection of this branch with the main family of Davenport, a large and distinguished family in Cheshire, has been clearly shown by A. Benedict Davenport, Esq., in his Genealogy published in 1851.

The family indeed was so numerous that Lower

(English surnames ii.–30) gives the proverb that in
" Cheshire there are as many Leighs as fleas, Massies
as asses, and Davenports as dog-tails." However, we
are not only assured of the correctness of the pedigree,
but we find by the Winthrop Papers that John Davenport used his family coat-of-arms which is as follows:
Argent, a chevron sable between three cross crosslets
fitchée of the second. Crest, a felon's head, couped at
the neck, proper, haltered or.

This crest was assumed as a badge of the office of
Grand Sergeant of Macclesfield Hundred. From Rev.
John Davenport is descended a highly respected family
of the name in Connecticut.

Another family of the same name, and probably of
the same original stock, is descended from Capt. Richard Davenport of Salem, who came from Weymouth,
co. Dorset. Eleazer, said to be the son of this Richard, m. Rebecca, daughter of Isaac Addington, and
had a son, Hon. Addington Davenport, born in 1670,
who m. Elizabeth, dau. of John Wainwright of Ipswich. He died in 1736, and his widow d. in 1756.
Her will (see Register, iv.–115, 116.) gives to " my grand-
daughter, Abigail Davenport, my silver salver, that has

her grandfather's coat-of-arms on it." We incline to think that these were the Davenport arms, since this son, Addington Davenport jr. used the arms. He was the first rector of Trinity Church, Boston, and married Ann Faneuil. He died 8 Sept. 1746; and a hatchment bearing his arms impaling Faneuil, was erected in the church. This has been preserved, perhaps the only remaining instance of such a memorial, and we understand that Bishop Eastburn has ordered its erection in a proper place in the church.

We hope hereafter to be able to show to what branch of the English family these Davenports belonged.

Gore has a copy of the arms of Isaac Addington, Secretary of Mass., dated 1717—impaling Norton.

HERALDIC NOTES & QUERIES.

IX.

In Burke's General Armory we read the following: "Hopkins, (Maryland; granted 1764). Sa. on a chev.— betw. two pistols, in chief or, and a silver medal, with the French King's bust, inscribed Louis XV. tied at the top with a red ribbon, in base,—a laurel chaplet in the centre, a scalp on a staff on the dexter, and a toma- hawk on the sinister, all ppr. a chief embattled ar. Crest. On a wreath, or. and sa. a rock, over the top a battery in perspective, thereon the French flag hoisted, an officer of the Queen's Royal American Rangers on the said rock, sword in hand, all ppr.; round the crest this *Motto* Inter Primos."

The soldier, to whom this remarkably overloaded coat was granted, cannot be said to be famous in American

History. He cannot positively be identified, but was probably the Capt. Hopkins, mentioned in the " Diary of the siege of Detroit," Munsell's Historical Series, No. iv. The Editor, Mr. F. B. Hough, appends a note that he " had charge of a company of Rangers, and in the numerous skirmishes and sorties that occurred during the siege, he is often mentioned as having had the command."   W. S. A.

X.

It has been said in other words, that the Signers of the Declaration of Independence need no ancestral honors. Probably but few of them inherited any claim to coat-armor. The right of Charles Carroll of Carrollton is among those which are undeniable. I have an old book-plate of "Charles Carroll of ye Inner Temple Esqr. Second Son of Daniel Carroll of Litterlouna Esqr. in the Kings County in the Kingdom of Ireland 1702." This Charles had emigrated to Maryland about 1686, and was grandfather of Charles Carroll, the Signer. The family arms are, Arg. two lions combatant gu. supporting a sword ar. hilt and pommel or. Crest. A falcon or.

W. S. A.

THE MILLER FAMILY.

Among the earliest settlers of Milton, in the Province of Massachusetts Bay, was Mr. Samuel Miller, who married Rebecca, daughter of Joseph Belcher of Boston.

He was a gentleman of good estate and was a large proprietor of "the Blue Hill lands," so called.

He was the father of several children, among whom

was a son Ebenezer, who entered Harvard College in 1718, and graduated in 1722.

On leaving college Ebenezer Miller, by the advice of his father who was an Episcopalian, determined to study for the ministry.

There being at that time in the Province no clergyman of the Church of England with whom he could pursue his studies, nor any Bishop under whose authority and sanction he could receive ordination, it was necessary that he should go to England for these advantages, and he sailed for London in the year 1723.

He remained in England until 1728. He was ordained Deacon in 1726, and Priest in 1727, by the Lord Bishop of London.

The certificate of his ordination has been seen by us, bearing the signature and seal of the Bishop. Immediately after his ordination he was appointed Chaplain of the Duke of Bolton, then Lord Warden of the Cinque Ports, &c., &c., as appears by his certificate of appointment which is now before us. In the same year he received the honorary degree of Master of Arts from the University of Oxford. The diploma, on parchment under the great seal of the University, has been shown us by his descendant, who has it in his possession.

In the year 1728 he was appointed by the " Ancient and Honorable Society in England for Propagating the Gospel in Foreign Parts," a missionary for New England, with an annual stipend of one hundred pounds sterling.

Early in 1728, before leaving England, he was married, at the Church of St. Martin in the Fields, to Martha Motram, of the family of Motram of Addlethorp, Lincoln.

On his return to the Province he proceeded to Braintree, then a prominent town, and caused an Episcopal Church to be erected, which was dedicated Christmas day, 1728.

He continued his ministry there uninterruptedly till 1763, when he died.

At the request of the Society in whose service he was, he returned to England in 1748. During this visit he received the Honorary Degree of Doctor of Divinity, from the University of Oxford. His diploma is quaintly expressed in Latin. The especial reason which is given for conferring on him this honor, is that he has been a long and faithful servant of the Lord in spreading the gospel, "præsertim inter barbaros in Nov-Anglia."

Besides the certificates and diplomas above mentioned, there is still in the possession of his great grandson, a large and beautiful silver tankard, which the writer has seen. It was a gift on the occasion of the marriage of Dr. Miller, 1728, as above stated. Upon it are engraved the arms of the Millers of Kent, impaled with those of the Motrams of Lincoln, viz. : E-mine, a fess gules between three wolf's heads erased azure, for Miller; and Sable, on a chevron argent, between three cross crosslets fitchy, as many quatre foils, for Motram. The Miller crest surmounts the whole, viz.: a wolf's head erased, collared ermine.

There are also other pieces of silver in the possession of the family bearing the same arms and dating back to about 1740.

Charles Miller, youngest son of Dr. Ebenezer Miller and Martha Motram, married Hannah Smith.

Edward Miller, son of Charles Miller and Hannah Smith, married Caroline Nicolson of Plymouth; from whom descend a son, Charles E. Miller of Quincy, now resident on the original estate, which has been in the family more than one hundred and thirty-four years, and by whom the coat-of-arms is presented to this work, and a daughter, Anna S. Miller, now the wife of the present Chief Justice of Massachusetts.

A. T. P.

THE SYMONDS FAMILY.

Among the early settlers of Massachusetts, who were sprung from the gentry of England, we count Samuel Symonds of Ipswich. His ancestors were long established,—Morant's Essex says, for twenty generations,—at Croft in Lancashire and Stratton in Staffordshire. Richard Symonds, a nephew of the emigrant, was a zealous antiquary as well as a devoted Royalist. His Ms. collections for the county of Essex are in the College of Arms. They contain the pedigree of the family, probably as far back as is certain; it was printed for the Camden Society in a volume of Symonds' heraldic collections. The emigration of Samuel, who was born in 1595, is mentioned also by Morant.

John Symonds of Croft, com. Lancastr. = dau. of Sir Wm. Lording, Kt.

Robt. Symonds, went into Staffordshire = dau. and h. of Congrave of Stratton.

John Symonds of Stratton=dau.of Gravener of Bellaport com.Salop,Esqre.

Thomas Symonds= dau. of Tho. Worth-   Robt. S., 2d son, married
of Stratton   ington, Gent.   and had issue.

John Symonds of Newport, com. Salop = Margaret, dau. of Thomas Maynard.

John Symonds of Newport, com. Salop = Ann, dau.of Thomas Bendbow.

Richard Symonds of the Poole, an = Elizabeth, ye 2d dau. of   William S.
antient seat in this parish,* came out | Robt. Plume of Yeld-   married and
of Shropsh. ; one of ye Cursitars | ham Hall, Gent; buried   had issue.
of ye Chancery ; buried in Yeldham | in Yeldham Church,   Roger S.
Church, July 8, 1627. | Jan. 27, 1611.

John S., eldest son   Thomas S.   Edward S. | Richard S.   Margaret S.

Samuel S., 4th son, one of ye Cursitars of the = ——, daughter of Tho.
Chancery, bought† ye place in Toppesfield in | Harlakenden of
Essex called Olivers, 100 per ann. ; went | Colne.
into New England.

Richard S. eldest son,   Dorothy   Samuel   Harlakenden   Elizabeth
Student of Greyes Inn.   which he carried with him to New England.

Harleian Ms., 1542, in the British Museum contains a pedigree of the family, with the following attestation

* Great Yeldham.

† He more probably inherited it.

of the arms. "The Auntiant Armes of Richard
Symonds of Great Yeldham in Com. Essex son
of John Symonds of Newport in Com. Sallop gent.
wth the guifte of this Creast all wch Sr Ri St George
Knt. Clarenceux King of Armes exempliffied by Lrs
pattent dated in the First year of King Charles the Xth
day of January ao 1625 to the said Richard Symonds
and to his posterity For ever."

The Church of Great Yeldham contains a fine brass
in memory of Richard Symonds, who married Eliz.
Plume. The arms are Symonds, quarterly of four, viz.:
1s' ard 4th, Azure, a chevron engrailed between three
trefoils slipped or., 2d, Three eagles displayed, 3d, On a
bend three eaglets displayed, impaling Plume, Ermine,
a bend vaire or and gules, cotised vert.

Dorothy Harlakenden, the first wife of Samuel
Symonds, was own cousin to Roger, of Earle's Colne,
who came to New England in 1635. He bore; Azure,
a fess ermine between three lion's heads erased or, and
quartered the arms of Willes, Londenoys and Oxenbridge.

There has till lately been great doubt as to the marriages of Samuel Symonds. His first wife has been mentioned. His second is clearly shown by the Winthrop Papers to have been Martha, d. of Edmund Reade of Wickford, in Essex, and widow of Daniel Epes. By her he had probably three or four children. His third wife, to whom he was a fourth husband, was Rebecca, dau. of Bennett Swayne, of a family long seated near Sarum in Wiltshire. Her will, on file at Salem, bears a seal with the family arms, Azure, a chevron between three pheons or.

MONUMENTAL INSCRIPTIONS.

I.

The old burying-ground at Charlestown furnishes ten coats-of-arms, and formerly contained more. Those remaining are nearly of a date, and with two exceptions are of one style of work. All are on stone, and nine are on the front of tombs built in the side of a slope.

the	Honbl.
JONATᴺ.	DOWS
Esqr.	1725.

It is by no means certain what arms are here impaled with those of Dowse. The Hon. Jonathan Dowse, son of Lawrence Dowse, married in 1693 Elizabeth Ballard, and in 1701 Catharine Herbert. The charge on the wife's coat is that of the Winslows, but the colors, which are of course wanting, may be different. Jonathan Dowse on his will, 1744, uses a seal on which the chevron alone can be seen.

II.

EZEKIEL   **CHEEVER**
Esqr. HIS   *TOMB* 1744.

This is probably the tomb of Ezekiel Cheever, called of Boston, when he married in 1715 Elizabeth Jenner of Charlestown. He was born in 1692, son of Thomas, and grandson of Ezekiel, the "famous school-master." According to Savage the family was from Canterbury, co. Kent.

Edmondson gives the arms of Cheytor of Durham, as Per bend dancetté ar. and az. three cinquefoils counterchanged. Crest, a stag's head erased lozengy ar. and az. the dexter horn ar. the sinister az.

III.

DAVID   WOOD
1762.

David Wood, whose name is on this tomb, was born in 1710, son of Joseph, and grandson of Josiah of Charlestown. We have here undoubtedly an instance of an occurrence which is often found, viz.: the appropriation by one family of the tomb of another. The arms engraved above are those of the family of our Governor, Sir William Phipps. Luckily we are not left without knowledge of the arms of Wood, as Josiah on his will, 1691, uses a seal bearing a lion rampant, which belongs to the name.

IV.

THOMAS   GREAVES.
Here Lyes Interr'd the Body of ye
Honble. THOMAS GREAVES Esqr.

Who Departed this Life in his Sleep
On the 19th of June 1747. Ætatis 63.
He was a Beloved *Physician,* an Upright
Judge, and a *Wise* and Good Man.
XC Psalm, 10th.   *It is Soon Cut of and wee Fly away*
A good account of the family may be read in Froth-
ingham's History of Charlestown.   The name is oftener
spelt Graves.

v.

Jonathan   *Lemmon*
Son of Mr   *JOSEPH* &
Mrs *ELIZABETH LEMMON,* Decd
July 16th, 1724, Ætatis 15 Mo.

Joseph Lemmon, first of the family in this country,
and grandfather of Jonathan, came from England
late in the seventeenth century.   He died in 1709, and
in his will, written in 1707, he mentions his honored
mother, Mary Jenkins of Dorchester, co. Dorset, England,
and his brother, Robert Lemmon of the same, cooper.
He uses a seal bearing the same arms as the tomb, but
the fess seems to be engrailed and vert, and the dolphins
are on so small a scale, as to be hardly recognizable.
The crest also is a wolf's head erased.

CORNELIUS WENDELL.

Copied from the Original in possession of the Wendell Family.

THE

HERALDIC JOURNAL;

RECORDING THE ARMORIAL BEARINGS AND GENEALOGIES OF
AMERICAN FAMILIES.

NO. IV.   APRIL, 1865.

THE WENDELL FAMILY.

We learn from the History of the Old Dutch Church
at Albany, that among the earliest church-members were
Evert Wendel, his wife Merritje, and his sons John and
Evert.   From a very interesting sketch of the family in
Bridgman's " King's Chapel Epitaphs " we learn that
of these sons John married Elizabeth Staats and had
nine children born in Albany.   The oldest, Abraham,
born in 1678, and the youngest, Jacob, born in 1691,
removed to Boston.

Abraham was the father of John who married
Elizabeth Quincy, and whose sister married Edmund
Quincy.

Jacob was one of the wealthiest merchants of Boston,
a member of the Council, etc., and died in 1761.   His
wife was Sarah, daughter of Dr. James Oliver; his
youngest daughter married William Phillips and was
the mother of John Phillips, the first Mayor of Boston,
whose son, Wendell Phillips, has rendered the name
familiar to the present generation.

Judge Oliver Wendell, son of Jacob, married in 1762 Mary Jackson, and had several children; of whom Sarah married Rev. Abiel Holmes of Cambridge and was the mother of Dr. Oliver Wendell Holmes.

The first settler at Albany, Evert Jansen Wendell, is said to have come from Embden in East Friesland in Hanover. The family was undoubtedly entitled to coat-armor, since it has been constantly and conspic- uously used in every generation here.

OFFICIAL SEALS.

The fourth Governor of Massachusetts was John Haynes of Copford Hall, co. Essex, a gentleman of considerable fortune. In the second series of the Win- throp papers (Mass. Hist. Society, 4th S. VII.) will be found a number of his letters and a fac-simile of his seal, which is here given on a larger scale.

To the kindness of J. Hammond Trumbull, Esq. we are indebted for the following account of the family. "John Haynes of Copford Hall, Lexden Hundred, co. Essex, (son of John Haynes of Old-holt, in the same hundred, esquire, by Mary Michell his wife) married Mary, daughter of Robert Thornton of Nottingham.

His eldest son, Robert, dying without issue in 1657, the manor of Copford Hall with his other estate in Essex, passed to the Governor's second son, Major-general Hezekiah Haynes, and successively to *his* eldest son John Haynes, and to *his* eldest son again of the same name, who d. s. p. 21 August, 1713. From the latter it passed to a younger brother Hezekiah, who was the owner of Copford Hall in 1768. The arms are given by Morant, (History of Essex, ii. 196) 'Argent, three crescents barry undée, azure and gules. Crest a stork rising, proper. This coat was confirmed to Nicholas Haynes, 4th son of Richard Haynes of Reading, by R. Cook, Clarencieux 1578.' "

John Haynes removed to Connecticut and was the first governor of that colony in 1639. His sons, Robert and Hezekiah, remained in England, and Roger returned there soon. By his wife, Mabel Harlakenden, he had Ruth, who married Samuel Wyllys, and Mabel, wife of James Russell of Charlestown, and also John, who returned to England, and Joseph of Hartford. The only son of the latter was John, a judge of the Supreme Court of Connecticut, with whose son the male line of the family in this country terminated, says Savage.

Of course many descendants in the female lines can be traced.

———

Of Sir Henry Vane, our next Governor, it is useless to say much ; as he was but a transient visitor. His arms will be found in any peerage under the title of his descendant, the Duke of Cleveland. They are azure, three sinister gauntlets gold. The engraving in the History of Boston is different and probably erroneous.

THE THORNDIKE FAMILY.

From the works of Herbert Thorndike, Prebendary of Westminster Abbey, the researches of Lord Monson, Messrs. H. G. Somerby and George Quincy Thorndike, and original documents, the following account has been prepared.

William Thorndike, the ancestor of the Thorndikes of New England, was born in the reign of Henry VII. He lived in the town of Little Carltọn, county of Lincoln, married there, and died 1539; in his will he mentions his six children.

The children of William[1] Thorndike were Herbert,[2] William,[2] John,[2] and three daughters.

Herbert[2] Thorndike, eldest son of William,[1] was Lord of the Manor of Little Carlton, and by his wife, Janet Thorndike, had five sons, Nicholas,[3] Richard,[3] Herbert,[3] James,[3] George,[3] and five daughters.

Nicholas,[3] eldest son of Herbert and Janet Thorndike, married Frances Southrey, and had two sons and two daughters.

The sons, Francis[4] and Herbert,[4] signed the pedigree for the first visitation of Heralds recorded in the family, in the year 1634.

Francis,[4] eldest son of Nicholas[3] Thorndike and Frances Southrey, married Alice Coleman, and left four sons, Francis,[5] John,[5] the first of the family in New England, Herbert,[5] Prebendary of Westminster Abbey, and Paul.[5]

John,[5] second son of Francis[4] and Alice (Coleman) Thorndike, came to New England in the year 1633, married here, and had one son, Paul,[6] and six daughters.

In the year 1668 John Thorndike[5] returned to England on a visit to his brother Herbert,[5] then Prebendary of Westminster Abbey, and took with him his son Paul,[6] and two of his daughters, Martha[6] and Alice.[6] He died in London not long after he arrived there, and was buried in Westminster Abbey Cloister, November 3d, 1668.

Paul Thorndike[6] returned to New England, but his sisters Martha[6] and Alice[6] continued to live with their uncle Herbert[5] until he died, when he provided for them in his will, on condition, however, "that they should neither return to New England their birthplace, nor yet remaining in England, marry with any who went to the Mass nor to the new Licenced Conventicles." Herbert Thorndike was one of the most profound and distinguished scholars in England during his life, as his numerous works not long since republished testify.

Paul Thorndike,[6] son of John, on his return to New England settled at Beverly, and married Mary Patch, and left three sons, John,[7] Paul,[7] and Herbert,[7] and four daughters.

John Thorndike,[7] eldest son of Paul[6] Thorndike and Mary Patch, married Joanna Larkin, and had Robert,[8] Paul,[8] John,[8] James,[8] Herbert,[8] Edward,[8] and two daughters.

James[8] Thorndike, fourth son of John and Joanna Thorndike, married Anna Ober, and had Hezekiah,[9] James,[9] Jeremiah,[9] Paul,[9] Herbert,[9] and three daughters.

Hezekiah[9] Thorndike, eldest son of James and Anna Thorndike, married Sarah Prince, and had Hezekiah,[10] Jeremiah,[10] and one daughter.

Hezekiah [10] Thorndike, eldest son of Hezekiah and Sarah Prince Thorndike, married Abigail Chamberlain, and had one son, John Prince [11] Thorndike.

John-Prince [11] Thorndike married Sarah Hill, and has John Hill Thorndike,[12] James F. Thorndike,[12] and George Quincy Thorndike,[12] who has kindly presented the engraving of the arms of the family. These are Argent, six guttées, three two and one, gules, on a chief of the last three leopard's faces gold. The crest is a damask rose ppr., with leaves and thorns vert, at the bottom of the stalk a beetle ppr.

S. Lothrop Thorndike, Esq.[12] of Beverly descends from John [7] Thorndike through Herbert,[8] Nicholas,[9] Nicholas Jr.,[10] and Albert.[11]

Augustus [12] Thorndike, son of Charles [11] and Mary Edgar Thorndike, descends from Paul,[6] Paul Jr.[7] Andrew,[8] Israel,[9] Augustus.[10]   A. T. P.

MONUMENTAL INSCRIPTIONS.

CHARLESTOWN, CONTINUED.

VI.

Here   Lyes
Interrd ye   Body of
Mrs. SARAH FOSTER, Wife to Mr.
RICHARD FOSTER, Junr.; who Decd.
November ye 16th, 1724.   Ætatis 29.   [A 5 Mo
Also Two of their Children; Richard A 15 Mo Katherine
Here lies Interred the Remains of
the Honble. RICHARD FOSTER, Esqr., who died
August 29th 1774, Aged 82 Years.
He sustained with reputation the office of High Sheriff
for the County of *Middlesex* for many Years, and
upon his resignation, was appointed a Justis of the
Court of Common Pleas for the same County,
in which office he continued untill his decease.
Mrs. MARY FOSTER, Second Wife
of the Honble. RICHARD FOSTER Esqr.
died October 26th, 1774.   Aged 72 Years.

———

The Hon. Richard Foster was grandson of William,
who was of Charlestown about 1650. He may have

been the passenger in the Hercules from Southampton
in 1634, and *he* may have been son of Richard Foster
of Romsey, baptized there 22 Jan. 1615.   William of
Charlestown is recorded as aged about 80 at his death in
1698.   Various articles of silver with the Foster arms
are still preserved.   Mr. Edward I. Browne of Boston
has a large tankard, on which they are beautifully
engraved, with the colors, viz.: argent, a chevron vert
between three hunting-horns sa.   It was inherited from
the marriage of Ann, sister of Hon. Richard Foster,
with Rev. Daniel Perkins of Bridgewater.   A watch
and a seal are in the hands of others.

VII.

JENNER   1725

Here lies Intomb'd the Body of
THOMAS JENNER, Esqr. Who died
June the 23d. 1765 Aged 72 Years.
From whence He Silently Speaks,
My Friend, Stop here & drop a Tear
As you are passing by
For you must dye as well as I
Think on ETERNITY.

  This Thomas Jenner was gr. gr. grandson of Rev.
Thomas Jenner of Weymouth.   Some account of the

family will probably soon appear in the N. E. Historical and Genealogical Register. The ornamentation of the border of the shield may be intended to represent it as engrailed, which it should be according to English works on Heraldry.

VIII.

Here lies Interr'd the Body of the Honble.
CHARLES CHAMBERS, *Esqr*, Who departed this Life *April* 27th *A. D.* 1743 in ye 83d Year of his Age. He was for many Years one of his Majestys Council, a Judge of the Court of Common Pleas & a Justice of the Peace for ye County of *Middlesex*, all which Offices he discharged with great Honour and Fidelity.

Here lies Interr'd the Body of the Honble.
DANIEL RUSSELL Esqr who departed this Life *Decemr*. 6th 1763 Aged 78 Years, who for upwards of 20 Years was a Member of his Majestys Council for this Province, He also serv'd the Province as Commissioner of Impost, and the County of *Middlesex* as Treasurer, for more than 50 Years, in the Discharge of all which Offices such was his Conscientious Fidelity and unsulled Integrity as procured him Universal approbation and Esteem.
In Public & Private Life his whole Conduct was such as Evidently shewed his Invariable desire and Endeavour to preserve a Conscience void of offence towards GOD and Man.

[NOTE. These two inscriptions are on the same stone —Russell married a daughter of Thomas Chambers and had a son Chambers Russell.]

HERALDIC NOTES AND QUERIES.

XI.

A valuable piece of additional evidence concerning the Colman arms has been obtained since the publication of the February number. Mrs. Samuel Appleton of Boston has an old silver bowl or cooler, on the inside of which the arms are thus engraved.

It formerly belonged to George Storer of this city, who died in 1838, and has on the bottom the initials T. B. Its pedigree is as follows. John Colman, brother of Rev. Benjamin, had a daughter Judith, who married in 1724 Dr. Thomas Bulfinch. Their son Thomas married Susan Apthorp, and had with other children Anna, who married in 1795 George Storer.

W. S. A.

XII.

The Second Church in Boston possesses the following articles of communion plate, with coats of arms engraved thereon.

1st. A large flagon, the gift of Mr. John Frizell who died April 10, 1723, bearing quarterly 1 and 4, argent three crowns; 2 and 3, azure three cinquefoils. These are the arms of Frizell or Frazer, but apparently reversed.

Still this may be in accordance with Scottish heraldry and mode of distinguishing cadency.

2nd. A flagon given by Rev. William Welsteed, 1753, bearing azure, a bend lozengy argent and gules. Crest a basket of fruit.

3d. A cup dated 1730, inscribed with arms, viz.: a fesse, and in chief three cross-crosslets fitchée. Crest a bird. Evidently given by a Goodridge.

4th. Three large dishes, two given in 1711 by Thomas and Edward Hutchinson and bearing their arms; the third no doubt belonged to their father in law, Col. John Foster, and has a coat of a chevron between three bugle horns.

5th. A baptismal basin given in 1706 by Adam Winthrop and bearing his well-known arms.

W. H. W.

THE WHITING FAMILY.

The Whitings in New England are descended from Rev. Samuel Whiting of Lynn, Mass. Cotton Mather says of him, he "drew his first breath at Boston, in Lincolnshire, November 20, A. D. 1597. His father, a person of good repute there, the eldest son among many brethren, an alderman, and sometime a mayor of the town, had three sons; the second of these was our Samuel, who had a learned education by his father bestowed upon him, first at Boston school, and then a the university of Cambridge. He had for his companion in his education, his cousin-german, the very renowned Anthony Tuckney, afterwards doctor, and master of St. John's College." He was chaplain to Sir

Nathaniel Bacon and Sir Roger Townsend; was settled at Lyn, co. Norfolk, and Skirbeck, co. Lincoln. " Having buried his first wife, by whom he had three children—two sons who died in England, and a daughter, afterwards matched with one Mr. Thomas Weld in another land—he married the daughter of Mr. Oliver St. John, a Bedfordshire gentleman of an honourable family, nearly related unto the Lord St. John of Bletso." He came to New England in 1636, settled at Lynn, and died 11 December, 1679. A tabular pedigree of his descendants will be found in Drake's History of Boston, p. 363. We may mention among them are Gen. John Whiting of Lancaster, a soldier in the Revolution, and Hon. William Whiting, Solicitor of the War Department, Washington.

As to the family and arms, we find but a brief account in Pishey Thompson's History of Boston, England. He says (p. 430) " The family of Whiting was very early connected with Boston and the neighborhood. William Whytynge of Boston, is mentioned in the Subsidy Roll of Edward III. (1333). William Whyting of Deeping, occurs in Dugdale under the date 1352, and John and Robert Whiting of Thorpe, near Wainfleet, are named by the same authority as living in 1560. The arms of the family were quartered with those of Hunston, Sutton, Stickney, Gedney, and Enderby, in a shield on a mantel-piece in the chantry of St. Laurence, at Leake; and in another shield in the same place, with those of Hunston, Sutton, Stickney, and Smith of Elsham.

He adds that John, father of Rev. Samuel, was Mayor in 1606 and 1608; that John, brother of Samuel, was Mayor 1626, 1633, 1644, and 1645, and James, another brother, in 1640.

Elizabeth, second wife of Rev. Samuel, was daughter of Oliver St. John, own cousin of Oliver Cromwell, and Chief Justice of England.

By the kindness of Mr. Drake we give a cut of the arms; which are emblazoned; Party per saltire, azure and ermine, in the fesse point a leopard's face gold, in chief three bezants. Crest, a lion's head erased.

[Note. William Whiting of Hartford, of another family, used a somewhat similar coat for his seal in 1687. Instead of being per saltire azure and ermine, it is azure two flanches ermine. Of this seal we shall soon give an engraving from a drawing by J. H. Trumbull, Esq.]

THE ORIGIN OF THE COLONISTS, AS RECORDED IN MATHER'S MAGNALIA.
(Continued.)

i.–321. " Mr. John Davenport was born at Coventry, in the year 1597, of worthy parents; a father who was mayor of the city, and a pious mother, who having lived just long enough to devote him, as Hannah did her Samuel, unto the service of the sanctuary, left him under the more immediate care of Heaven to fit him for that service."

i.–333. Thomas Hooker. "This our Hooker was born at Marfield in Leicestershire, about the year 1586, of parents that were neither unable nor unwilling to bestow upon him a liberal education."

i.–400. Mr. Peter Bulkly. "He was descended of an honorable family in Bedfordshire, where for many successive generations the names of Edward and Peter were alternately worn by the heirs of the family. His father was Edward Bulkly, D. D., a faithful minister of the gospel, the same whom we find making a supplement unto the last volume of our books of martyrs. He was born at Woodhil (or Odel) in Bedfordshire, January 31st, 1582."

"His first wife was the daughter of Mr. Thomas Allen of Goldington, a most vertuous gentlewoman whose nephew was Lord Mayor of London, Sir Thomas Allen. By her he had nine sons and two daughters. After her death, he lived eight years a widower and then married a vertuous daughter of Sir Richard Chitwood, by whom he had three sons and one daughter."

i.–429. "The life of Mr. Samuel Newman commenced with the century now running, at Bunbury, where he was born of a family more eminent and more ancient for the profession of the true Protestant religion than most in the realm of England."

i.–443. "It was at a small town called Lowton, in the county of Lancaster, anno 1596, that so great a man as Mr. Richard Mather was born of parents that were of credible and ancient families. And these his parents, though by some disasters their estate was not a little sunk below the means of their ancestors, yet were willing to bestow a liberal education on him."

i.–464. " Mr. Charles Chancey was an Hartfordshire man; born in the year 1589 of parents that were both honourable and religious."

i.–484. " Mr James Noyes was born, 1608, at Choulderton in Wiltshire of godly and worthy parents. His father was minister of the same town, a very learned man, the schoolmaster of Mr. Thomas Parker. His mother was sister to the learned Mr. Robert Parker, and he had much of his education and tutorage under Mr. Thomas Parker."

i.–488. " Mr. Thomas Thatcher was born May 1, 1620, the son of Mr. Peter Thatcher, a reverend minister at Salisbury in England : one whom, in a letter of Dr. Twiss to Mr. Mede, at the end of his works, we find joined with famous Mr. White of Dorchester, in a conversation, wherein the learned exercises of that great man made a grateful entertainment."

i.–497. " Mr. Peter Hobart was born at or near Hingham, a market town in the county of Norfolk, about the latter end of the year 1604."

i.–502. " Mr. Samuel Whiting drew his first breath at Boston in Lincolnshire, November 20, A. D. 1597. His father, a person of good repute there, the eldest son among many brethren, an alderman and sometime a mayor of the town, had three sons : the second of these was our Samuel, who had a learned education bestowed upon him, first at Boston school, and then at the university of Cambridge. He had for his companion in his education his cozen-german, the very renowned

Anthony Tuckney, afterwards Doctor, and master of St. John's Colledge."

i.–511. " Mr. John Sherman was born of godly and worthy parents, December 26, 1613, in the town of Dedham, in the county of Essex.

He was married twice. By his first wife the vertuous daughter of parents therein resembled by her, he had six children. But his next wife was a young gentlewoman whom he chose from under the guardianship and with the countenance of Edward Hopkins, Esq. the excellent governor of Connecticut. She was a person of good education and reputation and honourably descended; being the daughter of a Puritan gentleman whose name was Launce, and whose lands in Cornwall yielded him fourteen hundred pounds a year. He was a parliament-man, a man learned and pious, and a notable disputant; but once disputing against the English Episcopacy (as not being ignorant of what is affirmed by Contzen the Jesuite in his politicks ' That were all England brought once to approve of bishops, it were easier to reduce it unto the Church of Rome,') he was worsted by such a way of maintaining the argument, as was thought agreeable: that is, by a wound in the side from his furious antagonist; of which wound at last he died. The wife of that gentleman was daughter to the Lord Darcy, that was Earl of Rivers, a person of a Protestant and Puritan religion, though of a Popish family; and one that after the murder of her former husband Mr. Launce, had for her second husband the famous Mr. Sympson. But by the daughter of that Mr. Launce, who is yet living, Mr. Sherman had no less than twenty children added unto the number of six, which he had before."

THE

HERALDIC JOURNAL;

RECORDING THE ARMORIAL BEARINGS AND GENEALOGIES OF AMERICAN FAMILIES.

NO. V. MAY, 1865.

ON THE AUTHENTICITY OF AMERICAN COATS-OF-ARMS.

To prevent mistakes concerning the probable value of such coats-of-arms as may have formerly been in use in this country, we desire to remind our readers that such use can be considered only as an evidence that the bearer considered himself entitled to them. No person is now entitled to use arms in England, we believe, unless that he can prove his descent from some one authorized to this distinction. The first owner may have borne arms prior to the visitations, he may have had them recorded at the visitations, or he may have had a grant as recently as the last month from Heralds' College; but without some such endorsement by authority the claim is still unproved.

We make this point since we fear some of our readers may be inclined to regard the use of arms by our first colonists as a positive proof that they belonged to the families bearing such coats. Although our conviction is strong that none of our Puritan fathers would have made a claim which they knew to be wrong, still they were as liable as others to be the victims of mistake.

If English writers are correct in their idea that, prior to 1630, many individuals had assumed arms to which they could prove no right, we must allow that instances may be found among our examples.

Still the value of our collections will be made obvious by the fact that there is no official Register of Arms published, and that by following out the clue given by our examples we may trace families not recorded in modern books. Two examples, the Mather and Cheever arms, have already been given in this Journal, in which the coats are not in Burke, but are in a heraldic manuscript dated 1602–15.

Again the visitations are often lamentably imperfect, being intended mainly to show the elder line of each family. It is certainly a great aid to the genealogist to find that in 1650 his subject claimed to belong to a particular family, as it shows whither inquiry should first be directed. Of course we hold that our American *armigeri* should be placed in the same category as the English. There is always a chance for mistake where arms are used without a pedigree being traced; but we do not see any reason to suspect our ancestors more than their English relatives.

We conclude then that in the present disorganized state of information and rule concerning heraldry in England we ought to collect and report our instances; but should extended researches prove that the emigrant was mistaken, we must concede the error in a proper spirit. It is unnecessary for us to claim more for our ancestors than this; their temptation to such assumptions was less here than at home, and in both countries the percentage of error was probably small.

OFFICIAL SEALS.

Richard Bellingham, Governor of Massachusetts in 1641, was born about 1590, was bred a lawyer, and was chosen Recorder of Boston, England. Of his family nothing is known, and Pishey Thompson in his History was inclined to considered him as probably from Yorkshire. The visitation of Westmoreland made in 1615, records a distinguished family of the name in that county. Richard Bellingham of Naunton, co. Lincoln, son of Sir Robert B. (temp. Hen. VI.) had Richard, eldest son, whose son John Bellingham was of Groomby Wade, co. Lincoln, in 1562, and this John had a brother Richard. It seems probable that our Governor belonged to this family. His second wife was Penelope, sister of Herbert Pelham, but by his first wife he had a son Samuel. The arms here engraved are copied from a deed made in 1650 by this Samuel Bellingham and his wife, described in the Register, xix., p. 107, and now in the possession of W. S. Appleton.

Of the ancestry of John Endicott, who may be regarded either as the first or seventh Governor of Massachusetts, little seems to be definitely known. He was one of the original purchasers of the patent and held a leading place in all the enterprises of the company. We have been unable to obtain any example of arms used by him, and therefore place instead a copy of his personal seal, used on the letters published in the Winthrop Papers, for which copy we are indebted to the Massachusetts Historical Society.

THE SEWALL FAMILY.

Concerning the ancestry of this family we learn from a letter written in 1720 by Chief Justice Samuel Sewall, and printed in the Register, i.,111, that it commences with Henry [1] Sewall, a linen draper of Coventry, who was more than once Mayor of that city. His eldest son was Henry [2] Sewall, whose oldest son Henry [3] was sent over to New England in 1634. This last Henry [3] was the father of the writer of the letter, and the pedigree is therefore of the highest authority. Henry [3] Sewall, the third, married Jane, daughter of Stephen Dummer, and returning to England had a daughter Hannah,[4] bapt. at Tamworth, and Samuel,[4] bapt. at Bishop's Stoke, March 28, 1652. Removing to Badesly he had there three children born, John,[4] Stephen,[4] and Jane.[4] The family returned to New England in 1661.

Many members of this family have occupied important positions in Massachusetts. Samuel[5] was Chief Justice, and so was his nephew Samuel,[6] son of Stephen[5]. The first C. J. was father of the noted minister Rev. Joseph[6] Sewall, whose grandson was also Chief Justice of the Supreme Court. From John,[4] another brother of the first Samuel,[4] were descended Stephen,[6] Professor of Hebrew at Harvard College, and Jonathan Sewall, Attorney-General of Mass., a Loyalist, who went to Halifax, and whose sons were Stephen, Solicitor-General, and Jonathan, Chief Justice of Canada. To this branch also belonged Gen. Henry Sewall, Clerk of the District Court of Maine, and his brothers Rev. Jotham, and Daniel, Register of Probate for York, Maine.

These last were all descended from John[4] Sewall through his son Nicholas.[5] His son Samuel,[5] also of York, had seven sons by his second wife, viz.: Samuel, John, and Joseph of York, David, judge of the U. S. District Court, Dummer of Bath, Henry of Kennebunk, and Moses.[6] The latter had a son Moses,[7] father of Stephen, William, Moses, and Benjamin ; the last named Benjamin,[8] a merchant of Boston, has kindly furnished us with the following engraving which is an exact facsimile of the shield engraved by Nathaniel Hurd under his portrait of the Rev. Samuel Sewall of Boston.

The arms of the family more correctly emblazoned would be, sable, a chevron between three bees argent. Another blazon of the same terms the bees, butterflies. The engraving is worthy of notice as giving an example of Hurd's style, so often occurring on his book-plates.

HERALDIC NOTES AND QUERIES.

XIII.

In the Heraldic Register by Sir Bernard Burke, published in 1850, will be found, at p. 32, a blazon of arms granted in 1847 to Thomas Mather of Glyn Abbot, co. Flint, son and heir of Thomas Mather of Mount Pleasant, Liverpool, and grandson of Daniel Mather of Toxteth Park. These arms are quarterly argent and gules four scythes counterchanged; and are very appropriate since "mather" means a mower. It is strange to find however that the family is said never to have had arms; Ellis Mather, the first settler at Toxteth, being of a yeoman family long seated at Redcliffe and its vicinity. This branch claims to embrace also our New England Mathers, but, as heretofore shown, this family asserted a right to coat-armor. We trust therefore that the present representative of the Mathers will publish the record of the early generations, and will substantiate or refute the claims of Cotton Mather to a gentle ancestry.

XIV.

We have received from Dean Dudley, Esq., the following note of seals of arms from originals in his possession.

1st. Seal of Jonathan Bangs of Plymouth, 7 July, 1680, a rude representation of a blackamore's head, pierced with a spear.

2d. Seal on a deed of John Freeman, Sr., 7 July, 1680, witnessed by John Cotton, John Bradford, William Walker, Joseph Collins. The shield bears three garbs or wheat sheaves. It is surmounted by two crests, the one a garb, the other an antelope's head couped.

XV.

We have had the opportunity to examine some old silver in the possession of Dr. Jeffries bearing the following arms.

1st. A salver, hall-date A. D. 1752, with this coat, azure a heron gold : impaling gold, a chevron between three bird's heads erased sable. The birds are evidently sea-fowl.

2d. A basket inscribed A. W. A. with the same arms.

3d. A small salver, hall-date 1737, a lozenge bearing two chevrons between three trefoils slipped. Colors not marked.

4th. A tankard marked D. I. S. bearing seven mascles, three, three and one—impaling a shield of ten billets within a bordure bezantée. This last very probably is Quincy impaling Salter, there having been such an intermarriage.   w. h. w.

XVI.

The St. James's Magazine for April, 1865, contains an

article on "Heraldry, Past and Present," which adds something to Note ix., page 38. Among ridiculous crests the author mentions the one granted in 1764 to Joseph Hopkins of Maryland. This brings us a little nearer to indentification of the soldier to whom the former note referred.

Smith's MS. "Promptuarium Armorum," before quoted, contains the arms of Cheever, as engraved and described on page 46, and attributes the coat to Christofer Cheever of Butterby in Episcopatu Dunelm. In the Visitation of Durham he is called Christopher Cheytor.

W. S. A.

THE CHANDLER FAMILY.

The first settler in New England in this branch of the family was William [1] Chandler of Roxbury who came in 1637 with his wife Hannah, and several children. Of these, John,[2] born in 1635, married Elizabeth, daughter of William Douglas,* and removed with his family in 1686 to join in the planting of Woodstock, Conn. Here he died 15 Apr. 1703, aged about 68 years. His oldest son John,[3] born in 1665, married in 1692 Mary, daughter of Joshua Raymond of New London, resided several years in the place, and had four children born there, the first in 1693. He moved to Worcester, Mass., in 1731, and was appointed first Chief Justice of the Court of Common Pleas, and the first Judge of Probate

----

* William Douglas was of New London, and Miss Caulkins shows that his wife was "Anne Mattle, daughter of Thomas and sister of Robert Mattle of Ringstead, co. Northampton, England, both of whom died before 1670, leaving property to which she was the legal heir."

for that county. His son John,[4] b. 10 Oct., 1693, m. Hannah Gardiner 1716, and had a family of nine children. The oldest son, also named John,[5] b. 26 Feb., 1720, m. first 1741 Dorothy Paine, and secondly Mary Church of Bristol. By this latter wife he had Mary, wife of Wm. Sever of Kingston, whose daughter married Gov. Lincoln.

Other children of John Chandler [5] by this same wife were Gardiner,[6] born 27 Jan'y., 1749, Lucretia,[6] (wife of Aaron Bancroft D. D., and mother of George Bancroft, of Mrs. Lucretia Farnham, and of Eliza, wife of Gov. Davis) and Sarah [6] who married John Stanton.

Gardiner [6] Chandler m. Elizabeth Ruggles of Hardwick and had three children, of whom Elizabeth-Augusta married Francis Blake of Boston.

Sarah [6] Chandler and John Stanton had issue Francis, Sallie, John, and Mary Stanton; of these Sallie m. Joshua Blake, brother of Francis who married her cousin, and had John Stanton, Mrs. R. Austin, Mrs. Edward Clark, Mrs. George B. Blake, Francis, Charles, Mrs. Gardiner Hubbard, Mrs. Carr, and Joshua Blake.

Francis and Joshua Blake were sons of Joseph Blake of Boston, Rutland, and Hingham, one of the Milton branch of the Dorchester family of Blake. His other children were Joseph, John, George, Charles, and Mrs. Elijah K. Mills. Francis Blake's children were Francis and Harrison-Gray-Otis Blake.

The following wood cut of the Chandler arms, for which we are indebted to Miss Mary Stanton, is copied from the book-plate of John Chandler jr., son of the judge. The original was engraved by Hurd, presumably on good authority.

MONUMENTAL INSCRIPTIONS.

CHARLESTOWN, CONCLUDED.

IX.

In Memory of
SAMUEL CARY Esqr.
who deceas'd *Febry.* 28, 1740–1
Aged 58 Years.
Go; Traveler, Live to GOD. B. Colman.

The descent of Samuel from James of Charlestown is easily traced in the Genealogical Dictionary of New England. The carving of this stone is of a peculiar and elaborate style; T. B. Wyman jr., of Charlestown, furnishes the following extract from Richard Cary's account of administration on his father's estate.

To cash paid Mr. Emes for a stone and cutting my fathers Arms for his Tomb £50

Putting up 3

Irons, Trucking, &c. 1..12

———

£54..12

Here Lyes Buried The Body of
Capt. John Fowle Aged 74 Years
Died October ye 3d 1711.

This inscription enables us to correct a mistake in Savage's Dictionary, where John, who died in 1711, is supposed to have been grandson of George Fowle of Concord. Capt. Fowle must have been the son of George, and born in England about 1637. John, Charlestown, whom Mr. Savage calls eldest son of George, was more probably a brother. W. S. A.

WETHERSFIELD, CONN.

The following inscriptions have been kindly furnished us by J. E. Bulkley, Esq. Besides these there are two more tombs inscribed with arms, viz.: those of Samuel Wolcott, 1734, and Leonard Chester, 1648. We shall give transcripts of these hereafter.

I.

Hon Gershom Bulkley
Died Dec 2d 1713 aged 77.
He was honorable in his descent
Of rare abilities, extraordinary industry
excellent in learning
master of many languages
exquisite in his skill
in divinity, physic, and law
and of a most exemplary
and
Christian life

[This stone is in the Wethersfield yard. The Motto, which is not on the stone, is "Nec temere, nec timide."]

II.

Here lies interr'd the Body
of Capt. Edward Bulkley
Esqr who Departed this
Life August the 27 A. D
1748, In the 75th Year of
His Age.

[This stone is in that portion of the old town of
Wethersfield, which is now known as Rocky Hill.]

THE BULKELEY FAMILY.

The two tombstones copied in the last article belonged to the son and grandson of Rev. Peter Bulkeley
of Concord, Mass. He was born in Odell, co. Bedford,
in 1583, and was the son of Rev. Edward Bulkeley, D.
D., the incumbent of that place. English authorities
say that Edward, who married Alice Irby, was the son of
Thomas B. of Wore, co. Salop, descended from a family
settled at Bulclogh, co. Chester; yet this pedigree seems
to clash with Mather's account, as published on the 62d
page of this journal. As the whole pedigree however

will be hereafter published by one of the family who
has collected the necessary facts, we will only say that
it is evident that Peter Bulkley was of a family entitled
to coat-armor.   We have seen an impression of his seal
on a letter dated 1653, and we have the farther evidence
of the following seal, copied by J. Hammond Trumbull, Esq., affixed to a letter dated in 1676.   This letter,
now preserved in the files at Hartford, was written by
Rev. Gershom Bulkley of Wethersfield.

Peter Bulkley was one of the first settlers at Concord
and died there 9 March, 1659, in his 77th year.   Shattuck
says of him, "he was a thorough scholar, an elevated de-
votional Christian ; laborious in his profession ; and as
a preacher, evangelical, faithful, and of remarkable energetic, powerful, and persuasive eloquence."

His second wife, whose arms he impales, was Grace,
daughter of Sir Richard Chetwode.   By his first wife,
Jane, daughter of Thomas Allen of Goldington, he had
Edward, who succeeded him as a minister at Concord,
Thomas, and John,—by his second wife, Gershom and
Peter.   These sons all occupied good positions in the
community, and Edward was father of Peter who was

speaker of the Mass. House, Agent to England for the colony, and assistant for eight years.

Gershom Bulkley, born 2 Jan'y., 1636, H. C. 1655, settled as minister at New London and Wethersfield. In 1676 he served as Surgeon in the army raised against the Indians ; married 24 Oct., 1659, Sarah, daughter of Rev. Charles Chauncey, by his wife Catherine, daughter of Robert Eyre, Esq., of Sarum, co. Wilts. He was skilled in the law as well as medicine and divinity, and was the author of a pamphlet on Connecticut affairs as well as of the MS. "Will and Doom." His sons were Charles, Edward, Peter, and John. The latter was the minister at Colchester and was "classed by the Rev. Dr. Chauncey in 1768, among the three, most eminent for strength of genius and powers of mind which New England had produced. The other two were Mr. Jeremiah Dummer and Mr. Thomas Walter." Edward, who died in 1748, was father of Peter, and from him through Joseph, Edmund, and Julius H. is descended Joseph E. Bulkley of New York, before mentioned as the collector of the interesting documents from which this sketch is compiled.

THE ORIGIN OF THE COLONISTS, AS RECORDED IN MATHER'S MAGNALIA.

(CONTINUED.)

i.–522. "Mr. John Ward was born, I think, at Haverhil, on November 5, 1606. His grandfather was that John Ward, the worthy minister of Haverhil, whom we find among the worthies of England, and his father was the celebrated Nathanael Ward, whose wit made him known to more Englands than one."

i.–585. "Mr. Samuel Eaton. He was the son of Mr. Richard Eaton, the vicar of Great Burdworth in Cheshire, and the brother of Mr. Theophilus Eaton, the renowned Governor of New Haven."

i.–592. "Mr. Henry Whitfield. He was a gentleman of good extraction by his birth; but of a better by his new birth; nor did his new birth come very long after his birth. . . . . . His father being an eminent lawyer, designed this his youngest son to be a lawyer also, and therefore, afforded him a liberal education, first at the university, and then at the Inns of Court." "Okely in Surrey was the place where the providence of the Lord Jesus Christ now stationed him."

i.–505. Mr. John Woodbridge. "He was born at Stanton, near Highworth in Wiltshire, about the year 1613, of which parish his father was minister; and a minister so able and faithful as to obtain an high esteem among those that at all knew the invaluable worth of such a minister. His mother was daughter to Mr. Robert Parker."

i.–597. Mr. John Oxenbridge. "He was born in Daventry, Northamptonshire, January 30, 1608."

i.–616. Mr. John Bailey. "He was born on February 24, 1643, near Blackbourn in Lancashire; and of a very pious mother, who even before he was born, often, as Hannah did her Samuel, dedicated him unto the service of the Lord."

THE

HERALDIC JOURNAL;

RECORDING THE ARMORIAL BEARINGS AND GENEALOGIES OF AMERICAN FAMILIES.

NO. VI.   JUNE, 1865.

THE BRIGHT FAMILY.

Probably no other family in New England has been traced out in its original location in England, with so great diligence and success, as the Brights of Suffolk. The taste and liberality of one member of the family have resulted in the publication of a volume* giving a complete record of the portion of the family which remained in England as well as of the branch which settled here.

The supposed ancestor of the family was John[1] Bright of Bury St. Edmunds, co. Suffolk, living in 1538. We say supposed, since it is not exactly proved that he was the father of the next, Walter[2] Bright of Bury St. Ed. who d. about 1550.   Walter[2] was father of Thomas,[3] Alderman of Bury, who d. in 1587, who m. Margaret Payton and had, with other children, Henry[4] Bright who d. in 1609.   This last, by wife Marie, had Henry,[5] bapt. at Bury St. Ed. 29 Dec. 1602, who came to Watertown about 1630.

* The Brights of Suffolk, England, represented in America by the descendants of Henry Bright, Jr., who came to New England in 1630, and settled in Watertown, Mass. By J. B. Bright. For private distribution. Boston : 1858. Pp. 345.

The identification is made complete by the will of Elizabeth Dell, daughter of Henry[4] Bright, in which she leaves legacies to her brother Henry Bright of New England and his children.

The pedigrees show that from Thomas Bright issued two lines, one through his son Thomas of Talmach Hall, which ended in an heiress who married Thomas Dawtrey; the other through his son Robert of Netherhall, whose line ended in Mary, wife of Edmund Tyrell. The other branch was that of the emigrant.

The arms of the family are here given.

These were confirmed in 1615 to Thomas and Robert Bright, uncles of the emigrant; and it is most probable that they had been long the inheritance of the family.

Henry[5] Bright of Watertown, "aged 78 in 1680," married Anne Goldstone. He was a deacon in the church for many years, and held various town offices of trust. His son Nathaniel[6] Bright m., in 1681, Mary Coolidge, and had Nathaniel,[7] b. 1686, father of Nathaniel[8] and grandfather of John,[9] born in 1754. This John[9] Bright married Elizabeth Brown, and was father of Jonathan[10] Brown Bright, the author of the Genealogy.

Henry Bright, the emigrant, married Anne, daughter of Henry Goldstone of Wickham Skeith, co. Suffolk, an emigrant in 1634. Henry was son of William G., vicar of Bedingfield. We are led to notice a remark in the Genealogy on the fact, that several other families from this vicinity, in Suffolk, came to New England. "The Winthrops were from Groton, the Fiskes from Laxfield, Appletons from Little Waldingfield, Wards from Haverhill, Browne, Bond, and others, from Bury St. Edmunds, and numbers from different parts of that county, many of whom were among the earliest settlers of Watertown and Waltham, where the names of Bright, Goldstone, Fiske, Pierce, Mason, Brown, Spring, Kimball, Mixer, Barnard, Coolidge, Livermore, and others, are found in the records."

OFFICIAL SEALS.

Concerning the family of Governor John[2] Leverett, we have to confess almost total ignorance. His father was Thomas[1] Leverett, an alderman of Boston, co. Lincoln, who married Anne Fisher in 1610, and removed to New England with his friend John Cotton. Pishey Thompson, with his customary brevity, informs us that the family is one of great antiquity in Lincolnshire, and is recorded in the Heralds' Visitation of 1564, as bearing arms. We hope some of our English friends will give us the particulars of the pedigree there.

It is certain that the Governor used arms, and we give the following example of his seal from a document among the Ewer Papers, in the Library of the New England Historic-Genealogical Society.

Another example will be found on the tombstone of his grandson, as copied at p. 29 of this volume. The writer also possesses an old water-color painting of the arms, dated 1645, which was bought some 90 years ago, probably at Cambridge, by Mr. Monroe. The painting bore every evidence of having been made at the date inscribed on it.

The descendants of Gov. Leverett, bearing his surname, are very few. His sisters married Samuel Moseley, Penn Townsend, and Capt. Davenport; his daughters married Elisha Cooke, John Hubbard, Paul Dudley, Thomas Davis, James Lloyd, and Nathaniel Byfield. His only son, Hudson[3] Leverett, married Sarah Payton, and had John,[4] Judge Sup. Ct. and Pres. H. C., who left two daughters; and Thomas,[4] who had an only child, Knight.[5]

Knight had John[6] and Thomas[6]; of whom John had three sons and nine grandsons, and Thomas had two sons and four grandsons, recorded in the Leverett Genealogy.

Two of the grandsons of Thomas,[6] were Frederick[8]-Percival, the author of the Latin Lexicon, and Charles[8]-Edward, Rector of Prince William, South Carolina.

It may be further remarked, that Gov. John Leverett was knighted by King Charles II., though he never assumed the title.

THE WILKINSON FAMILY AND ARMS.

Communicated to the Heraldic Journal

By THEODORE A. NEAL.

The American family of Wilkinson, which is entitled to bear the arms at the head of this article, was established here by Lawrence Wilkinson, who was a Lieutenant in the army of King Charles I., and was taken prisoner at the surrender of Newcastle, October 22, 1644. His estates were sequestered and sold by Parliament,* and having obtained especial permission from Lord Fairfax, in 1652, he went with his wife and son to New England, and settled at Providence, Rhode Island, where he had lands granted to him, was made freeman in 1658, chosen Deputy to General Court in 1673, and died May 9, 1692. He was the son of William Wilkinson of Lanchester, in the county of Durham, by his wife Mary, sister of Sir John

---

* Sequestrations in Durham, 1645–47. Lawrence Wilkinson of Lanchester, Officer in Armes, went to New England.

Conyers, Bart., and the grandson of Lawrence Wilkinson of Harpsley House, Durham, to whom the above arms were confirmed, and the crest granted September 18, 1615, as appears by the following extract from a grant issued by Richard St. George, Norroy King at Arms. ". . . . . being now requested by Lawrence Wilkinson . . . . . . to make search for the antient Coate armor belonginge to that name and Familye, which I fynd to be Azure a fesse erminois betwene thre unicorns passant Argant; and for that I can fynd noe creast proper or belonging thereunto, as unto many Antient Coates at this day there is wanting, he hath further requested me to confyrme unto him such a one as he may lawfully beare . . . . . . I have likewise condescended unto and allowed him this Creast ensuinge (vide) a demy unicorne erazed erminoys standing on a murall crown gules; as more plainly appeareth depicted in the margent all which Armes and Creast I the said Richard St George Norroy doe give, grant, ratifye and confyrme unto the sayd Lawrance Wilkinson, and to the severall descendants of his bodye forever bearing their due differences."

Lieutenant Lawrence Wilkinson's grand daughter Ruth married Wm Hopkins, and among their sons were William Hopkins, Governor of Rhode Island and one of the signers of the Declaration of Independence, and Esek Hopkins, a Commodore in the American Navy. Another of Lieut. Wilkinson's descendants was Jemima Wilkinson, the " Prophetess."

Among the present representatives of the family is William Henry Wilkinson, born in Boston, August 29, 1822, for some years past a resident of Sydney, New South

Wales, at whose instance the "Genealogical History of the Family of Wilkinson," from which this sketch is mainly compiled, was very carefully traced and verified, both in England and this country, by that accomplished genealogist, H. G. Somerby, Esq.

Boston, April 14, 1865.

HERALDIC NOTES AND QUERIES.

XVII.

In the present number will be found the Emerson arms, as represented on a tombstone at Ipswich. By the kindness of W. G. Brooks, Esq., we have examined a very well executed painting of the same arms, which may be thus emblazoned: Per fesse indented gold and vert, on a bend engrailed azure, three lions passant argent. Crest a demi-lion vert, bezantée holding in his dexter paw a battle-axe gold, handled gules.

Underneath the shield is the following inscription: "The Arms and Crest above depicted were granted to Ralph Emerson of Foxton, in the County Palatine of Durham, by Thos. Wall, Garter Principal King of Arms, A°· 26 Hen. VIII.[i] Ita Testor Rob. Dale Fæcialis Titulo Suffolc[i]. Colegij Armor Registrar. . . Depositat. . . . 25 J . . . 1709."

This painting belonged to a gr. gr. dau. of Rev. Samuel Phillips of Andover, son of Samuel P. of Salem and his wife Mary, daughter of Rev. John and Ruth (Symonds) Emerson.

XVIII.

Dr. F. E. Oliver has in his possession a little silk flag,

which was probably used at the funeral of some noted
citizen of this colony.   It is about one foot square, and is
inscribed with a shield surrounded by a black border.
The arms are, 1. Gules a fesse wavy between three fleurs-
de-lys gold.   Impaling 2d, sable, on a bend argent,
three stag's heads erased proper.   No crest.

XIX.

We have seen a drawing of arms engraved on a tankard
made by Revere, about 1770, and formerly owned by
Thomas Avis of Boston.   The arms are, 1st, Per pale,
gules and argent a lion rampant.   Impaling 2d, sable on a
chevron gold—between three arrows in pale, points in
chief,—three roundles.   Crest a dexter arm embowed and
vambraced, holding a battle-axe.

XX.

In the Register, XIX., 147, is a copy of a letter written
by Sir William Pepperell, from which we make the following extract: "I must ask another favor of you, to
procure for me and send a handsome marble tomb-stone,
to put over my dece^d Father's Tombe, with proper marble
pillers or supporters to set it on.   I would have his Coat
of arms cut on it, which is three pine apples proper, but
you will find it in ye Herald's Office, it being an Ancient
Arms."

The Hon. Wm. Pepperell here referred to died Feb. 15,
1733, in his 87th year.   As the family continued to use
the arms, it would be satisfactory to find what proof was
given of them.

MONUMENTAL INSCRIPTIONS.

The hill-side, which forms the grave-yard of Old Ipswich, has fared quite as badly as others, whose situation
might have been thought much more exposed and preca-
rious. There are no stones there of a date nearly so early
as one would expect, and only four exist on which armorial
bearings are found. Several show that they once held
shields, by the hollows which the metal filled, evidence
generally supported by the use of the word Armiger, still
legible.

HERE LIES ENTOMBD THE BODY OF
COLONEL FRANCIS WAINWRIGHT ESQ
WHO DIED AUGUST Y 3 1711 ÆTATIS 47

& HIS VERTUOUS CONSORT MRS SARAH
WAINWRIGHT, WHO DIED MARCH Y 16
1709 ÆTATIS 38.

WITH THREE OF THEIR YOUNGEST
CHILDREN JOHN FRANCIS & JOHN
WHO DIED IN THEIR INFANCY.

Memoirs of Francis Wainwright, senior, and of his son here commemorated, may be found in Felt's History of Ipswich. Francis Wainwright, junior, left only three daughters, Sarah, wife of Stephen Minot of Boston, Elizabeth, and Lucy, who married Stephen Waldo of Boston.

The monument is a large one, of brick masonry, three or four feet in height. The top is a flat slab, with the arms and inscription.

HERE LYES Y BODY OF MR NATHANIEL
EMERSON WHO DIED DECEM^R Y
29, 1712 AGED 83.

He was son of Thomas, and of course born in England. This is evidently by the same hand as that of Wainwright, but it is on a simple perpendicular stone. In the

Notes and Queries in our present number will be found an
account of a painting of these arms, possibly the authority
upon which they are here inscribed. Our readers will
note that Nathaniel, as an Englishman, ought to have been
acquainted with his right to the arms he used.

DOMUS GRATA

In memory of
JOHN DENISON, A. M. only son
of Col. *JOHN DENISON;* grandson
to a minister of the same name;
a descendant from the renowned
MAJOR-GENERAL DANIEL DENISON.
An amiable young man, & worthy
of his ancestors. His genius, learning
and engaging manners, spoke him

the future joy & ornament of his native town.   But Heaven meant otherwise.
He died in his 25th year on the 25th of
Augt. 1747.   *He cometh forth like*
a flower & is cut down.   He fleeth also as
a shadow, & continueth not.

This model inscription leaves nothing to be said.   Near
by is the large square tomb of his father, from which the
arms are now gone.   A hollow shows their former existence, as well as the inscription, which begins,

Huic Tumulo mandatur quod erat mortale

D. JOHANNIS DENISON ARMIGERI.

etc.

THE TEMPLE FAMILY.

WE place here the seal of Sir Thomas
Temple, Knt. and Baronet, affixed to his will
of 14 Oct. 1671, on record at Boston.   He
had lived in Boston several years, was appointed by Cromwell Gov. of Acadie, and
had a renewal of the office from Charles II.   He died,
however, in London, and made a later will there, so that
this one was void.   In this he remembers " my brother
Edmond Temple's children," " my brother Robert Nelson,"
" cousin John Nelson," " cousin Temple Nelson," " cousin
Adolphe Andrews which was in New England," " cousin
Mrs. Katherine Wolverston, daughter of Mrs. Adolphea
Longfield"; and also " cozen Thomas Temple, i. e. Dr
Temple's son," and "cousin John Temple."

As the descendants of one brother settled here and
intermarried with other prominent families, we will give a

brief genealogy of the family—in which it is to be noted
that though the fact of the title of baronet has kept the
general record plain, the items are somewhat confused.

A high antiquity has been claimed for the family, as
any peerage will show, and arms have been used referring
to its presumed descent from the Earls of Mercia, but it
will be sufficient for us to commence in comparatively
modern times.

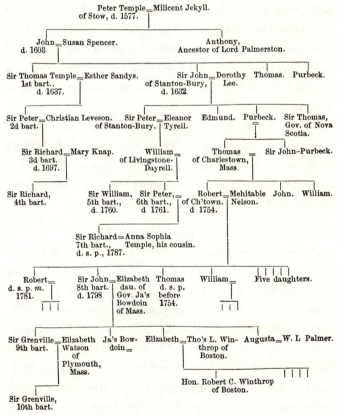

Note however that Burke would derive the American
branch from Edmund instead of Purbeck; and in a copy

of Johnson and Kimber's Baronetage, formerly owned and annotated by Sir John Temple, 8th bart., Purbeck is called son of the 2d bart. instead of cousin; yet the foregoing pedigree is most probable.

As to Edmund, I may say that Sir Thomas of Nova Scotia sold, in 1672, a house in Boston to "Stephen Temple of Selby in Northampshire, son and heir apparent of the late Colonel Edmund Temple." This may lead to a settlement of this branch, and we may add that in 1690 this house was sold by "John Temple of Sibbertoft in Northamptonshire, and Edmund Temple of the borough of Leicester, co. Leic." Edmund died about that time, as it is added "signed, sealed and delivered by Ellen, widow of Edmund Temple."

Lastly, the question arises, how did Sir Thomas Temple become a baronet? In 1656 he was styled Col. Thomas T., Esquire. It may be supposed that he was a baronet of Nova Scotia, as was also the eighth baronet, but neither are recorded in any list we have seen.

NELSON.

As to the Nelsons, it is said that Robert[1] Nelson of Gray's Inn, married Mary, sister of Sir Thomas of Nova Scotia, and had a son John[2] Nelson, who was in Boston as early as 1685. He married Elizabeth, daughter of William Tailer, Esq., of Boston, sister of Lt. Gov. Tailer. Her mother was sister of Lt. Gov. Stoughton. John[2] Nelson had a brother Temple, said to have died s. p. 1671. John had children, Temple and Pascal (the latter named for his uncle Edward Pascal, who m. Hester Temple) and four daughters, viz.: —— ——, who m. Capt. Thomas Steel, Elizabeth wife of Nathaniel Hubbard, Rebecca wife

of Henry Lloyd, and Mehitable who married her second
cousin, Robert Temple of Charlestown, Mass.

Temple[3] Nelson married Mary, daughter of Gov. John
Wentworth of New Hampshire, and had a son John, b.
1731, who died in Grenada, W. I.

The descendants of Rebecca Nelson and Henry Lloyd,
however, are still numerous.

EMMETT.

Rebecca Temple, dau. of Thomas Temple of Charlestown, married Dr. Christopher Emmett of Dublin. Their
children were Thomas and Robert, which Robert had
twelve children, the youngest being Robert Emmett, the
Irish patriot. The third son, Thomas-Addis Emmett,
came to America, as did the eldest son, Christopher-
Temple Emmett, who here married his second cousin,
Anne-Western, daughter of Robert Temple of Charlestown, and niece of the eighth baronet. Her sister married
Hans Blackwood, Lord Dufferin. Her mother was Harriet, daughter of Gov. Shirley of Massachusetts.

HERALD PAINTERS. NO. 3.

JOHN COLES.

Many families in New England possess old paintings of
their Coats of Arms, which appear all to have come out
of the same mill.

They are blazoned on a sheet of paper, about 14 inches
by 10. The shield generally (if not *always*) surmounted
by an esquire's, or closed, side-faced helmet, of blue and
gold, although an esquire's helmet should be plain steel.
Outside of the two lower corners of the shield are often

(if not *always*) two green branches. On the scroll, instead of motto, the words "By the name of Smith," and written under the whole "He beareth Argent a Lion rampant Azure, by the name of Smith," or whatever else the name and arms may be.

I have seen many of these drawings, but never considered them of any great value, because I believe they were painted by an artist who furnished arms in the same well-known manner as the modern herald painters.

Stott, an English engraver, living in Boston about 1840, told me that the first of these were the work of an Englishman in Boston, who was succeeded in the *trade* (certainly not *art*) by his son, who had then been dead he believed for half a century or more. He said they painted the helmets, shields and ornaments at their leisure, and filled them up when called for.

I have one in my possession which belonged to my mother's grandfather, a Bostonian, who died in 1776. It is mentioned in the Inventory of his effects, and is still in its original gilt frame. I know, however, that some must have been painted later than mine, as I have seen one in which the U. S. flag was introduced (queer heraldry) and we know the stars and stripes were only adopted in July, 1777.

With regard to the green branches below the shield, a gentleman once told me that his ancestors came from Wales. I inquired what reasons he had for saying so, as I knew, for a certainty, that they came from England. He said he had always heard so, and that there was an old painting of the family arms with *leeks* in it. I remarked that such was no proof and begged to see the drawing, and it was one of this kind.　　　　　　　　　　B. H. D.

Kilburn & Mallory, Engravers. A. Holland, Printer.

DIFFICILES SED FRUCTUOSÆ

Appleton,

Of Little Waldingfield,

And

Of Ipswich, Mass.

THE

HERALDIC JOURNAL;

RECORDING THE ARMORIAL BEARINGS AND GENEALOGIES
OF AMERICAN FAMILIES.

NO. VII. JULY, 1865.

THE FAMILY OF APPLETON.

Nearly all of this name in this country are descended
from Samuel Appleton, who settled at Ipswich in 1635.
He was born in 1586, at Little Waldingfield, Suffolk,
England, in and near which village his family had been
seated for many years. The earliest certain ancestor is
John Appulton, who was living in 1395. The family was
of gentle rank, and occupied the estate of Holbrook Hall.
The identification of the emigrant is perfect; perhaps the
most valuable evidence is the will of Robert Reyce, who
married his sister Mary, which mentions "my loving
Brother-in-Law Samuel Appleton, now dwelling at Ipswich in New England."

The shield, which accompanies this article, is copied
from several manuscripts in the British Museum, some of
them copies of the Heraldic Visitations of Suffolk. It
may be thus described: Quarterly of twelve ;—

    1. Appleton. Arg. a fess sa. between 3 apples gules,
        leaves and stalks vert.

7

2. Crane.   Arg. a fess between 3 cross-crosslets fitchée gules ; which brings

3.   1. Mollington.   Arg. a fess between 2 chevrons azure.

4.   2. Carbonel.   Gules, a cross arg in a border engrailed or.

5.   3. Boteler.   Arg. 3 covered cups per bend sa. cotised gules.

6. Mountney.   Azure, a bend between 6 martlets or.

7. Sexton.   Arg. 3 single wings gules 2 and 1.

8. Isaack.   Sa. a bend or, in sinister chief point a leopard's head of the second ; which brings

9.   1. Condy.   Barry wavy of 14 arg. and azure, over all 3 anchors or.

10.   2. Tuke.   Per chevron arg. and sa. 3 Cornish chough's heads erased counterchanged.

11.   3. Hawte.   Arg. a cross engrailed gules.

12.   4. Wheathill.   Per fess azure and or, a pale counterchanged, 3 lions rampant of the second.

Crests :*   Three pine-apples vert, the tops purfled or, in a crown ppr.

   An elephant's head couped sa. tusked and eared or, with a serpent entering his mouth vert.

On the monument of Sir Robert Crane, at Chilton, numbers four and five change places, seemingly for the better.   There appears also to be no doubt that two more

---

* It is difficult to say which of these crests has the greater authority. Both were in constant use in England, but the elephant's head has alone prevailed in this country.

coats should follow them, viz., Phelip—Quarterly gu. and arg. in the first quarter an eagle displayed or—and Erpingham—Vert, an inescutcheon in an orle of martlets arg.

An incomplete genealogy of the family may be found in the "Memorial of Samuel Appleton of Ipswich." Samuel, the emigrant, was fourth son of Thomas of Little Waldingfield. He married, at Preston, in 1615, Judith Everard, and seems to have had a second wife, Martha, before coming to New England. The male issue of his elder brothers is believed to be entirely extinct, in which case the technical head of the family is the present William Channing Appleton of Roxbury.

Among the epitaphs in the present number is a wood cut of the coat of arms on the tomb of Col. Samuel Appleton of Ipswich, a grandson of the emigrant. It presents a strange instance of false heraldry which cannot easily be explained. The execution is too good to be supposed the work of an ignorant country workman. Col. Appleton married Elizabeth Whittingham, and had two sons, Whittingham, of whom nothing is known, and Samuel, a merchant of Boston. He married Anna Gerrish, and at his death, in 1728, left an only child, Samuel, whose wife was Mary Wentworth of Portsmouth, and whose daughters, Anne and Rebecca, are presumed to have been his co-heiresses; *presumed*, as they had a brother Henry, of whom it is known that he lived to manhood, but not whether he married. Anne married Thomas Storrow, Captain in the British Army, who died at Boston about 1800, and Rebecca married Henry Barlow Brown of Woodstock, Vt.

RECENT FABRICATIONS OF ARMS.

In the May number of the Herald and Genealogist will be found a review of a book entitled "Popular Genealogists, or the art of Pedigree-making. Edinburgh: Edmondston and Douglas, 1865." Crown 8vo., pp 100.

From this article it appears that English genealogists are being aroused to the necessity of revising and correcting the published accounts of their prominent families, which have been repeated in a succession of popular books without verification. Any one who has tried to investigate the genealogy of any noted family, as of one of our Colonial Governors, or any of the prominent founders of these colonies, must have regretted not only that information was scanty but the authorities were at variance. It seems however that the case is even worse. Sir Bernard Burke, a compiler known to all our readers, has issued many volumes of a genealogical nature, and he seems to have been most egregiously deceived in the information given him.

His "Landed Gentry" has been especially examined by Americans, as giving particulars of those families in which a portion of our citizens hope to find their ancestry.

It is the only book which pretends to tell us about the great class of untitled *armigeri*, and it has been unhesitatingly quoted by most writers. The critic however thus deals with it—"The immense majority of the pedigrees in the Landed Gentry, including more especially the Scottish pedigrees, cannot, I fear, be characterized as otherwise than utterly worthless. The errors of the Peerage are as nothing to the fables which we encounter everywhere.

Families of notoriously obscure origin have their veins
filled with the blood of generations of royal personages of
the ancient and mythical world. There are not a few mi-
nute circumstantial genealogies of *soi-disant* old and distinguished families, with high-sounding titles, which families can be proved, by documentary evidence, never to
have had a corporeal existence. Other pedigrees contain
a small germ of truth, eked out with a mass of fiction, in
the proportion of Falstaff's bread and sack; while an
extreme minuteness of detail is often combined with reck-
less disregard of dates and historical possibilities."

In proof of this, the reviewer cites particularly, the
Coulthart pedigree, which has been pushed into all of
Burke's works, and even issued by itself, in magnificent
form. The family claimed to rank among the best Scottish families, and the claim was established by charters,
seals, and the other evidence. It now seems there never
was such a barony, clan or arms, and the pedigree maker
merely copied old charters from a printed book, altering
the names and localities to suit his pedigree. The family, probably, cannot be traced over four generations.

In aid of this fraud, these imaginary marriages have
been put into Peerages, and the arms have been copied
and quoted in so many books, that nearly every recent
writer has found a place for them. The arms are first
quoted by Burke in 1844, and since that date the impost-
ure has gone on unchallenged.

This little book has apparently created much discussion, and various plans are proposed for the prevention of
frauds hereafter. A writer in a late number of Notes
and Queries proposes a catalogue of persons, whose arms

or pedigrees are registered in the College of Arms. He adds that such a volume for Ireland was published by William Skey, St. Patrick Pursuivant, and Registrar of the Heralds' Office, with the title of "The Heraldic Calendar, a List of the Nobility and Gentry, whose Arms are registered, and pedigrees recorded in the Heralds' Office, Ireland. Dublin: 1846. 8vo."

It certainly seems strange that the only official lists should be closed to the public. Any one who examines the county histories will be surprised at the great changes wrought by the last two centuries; and it seems a good time now, to place on record the names of the old families, ere they be entirely overshadowed by the modern pretenders. To Americans such a work will be deeply interesting, as it cannot be doubted that many of the early settlers here have become the representatives of their families.

OFFICIAL SEALS.

These arms are on the seal of Governor Simon Bradstreet, who succeeded Leverett, in 1679. He was born, March, 1603, at Horbling, in Lincolnshire, where his father, Simon, was minister; was bred at Emmanuel College, Camb., A. B. 1620, and A. M. 1624. He came to New England in 1630, and was constantly in the government. He married first, Ann, dau. of Gov. Thomas Dudley, and secondly, Ann, dau. of Emmanuel Downing, and widow of Capt. Joseph Gardner. His descendants are numerous; though some of the name undoubtedly spring from Humphrey, who came from Ipswich, Eng., in 1634.

THE SCOTT FAMILY.

There are several reasons which lead us to believe that one or more branches of the Scotts of Scott's Hall, co. Kent, settled in New England. There are now extant two ancient manuscript pedigrees of the family, one of which expressly states the fact, and we will consider this first. This roll is now in the possession of Rev. Dr. Jenks, and contains several generations of the ancestors of Sir William[1] Scott, who married Anne, daughter of Reginald Pimpe.

He had several sons, of whom we mention Sir Reginald[2] and Richard.[2]

Sir Reginald[2] Scott, by his second wife Mary, dau. of Sir Brian Towke, had Sir William,[3] Ambassador to Turkey and to Florence, who married Mary Howard, daughter of Charles, Earl of Nottingham. Their children were, Hon. John[4] Scott, Surveyor General to Charles I., and Sir Edward[4] Scott of Scott's Hall, who died about 1645, leaving a son, Edward[5] Scott, married to Katherine, dau. of George, Lord Goring.

Hon. John[4] Scott married a daughter of Sir George Wortup, and had sons, John,[5] Joseph,[5] (who d. *s. p.*), and Thomas, (living 1665), of these, John[5] married Deborah, daughter of Thurston Rayner of Suffolk, and lived at Ashfordun, Long Island. On the Pedigree, the arms of this John impale Rayner, viz., argent, on a chief azure, two estoiles gold. We do not find that he married here, but Thurston Rayner was from Ipswich, co. Suffolk, aged 40 in 1634, and these arms may enable us to trace his family.

In the Hutchinson Papers, p. 380, (old edition), is a copy of a petition from this John Scott, in which he says that his father sold an estate of £2200 pr. ann., in 1641, and lent £14,300 to the King, and lost his life in the service. Also, that he himself was arrested, and, after paying £500, was sent to New England, under charge of "one Downing." Further, that he lived on Long Island, and bought near one third part of it. The King, in 1663, accordingly ordered inquiry to be made to see what could be done for Scott, who desired to be made Governor. It seems Scott afterwards claimed the place or the land, and was imprisoned therefor; but the dispute was settled, as the island was included in the grant to the Duke of York.

On this MS. is a shield of eight quarterings, viz:

1. Argent, three Catherine wheels sable, a bordure engrailed gules.
2. Barry of six, argent and gules, a chief vaire.
3. Purpure, a lion rampant and crowned, gold.
4. Chequy, gold and azure.
5. Argent, guttée de sang, a saltire sable.
6. Argent, a bend double cottised, gules.
7. Gules a fesse between six cross-crosslets fitchée, argent.
8. Gules, a chevron between three trefoils argent.

A second manuscript is in the possession of the descendants of Judge James Scott of Newport, R. I. In this the pedigree is continued, in the line of Richard² Scott, third son of Sir John Scott and Anne Pimpe.

This Richard[2] Scott married a dau. of George Wetten-
hall of East Pelham, and had several sons; of whom
Edward,[3] third son, married Mary, dau. of John Warren.
Their son was Edward[4] Scott of Glemsford, co. Suff., who
m. Elizabeth Grome of Suff., and had Edward[5] and
Richard.[5] Edward[5] Scott of Glemsford m. Sarah, sister of
Richard Carter of Brookhall, co. Essex, and had Edward,[6]
Richard,[6] Frederick,[6] and Matthew.[6] It is thought that
Judge Edward Scott was the son of one of these last
named four brothers; he came to Newport, about 1710.

It has also been thought that Richard[5] Scott, son of
Edward[4] S. of Glemsford, was the person who came to
Boston, in 1634, and married Catherine, dau. of Rev.
Edward Marbury, sister of the famous Anne Hutchinson.
He was a quaker and removed to R. I., where his descend-
ants have been in good standing. However, these affil-
iations need confirmation by researches in England; as
the name is common both in England and this country.

We may further note that Thurston Rayner came from
Ipswich, co. Suff., in 1634, and in the same ship came
Thomas Scott, aged 40, his wife Elizabeth, and children,
Elizabeth, aged 9, Abigail, 7, and Thomas, 6. These
were possibly relatives of John Scott of Long Island.

In the same ship were Martha Scott, aged 60, supposed
to be mother of Thomas, and Richard Kimball, aged 39,
whom Thomas in his will calls "brother."

Richard Kimball, aged 39, had wife Ursula, children
Henry, aged 15, Richard, 11, Mary, 9, Martha, 5, John,
3, Thomas, 1. An Elizabeth Kimball, aged 13, also a
passenger, was under the care of Thomas Scott. By this
vessel also came Henry Kimball and his family.

The following cut is from the MS. belonging to Judge Edward Scott. It differs slightly in the quartering from the Long Island MS.

MONUMENTAL INSCRIPTIONS.

MARBLEHEAD.

In this yard we find but one coat of arms, viz., that on the upright tombstone of John Legg. The inscription is all within a heart-shaped border, and reads thus:

John Legg Esq[r]. died y[e]
8th of Octob[r] in y[e] 74th year of
his age.

The will of John Legg, on file at Salem, mentions his daughters, Mary, wife of Edward Brattle, and Elizabeth Browne. He probably had no sons. The will bears a fine impression of his seal, with the same arms here given, a stag's head cabossed, and having a helmet and wreath but no crest.

IPSWICH. (CONCLUDED.)

IV.

HERE LYES INTERRED
THE BODY OF COL^{ONL}
SAMUEL APPLETON ESQ^R
WHO DEPARTED THIS
LIFE OCTOBER 30 MDCCXXV
ÆTATIS SUÆ LXXI.

HERALD PAINTERS. NO. 3.

JOHN COLES.

In our last number we published a letter in reference to this artist. He and his son continued to practice the art, for many years, and the greater number of paintings now extant in New England are by them.

It is hardly necessary for us to say, that these are totally worthless, and in fact, any arms which were not in use prior to 1750 or 1760, should be summarily dismissed, as a rule. We may make a few exceptions, when the position of a family in the preceeding generations render the possession of arms probable, but it is evident that Coles established a fashion for these pictures, and after that date everything is highly suspicious.

We may add to this the following note, from Rev. Dr. Jenks of Boston. " With respect to your question concerning Mr. Coles, I can reply that I knew him in early life, and often called on him, as I remember, in making inquiries about heraldry." " Mr. Coles's authorities for his drawings of coats of arms were very scanty, being, as I have supposed, confined to Guillim's folio volume. And he was in the habit of giving arms to applicants, whenever he found them assigned in that book to the family name of his employer, without much, if any, genealogical research or inquiry. If no crest were found in Guillim, he did not hesitate to raise on the torse our national flag. His charge for furnishing such drawings, of folio size, was I recollect, a guinea."

In the Boston Directory for 1800, we find the name of " John Coles, Heraldry painter," and it continues until

1813, and possibly a little later. From 1806, also, we find John Coles, Jr., a miniature and portrait painter. Both disappear in 1826.

THE BOWES FAMILY.

 In the Genealogical Register, X. 82, will be found a letter in relation to this family. The pedigree begins with Nicholas[1] Bowes, who d. in 1721, leaving by his wife, Martha Remington, a son Nicholas,[2] b. 1706, minister at Bedford, Mass., who married Lucy Hancock, daughter of Rev. John H. of Lexington. Their son, William,[3] b. 1734, married Mary, dau. of William Stoddard, and had William,[4] b. 1771, who married Harriet, dau. of Rev. John Troutbeck. William[3] was a Loyalist, and died in London, where his descendants now live.

The letter speaks of seals and a book plate of arms still preserved. We are happy to confirm this by the above cut, copied from the seal on the will of the first Nicholas Bowes, now on record at Boston. In it he mentions his wife, Martha, and her brother Jonathan Remington, Esq., sons William and Nicholas, (to which latter he leaves his seal ring,) daughter Dorcas, &c.

The seal has the field of the Bowes arms ermine.

HERALDIC NOTES AND QUERIES.

XXI.

The following notes on N. E. Heraldry are taken from "Prestwich's Respublica, &c., &c., &c." In Chap. VIII.,

"The Armorial Bearings belonging to the sundry Commanders or Captains of Companies, &c., that bare coronets, flags, and pennons, as of English, Scotch, Irish, American, and French, in the Armies of the Commonwealth," we find CXXII., Captain-major Benjamin Cayne, of New England. Azure; an eagle displayed Argent; crest, on a wreath Argent and Azure, a demi griffin issuant, with wing raised and but one talon, brown colour.

In another part of the volume, also, Colonel John Dixwell, Governor of Dover Castle. Arms, Argent; a chevron Gules, between three fleurs-de-lis Sable.

The former of these is evidently the son of Robert Keayne of Boston, of whom Savage says that he "was a major, went home," i. e., to England.

The other is the regicide, and the only one of the three refugees in this country, who is known to have left descendants here.   W. S. A.

XXII.

I have recently seen a deed of Stephen Minot, dated in 1728, witnessed by Addington Davenport and Christian Wainwright, which has a seal bearing the Wainwright arms as already described (p. 89), from the Ipswich graveyard. This seal is of interest, not only as another example of the use of arms by this family, but because it adds the crest, viz., a lion rampant holding a halbert upright.

A. C. G., JR.

XXIII.

The following letter, copied from the New York Herald, seems to merit preservation:

Lowville, Lewis county, N. Y., June 26, 1865.

The letter, of which I enclose a copy, contains a few items of family history interesting at present in connection with the public and personal history of its writer, now an applicant for the national pardon. The facts, I think, have not appeared, and the copy is at your service. The envelope bears the frank of Alexander, as a member of Congress.   Yours, truly

W. HUDSON STEPHENS.

LETTER FROM MR. STEPHENS.

Washington, D. C., Feb. 11. 1854.

Dear Sir—Your letter of the 6th inst., was received yesterday. All the information I can give you on the point is this; my grandfather's name was Alexander Stephens; he was born in 1720, somewhere in England, but where I do not know; he emigrated to this country about 1745 and settled in Pennsylvania, or at least he lived in that State just before and during the Revolutionary war. He married the daughter of Andrew Baskins, who owned the place at the mouth of the Juniata river, a very noted stand. After the war he moved to Georgia, where he lived until 1813; he died at ninety-three years of age. If he had any relatives in this country I am not aware of it. The "Stevens" are Welch, I think; but whether originally from the same stock as the "Stephens," I am unable to give an opinion. The name Stephens appears early in English history. Yours, respectfully,

ALEXANDER H. STEPHENS.

W. H. Stephens, Copenhagen, N. Y.

XXIV.

Of the many seals on the wills at the Suffolk Probate Office, hardly one is more peculiar than the one of which we here present a fac-simile. It occurs on two wills, both of Dorchester people, and both dated in 1700.

The first is that of James Blake, and the witnesses are

Nathaniel Clap,	Ebenezer Clap,
Humphrey Atherton,	Benjamin Blackman,
Noah Beeman,	Hannah Bartlett.

The other will is that of Isaac Jones, witnessed by

John Capen,	Dorcas Davenport,
Ebenezer Williams,	Amos Gates.

It will be noted that no witness is common to both wills, nor is the handwriting of both documents the same.

We are therefore left without a clue to the probable owner of the seal; which seal, we may remark, is beautifully cut, and clearly heraldic.

We can find no English coat-of-arms resembling this, and presume it must have belonged to some foreign resident at Dorchester at the time. A search on the records of the town might possibly afford a clue.

————

We may add that this seal and that of Nicholas Bowes are a portion of those found at the Suffolk Probate Office by our associate, Mr. Perkins. It is intended to continue the publication of these valuable evidences, and, wherever practicable, to annex engravings of the seals.

THE

HERALDIC JOURNAL;

RECORDING THE ARMORIAL BEARINGS AND GENEALOGIES
OF AMERICAN FAMILIES.

NO. VIII. AUGUST, 1865.

THE GORE ROLL OF ARMS.

We propose to lay before our readers a transcript of a very valuable collection of the arms of New England families, made during the last century. The original MS. is at present inaccessible, but we have the advantage of a very careful copy, painted by Isaac Child, Esq., a gentleman well versed in the rules of Heraldry, and his transcript may be accepted as entirely authentic.

The earliest coats recorded are dated in 1701 and 1702, the latest in 1724; it seems highly probable that the dates refer to the time when the memoranda were made, because there is no other reason for affixing a special date. Thus the first coat is that of Deane Winthrop of Pulling Point, 1701. Certainly this was not the first appearance of the Winthrop arms, nor was Deane the head of the family at the time. Again, the arms were probably recorded at the dates affixed, since the earliest name of the Gores entered in the book was that of Samuel Gore, or John Gore, both born after 1750, and at this late

8

date he could hardly have collected the information placed under the shields. These inscriptions are also peculiar, since they give only the rank of the bearer at the time named. For example, Spencer Phips, 1710, is called one of the Council and Justice of the Peace. Would any one in 1778, have omitted the fact that Phips became Lieut. Governor of the State in 1734?

It is then desirable to know who was the artist at so early a date. Mr. Child's copy says, made by *John* Gore, but it is certain that an English heraldic MS. which was preserved with this book, had inscribed in it the name of *Samuel* Gore. Mr. Drake has also a bill dated in 1783, from Samuel Gore to Gov. John Hancock, in which these items occur:

> To painting chariot body and wheels,   £15
> " painting sett of coach wheels,   1.4
> " drawing arms on paper,   3

From this we may argue that Samuel[5] was probably the painter. I presume he was the son of John[4] and Frances (Pinkney) Gore, who were married in 1743, and that John was the son of Obadiah[3] and Sarah (Kilby) Gore, and born 29 Dec., 1718. Savage records that the first of the name here was John[1] of Roxbury, 1635, who d. 1657. His son Samuel[2] m. Elizabeth Weld, and died in 1692, leaving sons Samuel[3] and Obadiah,[3] the latter b. 1688. This Obadiah[3] was grandfather of the presumed artist. The successive generations seem to have been carpenters and housewrights, nor can we learn from the inventories any mention of this book.

The only suggestion we can make is, that since the dates under so many of these shields coincide with the

death of the bearers, the painter may have been employed
to engrave the coffin-plates, or to furnish hatchments or
banners, both of which we know were used here at the
funerals of noted citizens.

We give the arms as they stand in Mr. Child's copy,
though many of them are of families not resident here, as
this may show the amount of credit to be given to the
artist. Several of the coats were left unfinished, and
probably some were not distinguishable. Such as it is,
however, the roll constitutes a very valuable addition to
our sources of information, and research seems to confirm
its correctness.

GORE'S LIST.

1. Dean Winthrop of Pulling Point, co. Suffolk, 1701.
   Argent, three chevrons gules, over all a lion rampant
   sable.
   Crest, on a mount vert, a hare courant ppr.
   [Note. Deane was the sixth son of Gov. John
   Winthrop of Mass., and died in 1704.]

2. Capt. Henry Crafts, son of the late Duke of Mon-
   mouth, Commander of her maj^y ship Gosport, 1702.
   Lozenzy, argent and azure, a crescent for difference.
   Crest, a demi-lion, gules.

3. Richard Midcot of Boston, Esq., county of Suffolk.
   One of his Majesty's Council of the Province of
   Mass., 1702.
   Azure, an eagle displayed argent; on a chief gules,
   three escallops gold.
   Crest, a demi-eagle displayed, holding in the beak
   an escallop.
   [Note. Richard Middlecott came from Warminster,

co. Wilts, and died in 1704. BURKE gives these
arms to a Lincolnshire family.]

4. Dr. John Owen of the Island of Antigua, 1702.
    Gules, a boar argent, collared and chained to a holly
        bush, on a mount in base ppr.
    Crest, a boar's head palewise, couped.

5. Anna, wife of Peter Sargent, Esq., of Boston, 1702.
        Sargent and Shrimpton. The shield is Sargent
        (See No. 31) impaling.
    Argent on a cross sable, five escallops of the field.
    Crest, a demi-lion azure, holding in his paws an
        escallop.

6. John Jay (or Joy) of Medford, county of Middlesex,
        1702.
    Argent, a chevron azure, on a chief of the second
        three martlets of the field.
    Crest, a cormorant's head.
        [This gentleman has yet to be traced.]

7. John Legg of Boston, Esq., county of Suffolk.
    Sable, a buck's head, cabossed argent.
    Crest, out of a coronet gold, five ostrich feathers azure.
        [This family was of Marblehead, as will be seen
    by the Epitaph published in our July number.]

8. Madame Anna Leverit, widow of John Leverit, Esq.,
        Gov. of the Colony of Mass., 1682.
    1st Argent, a chevron between three leverets, sable.
        Impaling, 2nd, Gold, on a cross gules, five bells
        argent.
    Crest, a scull.
        [Note. The arms impaled are certainly those of
    Sedgewick. Savage says Leverett married *Sarah*
    Sedgewick, dau. or sister of Major Robert S.]

9. Edward Brattle of Marblehead, county of Essex. Brattle and Legg, 1707.

Gules, a chevron, gold, between three battle axes, argent.

Crest, a dexter arm, vambraced and embowed, grasping a battle-axe.

The impalement is of the Legg arms, described in No. 7.

[Note. This Edward was a younger brother of Thomas, (see No. 30,) and married Mary, daughter of John Legg.]

10. Anna, wife of John Richards, Esq., one of his Majesty's Councillors of the Province of Mass. Richards and Winthrop, 1707.

Argent, four lozenges conjoined in fesse, gules, between two bars, (sable?). Impaling, Winthrop, as in No. 1.

No crest.

[John Richards who used a seal in 1685, was son of Thomas Richards of Dorchester, whose widow Welthian also used them on her will in 1679.]

11. Charles Frost of Boston, 1707. Frost and Davis. The shield is impaled, being

1, Frost. Argent, a chevron gules, between three trefoils slipped.

2d, Davis. A stag trippant gold.

Crest, a head, within sprigs of (laurel?).

[This was Charles Frost, b. 1683, son of John and grandson of Nicholas F. of Kittery, who was born at Tiverton, co. Devon, about 1595.]

12. Nathaniel Norden, Esq., of Marblehead, one of his Majesty's Council. Norden and Lat . . . . .

Argent, on a fesse gules between three beavers
passant, a crosslet fitchée between two fleurs-de-
lys, gold.

Crest, a demi-beaver, holding in his mouth a branch
of leaves.

The impalement is Gules, a cross patonce argent.

[This is the Latimer arms, and I find he married
Mary, daughter of Christopher Latimer, or Lattimore
of Marblehead.   Norden died in 1727.]

13. Lady Mary, formerly wife to Sir William Phips,
Knt., Governor of the Province of Mass., ...
of Peter Sargent, Esq., of His Majesty's Council.
Sargent and Spencer, 1705.

The shield is Sargent (See No. 31) impaling quarterly
argent and gules—in the second and third quarters
a fret gold—over all, on a bend sable, three escallops gold.

Crest, out of a ducal coronet a griffin's head, gorged
with a bar gemelle, gules between two wings
expanded.

[Note. Peter Sargent came from London, 1667,
and though Savage does not record his first wife,
she would seem to have been Anna Shrimpton.
His second wife, the widow of Gov. Phips, was
daughter of Roger Spencer of Saco, Maine, 1652.
Another daughter m. Dr. David Bennett, and had
Spencer Bennett, who took the name of his uncle
Phips, and is recorded in the next article.

As to the Sargent arms we may note that Peter
used them in 1693, as appears by his seal on a power
of attorney, now at Salem.]

14. Anthony Chickley, Esq., Attorney-General of the
Province of Mass., 1706.

Azure, a chevron between three mullets, gold.

No crest.

[He died in 1708. He was bapt. 31 July, 1636,
at Preston-Capes, North-Hants, England, and was the
son of William and Elizabeth Checkley. From the
arms the family may have been related to that of the
famous Archbishop Chichele.]

15. John Chamberlain, Esq., of the Island of Antigua,
1707.

Gules, an inescutcheon between eight mullets in orle,
argent.

Crest, out of a ducal coronet gold, an ass's head,
argent.

16. John Paul of Boston, Mass., 1709.

Azure, a lion rampant, argent, between eight fleurs-
de-lys in orle, gold.

Crest, a stag's head, cabossed gules.

[Note. This is evidently the arms of John Pool,
or Poole. See Dorchester Epitaphs, ante, p. 9.]

17. Edward E   , Esq., of Pembrouck in Wales.
Gov. of the Province of Pennsylvania, 1705.

Azure, a winged antelope, gold.

Crest, a stag's head erased, gold.

18. William Skinner of London, merchant, 1707.

Sable, a chevron, gold, between three griffin's heads,
erased argent, a crescent for difference.

Crest, a griffin's head erased, argent, holding in the
beak a hand couped gules.

19. Henry Harvie, Fort Major of Provence Newfoundland, 1708.

Gules, on a bend argent, three trefoils slipped, azure.
Crest, a leopard ermine, holding in the dexter paw a
trefoil slipped, azure.

20. Widow Mary Apthorp, widow of Charles Apthorp
of Boston, 1709.

1st, Per pale nebuly argent and azure, in fesse two
mullets, counterchanged. Impaling 2d, Quarterly, —— and ——, four eagles displayed gules.
No crest.

21. Spencer Phips, Esq., of Cambridge, county of Middlesex, one of His Majesty's Council, and Justice
of the Peace for the County, 1710.

Sable, a trefoil slipped ermine, between eight mullets,
argent.

Crest, a bear's paw, sable, holding a trefoil slipped
ermine.

[Note.   These arms were used by Sir Wm. Phips,
and very probably were granted him. The same
are borne by the Marquess of Normanby, but despite
the assertions of the Peerages, his ancestor, Constantine Phipps, was not a son of our Governor, and
probably only most remotely connected. We hope
our English friends will explain this matter more
satisfactorily.]

22. John Foster, Esq., Col. of the Life to the Earl of
Bellemont, Governor of the Province of Mass.,
Justice of the Common Pleas for the County of
Suffolk, and one of His Majesty's Council, 1710.

Argent, a chevron vert, between three bugle-horns,
stringed, sable.

Crest, a dexter arm embowed, the hand grasping a
spear.

23. Susannah, widow of John Foster, Esq., of Boston. Foster and Hawkins, 1710.

1st, Foster, as in No. 22.

Impaling 2nd, Argent on a saltire sable, five fleurs-de-lys, gold.

Crest, on a mound vert, a hind lodged ppr.

[This seems to be an error in the Christian name. *Abigail*, dau. of Thomas Hawkins, married John Foster, and died in 1711.]

24. Gurdon Saltonstall, Esq., Gov. of the Colony of Connecticut, 1742. Saltonstall and Whit . . . . . (Whittingham).

1st, Gold, a bend between two eagles displayed, sable.

Impaling 2nd, Argent, a fesse (azure?) over all a lion rampant, gules.

Crest, out of a ducal coronet, gold, a pelican's head, vulning its breast.

[Note. Gov. Saltonstall, son of Nathaniel, and grandson of Richard Saltonstall, Jr., and Meriell Gurdon, married, for his third wife, Mary, dau. of William Whittingham, and widow of Wm. Clarke. The grandfather was John W., who was son of Baruch W., and grandson of the distinguished Reformer, William Whittingham, Dean of Durham.]

25. Samuel White of Boston, merchant, 1712.

Gules, a chevron between three boar's heads, couped, argent.

Crest, out of a mural coronet gules, a boar's head argent.

[This has also to be identified.]

26. William Taylor, Esq., Col. of the Second Regiment of Foot, at the taking of the Government of Port Royal, afterward Lt.-Gov. of the Province, and one of the Council, 1711.

Per saltire, gold and gules, an eagle displayed.

Crest, a demi-eagle displayed, gules, double headed, and in each beak a cross-crosslet.

[William Taylor was the son of William Taylor, by his wife Rebecca Stoughton. He died in 1732. These arms were used by him on his seal.]

27. James Cutting of Barbadoes, merchant, 1712.

Azure, two swords argent in saltire, hilted gold—on a chief of the second, three lions rampant of the field.

28. Elizabeth, wife of Simeon Stoddard, Esq., of Boston, merchant, 1712. Stoddard and En . . . (Evance?).

1st Sable, three estoiles within a bordure, argent.

Impaling 2d, Argent, a chevron between three fleurs-de-lys, sable.

Crest, a sinister arm, embowed, habited gules, holding in the hand the stalk of a flower.

29. Gillis Dyer, Esq., Colonel of the Life-guard to his Excellency Joseph Dudley, Esq., Governor of the Province; Sheriff of the County of Suffolk, 1713.

Argent, on a bend cottised azure, three crescents gold.

Crest, a mailed arm, gauntleted, holding a dagger upright, hilted gold.

[Giles Dyer died 12 August, 1713.]

30. Thomas Brattle, Esq., Treasurer of Harvard College, and Fellow of the Royal Society, at Boston, in the County of Suffolk, 1713.

Gules, a chevron gold between three battle-axes, argent.

Crest, a dexter arm, embowed, vambraced, holding in the hand a battle-axe, gold.

[He was son of Thomas Brattle of Charlestown, who died in 1683, the wealthiest man probably in the Colony, says Savage.]

31. Peter Sargent, Esq., one of His Majesty's Council for the Province of Mass., 1714.

Argent, a chevron between three dolphins embowed, sable.

Crest, a bird rising.

[He was from London, 1667, and d. *s. p.* 1714. See No. 13.]

32. Elizabeth, wife of Simeon Stoddard, Esq., of Boston, 1714. Stoddard and Roberts.

Stoddard impaling—Per pale argent and gules, a lion rampant, sable.

Crest, a stag's head erased, per fesse (argent and gules).

[These impalements are difficult of explanation. Simeon was son of Anthony Stoddard, and married 1st, Mary ———, who d. 1708. He m. 2d, May, 1709, Elizabeth, widow of Col. Samuel Shrimpton, who d. April, 1713. Third, in May, 1715, Mehitable (Minot) widow of Peter Sargent. His second wife, the widow Shrimpton, was dau. of widow Elizabeth Roberts of London.]

33. Capt. Thomas Richards of Boston, in the county of Suffolk, 1714.

Argent, four lozenges, conjoined in fesse gules, between two bars sable.

No crest.

[This was probably the son of James Richards of
Hartford, and nephew of John R. (shield No. 10,
ante.) He died December, 1714. James Richards'
tomb at Hartford, we are informed, bears these arms.]

34. Isaac Addington, Esq., Secretary of the Prov. of
Mass., Judge of Probate for county of Suffolk,
Justice of the Peace, and one of his Majesty's
Council, 1715. Addington and Norton.

1. Per pale ermine and erminois, on a chevron,
counterchanged, four lozenges, between three
fleurs-de-lys.

Impaling, Gules a fret argent, over all a bend vairy
gold and gules.

Crest, a wild-cat? ermine.

[Isaac Addington was son of Isaac Addington by
his wife Anne Leverett. He married, first, Elizabeth, dau. of Griffith Bowen of London, and secondly, Elizabeth, widow of John Wainwright, and dau.
of William Norton. She was niece of Rev. John
Norton, and this branch was from the Nortons of
Sharpenhow, co. Bedford.]

35. Elizabeth, wife of Elisha Cook of Boston, Esq.
Cook and Leverett, 1715.

Cook (as in No. 36) impaling Leverett.

[She was daughter of Gov. John Leverett.]

36. Elisha Cook of Boston, Esq., one of his Majesty's
Council of the Province of Mass., 1715.

Gold, a chevron chequy azure and of the field,
between three cinquefoils of the second.

Crest, a unicorn's head, gold, between two wings
endorsed, azure.

[Elisha Cook was son of Richard of Boston, said
to have come from Gloucestershire. He died Oct.
1715. His son, of the same name, married the dau.
of Richard Middlecot.]

37. Andrew Belcher, Esq., Commissary General of the
Province of Mass., and one of his Majesty's
Council, 1717.

Gold, three pales gules, a chief vair.

Crest, a greyhound's head erased, ermine, with a
collar gules, and ring, (gold?).

[Andrew Belcher, a settler here in 1639, married
Elizabeth, daughter of Nicholas Danforth, and had
Andrew, the person here recorded, who married Sarah, daughter of Jonathan Gilbert of Hartford. He
died in Oct., 1717, having acquired a large fortune.
His son Jonathan was the Governor of Mass. These
arms are on Andrew Belcher's seal on his will.]

38. Joseph Lemon of Charlestown, in the County of
Middlesex, 1717.

Azure, a fesse between three dolphins embowed,
argent, an annulet for difference.

Crest, a pelican in her nest, feeding her young.

[At p. 48 will be found a notice of the Lemmon
family.]

39. George Caldwell of London, merchant, now of Boston,
co. Suffolk, 1717. Caldwell and Mane.

The first coat is quarterly, viz.: 1. Per pale crenellé
gules and argent, three bear's paws erased.

2. Three fleurs-de-lys.

3 and 4. Argent, a galley sable.

Over all a pallet ermine.

Impaling. Per chevron flory, sable and gold, in chief three bezants, in base the stump of a tree? sable.

Crest, a hand gauntleted, holding a bear's paw erased.

[This must be a foreign coat, the style being so strange.]

40. Elisha Hutchinson, Esq., Col. of the First Regiment of Foot in the co. of Suff., Capt. of Castle William, Chief Justice of the Court of Common Pleas in the co. of Suff., and one of the Council, 1717.

Per pale gules and argent, a lion rampant, argent, between eight crosses-croslet gold.

Crest, out of a ducal coronet, gold, a cockatrice vert, combed gules.

[He was the son of Edward Hutchinson of Boston, co. Linc., and of Boston, N. E. He died Dec., 1717. His grandson was Governor of Massachusetts.]

41. Waight Winthrop, Esq., Maj.-General of the Province of Mass., Chief Justice of the Court of Assize, and one of his Majesty's council, 1717.

Arms as No. 1. Motto, Spes Vincit Thronum.

[Wait-Still Winthrop was son of Gov. John W. of Conn., and grandson of Gov. John of Mass., hence nephew of Deane Winthrop, (shield No. 1.) He died November, 1717.]

42. Nicholas Paige of Rumney Marsh, Col. of the Second Regiment of Foot in the County of Suffolk, 1717.

Argent, on a bend, three eagles displayed.

Crest, a demi-eagle, displayed.

[He was from Plymouth, co. Devon, 1665, and married Anne, widow of Edward Lane, niece of Gov. Joseph Dudley. He died late in 1717.]

43. John Huse, Esq., of Salem, in the County of Essex, merchant, 1717.

Argent, an estoille of sixteen points, gules.

Crest, three trees proper.

44. Capt. John Browne of Salem, in the County of Essex, merchant, 1718.

Argent, on a bend double cottisid, three eagles displayed, a crescent for difference.

Crest, an eagle displayed.

[This John Browne has not yet been distinguished from others of the name.]

45. Daniel Wibond of Boston, Capt. of Marines on board his Majesty's ship Chester, 1717.

Sable, a fesse (gold?) between three swans argent, membered gules.

Crest, a dragon's head, apparently.

[These arms are those of Wyborn, co. Kent.]

46. Eliakim Hutchinson, Esq., one of his Majesty's Council for the Province of Mass., 1718.

Arms as in No. 40, but with a label of three points, argent, over all.

[Eliakim was son of Richard Hutchinson, a wealthy ironmonger of London, and cousin of Edward of Boston. He died in 1718, probably.]

47. Robert Barker of Ipswich, co. of Suffolk, Great Britain, 1718.

Per fesse nebuly, azure and sable, three martlets, gold, a canton ermine.

Crest, a hind, lodged?

[See No. 62.]

48. Sir Thomas Lucas of Colchester, Great Britain, 1718.
   Argent, a fesse between six annulets, gules, three in
   chief, as many in base.
   Crest, out of a ducal coronet, gold, a demi-griffin,
   with wings expanded, gules.
   [See No. 62.]

49. John Britton of Tollingham, Great Britain, impaled
   on the dexter side with Choute, 1718.
   1st, Chute, viz., Gules, three swords bar wise, the
   points to the dexter, argent.
   Impaling 2d, Britton: Quarterly, per fesse indented,
   argent and gules, in the first quarter, a mullet sable.
   Crest, a demi-lion collared, therefrom a cord, bowed,
   and held in the dexter paw.
   [See No. 62.]

50. John Wood of Westlitton in Yorkshire, Great Britain,
   1718.
   Sable, on a bend argent, three fleurs-de-lys of the
   field, a crescent for difference.
   Crest, a wolf's head erased, sable, collared gold.
   [See No. 62.]

51. Edward Sturton, Esq., Great Britain, 1718.
   Sable, a bend gold between six plates.
   Crest, a demi-friar, holding in the dexter hand a
   whip with three lashes.
   [See No. 62.]

52. Robert Chichester of Raley, in the co. of Devon in
   Great Britain, 1718.
   Chequy gold and gules, a chief vairy gold and gules.
   Crest, a heron rising, holding an eel in the beak.
   [See No. 62.]

THE
HERALDIC JOURNAL;

RECORDING THE ARMORIAL BEARINGS AND GENEALOGIES
OF AMERICAN FAMILIES.

NO. IX. SEPTEMBER, 1865.

THE GORE ROLL OF ARMS.

[Concluded.]

53. Joshua Gee of Boston, co. Suffolk, shipwright, 1720.
Gee and Thatcher.

1st, on a chevron, between three leopard's faces, as
many fleurs-de-lys.

2d, a cross moline, on a chief three grasshoppers.

Crest, a wolf stataut reguardant, ermine.

[Joshua Gee was son of Peter Gee of Boston, 1667.
Savage seems to make some confusion in the marriages, by saying that Joshua m. Elizabeth, dau. of
Rev. Thomas Thornton, but it seems that he married
Elizabeth, dau. of Judah Thatcher, and gr. dau.
of Thornton. She afterwards became the third
wife of Rev. Peter Thatcher of Milton, her second
cousin.

The relation was this, Thomas Thatcher of Plymouth, Mass., was son of Rev. Peter, rector of St.
Edmund's, Salisbury, co. Wilts, and nephew of

9

Anthony; Judah was son of Anthony Thatcher, and
cousin of Thomas; Rev. Peter, son of Thomas, and
Elizabeth, dau. of Judah, were thus second cousins.
These Thatcher arms are confirmed by the Suffolk
Wills, hereafter to be printed.]

54.   Wigglesworth Sweetser of Boston, co. of Suffolk,
1720.

Argent, on a fesse azure, three saltires couped, gold.

[Seth Sweetser came in 1637, aged 31, from
Tring, co. Hertford. His son Benjamin m. Abigail,
probably dau. of Edward Wigglesworth, and had a
son Wigglesworth Sweetser, who had a son of the
same names.]

55.   Sir John Barkley of Stratton in Somersetshire, Gr.
Britain, 1719.

A chevron between ten crosses pattée.

Crest, a unicorn passant.

[See No. 62.]

56.   George Whithouse of Kingston, Island of Jamaica,
1719.

Per chevron flory sable and argent, in chief two
escallops, and in base a tower, all counterchanged.

Crest, five spears, one in pale and four in saltire.

[Note. This is evidently the coat of Whitehorn,
though it is precisely reversed from Burke's description.]

57.   Samuel Brown, Esq., of Salem, Justice of the Court
of Common Pleas, Col. of the First Regiment of
Foot, co. of Essex, and one of his Majesty's
Council.

Arms the same as No. 44.

[William Browne of Salem, son of Francis B. of Brandon, co. Suffolk, came here in 1635, aged 26. His son William married Hannah Curwin, and had Samuel, the one here recorded.]

58. Francis Brinley of Newport, Colony of R. I., now of Boston, 1719.

Per pale sable and gold, a chevron between three escallops, counterchanged, within a bordure argent, charged with eight hurts.

Crest, an escallop, gules.

[He was son of Thomas of Datchett, co. Bucks, was of Newport, an Assistant in Rhode Island, and died in 1719. We shall say more of this family when we come to the King's Chapel (Boston) Inscriptions.]

59. Sir Thomas Culpepper, Baron of Thornsway, co. of Kent, G. Britain, 1719.

Azure, a bend engrailed gules.

Crest, a falcon, with wings expanded.

[Note. This coat is clearly wrong, being color on color. It should be *argent*, a bend engrailed gules. See also No. 62.]

60. Joseph Dudley of Roxbury, co. of Suffolk, Esq., Gov. of the Province of Mass. Bay, New England, and New Hampshire, 1720.

Gold, a lion rampant, azure, the tail forked.

Crest, a lion's head erased.

[This was the son of Gov. Thomas Dudley. See pp. 35–6. We may note that the Dudley lion was usually *vert*, instead of azure.]

61.   John Mansale of Bristol, merchant, 1710.

Argent, a chevron between three maunches, sable.

Crest, a griffin's head, couped.

[See No. 62.]

62.   Thomas Chute of Marblehead, co. of Essex, 1719.

Gules, semée of mullets, gold, three swords argent, hilted, or barways, the centre sword encountering the other two; a carton argent and azure (vert?), thereon a lion of England.

Crest, a dexter cubit arm in armor, the hand grasping a broken sword.

[In the Register, XIII., 123, it is stated that Lionel Chute of Ipswich was son of Anthony Chute, and the descendant of Alexander Chute of Taunton, co. Somerset, A. D. 1268. Lionel's son James married an Epes of Ipswich, and had a son Thomas, born in 1692, the one here mentioned.

The MS., which was then copied for the Register, comes down only to this generation of Thomas Chute. It had evidently been seen by the author of this "Gore" list, since the arms pricked on it are those of Sturton (51), Bartley (55), Lucas (48), Gee (53), Colpepper (59), Baker (47), Wood (50), Brittan (49), and Chittester (52), which are Nos. 47, 48, 49, 50, 51, 52, 53, 55, and 59 in this List, except that Bartley, Baker and Chittester should be Barkley, Barker and Chichester, as given by us. Mansale (No. 61), also occurs in the marriages.]

63.   Samuel Phillips of Boston, co. of Suffolk, 1721.

Argent, a lion rampant, sable, collared and chained.

Crest, a lion, as in the shield, collared and chained, gules.

[This was very probably Samuel Phillips, gold-smith, of Salem, son of Rev. Samuel P. of Rowley, who was son of Rev. George P. of Boxford, co. Suffolk, and Watertown, Mass. George was son of Christopher Phillips of Rainham, St. Martin, co. Norfolk, and was born about 1593.]

64. William Hutchinson, Esq., of Boston, co. of Suffolk, Justice of the Peace, 1721.

Arms as in No. 46, but without the label, and identical with No. 40.

[He was the son of Eliakim Hutchinson, and died in 1721.]

65. Edward Pell of Boston, co. of Suffolk, 1720. Pell and Clarke.

Quarterly, 1 and 4, ermine, on a canton —— a pelican, vulning herself, gold.

2 and 3, Gules, three swords, argent, hilted gold, erect, in fesse.

Crest, on a chaplet vert, a pelican, vulning herself.

66. Thomas Savage, Esq., of Boston, Col. of the First Regiment of Foot, co. of Suffolk, 1720.

Argent, six lioncels, sable.

Crest, out of a coronet, gold, a bear's paw erased, sable.

[These arms will be fully treated hereafter, under "Monumental Inscriptions." They are on the tomb-stone of Major Thomas Savage, in the King's Chapel Yard, Boston.]

67. Elizabeth, wife of John Yeomans, Esq., of the Island of Antigua. Yeomans and Shrimpton, 1721.

1, Sable, a chevron between three spears, upright.

2, Argent, on a cross, gold, five escallops of the field.

Crest, a dexter arm, in armor, embowed, the hand
grasping a spear.

[John Yeomans was grandson of John Y., Lieut.-
Governor of Antigua. Elizabeth was daughter of
Samuel Shrimpton, Jr., and great-grand-daughter of
Henry Shrimpton.]

68. Zechariah Tuttle of Boston, co. of Suffolk, Lieutenant
of Castle William, 1721.

Azure, on a bend argent, double cotised gold, a lion
passant, sable.

Crest, a bird (Cornish chough?) holding in its beak
a branch of olive.

[These arms are those of Tothill.]

69. Mrs. Anna Wade of Medford, co. of Middlesex, 1721.

Azure, a saltier between four escallops, gold.

Crest, a hippopotamus.

[The Wades of Medford were sons of Jonathan of
Ipswich, Mass., who owned lands in Denver, co.
Norfolk. This Anna may be the dau. of Nathaniel
Wade and Mercy Bradstreet, born in 1685.]

70. Jonathan Mountfort of Boston, co. of Suffolk, 1722.

Bendy of eight, gold and azure.

Crest, a lion's head, couped.

71. Daniel Stoddard, a naval officer of the Port of Boston, 1723.

Sable, three estoilles within a bordure argent, a crescent for difference.

Crest, a demi-horse ———, erased, environed round
the body with a coronet, gold.

72. Widow of Joseph Dudley, Esq., of Roxbury, co. of
Suffolk, 1722.

1st, Gold, a lion rampant (azure ?). Impaling, ——
on a bend double cotised, three martlets.

Crest, a wolf's head, erased.

[This is evidently Rebecca, daughter of Edward
Tyng, and wife of Gov. Joseph Dudley. She survived her husband, and died Sept., 1722. These
arms of Tyng are on old plate, still preserved in the
family. See, also, No. 79.]

73. Mary, widow of Francis Brinley of Newport, in the
Colony of Rhode Island. Brinley and Borden,
1722.

1st, Per pale argent and gold, a chevron between
three escallops, counterchanged, within a bordure
argent, charged with eight hurts. Impaling, argent, three cinquefoils, azure.

Crest, an escallop gules.

74. John Jekyll of Boston, Esq., Collector of the Customs for the Counties of Suffolk, Middlesex, Plymouth, Barnstable, and Bristol, 1723.

Gold, a fesse between three hinds trippant, sable.

Crest, a horse's head couped argent, maned and
bridled, sable.

75. Capt. Henry Burn of the Island of Christophers, 1723.

Gold, a chevron between three pelican's heads erased
azure.

Crest, out of a ducal coronet of gold, a pelican's head.

76. Benjamin Pickman, Esq., of Salem, co. of Essex,
1723.

Gules, two battle-axes in saltire gold, between four
martlets, argent.

No crest.

[Benjamin Pickman of Salem, says Savage, was third son of Nathaniel of Bristol, England, where he was baptized at Lewen's Mead, (Bristol) in 1645, had a son Benjamin, who died in 1718, leaving a son Benjamin, born 1708. These arms are also in the Salem Churchyard.]

77. William Dummer, Esq., of Boston, co. of Suffolk, Lieut.-Gov. of the Province of Mass., one of the Council, and Capt. of Castle William, 1723.

Azure, three fleurs-de-lys, gold, on a chief of the second, a demi-lion of the field.

Crest, a demi-lion azure, holding in the dexter paw a fleur-de-lys, gold.

[We shall speak more of this coat under "Official Seals."]

78. John Waire of the Island of Jamaica, merchant, 1723.

Gules, two wings conjoined in lure argent, over all a bend azure.

Crest, an ostrich's head, with wings elevated, holding in the beak a key.

[The arms are those of Warre.]

79. Jonathan Tyng, Esq., of Woburn, co. of Middlesex, Colonel of the Second Regiment of Foot, Justice of the Court, 1724.

Argent, on a·bend cotised sable, three martlets, gold. No crest.

[He was son of Edward Tyng, and died in January, 1724. The family was one of the most prominent in Massachusetts, and was connected by marriage with many of the families already noted as using arms.]

80. James Tilestone of Boston, co. of Suffolk, 1724.

Azure, a bend cotised between two garbs, gold.

Crest, out of a mural coronet gules, a greyhound's head.

[These are the arms of Tillotson.]

81. John Frizell of Boston, merchant.   Frizell and Fowle.

1st, Quarterly, 1 and 4, Argent, three antique crowns, gules.

2 and 3, Azure, three cinquefoils, argent.

Impaling 2d, Argent, three trees proper.

Crest, a stag's head, between two halberts.

[We have already mentioned these arms of Frizell or Frazer.   See p. 58.]

82. Henry Roswell of London, merchant, 1723.

Per pale, gules and azure, a lion rampant, argent.

Crest, a lion's head couped argent, langued gules.

83. John Sil * * n of the North of England, Great Britain, 1723.

Argent, on a bend cotised sable, three annulets of the field.

Crest, two bear's paws erased, the dexter one gules, the sinister proper, holding a branch upright(?) gules.

84. Richard Waldron, Esq., of Portsmouth in Piscatequa, alias New Hampshire, 1724.

Argent, three bull's heads cabossed, horned gold.

85. Boarland.

Argent, two bars, gules, over all a boar, rampant, (Azure?).

Crest, a broken lance.

Motto, Press Through.

[These arms are used by a Scotch family, and also by the Borlands of Boston, Mass.]

86. Cushing.

Quarterly, 1 and 4, An eagle displayed.

2 and 3, two dexter hands, open, couped, a canton chequy.

Crest, two bear's paws, holding a ducal coronet, from which is suspended a heart.

[No colors or name are marked on this sketch. The family, however, is a distinguished one here, and the pedigree will be found in the New England Historical and Genealogical Register, for 1865.]

87. Paddock of Gloucester.

[An unfinished sketch.]

88. Sir Edward Sprague, Knt.

Gules, a fesse between three trefoils.

Crest, out of a naval crown a demi-lion, crowned.

89. Lathrop.

Gyronny of eight azure and gules, an eagle displayed, argent.

Crest, a game-cock.

90. Joshua Winslow, Esq.

Argent, on a bend gules eight lozenges conjoined, gold.

Crest, the stump of a tree.

[More correctly the bend should be gules lozengy gold, but I give it as it is painted.]

91. Sayward of York.

Gules, on a fesse argent, between two chevrons ermine, three leopard's faces of the field.

Crest, a tiger's head, couped.

[Henry Sayward was of York, Me., 1664.]

92. Scolly.
    Three shovellers. [No colors.]
93. Whitwell.
    (Gules?), a fesse chequy, gold and sable, between
    two bars—gemelles.
94. Thomas Kneeland of Essex.
    A lion rampant, gold, holding in the dexter paw an
    escutcheon, charged with a cross formée.
    Crest, a demi-lion.
95. Argent, a chevron gules between three pine apples,
    vert, on a canton a fleur-de-lys, in the centre point
    a Baronet's badge.
    Crest, out of a ducal coronet a mailed arm embowed,
    the hand grasping a staff; thereon a flag.
    Mottos, " Peperi " and " Virtute."
    [These arms, though not clearly emblazoned, are
    certainly those of Sir William Pepperell.]
96. Beach.
    Gules, three lions passant, gold, over all a bend
    charged with three stag's heads, cabossed.
    Crest, a bird rising.
97. Bell of Boston.
    Azure, a fesse ermine, between three bells, gold.
    [It will be noticed that the last thirteen coats are
    not finished in the drawing, and the names of the
    owners are not all specified.]
98. Christopher Kilby, Esq.
    Argent, three bars azure, in chief as many annulets
    of the last.
    Crest, an ear of maize, stripped open.
    Mottos, "Persisto," and "Gratia Gratiam Parit."

99.   Gilbert McAdams.   McAdams, Kilby and Clark.

Gules, three crosses-crosslet fitchée, argent.

On an escutcheon of pretence Kilby (as in No. 82),
    quartering Clarke, viz., a bend raguly and trunked
    between three roundles.

[I presume that this Christopher Kilby and Gilbert
McAdams were brothers-in-law. At all events, in
1760, Christopher Kilby of London, then of New
York, and Gilbert McAdams of New York, joined in
a sale of land in Boston. A certain Christopher
Kilby married Sarah Clarke, 18 August, 1726,
which may account for the quartering of the arms
on the above shield. It will also be noted that the
Gores and Kilbys intermarried.]

OFFICIAL SEALS.

Following Bradstreet in our series of the Governors of
Massachusetts, we find Sir Edmund Andros. It is not
improbable that his desire for change in the forms of the
government caused the adoption of the mode of using a
small seal for documents issued by the Governor. It is
believed that prior to his time no such rule was in force,
but since then, even to the present time, in some of our
States, documents not issued by the authority of the
Legislature, are stamped with the Governor's privy seal,
and not with the great seal of the State. Thus we find
that the Provincial Governors used a seal bearing their
respective arms for commissions in the military forces, but
on commissions of justices of the peace, judges, &c., the
seal of the Province.

The seal of Sir Edmund Andros here given is of frequent occurrence, and the following reply to an interrogation made in Notes and Queries last year, gives us some valuable information about a peculiarity in the arms.

"Sir Edmund Andros, of Guernsey, bore for arms: Gules, a saltire gold, surmounted of another vert; on a chief azure, three mullets sable. *Crest*, a blackamoor's head in profile, couped at the shoulders and wreathed about the temples, all proper. *Motto*, "Crux et præsidium et duces."

In 1686, he made application to the Earl Marshal to have his arms "registered in the College of Arms in such a manner, as he may lawfully bear them with respect to his descent from the ancient family of Sausmarez in the said Isle" (Guernsey.) In this petition it is set out that—

"His Great Grandfather's Father, John Andros al[s] Andrewes, an English Gentleman, born in Northampton-shire, coming into the Island of Guernsey, as Lieutenant to Sir Peter Mewtis, Knt., the Governor, did there marry A° 1543 with Judith de Sausmarez, onely Daughter of Thomas Sausmarez, son and heir of Thomas Sausmarez, Lords of the Seignorie of Sausmarez in the said Isle," &c.

The warrant, granting the petition, is dated September 23, 1686; and from this time Sir Edmund Andros and his descendants, as Seigneurs de Sausmarez, quartered the arms of De Sausmarez with their own, and used the crest and supporters belonging thereto, as depicted in the margin of the warrant. These arms are thus blazoned:—
Argent, on a chevron gules between three leopard's faces

sable, as many castles triple-towered, gold. *Crest*, a falcon affrontant, wings expanded, proper, belted, gold. Supporters: Dexter, a unicorn argent, tail cowarded; sinister, a greyhound argent, collared gules, garnished gold." This reply by Edgar Mac Culloch, Esq., of Guernsey, is in Notes and Queries, 3d Series, V., 425. The grant seems unusual, since Andros thereby acquired the right to supporters, and we presume that this must have been in consequence of his inheriting a Seignory.

Sir Edmund was Governor of New York, and afterwards, in 1686, was made Governor of New England. He was driven from here in 1689, and was afterwards made Governor of Virginia.

His wife died at Boston, in February, 1688, and he died in England, in February, 1714.

PEDIGREE OF CHUTE, OR CHEWTE.

As we have in the present number referred to a parchment pedigree of the Chutes, we here reprint the account given in the New England Historical and Genealogical Register, XIII., 123. The original is in the possession of Ariel P. Chute, Esq., of Lynnfield, Mass.

"Alexander[1] Chute of Taunton, in the county of Somerset, A. D., 1268, had issue: John[2] of the same town, m. Jane, dau. of Sir John Bromfield; and Richard,[2] *temp.* Edw. I. 1274.

John[2] and Jane had a son Edward,[3] m. Christiana Chiddiock, dau. of Sir John C., and had issue, *temp.* Edw. III. 1308, the three following sons:

Phillip[4] of Taunton, m. the dau. of Sir John Brittan; James[4] m. the dau. of Richard Greenfield; Anthony[4] m. Anna Indford, and d. *s. p.*

Phillip[4] had issue, George[5] m. the dau. of Thomas Faril, Esq., about 1344, and Jane[5] m. Sir John Cameron.

George[5] had Ambrose[6] of Taunton, m. Amabel Chittester, daughter of Sir John C., and had Edward[7] and Christian.[7] The former m. about 1379, Dionis, daughter of Henry Stourton, the latter (Christian[7]) m. Ralph Mansell, Esq.

Edward[7] and Dionis had Henry,[8] 1420, m. the dau. of Edward Hasherfield, Esq.; William[8] m. ——, and d. *s.p.*; Anthony[8] m. the dau. of Sir John Clifton, and had Christopher[9] of Hertfordshire, who m. the dau. of Richard Wellgrave, Esq., and Robert,[9] sergeant at law, and later Baron of the Exchequer, *temp.* Henry VI.

Henry[8] had issue, Robert[9] of Taunton, who m. Alice, dau. of Mark Bartley, Esq.; and Anna,[9] who m. John Stanley.

Robert[9] (1438) had Charles,[10] who m. the dau. of Sir John Chang (?), and about 1480 had a son Edmond,[11] who sold the manor of Taunton to Lord Donhare (?), about 1502. His son and heir Robert[12] m. Jane Lucas, dau. of John L., and had issue; Oliver[13] m. the dau. of Relide. Charles[13] m. the dau. of John Crips of the Isle of Guernsey; and William[13] m. the dau. of John Braddelson of Turbridge.

Charles[13] (1580) had issue; Anthony[14] m. the dau. of William Gee, and Phillip[14] m. the dau. of —— Coolpepper, and had George,[15] m. a lady of Kent, Edward,[15] and Anthony.[15]

Anthony,[14] son of Charles,[13] had issue; Anthony,[15] William,[15] Christopher,[15] and Lionel,[15] who m. the dau. of Stephen Greene, and had five children, viz., Lionel,[16] George,[16] Charles,[16] Judith,[16] who m. John Edmonson, and one[16] unnamed in the record.

Lionel,[15] Jr., m. the dau. of Robert Barker, and had a son James,[17] who came with his father from England, about 1635, and settled at Ipswich, Mass., where he m. the dau. of ———— Epes, Esq., of that place, and had James,[18] who m. the dau. of ———— Wood, and had issue, Lionel[19] m. Hannah Cheney; James[19] m. Mary Thurston; Thomas[19] m. a dau. of Mr. Clarke of Boston, and had issue; Mary[19] m. John Cheney of Newbury; Elizabeth[19] m. Andrew Stickney of Newbury; Anne[19] m. Thomas Brown of Newbury; Martha[19] m. Josiah Smith of Newbury; Ruth[19] m. John Hurd of Marblehead; and Timothy[19] of Newbury."

On the pedigree, besides the arms of Chute, there are impalements of those of Stourton, Barkley, Lucas, Gee, Culpepper, Barker, Wood, Brittan and Chichester.

Lionel[16] Chute was the first schoolmaster at Ipswich, Mass., and died in 1645. His son James married undoubtedly the step-daughter of Samuel Symonds, and from this we may argue that the family occupied a good position.

THE

HERALDIC JOURNAL;

RECORDING THE ARMORIAL BEARINGS AND GENEALOGIES
OF AMERICAN FAMILIES.

NO. X.   OCTOBER, 1865.

ARMS OF THE CURWENS OF SALEM.

 The engraving accompanying this article is intended for an exact representation of an impression, in wax, of arms upon a seal-ring formerly used by the Curwens of Salem, and known to have been in existence as late as the year 1802, as the following memorandum, from a MS. by Daniel Ward of Salem, will show : " Salem, July 28th, 1802. Then I bought of Colonel Benjamin Pickman a ring which belongd to George Curwen, and was on his finger at the time he was taken in portrait about 1675—it has the arms of the family of Curwen and [is] of very antient fashion * * * * it is my wish that it may be kept, after my death, as long as possible in the family."

George Curwen, here alluded to, was the founder of a family which, for several generations, was prominent among the leading families of New England, though it is now extinct in an uninterrupted male line except in the branch represented by the Hon. Thomas Corwin of Ohio. Curwen came to this country, according to tradition, in 1638. His portrait above mentioned is preserved and is now in the possession of George R. Curwen, Esq., of Salem, who has, likewise, the cane and scarf or band worn by the first George when he set for his picture.

The seal-ring came to the hands of Pickman as administrator of the estate of Samuel Curwen, the loyalist refugee, whose journal and letters, edited by his kinsman, the late George Atkinson Ward, Esq., are widely known.*

The present Curwens of Salem are descended, in a female line after the fourth generation, from the first George; the name of Curwen having been assumed by Samuel Curwen Ward, under a special act of the Legislature of Massachusetts, in the year 1802.

A genealogical account of this family may be seen in "The Giles Memorial," a valuable genealogical collection, by John Adams Vinton,—published at Boston, in 1864.

It is proposed to give here an account of the earlier instances of the use of these arms by members of the family; and first in order is,

I. (1675). The portrait already mentioned, with the seal-ring worn upon a finger of the right hand.

II. (1688–9). An impression, upon wax, on a deed, dated March 21, 1688–9, from George Curwen, Sheriff of Essex County, and grandson of George, above-named. This impression is sharply and clearly made; but the arms bear no crescent in the chief.

---

* The Journal and Letters of Samuel Curwen, an American in England, from 1775 to 1783; &c. 4th ed. Boston: Little, Brown & Co., 1864. See also "Household Words," for May and June, 1853, for a notice of this book.

III. (1690–1). Another impression of the same, on a deed by the same grantor, dated Jan. 27, 1690, who writes his name in this instance, "George Corwin."

IV. (1690). A still better impression of another seal. This appears to have been made with the seal-ring above mentioned. It bears the crescent. The deed to which this seal is affixed was executed by Hon. Jonathan Corwin, son of the first George, and a magistrate and citizen of distinction. It is dated 15th Sept., 1690.

V. (1698). A pen-and-ink drawing in a MS. in the collection of the American Antiquarian Society, at Worcester, of the arms of Curwen impaling Sheaf;—signed "*testis*, Geo. Curwin, 1698." This was the Rev. George, born May 21, 1683, son of Jonathan above-named; and the sketch was made, probably, while he was a student at Cambridge.

VI. (1714–1717). A portrait of the Rev. George Curwen last named, taken in his clerical garments. As he was ordained pastor of the First Church in Salem in 1714, and died 23 Nov., 1717, his portrait must have been painted at sometime between those dates. His picture was recently cleaned and rebacked, which process brought to light the Curwen arms, in their proper colors, thereon, *with the crescent in the chief.*

VII. (1755). A fragment of still another seal, bearing the same arms, on a letter of June 16, 1755, from several Corwins of New Jersey to Samuel Curwen of Salem. This letter contains genealogical facts establishing the connection of the families in Salem and New Jersey.

VIII. (1775–83). Arms, in which a field fretty is substituted for the fret and mascle of the older seals hereinbefore noticed. These arms were cut by " Jno. Barnes, Coventry St., London," for Samuel Curwen above-mentioned. The original seal is lost, but the artist's proof is still preserved in a box labelled with his name and number as given above.

IX. In addition to the foregoing, a silver seal, bearing the Curwen arms, without the crescent, is now in the possession of James Barr Curwen, Esq., of Salem. This was found among the effects of Samuel Curwen, above-named, at his decease. Its age is not known, but it is believed, by members of the family, to be very ancient.

George Curwen, the first, was born 10 Dec., 1610, and died, at Salem, Mass., 3d Jan., 1685. His first wife was Elizabeth (Herbert) White of Northampton, Eng., widow of John White. His second wife was Elizabeth Brook, widow of Robert Brook, and youngest child of Gov. Winslow of Plymouth Colony. He was often charged with the highest public trusts, was connected by marriage with many leading families, and, at his death, he left one of the largest estates ever administered upon in the Colony. By the early death of all his descendants of the third generation, the children of the fourth generation were all left orphans in extreme infancy, and, although one of these (Bartholmew) was twenty-five years old at the death of his uncle Jonathan, the survivor of the second generation, yet he moved with his family, to Amwell, New Jersey, and all traditions which he may have received from his uncle and other relatives, were thereby lost to those who remained in Salem. Many of his family papers were destroyed by fire, and thus his descendants are possessed of but a few unimportant genealogical facts, and these are of comparatively recent date.

Since the death of Samuel Curwen, the loyalist, no serious effort has been made to trace this family back to the place of its origin in Great Britain. What the author of the "Journal and Letters" attempted, in this direction, may be learned from the following extract from his diary, under date of 4 April, 1777:

"Friday, 4th. Cloudy, raw morning. Walked with W. C. to the Herald's Office: examined the books and took out an exemplar of my arms, or at least those belonging to the Workington family, who are in the table of Sir William Dugdale's book entd to a Thomas Curwen (and by him signed) son of a Sir Henry, 1663, dated Egmond Allerdale, descended from an Elfrida; but who her father was I know not. In the table stands a George, from whom are descendants, but not herein placed, *temp.* Henry 8.

There are two other families descended from this: one of Helsington, distinguished by a crescent in the chief, denoting a second son, and one at Camberton who married an heiress of the name of Lloyd, if I have not mistaken (or say forgotten) and quartering her arms. Ours, or those I have from my ancestors assumed, are frette and may consist of 4, 6, or 8 whole lozenges, according to the bigness of the field, as the Norroy King of arms informed me: ye word importing as many as fancy or convenience shall direct. Passed the P. M. at home &c."

It seems highly probable that a little pains in examining the record of the Helsington branch, would give us the pedigree of the emigrant.   A. C G., JR.

REVIEW.

Genealogy of the Gilman Family in England and America: traced in the line of the Hon. John Gilman of Exeter, N. H. By Arthur Gilman, of Glynllyn. Albany: J. Munsell, 1864.

This little book of 24 pages has been issued by Mr. Gilman, for the purpose of correcting errors and obtaining further information in regard to the English portion of the family. A similar outline sketch was prepared for the family here some time since, and the author intends, with the information thus obtained, to prepare a complete record of the family.

The main interest to us in this book is contained in the indentification of the emigrant hither, and his probable right to coat-armor. We extract the following outline:

Edward[1] Gilman of Caston, co. Norf., was married 22 June, 1550, to Rose Rysse. By her he had four sons and five daughters, to whom at his death, in 1573, he devised his house and estates. Of these sons, Robert[2] of Caston m. Mary ——, and died in 1618, leaving sons, Robert,[3] Edward,[3] Lawrence,[3] and John.[3]

Edward[3] Gilman of Hingham, co. Norf., m. 3 June, 1614, Mary Clark, and "with his wife, three sons, two daughters, and three servants, came, in 1638, and settled in this Town of Hingham, Mass.," as Daniel Cushing records. (See N. E. Hist. and Gen. Register, XV., 26.) At the same time "John Foulsham and his wife and two servants came from old Hingham." By this Genealogy we learn that Mary,[4] dau. of Edward[3] Gilman, was baptized at Hingham, Eng., in 1615, and married John Foulsham. The other dau. was Lydia, who was married in England to Daniel Cushing. The three sons were, Edward,[4] bapt. 1617, John,[4] bapt. 1626, and Moses,[4] bapt. 1630.

Robert[3] Gilman of Hingham, brother of the emigrant, died in 1658, leaving a son, Samuel,[4] bapt. 1644, who died in 1698. This Samuel[4] had a son Samuel[5] who m. first, at Wymondham, 1701, Hester, daughter of William Le Neve, and secondly, Anna Francis Amyas. In the chancel of the church of Hingham are tablets to his memory and his wives', on which are the Gilman arms. His son Samuel[6] married Francis, dau. of Edward Heyhoe, and had Samuel,[7] father of the late Samuel[8] Heyhoe Le Neve Gilman of Hingham, Eng.

We place here an engraving of the Gilman arms, presuming that the use can be shown, antecedent to the time of the emigrant. Of the family here it is enough to say that it has occupied a prominent position in New Hampshire. Edward's son John was of Exeter, and there had Nicholas, Judge S. C., whose son Samuel was also a Judge of the same Court. Another son of Judge Nicholas was the Rev. Nicholas of Kingston, and a brother of the Judge was Col. John Gilman, whose son, Hon. Peter Gilman, was speaker of the Assembly, member of the Council, &c.

We presume that the Genealogy when completed will be very extensive, and that the English portion will receive special notice.

OFFICIAL SEALS.

 Next to Andros, among the regularly constituted Governors, may be placed Sir William Phips. Of him we have a wonderful biography, prepared by Cotton Mather. It will be sufficient, however, to say that his father was James Phips, a gunsmith of Bristol, Eng., who settled in Maine, before 1649. His family is said to have embraced twenty-six children, a story almost incredible, especially as we can find traces of so few in our records.

William was born 2 Feb., 1650, became a ship carpenter and builder, and in 1683 he commanded a vessel in the West Indies, fitted out to recover a Spanish treasure-ship formerly wrecked there. Succeeding in securing much bullion and other valuables, he was knighted on his return to England, in June, 1687, and returning here was made sheriff. In 1690, he commanded the expeditions against Nova Scotia and Quebec; and in 1692, being in London, he was appointed Governor, under the new charter, on the recommendation of Increase Mather.

His administration was especially unfortunate, in that it was marked by the Witchcraft delusion. He died in London, 18 Feb., 1695, and was buried at St. Mary Woolnoth.

Sir William Phips married, as Mather says, "a young gentlewoman of good repute, who was the widow of one Mr. John Hull, a well-bred merchant, but the daughter of one Captain Roger Spencer, a person of good fashion, who, having suffered much damage in his estate, by some unkind and unjust actions, which he bore with such patience, that for fear of thereby injuring the public, he would not seek satisfaction, posterity might afterwards see the reward of his patience, in what Providence hath now done for one of his own posterity."

His wife survived him and married Hon. Peter Sargeant, Oct., 1701, and died within five years after. In the Gore list (*ante*, p. 118) we are informed that she claimed and used the Spencer arms. Capt. Roger Spencer seems to have left three daughters only, the wife of Freegrace Norton, Mary Phips, and Rebecca, wife of Dr. David Bennet.

Gov. Phips had no children, but his wife's nephew Spencer Bennet was adopted by her and assumed the name and arms. As Spencer Phips he occurs as Lieutenant Governor of Massachusetts (see p. 120).

It may be noticed that there was another family of Phips here, beginning with Solomon of Charlestown, 1641, whose sons were Solomon, who married Mary, daughter of Dept. Gov. Thomas Danforth, and Samuel, who was Register of Deeds for Middlesex, Mass. This latter *seems* to have used a seal of a chevron between three bunches of grapes, at least this seal is found on many papers signed by him.

The coat of arms here engraved is copied from the seal on Sir William Phips's will, in the Suffolk Registry. He also had a large privy seal for public documents during his term of office, but the impressions which we have seen are on paper and a wafer, and we can only say that this seal was about the size of that of the Earl of Bellemont, and other governors.

It is highly probable that the arms were granted to Sir
William, and that the arms of the Marquesses of Normanby were assigned to them at even a later date. There is
no known connection between the families,—as we have
already said.

In the excellent edition of Collins's Peerage, edited by
Sir Egerton Brydges in 1812, under the title of Lord
Mulgrave, he prints the following epitaph, remaining in
the church of St. Mary Woolnoth, London:

Near this place is interred the body
Of Sir William Phipps, Knight, who in the year
1687, by his great industry, discovered among
The rocks, near the banks of Bahama, on
The north side of Hispaniola, a Spanish plate-
Ship, which had been under water 44
Years, out of which he took in gold and
Silver to the value of three hundred
Thousand pounds sterling, and with a
Fidelity equal to his conduct, brought it
All to London, where it was divided
Between himself and the rest of the adventurers; for
Which great service he was knighted by his
Then Majesty King James II. and afterwards
By the command of his present Majesty,
And at the request of the principal inhabitants
Of New England, he accepted the Government
Of the Massachusetts, in which he continued to
The time of his death; and discharged his trust
With that zeal for the interest of his country,
And with so little regard to his own private advantage,
That he justly gained the good esteem and affections

Of the greatest and best part of the inhabitants of that
Colony.
He died 18th February, 1694,
And his Lady, to perpetuate his memory,
Hath caused this monument to be erected.

Sir Egerton then gives Sir Constantine Phipps as his
son; but in the appendix he says that since writing the
article he has met with the "Life of Sir William Phips,"
written by *Nath.* Mather, meaning Cotton Mather. He
notes that the book says Phips "not having any children
of his own, adopted a nephew of his wife to be his heir."
He adds " it appears that Sir William Phips was not himself the ancestor of Lord Mulgrave, though I had followed the Irish Peerage by Archdall, in asserting him to
be so. The adopted nephew of his wife was probably the
true ancestor."

As this nephew was born in 1685, he certainly was not
the father of Sir Constantine, who was Lord Chancellor
of Ireland in 1710, and whose son was married in 1718.

It is curious to trace back this popular error, to its
source, and to notice how the text has been repeated,
whilst even the imperfect correction has been neglected.

MONUMENTAL INSCRIPTIONS.

Communicated by J. HAMMOND TRUMBULL, Esq.

HARTFORD, CONN.

The only remaining coat of arms in the ancient First
Church Burying Ground at Hartford, is the following:

HERE LIETH

THE BODY OF JAMES RICHARDS

ESQ. LATE ONE OF THE ASSISTANTS

OF CONECTICOT. WHO DEPARTED

THIS LIFE THE 11 DAY OF IVNE 1680

ÆTATIS SUÆ 47.

IN THE FIRME HOPE OF THE GLORIVS

RESVRECTION.

Hon. James Richards of Hartford, ("son, perhaps, of Thomas of Dorchester," as Mr. Savage thinks,) was an Assistant from 1664 until his death, and was a prominent actor in public affairs of the colony. His widow, Sarah (a daughter of William Gibbons) married Humphrey Davie, Esq., of Boston, and afterwards of Hartford, whom surviving, she married Col. Jonathan Tyng of Dunstable. One of the daughters of Mr. Richards married the Rev. Gurdon Saltonstall, afterwards Governor of Connecticut, and another married John (son of her step-father Humphrey) Davie, who succeeded to the title and estate of his uncle Sir John Davie of Creedy, co. Devon, Baronet, and removed to England. Thomas, the only son of James Richards, died without male issue.

Burke has the arms of " Richards (of Rew, co. Devon ; Isleworth, co. Middlesex; and Somersetshire), Argent, a fesse fusily sable, between two cotises gules," and " Richards (East Bayborough, co. Somerset) Argent, five lozenges, conjoined in fesse gules, between two bars sable."

We do not find the colors of the arms of James Richards, but the coat is clearly one of these here described, which are so nearly alike in form as to indicate a common origin.

See also, *ante*, pp. 121 and 123.

HERALDIC NOTES AND QUERIES.

XXV.

In the Reports of Cases before the Superior Court of Massachusetts, 1761–1772, by Josiah Quincy, Jr., lately published in Boston, we find a decision of some little interest to our readers. In 1767, in the case of Bromfield *vs.* Lovejoy, it seems that the latter was termed Yeoman, although he bore a Captain's commission and hence claimed the style of gentleman.

Mr. Otis claimed "Lovejoy is certainly no Gentleman by Office ; for no Commission from any Governour whatever, can make a Man Gentleman by Office. Lovejoy is then a Gentleman, if any way, by Curtesy or Reputation, and ' Gentleman ' would be a good Addition ' but if he be named Yeoman, he cannot abate the Writ. ' Yeoman or Gentleman are Additions *ad Placitum* and *ad Libi-*

tum, are no Part of Name, but Additions *ad Libitum* as People please to call them.'

The Court took a Distinction between Gentleman by Curtesy, and Reputation, and seemed to be of Opinion that if a Man was Gentleman by Curtesy, Yeoman was not his due addition; *aliter* of Gentleman by Reputation only. In the present Case they were of Opinion, that Lovejoy was a Gentleman both by his Commission and by Curtesy. Therefore they ruled that the Writ abate, though they said it was a very great Hardship upon the Bar."

XXVI.

In 1807, the notorious Rev. Samuel Peters published a History of the Rev. Hugh Peters, and in the Appendix favored his readers with some startling pedigrees. Thus (p. 128) he says that after Cromwell's time "New-England and especially Connecticut was filled with emigrants of high families and science from New England." He instances Thomas Seymour "a younger branch of the family of the Duke of Somerset;" also " three brothers of the then Lord Stanley, Earl of Derby;" "William Russel a younger branch of the family of the duke of Bedford." Pierrepont, a clergyman of New Haven, is reported to have a grand-son, "the legal heir of the estate and title of the Duke of Kingston. He also gives us Montague, "of the family of the Earl of Sandwich;" Graham, "of the Duke of Montrose's family;" Clinton "of the family of the Earl of Lincoln," and several representatives of the gentry.

Such idle fables have been very prejudicial to the study of the science of genealogy here, but it has been fully matched by recent publications here. We may especially mention an absurd display made in New York at the funeral ceremonies of our lamented President, and afterwards defended in an article in the New York Herald.

CONNECTICUT SEALS.

Communicated by J. HAMMOND TRUMBULL, Esq.

I.

 GUY and EDWARD PALMES were merchants or traders at Milford, in 1658. The next year Edward was at New Haven, whence he removed, before Dec., 1660, to New London. He married Lucy, dau. of Gov. John Winthrop; was a representative in the General Court, 1671–4 and 1677; major commanding the military force of New London county, in the Indian war of 1675–7; a supporter of the administration of Andros in 1687–8, and opposed to the resumption of charter government in 1689, without express warrant from the Crown. (See Conn. Records, iii., 388–9.) He died at New London, March 21, 1714–5, æ. 78.

His seal, of which several impressions are preserved on letters in the Conn. Archives ("War," 1, 39, &c.), bore the arms—with a crescent for cadency—of the ancient family of Palmes of Naburn, Yorkshire, "enjoying its estate, from sire to son, since 1226," long prior to which date it had been settled at Taunton-Dean, co. Somerset. Burke has the arms, Gules, three fleurs-de-lys argent, a chief vairé, as above engraved. On the seal the chief is counter vair, probably by fault of the engraver, and the colors are not marked.

II.

At p. 61 of this volume, mention is made of the arms of WILLIAM WHITING, of which an engraving is here given. He was one of the first proprietors of, and an early settler at Hartford, a wealthy merchant, an associate of Lord Say and Sele, Lord Brook, George Wyllys, Robert Saltonstall, and others, in the purchase of two patents for lands on the Piscataqua (see Mass. Rec., I., 324) and one of the most efficient promoters of the trade and commerce of Hartford. He was a deputy in the first General Court, in 1637; chosen an Assistant in 1641, and Treasurer of the Colony from 1643 till his death, in 1647. His will is printed in the Col. Rec. of Conn., I., 493. His oldest son, William Whiting, was a merchant in London, and for some time the agent of the colony, by appointment of the General Court, in 1686. Several of his letters written in 1687, now in the State Archives (Foreign Correspondence, 11, 14, 15, 17), are sealed with his arms as above given. The shield is surmounted by a helmet, but no crest can be made out.

[It will be noticed that this coat differs slightly from that of the Whitings of Boston; both are found in heraldic works as belonging in the name, and though different branches of the family may have adopted these slight changes for distinction's sake, it seems more probable that they are accidental varieties caused by imperfect transcript of the original arms. ED.]

THE

HERALDIC JOURNAL;

RECORDING THE ARMORIAL BEARINGS AND GENEALOGIES
OF AMERICAN FAMILIES.

NO. XI. NOVEMBER, 1865.

THE SALTONSTALL FAMILY.

In Bond's History of Watertown will be found a very elaborate account of the Saltonstalls, from which we prepare the following sketch. The pedigree here cited commences with Gilbert[1] Saltonstall of Halifax, co. York, who purchased Rookes, in Hipperholmes. He had two sons, Samuel[2] of Rookes and Huntwick, and Sir Richard,[2] Lord Mayor of London in 1597, who died in 1600. Samuel,[2] by his first wife Anne, dau. of John Ramsden of Longley, had Sir Richard[3] Saltonstall of Huntwick and Ledsham, who m. Grace, dau. of Robert Kaye of Woodsome. He was one of the Associates in the Massachusetts Colony, an Assistant, and in 1630, he

11

came with his family to New England, where he remained about a year. In 1644 he was Embassador to Holland, and he died probably in 1658.

Of his children, the eldest son, Richard[1] Saltonstall, born at Woodsome, co. York, in 1610, was of Emmanuel College, Camb., and married Meriell, dau. of Brampton Gurdon, Esq., of Assington Hall, co. Suff. (Burke's Commoners, I., 396.)

He settled at Ipswich, Mass., was a Deputy and Assistant. He died in 1694, and the records show that his influence in the Colony had been largely exercised in behalf of those who sought to give a liberal tone to our government.

His children were Meriell,[5] who m. Sir Edward Moseley of Hulme, co. Lanc.; Abigail,[5] wife of Thomas Harley of Hinsham Court, co. Hereford; Elizabeth[5] m. Hercules Horsley; Richard,[5] who d. *s. p.*; and Nathaniel.[5]

Col. Nathaniel[5] Saltonstall of Ipswich, Mass., m. 1663, Elizabeth, dau. of Rev. John Ward; was an Assistant and one of the Council. He was appointed one of the Witchcraft Judges, but refused to act.

His sons were Gurdon,[6] Richard,[6] Nathaniel,[6] and John.[6] Of these, Gurdon[6] was a minister at New London, but was elected Governor of Connecticut in 1707, and held that office till his death in 1724. He married thrice; first, Jerusha, dau. of James Richards; secondly, Elizabeth, dau. of William Rosewell; thirdly, Mary, dau. of William Whittingham, and widow of William Clarke. Three sons survived him, all by the second wife, viz., Rosewell,[7] whose line ended in heiresses, Nathaniel,[7] who went South, and Gen. Gurdon[7] Saltonstall.

This last, Gurdon,[7] m. Rebecca Winthrop, and left a numerous posterity; of whom we may note Commodore Dudley Saltonstall of the Revolution.

We will now revert to Col. Richard,[6] brother of the Governor, who m. 1702, Mehitable, dau. of Capt. Simon Wainwright, and had Richard,[7] who was a Colonel, and afterwards Judge of the Superior Court of Massachusetts.

This Richard[7] had three wives, by the third of whom, Mary, dau. of Elisha Cooke, he had Nathaniel[8] and Leverett.[8] By his first wife he had a son, Col. Richard,[8] who was a Loyalist, and died *s. p.*, and his half-brother Leverett,[8] also a Loyalist, was a Captain under Cornwallis, and d. *s. p.*, aged 28.

The only male heir of this branch remaining here, was Dr Nathaniel[8] Saltonstall of Haverhill, who remained "true to those principles of civil liberty and humanity which he inherited from his worthy ancestor, Sir Richard Saltonstall, and his not less worthy son, Richard of Ipswich." He married in 1780, Anna White, and had Leverett,[9] Nathaniel,[9] Anna,[9] Mary,[9] Sarah,[9] Richard,[9] and Matilda,[9] all of whom married and left issue.

Hon. Leverett[9] Saltonstall in the past generation fully revived the reputation of the family in Massachusetts. He was Speaker of the Mass. House of Representatives, President of the Senate, and Representative in Congress. He was also President of the Bible Society, and filled many other important and honorable offices. His only surviving son, Leverett[10] Saltonstall, is one of the officers of the Mass. Historical Society.

We may note that Sir Richard,[2] the Lord Mayor, had sons, Sir Richard[3] of North Ockendon, co. Essex, Sir

Samuel,[3] and Sir Peter of Berkway, co. Herts, all of whom left issue. How far back the use of the family arms can be traced is not known to us—it is sufficient to say that they were used by Sir Richard on his seals— (Mass. Hist. Collections, 4th S., Vol. VII., Plate V.) both simply as above, and impaling a coat apparently of three stag's heads cabossed.

BARONETS OF NEW ENGLAND.

Three of our colonists became baronets, viz., Sir George Downing, Sir John Davie, and Sir William Pepperrell. We will give a brief sketch of each family, thus ennobled.

Sir George[2] Downing, son of Emmanuel[1] Downing by his wife Lucy, dau. of Adam Winthrop and sister of Gov. John W., was born probably in 1623–4, was graduated at Harvard in 1642, went to England, was a chaplain in Okey's regiment, was appointed by Cromwell resident at the Hague, and after the Restoration became Secretary of the Treasury, Teller of the Exchequer, and one of the Commissioners of Customs. He was created baronet in 1663, and married Frances, daughter of Sir William Howard. He d. in 1684, leaving sons, Sir George,[3] Charles,[3] and William,[3] the latter of whom d. *s. p.*

Sir George[3] Downing m. Catherine, dau. of James, Earl of Salisbury, and had an only son, Sir George,[4] who m. a daughter of Sir William Forester, and d. *s. p.* in **1749.**

His cousin, Sir Jacob[4] Downing, son of Charles,[3] succeeded to the title, and m. a Miss Price, but d. *s. p.* in
1764, when the baronetcy became extinct.

The English books all assert that the first Sir George
was son of Rev. Calybut Downing, of Hackney, co.
Middlesex. *This is an error, without doubt.* Winthrop
expressly says, that he was a son of Emmanuel, and as his
uncle, may be esteemed good authority.

As to Emmanuel, Savage says he was a lawyer of the
Inner Temple, and lived in the parish of St. Michael,
Cornhill Ward, and probably was son of Rev. Emmanuel
Downing.

Against this opinion may be set that printed in Mass.
Hist. Collections, 4th S., VI. 40[1], which is that Emmanuel
was bapt. 1 January, 1585, at the church of St. Lawrence,
Ipswich, and was the son of George D., a schoolmaster
there. Certain it is, from the same letter, that his first
wife was Anne, daughter of Sir James Ware. This Sir
James was father of Sir James, author of " Works concerning Ireland," one of the Privy Council in 1639, &c.

The seal above given is that used by Emmanuel Downing, (see Winthrop Papers before quoted). The follow-
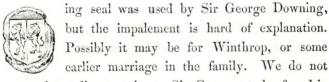
ing seal was used by Sir George Downing,
but the impalement is hard of explanation.
Possibly it may be for Winthrop, or some
earlier marriage in the family. We do not
repeat the pedigree, prior to Sir George, to be found in
Burke and other writers' books, since we have shown
that they are totally wrong. One would think that as
the family so generously endowed Downing College, at
Cambridge, some of our English friends would follow
our traces and give the true pedigree of their benefactors.

OFFICIAL SEALS.

John Coote, Earl of Bellomont in the Peerage of Ireland, was appointed, in 1695, Governor of New York, Massachusetts and New Hampshire. During his absence the Lieutenant Governor William Stoughton acted here, but in 1698, the Earl proceeded to New York, and in May, 1699, he arrived in Boston. He remained here one year, and returning to New York died there, 5 March, 1701.

The seal here given is copied from that on the commission of John Lane of Bedford. It has been compared with one engraved in the Historical Magazine, X., 176, which enables us to give the following emblazonment. It is a shield of eight quarterings, having, on an escutcheon of pretence, the quartered coat of the Nanfans, to which family the Earl's wife belonged. The main shield is:

1. Argent, a chevron sable between three coats proper, for Coote.
2. ——, a fesse between two cotises dancetté.
3. ——, a chief ——,
4. Chequy, —— and ——, a fesse ermine.
5. Ermine, on a chief three crosses.
6. ——, Two lions passant in pale.
7. ——, on a bend dancetté (three fleur-de-lys,) Cuffe.
8. Coote, as in the first quarter.

On the escutcheon of pretence, we have:

1. A chevron between three wings, for Nanfan.

2. ——, a maunch.

3. A coat illegible in our seal, but described in the Hist.
Mag. as a quartered coat, 1 and 4, three crosslets;
2 and 3, three lions passant; the whole charged with
a label of three points.

4. Per pale —— and ——, a saltire, ——.

Inasmuch as very few sources of information are
open to us in regard to the Coote family, we will transcribe the account, in Lodge and Archdall's Peerage of
Ireland, (Dublin, 1789).

The family is traced from Sir John[1] Coote of Devonshire, who m. a dau. of Sir John Fortescue, and had
Sir William,[2] who m. the dau. of Thomas Mansel. His
son, Sir William,[3] m. the heiress of —— Worthy of
Worthy, and had Sir John,[4] who m. —— Sacheveral,
and had Robert.[5] Robert[5] Coote, m. ——, dau. of Grantham, and had Thomas,[6] who m. —— Darnell, and had
Sir John[7] whose wife was a Tyrwhit, and his two sons
were Robert,[8] Abbot of St. Albans, and John.[8]

This John[8] m. the dau. of Fotherby, and had John,[9]
who m. Margaret Drury and had four sons, whereof
Francis[10] Coote of Eaton, co. Norf., m. Anne —— and
had Sir Nicholas,[11] living 1636.

The two sons of Sir Nicholas[11] were Sir Charles,[12] and
Rev. William[12] Coote, Dean of Downe.

Sir Charles Coote[12] settled in Ireland, was of the Privy
Council in 1620, and in April, 1621, made a baronet. He
married before 1617 Dorothea, co-heir of Hugh Cuffe, of
Cuffe's wood, co. York, whose father was from co. North-
ampton. His children were Charles,[13] created Earl of
Mountrath, Chidley,[13] Richard,[13] created Baron Coote of
Coloony, and Thomas.[13]

Richard[13] Coote, created Baron of Coloony, Sept. 1660, m. Mary, dau. of Sir George St. George, by whom he had five daughters, and two sons, Charles,[14] who died in infancy, Richard,[14] second Baron; Chidley,[14] and Thomas.[14]

This Richard[14] Coote, being on the side of King William in 1688, was made Treasurer to Queen Mary, and in 1696 created first Earl of Bellamont. He married Catherine, dau. and heir of Bridges Nanfan of Bridgemorton, co. Worcester, and had sons Nanfan,[15] and Richard.[15] He died in New York in 1700, and his wife (who m. 2dly, Admiral Coleville, 3d, Samuel Pytts of Kyre, and 4th, Alderman William Bridgen) died in 1737, aged 72.

Nanfan[15] Coote left an only daughter, and the title went to his brother Richard, who had three sons who died without issue, and the Earldom became extinct in 1766. The Barony however went to Charles,[15] son of Charles,[15] and grandson of Thomas,[14] brother of the first Earl. This Charles was made Earl of Bellamont, by a new creation in 1770, but left no son to succeed to the title.

THE MINER FAMILY.

The following very curious document was printed in the N. E. Hist. and Gen. Register, XIII., 161–4, but it seems to deserve republication here, in order that its statements may be verified. The copy was made by J. Hammond Trumbull, Esq., and he has kindly furnished the following additional note.

In Thomas Miner's manuscript diary, under date of April 24, 1669, he writes:

" I Thomas Minor am by my accounte sixtie one yeares

ould. I was by the Towne [of Stonington, Conn.] this yeare chosen to be a Select Man, the Towne Treasurer, the Townes Recorder, the brander of horses,—by the Generall Courte recorded the head officer of the Traine band,—by the same Courte one of the Fouer that have the charge of the Malishia of the whole Countie, and chosen and sworne Commissioner, and one to assist in keeping the Countie Courte."

About 1683, he procured from his cousin William of Bristol, Eng., a copy of the family pedigree here printed.

The arms and crest are found on the tablets which cover the graves of Ephraim Minor, Esq., [1724], Dea. Thomas Minor, [1734], and Dea. Manasseh Minor, [1728], three of the sons of Lieut. Thomas: the first in the burying-ground at Togwank, the last two at Wicke-taquoc, in Stonington.

———

AN HERAULDICAL ESSAY UPON THE SURNAME OF MINER.

It is more praise worthie in noble and excellent things to know something, though little, than in mean and ignoble things to have a perfite knowledge. Amongst all those rare ornaments of the mind of man, Herauldrie hath had a most eminent place; and hath been held in high esteem, not only at one time and in one climate, but during all times and through those parts of the world where any ray of humanitie and civilitie hath shined: for without it all would be drowned in the Chaos of dissorder. Neither is she so partial that money shall make the man. For he ought not to be accounted a perfite Herauld except that he can discerne the difference betwixt a Coat armoriall obtained by valour or purchased by money. *Scutum*

Gentilitium Palud [*amentum et Cristatum*] honorable not mercenary as appears by this coat of the MINERS.

The reason (as GARCILLASSO sayeth, Page 432) is this;—Edward the third going to make warre against the French, tooke a progresse through Somersett; and coming to *Mendippi Colles Minerarij,*—Mendippe hills in Somersett, where lived one HENRY MINER, his name being taken both *a denominatione loci et ab officio* who with all carefullness and Loyalltie having convened his domesticall and meniall servants, armed with battle axes, proffered himself and them to his masters service; making up a compleat hundred. Wherefore he had his coat armorial GULES (signifying *Minius,* red, another demonstration of the original surname: A FESSE (id est, *cingulum militare,* because obtained by valour) BETWIXT THREE PLATES ARGENT, another demonstration of the arms: for there could be no plates without MINES. It is folly to suppose such a surname as MINOR to have any coat of armes, It being contrary, yea contradictory, in termes—that *Minors* can obtain paternal coats or achievements unlesse it be presupposed that *Major* was his father.

BARTAS, a French Herauld, says MINER is a word contracted in Dutch—𝔪𝔦𝔫-𝔥𝔢𝔦𝔯, that is *my Master,* or *Lord,* and gives his reason for the plates to be dollars, or pieces of eight, abundance of which will make any Hollander (albeit born upon a Dunghill) to be titled 𝔪𝔦𝔫-𝔥𝔢𝔦𝔯; but ye crest, reason aforesaid and chronologie proves the first. And albeit Heraulds differ in the descriving (says FORDON, page 342) of this surname of MINER, and time with the various dialects of severall counties, have almost made it to be another name; yet if ignorance would strive to eradicate *Ancestrie*, it cannot do it in this coat, the name and colors making so much proofe, with the place (sayes Baker) 1. the place where the original came from,—MENDIPPI COLLES MINERARIJ. 2^{ly} The field MINUS. 3^{ly} The charge MINERALL. [4^{ly}] The circumstances and actions upon record relative to the crest, being a battle axe, armed at both ends MINERALL.

HERAULDRIE is a thing not of yesterday, or which may be otherways found out, being already condescended upon by all nations, and as it were, established, *Jure Gentium*, among the GREEKS, ROMANS, GERMANS, FRENCH, SPAINIARDS, ENGLISH, SCOTS, DANES, and HUNGARIANS, &c. Fordon, the great Antiquarian, sayeth, that the King's Secretary returned the for's'd HENRY MINER, a compliment for his loyaltie, in these words, " OCEANUS (QUAMVIS MAGNI FLUVIJ MULTIQUE TORRENTES SINT EI STIPENDARIJ) NON DEDIGNATUR RECIPERE *minores* RIVULOS &c.," *id est*,

The ocean (though great rivers with many currents pay him tribute) disdains not also to receive the Lesser if loyall brooks which by one only Urne pour themselves into its bosom.

This Henry died in the year 1359, leaving behind him HENRY, EDWARD, THOMAS, and GEORGE, MINERS, of whom little is to be said, save only that Henry married one Henreta Hicks, [A] daughter to Edward Hicks of Glocester, of whom, as appears by the paling of their armes, are the Hicks of BEVERSTON CASTLE in Glocester descended; and had issue WILLIAM and HENRY. WILLIAM married one HOBBS [B] of Wiltshire, and had issue THOMAS and GEORGE. Henry, the 2^d son, served RICHARD the second, *anno* 1384. THOMAS, 1399, married one —— GRESSLEYS, [C] daughter of COTTON, in the Countie of Stafford, and had issue LODOVICK, GEORGE, and MARY. LODOVICK married ANNA DYER, daughter of THOMAS DYER [D] of Stoughton in the *Com*. Huntington, and had issue—Thomas borne 1436, and after that twins, being 22 years after the birth of the said THOMAS; and the twins GEORGE & ARTHURE, who both served the house of AUSTRIA, the younger married (as Philipe Cormine relates) one HENRETTA DE LA VILLA ODOROSA. THOMAS married BRIDGET, second daughter to SIR GEORGE HERVIE [E] *de* St. Martins in *Com*. Middlesex, and died 1480, leaving his son WILLIAM, and daughter ANNA MINER, in tutorage to their mother BRIDGET whom she resigned to her father, and turned to a monastericall life in Datford, where she remained during her life. WILLIAM married ISABELLA HARCOPE [F] *de* Frolibay, and lived to revenge the death of the 2 young princes murdered in the tower of London, upon their inhuman uncle Richard the 3d. It was said of this WILLIAM MINER that he was "*Flos Militiæ,*" the flower of chevallrie. He left behind him 10 sons, WILLIAM, GEORGE, THOMAS, ROBERT, NATHANIEL, and JOHN; the rest are not recorded. The 2 last went over to Ireland, 1541, when King Henry the 8 was proclaimed I king of Ireland. NATHANIEL married one FITZMAU-RICE neigh Catherlough, in the province of Leinster in Ireland. John married to JOSELINA O'BRYAN, daughter to TEIG O'BRYAN of Innis in the county of Clare; whose posteritie remains there, in the name of MINER, bearing the same coat. GEORGE married and lived in Shropshire. THOMAS in Hereford. WILLIAM, the eldest son, had

issue—CLEMENT and ELIZABETH MINERS, and was buried
at Chew-Magna, the 23 day of February, *Anno Domini*,
1585; and lies interred in the Priests Chancell, about four
foot from the wall, with this inscription 𝔥𝔢𝔦𝔯——𝔠𝔱𝔥——
𝔪 𝔪𝔶𝔫𝔢𝔯——𝔬𝔣——𝔭𝔰𝔥——𝔬𝔳𝔦𝔦𝔱 𝔯𝔯𝔦𝔦𝔦 𝔣𝔢𝔟𝔯𝔲' 𝔪𝔡𝔩𝔯𝔯𝔯𝔳:
this and no more legible upon the stone, with the coat
expressed in the margin, at this sign*, but by the records
and registers of the said church, it is evident, that his

 name was WILLIAM MINER, they
both agreeing in the same date and
place, and must needs have been the
head of the same family, as by the
paternal coat clearly appears. CLEM-
ENT his son succeeded his father in
heritage, and married —— and had

issue CLEMENT, THOMAS, ELIZABETH, and MARY MI-
NERS; and departed this life the 31 of March, 1640, and
lyes interred in Chew-Magna in the countie of Somersett.
CLEMENT the eldest brother married SARH POPE [G]
daughter of John POPE of NORTON-SMALL-REWARD, in
the countie of Somersett, and had issue WILLIAM and
ISRAEL. This Clement was buried at Burslingtown in
the Countie of Somersett. THOMAS his brother is now
alive at STONINGTOWN, in CARNETICUTE COLLONEY, in
NEW ENGLAND, *Anno Domini* 1683, and has issue, JOHN,
THOMAS, CLEMENT, MANASSAH, EPHRAIM and JUDAH
MINERS, and two daughters MARIE and ELIZABETH.
WILLIAM MINER, eldest son of CLEMENT MINER, mar-
ried SARAH, daughter of JOHN BATTING [H] of Cliffon
in Gloucestershire, and lives *Anno* 1683, in Christmas
Street in the city of Bristol, and has issue WILLIAM and

Sarah Miners. Iseraell, the second son, married
Elizabeth, daughter of Thomas Jones [I] of Burslingtown in the Countie of Somersett, and has issue Clement,
Thomas, Sarah, Jean, and Elizabeth Miners, *Anno*
1683. And now having done with the description Gene-
alogicall I hope that

*   *   *   *

Even every ingenious stranger makes mention

*   *   *   *

and if I have used any old or ancient words, yea words
now differently syllabicated, I may excuse myself with
Quintilianus, '*verba a vetustate repetita, non solum
magnos assertores habent, set etiam afferunt orationi
majestatem aliquam, non sine delectatione,*' and for the
Ingenious Reader I am; not caring that every peasant
should venture his sick-brain'd opinion upon this essay,
knowing well that *ars nominen habet inimicum præter
ignorantum*, but if he will take this council*

*   *   *   *

*   *   *   *

and keeping himself silent, he may parse for a wit; while
on the contrary his too much garrulity shows his naked-
ness, as much as *Prester John*† who describes himself
from the loijns of Solomon, or Frithulf from Seth:
but I shall be very much beholden to the learned reader,
who if he can give more satisfaction in this essay would
for the honor of antiquitie (who now lyes *in profundo
Democratis Puteo*) mend the errata Chronologicall, and

---

* [In the margin]   If thou hast no taste in learning medle no more with
what thou understandest not.   [The Greek, of which this is a translation, is
nearly illegible in the manuscript.]
† Damian. a Goes "De moribus Æthiopum."

see if he can describe the surname from a longer time ;
it being supposed that HENRY MINERS name before the
Kings Progresse in Somersett was BULLMAN, but how
certain however I know not, but leave it to some other
whose experience and learning exceeds mine; desiring
nothing more than herauldrie should be restored to its
pristine splendor and truth, and not to be abused by every
common Painter and Plasterer, who before they will
lose a fee will feinzie a coat of armes to the loss of the
estates, goods and sometime their very name

    "*Quid non mortalia pectora cogis auri sacra fames.*"
But—

"*Emblemata ad voluntatem Domini Regis sunt portanda
et non alias,*"

and Herauldrie stands in need of the doze   *   *   *   and
now I will conclude, with RALPH BROOKE, Esquire, and
York Herauld,

> " To make these names alive again appeare
> Which in oblivion well neigh buried were,
> That so our children may avoid the jarres
> Which might arise about their ancestors,
> And that the living might those titles see
> With which their names and houses honored be ;
> Yet I have hope of more acceptance from
> Those future times that after me shall come,
> For when beneath the stroke of death I fall
> And those that live these lives examine shall,
> Detraction dying, you that doe remain
> Will credit me and thank me for my pain.
>
>   Virg. ———si quid novis rectius
>   Candidus imparti : si non, his utere **mecum.**"

[A marginal note on the original is as follows :—
"This Coat of the Miners of Chew I attest to be en-

tered at Bath in Somersett by Clarenceux the 4 of K.
James the first, which visitation is in custody of me, 1606.

Alex: Cunninghame."

[NOTES.—The Miner arms are impaled with those of
the following families at the sides of the pedigree against
the places where we have inserted the respective letters:

A. "With *Hicks*,"—gu. a fesse wavy or, between
three fleurs-de-lis of the second.

B. "With *Hobbs*,"—ar. two bars sable, in each of the
three compartments, three birds gu. [Burke gives Hobbes,
of Sarum, co. Wilts, "sa. on a chev. or, betw. three *swans*
ar. as many lions' heads erased." Perhaps the artist designed to represent swans, in this sketch,—but swans
gules would be *raræ aves*,—and the birds do not look
swan-like, though they might pass for *ducks*.]

C. "With *Gressley*,"—barry of six, gules and ermine.
[Gresley, of Coulton, co. Stafford, "*Vaire* gu. and erm."
Burke.]

D. "With the *Dyers*,"—Per fesse indented, gu. and
or. [I have little doubt that this *ought* to have been,
Or, a chief indented, gu.; but the drawing is as I have
given it.]

E. "With the *Hervies*,"—gu. on a fesse ar. three trefoils slipped.

F. "With the *Harcops*,"—sa. a chevron betw. three
lions (?) rampant ar.

G. "With the *Popes*,—per pale or and az., on a chev.
between three griffins' (?) heads erased, as many fleurs-
de-lis, all countercharged.

H. "With the *Battings*,"—ermine, a fesse sable.

I. "With *Jones*," ermine, a chevron sable.]

THE

HERALDIC JOURNAL;

RECORDING THE ARMORIAL BEARINGS AND GENEALOGIES
OF AMERICAN FAMILIES.

NO. XII. DECEMBER, 1865.

THE ELLERY FAMILY.

William[1] Ellery, the emigrant ancestor of the family, is said to have come from Bristol, Eng.

He was settled in Gloucester, Mass. Bay, as early as Oct. 8th, 1663, which is the date of his marriage to Hannah, dau. of William Vinson. She died Dec. 24th, 1675. He again married, June 13, 1676, Mary, dau. of John Coit and Mary Stevens, and grand dau. of "Mr. John Coit."

William Ellery was admitted freeman May 15, 1672; was a Selectman a few years; and a Deputy to General Court in 1689. His residence was near that of his father-in-law's; at Vinson's, or, as it was sometimes called, Ellery's Cove. He died Dec. 9, 1696. By his two wives he had thirteen children, six sons and seven daughters, all born in Gloucester.

Benjamin[2] Ellery, Esq., born Sept. 6, 1669, went to Bristol, R. I., but finally settled at Newport, R. I. He married, July 30 1696, Abigail, daughter of John Wilkins, who was from Wiltshire, Eng.

12

Mr. Ellery had a letter of marque from George of Denmark, consort of Queen Ann, in 1702. He bore the title "Capt.," but nothing is known of his services at sea. He became a very wealthy merchant of Newport, and was a Deputy of Newport in the Colonial Assembly, Judge of the County Court, and Assistant of the Colony. He died July 26, 1746, disposing by will of a large estate, of which, were portraits of himself, wife and sons, which are still in possession of a descendant.

John² Ellery, born June 25, 1681, also went to R. I., but is supposed to have finally settled in Conn., from the "following" (which undoubtedly is a record of his marriage) "taken from an old manuscript found among the papers of the late William Ellery, Esq., of Hartford, Conn., in possession of his dau. Jane Seymour, mother of Gov. T. H. Seymour:"

"Jane Bonner and John Ellery of Boston was married the 31 Aug. 1710." This branch of the Ellery family was connected with many of the leading families in Connecticut.

Capt. Nathaniel² Ellery, born March 31, 1683, first married "Abigail Norwood; she survived the union only three months." He next married, Feb. 16, 1721, Ann, dau. of William Sargent, 2d, and great-grand-daughter of Deputy Gov. Symonds. Madam Ellery died, Oct. 8, 1772, aged ninety years. A fine portrait of her by Copley is in possession of a descendant.

Mr. Ellery's title, "Captain," was derived from military service. He was a prominent and public spirited citizen of Gloucester; was a Selectman several years; and in 1732 Town Treasurer. He and his brother, Capt. William² Ellery, with five other prominent citizens, built at their own expense the First Parish Meeting house. They also with others projected the first school house in the Harbor Parish.

Mr. Ellery was a merchant, and died May 30, 1761, possessed of a large estate. His dau. Mary m. Rev. John Rogers of Gloucester.

Capt. William[2] Ellery, born March 17, 1694, married, May 22, 1719, Dorcas Elwell, who died Feb. 13, 1733. He next m. Abigail Allen, dau. of "Squire" Allen, Oct. 1, 1739.

Mr. Ellery is supposed to have been a sea captain in early life. He was also engaged in trade, and was a Selectman a few years; he died Sept. 20, 1771. His dau. Lucy married Rev. Samuel Foxcroft, first minister of New Gloucester, Me.

Capt. Dependence[2] Ellery, born Jan 24, 1697, married Jan. 4, 1722, Sarah Warner. They had eleven children of whom little is known.

Hon. William[3] Ellery, son of Benjamin,[2] was born at Bristol, Rhode Island, Oct. 31, 1701; was grad. at Harvard College in 1722; married Elizabeth, dau. of Job and Ann Almy, Jan. 3, 1722. He was a wealthy merchant of Newport, and Judge, Deputy, Assistant, and Deputy Governor of the Colony. He died March 15, 1764.

Mr. Nathaniel[3] Ellery, Jr., son of Nathaniel,[2] born Oct. 20, 1726, married, Oct. 20, 1747, Rachel, dau. of Colonel John Stevens. She died July 1, 1750. He again married, Sept. 17, 1751, Mary, dau. of Deacon William Parsons.

Mr. Ellery was an eminent merchant of Gloucester, and extensively engaged in commerce. His son, John

Stevens[4] Ellery, married Esther, dau. of Winthrop Sargent and Judith Sanders, and had a son, John Stevens[5] Ellery, Jr., who became a very wealthy merchant of Boston.

Nathaniel[3] also had a son Nathaniel,[4] born Feb. 13, 1753, was grad. at Harvard in 1772; married Dec. 11, 1788, to Sarah, dau. of John Cunningham. He served as an officer during the revolution. His only son, William,[5] became a merchant of Gloucester; m. Harriet Foster, dau. of Capt. Daniel Sayward. Capt. William[3] Ellery, son of Nathaniel,[2] born in July, 1730, m. Abigail Foster of Boston, Aug. 1, 1765. He was a few years a Selectman, and in 1776 a Representative to General Court. He was a sea captain, by which profession he acquired a large fortune. He afterwards became a merchant of Gloucester.

Benjamin[4] Ellery, son of Hon. William,[3] born Feb. 5, 1725; married, Nov. 22, 1749, Lucy, widow of Col. John Vassal, and only dau. of Jonathan Barran of Chelmsford. She died Oct. 19, 1752. He next married, Jan. 22, 1769, Mehitable, only dau. of Abraham Redwood, Esq., the founder of the Redwood Library in Newport.

Hon William[4] Ellery, son of Hon. William,[3] was born at Newport, Dec. 22, 1727; was grad. at Harvard College in 1747. He married, Oct. 11, 1750, Ann, dau. of Hon. Jonathan Remington of Cambridge. She died Sept. 7, 1764. He next married, June 28, 1767, Abigail, dau. of Col. Nathaniel Carey. She died in 1793. Mr. Ellery became a wealthy merchant of Newport. He was appointed Naval Officer of the Colony of R. I., in 1757; and in 1768–9, was Clerk of the Court of Common Pleas

for the county of Newport. In 1770 he commenced the
practice of law. In 1776 he was elected Delegate to
the Continental Congress, and the same year signed the
Declaration of Independence. He was appointed Loan
Officer of R. I., in 1786, in which office he continued till
1790, when he received the appointment of Collector of
Customs for the district of Newport, which he held till
his death, Feb. 15, 1820. His dau. Elizabeth,[5] m. Hon.
Francis Dana, Chief Justice of Mass. Lucy[5] m. William
Channing, Esq., Attorney General of R. I., and was
mother of the famous divine, William Ellery Channing,
D. D. Almy[5] m. Hon. William Stedman. His son,
George Wanton[5] Ellery, is now Deputy Collector of the
customs for Newport. Mr. Ellery was one of the trus-
tees of Brown University, and was also Chief Justice
of R. I. in 1785.

Christopher[4] Ellery, Esq., son of Hon. William,[3] was
born in Newport, April 22, 1736 ; m. Mary, dau. of Samuel Vernon and grand-dau. of Gov. Ward. Mr. Ellery
was a Deputy in the Colonial Assembly, a Justice of the
Court of Common Pleas, and an Assistant of the Colony.
He died in 1789. His son, Hon. Christopher[5] Ellery,
was in the majority of the National Senate, during the
first four years that Thomas Jefferson was President of
the United States. His son, Frank, has been an officer in
in the Navy (regular service) since 1812.

Abraham Redwood[5] Ellery, Esq., son of Benjamin, born
May 24, 1773, was grad. at Harvard. He married Charlotte, dau. of Capt. Charles Frederick Weissenfels, and
grand-dau. of Col. Frederick Henry Weissenfels, of West
Prussia, a descendant of Baron Von Weissenfels. Mr.

Ellery entered the office of Chief Justice Parsons, for the study of law. When the army was raised under the Presidency of John Adams, Mr. Ellery was appointed Capt. on Gen. Hamilton's staff. He was soon made Assistant Adjutant General. After leaving the army he went to New Orleans, and pursued his profession. He died at the Bay of St. Louis, Nov. 1, 1820.

ARMS.

A number of old book-plates in old books are in possesssion of different descendants, also an old silver seal inscribed B. E., 1749.

It will be noticed, that the style of this coat is very different from the English mode. It is highly probable that the family is of French origin, and that we are to look in the French armorials for the arms.

H. E.

BARONETS OF NEW ENGLAND.

Sir William Pepperrell was created a Baronet, 15 Nov. 1746. The Baronetage before cited says only that he was descended from a family in Cornwall. His father, William[1] Pepperrell, was a native of Tavistock, near Plymouth, co. Devon; we have already (p. 88) printed a letter from which it would seem that the family claimed arms, and the baronet received an augmentation to the coat. He lived at Kittery, and acquired a very large fortune as a merchant there. He m. Margery, dau. of John Bray, and had sons Andrew[2] and William,[2] besides six daughters. His son William, also a distinguished merchant, was a member of the Council for thirty-two years, and for his success in capturing Cape Breton, in 1745, was created a baronet. He died in 1759.

His only son, Andrew,[3] died in 1751, and the title thus ceased with the first possessor. His only daughter, Elizabeth,[3] m. Nathaniel Sparhawk of Boston, and their son, William,[4] assumed the name and arms of Pepperrell, and was created a Baronet, 9 Nov., 1774. He married Elizabeth, dau. of Hon. Isaac Royal, of Medford, Mass., and had only one son, William[5] Royal Pepperrell, who d. in 1798. The second baronetcy, accordingly, expired again in 1816, at the death of Sir William, though his three daughters all married. Descendants through the female line from William Pepperrell still remain here.

These arms of Sir William are thus emblazoned, Argent, a chevron gules, between three pine-apples vert; together the augmentation of a canton of the second, charged with a fleur-de-lys of the first. Crest, an armed arm embowed, proper,—grasping a staff, thereon a flag argent,—issuing out of a mural crown, with three laurel leaves between the battlements proper; over the crest on a scroll the word PEPERI. Motto: *Virtute parta tuemini.*

Sir John Davie, of New London, Conn., succeeded to the title about A. D. 1706. Kimber and Johnson's Baronetage is our authority for the following sketch. The family was originally of Devonshire, and called De-la-Wey; a high antiquity is claimed for it prior to John[1] Davie, *the younger,* (i. e., of two brothers of the same Christian name,) who was thrice Mayor of Exeter, first in 1584. His son, John[2] Davie, of Creedy, co. Devon, was created a baronet in 1641, and had sons, Sir John,[3] William,[3] Robert,[3] and Humphrey.[3] Sir John,[3] the second baronet, had a son Sir John,[4] High Sheriff of Devon, as was his father, who d. unm. The fourth baronet was Sir William,[4] son of William,[3] who had only three daughters. Robert[3] had two sons who died unm., so the title fell to Sir John,[4] fifth baronet, who was son of Humphrey[3] Davie.

Humphrey[3] Davie married the sister of Edmund White of Clapham, co. Surrey, and had John.[4] He removed to New England, settled at Billerica, was an Assistant, 1679–86. He married here, Sarah, widow of James Richards of Hartford, and died in 1689. His son, John, married his step-sister, Elizabeth Richards, and lived at Groton, Conn., till his accession, when he returned to England, with his family of three sons and three daughters.

Though the family thus ceased to be connected with New England, in the main line, one branch *may* yet remain. In the REGISTER, I., 169, it is said that Humphrey of Boston had a son, Humphrey of Dorchester, whose daughter, Elizabeth, m. James Butler, and died in 1739.

OFFICIAL SEALS.

Our next example of the seals of the Governors of Massachusetts is that of Joseph Dudley, who was appointed in 1702, and served till 1715. As is well known, he was the son of Gov. Thomas Dudley, whose seal we have given at p. 35. Of course the right to arms is the same in each case, but it will be noticed that in this seal the lion is delineated with a forked tail (queue fourchée) and the mark of cadency, the crescent, is omitted. Our English friends have devoted some time to an examination of the pedigree of these Dudleys, but without arriving at any certain origin. In the last number of the "Herald and Genealogist," (Part XVI., pp. 308–315,) is an article on the families of Nicolls, Purefoy, and Dudley, from which we propose to make some extracts.

Cotton Mather says that Thomas Dudley "became a clerk unto Judge Nichols, who, being his kinsman by his mother's side, therefore took the more special notice of him." Mr. Adlard (The Sutton-Dudleys of England, &c.) prints a MS. belonging to Mr. Thornton, stating that Dudley was educated by the care of one Mrs. Purfroy. Mr. Adlard, finding a marriage of Dorothy Purefoy with —— Nicols, somewhat hastily assumed that the Judge was a relative of Dudley's protectress.

The writer in the "Herald and Genealogist" does indeed prove a connection, but in a different mode. The Judge Nicols was undoubtedly Sir Augustine Nichols, Justice of the Common Pleas, 1612—1616. His grandfather was William[1] Nichols of Clay Coton, in Northamptonshire, whose son Thomas[2] was a lawyer, and acquired a considerable estate. Thomas[2] married Anne, dau. of John Pell of Eltrington, co. Northampton, and died, 29 June, 1568, leaving four sons and three daughters. His widow married Richard Purefoy, probably the third son of Edward Purefoy of Shalston, co. Bucks. She was probably Dudley's friend.

It is probable, therefore, either that Dudley's mother was a kinswoman to Judge Nichols, or that his mother, Anne Pell, was related to the Dudleys.

Unfortunately the will of Mrs. Anne (Pell) Purefoy has not been found, and Nichols's will bequeathes legacies according to a schedule, which schedule is missing.

———

Of Gov. Joseph Dudley there is little for us to write here. He was unusually gifted by nature with advantages, and he occupied a conspicuous place in our colonial history. The relation of his life must be sought in Hutchinson's and Palfrey's histories.

He was born 23 Sept., 1647 ; m. Rebecca, dau. of Edward Tyng, and had thirteen children. Of his sons, Paul was Chief Justice, and William was Speaker of the House of Representatives.

THE CHAUNCEY FAMILY.

" Charles Chauncey, the second President of Harvard College, was the emigrant ancestor of all who bear the name of Chauncey in the United States. He was the fifth son of George Chauncey of Newplace and Yardley-Bury in Hertfordshire, who died in 1627, and the third of his second wife. His mother, Agnes, was the daughter of Edward Welsh of Great Wymondly, and the widow of Edward Humberstone. He was baptized and registered 5 Nov., 1592, in Yardley-Bury Church, Hert."

This citation, from the "Memorials of the Chaunceys," by William Chauncey Fowler, (Boston, 1858,) indicates our authority for the following sketch.

The family is traced to William de Chauncey, Baron of Skirpenbeck, from whom in successive generations were Walter, Aufrid, Roger, Robert, Thomas, William, and Thomas. This last, who died 49 Edw. III., (1376) had a son, Sir William de Chauncey, Baron of Skirpenbeck, who married Joan, dau. of Roger Bigod, and, in 1399, obtained a license to alienate his manor of Skirpenbeck with the title.

His son, John[1] Chauncey, m. Margaret, dau. of William Gifford, and had John,[2] who m. Ann, dau. of John Leventhorp, and was by her the father of John.[3] John[3] Chauncey m. a dau. of Thomas Boyce, and had John,[4] who m. Elizabeth, dau. of John Proffit and widow of Richard Mansfield. He d. 4 June, 1546, and his heir, Henry,[5] by wife Lucy had George[6] of Newplace and Yardley-Bury.

This George[6] Chauncey m. first, Jane, dau. of John Cornwall of Yardley, and had several children; by his second wife, as we have seen, he was the father of Rev. Charles[7] Chauncey.

Charles[7] Chauncey was of Trinity College, Cambridge; Master of Arts, 1617; a Fellow, and Bachelor of Divinity, in 1624. In 1627, he became Vicar of Ware, and in 1637 he came to New England, where he preached for three years, at Plymouth, with Rev. John Reyner. In 1641 he succeeded Rev. John Lothrop at Scituate, but not being suited there he was about returning to England, in 1654, when he was offered the post of President of Harvard College. He died in office, 19 Feb., 1671–2.

His wife was Catherine, daughter of Robert Eyre of Sarum, Wilts, by his wife Agnes, daughter of the famous John Still, Bishop of Bath and Wells. This family was one of note in Wiltshire for several centuries.

Of the children of Rev. Charles Chauncey, four settled here, viz., Nathaniel,[8] of Hatfield, Mass.; Elnathan,[8] of Boston, (d. *s. p.*); Israel,[8] of Stratford, Conn.; and Sarah,[8] who married Gershom Bulkeley.

The oldest son, Isaac,[8] was graduated at Harvard, but returned to England and died in 1712. He was a voluminous writer. His son, Charles,[9] born in England, settled in Boston, and here m. Sarah, dau. of John Walley. His son, Rev. Charles[10] Chauncey, D. D., b. in 1705, became the minister of our First Church, in 1727, and died, after a most active and useful ministry, in 1787.

He married three times; by his first wife, Elizabeth, daughter of Grove Hirst, he had an only son, Charles.[11] Samuel,[12] son of this last Charles,[11] left a son, Charles William,[13] the only remaining descendant of the name in this line.

Of the other children of President Chauncey, Elnathan[8] was a clergyman at Windsor, Conn., and Hatfield, Mass. His son, Rev. Nathaniel,[9] was settled at Durham, Conn., whose son, Elihu,[10] was a Colonel in the French War, and was the father of Charles[11] Chauncey, J. S. C., Conn. A son of this last, Charles[12] Chauncey, Jr., was a noted lawyer in Philadelphia.

Rev. Israel[8] Chauncey, the only other son of the President to be traced, was settled at Stratford, Conn. His son, Charles,[9] was ordained at Bridgeport, Conn., and by his second wife, Sarah, dau. of Henry Wolcott, had several children, of whom Robert[10] had an only son, Wolcott,[11] whose son was Isaac[12] Chauncey, Commodore in the Navy.

Another son of the Rev. Israel[8] Chauncey was Rev. Isaac[9] Chauncey of Hadley, Mass.

It will be noticed in this brief sketch, that the family was not only of honorable parentage in England, but that it has been highly esteemed here. Like many of our "Brahmin families," the clerical element has been predominant in every generation, but Mr. Fowler's volume shows, also, that those members who were not devoted to that service have been useful and respected members of society wherever placed.

HERALDIC NOTES AND QUERIES.

XXVII.

 The seal of famous Rev. Hugh Peters here copied from the first volume of the Winthrop Papers, serves to open a discussion as to his family.

Savage says that he was born in 1599, at the parish of St. Ewe, or, as commonly said, in the town of Fowey, Cornwall; was bred at Trinity College, Cambridge; preached in London, Rotterdam, and finally at Salem, Mass.

As to his family, it will be noticed that he uses the arms of the family of the Lords Petre, of Writtle, in the county of Essex. The curious but most incorrect "History of the Rev. Hugh Peters," by Rev. Samuel Peters, (New York, 1807,) says "the family, of which Hugh Peters had his descent, came from Normandy into England, with William the Conqueror, in 1066, and John Peters was knighted by Henry VIII., and his grandson, John, was created a Baron by King James I., in 1603." William, fourth son of Sir John Petre, Knt. of Exeter, is said to have been father of Hugh, but it is not expressly said that this Sir John of Exeter was the grandfather of the first Lord, though it is implied.

On the other hand, Burke (Commoners, I., 29) says that Hugh was the son of Thomas Dykewoode Peters, whose father, Thomas Dykewoode, (of a family which had been driven from Antwerp, on account of its religion,) first assumed the name of Peters.

Thus much is clear, from Collins's Peerage and Burke: William[1] Petre (12 Edw. IV.) had a son John[2] of Torre Brian, co. Devon, who had a daughter married to John Petre of Exeter, as also six sons, of whom William,[3] born at Exeter, who became Secretary of State and held other high offices. This Sir William had an only son John, created a Baron by the title of Lord Petre of Writtle, in 1603, who had four sons, and the succession has continued to the present time.

A sister of Sir William married her cousin, John Petre of Bowhay, near Exeter, and had a son Thomas, whose grandson, Henry Peter, married Deborah, dau. of John Treffry of Place. Her sister Martha seems to have married Thomas Dykewood Peters, and have been the mother of our Hugh.

It will be noticed that Sir William Peters, who was born about 1510, must have been somewhat older than this Thomas Dykewoode, who was the grandfather of Hugh, and who assumed the name of Peters. It seems also that he assumed the arms, and his son married in the same family as Sir William's relative. As Sir William was a man of so much note, having been "Secretary and of the Privy Council to four Kings and Queens of this realm, and seven times Ambassador abroad in foreign lands," it would be interesting to find who this Thomas Dykewoode was, who was thus, by name and arms, enrolled in so prosperous a family.

Of Hugh Peters himself it is unnecessary to say much. He married, first, widow of Edmund Reade of Wickford, co. Essex, and was thus the step-father of the wife of John Winthrop, Jr. He m. secondly, at Boston, Deliverance Sheffield, and had one daughter. His brother Thomas came here but returned. The mendacious "Life," before quoted, adds another brother, William of Boston, said to be father of John, Andrew, Thomas, William, Samuel, and Joseph. On this point Savage writes, "after diligent search no William is found, either in Boston or its vicinity, and I suppose this may be regarded as one of the many inventions of the book."

Truly there was an Andrew of Boston, who seems to have been the progenitor of most of those recorded in the "Life," but there is no reason to connect him with Hugh Peters.

XXVIII.

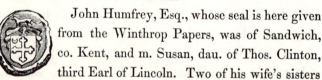 John Humfrey, Esq., whose seal is here given from the Winthrop Papers, was of Sandwich, co. Kent, and m. Susan, dau. of Thos. Clinton, third Earl of Lincoln. Two of his wife's sisters m. Isaac Johnson, and John, son of Sir Ferdinando Gorges.

Here Humfrey was in high position, yet, having lost his property, he went home in 1641. His children are said to have been, Theophilus, Thomas, Joseph, John, Lydia, Ann, (who m. William Palmes,) and perhaps others.

Although we have given the seal as engraved in the Mass. Hist. Society's Collections, it is possible that the cross should be charged either with escallops or pellets, as it is in the arms of some families of the name. Still the crest differs from those in Burke, except one coat in which the cross is plain, but is a cross patonce instead of boutonné.

THE

HERALDIC JOURNAL;

RECORDING THE

𝕬𝖗𝖒𝖔𝖗𝖎𝖆𝖑 𝕭𝖊𝖆𝖗𝖎𝖓𝖌𝖘 𝖆𝖓𝖉 𝕲𝖊𝖓𝖊𝖆𝖑𝖔𝖌𝖎𝖊𝖘

OF

AMERICAN FAMILIES.

VOLUME II.

BOSTON:
WIGGIN & LUNT, PUBLISHERS,
13 SCHOOL STREET.
1866.

PREFACE.

In presenting our readers with the fourth part of our second volume, we are tempted to recapitulate a few of the more salient features of this year's publication. In the first place, the change in form has rendered it possible to treat the different topics more at length, and to attain a completeness from which we were before debarred. This advantage has counterbalanced the inconveniences of a change in the plan as originally announced.

In the present volume will be found some articles of more than local interest. The explanation of the system of " Hall Marks on Plate," which enables us to determine the age of many heir-looms, can hardly be accessible elsewhere to many of our readers. The review of Mr. Shirley's " Noble and Gentle Men of England" presents a catalogue of the names of the true " County Families" widely at variance with the ideas commonly entertained here. The importance of the Washington pedigree will justify the space accorded to it, and we have been able to present not only the genealogy of the family here, but the elaborate correction of errors in the English accounts, made by the industry of Mr. Chester.

In genealogy, the Hutchinson, Jeffries, Pynchon, Browne, Norton, Montgomery, Bolton and Amory families have been carefully traced, and thus the field covered by the second portion of our title has been improved.

In this volume also will be found transcripts of all the armorial tombstones in the three Boston grave-yards, a work never before attempted, but certainly of interest to antiquarians. The examples remaining at Salem have also been carefully copied and anno-tated by our associate, Mr. Goodell.

As was promised at the close of our first volume, we have this year made considerable progress in the publication of the seals on early documents recorded at the Suffolk Probate Office. Forty-nine are herein copied, and this is but a portion of those collected by Mr. Perkins. The series will be continued in the next volume, and the other Probate Offices of the State will be thoroughly examined. As these wills are generally of a later date than the period covered by Mr. Savage's labors, the genealogist will find new matter in the accompanying notes.

During the present year the interest in genealogy and heraldry has apparently been increasing in Eng-land. The "Herald and Genealogist" has com-pleted its third volume, and a new quarterly, the

"Miscellanea Genealogica et Heraldica," edited by Dr. Joseph Jackson Howard, was commenced in July. Both of these magazines deserve a liberal support on this side of the Atlantic, as discussing subjects in which we claim a common interest with our English cousins. To the "Herald and Genealogist" we are especially indebted, for not only has Mr. Nichols given copious extracts from the pages of this journal, but in several cases he has devoted much space to the history of families in which we feel the greatest interest. We may instance the Dudley, Norton, Lowell, Washington and Temple families, concerning all of whom new and interesting facts have been discovered.

During this year two or three new Heraldic Manuals have been issued in England,—Clark's, Cussans' and Elvin's,—and the writer may be pardoned for mentioning that the first heraldic treatise, especially prepared to meet the requirements of American students, has been published in this city. It is hoped that the "Elements of Heraldry" may prove to be adapted to the special wants of our public.

We have recently taken occasion, in another magazine, to review the present position of the study of heraldry in this country, and the following points may not be unworthy the consideration of our readers: "Here in America, there is a common mistake in the supposition that certain coats-of-arms belong to certain families. As a supplement, it is supposed that all of the same surname constitute one family, and are hence entitled to the arms. This idea is clearly erroneous. Identity of surname raises no presumption of identity of origin." " It cannot be too strongly asserted, that there is no such thing as *family* arms, and that the only right an American can have to a coat-of-arms is contingent on the proof of his descent from a person entitled to it." " The right to use arms, by inheritance, is dependent entirely upon a well-authenticated pedigree. A coat-of-arms, whether obtained by grant or by recognition of the Heralds as of sufficient antiquity, is a species of property. It is inherited by the descendants of the first lawful possessor, and by them only. Whoever seeks to establish a claim on the ground of inheritance, must prove his descent precisely as he would in claiming a title or a piece of land."

These points being conceded, we must again solicit the co-operation of our readers in the collection of all authenticated pedigrees and instances of the use of coat-armor. We hope in the coming year to obtain much from the other Atlantic States, and would here repeat our readiness to publish any authenticated examples occurring in the entire country. Our own collections are necessarily limited in their field, but as the only existing journal here devoted to heraldic discussions, this magazine may invite a wide circle of contributors.

Finally, the editor of these first two volumes may ask the indulgence of his readers for all mistakes and deficiencies on the ground, first, of this being a pioneer work, and secondly, of having been deprived during the past year, by the absence of his colleagues, of those opportunities for consultation which would have doubtless rendered his duties lighter and more certain of fulfilment.

W. H. W.

GENERAL INDEX.

Arms, engraved:

Amory, 101; Apthorp, 14; Avery, 184; Belcher, 62; Bolton, 111, 115; Bonner, 120; Borland, 89; Bowdoin, 135; Brinley, 31; Browne, 23; Burnet, 60; Byfield, 126; Checkley, 131; Chester, 44; Cheseborough, 86; Clarke, 74, 169; Coggeshall, 45; Curtis, 116; Cushing, 123, 124; Davenport, 179; Dummer, 34; Eells, 9; Faneuil, 121; Fitch, 46; Franklin, 97; Freke, 130; Gedney, 20; Gee, 77; Goodridge, 81; Greene, 22; Greenwood, 78; Hancock, 99; Holyoke, 180; Hubbard, 134; Hutchinson, 83, 183; Jackson, 140; Jeffries, 166; Jones, 42; Lasinby, 129; Leete, 47; Lidgett, 169, 183; Lloyd, 88; Lord, 43; Lynde, 29, 91; Martyn, 7, 81; Mascarene, 125; Mather, 7; Moseley, 181; Mountfort, 79; Newton, 10; Norton, 1; Noyes, 84; Oxenbridge, 178; Pain, 19; Payne, 134; Peck, 41; Pickman, 26; Savage, 22; Sears, 137; Shirley, 116; Snelling, 10; Southac, 138; Steele, 20; Townsend, 21; Trail, 18; Tuthill, 132; Usher, 168; Vassall, 15; Wanton, 46; Wheelwright, 19; Wilson, 182; Winslow, 21; Woodhull, 116; Wyllys, 40.

Arms, engraved, but not identified: 8, 9, 90, 128, 179, 181, 183, 184.

Arms of families in West Chester Co., New York:

Allaire, 191; De Lancey, 191; Heathcote, 191; Jay, 191; Morris, 192; Pell, 192; Phillipse, 192; Van Cortlandt, 192; Wetmore, 192.

County Families of England:

Review of Shirley's Noble and Gentle Men, 53, 144.

Essex Wills, 141–143.

Genealogies:

Amory, 101; Bolton, 110; Bowdoin, 136; Brinley, 31; Browne, 24, 95; Clarke, 75; Digby, 92; Franklin, 97; Hutchinson, 171; Jeffries, 166; Kilby, 48; Montgomery, 63; Mountfort, 80; Norton, 1; Pickman, 26; Pynchon, 49; Sears, 137; Shirley, 117; Shute, 32; Vassall, 17; Washington, 66, 145; Woodhull, 113.

Hall Marks on Plate, 35.

Herald Painters:

James Turner, 94.

Monumental Inscriptions:

Boston, King's Chapel, 11–22; Copp's Hill, 74–84, 119; Granary, 120–140; Salem, 23–30; Stonington, Conn., 84–88.

Notes and Queries:

James Turner, 93; Fairfax family, 94; Browne family, 95.

Seals of the Governors of Massachusetts:

Dummer, 34; Burnet, 60; Belcher, 62; Shirley, 116.

B

Seals of Connecticut gentlemen :
  George Wyllys, 40; John Mason, 41 ; William Jones, 42; Thomas Lord,
  43; Leonard Chester, 44; John Coggeshall, 45 ; John Wanton, 46;
  Thomas Fitch, 46 ; William Leete, 47.
Suffolk Wills, 6, 177.
Temple Family, 186.
Washington Family in England, 145.

INDEX OF NAMES.

[Note. The list of the County Families of England, p. 57–60, being alphabetically arranged, is not incorporated herein.]

Adams, 8.
Addington, 181.
Allaire, 191.
Allen, 184.
Amory, 100–110.
Andrews, 141.
Apthorp, 14.
Arnold, 142.
Avery, 184.

Beal, 143.
Belcher, 61, 62, 176.
Bigg, 179.
Blake, 88, 179.
Bollan, 13.
Bolton, 110–115, 190.
Bonner, 120.
Borland, 89.
Bowdoin, 135–6.
Bowes, 179.
Boyes, 88.
Bradstreet, 6.
Bridges, 142.
Brinley, 31–2.
Browne, 23–6, 95–6.
Burnet, 60–1.
Byfield, 127.

Checkley, 131.
Cheseborough, 84–87.
Chester, 44, 145, 163.
Clarke, 74–6, 131, 169.
Coggeshall, 45.
Cole, 143.
Collins, 143.
Coward, 90.
Cranston, 176.
Crawford, 9, 179.
Croade, 143.
Cromwell, 90, 142.
Crossweight, 181.
Curtis, 111.
Cushing, 123.
Cussans, 144.

Dammer, 184.
Davenport, 179.

Dawson, 181.
De Lancey, 191.
Dennison, 141.
Derby, 142.
Digby, 91–3.
Dummer, 34.

Eckley, 128.
Eells, 9.
Eliot, 10, 91, 119.
Endicott, 141.
Epes, 143.

Fairfax, 94–5.
Faneuil, 121, 177.
Felton, 142–3.
Ferniside, 8.
Fitch 46, 47.
Foster, 142.
Francis, 179.
Franklin, 97–9.
Frary, 91.
Freke, 130.
Fuller, 142.

Gardner, 177.
Gedney, 20, 143.
Gee, 77.
Gerrish, 142.
Gibbs, 90, 143.
Goodrich, 81–2.
Grafton, 90.
Greene, 22.
Greenwood, 78.
Griggs, 143.
Groves, 182.

Hale, 178.
Hancock, 99, 100.
Hanscombe, 141
Hardie, 143.
Harris, 10.
Hawkins, 184.
Hayward, 143.
Heathcote, 191.
Hendley, 189.
Henshaw, 177.

Higginson, 184.
Hill, 176, 177.
Hirst, 143, 184.
Hoare, 143.
Horner 183.
Holyoke, 26, 180.
Hubbard, 134.
Hunt 179.
Hutchinson, 83–4, 170–6, 182.

Jackson, 140.
Jaffrey, 170.
Jay, 191.
Jeffries, 166–7.
Johnson, 76.
Jones, 42, 88.

Kilby, 48.
Kimball, 179.
Knight, 179.

Lasinby, 129.
Leete, 47.
Leverett, 8.
Lidgett, 169, 182.
Lindall, 143.
Lloyd, 88.
Lord, 43.
Lyde, 126.
Lynde, 29, 91, 179.

Macmillan, 143.
Marion, 177.
Martyn, 7, 8, 81.
Mascarene, 125.
Mason, 41, 176.
Mather, 7.
Michell, 143.
Moers, 142.
Montgomery, 63–66.
Morris, 192.
Moseley, 181.
Mountfort 79, 80.

Nash 179.
Nelson, 187.

Newton, 10.
Norton, 1, 176.
Noyes, 142.

Oliver, 181.
Oughlin, 90.
Oxenbridge, 178.

Pain, 19, 181.
Palmer, 8.
Parsons, 9.
Payne, 134.
Peck, 41.
Pell, 192.
Perkins, 125.
Philipse, 192.
Phillips, 143.
Philpott, 1.
Phips, 7.
Pickman, 26–28.
Pollard, 143.
Price, 90.
Prytherch, 142.
Pynchon, 49–53, 142.

Quincy, 90.

Raisin, 78.

Rawlins, 178, 184.
Read, 142.
Richard, 7.

Savage, 7, 22, 184.
Scottow, 7.
Sears, 137.
Sewall, 91.
Shaller, 90.
Shattuck, 142.
Sherwin, 181.
Shirley, 12, 53, 116–118, 144.
Short, 142.
Shute, 32–4.
Smith, 141.
Snelling, 10, 11.
Southac, 138–9.
Sparke, 142.
Staniford, 142.
Steele, 9, 20.
Stoughton, 6.

Temple, 176, 185–190.
Thayer, 183.
Townsend, 21, 90.
Trail, 18.

Turner, 94.
Tuthill, 132–3.

Usher, 168.

Van Cortlandt, 192.
Vassall, 15, 177.
Veren, 142.

Wainwright, 184.
Wanton, 46.
Washington, 66–74, 145–165.
Watson, 181.
Watts, 119.
Wetmore, 192.
Wheelwright, 19.
White, 187.
Willard, 185.
Williams, 143.
Wilson, 182.
Winchcombe, 10.
Winslow, 21, 120.
Winthrop, 6, 177.
Woodhull, 113–4.
Worcester, 184.
Wyllys, 40.

THE

HERALDIC JOURNAL;

RECORDING THE ARMORIAL BEARINGS AND GENEALOGIES
OF AMERICAN FAMILIES.

NO. XIII.   JANUARY, 1866.

THE NORTON FAMILY.

 In the New England Historical and Genealogical Register (XIII., 225) we published a transcript of an old MS. pedigree of the Norton family, tracing the line to Rev. John Norton of Boston, and his brother William. This pedigree was undoubtedly the work of John Philepott, Somerset Herald, in 1632, and he makes the following indorsement upon it:—" This Genealogie of the Norton of Sharpenhow in Bedfordshire, beginning at NORUILE that married into the house Valois, and came into England with Kinge William the Conquer and was his Constable; whose posteritie, long time after, assumed the English name of NORTON, being the same in signification that NORUILE is in French. For the proof whereof it is to be understood that this pedigree agreeth with records remaining in the office of Armes . . . . in one book of pedigree, late William Haruie's. Clarencieux King of Armes, couered in Read, and set forth in trick as far as Noruile, wch. was sonn of Sr. John Noruile, alias Norton.

and married with the daughter of Montchensie, and to Joan daughter of Sr. John, and her issue."

The pedigree is then traced for eight generations to Sir John Norton, whose son John was of Sharpenhow, co. Bedford.

This genealogy, having been reprinted from the Register, was recently reviewed in the "Herald and Genealogist," (Part XV., pp. 276–280,) and we therefore avail of the criticisms of the learned editor. He regards the pedigree " as evidently tainted with the romantic ingredient to which even the official heralds condescended at that period," and is disposed to regard all as imaginary prior to the Sir John Norton we have mentioned. He adds : "this pedigree of Norton of Sharpenhoe is the more remarkable because it is the hitherto unrecognized genealogy of Thomas Norton, the Elizabethan poet, one of the metrical translators of the Psalms, and joint-author of *Gorboduc*, with Thomas Sackville, afterwards Lord Treasurer and Earl of Dorset. When Mr. W. Durrant Cooper, F. S. A., prefixed a memoir of Norton to the edition of *Gorboduc*, printed for the Shakespeare Society in 1847, he failed to discover any pedigree, though there actually is one, signed by his son Robert Norton, in the Visitation of Hertfordshire, of 1634, and another signed by his nephew Graveley Norton, in the Visitation of Bedfordshire, in the same year."

From these three sources, therefore, we proceed to prepare the following sketch.

John[1] Norton of Sharpenhoe had a son, John,[2] who married twice, and left issue probably only by his second wife, Jane, daughter of John Cowper, by whom he had seven children. We will trace the families of two of his sons, viz., Thomas,[3] and Richard.[3]

Thomas[3] of Sharpenhow by his first wife, Elizabeth, dau. of Robert Merry of Northall, had a son, Thomas,[4] the noted writer, born in 1532.

This Thomas[4] Norton was one of the members in Parliament for London, from 1571 to 1582, and Remembrancer of the City, 1570–1. "He most exactly translated into English that excellent booke of Master Calvin's, *Institutions of Christian Religion*, and was the greatest helpe Mr. John Foxe had in compiling his large volume of *Acts and Monuments*."

He "attained the noted name of 'Master Norton the Parliament man,' and hath left even to this day a pleasing impression of his wisdome and vertue in the memories of many good men."

Thomas[4] Norton married first, Margaret, dau. of Archbishop Cranmer, who d. *s. p.*, and secondly, her cousin, Alice, daughter of Edmund Cranmer, by whom he had six children. Of these, Robert[5] Norton was of Market Cell, near Dunstable, and in 1634 had four sons and one daughter.

Luke[4] Norton, half-brother of Thomas[4] (being the son of Thomas[3] by his second wife, Elizabeth, daughter of Robert Marshall of Hitchin, co. Hertford,) married Lettice, daughter and heiress of George Graveley, and had three sons and six daughters in 1634. We need mention only Graveley[5] Norton, who signed the Visitation.

We will now revert to Richard[3] Norton, son of John,[2] and uncle to the noted Thomas. He married Margaret Wingate and had sons, Thomas,[4] and William.[4] The

industry of Mr. Nichols has brought to light the will of
this Margerie Norton, proved in 1572, in which she mentions her son Danyell, daughters Hill and Winshe, son
William Norton, brother Edward Norton, brother Wingate. Executors, her son William Norton, and son-in-law
William Winshe.

William[4] Norton, son of the preceding, married first,
Margerie, dau. of William Hawes, and had a son, William.[5] He married, secondly, Dennis Cholmley, niece to
Sir Nicholas Hare, Master of the Rolls, and had six sons
and two daughters.

William[5] Norton married Alice, daughter of John
Browest, and had six children, of whom John,[6] and William,[6] came to New England.

————

It will be noticed that William,[5] father of the emigrants,
was second cousin to Robert,[5] son of the Remembrancer
Thomas.[4] A note on the pedigree states that it was
" continued downe to this present yeare 1632 by the
informacon of Mr. Robert Norton the elder, sonn of the
said Mr. Thomas Norton the younger." This Robert was
evidently a man of letters, and the third edition of Camden's Annals of *Queen Elizabeth*, (Folio, 1635) was
translated by him. In it occurs a tribute to his father's
memory, from which we have already made an extract.

We have already (H. J. 1, 32) quoted Cotton Mather's
account of the birth of Rev. John Norton, son of William[5]
and Alice (Browest) Norton. We will however add a
few particulars from the Magnalia. He was born 6 May,
1606, studied at Peterhouse, Cambridge, was A. M., 1627,
but "an extreme disaster befalling his father's estate, he

quitted the University, and became at once usher to the school, and curate in the church at Starford." "In the year 1634, having married a gentlewoman both of good estate and of good esteem, he took shipping for New England." Disappointed by a storm which drove back his vessel, he carried out his plan in the following year. He was settled at Ipswich, and succeeded Rev. John Cotton at Boston. He died 5 April, 1663, leaving a widow, Mary, who died 17 January, 1678, but no children.

William[6] Norton, brother of Rev. John, was born in 1610, and settled at Ipswich, Mass. He married Lucy, daughter of Emmanuel and Lucy (Winthrop) Downing, and died 30 April, 1694, leaving sons, John[7] and Bonus,[7] and dau. Lucy, who m. John Wainwright, and afterwards Isaac Addington. Both sons left issue. John[7] was of H. C. 1671, and was settled as minister at Hingham, Mass. By wife Mary, dau. of Arthur Mason, he had Elizabeth,[8] who married Col. John Quincy, and one son, John.[8] Capt. John[8] Norton married Elizabeth, daughter of Col. John Thaxter, and had John,[9] William,[9] and Samuel.[9]

John[9] Norton m. Anne, dau. of Jeremiah Belknap, and had Samuel,[10] who married Jane, daughter of Joseph Andrews. This last Samuel[10] had Andrews[11] Norton, late Professor of Sacred Literature at Harvard College (b. 31 Dec. 1786, d. 18 Sept. 1853) who, by his wife Catherine, dau. of Samuel Eliot, had four children, one of whom is Charles[12] Eliot Norton, the well-known author, and co-editor of the North American Review.

SUFFOLK WILLS.

In presenting the following copies of the Seals preserved upon Wills in the Probate office for the county of Suffolk, it has not been found practicable to preserve a chronological arrangement. Owing to the insufficient space provided for the older files of papers, we have been obliged to examine them as they came to hand; and as the examination has not been completed yet, it follows that no regular order can be maintained in these notes.

It has been observed that whilst many of these seals evidently belonged to the persons using them, others belonged to the notaries or attesting witness. Moreover, these notaries seem each to have possessed several seals, and it is difficult always to decide upon the ownership. With all these disadvantages, however, it is felt that the publication of all the remaining examples will be the safest and most feasible plan to adopt.

We will begin by mentioning a few seals already engraved or described in this Journal.

1. Lt. Gov. William Stoughton used a seal with the same arms that are engraved on his tombstone (H. J. 1, 10), and on his will in 1701; as did also his sister Rebecca and others on a deed concerning her husband, William Tailor's property in 1682–3 : Thomas Cooper, who m. Mehitable Minot, niece of the Governor, on a paper dated 1705.

2. Adam Winthrop, (will dated 1700,) son of Adam, and grandson of Gov. John, used the well-known arms of his family on his seal.

3. Gov. Simon Bradstreet, on his will 1697, uses a seal of the arms engraved on p. 102 of our first volume.

4. In 1679, Welthian, widow of Thomas Richards, uses the arms described, (H. J. 1, 123,) and engraved on the tomb of her son James of Hartford, (H. J. vol. 1, 156.)

5. Sir William Phips, on his will 1695, uses the seal of which a fac-simile is engraved on p. 152 of our first vol.

6. Joshua Scottow, 1697, uses the seal belonging to his father-in-law, Major John Savage, being the arms engraved in the present number—" Inscriptions from King's Chapel, &c." In 1705, Thomas Savage uses the same seal, and bequeaths to son Habijah, " my seal-ring that was my father's."

7.

The accompanying cut represents the very curious seal on the will of Rev. Increase Mather, (1701,) the witnesses being Jonas Clarke, Edmund Wilder, and Joseph Woodwell. It seems to be armorial, yet it does not relate to either of these names. Mather often wrote his name Crescentius Mather, and but for the armorial character of the seal, it might be supposed to be a personal device, such as his son Cotton would have devised with delight. As it stands, it requires farther search to determine its character.

8.

We here present the seal of Michael Martin, of Boston, dated 23 Oct. 1700, proved 14 Nov. following. SAVAGE gives but the most meagre account of him, so that we will give some genealogical facts from the will.

He describes himself as the " only surviving son of Rich-

ard Martyn, of Portsmouth, in Piscataqua in New England, and after mentioning wife Sarah and son Richard
Martyn, he proceeds to make bequests to his three sisters
and their husbands, to his cousin Edward Martyn of Boston, and to his nephews and nieces. His sisters were
Sarah, wife of Richards Cutt; Elizabeth, wife of Edward
Kennard, and Hannah, wife of Richard Jose. His "three
sisters' oldest sons" were John Cutt, John Kennard, and
Thomas Jose. He mentions also Sarah, Mary and Elizabeth Cutt, daughters of his sister, and "cousins" Margaret Cutt, Judah Cutt, Susanna Martyn, (to whom he
gave his gold seal ring,) Joanna Jose, and Michael Kennard, (to whom he gave his silver seal.) There can be no
doubt from these two entries that the seal here shown was
his own.

His "cousin" (nephew?) Edward Martyn of Boston, in
his will of 1 May, 1717, mentions wife Sarah, and children
Mary, Sarah, Edward, Richard, John, Susanna, Nathaniel,
Elizabeth and Abigail. He gives a piece of plate to the
North Church, and probably he or Michael owned the
tomb in the Copp's Hill grave-yard, on which are the
Martyn arms, hereafter to be printed.

9.

This seal is on the will of Lisley Palmer,
who died 12 Feb. 1682–3, aged 33, and
was buried in the Granary burying
ground. The arms do not seem to belong to Palmer, nor to either of the three
witnesses, Hudson Leverett, John Ferniside, and David
Adams.

This seal, therefore, is yet to be appropriated.

10.

On the will of Samuel Eells of Hingham, dated 1 Aug. 1705, proved 15 June, 1713, we have one of those coats which reveal at once the owner's name. SAVAGE says that this Samuel was probably son of John of Dorchester and Newbury, and that he married Ann, daughter of Rev. Robert Lenthall of Newport. He was of Milford, Fairfield and Hingham, an officer in King Philip's war, and a representative in 1705 and 1706. His will gives the following particulars. Wife Sarah, (widow of Joseph Peck, says Savage,) on whom he says he settled certain lands at his marriage, by an indenture dated 28 July, 1689. Son Samuel of Milford, his wife Martha, and children Elizabeth, Frances and Anna Eells. Son Nathaniel Eells of Scituate, and daughter-in-law Frances Eells, widow. He bequeaths "my silver seal" and "great gold ring."

The same seal is on the wills of Thomas Steel and Susanna Crawford, but there can be no doubt as to the true ownership.

11.

The will of William Parsons, 1702, witnessed by John Hill and Moses Bradford, has another of these untraced coats-of-arms. It bears a faint affinity to a Bradford coat, of three stags' heads, couped, on a fesse, but we cannot build a theory on so slight foundation. Parsons mentions his grand-daughter Susanna Young, but no other relatives.

12.

Thomas Newton, evidently a notary public here, used two seals, one being a quartered shield. Impressions are found on wills witnessed by him, as those of Sarah Harris, 1702; John Eliot, 1707; Mary Winchcombe, 1717, and finally on his own in 1721.

There can be little doubt that this was the Thomas Newton, who, as Savage says, came from New Hampshire, where he was Secretary until 1690, and here was Controller of the Customs, Judge of the Admiralty, and Attorney General in the witchcraft prosecution.

At all events, this Thomas Newton is termed Esquire in his will, dated 6 March, 1720, proved 5 June, 1721, in which he mentions wife Christian, son Hibbett Newton, and daughters Elizabeth, Christian and Hannah.

His wife's will, proved 10 Feb. 1730, mentions dau. Thompson, dau. Christian Wainwright, and Elizabeth Newton. She also mentions her estate at "Plastow in Old England," and says her son Hibbett had had his share therein, which property she received from her father. She also mentions grandson Thomas Newton.

13.

The seal of William Snelling, on his will proved in 1674, enables us to fix his pedigree almost beyond doubt. He was a physician of Newbury, 1651, but died in Boston, and his will describes him as " the youngest son of the late Thomas Snelling of Chaddlewood, in Plimton Mary in the county of Devon."

In Tuckett's "Devonshire Pedigrees," (II. 21,) we find the following account of the family.

William[1] Snellinge of Chaddlewood in Plympton, S[t]. Mary, mar. Jane, dau. of —— Specot of Thornborough, and had Thomas[2] Snellinge of Chaddlewood, living in 1620, who m. Jane, dau. and heir of —— Elford, and had sons John[3], Thomas[3], Emmanuel[3], and William[3], and daus. Jane[3], Welthian[3], Mary[3], Florence[3], and Dorothy[3].

John[3] Snelling m. Frances, dau. of Walter Hele of Holbeton, and had George, Sampson, John, Elizabeth, Mary, Frances, Joane, and Jane, living in 1620.

We presume that Thomas[3] was father of William and John who came to New England, though therein we differ from the pedigree in Bridgman's Copp's Hill Epitaphs, p. 214. A. T. P.

MONUMENTAL INSCRIPTIONS.

BOSTON.

We shall commence our description of the monuments remaining in Boston, with those preserved in the King's Chapel and the adjacent yard. It is hardly necessary for us to say that the collections published by the late Thomas Bridgman contain many coats-of-arms which are not found in the localities described. We propose to copy those actually existing—and we will first give those within the Chapel.

I.

This coat-of-arms is on the tablet dedicated to the memory of Frances, wife of Gov. William Shirley, and is accompanied by the following inscription:—

M. S.

FRANCESCÆ SHIRLEY,

Quam Virginem

Omnium Admirationi commendavit

Eximius Formæ Nitor

Familiarum vero etiam Amori

Gratior veniens in pulchro Corpore virtus:

Quam Nuptam

Fides intemerata, Amor sincerus

Rerum Domesticarum prudens Administratio

Indoles suavissima,

In tantum Marito devinxerunt,

Ut Cor ejus in illa tutissime confiderit:

Quam Matrem

Nulla prius habuit Cura

Quam ut Liberorum Animos præstantissimis moribus imbueret

Quod et strenuit laboravit et feliciter:

Quam Demun

In omni Vitæ statio et Conditione,

Summæ Ingenii Elegantia

Quicquid Decorum atque Honestum diligenter excolentis

Quicquid Vanum contra et Leve serio aversantis

Morum Simplicitas candida

Pietas infucata

In Egeno Liberalitas in omnes Benevolentia,
Dolorum Tolerantia, Voluptatem Temperantia,
Omnes denique et omnimoda Virtus
Ut amabilem fecerunt omnibus
Ita Amorem ipsum et Delicias hujus Provincæ Vivam
Desiderium Triste et insolabile reddiderunt mortuam.
Maritum habuit Gulielmum Shirley hujus Provinciæ
Præfectum,
Quem Filiis quatuor, Filiabus quinque beavit
E Stirpe Generosa nata est Londini MDCXCII
Dinata Dorcestriæ Massachusettensium prid : Kal. Sept.
MDCCXLVI
In communi hujus Oppidi Cæmeterio conditæ ipsius Exuviæ
Felicem ad meliorem vitam Reditum expectant.
Juxta hanc Prœstantissimam Matrem positum est
Quicquid Mortale fuid Filiæ Natu secundæ FRANCISCÆ
BOLLAN
GULIELMI BOLLAN Armigeri
In Curia Vice Admiralitatis apud Massachusettensis
Regii Advocati,
Nuper Uxoris,
Quam Virtus et Formæ excellens,
Prudentia et Ingenium excultum
Pietas et Mores suavissimi,
Dilutissimam omnibus, dum in vivis fuit finxerunt.
Spatiolo Vitæ (heu brevi) percurso,
Annum quippe vix quartum supra vicissimum attigit,
Primo in Partu diem obiit supremum XII Kal. Martias
MDCCXLIV
Marito, Parentibus, Amicis
Ingens sui Desiderium relinquens.

[As we shall hereafter have to trace the family of William Shirley, in his place among the Governors, it will be sufficient to say that the arms are Shirley, impaling Barker.]

The next monument is that of Charles Apthorp, son of John and Susan (Ward) Apthorp, who was born in 1698. Charles Apthorp was a merchant here, paymaster and commissary of the English troops. He married, 13 Jan. 1726, Griselda, dau. of John Eastwicke, by his wife Griselda, dau. of John Lloyd, (called by Bridgman Sir John Lloyd of Somersetshire.) The Apthorps were numerous here, and very well connected. Of the children of Charles, Griselda m. Barlow Trecothick, Lord Mayor of London; John m. Alicia Mann, sister of Sir Horace Mann, British minister at Florence. Rev. Dr. East Apthorp m. a dau. of Foster Hutchinson, &c.

We cannot explain the arms here given, which should be Apthorp impaling Eastwicke.

M. S.

CAROLI APTHORP

QUI

PATER FAMILIAS PRVDENS ET LIBERALIS

MERCATOR INTEGERRIMVS

INSIGNI PROBITATE CIVIS,

INTER HVIVS ÆDIS INSTAVRATORES

PRÆCIPVE MVNIFICVS,

SINCERE FIDE ET LARGA CARITATE

CHRISTIANVS,

OBIIT SEXAGENARIVS

XI NOVEMBR. MDCCLVIII

REPENTINA

ET SVIS IMMATVRA

MORTO PRÆREPTVS

NE

TANTARVM VIRTVTVM

MEMORIA ET EXEMPLVM

OBSOLERET,

VIDVA ET XV LIBERI

SVPERSTITES

HOC MARMOR

ARMORIS ET PIETATIS MONVMENTVM

PP.

The third of the old monuments is that of the Vassall family, which bears the following

Sacred to the Memory of

SAMUEL VASSALL, Esq., of LONDON, Merchant,

one of the original proprietors of the lands

of this Country;

a steady and undaunted
asserter of the Liberties of England
in 1628.
He was the first who boldly refused to submit to the tax
of Tonnage and Poundage,
an unconstitutional claim of the Crown
arbitrarily imposed ;
For which (to the ruin of his family)
his goods were seized and his person imprisoned by the
Star Chamber Court.
He was chosen to represent the City of
LONDON
In two successive Parliaments which met Apr. 13 and
Nov. 3, 1640.
The Parliament in July, 1641, voted him
£ 10445,, 12,, 2
for his damages,
and resolved that he should be further considered
for his personal sufferings ;
But the rage of the times and the neglect of
proper applications since,
have left to his family only the honour of that
Vote and Resolution.
He was one of the largest subscribers
to raise money
against the Rebels in IRELAND.
All these facts may be seen in the Journal
of the House of Commons.
He was the Son of
the gallant JOHN VASSALL
who in 1588
at his own expense fitted out and commanded two Ships

of War,
with which he joined the Royal Navy
To oppose
The Spanish Armada.
This monument was erected by his great grandson
FLORENTIUS VASSALL, ESQ.,
of the Island of JAMAICA now residing in ENGLAND
May, 1766.

In the Register, (XVII. 56, 113,) will be found a most careful genealogy of the Vassalls, from which and from Burke's "Commoners" we make a few notes.

Samuel[2] Vassall, the Patentee, had a brother William[2], who came here and resided at Scituate, but afterwards went to Barbadoes. He had a son John[3], of whom nothing more is known than that he sold his estate in 1661, and was afterwards in North Carolina. The daughters of William[2] married here Resolved White, James Adams, and Joshua Hubbard.

John[3] Vassall, only son of Samuel, lived in Jamaica, and had sons William[4] and Leonard[4]. William[4] was the father of Florentius[5] Vassall, the gentleman who erected the above monument. His children were Elizabeth[6] and Richard[6], which last had an only daughter Elizabeth, wife of Henry Richard Fox, third Lord Holland.

Leonard[4] Vassall married first Ruth Gale of Jamaica, and had seventeen children; and secondly, widow Phebe Gross, and had one daughter. Four sons, Lewis[5], John[5], William[5] and Henry[5] survived. These children all resided in Boston and its vicinity, and have left descendants in the female line. The family, however, took sides with the

Crown at the time of the Revolution, and the present inheritors of the name are to be found in England.

The arms above given are the original coat of the family.
Burke, however, gives an augmentation granted to Col.
Spencer-Thomas[7] Vassall, grandson of John[5] and Elizabeth,
(dau. of Gov. Spencer Phips,) and son of John[6], by his
wife Elizabeth, sister of Lt. Gov. Thomas Oliver. The
augmentation consists of a fesse gold   thereon the
breached bastions of a fortress, above which the words
Monte Video; and a canton argent thereon the number
38th, within a branch of cypress, and another of laurel,
the stems united in saltire.

In the burying-ground beside the Chapel will be found
stones adorned with arms. The first we will examine

bears the following coat, inscribed Trail.
The family which owned this tomb is
not mentioned by DRAKE or SAVAGE,
and doubtless was of comparatively
recent settlement here. We have been
able to learn but little of them, except
that John Trail, merchant, was a sub-
scriber to Prince's Chronology in 1736,* and was probably
the man whose will, dated in 1757, leaves estate to his
widow and the heirs of his brothers and sisters, George
and William Trail, both deceased, Isabella Coventry and
Margery Stuart.

His brother George Trail m. 29 Jan. 1751, Jane Wendell, and died in the same year. His will mentions real
estate in Rowsay in the Orkneys in North Britain, and
appoints as overseer his friend Thomas McKenzie, of Kirk-

wall, in the Orkneys. Robert Trail, perhaps a relative, m. Mary Whipple, 1 Sept. 1748, (Reg. X. 48) ; Henry Trail m. Jennett Orr, 14 Jan. 1755 ; and Isabella Trail m. William Thomas, 4 March, 1754.

HERE LYES
YE BODY OF
ELIZABETH
PAIN, WIFE
TO SAMUEL
PAIN, AGED
NEAR 52
YEARS, DEPARTED
THIS LIFE NOVEMBER
YE 26, 1704.

We have failed to learn anything concerning this Samuel Pain or his wife. The stone is a small upright one, on the westerly path, near the Chapel.

Next to the Trail tomb, and in the same row, is one decorated with the accompanying arms, and inscribed John Wheelwright, 1740. It is highly probable that this John was descended from Rev. John[1] Wheelwright, who m. Mary Hutchinson, and was concerned in the Antimonian troubles here. He went to Exeter, N. H., and died at Salisbury in 1679. He had sons John[2], (who remained in England,) Thomas and Samuel ; and a grandson John[3], of Boston and Wells, Me., though by which son is not determined. This last John[3], who died at Wells,

13 Aug. 1745, aged 81, (Drake, Hist. Boston, 436,) **was** probably the father of the John[4] Wheelwright who owned the tomb. This John[4] had children Thomas[5], (who died before him in 1750, when his father administered on the estate,) Jeremiah, Nathaniel and Joseph, and a granddaughter Mary, who m. Rev. John Greaton. John's will, dated 10 Aug. 1751, was proved 31 Oct. 1760, and mentions also his daughter-in-law (step-daughter) Elizabeth Weeks, and an agreement made 2 Oct. 1741, before his marriage with her mother.

The Gedney tomb has these arms upon it. This was a branch of the Salem family, which commenced with John, who had sons John, Bartholomew, Eleazur, and Eli.

The tomb bearing the following arms is inscribed, Capt. John Steel, and was no doubt the property of the gentleman who died July 18, 1768, "far advanced in years," as his will states. He was in 1750 the Captain of

the North Battery, and was doubtless the son of the Thomas Steele who died 8 Jan. 1735–6, aged 71, upon whom Rev. Benj. Colman preached a funeral discourse. Of this Thomas Steele the minister writes, "he was an Honour to the Kingdom and Church of Scotland where he was born and educated, and to the University that adorned him with Letters. His father was a Gentleman of superior Wisdom and Virtue, of whom I had a very high Character sent me by the late Reverend Mr. Woodrow of Eastwood, near Glasgow." The sermon is dedicated to the widow, and mentions the children by a former wife. This wife was Mary, who died 26 Jan. 1722–3, aged 42, on whom Colman also preached a sermon.

Capt. John Steel's will mentions a son-in-law Joseph Turrell, and an only surviving child, Mary, wife of Royall Tyler.

———

The Townsend tomb possibly belonged to the family descended from William Townsend, who married Hannah Penn, and had sons James, Penn and Peter here. Of these, the most noted was Penn, who married Sarah Addington, Mary Leverett and widow Hannah Jaffrey, and held many high offices here. Penn Townsend died in 1727, leaving several children.

In this case as in several of the others it is extremely difficult to trace out the ownership of the tombs, and we must leave the task to those interested, having discharged our duty in recording the existence of the stones.

———

The Winslow tomb has a stone bearing these arms, but without other inscription. We shall hereafter refer to earlier examples of the use of the arms.

———

The tomb thus decorated was undoubtedly that of the Greene family, though it is not easy now to trace the ownership. The next tomb is said to have been theirs, but this is a mistake or they owned both. The same arms are on the book plate of Gardiner Greene, (b. 1753,) son of Benjamin, and grandson of Nathaniel and Anne Greene of Boston.

The last example is the following:

Here lieth Interred
the body of Major
Thomas Savage
aged 75 years dec^d
the 15 of February 168$\frac{1}{2}$

We have already (p. 7) given other examples of the use of these arms by the family. Among the descendants of Major Thomas may be mentioned Hon. James Savage, the greatest genealogist of New England.

SALEM.

The old graveyards of Salem have suffered as much dilapidation as any of their neighbors, and at present we can report but three tombs remaining with armorial insignia. These are the resting places of the Browne, Lynde, and Pickman families, and we will add to the transcript of the epitaphs some genealogical notes.

I.

<table>
<tr><td>

Here lyeth
interred y^e Body of
William Brown, Esq
aged 79 years
[Departed this Life
the 20th of January
1687.]

</td><td>

Here lyeth
interred y^e Body * *
Mrs. Sarah Brown
wife of Willliam * * *
 * * * * aged about
 * * * * * * *

</td></tr>
</table>

It will be noticed that these inscriptions are very imperfect, and we have completed that of William from a copy published in 1849, in the N. E. Hist. and Gen. Register, III. 128.

Though there were many families of the name in Massachusetts, this particular family, descended from Wil-

liam of Salem, has been easily distinguished by its high
social position. The emigrant ancestor, William, is said
to have been born 1 March 1607–8, and was a son of
Francis[3] Browne of Brandon, co. Suffolk, who was the
second son of Thomas[2] and Margaret Browne of Brandon,
and grandson of Simon[1] Browne of Browne Hall, co.
Lanc. The first wife of William[4] Browne was Mary
Young, and his second, Sarah Smith. His children were
William[5]; Benjamin[5]; Joseph[5] (who m. Mehitable, dau. of
Gov. Brenton, and prob. d. *s. p.*) ; Sarah,[5] wife of Thomas
Dean ; Mary[5] wife of Waitstill Winthrop ; besides three
sons who died young.

It will be noticed that the above epitaph is of this
William Browne, who was Representative and Assistant.

Benjamin[5] Browne m. Mary, dau. of Rev. John Hicks,
was of the Council, &c., and died 7 Dec. 1708, having
had no sons ; the name was therefore continued only in
one line, that of Major William[5] Browne.

This William[5] Browne was one of Andros's Council,
and of the Council of Safety afterwards. He m. 1st,
Hannah, dau. of George Curwen, and had sons, Samuel[6]
and John,[6] daughters Mary,[6] wife of Ch. Justice Benj.
Lynde, and Sarah,[6] as well as three children who died
young. He died 23 Feb., 1716. We will trace first the
descendants of his son, Col. Samuel[6] Browne, who was a
Counsellor and Judge, m. 1st, 19 March, 1695–6, Eunice,
sister of Col. John Turner who d. *s. p.* He m. 2d, 21
Feb., 1705–6, Abigail Keatch of Boston, and had Samuel,[7] b. 7 April, 1708; William,[7] b. 7 May, 1709; and
Benjamin,[7] b. 1715–6, d. unm. 14 Aug. 1737. Col. Samuel[6] died in 1731 ; his wife died 18 Feb. 1724.

Samuel[7] Browne, H. C. 1727, married 30 March, 1732, Katherine, dau. of John Winthrop, and had five children, Samuel,[8] Benjamin,[8] Anne,[8] Abigail,[8] and William.[8] He died 26 Nov., 1742, and his widow m. Col. Epes Sargent, to whom Mr. Adlard (Sutton-Dudleys of England, p. 120,) assigns three children.

Hon. William[7] Browne, brother of this last, m. 14 Nov. 1737, Mary, dau. of our Gov. William Burnet, and gr. dau. of the noted Bishop. By her he had William[8] Burnet, b. 7 Oct. 1738 ; Mary,[8] b. 27 Feb. 1743, d 1769 : Sarah,[8] b. 13 July, 1745, d. 2 Nov. 1756; Samuel,[8] b. 1739, d. 20 Oct., 1754 ; Benjamin,[8] b. Dec. 1740, d. 1762 ; and Thomas,[8] b. 1742, d. 1756. His wife died 1 Aug., 1745, and he m. 2d, Mary, dau. of Philip French of New Brunswick, New Jersey ; by whom he had Philippa,[8] b. 1750, d. 20 July, 1763, and Francis,[8] b. 1752, d. 30 Oct. 1756. His wife d. in 1761, and he died 27 April, 1763.

William,[8] son of Samuel,[7] H. C. 1755, was Judge of Sup. Court, 1775, was a Loyalist and afterwards Governor of Bermuda. He d. in 1802.

To return to the junior branch, Capt. John[6] Browne son of Major William,[5] born 21 Nov. 1672, m. Sarah, dau. of Francis Burroughs, who died 24 Nov., 1715. Their children were Sarah,[7] b. 27 Oct. 1701, wife of Col. Ichabod Plaisted ; William,[7] b. 10 July, 1711, d. unm. 1 June, 1755, and Benjamin,[7] b. 25 July, 1706. He m. 2d, Mary, widow of Col. Ichabod Plaisted of Berwick, but had no children by her.

Col. Benjamin[7] Browne, H. C. 1725, m. 19 June, 1729, Eunice, dau. of Col. John Turner, and had John,[8] b. 10

July, 1735; Hannah,[8] b. 12 July, 1730, d. 1754; Eunice, b. 13 Sept. 1731; and Benjamin, b. 5 Aug. 1733, d. Dec. 1749. He died 3 Feb., 1749–50.

Among the evidences of the use of these arms we may refer to Gore's Roll, Nos. 44 and 57, where they are assigned to Samuel[5] and John[6], the grandsons of the emigrant; and after the death of Samuel,[7] son of this Samuel,[6] it appears from the following, that a hatchment was placed on his house: "1744, July 16, Took down Mr. Brown's escutcheon from the front of his house." (James Jeffrey's Diary, printed in Hist. Coll. Essex Institute, II. 66.) We believe also that there are some early impressions of seals used by members of the family.

II.

JUDITH, wife of E. A. HOLYOKE, ESQ. died Nov[r] y[e] 19, 1756 Aged 19 years.

ELIZABETH wife of	SAM[L] PICKMAN ESQ[R]
died Decem[r] y[e]	16, 1761 Aged 47
William Eppes	Esq[r] died Oct[r]
y[e] 1st 1765	Aged 39 years.

The first of the Pickmans of Salem was Nathaniel, *said* to have come from Bristol, with wife Tabitha and several children. His will dated 23 Sept., proved 25 Nov. 1684, and the deeds on record mention children Nathaniel,[2] Bethia,[2] (m. John Silsbee, and 2d, Alexander Cole,) Mary,[2] (m. Robert Hodges,) Hannah,[2] wife of John Saunders, and Tabitha,[2] wife of Edward Feveryear of Boston.

The will of John Pickman, dated 23 Aug. 1671, proved 29 June, 1683, mentions my brother Nathaniel's children, brother Samuel's children, bro. William's children, "now in England," bro. Benjamin's children, sister Anne Joons in England, wife Hannah.

It may be fairly presumed that all these were the children of the first Nathaniel, unless it be thought more probable that the father did not come over.

Benjamin[2] Pickman (bapt., says Savage, at Lewen's Mead, Bristol, Eng., in 1645) m. Elizabeth Hardy, and had a large family; the youngest daughter was named Elizabeth, b. 18 Aug. 1687, and m. Richard Pike. Of the sons, we find descendants only of

Benjamin,[3] b. 30 Jan. 1671–2, m. 1st, —— Hasket, and 2d, 26 Oct. 1704, Abigail Lindall. By his first wife, he had John[4] of Boston; by his second he had Abigail,[4] b. 9 Feb. 1706, wife of Nathaniel Ropes; Benjamin,[4] b. 28 Jan. 1708; William,[4] b. 1 Oct. 1710, d. 10 April, 1735; Samuel,[4] b. 19 Jan. 1711–2, deputy-governor of Spanish Town, d. 25 Aug. 1772; Elizabeth,[4] b. 22 Jan. 1713–4, m. John Nutting; Caleb,[4] b. 10 June, 1715, d. 4 June, 1737; Rachel,[4] b. 25 July, 1717, m. Ebenezer Ward; and Sarah,[4] b. 1 Dec. 1718, m. George Curwen. He was one of the council.

Hon. Benjamin[4] Pickman m. October, 1731, Love Rawlins, and had sons Benjamin,[5] b. 7 Nov. 1740; Clark Gayton[5], b. 30 July, 1746, and William,[5] b. 12 March, 1748, besides daus. Love,[5] (wife of Peter Frye,) Abigail,[5] who m. William Eppes, and Judith,[5] wife of Dr. Edward A. Holyoke.

He d. 20 Aug. 1773; his wife d. 9 June, 1786.

Of the two sons who continued the name, Col. Benjamin[5] m. 22 April, 1762, Mary, dau. of Dr. Barzillai Toppan, and had sons Benjamin,[6] b. 30 Sept. 1763; Thomas,[6] b. 10 May, 1773, (who m. Sophia Farmer, and had a dau. Mary T., wife of Dr. George B. Loring,) and William,[6] b. 25 June, 1774, and two daughters. He d. 13 May, 1819.

His son, Col. Benjamin[6] Pickman, H. C. 1784, member of Congress, &c., m. 20 Oct. 1789, Anstis Derby, and had children Benjamin, Clark Gayton, Anstis Derby, Hasket Derby, Elizabeth Derby, Mary-Ann, Martha, and Francis Willoughby; this last, Francis W., is the father of Rev. Wm. R. Pickman.

William[5] Pickman, uncle of Benjamin[6], was Naval Officer of Salem, m. Elizabeth, dau. of Rev. Dudley Leavitt, and had a dau. Elizabeth,[6] and sons William,[6] (who died unm.) and Dudley L.[6]

Hon. Dudley Leavitt[5] Pickman m. Catherine Saunders, and had Catherine S.[7] (wife of Richard S. Fay), Elizabeth,[7] (wife of Hon. Richard S. Rogers), and William Dudley,[7] who m. 12 June, 1849, Caroline Silsbee.

It may be added here, that, though the name of Pitman has been long kept as distinct from Pickman at Marblehead, yet the two were often used indiscriminately in the records.

The main tablet of the Pickman tomb was of freestone, and the inscriptions have nearly disappeared. That which we have copied is on a slate tablet inserted in the other, and of course more recent than the date of the original erection of the tomb.

III.

Hic Depositæ Sunt

Reliquæ Benjaminis Lynde, Armigeri
Prov Mass Justic. Capitatis Ob^t. 28 Jan. 1744 Ætat 79
et Mariæ Lynde *Conjugis suæ*
Hon° Gulielmi Browne *Armigeri Filiæ*
quæ obiit 12mo. *Julii* A. D. 1753 *Ætat.* 74.
Mr William Lynde *Merch^t*
died the 10th *May* 1752 *Ætat* 37

On the opposite side of the tomb is the following inscription:

Sacred to ye Memory
of the Honble Benj Lynde Esqr
Who sustained, with usefulness & Dign-
-ity in his native Province
The high Offices of
A Representative, a Counsellor &
One of ye justices of ye superior Court
In which Last Capacity
His Honored Father & He com-

pleated beyond Example no less
a Period than Sixty Years
He was born in the year 1700 & on
ye 3^d of october 1781 with an hope
full of Immortallity He resigned his
spirit Into ye hands of his Redeemer.
Reader, wouldest thou know all his worth
Thou must inspect ye registers of heaven.

Concerning the Lynde family I may add, that this branch is descended from Simon Lynde of Boston, 1650, born, says Savage, in London, 1624, son of an Enoch, who d. there 23 April, 1636, and of Elizabeth, who long survived. Simon m. Hannah, dau. of John Newgate, and their son Benjamin, born 22 Sept. 1666, m. Mary, dau. of William Brown, by whom he had Benjamin, 5 Oct. 1700. These two, father and son, were the Chief Justices here mentioned. As another proof of the arms, we may mention an old painting now in the possession of Dr. T. E. Oliver, with a curious endorsement, which we shall hereafter copy.

We may also add from Alden's Epitaphs (Vol. I., p. 71,) the following epitaph on Gov. Bradstreet.

" SIMON BRADSTREET, armiger, ex ordine senatoris, in colonia Massachusettensi ab anno 1630, usque ad annum 1673. Deinde ad annum 1679, vice-gubernator. Denique ad annum 1686, ejusdem colonia communi et constanti populi suffragio, gubernator. Vir, judicio lynceario preditus, quem nec numma nec honos allexit. Regis authoritatem et populi libertatem, æqua lance libravit. Religione ornatus, vita innocuus, mundum et vicit, et deseruit, 27 die Martii, A. D. 1697, ætatis 94."

A. C. G., JR.

THE BRINLEY FAMILY.

Although, in our account of the arms in the King's Chapel and yard, we confined ourselves to the examples now remaining, we may say that there is but little doubt that the Brinley tomb was formerly thus adorned. There still remains a space in the slab whence an inscription has been taken; and from other examples we are convinced that this place once held an armorial tablet. At all events, the arms above engraved are on the will of Francis Brinley who died in 1719. From a very good account of the family in Bridgman's King's Chapel Epitaphs, we copy the following:

It is said that Thomas[1] Brinley, Esq., was Auditor-General of the Revenues of Kings Charles the First and Second; was born in the city of Exon, married Ann Worse of Pettwork, co. Sussex, had five sons and seven daughters, and was buried at Datchet, near Windsor, in 1661, aged over 70 years.

Of these twelve children, one daughter m. William Coddington, and another Griselda, m. Nathaniel Sylvester. One son, Francis[2] Brinley, b. in 1632, came to Newport, R. I., married Hannah Carr, and had two sons, Thomas[3] and William.[3] William,[3] d. *s. p.*, but Thomas[3] m. Mary Apthorp, and had Francis[4] and William,[4] besides a daughter, Elizabeth,[4] who m. William Hutchinson.

Francis[4] Brinley, was born in London in 1690, and was educated at Eton. He settled in Roxbury, Mass., and married Deborah Lyde in 1718, by whom he had five sons and two daughters, viz.: Thomas,[5] Francis,[5] Edward,[5] Nathaniel,[5] George,[5] Deborah,[5] (wife of Col. John Murray,) and Catherine,[5] (wife of Hon. Godfrey Malbone).

Of these Thomas,[5] was a refugee, m. Elizabeth Cradock, and d. *s. p.* in 1784.

Francis[5] Brinley m. Aleph, dau. of Hon. Godfrey Malbone, and had four sons and three daughters.

Edward[5] Brinley m. Sarah Tyler, and left two sons who married, and had issue.

Nathaniel[5] m. Catherine Cradock, and had one son, Robert, and one grandson, Nathaniel.

George[5] Brinley m. a sister of Sir John Wentworth, was Commissary-general and a refugee ; two of his sons were in the British army, and his daughter Mary married Mr Moody of London, and was the mother of the distinguished authoress, Mrs. Gore.

Among the American descendants, we may mention George of Hartford, and Francis of Tyngsborough, both distinguished as antiquaries.

OFFICIAL SEALS.

MASSACHUSETTS.

The Governor who succeeded Joseph Dudley was Samuel Shute, of whom Hutchinson says, (II. 215,) " Colonel Shute's family were generally dissenters; his father, an eminent citizen in London; his mother, daughter of Mr. Caryl, a dissenting minister of great note. His brother, afterwards Lord Barrington, was then a member of Parliament, and at the head of the dissenting interest. The Colonel began his education under Mr. Charles Morton, who, about the year 1684, came to New England and was minister of Charlestown. After tuition under him, he was sent to Leyden. He went, after that, into the army under King William, who made him a captain, served under the duke of Marlborough, was a lieutenant-colonel, and wounded in one of the principal battles in Flanders." He arrived at Boston, Oct. 4, 1716, and he sailed for home Jan. 1, 1723. His acting successor was the Lieutenant-Governor William Dummer, who held the place till the arrival of Burnet, 13 July, 1728.

As very little is said by our standard authorities about the family of Shute, we copy the following from Lodge's Irish Peerage:

" The family hath long been seated in the counties of Leicester and Cambridge, in the latter of which, at Hockington or Hogginton, resided Christopher Shute, Esq.," whose son Robert[2] was in 1579 created second Baron of the Exchequer. He married Thomasine, dau. of Christopher Burgoyne, and had sons Francis,[3] John,[3] Christopher[3] and Thomas.[3]

Francis[3] Shute of Upton, co. Leicester, m. Frances, dau. of Hercules Meautys, and had several children, of whom Francis[4] married, and had James,[5] Samuel,[5] (sheriff of London, 1681,) and Benjamin.[5]

Benjamin[5] Shute m. Elizabeth Caryl, and died in 1683, having had three sons and three daughters. These sons were Samuel[6] (Gov.), John[6] (viscount Barrington), and Benjamin.[6]

The Governor, Samuel,[6] d. unm. 15 April, 1742, aged 80; his brother Benjamin[6] d. unm. in 1714. John[6] Shute in 1710 received by will the property of John Wildman of Becket, co. Berks, though not a relative. Some years afterwards he received another estate, from Francis Barrington of Tofts, who m. Elizabeth, dau. of Samuel[5] Shute. He was in Parliament, and in 1720 was made Baron Barrington of Newcastle, and Viscount Barrington of Ardglass. His son John married a daughter of Florentius Vassall. A sister of Gov. Samuel, Mary Shute, married Henry Yeamans, concerning whom much is narrated in Sumner's History of East Boston.

Lord Barrington took the arms and name of Barrington, but Burke gives the arms of Shute of Hollington, co. Camb., as "per chevron sable and gold; in chief two eagles displayed of the last. *Crest*, a griffin sejant gold, pierced in the breast with a broken sword-blade argent vulned gules."

We have not yet seen an example of Gov. Shute's seal, though such are presumably in existence.

The official seal of William Dummer, who was acting Governor of the Colony from 1723 to 1728, is here given. Of his three predecessors in the office of Lieutenant-Governor, two, William Stoughton and William Tailor, were certainly entitled to arms. The third, Thomas Povey, was an Englishman, and never came here.

William[1] Dummer was the grandson of Richard[2] Dummer of Bishopstoke, Hants, the second son of John[1] D., born there in 1599. Richard[2] came to N. England in 1632, returned to England, and came again in 1638, with brothers Stephen[2] and Thomas[2]. Here the family prospered, and his sons Jeremiah,[3] Richard[3] and Rev. Shubael[3] occupied prominent positions. He died 14 Dec. 1679.

Jeremiah[3] Dummer was a goldsmith; married in 1672 Hannah Atwater, and had sons Jeremy,[4] William,[4] and Samuel.[4] Of these, Jeremy[4] was the agent of the colony in England from 1710 to 1721. He possessed great abilities, and obtained the favor of Lord Bolingbroke. The works by which he is best remembered here are a Defence of the New England Charters, and a Letter concerning the Expedition to Canada. He died 19 May, 1739, aged about 60.

William[4] Dummer, the acting Governor, married Katherine, dau. of Gov. Joseph Dudley, but died s. p. 10 Oct. 1761, aged 84. His will mentions the children of his sister Anna Powell, kinsmen Nathaniel Dummer and William Vans. By his will also he established the school at Byfield, now called Dummer Academy.

HALL MARKS ON PLATE.

During the Colonial period of our history, our ancestors were obliged to depend largely upon the mother country for articles of luxury. As wealth increased it became the fashion to use silver plate, and the inventories of the prominent merchants contain often quite large amounts. Notwithstanding from the time of John Hull, the mint-master, there have always been goldsmiths here, it is probable that much of the plate used here was imported. As it is sometimes desirable to ascertain the exact date when such articles were made, we have prepared the following account

of the marks on English plate, from a book entitled "Hall
Marks on Gold and Silver Plate, with Tables of Annual
Date Letters," &c. &c., by W. Chaffers, F. S. A., Lon-
don, 1863.

Acting under different statutes the Goldsmiths' Company
of London have long been charged with the assaying of
articles of gold and silver plate, except such small articles
as could not be marked without injury. The marks thus
placed, by means of little punches, are of different devices,
and have varied from time to time, as we shall show.

The most important mark is what is termed the Date
mark. "The assay marks used at the Goldsmiths' Hall
of London, were ordered to be letters of the alphabet,
changing every year. We do not know with certainty
when this plan was first adopted, but it was probably as
early as the time when the Goldsmiths' Company were
empowered to assay the precious metals, which, according
to their ordinances, was in the year 1300. We can trace
these letters back with a degree of certainty to the fifteenth
century."

"The Goldsmiths' Hall of London employ the letters
A to U inclusive, (omitting J,) forming a cycle of twenty
years, the character of the alphabet being varied every
succeeding cycle. These letters are changed on the 20th
of May, in every year; each letter is therefore used during
the moieties of two calendar years."

We may here add, that though the letters are changed
in each cycle from the one preceding, still the same letters
have been used in different cycles, and therefore the shape
of the shield of the punch must be carefully noted. Thus,
Roman capitals were used twice in cycles 15 and 19,

(1697–1717, and 1796–1816,) and Roman small in cycles 16, 18 and 20, (1717–1737, 1756–1776, and 1816–1836,) but the shield in each case was distinct. Also, since 1784, five stamps have been used, and before that only four.

We will describe these other marks, which, on distinct stamps, always accompany the Date mark, commencing, for convenience, with A. D. 1600. From 1600 to 1697, the first stamp is a leopard's head, the second a lion passant, the third the Date mark, the fourth the maker's mark, which consisted of his initials generally.

From 1697 to 1716, the first and second of these marks were changed to, 1st, Britannia; 2d, a lion's head erased; but this arrangement lasted only twenty years, and from 1716 to 1784, the old four styles were used.

From 1784 to the present time, an additional stamp has been used, consisting of the king or queen's head. Since 1823, the first stamp, the leopard's head, is without a crown.

We will now describe the Date marks since A. D. 1600. Cycle No. 9, 1598 to 1618, has the four stamps, of which the Date mark is Lombardic capitals in a shield of straight top and sides and rounded bottom.

Cycle No. 10, 1618–1638, four stamps; Date mark, small italics in a pentagonal shield, of straight lines and pointed bottom.

Cycle No. 11, 1638–1658, four stamps; Date mark, court hand in a shield, as in Cycle No. 9.

Cycle No. 12, 1658–1678, four stamps; Date mark, black letter capitals in pointed shield, as in Cycle No. 10.

Cycle No. 13, 1678–1698, four stamps; Date mark, black letter, small, in same shield.

Cycle No. 14, 1698–1716, four stamps; Date mark, court hand, as in the following alphabet, in the same pointed shield :—

𝕬	March to May 1697	𝕭	1703–4	𝕷	1710–1
𝕭	1697–8	𝕯	1704–5	𝕶	1711–2
𝕮	1698–9	𝕰	1705–6	𝕷	1712–3
𝕾	1699–0	𝕻	1706–7	𝕹	1713–4
𝕰	1700–1	𝖂	1707–8	𝕼	1714–5
𝕱	1701–2	𝕷	1708–9	𝕽	1715–6
𝕲	1702–3	𝕺	1709–0		

Cycle No. 15, (1716–1736,) four stamps, Date mark, Roman capitals, as follows, in a pointed shield :

A	1716–7	H	1723–4	P	1730–1
B	1717–8	I	1724–5	Q	1731–2
C	1718–9	K	1725–6	R	1732–3
D	1719–0	L	1726–7	S	1733–4
E	1720–1	M	1727–8	T	1734–5
F	1721–2	N	1728–9	V	1735–6
G	1722–3	O	1729–0		

Cycle No. 16, (1736–1756,) four stamps, Date mark, Roman small in a curved shield, except four which are marked in their place; all the others are like c :

a 1736–7		h 1743–4		p 1750–1	
b 1737–8		i 1744–5		q 1751–2	
c 1738–9		k 1745–6		r 1752–3	
d 1739–0		l 1746–7		**ſ** 1753–4	
e 1740–1		m 1747–8		t 1754–5	
f 1741–2		n 1748–9		**u** 1755–6	
g 1742–3		o 1749–0			

Cycle No. 17, (1756-1766,) four stamps, Date mark, black letter capitals in a shield, as here shown:

A 1756–7		**H** 1763–4		**P** 1770–1	
B 1757–8		**I** 1764–5		**Q** 1771–2	
C 1758–9		**K** 1765–6		**R** 1772–3	
D 1759–0		**L** 1766–7		**S** 1773–4	
E 1760–1		**M** 1767–8		**T** 1774–5	
F 1761–2		**N** 1768–9		**U** 1775–6	
G 1762–3		**O** 1769–0			

The next cycle, and all subsequent ones, use five stamps, so we may here stop our account, saying only that the Date marks are as follows:

1776–1796: Roman small letters, but in the oblong shield used in Cycle No. 17.

No. 19, 1796–1816: Roman capitals in same shield.

No. 20, 1816–1836: Roman small, in a shield with a rounded bottom, thus,

No. 21, 1836–1856: Black letter capitals in the following shield:

No. 22, 1856–1876: Black letter small, in the shield of No. 20.

To recapitulate somewhat. If a piece of silver have five stamps, it was made since 1784. If only four, if the first be a figure of Britannia and a lion's head erased, , it belongs to cycle No. 14; otherwise, if it bear the leopard's head erased and the lion passant, it belongs to one of the cycles prior to No. 18, and the date mark must be examined.

We repeat; as the same alphabets were used in different cycles, the shape of the punch must be carefully compared with our examples.

CONNECTICUT SEALS.

Communicated by J. HAMMOND TRUMBULL, Esq. (Continued from Vol. I. p. 160.)

III.

GEORGE WYLLYS, born at Fenny Compton, co. Warwick, came to New England in 1638, and settled in Hartford, where he was the largest landed proprietor in 1639. He was a partner of Robert Saltonstall, William Whiting and others, in the Hilton's Point, or Dover, and the Piscataqua patents, and joined in the surrender of jurisdiction of these lands to Massachusetts, in June, 1641, (Mass. Rec., I. 324.) He was chosen an assistant in 1639, deputy governor in 1641, and governor in 1642. He died 9 March, 1645. See his will in Col. Reg. of Conn., I. 468–72.

His oldest son, George, remained in England. A dau., Amy, married Major John Pynchon of Springfield, Nov. 6, 1645. His second son, Samuel, married Ruth, dau. of Gov. John Haynes. He was a graduate of Harvard College in 1653; was an enterprising merchant, largely engaged in trade with the West Indies; chosen an assistant in 1654, and the first named assistant in the Connecticut charter in 1662.

His arms, as above, are copied from an impression of a seal used by Samuel Willis, on a bond given in 1684, now in the Connecticut Archives, and from the portrait of his grandson, George, who was Secretary of the Colony from 1735 to 1796, which is now in the Hall of the Conn. Hist. Society. In the former, the chevron seems to be voided; on the portrait, the arms are argent, a chevron between three mullets gules.

IV.

 A letter from Major JOHN MASON, in the Mass. Archives, (Indians, vol. 1, No. 31,) has a seal in wax with the accompanying arms. Another impression of the same seal is on a letter from Major Mason in Conn. Archives, (Col. Boundaries, I. 75,) dated 3 Aug. 1670. The arms are probably those of the family of Mason's second wife— Peck.

Burke gives the arms of Peck of Sandford Hill, co. Essex, and Wood Pelling and Methwould, co. Norfolk, temp
Charles II. " Or, on a chevron gules, three crosses formée
of the field.   Crest, two lances or, in saltire, headed argent, pennons hanging to them of the first, and charged
with a cross formée gules, the spear enfiled with a chaplet
vert." Peck of Leicestershire and Lincolnshire: " Argent, on a chevron engrailed gules, three crosses formée
of the field."

v.

 WILLIAM JONES, born about 1624, arrived
at Boston from London, 27 July, 1660, in the
same ship with the regicides, Whalley and
Goffe.   The year previous he had married in
London, Hannah, youngest daughter of Theophilus Eaton, Governor of New Haven, his second wife.
He was elected an assistant in New Haven Colony in 1662;
deputy governor in 1664, and in 1665 an assistant of the
colony of Connecticut.   He died 17 Oct. 1706, aged 82.
(Savage, s. n.; Col. Rec. of Conn.)

The arms, as above, are from the impression of a seal on
a letter addressed by Mr. Jones to the council at Hartford,
27 Aug. 1675, in Conn. Archives. (War. I. 15.)

Of the charge in base, I cannot certainly determine the
character.   It appears like a snake, head and tail elevated.
The birds in chief are plainly Cornish choughs or crows,
which are among the bearings of several families of the
surname, and of Johns, Johnes, &c., of Cornwall and
Wales.

VI.

Thomas Lord, with wife Dorothy and seven children, embarked in the Elizabeth and Ann, from London, 29 April, 1635. His eldest son, Richard, had preceded him, and was a proprietor at Newtown, (Cambridge, Mass.) in 1632, and admitted freeman of Mass., 4 March, 1635. Both the father and son removed to Hartford, among the earliest settlers, and were proprietors there in 1636.

Richard was a prominent man in the town and colony, a merchant of considerable fortune, and much engaged in commercial enterprise. He was the captain of the first Connecticut troop of horse, " the bright starre of our cavalrie," as his epitaph has it. He died in 1662, and is buried at New London. The inscription on the crumbling and mutilated stone which marks his grave, is printed by Miss Caulkins, Hist. of New London, 153. His brother Thomas, of Wethersfield, Conn., was a physician and surgeon. (See Col. Rec. of Conn., I. 234.) He died in 1661 or 1662.

Thomas Lord, the father, died probably before 1661. His widow, Dorothy, executed her last will 8 Feb. 1669-70. It was witnessed by (Secretary) John Allyn, and Steven Hopkins, and was sealed with arms nearly as drawn above. The seal was doubtless one which had been her husband's, and the arms correspond exactly with those of Laward, *alias* Lord, as given in Berry's Encyclopædia and Burke's Armory, *s. n.*

" Laward, *alias* Lord. Argent on a fesse gules between three cinquefoils azure, a hind passant *inter* two pheons or. Crest, a demi bird sable, on the head two small horns or, the wings expanded, the dexter outside gules, inside or, the sinister outside of the last, inside of the third."

"Laward. Argent, on a fesse gules, between three cinquefoils pierced azure, a hind trippant of the field between two pheons or."

The seal is too small, and the impression not sufficiently distinct to permit the crest to be clearly made out. I have marked the colors from Burke's blazon, they not being indicated in the impression from the seal.

VII.

LEONARD CHESTER, from Blaby, co. Leicester, was the son of John Chester, and Dorothy, sister of Rev. Thomas Hooker. He removed from Watertown, Mass., to Watertown, (now Wethersfield,) Conn., where he was one of the first settlers and a large proprietor. He died Dec. 11, 1648, and was buried at Wethersfield. The pedigree of the Chesters of Blaby, showing the descent of Leonard from William Chester of London, and of Barnet, co. Hertford, is given in Nichols's History of Leicestershire, (vol. 4, pt. 2, p. 52,) and copied in Bond's Genealogies of Watertown, p. 736. The arms as given by Nichols, viz., "Ermine, on a chief sable a griffin passant or, armed argent," are rudely carved on the stone which marks the grave of Leonard Chester.

As drawn above, they are copied from an impression of the seal used by Col. John Chester, distinguished for good service in command of a company at Bunker Hill, and supervisor of the revenue for the district of Connecticut, 1791–1802; who was the eldest son of John, eldest son of John, eldest son of John, eldest son of Leonard. The seal is appended to his official seal, as supervisor, in 1799, on a document in the Conn. Hist. Society's Library.

The Chesters of Blaby trace their descent from an uncle of Sir Robert Chester of Royston, co. Cambridge, one of the gentlemen of the privy council to Henry VIII. The crest is a dragon passant, *or*.

VIII.

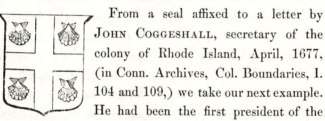 From a seal affixed to a letter by JOHN COGGESHALL, secretary of the colony of Rhode Island, April, 1677, (in Conn. Archives, Col. Boundaries, I. 104 and 109,) we take our next example. He had been the first president of the colony under the patent, 1647–8, and had filled various other offices of honor and trust. Burke gives the arms of Coggeshall of Milton and Bengall, co. Suff. " Argent, a cross between four escallops sable. Crest, a stag lodged sable, attired or."

The Suffolk Coggeshalls were descendants of a younger brother of Sir John de Coggeshall, of the manor of Codham, Wethersfield, co. Essex, knighted by Edward the Black Prince, in 1337. The common ancestor, Sir Thomas de Coggeshall, held the manor of Little Coggeshall Hall, co. Essex, in the reign of King Stephen, "whose posterity long flourished, and enjoyed several very considerable estates in this county." (Morant's Essex, II. 162.) In a note, p. 371, Morant gives the arms of Coggeshall, as above: " Argent, a cross between four escallops sable."

Berry gives the arms of Cockshall, co. Essex, as above, and otherwise for the same name : "Sable, a cross between four escallops argent."

IX.

JOHN WANTON, Governor of Rhode Island, 1734–40, used a seal bearing the arms of the ancient family of Wanton, (de Walton, de Wanton, or Wanton,) of Essex. "Azure, a chevron sable." Morant's Essex, II. 541, 558. An impression of this seal is found with his signature to a certificate of the commissioners for determining the New York boundary, Dec. 2, 1738, in Conn. Hist. Society's Library. A similar seal was used by his son, Governor Gideon Wanton, in 1745 ; but in the imperfect impression which I have seen, for the chevron are substituted two chevronnels apparently.

[Note. As this form often occurs on seals, it seems very probable that it was the mistake of the seal engraver, who, instead of giving the whole chevron in relief, gave only the two angular lines, by which, in drawing, the chevron is marked. We see the same result in the usual style of wood cuts, wherein the tincture of the chevron is not represented.]

X.

The accompanying cut is from an impression of the seal of THOMAS FITCH, Governor of Connecticut, 1754–66. The instrument to which it is attached bears date 1757. The arms,— " Vert, a chevron between three leopards' heads, or. Crest, a leopard's head cabossed, or, in the mouth a sword proper hilt gules,—are given by Burke as those of Fitch of Head-all and Woodham Walter, co. Essex, and Eltham and Mount Mascul, co. Kent. Morant states that the Fytch family bought several estates in the county of Essex about the middle of the sixteenth century; one branch of the family settling at Brazen-Head, in Lindrell, the other, and principal branch, at Little Cranfield, a few miles distant. (Hist. Essex, II. 446, 463.) The Rev. James Fitch, first minister of Norwich, Conn., was born at Bocking, co. Essex, as was probably his brother Thomas, from whom Governor Thomas descended. A branch of the Fitch family was settled at Bocking as early at least as 1569, when John Fitch, gent., held the manor of Boones and messuage of Lyons, in that parish. Morant, II. 387.

XI.

 We add, under this head, the following example of the arms of Governor WILLIAM LEETE, copied from the Winthrop papers, published by the Massachusetts Historical Society. Of him, Cotton Mather writes: "He was by his education a lawyer, and by his imployment a register in the Bishop's Court. In that station, at Cambridge," he saw certain transactions which led him finally to come to New England in 1639. After holding other offices, he succeeded Winthrop as governor of Connecticut, and "until his own death, the annual election, for about a decade of years together, still made him governor."

He died 16 April, 1683. Savage credits him with three wives and numerous children, and as his sons were also blessed with issue, it is very probable that descendants of the name still continue.   ED.

CHRISTOPHER KILBY.

In the Gore Roll of Arms, (H. J., I. 140,) we noticed the arms of Gilbert McAdams and his wife, but could not give much genealogical information. We are indebted to Isaac J. Greenwood, Jr., of New York, for the following facts.

Christopher Kilby, born in 1704, was the son of John and Rebecca (Simpkins) Kilby, who was one of the founders of Brattle Street Church, and died in 1722. Christopher married Sarah, oldest dau. of Hon. William Clarke, 18 Aug 1726, was a merchant, and in 1739 went to England as the Provincial Agent. He returned to New York, where he was a freeman in 1758, but soon went to England. He lived at Tranquil-dale, in Betchworth, co. Surrey. His will, dated 5 Oct. 1771, proved 29th same month, mentions widow and executrix Martha Kilby, and grand children, but leaves, out of an immense estate, to his only daughter, Mrs. Sarah McAdams, "the sum of one shilling and no more."

This daughter, Sarah, m. first, —— Cunningham, and secondly, Gilbert McAdams; the date of their marriage bond in New York being 24 Sept. 1757. McAdams was in 1771 living in Ayr, Scotland.

These facts fully explain the before-mentioned shield in Gore's Roll. The Clarke arms will be hereafter given in our Monumental Inscriptions from the Copp's Hill yard.

THE

HERALDIC JOURNAL;

RECORDING THE ARMORIAL BEARINGS AND GENEALOGIES
OF AMERICAN FAMILIES.

NO. XIV.   APRIL, 1866.

THE PYNCHON FAMILY.

William Pynchon, whose seal is
here presented, was one of the Patentees of the Massachusetts Colony, an
Assistant, Treasurer, &c. He came
over with Winthrop, and, about 1636,
he removed to the western part of the
State, where he founded the town of
Springfield. He unfortunately became involved in religious controversies and returned to England, where he
died in 1662. His descendants however remained here :
to one of whom, a gentleman of Boston, we are indebted
for the following genealogy, prepared from English records
and family papers.

From the Visitations of Essex, 1558 and 1612, it seems
that Nicholas[1] Pinchon of Wales, Sheriff of London in
1532, had a son, John[2] Pinchon of Writtle, co. Essex,
who m. Jane, heiress of Sir Richard Empson, and d. 29
Nov., 1573, leaving six children. His widow married
Dr. Thomas Wilson, Secretary of State.

John[2] and Jane Pinchon had
I. William.[3]
II. John,[3] of whom presently.
III. Sir Edward.[3]
IV. Agnes,[3] m. Thomas Chicele of Hingham Ferriers.
V. Elizabeth,[3] m. Geoffrey Gates of St. Edmund's Bury.
VI. Jane, m. Andrew Paschal of Springfield.

The oldest son, William[3] Pinchon, m. Rose, dau. of
Thomas Reding of Pinner, in Middlesex, and had—

Peter,[4] (died aged 15), Sir Edmund,[4] Henry,[4] Christo-
pher,[4] (who m. Mary Vincent, and had a son Edward,[5])
Elizabeth,[4] and Anne,[4] wife of Richard Weston, Earl of
Portland.

William[3] died 13 Oct., 1592; his heirs at Writtle were
Sir Edmund,[4] who m. Dorothy, dau. of Sir Jerome Weston of Skreens, in Roxwell, and had an only son, John,[5]
and three daughters, Mary,[5] wife of Walter Overbury,
Elizabeth,[5] and Anne,[5] wife of John Wolfe.

John[5] Pinchon m. 1st, Elizabeth, dau. of Thomas
Cornwallis, and died 30 July, 1654, leaving a son, Edward,[6] who d. Feb., 1672, and a daughter, Bridget,[6] who
was the second wife of William Petre, fourth Baron
Petre.

The only child of Lady Petre was Mary, born 25
March, 1679, m. George Heneage of Hainton, co. Linc.

———

Here the older branch seems to terminate, and we
return to John[3] Pinchon, son of John,[2] who settled at
Springfield, co. Essex, and m. ——, dau. and heir of ——
Orchard.

His son was William[4] Pynchon, the emigrant, who by
his first wife had—

John,[5] b. 1621.

Anne,[5] m. Henry Smith.

Margaret,[5] m. William Davis.

Mary,[5] m. Elitzur Holyoke.

His wife died here in 1630, and he married Frances Sanford. He died at Wraisbury, Oct. 1662, aged about 72. His second wife d. there 10 Oct., 1657.

John[5] Pynchon of Springfield, Mass., m. 30 Oct. 1645, Amy, dau. of Gov. George Wyllys, and had—

Joseph,[6] b. 26 July, 1646; d. unm. 30 Dec. 1682.

John,[6] b. 15 Oct. 1647.

Mary,[6] b. 28 Oct. 1650, m. Joseph Whiting.

William,[6] b. 11 Oct. 1653; d. 15 June, 1654.

Mehitable,[6] b. 22 Oct. 1661; d. 24 July, 1663.

He was "the chief man in the western part of the State," a Councillor, Colonel, and Judge of Probate. He d. 17 Jan. 1703. His wife d. 9 Jan. 1699.

The only heir, John[6] Pynchon, m. Margaret, dau. of Rev. William Hubbard, the Historian, and had—

John.[7]

Margaret,[7] m. Capt. Nathaniel Downing.

William,[7] b. 1689; of whom hereafter.

John,[6] died 25 April, 1721; his wife d. 11 Nov. 1716.

Col. John[7] Pynchon married twice and had a large family. He d. 12 July, 1742. By his first wife Bathshua, dau. of Rev. —— Tailer, of Westfield, he had—

1. Eliza.[8]

2. William,[8] b. 11 Nov. 1703, m. Sarah, dau. of Pelatiah Bliss, and had—

i. William, m. Lucy Harris.

ii. John.

iii. Sarah.

3. Mehitable,[8] m. Benj. Cotton.

4. Joseph,[8] } twins, b. 7 Feb. 1704–5;

5. John,[8] } m. and d. *s. p.* 6 April, 1754.

6. Mary,[8] m. Gen. Joseph Dwight.

7. Bathshua,[8] m. Robert Harris.

His wife dying 20 June, 1710, he m. Phebe ——, who d. 17 Oct. 1722, and had—

8. Edward,[8] m. a widow Bliss, and d. *s. p.*

9. George,[8] m. twice, and had ch. George, Louisa, Nathaniel, Peter, Peter, and Henry.

10. Charles,[8] m. Anne Dwight, and had two daughters.

———

We return to William[7] Pynchon, Judge C. C. P., who m. Catherine, dau. of Rev. Daniel Brewer, and had—

Sarah,[8] b. 17 Aug. 1721; m. Josiah Dwight.

William,[8] b. 12 Dec. 1723.

Margaret,[8] b. 24 Nov. 1727; m. Elijah Williams.

Daniel–John,[8] b. 7 Oct. 1733; d. 22 April, 1754.

Joseph,[8] b. 30 Oct. 1737; m. Sarah Ruggles.

William died 1 Jan. 1741; his widow d. 10 April, 1747.

William[8] Pynchon, son of the last named, was an eminent lawyer of Salem, where he m. Catherine, dau. of Mitchel Sewall, and had—

Elizabeth,[9] b. 26 Jan. 1752; m. Timothy Orne.

Katharine,[9] b. 25 Feb. 1754; m. William Wetmore.

Sarah,[9] b. 6 Feb. 1757; m. Rev. Thomas Fitch Oliver.

William,[9] b. 24 July, 1759 ; m. but d. *s. p.*

John,[9] b. 27 Nov. 1766 ; d. unm.

William[8] died 14 March, 1789, and this branch is extinct in the male line.

THE COUNTY FAMILIES OF ENGLAND.

The Noble and Gentle Men of England : or Notes touching the Arms and Descents of the Ancient Knightly and Gentle Houses of England, arranged in their respective Counties. Attempted by Evelyn Philip Shirley, Esq., M. A., one of the Knights of the Shire for the county of Warwick. Westminster : John Bowyer Nichols and Sons, 1859. Pp. 315.

Any casual reader who may take up a book like Burke's General Armory, with its thousand pages and about sixty thousand coats-of-arms therein recorded, would be apt to imagine that England, like Virginia, was a land of " First Families" and no others. On examination he would be somewhat reassured first by finding that this miscellaneous collection was totally without authority, secondly without any chronological plan, and thirdly replete with duplications. On these points we may say now in detail,—first, that the only authentic *record* of arms is that of the Heralds' College, though many families have a prescriptive right which cannot be challenged ; secondly, the arms here recorded are the accumulations of many writers, and besides being without authority are of all dates, from the earliest period

when armorial bearings were used ; thirdly, the number
of coats-of-arms is greatly multiplied by their repetition
under different spellings of the name, and by the insertion
of numerous varieties of one coat, caused, as is very probable, by mistakes in transcribing, errors of artists, or even
unwarranted vagaries of individuals. It would, perhaps,
be possible to reduce Burke's list one half, and yet record
all the distinct coats which have been borne by distinct
families for more than one generation. We are not aware
that any attempt has been made to ascertain the number
of coats preserved in the Heralds' Visitations at the College, but in Sims' Index to the Visitations, preserved at
the British Museum, we have three hundred and thirty
pages of names, with perhaps an average of fifty families
on each page, which would give some fifteen thousand to
twenty thousand authentic coats.

It would seem therefore still possible for English Heralds to construct a list of all the authorized arms which
have been borne in that country by persons who established families. To be really valuable, however, it would
be necessary to adopt a chronological form, or to mark
with each blazon the date of its first appearance.

Such a list would possess the greatest interest to Americans, because it would throw a light upon such examples
of arms as are recorded in this Journal. Mr. Shirley's
volume, as we shall show, proves the immense changes
which have taken place in the social position of families
in England. An examination of the Peerages shows the
rapid extinction of families there, especially in the male
line. Thus Sir Egerton Brydges, writing in 1798, says :

James I. created 204 baronetcies, and 128 were then extinct;

Charles I.	"	247	"	" 184	"	"
Charles II.	"	437	"	" 307	"	"
James II.	"	20	"	" 16	"	"
William	"	37	"	" 25	"	"

so that out of 945 baronetcies, only 285, or about 30 per cent., remained after a century had elapsed.

In 1798, the peerage consisted of two hundred and sixty-four members, exclusive of the royal family, and of these Brydges says, " the ancestors of about twenty-six or twenty-seven possessed their peerages in the male line in the reign of Queen Elizabeth." Of course, the present number of peers of ancient lineage is no greater.

It must be remembered, however, that many peèrages have been inherited by females; so that the total extinction of families is not so great as the above facts would argue at first sight. It may not unfairly be urged, also, that though of late years the peers have been noted for longevity, and even for numerous issue, such was not the case in the seventeenth and eighteenth centuries.

Whoever examines the statistics of American families will be astonished at the fertility of the English race in this country. A moderate competency seems more favorable to the increase of a family than great wealth or high station. May we not hence infer that in England the same rule formerly held true, during the period when small freeholders occupied the land, and before the great cities attracted their unhealthy crowds? Few points seem less investigated than the origin and position of the farmers and merchants of England after the cessation of the Wars of the Roses. We find repeated instances of gentlemen by birth engaging in the commerce and manufactures of the larger cities. We find many examples of the division of lands, whereby the younger sons of good families became freeholders, and thus dropped socially a grade. to the rank of yeomen. We are still without data, however, to show whether these were the rule or the exception.

To us, as we have said, the question is an important one. The great emigration hither was that led by Winthrop, and, as we are trying to prove in each number of this Journal, it contained a considerable proportion of gentry, recognized as such prior to their removal. The remainder of the colonists were undoubtedly yeomen, tradesmen and mechanics, but most evidently not of the lowest class. In fact, if we were to accept Macaulay's picture of the country gentlemen of the day we should consider them as of the superior class. A large majority of them, as witnessed by our early county records, could read and write ; they were capable of self-government, and were prompt to devise satisfactory solutions for the problems presented by their new life. We doubt if as much could be said of five thousand colonists now to be taken from the lower classes of England.

Hence our abiding faith that the result of all investigation in England will result to the credit of our ancestors, will establish the value of their heraldic evidences, and free them from the suspicion of that weakest form of vanity, the assumption of a false social position.

We have said that Mr. Shirley has shown how rapidly the landed gentry of England have been overwhelmed by the variations of fortune.

He proposes to give a list of all existing families now represented in the male line, descended from those established as knightly or gentle houses prior to A. D. 1500, and still possessing landed property in their original county or elsewhere in England.

He omits those still existing who have lost their lands, and also those proprietors whose families can be traced to A. D. 1500, but were then obscure. In brief, he asks how many of the "county families" of that date still hold the same position.

Of course, the first edition of such a work is apt to err through omissions, and we learn that a new and enlarged edition is now in preparation. Our first impression of the following list, however, is one of amazement at its brevity. Three hundred and thirty names, it seems, is all that his diligence has yet collected. The list is as follows:

Abney,	Astley,	Bendyshe,	Bracebridge,
Acland,	Babington,	Berington,	Bray,
Acton,	Bacon,	Berkeley,	Brisco,
Acton,	Bagot,	Betton,	Brooke,
Aldersey,	Baldwin,	Biddulph,	Brooke,
Alington,	Bamfylde,	Bingham,	Broughton,
Anne,	Barnardiston;	Blois,	Brudenell,
Annesley,	Barnston,	Blount,	Butler,
Antrobus,	Barttelot,	Bodenham,	Bunbury,
Arden,	Bastard,	Bond,	Burdet,
Arundell,	Baskervyle,	Borough,	Burney,
Ashburnham,	Beaumont,	Boscawen,	Burton,
Ashurst,	Bedingfield,	Boughton,	Byron,
Assheton,	Bellew,	Boynton,	Carew,

Cary,	Curzon,	Floyer,	Hazlerigg,
Cave,	Davenport,	Forester,	Heigham,
Cavendish,	Dawnay,	Fortescue,	Heneage,
Chadwick,	Dayrell,	Frampton,	Hervey,
Chetwode,	Dering,	Fulford,	Hesketh,
Chetwynd,	De Grey,	Fursdon,	Hill,
Chichester,	Digby,	Gage,	Hoghton,
Cholmondely,	Disney,	Gatacre,	Honywood,
Clarke,	Dod,	Gent,	Hornyold,
Clavering,	Drewe,	Gerard,	Hotham,
Clifford,	Dukinfield,	Giffard,	Howard,
Clifton,	Dykes,	Glanville,	Huddleston,
Clifton,	Dymoke,	Goring,	Hulton,
Clinton,	Eccleston,	Gower,	Irton,
Clive,	Edgcumbe,	Gregory,	Isham,
Clutton,	Edwardse,	Grenville,	Jenney,
Codrington,	Egerton,	Gresley,	Jerningham,
Colville,	Estcourt,	Greville,	Jocelyn,
Coke,	Eyre,	Grey,	Kelly,
Coker,	Eyston,	Grey,	Kendall,
Compton,	Eyton,	Grimston,	Kingscote,
Congreve,	Fairfax,	Grosvenor,	Knatchbull,
Cope,	Fane,	Gurney,	Knightley,
Corbet,	Farnham,	Haggerston,	Kynaston,
Cornewall,	Feilding,	Hamerton,	Lambton,
Cotes,	Ferrers,	Hanford,	Lane,
Cotton,	Filmer,	Harcourt,	Lascelles,
Cotton,	Finch,	Harington,	Lawley,
Courtenay,	Fitzherbert,	Harley,	Lawton,
Courthope,	Fitzwilliam,	Harpur,	Leche,
Croke,	Fleming,	Harries,	Lechmere,

Leigh,	Neville,	Roundell,	Swinburne,
Leigh,	Noel,	Rous,	Talbot,
Leigh,	Northcote,	Russell,	Tancred,
Leighton,	Norton,	St. John,	Tatton,
Leicester,	Oakeley,	Salvin,	Thornes,
Lingen,	Oglander,	Salway,	Thornhill,
Lister,	Okeover,	Sandford,	Thorold,
Loraine,	Onslow,	Savile,	Throckmorton,
Lowther,	Ormerod,	Scrope,	Thynne,
Lumley,	Oxenden,	Scudamore,	Tichborne,
Luttley,	Palmer,	Sebright,	Toke,
Lyttleton,	Palmes,	Selby,	Townley,
Malet,	Parker,	Seymour,	Townshend,
Maineraring,	Pelham,	Sheldon,	Trafford,
Manners,	Pennington,	Shelley,	Trefusis,
Markham,	Percival,	Sherard,	Tregonwell,
Massie,	Pigott,	Shirley,	Trelawney,
Mainwaring,	Pilkington,	Shuckburgh,	Tremayne,
Manners,	Plowden,	Skipwith,	Trevelyan,
Markham,	Pole,	Sneyd,	Trye,
Massie,	Polhill,	Speke,	Turvile,
Maunsell,	Polwhele,	Spencer,	Twysden,
Meynell,	Popham,	Stanhope,	Tyrell,
Meynell,	Poulett,	Stanley,	Tyrwhitt,
Middleton,	Prideaux,	Starkie,	Vernon,
Mitford,	Radclyffe,	Staunton,	Villiers,
Molesworth,	Rashleigh,	Stonor,	Vincint,
Molyneux,	Rawson,	Stourton,	Vyvyan,
Monson,	Ridley,	Strickland,	Wake,
Mordaunt,	Rokeby,	Stroude,	Walcot,
Musgrave,	Roper,	Sutton,	Waldegrave,

Wallop,	Weston,	Winnington,	Wrottesley,
Walpole,	Whichcote,	Wodehouse,	Wybergh,
Walrond,	Whitgreve,	Wollaston,	Wykeham,
Waterton,	Whitmore,	Wolryche,	Wyndam,
Welby,	Wilbraham,	Wolsely,	Wyvill.
Weld,	Willoughby,	Wombwell,	
West,	Wingfield,	Wrey,	

Our last reflection on this list is the omission of so many names which have been commonly supposed to belong to the best families. De Grey is the sole representative of the French form so often used, and Fitzherbert and Fitzwilliam represent the other form. We trust the new view thus opened of the real aristocracy of England will repay our readers for the trouble of searching these lists.

OFFICIAL SEALS.

(Continued from p. 32.)

Succeeding Gov. Shute, our Province was favored with a ruler in the person of William Burnet, who was appointed in 1728. He was the oldest son of the celebrated Bishop Burnet, and was born in 1688. In 1720, he was appointed Governor of New York and New Jersey, which place he held until transferred to the eastward.

He died 7 Sept. 1729, leaving by his second wife * (a

---

* His first wife was a dau. of Dr. George Stanhope, Dean of Canterbury.

Miss Vanhorne) two sons and a daughter, says ELIOT. One of them, Mary, m. William Browne of Salem.

Concerning the family and arms, NESBIT writes, (Heraldry, p. 404–5) : " Leaves, of what Kind I know not, frequently called Burnet-leaves, are carried by the Name of Burnet, as relative to the Name, which is ancient with us." " There are two principal families of the Name, in the South and North of Scotland, who have contended for Chief-ship ; that in the South in the Shire of Peebles, is Burnet of Burnetland, or of that Ilk, so designed of old, and of late, of Barnes."

" The other principal family of the Name is Burnet of Lees in the County of the Merns, honoured with the title of Knight Baronet in the Year 1626. This Family, says Sir George Mackenzie, got a Charter of the Lands of Lees from King Robert Bruce, and carries Argent, three Hollin leaves in Chief Vert, and a Hunting-horn in Base Sable, garnished Gules. Crest, a Hand with a Knife pruning a Vine-tree proper. Motto, Virescit vulnere virtus.

" Dr. Thomas Burnet, Physician in Ordinary to His Majesty, descended of a third son of the Family of Lees, carries as Lees, with a Mullet for difference, and his brother, Dr. Gilbert Burnet, late Bishop of Sarum, carries the same."

The next Governor of Massachusetts was Jonathan Belcher, a native of the Colony. He was the grandson of Andrew Belcher of Sudbury, who m. Elizabeth Danforth, and son of Andrew Belcher of Cambridge, who m. Sarah Gilbert.

Jonathan Belcher was born 8 Jan. 1682. Hutchinson

writes of him (Hist. ii., 369), "being the only son of a wealthy father he had high views from the beginning of life. After an academical education in his own country, he travelled to Europe, was twice at Hanover, and was introduced to the court there, at the time when the princess Sophia was the presumptive heiress to the British crown. The novelty of a British American, added to the gracefulness of his person, caused distinguishing notice to be taken of him, which tended to increase that aspiring turn of mind which was very natural to him."

He married first Mary Partridge, and secondly, in New Jersey, Mary Louisa Emilia Teal. By his first wife he had sons Andrew and Jonathan, the latter of whom was Lt. Governor and Chief Justice of Nova Scotia, whose son Andrew was a member of the Council there. Sarah, daughter of Gov. Belcher, married Byfield Lyde of Boston.

As to the arms, Gov. Belcher used an official seal, of which we have seen an impression on a commission.

The cut here given is copied from the book-plate of the Governor's son, Jonathan. We may further note, however, that the will of Andrew Belcher, the second of the name, bears the same arms on its seal, although the impression is so broken as to hardly repay copying.

REVIEW.

A Genealogical History of the Family of Montgomery, including the Montgomery Pedigree. Compiled by Thomas Harrison Montgomery. Philadelphia: printed for private circulation, 1863. Pp. 158.

This very interesting volume has attracted much attention in England, as well as here, from the well-substantiated claim put forth therein, that the representative of the ancient family of Montgomery is to be found in the branch existing in America.

The family is of Norman origin, the first of the name being Roger,[1] Count of Montgomerie in A. D. 912. The sixth Count, Robert,[6] concerning whom the historians narrate many particulars, joined the army of William the Conqueror, and received great rewards for his services in England. He was created Earl of Shrewsbury, and died in 1094. His sons were Robert,[7] Count of Montgomerie, whose grandson Guy, Count of Ponthieu, had a grandson, William, the last male of this oldest branch. (William's granddaughter m. Ferdinand III., King of Castile.) Roger,[7] Count of Marche, whose line became extinct in 1181; and Arnulph[7], Earl of Pembroke, ancestor of the present family.

This Arnulph[7] had a son Philip[8] de Montgomerie, who settled in Scotland, and there had a son Robert[9] of Eaglesham and Thorntoun. From him (through John,[10] Alan,[11] John,[12] John,[13] and Alexander[14]) was descended Sir John[15] de Montgomerie, who m. in 1361 the heiress of Sir Hugh Eglinton.

His son, Sir John,[15] was the father of Alexander,[17] Lord Montgomerie, so created about 1448. His great-grandson Hugh,[20] 3d Lord Montgomerie, was created Earl of Eglinton in 1508. The third son of this Earl was Sir Neil[21] Montgomerie of Lainshaw.

In the main line, Hugh, 5th Earl of Eglinton, died in 1612, when the title went, by reason of a new charter which he had obtained, to his cousin, Sir Alexander Seton, son of his aunt, Margaret, Countess of Winton.

The representation of the family now devolved upon the Lainshaw branch. Sir Neil's son Neil[22] married the heiress of Lord Lyle, and had Neil,[23] who died before 1621. This last Neil[23] married Elizabeth, dau. of John Cuninghame, and had

> Neil[24] of Lainshaw,
> William[25] of Brigend,
> James[24] of Dunlop,
> John[24] of Cockilbie.

Of these, Neil and his son John, in 1654, sold their estates at Lainshaw to his brother John of Cockilbie, and this younger branch thus usurped the place which belonged to the Brigend branch, as representatives of the family.

William[24] Montgomerie married a lady of the same family name, though of what branch is unknown, viz., Jean, dau. of James Montgomerie of Brigend, in Ayrshire. He had four sons, of whom the second and third died without issue, and the youngest, Hugh,[25] became ultimately the owner of Brigend.

John[25] Montgomerie, oldest son of William of Brigend, had a son Hugh,[26] styled in the deeds as of Brigend in

1654, who married Katherine, dau. of Sir William Scott of Clerkington, and had two sons and two daughters.   He died 6 May, 1710, aged over 80 years.   In 1692, he had joined his son William[27] in a sale of Brigend to their cousin John.   His other son James[27] had a family, but none of the sons left issue.

The oldest son and representative of the family was William,[27] who married, 8 January, 1684, Isabel, dau. of Robert Burnett of Lethintie, co. Aberdeen, and in 1702 he removed to East Jersey, where his father-in-law had a large estate.   Here he settled on an estate which he named Eglintoun, and from this time the family is to be considered as American.

The volume under notice has a very full account of the descendants of William, the emigrant, but we will confine our extracts to the line of representation.

William's oldest son Robert[28] m. Sarah Stacy in Feb. 1709–10, and his heir was James,[29] who m. Esther Wood in 1746.   Their son Robert[30] of Eglintoun m. Margaret Leonard in 1771, and was succeeded by Austin[31] Montgomery, son of John.[30]   This Austin[31] died s. p. in 1855. His brother the Rev. James[31] Montgomery, Rector of Grace Church, New York, and St. Stephen's, Phila., had a son James[32] T. Montgomery, a lawyer of Philadelphia, who is the present representative of the family.

In reviewing the vicissitudes of the family, we notice two salient points.   In the first place, the title passed from the Lainshaw branch in consequence of a family feud, carried even to the murder of the fourth Earl of Eglintoun by the family of the wife of his nearest male heir, Sir Niel Montgomerie of Lainshaw in 1586.   Thus this line was shorn of its honors and estates. Again, Hugh of Brigend, father of the emigrant, seems to have inherited a valuable property, but he lost it all, as letters remaining show, by a lack of business ability, and very possibly by adopting the losing side in religious matters.

Thus, though quite a number of family papers were brought here to America, the knowledge of the rights of this branch was forgotten and ignored in Scotland, and various junior branches have from time to time claimed the representation.

After a careful examination of the evidence here presented, it seems plain that the case has been made out by the claimants here, and, so far as it is a matter of interest to the family, they may be congratulated on their undoubted right to be considered the main line and representatives of a very ancient and distinguished family.

THE WASHINGTONS: a Tale of a Country Parish in the 17th Century, based on authentic documents. By John Nassau Simpkinson. Rector of Brington, Northants. London: Longmans, &c. 1860. Pp. 326, 89.

This very interesting volume may serve us as an excuse for some remarks upon the pedigree of the Washington family, the only genealogy, perhaps, possessing a national importance.

It has been assumed by Sparks and other writers that John and Lawrence Washington, who were the emigrants to Virginia, were descended from the family settled at Sulgrave. Mr. Simpkinson, finding that Lawrence W., of Sulgrave, who sold that estate, had settled at Brington, has brought together all the facts obtainable in reference to the residence there, in the belief that this Lawrence was the father of the emigrants. From the household books of the Earls Spencer of Althorp, in the same parish, he has gleaned many curious items in regard to the intimacy of the two families, and by giving his narrative the form of fiction, he has produced a book at once instructive and entertaining.

He has shown that Lawrence Washington was buried at Brington, 13 Dec. 1616, having had by his wife Margaret Butler, married in 1588, 8 sons and 9 daughters. He farther shows that of these sons, three were Sir William, Sir John and Lawrence, and following Heard and Sparks, he assumes that this Sir John and Lawrence were the two emigrants.

We find serious reasons however for doubting the accuracy of this identification. We hope in our next number to lay before our readers the result of very extensive searches in England, which we are assured will prove positively the impossibility of these being the emigrants. In the meantime we will point out a few awkward points in the evidence here presented.

In the first place, after January, 1623, John Washington is always termed Sir John in the Althorpe books: yet there is no record in Virginia of the emigrant's bearing such a title. It is hardly possible that in Virginia, at that date, he would have forborne to use his proper title. Again it is as fairly proved as such a fact can be, that this Sir John was the husband of Mary Washington, daughter of Philip Curtis, who was buried in Islip, Northants,

1 Jan. 1624, having had three sons, Mordaunt, John, and Philip.

It seems quite sure therefore that Sir John was married as early as 1620, and probably was born as early as 1600, very possibly a few years earlier. Yet we are informed that this Sir John, dropping his title, came over in or about 1657, and then, at the age of sixty at least, was a leader in the Indian wars. He must also have lost or left behind him his children by his first wife, and have had another family by a second wife.

In the N. E. Hist. Gen. Register for July, 1863, pp. 249 –51, is a correspondence between Mr. Simpkinson and Mr. Greenwood of New York, in which the latter brings the following objections, that John brought with him to Virginia, a wife who was buried there, and afterwards married Ann Pope. Mr. Simpkinson writes in reply: " I have been too ready to take it for granted that Sir Isaac Heard, Washington himself, his American biographers and our Northants county historian, Baker, had between them identified the emigrant. And though my own deductions about him could not but raise some suspicion as to his identity, I did not presume, and certainly was not disposed to question, what seemed to rest on such high authority. Your statements, however, have convinced me that the conclusions hitherto accepted are extremely questionable. There is an end, of course, to my conjecture that it was John, *son* of the emigrant, that married Ann Pope, and though the facts cited in the will do not absolutely contradict our received theory about the emigrant, and still make it possible that he may have been that John Washington, son of Lawrence, whose first wife lies buried at Islip, yet I confess that the improbabilities appear very great. It is very unlikely that two brothers, emigrating in advanced middle age, should have both married a second time in America; both have delayed making their wills till so late in life, and both have contemplated the likelihood of the other surviving, and acting as executor."

When we turn to the original authority for the origin of the family, viz., the letters of George Washington, we find but small foundation for recent assumptions. In 1792, Washington wrote to Sir Isaac Heard, (Sparks' Life, I., 546) : "In the year 1657 or thereabouts, and during the usurpation of Oliver Cromwell, John and Lawrence Washington, brothers, emigrated from the North of England, and settled at Bridge's Creek, on the Potomac River, in the County of Westmoreland. But from whom they descended, the subscriber is possessed of no document to ascertain." "John Washington was employed as general against the Indians in Maryland, and, as a reward for his services, was made a colonel; and the parish wherein he lived was called after him. He married Anne Pope, and left issue two sons, Lawrence and John, and one daughter, Anne, who married Major Francis Wright."

He also writes: "I have often heard others of the family, older than myself, say, that our ancestor, who first settled in this country, came from some one of the northern counties of England; but whether from Lancashire, Yorkshire, or one still more northerly, I do not precisely remember."

It seems hardly necessary now to point out that this family tradition, fully as vague as those preserved in a score of families here, who, like the Washingtons, still use coat-armor, is far from warranting the positive identification hitherto made.

We may add one curious result of Mr. Simpkinson's publication. Early in 1861, Hon. Charles Sumner sent to Mr. Sparks two stones, fac-similes of those at Brington, in memory of Lawrence Washington, (*presumed* father of the emigrants,) and of his brother Robert. With Mr. Sumner's assent, these stones were presented to the Mass. House of Representatives, and in accordance with a Resolve "In relation to certain Memorials of the Ancestors of Washington," they were ordered to be placed "in some convenient place in the Doric Hall of the State House, near the statue of Washington."

We will now give the Washington pedigree in this country, as recorded by Sparks and others.

1. John[1] Washington m. 1st, ——; 2dly, Ann, sister of Thomas Pope. His will is dated 27 Sept. 1675, and proved 6 Jan. 1677. Children—

John.[2]

3. Lawrence.[2]

Anne,[2] m. Maj. Francis Wright.

2. Lawrence[1] Washington, brother of John,[1] m. 2dly, ——, prob. dau. of Capt. Alex. Fleming. His will is dated 26 Feb. 1675, and proved 10 Jan. 1677. He had

Mary,[2] by first wife, living in England.

John,[2] ⎱
Anne,[2] ⎰ not of age in 1675.

SECOND GENERATION.

3. Lawrence[2] Washington m. Mildred, dau. of Col. Augustine Warner, and died in 1697. His children were

4. John.[3]

5. Augustine.[3]

Mildred,[3] m. —— Gregory, and 2d, Col. Henry Willis.

THIRD GENERATION.

4. John[3] Washington m. Catherine Whiting, and settled in Gloucester county. His children were—

6. Warner.[4]

7. Henry.[4]

Mildred,[4] m.

Elizabeth,[4] d. unm.

Catherine,[4] m. Fielding Lewis.

5. Augustine[3] Washington m. 20 April, 1715, Jane, dau. of Caleb Butler, who d. 24 Nov. 1728; and had—

      i. Butler,[4] d. young.

8.   ii. Lawrence.[4]

9.   iii. Augustine.[4]

      iv. Jane,[4] d. young.

He then married 6 March, 1730, Mary Ball, and had

10.   v. George,[4] b. 11 Feb. 1732.

      vi. Elizabeth,[4] b. 20 June, 1733; m. Fielding Lewis. (2d wife.)

11.   vii. Samuel,[4] b. 16 Nov. 1734.

12.   viii. John Augustine,[4] b. 13 Jan. 1735.

13.   ix. Charles,[4] b. 1 May, 1738.

      x. Mildred,[4] b. 21 June, 1739; died 28 Oct. 1740.

He died 12 April, 1743, aged 49.

FOURTH GENERATION.

6. Warner[4] Washington m. 1st, Elizabeth, dau. of Col. Wm. Macon, and had—

      i.   Warner,[5] who m. —— Whiting, and had a large family, the oldest being Warner.[6]

By a second wife, Hannah, dau. of Hon. William Fairfax, he had—

      ii.   Mildred,[5] m. —— Throckmorton.

      iii.   Hannah,[5] m. —— Whiting

      iv.   Catherine,[5] m. —— Nelson.

      v.   Elizabeth.[5]

      vi.   Louisa.[5]

      vii.   Fairfax.[5]

      viii.   Whiting.[5]

He removed to Frederick county, and died in 1791.

7. Henry[4] Washington m. a dau. of Col. Thacker, and had, besides two or three daughters,

      Thacker,[5] who m. the dau. of Sir John Peyton, and had several children.

8. Lawrence[4] Washington m. 19 July, 1743, Anne, dau. of Hon. Wm. Fairfax, and had—

      Jane,[5] b. 27 Sept. 1744 ; d. Jan. 1745.

      Fairfax,[5] b. 22 Aug. 1747 ; d. Oct. 1747.

      Mildred,[5] b. 28 Sept. 1748 ; d. 1749.

      Sarah,[5] b. 7 Nov. 1750 ; d. young.

He died in 1752, aged about 34.

9. Augustine[4] Washington m. Anne, dau. of Wm. Aylett, and had—

      Elizabeth, m. Alex. Spotswood.

      Anne m. Burdet Ashton.

William m. Jane, (his cousin,) dau. of John
Augustine Washington, and had four children.

10. George[4] Washington, first President, m. 6 Jan.
1759, Martha, widow of Daniel Parke Custis, and dau. of
John Dandridge.

He died 14 March, 1799, without issue.

11. Samuel[4] Washington m. 1st, Jane, dau. of Col.
John Champe; 2d, Mildred, dau. of Col. John Thornton,
and had—

    i. Thornton,[5] who m. twice, and left three sons.

3d, he married Lucy, dau. of Nath. Chapman; 4th,
Anne, dau. of Col. Wm. Steptoe, widow of Willoughby
Allston, and had—

    ii. Ferdinand, m. but d. *s. p.*

    iii. George Steptoe.

    iv. Lawrence Augustine.

His 5th wife was a widow Perrin. He died in 1781.

12. John[4] Augustine Washington m. Hannah, dau. of
Col. John Bushrod, and had—

    i. Jane,[5] m. William Washington.

    ii. Mildred,[5] m. Thomas Lee.

    iii. Bushrod,[5] m. Anne Blackburn.

    iv. Corbin,[5] m. ——, dau. of Richard Henry
Lee, and had three sons.

13. Charles[4] Washington m. Mildred, dau. of Col.
Francis Thornton, and had—

    i. George Augustine,[5] m. Frances Bassett,
and had—

        Anna Maria.[6]

        George Fayette.[6]

        Charles Augustine.[6]

    ii.   Frances m. Col. Burgess Ball.

   iii.   Mildred.

   iv.   Samuel.

It will be noticed that this account is far from complete, but it is to be hoped that enough of the archives of Virginia have escaped the perils of war to enable genealogists now to revise and correct it.

MONUMENTAL INSCRIPTIONS.

BOSTON.

COPP'S HILL YARD.

We will continue our description of the Boston yards by copying the examples found in that at Copp's Hill. The remaining tables are those of Greenwood, Gee, Goodrich, Mountfort, Martyn, two Clarks, and two Hutchinsons, besides one of unknown ownership. It is probable that others have been destroyed.

I.

HERE LYES THE MORTAL PART OF
WILLIAM CLARK Esq[r]
AN EMINENT MERCHANT OF THIS TOWN, AND
AN HONORABLE COUNSELLOR FOR
THE PROVINCE:
Who Distinguished Himself as a Faithful and Affectionate
Friend, a Fair and generous Trader,
LOYAL TO HIS PRINCE,
Yet always Zealous for the Freedom of his
Countrey. A Despiser of
SORRY PERSONS
and little Actions, An Enemy to Priestcraft and
Enthusiasm, Ready to relieve and help the Wretched.
A Lover of good Men of
Various Denominations, and a
Reverent Worshipper
Of the DEITY.

II.

[Arms as in the preceding.]
Reliquæ
JOHANNIS CLARKE, ARMIG:
laudasissimi Senatoris et Medicinæ Doctoris ;
Probitate Modestia
et Mansuetudine præclari
Terram reliquit Decem 5, 1728, ætat. 62
Nomen et Pietas manent post Funera.
This Dr. John[3] Clarke was the grandson of John Clark
of Newbury, a physician, who m. Martha, sister of Sir
Richard Saltonstall, and died Nov. 1664. His only son,
John, also a physician, m. Martha, dau. of John Whit-

tingham, had John, William, and Samuel, and died 19
Dec., 1690.

Dr. John,[3] as above, third of the name and profession,
m. Sarah, dau. of Sarah Shrimpton, and had, with several
daughters, an only son, John, b. 15 Dec., 1698. He
m. secondly, Elizabeth Hutchinson; and thirdly, Sarah
(Crisp), widow of John Leverett. His son, Dr. John[4]
Clark, the fourth, was born 15 Dec., 1698, and died 6
April, 1768. He had three children, John,[5] William,[5]
and Elizabeth,[5] wife of Rev. Jonathan Mayhew.

Dr. John[5] Clark, who died before his father, had a son,
Dr. John[6] Clark, who m. Abigail Tailer, and died at
Wrentham, 29 July, 1788.

Dr. John[7] Clark, son of John[5] and Abigail, b. 1778,
H. C. 1799, died at Weston, 21 April, 1805, aged 27.
His only daughter, Emily[8] Clark, b. 8 May, 1804, m. first,
Joseph Merriam of Lexington, by whom she had three
sons and one daughter, and secondly, George I. Soren.

————

There can be no doubt that William Clarke was the
brother of Dr. John, whose epitaph has been quoted.
Aug. 4, 1742, administration was granted on the estate of
Hon. William Clark, merchant, to his widow Sarah.
The inventory was very extensive, and among other items
in the accounts we find the following (Vol. XXXVII., p.
61) :—

Paid Johnson for escutcheons and coat of arms and
      (stock[n] for House) ?   £ 57

" Codner for a tombstone and coat of arms   40

In August, 1749, an agreement concerning the property
was made by the heirs, viz., Benjamin Clark, Rebecca

Winslow, and Thomas Greenough, whose wife Martha was a daughter of William Clarke. The papers also mention Robert Clark, the oldest son, as *non compos mentis*, and under guardianship, and a grand-daughter, Sarah Kilby, whom we have mentioned before (p. 48).

III.

THE
ARMES AND TOMB
BELONGING
TO THE FAMILY OF
GEE.

This family, according to Savage, commences with Peter, who, by wife Grace, had sons, Thomas, John, and Joshua. The last named, Joshua, m. Elizabeth, dau. of Rev. Thomas Thornton, and widow of Rev. Peter Thatcher, and had children, Samuel, Joshua, John, Ebenezer, and Elizabeth, and perhaps others. This Joshua Gee, Jr., H. C. 1717, was chosen a colleague with Cotton

Mather, at the Second Church in Boston, and ordained there 18 Dec. 1723.

He m. a dau. of Rev. Nathaniel Rogers of Portsmouth, who d. in 1730. Their children were, Mary, Joshua, Sarah, Elizabeth, Margaret. By a second wife he had, Anna, John, and Susanna. He d. 22 May, 1748.

IV.

GREENWOOD.

We are not able positively to identify the owner of this tomb, but we believe all of the name here were relatives.

Nathaniel Greenwood, said to be the son of Myles G. of Norwich, Eng., died in 1684, and was buried in this yard. His sons were Samuel and Isaac. Samuel m. Elizabeth, dau. of Richard Bronsson, and had Samuel, Isaac, Miles, Nathaniel, and Joseph, of whom Isaac, born in 1702, was Professor of Mathematics at Harvard, who d. 12 Oct. 1745.

Prof. Isaac G. m. Sarah, dau. of Hon. John Clarke, M. D., and had Isaac, John, Thales, and two daughters. Of these, Isaac, b. 9 May, 1730, was grandfather of Hon.

John G. of Brooklyn, Dr. Isaac J. of New York, Rev. Francis W. P. of Boston, Rev. Alfred of Barnstable, and Edwin of Boston. A longer account of the family will be found in Vol. XIV. of the N. E. Hist. and Gen. Register.

v.

MR. JOHN MOUNTFORT,

ÆTATIS LIV. OBT

JAN^{RY} VI.

MDCCXXIV

BENJAMIN MOUNTFORT

SON OF

JOHN AND MARY MOUNTFORT

ÆTATIS XXV.

OBT. MARCH X. MDCCXXI

The Mountfort family here springs from Edmund[1] M., who was a merchant of London, and settled in Boston in 1656. He was accompanied by his brother, Henry,[1] aged about 19, and in 1675 another brother, Benjamin,[1] joined them. Henry[1] died 29 March, 1691, aged 54, leaving an only son, Ebenezer,[2] who died in 1716. Benjamin married but had no children.

Edmund[1] Mountfort m. in 1663, Elizabeth Carwithy Farnham, and had with other children, Edmund,[2] ancestor of the Mountforts of Portland, and John,[2] b. 8 Feb., 1670, whose epitaph is given above.

John[2] Mountfort m. 17 January, 1693, Mary, dau. of Joseph Cock, and had several children, one of whom doubtless is the Benjamin[3] above recorded. The fifth son was

Joseph[3] Mountfort, born 12 April, 1713; m. in 1736, Rhoda J. Lambert, and had a large family. He died in 1775.

Joseph[4] Mountfort, fourth son of Joseph,[3] was born 5 Feb., 1750. He m. 16 Feb., 1777, Sarah Giles, by whom he had a large family. He served in several privateers during the Revolutionary War, and was twice taken prisoner. He died 11 August, 1838.

Napoleon-Bonaparte[5] Mountfort, fourth son of Joseph,[4] born 19 Dec., 1800, was a merchant of Boston, where he m. 2 January, 1825, Mary, dau. of Ezra Trull. He removed to New York, studied law, and was afterwards Judge of the Police Court.

George[5] Mountfort, fifth son of Joseph,[4] was long resident in New York, and in 1850 was Consul at Candia. In 1858 he resigned, and has since been resident in Boston.

VI.

MARTYN.

There is no inscription besides the name to inform us of the date of the erection of this monument. We presume, however, it was erected by the family of which we gave quite a full account in our last number (Vol. II., 7).

VII.

Isaac Dupee   Heir to Goodridge.

[The following inscription is placed around the tomb:

Erected by Isaac Dupee Grandson to G. Aged LXXV.
August 31. A. D. 1846.

It is by no means clear that the arms were then cut.
On the contrary, they seem at least as old as the Martyn
arms, and were probably replaced when the tomb was
rebuilt.]

In regard to the Goodridge or Gutteridge, or, as now
spelt, Goodrich family, we have to note, that there were
several families of the name. This tomb undoubtedly
belonged to Walter Goodrich, who was a member of Rev.
Mr. Welsteed's church, and gave a piece of plate in 1730
inscribed with these arms. (See Vol. I., page 59.)   Concerning him we find that Walter Gutridge m. Anna Gross,
12 Nov. 1696, and had

Hannah, b. 21 March, 1698 ; m. James Halsey.

Elizabeth, b. 30 March, 1699; d. young.

Walter, b. 9 July, 1701.

Elizabeth, b. 14 July, 1703 ; m. 1st, Foxwell Curtis,
30 July, 1724 ; 2d, John Grant, 26 Sept. 1734.

Thomas, b. 19 Nov. 1706.

Mary, b. 26 Oct. 1707 ; m. Elias Dupee, 12 July, 1725.

Katherine, b. 21 March, 1711–2 ; d. young.

This Walter was a mariner, and his will, dated 14
March, 1735, proved 25 Feb. 1745, mentions only his wife,
three daughters and their husbands. Of his two sons,
Walter was a captain, and his will, of 9 Feb. 1728, mentions wife Mary, bro. Thomas, and three sisters, Elizabeth
being then called *Curtis*, but in her father's will *Grant*,
having remarried. He seems to have had no children.

Thomas Goodrich, the other son, m. Grace Jackson, 6
Aug. 1730, and his will is dated 18 March, 1734, but

mentions no children. His widow no doubt married, 15 Jan. 1735, John Gardner.

VIII. AND IX.

These two stones are now used in the yard, one being appropriated by some other family, the other also inscribed with a name, but lying broken near the house in the yard.

There can be no doubt that both formerly adorned Hutch-inson tombs, the arms being those of that family, and there remaining no other evidence of its burial place. We know that this most distinguished family always claimed arms, and there can be little doubt that, like the other families residing near this graveyard, they possessed a tomb here. In too many instances after the extinction of a family here by death or removal, a culpable neglect has been evinced in transferring tombs to strangers.

WICKETAQUOC, STONINGTON, CONN.
(Communicated by J. HAMMOND TRUMBULL, Esq.)

1.

In Expectation
of a Joyful Resurrection
to eternal life,

Here lyeth interred y^e body
of the Rev^d Mr JAMES NOYES
aged 80 years,
who after a faithful serving
of the Church of Christ
In this place
For more than 55 years,
deceased Decr y^e 30, 17$\frac{19}{20}$
Majesty, Meekness, & Humility,
Here meet in one with greatest Charity.

This inscription, with the arms of Noyes, nearly as represented above, is from the slate tablet which covers the
grave of the first minister of Stonington, Conn., in the
ancient burying-ground (at Wicketaquoc) in that town.

Rev. James Noyes of Stonington was a son of the Rev.
James Noyes of Newbury, who was born at Choulderton,
Wiltshire, in 1608, and came to New England with his
brother Nicholas, and cousin Rev. Thomas Parker, in 1634.
James, the son, was born 11 March, 1640, H. C. 1659;
" much honor attaches to his name for so long faithful
fulfilment of his ministry, as in a most judicious funeral
sermon by (Rev. Eliphalet) Adams of New London, is
shown ; and equally so for service in the foundation of
Yale College, standing there as first on the list of Fellows."
—*Savage's Geneal. Dict.*

2.

[Arms as in No. 3.]
In Memory of
DAVID CHESEBROUGH ESQ^R
of Newport Rhode Island

Who was born at Stonington
Educated in Boston
For many Years an eminent Merchant
in Newport
Where he settled & liv'd till 1776
When driv'n off by the Enemy
He sat down on his Estate
In Stonington in Connecticut
Where he dy'd Feby 27 1782 Æt. 80
He was for many Years a Member &
Pillar of the 2d Congregational Church
In Newport.
Of exemplary Piety & Virtue

3.

In Memory of
MRS MARGARET CHESEBROUGH

Who departed this Life March 27, 1782
Aged 62
Thou tender Mother and thou best of Friends
Farewell.

This David Chesebrough was the son of William and Mary (McDowell) C. of Stonington, and great-grandson of William Chesebrough, the emigrant, of Boston 1630-9, then of Braintree and Rehoboth, and finally of Stonington, where he was the first settler.

These stones were erected through the agency of President Stiles, who wrote the inscriptions for both. Mr. Chesebrough " was for many years a member and pillar of the Second Congregational Church in Newport," of which Dr. Stiles was then pastor. David's wife was the daughter of —— Sylvester, Esq., of Shelter Island, and their only child Abigail, b. 16 May, 1734, married about 1761 Alexander Grant, Esq., a nephew of Sir Alexander Grant, Bart., of London.

They removed to Halifax, and subsequently to England, where, in 1783, they had four children living.

Thomas Chesebrough, next younger brother to David, grad. H. C. 1726, died at Stonington, 11 Dec. 1754, aged 48, and is honored on his tombstone as " a good scholar, a great historian, and well acquainted with the liberal arts and sciences."

On a label below the shield is the motto, " Virtue is true greatness," which has a home-like sound, more like the " Second Congregational Church" than the Herald's College. In England the motto is recorded as " Fidei coticula crux." Possibly, staunch Protestants may have found too strong a savor of Romanism in this recognition of the Cross as "the touchstone of faith," and have avouched their republicanism by the substitution of " Virtus vera nobilitas," or its more homely equivalent.

SUFFOLK WILLS.

(Continued from p. 11.)

In our last article we omitted mention of·two examples already published in our first volume, being

14. The seal of Nicholas Bowes, (Vol. I., p. 109), and

15. The curious seal used on the wills of James Blake and Isaac Jones, both of Dorchester, (Vol. I., p. 112.)

16.

Our next example is taken from the seal attached to the will of James[1] Lloyd, dated 10 April, 1684, and proved 21 Sept. 1693. This gentleman is said to have removed hither from Bristol, England, and had an estate at Oyster Bay, Long Island. He married first, Griselda, daughter of Nathaniel Sylvester, and secondly, Rebecca, dau. of Gov. John Leverett. His will mentions a brother Joseph Lloyd, though we are not informed of his settlement in this country.

James[1] had sons Henry[2] and Joseph,[2] of whom Henry[2] m. 23 Nov. 1708, Rebecca Nelson, and had ten children. Of these the youngest child, Dr. James[3] Lloyd, b. 24 March, 1728, m. Sarah Corwin, and died in 1810, leaving only two children, Hon. James[4] Lloyd, b. 1769, d. 1831, s. p., and Sarah, (b. 1766, d. 1839), wife of Leonard Vassall Borland, and had an only son John Borland.

The family here is represented in the line of John[3]
Lloyd, second son of Henry,[2] who m. Sarah Woolsey in
1742, and had a son John[4] Lloyd, who m. Amelia White,
and was the father of John Nelson[5] Lloyd, of Lloyd's
Neck, L. I.

17.

The will of John[1] Borland, 1726, gives
us an example of his arms, which are
described also in Gore's Roll. This will
gives us the following interesting particulars. He mentions his wife Sarah and
only son Francis[2] Borland ; also his three
nieces, Cecil, Anna, and Euphamie, daughters of his
brother Francis Borland, late of Glasford, in North Britain,
clerk, deceased. Also his brother's other daughter by
his second wife. Sister Anne Borland *alias* Mitchel,
widow. Niece Jannet, dau. of sister Jannet Borland,
alias Canady. Susanna Maxwell, dau. of sister Elizabeth
Maxwell. John[1] d. 30 March, 1727, aged 68 ; his widow
d. Sept. 1727, aged 63.

The only son, Francis[2] Borland, m. 22 Sept. 1726, Jane
Lindall, and had John,[3] b. 5 Sept. 1728, Jane,[3] b. 24 April,
1732, and Francis Lindall,[3] all three mentioned in their
father's will. Francis[2] Borland died 16 Sept. 1763, aged
72, and left a widow, (second wife), Phebe ——, who d.
3 April, 1775, aged 80. His dau. Jane m. 4 Sept. 1750,
John Still Winthrop, father of the late Lt. Gov. Thomas
L. Winthrop.

John[3] Borland, son of Francis,[2] m. 20 Feb. 1749-50,
Anna Vassall, and had twelve children, of whom we will
enumerate a few. John L. was a royalist ; Francis was a

physician at Somerset, Mass., and left issue; Samuel died at Hudson, N. Y., leaving issue; Jane m. Jonathan Simpson; Leonard Vassall m. Sarah Lloyd, as mentioned in the preceding article.

18.

The seal affixed to a power of attorney, dated in 1666, by John Gibbs and Dennis his wife, is probably that of one of the three witnesses, Jeremiah Ouglin, Richard Price, and John Grafton, Jr. We presume it to be that of Richard Price, since Burke records as the arms of Price of Westbury, co. Buckingham, argent, three Cornish choughs sable, beaked and legged gules. This Richard Price married the daughter of the famous buccaneer, Thomas Cromwell, but if this be his seal, the impalement is for an intermarriage in an earlier generation.

19.

The very handsome seal on the will of Richard Loft, 25 April, 1690, remains without a claimant. The witnesses were Michael Shaller, Peter Townsend, and John Herbert Coward, the last being the notary.

20.

A similar puzzle is found on the will of Daniel[4] Quincy, 14 Aug. 1690, who was son of Edmund[3] and Joanna (Hoar) Quincy, and grandson of Edmund[2] and Judith (Pares) Quincy. This last Edmund[2] was the son of

Edmund[1] and Ann (Palmer) Quincy, of Wigsthorpe in Northamptonshire, and was baptized 30 May, 1602.

The witnesses to the will are Jacob Eliot, Theophilus Frary, and Samuel Sewell.

21.

The seal on the will of Simon Lynde, 1685, is very interesting, as the impalement enables us to trace the family. The fleur-de-lis is the arms of the noted family of Digby, and, as we shall show, the mother of Simon Lynde was Elizabeth Digby. Hence, this was his father's seal.

Simon[1] Lynde, born at London, June, 1624, was a merchant there, and removed to Boston in 1650. In Feb., 1652, he m. Hannah, dau. of John Newdigate, and had a large family, of which we will mention three. These were Samuel,[2] b. 1 Dec. 1653, (m. Mary, dau. of Jarvis Ballard, who d. Dec. 1697, and at his death, 2 Oct. 1721, left an only dau., Mary,[3] wife of John Valentine,) Nathaniel,[2] b. 22 Nov. 1659, and Benjamin,[2] b. 22 Sept. 1666.

This Benjamin[2] Lynde m. Mary Brown, and had, besides William,[3] who d. s. p., Benjamin,[3] b. 5 Oct. 1700, who m. Mary Bowles and had three daughters, viz., Mary, wife of Andrew Oliver, Hannah, and Lydia, wife of Rev. William Walter, of Trinity Church, Boston.

Both of these Benjamins were members of the Council, and Chief Justices of the Province.

The line of Nathaniel[2] seems to have ended very soon in co-heiresses.

THE DIGBY FAMILY.

Concerning the Digby family, with which the Lyndes intermarried, as is evidenced by their arms, we have the following account:—

Sir Egerton Brydges, in " Collins's Peerage," says that this family was originally termed Tilton, but removing to Digby, co. Lincoln, took their name thence. John Digby was buried there in the time of Edw. I., and from him came Everard[1] Digby, M. P. for the county of Hunting-ton, *temp.* Hen. VI., who had seven sons. Three of these branches are worthy of mention.

From the eldest Everard,[2] was descended (through Everard,[3] Everard,[4] Kenelm,[5] Everard,[6] Everard[7]) Sir Kenelm[8] Digby, the famous author, soldier, and statesman.

From the second son, Simon,[2] came (through Reginald[3] and John[4]) George[5] Digby of Coleshill, whose son John[6] was born in 1580, and became Earl of Bristol. His older brother Robert[6] was father of Robert,[7] and was created Earl of Digby.

The third son, Sir John[2] Digby, of Eye-Kettleby, co. Leicester, m. Catherine, dau. of Sir Nicholas Griffin, and had sons William[3] and Simon.[3] Burke (Commoners, IV. 464) traces the descendants of Simon,[3] who was of North Luffenham, and whose last male heir died in 1811. He follows Brydges in saying that William[3] died without issue.

Our information, however, which purports to be founded on the original visitations of the county of Lincoln, states as follows:—

William[3] Digby married secondly, Helena, dau. of John
Ross, widow of Sir Edward Montague, and had,

    iii. William,[4] d. *s. p.*

    iv. . . . . .[4] (a dau.) m. . . . . . Field.

    v. Margery,[4] m. Thomas Mulsho of Thornham, co.
        Kent.

    vi. Isabella,[4] m. Sir Bryan Laffrells, Knt.

By his first wife, Rosa, dau. of William Perwick of Lub-
enham, he had,

    i. John,[4] who m. Mary, dau. of Sir William Parre,
       and had William,[5] Francis,[5] and Thomas,[5] all of
       whom d. *s. p.*

    ii. Simon.[4]

This Simon[4] Digby, of Bedale, co. York, m. a dau. of
Reginald Gray, and had,

    i. Roland,[5] who m. Jane, dau. of Henry Clapham,
       and had Francis,[6] m. . . . . . Wright; Maria,[6] m.
       John Baptist of Antwerp.

    ii. Everard,[5] who m. Katherine, dau. of . . . . Stock-
       bridge, and had Elizabeth[6] Digby, who m. Enoch
       Lynde, and was mother of Simon[7] Lynde.

HERALDIC NOTES AND QUERIES.

(Continued from Vol. I., p. 192.)

XXIX.

We have been favored with the following copy of a bill
found among the Curwen papers. It adds another Herald
Painter to our list.

The hon^{ble} Benj. Lynde Esqre, Samuel Curwin, Esqr and Mr Henry Gibbs, executors to the last Will & Testament of Mr. W^{m}. Lynde, dec^{d}.

To James Turner,   Dr.

1752 May 14. To 8 escutcheons for ye Funeral of
                 ye Dec^{d} at 8 s ap^{s}   £ 6.
             To an Inscription on ye Breastplate
                 of ye Coffin   „ 8.
   June 6   To 9 Enamell Rings for do. w^{t.} ⎫
               13 dwt. 23 gr   ⎬
             To fastening ditto at 9s 4 ap^{s} ⎭   4 „ 4
       9   To adding a Crescent for Differ-
               ence to each of the escutcheons
               at 2 s ap^{s}.   11 „ 0.

Marblehead, Sep. 2, 1752.

Concerning this James Turner, we now know only that he engraved a series of psalm music, and we have also seen a Franklin coat-of-arms engraved as a book plate, which displays considerable facility of execution.

XXX.

As there is now a chance of learning something about Virginia families, we desire to call attention to the Fairfax family, representing the Barons of that name.

It seems by the Peerages that the family was long resident in Yorkshire, and Thomas, first Baron Fairfax of Cameron, in the peerage of Scotland, died in 1640.

His son Ferdinando, 2d Baron, was on the parliamentary side, and *his* son Thomas, 3d Baron, was the famous parliamentary commander-in-chief. This Thomas died in 1671, leaving an only daughter, Mary, wife of George Villiers, Duke of Buckingham.

The title being limited to heirs male, went to Henry, his cousin, 4th Baron, whose son Thomas, 5th Baron, had sons Thomas and Robert, successively 6th and 7th Barons.

Of these, Thomas lived in Virginia, and died in 1782, Robert lived in England, and died in 1793.

The title then passed to the Rev. Bryan Fairfax, great-grandson of Henry, 4th Baron, being grandson of Henry Fairfax of Tolston, co. York, and son of William Fairfax, who had been a government officer at Salem, Mass., but who removed to Virginia. William Fairfax m. at Salem Deborah Clarke, but his first wife was Sarah Walker.

William's children were George William, (d. *s. p.* 1787), Thomas, (d. *s. p.* 1746), and Bryan.

It seems that Rev. Bryan Fairfax returned to England, and was confirmed in 1800 in his position as eighth Baron Fairfax of Cameron. He m. Elizabeth Cary, and had several children, but here our knowledge ends, except that in "Notes and Queries," (1st series, x. 74), it is stated that in 1854 the representative of the family was Charles Snowdon Fairfax, then of California, and Speaker of the H. Rep. of that State.

Our query is, if any of our readers can supply a record of Rev. Bryan Fairfax's descendants?

XXXI.

THE BROWN FAMILY.

In our last number, (pp. 23–26,) we gave an account of the Browns of Salem. Since that article was written, we have had an opportunity to examine a pedigree preserved in the family, from which we add the following particulars.

The pedigree commences with

Simon[1] Browne, who came from Browne Hall in Lan-

cashire, to. Brandish, co. Suff., about A. D. 1540. His
widow Elizabeth died 30 Aug. 1584. Their son Thomas,[2]
who d. 1 May, 1608, by wife Margaret, (who d. 1 May,
1605,) had,

Francis[3] Browne of Weybred Hall, who d. 9 May, 1626.
His son William[4] Brown, b. 1 March, 1607-8, served an
apprenticeship to a merchant in Southold, co. Suff., and
came to Salem, Mass., in 1635. His first wife was Mary,
dau. of Rev. Mr. Young of Long Island; his second, Sarah, dau. of Samuel Smith of Yarmouth. They had,

Hon. William.[5]

> John,[5] d. 1634.
> Samuel,[5] d. 1655.

Rev. Joseph,[5] minister at Charlestown, m. and d. *s. p.*
Hon. Benjamin.[5]

> Sarah,[5] m. Thomas Dean of London.
> James,[5] d. *s. p.*
> Mary,[5] m. Waitstill Winthrop.
> James[5] d. young.

Col. Samuel[6] Brown's wife, Abigail, was the dau. of Mr.
John Kech, of Bristol, Eng., and was born in 1685.

In the junior branch we have seen that Capt. John[6]
Browne had a second wife, Mary, widow of Col. Ichabod
Plaisted, and his dau. Sarah[7] Browne m. her step-brother
Ichabod Plaisted, jr. The issue was Mary[8] Plaisted, who
m. Joseph Sherburn of Boston, and Ichabod Plaisted, 3d,
who m. his own cousin, Eunice[8] Brown, dau. of Col. Ben-
min[7] and Eunice (Turner) Brown, and had two children,
Ichabod[9] Plaisted, 4th, b. 9 July, 1752, and Benjamin[9]
Browne Plaisted, b. 1754. He d. 2 Nov. 1755, and his
widow m. Timothy Fitch, and had three children.

THE

HERALDIC JOURNAL;

RECORDING THE ARMORIAL BEARINGS AND GENEALOGIES OF AMERICAN FAMILIES.

NO. XV. JULY, 1866.

THE FRANKLIN FAMILY.

EXEMPLUM IPSE HOMO ADEST

John Franklin,

Boston, New England.

The kindness of a friend has supplied us with the accompanying facsimile of the bookplate of John Franklin, the elder brother of the famous Benjamin. It is inscribed "J. Turner Sculp.," evidently the person mentioned in our last number, p. 94. This coat-of-arms, which was used by Dr. Benjamin Franklin on his seal, as in the facsimile on the copies of his famous letter to Strahan, is recorded by Burke as having been used also by William Franklin, the Governor of New Jersey.

We find it thus used by two brothers and the son of one of them, two of them being men in high positions and liable to a severe scrutiny of their pretensions. It therefore seems very probable that Benjamin Franklin may have obtained a grant of these arms, perhaps at the time when he began to hold prominent offices. It is strange, however, that arms should have been conceded to him so closely resembling those of families of the same name in other counties.

It is hardly possible that he could have enjoyed them by hereditary right. From the last and most interesting biography of the Philosopher which has appeared, we transcribe the following facts, which seem to show that the family for some generations had not risen above the rank of yeomen.

Thomas[1] Franklin of Ecton, Northamptonshire, was a blacksmith, and was living in Henry VIII's time. His grandson, Thomas,[3] was born 8 October, 1598, and married Jane White, niece of Col. White of Banbury, and had nine children. He died 21 March, 1681. Of his children, four were Thomas,[4] John,[4] Benjamin,[4] and Josiah.[4]

Of these, Thomas[4] was "something of a lawyer, Clerk of the County Court, and Clerk to the Archdeacon," and acquired considerable property. John[4] was a dyer, and probably a thriving man, for his two younger brothers afterwards learned the same trade.

Josiah,[4] the father of our Benjamin, was born at Ecton in 1655. By his first wife, Ann, he had, in England,

Elizabeth, Samuel, and Hannah; and he came with his family to Boston about 1683. Here he had Josiah, Anne, and two Josephs. His wife dying he m. Abiah, dau. of Peter Folger, and had John, Peter, Mary, James, Sarah, Ebenezer, Thomas, Benjamin, Lydia, and Jane; all of whom are duly recorded by Savage. Notwithstanding this numerous progeny, it is believed that the family is extinct in the male line. Descendants of Benjamin through females are quite numerous.

In regard to the arms, we repeat that it seems improbable that the two prominent bearers of the name would have assumed them unchallenged, and that it is more probable that a search at Heralds' College would show a grant to Benjamin or his father.

THE HANCOCK FAMILY.

 We have joined the Hancocks with the Franklins because they seem both to be in the same class of assumptions, or recent acquisitions, of arms, by persons in high official station. In neither case do we find any reason to imagine that the arms had been used by any of the family in this country, until the generation in which the bearer of the name had made it conspicuous.

Gov. John[5] Hancock, whose arms are here copied from a bill of exchange, whereon it was engraved as a sort of seal, was born in 1737, and was the son of Rev. John of Braintree. This John[4] was son of a more noted minister, Rev. John[3] Hancock of Lexington, who was son of Nathaniel,[2] and grandson of Nathaniel[1] Hancock, both of

Cambridge, Mass. This last Nathaniel died before 1652, and we have no reason to think that he claimed arms or was esteemed above the rank of a yeoman.

The true rise of the family commenced with Rev. John[3] of Lexington, a clergyman highly esteemed by his contemporaries. His son, Thomas,[4] was a bookseller, and afterwards a very distinguished merchant of Boston. He was largely engaged in supplying the British garrisons and armies here, as well as in carrying on an extensive commerce. He acquired a large fortune, and dying *s. p.*, in 1764, left the bulk of it to his nephew, John.[5]

This latter, as is well known, espoused the popular side in the Revolutionary war, was President of the Congress of 1776, and signed the Declaration of Independence. He was also Governor of Mass., 1780–1785 and 1787–1793. He died 8 Oct. 1793, and having lost his children, much of his estate devolved on his nephew John[6] Hancock, who survived till within a few years.

In the case of Thomas Hancock, the wealthy merchant, as in that of Benjamin Franklin, there is no improbability that he may have incurred the trifling expense of taking out a grant of arms; but we do not care to point out more than the possibility of their being thus acquired.

In our present number will be found the arms of James Bowdoin, Hancock's great rival, for which we cannot claim a much higher authority.

AMORY ARMS.*

This coat was received in 1864 from the Ulster Herald Office, annexed to the pedigree given below of a family now extensively multiplied in Boston and its vicinity. The pedigree extends down to generations in the present century, and must have consequently been entered in that office at a comparatively recent period. It was probably prepared by some member of the Bourchier family, set forth therein in full, as descended from Lucy, g. g. daughter of Robert Amory, described as of Bunratty, a castle still standing on the banks of the Shannon, and formerly a principal seat of the O'Briens, Earls of Thomond.

This Robert, born about 1600, and mentioned in the will of his eldest son, Thomas of Galy, which bears date 1666, as a legatee, married a sister of Robert Eliott. His son was, in 1649, Sheriff of Bristol, possessed estates in Somersetshire and Kerry, represented Dingle in Parliament in 1656, and was Purveyor of the navy for Ireland after and possibly before the Restoration. He married, as early as 1653, Elizabeth Fitzmaurice, daughter of Patrick, nineteenth Lord Kerry, and died 1666. His

---

* Barry of six argent and gules, on a chief of the first a lion passant of the second armed B.   Crest, eagle's head erased.

son of the same name resided at the Castle of Bunratty, and
died in 1728, leaving a large estate to his son Thomas, an
author of some reputation, and his daughter Lucy, before
mentioned, who married in 1724 Terence McMahon of
Crottola. The male line of Thomas of Galy terminated
about 1820, in his g. g. son Thomas, a Major in the
British Army.

Jonathan, the youngest son of Robert, married Rebecca,
sister of George Houston, and after her death in the West
Indies, removed to Carolina where he again married.
He received from King William a commission as Advocate General of that province, was appointed Treasurer
by the Proprietors, and chosen Speaker of its Assembly.
He died in 1699, leaving a considerable estate; his death
being shortly followed by that of Martha, his widow.
His daughter Sarah married, in 1707, Governor Arthur
Middleton, and died in 1722; another, Ann, married
James Ramsay. His son Thomas, who had been sent
before the death of his father, to England, for his education, to the care of his cousin Thomas of Bunratty, was
placed at Westminster School, and afterwards became
English and Dutch Consul at the Azores. He remained
there, making one or more visits to England, till 1719,
when he went to South Carolina. After travelling
through several of the Colonies he came to Boston, where
he married Rebecca, the daughter of Francis Holmes,
who owned several plantations and other property in Carolina, though originally from Massachusetts. Here he was
engaged extensively in commerce with Europe, the Azores,
and Carolinas, till his death in June, 1728, the year and
month that his cousin died at Bunratty, of whom, with

his uncle John, then ninety years of age, he was heir in
tail of extensive estates in Clare and Kerry, as also of St.
Ann's and other property in Somersetshire, under the
will of his eldest uncle. The entail had been docked, but
his cousin, in resettling his property upon his children,
vested in him and his heirs the remainder, on failure of
any descendants of his own of the name. From his sons,
Thomas, born 1722, a graduate of Harvard College in
1741, who married Elizabeth, daughter of William Coffin,
and died in 1784; and John, born 1728, who married
Catherine, daughter of Rufus Greene, grandfather of the
late Gardiner Greene of Boston, and died in 1804, are
derived all the descendants of Robert of the name in
Europe or America.

From repeated changes of abode from England to Ireland, West Indies, Carolina, Azores, and finally here, long
separation from kindred, infrequent correspondence, and
comparative estrangement, from early deaths in two generations leaving children in their minority in a strange
land, the chain of tradition was disturbed. This is no
unusual occurrence in American family history, and serves
to explain much of the interest taken in working out
genealogical problems, often attractive in proportion to
their difficulty. In many instances their solution is the
less easy, that busily occupied with absorbing cares, or
stirring political excitements, and educated to attach little
importance to what savored in their minds somewhat of
vanity, less attention was paid by former generations to
heraldic distinctions. These were occasionally used for
seals or hatchments, but not to the extent that has become
common since, when they are made useful or ornamental

for many purposes, such as books, equipages, plate or porcelain, and often paraded with an ostentatious display that provokes ridicule

When our Revolution emancipated us from the jurisdiction of the Earl Marshal, arms, mottoes and devices were in some instances adopted according to individual caprice. This naturally led to confusion, and when more sensible ideas prevailed upon the subject, resort was had again to the Herald's College. Whenever application was made for their proper arms by members of this branch, those generally adopted here, barry of six, argent and gules with a bend azure, and for crest, a talbot's head in a mural coronet, were invariably assigned. The shield is the same attached, except that the bend is sable, six hundred years ago, to the name in the lists of the Knights of Oxfordshire, and the same substantially which has been since used throughout its various branches in Gloucester, Essex, Devon, and Dorset, by the Earls of Dorchester, extinct in 1808, by Heathcoat Amory of Bolham Park, Devon, and Rev. Thomas Amory, Vicar of St. Teath, Cornwall, all of whom are believed to have descended from a common line of ancestry. It has been adopted here so generally, that it seems hardly worth while to change it, especially as the source of information, from which the arms annexed were taken, may not have been absolutely reliable, and they do not essentially differ. The coat, as represented above, has the barry of six argent and gules common to all, but is without the bend, and has in chief a lion passant, and instead of the talbot's head for crest, an eagle's head erased. In Vol. 10th, Genealogical Register, page 56, is a coat taken from a tankard, supposed to have descended from generation to generation for two centuries, which is wholly dissimilar from the arms so long connected with the name, and may be presumed to have belonged to some family with which an ancestor intermarried.

If we knew positively that the arms annexed were borne by the progenitors of Robert, mentioned in the pedigree, there would be more reason for adopting them. Unfortunately we know very little concerning him or his immediate ancestors. Numerous individuals of the same name as himself are found in Parish Registers, Probate Archives, State Records of different conditions and localities, one contemporary Robert being recommended by the Marquis of Winchester, Earl of Cleaveland, and other persons of note, to Charles II. for a baronetcy in consideration of military service and losses during the Rebellion. As his two sons had perished in the war, he requests that it may be conferred on such person as he may designate.

Whether this application was attended with success does not appear. There may exist in the Clare records what may indentify Robert of Bunratty, mentioned in the pedigree, but in the absence of more direct proof we have to rely on the statement of his descendant, Dr. Robert Amory, in the St. James Chronicle in 1788, when correcting a notice of his father, whose publications and extreme age of ninety-seven had then recently attracted attention, that his ancestor was a brother of Col. Damer, an officer of cavalry under Cromwell, whose immense estates, left to his nephews, when he died in 1720, at the age of ninety, were the foundation of the prosperity of his family. This statement was obviously inaccurate, but may have been an approximation to the truth. Robert D'Amory of Chapel, born 1571, grandfather of Col. Damer, may have been the common ancestor. If this hypothesis be the true one, the line may be traced back, by aid of the visitations, to the thirteenth century, and by other records, with an average degree of exactitude, to the conquest of England by the Normans.

At that time, one Gilbert of the name established himself near Oxford, in possession of Bokenhall, Hedynton, and other manors, granted him according to Dunkin and Skelton, the county historians, for his services at the battle of Hastings. Whence he came, Hooker intimates in dedicating his Translation of Hollinshed to Raleigh, his descendant through Sir Roger, who married the Lady Elizabeth de Clare, g. daughter of Edward I., born 1292, deceased 1360, by the statement that his ancestors were certain Earls of the name in Brittany, nearly allied to the Montforts. This Gilbert, and a succession of other Gilberts, Rogers and Roberts, flourished in Oxfordshire for the next three centuries, leaving frequent mark of their existence on the records of Bicester and other religious establishments which they founded or endowed. Another Gilbert is mentioned by Dugdale in his Baronage, as father of Sir Roger mentioned above, who was a Baron of the realm, but died in 1324, in rebellion against the Spencers, the unworthy favorites of Edward II., and of Nicholas, whose son, Sir Richard, who died 1332, was summoned to Parliament as a Baron. His g. son, Sir Richard, distinguished himself in the wars of Edward III., was the friend and by Dugdale is stated to have been the kinsman of the famous Sir John Chandos, and died in 1376.

By the marriage of his daughters with Bardolph and Raleigh, the estates of Sir Roger passed into those families, while those of Sir Richard appear to have been alienated to meet the expenses attending his military services.

Another Sir Richard, third son of Gilbert, held lands also in Oxon and was succeeded by his son Robert, father of Roger, whose son Robert had lands in Oxon and Berks, and was father of John of South Molton in Devon, who married the daughter of Eyre of Atherington, and had three sons, George, Robert, who married the widow of Sir John Pollard of Comb Martin, and Anthony. George had three sons, John, his heir, William, who married the daughter of Leigh of Ridge, and Anthony.

In 1580, John, by marriage with Miss Thomas, acquired the manor of White Chapel, which passed a century later by another marriage, that of their g. g. daughter, born 1657, died 1707, to Edward Gibbon. His brother Anthony was settled over the parish of Ashot, in Somerset, for forty-two years, from 1578 to 1620, and is said to have been the g. father of Robert, born 1571.

It would hardly be safe to attach too much faith to what concerns private individuals, at periods so remote. Exact information, even if to be procured on these subjects, is perhaps very justly regarded by many as of less than no value. But if inquiry is pursued in the right spirit, to give pleasure and not pain, and in the well grounded assurance that the farther one penetrates into the distant past the more insignificant become the paltry distinctions which alienate man from man, the more equal all are found to be in the presence of their innumerable ancestors, it has its use. Every name has antiquities interesting to all it serves to designate, and of these the heraldic emblems which marked them in the field, or distinguished their sepulchres, are worth an occasional thought.

Crests are of more recent origin than shields, and were more frequently varied as individuals chanced to prefer ; that of Robert de Aumari, Judge of Chester, in the fourteenth century, was a bunch of plumes. The lion, wolf, horse, talbot, eagle and other birds are found attached as crests to the shield, barry, nebuly or wavy, of six argent and gules. The earliest known record of the talbot's head as a crest, is in a visitation of Gloucestershire, 1591, as belonging to a family of the name, possessed for many centuries, and down to as late a period as 1620, of the manor of Yatte, in that county, from whom are derived a branch lately residing at Park Place, Stourbridge, mentioned in Burke's Landed Commoners.

Having, in the article alluded to in the Register, had the arms on the tankard engraved, in the hope that it might suggest some clue to their origin, it seems proper to correct any misapprehension which may have been given by this later information. It is convenient to have in a work of this nature, likely to be accessible to many generations, all the heraldic lore which can prove interesting to families residing where it is published. Enough has been said to satisfy the most scrupulous that the shield which has been so long in use here, and commonly borne by the different branches of the name in England, had better be retained as it is.

The tabular pedigree from the Ulster Office, before referred to, is here given, the statements in brackets having been supplied from other sources of information.

Robert[1] Amory of Bunratty, Esq., m. Miss Eliott, and had Thomas;[2] John[2] (who d. 1730, aged 90;) Robert[2] of Antigua, planter, will dated 26 May, 1702; Henry;[2] Jonathan[2] of Dublin, merchant, 1675; Anne,[2] wife of Chappell; Mary,[2] wife of William Hoskins of Galway, *s. p.* 1686; Elizabeth,[2] wife of Thomas Conyers, d. 1730.

Of these, John,[2] the second son of Robert, had issue, Thomas, d. *s. p.* Jonathan,[2] the youngest, had a son Thomas of Boston, in America. Thomas,[2] the eldest, was of Galy, co. Kerry; his will is dated 3 Aug. 1666, proved 2 Aug. 1667. He married Elizabeth Fitz-Maurice, d. of Patrick, Baron Kerry. She re-married Charles O'Connor, Kerry. Their children were Lucy,[3] d. unm: Elizabeth,[3] m. 1st, Richard Hart of Grangebridge, co. Limerick; [and 2d, Croker]; and Thomas,[3] an only son, of Bunratty, co. Clare, a minor in 1667. The first wife of Thomas[3] [was Mrs. Luttrell]. His second, married 24 Aug. 1717, was Elizabeth Dunroy. His will is dated 8 Aug. 1726, and proved 22 Nov. 1728.

The two children of Thomas[3] were—

Thomas[4] who d. 1788, aged 97. He married Elizabeth, dau. of Rev. John Vandeleur, Rector of Kilouth, and had an only son Robert,[5] who had a son Thomas,[6] a major in the army, [as well as two other sons holding commissions, one in the army and the other in the navy, all of whom were severely wounded in action, and] who d. *s. p.*

Lucy[4] who m. Terence McMahon of Bally Kilty and Crottola in Clare, had Thomas,[5] Cornelius,[5] Edward,[5] and Elizabeth,[5] all d. *s. p.*, and Lucy,[5] wife of John Bourchier of Elm Hill, co. Clare, who d. 1789. Their son was John,[6] who m. Mary, dau. of Thomas Macnamara of Ardloney, co. Clare, and had Daniel,[7] Major in the Artillery, who m. Mary Wilson of Dunboyne, co. Meath, and had John,[8] James,[8] Thomas,[8] Daniel,[8] and Mary.[8]

REVIEW.

Genealogical and Biographical Account of the Family of Bolton : in England and America. Deduced from an early period, and continued down to the present time. Collected chiefly from original papers, and records. With an appendix. By Robert Bolton, A. M. &c. New York : John A. Gray, 1862. Pp. 222.

Of this family history, prepared by the well known historian of West Chester County, but fifty copies were printed, and of course it possesses nearly the rarity of a manuscript work. As we find herein the record of a family entitled to coat-armor, we have prepared an abstract of its contents.

The first of the name in this country was Robert[5] Bolton, born in the parish of St. John's Wales, co. York, in 1688, who settled in Philadephia in 1718.

He was the son of John[4] Bolton, of the above-named parish, and grandson of John[3] Bolton of Brookhouse, in Blackburn, co. Lanc., who died in 1688. This John,[3] Sen., was son of Giles,[2] and grandson of Adam[1] Bolton of Brookhouse, in 1570.

Another son of Adam[1] Bolton, was Rev. Robert[2] Bolton, Rector of Broughton, "a great and shining light of the

Puritan party," "justly celebrated for his singular learning and piety." He was quite a voluminous author, the titles of sixteen of his works being given in this book.

Another brother, James[2] Bolton, was grandfather probably of Rev. Samuel[1] Bolton, Master of Christ's College, Cambridge.

It seems pretty well established that Adam[1] Bolton, who was the son of Richard who held Brookhouse in 1537, was descended from a race of gentry, taking their name from the manor of Bolton by Bowland.

In regard to the arms, we may say that it seems clear that the emigrant was a relative of Rev. Robert Bolton, whose son, Rev. Samuel Bolton, Prebendary of Westminster, sealed his will in 1668, with these following arms, sable, a falcon close, argent, as in the cut at the end of this article.

The annexed cut is copied from another seal of the Rev. Samuel Bolton, used in 1651. The quartering is three wolves' heads erased.

We have seen that Robert[5] Bolton came to Philadelphia in 1718, where, in 1721, he married Ann, dau. of Winlock Curtis, and granddaughter of John Curtis of Kent County, Delaware. She was the widow of Robert Clay of Philadelphia. Her family is said to have been long settled at Appledore, co. Kent, Eng. Her only brother was Hon. John Curtis, Speaker of the Assembly, Judge of the Supreme Court, Pa., &c. In a diary still remaining she writes, alluding to the strict piety and virtue of her husband's sister, "For of such a stock indeed my dear Mr. Bolton and his sister came, as appears by a treatise written by their *great uncle*," Robert Bolton, "called a 'General Direction for a Comfortable Walk with God.'"

Robert[5] and Anne had nine children, of whom the oldest was Robert,[6] born 1 Jan. 1722, who married in 1747, Susanna, dau. of Mathew Mauve. He resided at Savannah, Geo., and was especially noted for his advocacy of the right of permitting religious instruction to the slaves. His brother, John[6] Bolton, was the progenitor of the family in Maryland and New York City.

Robert[7] Bolton, only son of Robert[6] and Susanna, was born in 1757, was a soldier in the Revolutionary army. and married Sarah McClean of Chestertown, Md. Returning to Savannah, he became one of the most distinguished merchants of his day, acquiring a large property. He died in 1802, leaving eight children.

Robert[8] Bolton, eldest son of the last named, was born in 1788. He was by his father's will made a partner in the mercantile house, and established himself in Liverpool.

In 1811 he married Anne, daughter of Rev. William Jay of Bath, Eng. For several years he was very successful in business, but the commercial crisis of 1820 overwhelmed him. Resigning his business, he turned his thoughts to the ministry, to which he had long felt a strong attraction. In 1824 he received a call to become the pastor of the Independent chapel at Hurley-upon-Thames. In 1836 he returned to New York, and was settled as the Episcopalian clergyman at East Chester, New York. Afterwards he organized and established a church at Pelham. In 1850 he visited England, and was appointed chaplain to the Earl of Ducie. He died 19 Nov., 1857, at Cheltenham.

His children were fourteen in number. The eldest was Robert[9] Bolton, the compiler of the book under examination, widely and favorably known as the author of the History of West Chester County, and of the History of the Episcopal Church in the same county. He married, first, Elizabeth Rebecca, daughter of James Brenton of Newport, R. I., and secondly, Josephine, dau. of Brewster Woodhull of Brookhaven, L. I., by which latter he has issue, five children.

WOODHULL FAMILY.

We find in this Genealogy some very interesting particulars in regard to the Woodhull family. The emigrant was Richard[1] Woodhull of Jamaica, Long Island, afterwards of Setauket, who died in 1690. His son Richard,[2] born in 1649, was father of Richard,[3] b. in 1691. This last-named m. Mary Homan, and had Richard,[4] b. 1712, who by wife Margaret Smith had Stephen,[5] b. 1732. Stephen[5] Woodhull m. Hannah Cooper, and had John,[6] b. 1759, father of Brewster[7] Woodhull, already mentioned.

It seems that Richard[1] Woodhull, the emigrant, was born at Thenford, in Northamptonshire, 13 Sept. 1620. His father, Lawrence Woodhull, was the son of Fulke Woodhull by his wife Alice, dau. of William Coles of Leigh. Still farther back the family is traced to Walter de Wahull, who was summoned to Parliament in 1297 as a Baron, but whose descendants did not continue to enjoy the title. His descendant in the seventh generation was Sir Nicholas Woodhull, who by his second wife Elizabeth, dau. and coheir of William Lord Parr, had the Fulke Woodhull already mentioned as of Thenford.

An original letter here printed shows that Richard Woodhull, the emigrant, was acknowledged as a relative by Thomas, second Baron Crewe of Stene. It adds one or two particulars to Brydges' account, in his edition of Collins' Peerage:

"Sir:

I was heartily glad to find by y^r letter that it had pleased God to blesse and prosper your family, and that you received the small present * I sent you, wh. I thought had been lost. For our country news, take this account. My father departed this life Dec. 12, 1679, and as he lived well, soe he had great joye at his death, with a longing to leave this world. I have six children, but noe sonne, it having pleased God to take him in ye fifteenth yeare of his age, a man growne and very hopefull. God's will be done. My brother Walgrave hath left one sonne, who stands heire both to ye Bishop of Duresme, and

---

* This present, says Mr. Bolton, was a painting of the family arms on a panel nearly four feet square, and it is still preserved at Setauket. The arms are,

1. Woodhull; Or, three crescents, gules.
2. Foxcote; Argent, on a cross azure, five escallops, or.
3. Chetwode; Quarterly, arg. and gules, a cross formée counterchanged.
4. Sounde; Or, fretty sable a bar ermine, on a chief gules three leopards' faces of the field.
5. Hoccliffe; Or, a fesse between three lozenges, gules.
6. De Lyon; Arg. a lion rampant gules.
7. Newenham; Arg. a cross gules, over all a bend azure.
8. Parr; Arg. two bars azure, within a bordure engrailed, sable.
9. Ros; Or, three water-bougets, sable.
10. Crophull; Argent, a saltire gules, frettée or.
11. Verdon; Or, a fret gules.
12. Fitz-Hugh; Azure, three chevrons braced in base or, a chief of the second.
13. Gernegan; Barry of twelve or and azure, an eagle displayed gules.
14. Furneaux; Gules, a bend between six cross crosslets or.
15. Gray; Barry of six arg. and azure, over all on a bend gules, three martlets or.
16. Marmion; Vairé, a fesse gules.
17. St. Quintin; Or, three chevrons gules, a chief vairé.
18. Salusbury; Gules, a lion rampant or, between three crescents arg.
    Crest. Two wings endorsed gules, issuing out of a ducal coronet.

myself for Thenford.   Yr cozen Woodhull lives very
well, is a justice of peace, and very well beloved.   The
three brothers live all together with the greatest kindnesse
that can bee.   My uncle Sal" (i. e. Salathiel) "died last
yeare, and is buried at Hinton; my uncle Thomas, a
yeare before; my uncle Nathaniel is still living.   I have
enclosed the papers you desire.   My service to all my
cozens.   I rest your loving friend and kinsman.

Steane, Sep. 5, 1687.   CREWE.

For my Loving Kinsman, Richard Wodhull, Esq."

_____

By the kindness of Mr. Bolton, we present the follow-
lowing examples of the engravings in his volume:

BOLTON.

CURTIS.   WOODHULL.

OFFICIAL SEALS.

WILLIAM SHIRLEY, who suc-
ceeded Jonathan Belcher in 1740,
as Governor of Massachusetts, was
undoubtedly a descendant of the
family ennobled under the title of
Ferrers.   With the uncertainty
which overshadows so many English pedigrees, we cannot positively
state his father's name. Burke (Extinct Baronetcies)
calls him son of "William, who d. in 1701, by Elizabeth,
his wife, dau. of John Goodman, deriving (it is stated)
his descent from the Shirleys of Wisterton."   Drake,
however, (Register, X., 47) states that he was the son of
Thomas of Preston, co. Sussex, and grandson of Sir
Thomas Shirley of Wiston, in the same county. As it
seems tolerably certain that he was of the Wiston branch,

we will give a brief sketch of the family from Brydges' " Collins' Peerage."

The family is derived from Sewallus de Etingdon, who d. about A. D. 1085. After several generations we come to Sir Ralph Shirley, a noted warrior under King Henry V., who d. in 1443. His son Ralph had two sons, John and Ralph. From John was descended Sir Robert Shirley, created, in 1711, Viscount Tamworth and Earl Ferrers, who m. Elizabeth, dau. of Lawrence Washington of Caresden, co. Wilts. This title is still held by his descendants.

Ralph, the second son of Ralph, above noted, was Esquire of the Body to King Henry VII., and inherited Wiston, which had belonged to his grandmother. His son Ralph had William of Wiston, who d. in 1551, leaving Sir Thomas his heir, and Anthony of Preston, whose gr. gr. son was created a baronet. Sir Thomas, eldest son and heir, had three sons, of whom, Sir Anthony and Sir Robert were famous travellers. The eldest brother, Sir Thomas, m. Frances Vavasor, and had a son, Sir Thomas Shirley, M. D., who suffered much for his loyalty, and had his estate at Wiston taken from him. This last would seem to be the grandfather of our Governor, according to Drake's account.

Of William Shirley, Hutchinson writes that he " was a gentleman of Sussex, bred in the law, and had been in office in the city, but, having prospect of a numerous offspring, was advised to remove to Boston, in the Massachusetts, where he had resided six or eight years, and acquired a general esteem."

His first wife was Frances, dau. of Francis Barker, and

the arms on her monument (Vol. II., p. 12) show she was probably of the Yorkshire family of the name. By her, Shirley had William, Secretary to Gen. Braddock, and killed with him in 1755; John, a Captain in the army, d. at Oswego; Ralph d. young; Thomas; Judith d. young; Elizabeth m. Eliakim Hutchinson; Frances m. William Bollan; Harriet m. Robert Temple; and Maria m. John Erving.

Gov. Shirley d. 24 March, 1771, aged about 77. His only surviving son, Thomas, Governor of the Leeward Islands, Major-General, &c., was created a Baronet in 1786, and m. Anne, dau. of Thomas Western, by Margaret, dau. and coheir of Sir Richard Shirley, bart. of Preston. Sir Thomas d. in 1800, and his only son, Sir William Warden Shirley, bart., d. *s. p.* in 1815, when the baronetcy became extinct.

[NOTE. In our cut, copied from the History of Boston, the baronet's badge is added, but of course does not appear on the Governor's seal.]

MONUMENTAL INSCRIPTIONS.

BOSTON.

COPP'S HILL YARD.

(Continued from p. 84.)

X.

This very beautifully executed monument is to be found on a stone since appropriated to the epitaph of Rev. Andrew Eliot, which is inscribed on its reverse. By the kindness of a descendant, I learn that it was bought by the Eliots in 1770, as the following bill shows:

Oct. 1770.	Paid Mrs. Watts, £6.6,	£63	old tenor.
"	Mr. Rumney,	3	
"	Capt. Atwood, $1,	2. 5	
"	Mr. Cade, sexton,	4.10	
"	box for ashes, &c.,	15.6	
"	for cart⁴, &c.,	1. 4	
"	" nails,	6	
"	Mr. Homer for altering		
	stone,	2. 3	

£77. 3.6 old tenor.

These arms are not those of the Watts, we believe, but
Samuel Watts is in Prince's list of Esquires, and the
family may have obtained the stone and tomb by intermarriage with some family entitled to this coat.

GRANARY BURYING GROUND, BOSTON.

I.

Mary Winslow died Aug^st y^e 28th 1753, Ætatis 29.
Samuel Bonner Ob^t June 9th
1804, Ae: 67.

There can be little doubt that this was the tomb of
Capt. John Bonner, the designer of the early map of
Boston. We find that John and Sarah Bonner had
Ruth, b. 12 March, 1731, and Thomas, 9 August, 1735.
Other children we learn of from different sources; thus, 4
March, 1750, Ruth chose Joseph Winslow as her guardian,
and 8 July, 1754, Samuel, aged less than 14 years, chose
the same. At this latter date, also, administration was
granted on Capt. John Bonner's estate to his son-in-law,

Joseph Winslow, brazier, and our records say that Joseph Winslow and Mary Bonner were married 29 Jan. 1746. These two children were the ones here recorded.

From a record printed in the Register, V., 174, it seems most probable that Capt. John Bonner was born at Cambridge, Mass., 1693, and was the son of John Bonner of Boston, Cambridge and London, who perhaps died at Boston, 20 January, 1725, aged 84. If so, John Bonner, Jr., m. Sarah, dau. of Samuel Marsh, 17 November, 1715, and had Jane and Sarah, both of whom died young.

The arms here depicted are doubtless meant for those of the Bonners of Lincolnshire, viz., Quarterly gules and sable, a cross pattée, quarterly ermine and gold; on a chief of the last a demi rose, streaming rays, between two pelicans, vulning themselves, of the first.

II.

The accompanying coat is inscribed on the tomb of the Faneuils, which was probably erected by Andrew F., who died in 1737. This family, whose name is indelibly associated with Boston, was of Huguenot origin, and we propose to condense a portion of the abundant material in regard to their history, collected by L. M. Sargent, Esq., and published in 1856, in his

"Dealings with the Dead." It seems that in 1685, there were living in or near Rochelle, in France, three brothers and two sisters of the Faneuil family. These were Benjamin, Andrew, John, Susanna and Jane; of whom John and Susanna were Catholic, and remained at Rochelle, Jane was a Huguenot, married Pierre Cossart, and died in Ireland. Andrew settled in Boston, as early as 1709, was married, but had no children. He acquired a large fortune by commerce, which was left, at his death, in 1737, to his nephew Peter.

Benjamin Faneuil, the other brother, was married in 1699 to Anne Bureau, and settled at New Rochelle, N. Y., by whom he had eleven children. Of these the survivors were Peter; Benjamin; Anne, who m. Rev. Addington Davenport; Mary, wife of Gillam Phillips; Susanna, wife of James Boutineau, and Mary Anne, wife of John Jones.

Peter Faneuil, so well known for his gift to the town of the public hall which bears his name, died unm. in 1743.

Benjamin Faneuil, his brother, married, and had Benjamin, Peter, and Mary, wife of George Bethune. He died October, 1785.

In regard to the arms here figured, we may note first, that they are on Andrew Faneuil's will, and in that will he directs three pieces of plate to be given the French Church in Boston, "with the coat of arms and name of the donor engraven upon each of them." Peter Faneuil also had these arms painted on his chariot, and engraven on his silver. With this distinct claim to a right we must remain content.

III.

"The Armes and Tomb belonging to the Family of Cushing."

We learn from an article in the Register, XIX., 39, that this family has been traced to Thomas Cushing, a gentleman having large landed property in Hardingham, Hingham, and other parts of Norfolk.

From him was descended, by steps fully traced, Peter Cushing of Hardingham, who m., in 1583, Susan Hawes, and had, with other children, Mathew. This Mathew[1] Cushing went to Hingham, co. Norfolk, and m., in 1613, Nazareth Pitcher, by whom he had four sons, who accompanied him to Hingham, Mass., and all left descendants here.

The family held a high position from the first, a result mainly due, doubtless, to the commanding abilities of its members in successive generations.

John[2] Cushing, youngest son of the emigrant, was an Assistant and Colonel of the Plymouth regiment. His eldest son, John,[3] was a member of the Council, and Justice of the Supreme Court, and *his* son John,[4] 3d, was also Judge of the Supreme Court of Massachusetts, and father of William,[5] Judge of the Supreme Court of the United States. The first John,[2] also, by his son Joseph,[3] had a gr. grandson, Nathan,[5] Judge of the Supreme Court of Massachusetts. Thomas,[3] son of this John,[2] was member of the Council, and had a son Thomas,[4] Speaker of the Massachusetts House of Representatives, whose son Thomas[5] was also Speaker, member of the Philadelphia Congress of 1774, and Lieutenant-Governor of Massachusetts, 1780–88.

In the inventory of Thomas[3] Cushing is mentioned his coat-of-arms, and this branch is the one which owned this tomb. The arms engraved on the tombstone differ in some particulars from those used by the family in England, of which we here give an example.

John[5] Cushing, son of John,[4] before mentioned, was father of Robert,[6] and gr. father of John[7] Perkins Cushing, a distinguished merchant of this city, who died some four years ago.

IV.

"This tomb repaired by Thomas Perkins."

These arms are undoubtedly those of Jean Paul Mascarene, a Huguenot refugee. From a letter, written to his
son by a relative in France, published in the Register,
IX., 339, we learn that Jean Paul was born in Languedoc
in 1684, and was the son of John Mascarene of Castras.
This John was son and grandson of two Johns, and the
last was son of Martin Mascarene, born 1535.

John Mascarene, father of our colonist, was a Protestant,
and suffered imprisonment after the Revocation of the
Edict of Nantes. His son, Jean Paul, escaped to Geneva,
afterwards went to England, where he was naturalized in
1706. He entered the army, and came to America in
1711. He married Elizabeth Perry in 1714, and being
sent to Nova Scotia, with his regiment, he was one of the
Council there, and acting Commander-in-chief of the
Province. In 1750 he obtained leave to retire to Boston,
but was advanced to the rank of Major-General. He died
22 January, 1760.

His only son, John, left a son, who was the last of the name. The daughters of Gov. Mascarene were Margaret, who m. Foster Hutchinson; Elizabeth, who m. Thomas Perkins, and Joanna, wife of James Perkins.

We have a copy of Gov. Mascarene's memorandum for entering his arms at Herald's College, and they are thus described: Argent, a lion rampant gules, a chief azure charged with three mullets or, and a mullet of the same for crest.

V.

This stone has cut across it the name of Lyde, but the arms are those of Byfield. The following account explains the reason of this appropriation of the tomb:

"Nathaniel Byfield, it is said, was b. 1653, at Long-Ditton, &c." The funeral sermon,* preached by Rev.

* Nathanael's Character Displayed. A Sermon Preached the Lord's Day after the Funeral of the Honourable Nathaniel Byfield, Esq , Late Judge of the Vice-Admiralty, and one of His Majesty's Council for this Province. Who died at his House in Boston, on the 6th of June, 1733, in the 80th Year of his Age. By Charles Chauncy, M. A. One of the Pastors of the Old Church. Isa. iii, 1–3. Printed in the Year 1733.

Charles Chauncy, 1733, has at the close an account at the end taken from the Weekly Newsletter, a sufficient authority, from which we copy as follows:

" His immediate descent was from the Rev. Mr. Richard Byfield, the laborious, faithful pastor of Long-Ditton in Surrey, one of the Divines in the famous Westminster Assembly. His mother being of the noted family of the Juxons. He was the youngest of one and twenty children, and one of the sixteen that have sometimes followed their pious father to the Place of publick Worship. He was born in 1653, arrived at Boston in New England in 1674, and conceiving a Love to this Country, resolved to settle here;—and accordingly married the following year, Mrs. Deborah Clark, by whom he had five children, three whereof died in infancy; the other two lived to be married,—the youngest to the late Honourable Lieutenant-Governor Tailer, who quickly departed, without issue; the other to Edward Lyde, Esq., by whom she had five children, two of whom dying young, three only are now surviving, a son and two daughters."

" He lived with the Wife of his Youth till 1717, upwards of forty years; and the following year married Mrs. Sarah Leverett, youngest daughter of the Honourable Governor Leverett, with whom he lived till 1730,* when he was again left a sorrowful Widower. He has left his grandson, Byfield Lyde, Esq. (son-in-law to His Excellency Governor Belcher) Heir to the Bulk of his Estate."

This adds one or two facts to Savage's account.

---

* Charles Chauncy preached a funeral sermon on her death. It only mentions that she was born 13 July, 1673, m. 17 April, 1718, and died 21 December, 1730.

VI.

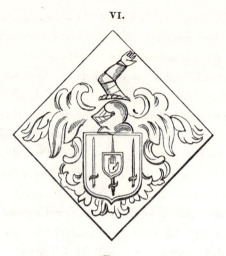

Rev.
Joseph
Eckley.

"The Rev. Joseph Eckley, D. D., was born in London, 22 Oct., 1750.   His father removing to New Jersey, about 1767, he was graduated at Princeton in 1772.   He was ordained as the successor of Mr. Hunt at the Old South Church in Boston in 1779, and remained there till his death, 30 April, 1811."   Dr. Allen's account, from which we collect these facts, furnishes other particulars of his ministerial labors.

Mr. Eckley married Sarah Jeffries, and had three sons, Joseph, Thomas, and David.

Joseph died unm. at Marblehead, about 1860.

Thomas m. his cousin of the half blood, Julia Ann Jeffries, and had Julia Ann, now deceased; Sarah, wife of Prof. H. L. Eustis of Harvard College, and Elizabeth, wife of Thomas Rhett.   David Eckley m. Caroline S.,

daughter of Jonathan Amory of Boston, and had Joseph
S. of Buffalo, David, Edward (deceased), John L.,
William (deceased), Henry of Framingham, Arthur A.
and Frances A. Mrs. Eckley died in June, 1866.

VII.

Mr. Joseph Lasinby
Died Sept. 9th 1774
Aged 80 years.

The family of Leasonbee, Lasenbee, Lasinby, or however the name may be varied, is, we believe, not recorded
by Savage. Still, Thomas and Mercy L. of Boston had
born here, Thomas, 21 January, 1688; Benjamin, 27
August, 1691; Joseph, 20 August, 1694; Mary, 22
April, 1696, and Margaret, 5 March, 1699. Thomas probably d. about 5 April, 1707, when his will is dated. His
widow Mercy survived till near 30 December, 1732, when
the heirs signed a division of their father's estate. These
were Thomas L. and Zeruiah his wife, Joseph L. and
wife Elizabeth, widow Mercy Bant, and Mary, wife of
Alexander Chamberlain.

Thomas and Zeruiah Lazenby had a son Thomas, born 31 March, 1725, who died apparently in 1746, when his father administered on his estate.

Joseph Lazenby m. 1st, Mary Proctor, 29 April, 1719, and had Joseph, b. 6 February, 1720; Mary, 26 May, 1721; Mary, 29 December, 1722; Benjamin, 10 June, 1724; Benjamin, 26 March, 1726; Elizabeth, 3 June, 1727; Samuel, 19 June, 1728; Mary, 11 August, 1729. His wife d. 6 November, 1730, aged 37. He m. 2d, Elizabeth Farmer, 1 July, 1731, and had Benjamin, b. 29 September, 1732; Thomas, b. 19 February, 1733–4; Mary, 3 October, 1735.

He died, as above shown, 9 September, 1774.

VIII.

"The Armes of John and Elizabeth Freke."

An examination of this stone satisfies us that the impaled coat is "on a bend, between three roundles as many swans," which arms were borne by many families of Clarke. Hence we identify the persons here commemorated as John Freke, who m. in 1661, Elizabeth, dau. of

Capt. Thomas Clark, by whom he had several children. He was a merchant, and was killed by an explosion on board a ship in Boston harbor, 4 May, 1675, aged less than 40 years. His widow m. Elisha Hutchinson.

IX.

RICHARD CHECKLEY, 1737.

Hocce meum Corpus de Funere viq. Sepulchri
  Saluatoris Jesus. Sarciet ille meus
Christus erit pestes Mors Frigida Tuq. Sepulchrum
  Exitium certum. Mox erit ille Tuum.

This Richard Checkley, who d. 7 May, 1742, was the son of Col. Samuel Checkley. Samuel was born at Preston-Capes, in Northamptonshire, 14 Oct., 1653, and was the son of William and Elizabeth C. His half-brother, Anthony C. (bapt. 31 July, 1636) came here with their uncle John Checkley, and was Attorney-General here. Samuel m. Mary Scottow, was a Representative from Boston, County Treasurer and Town Clerk. He died 27 Dec., 1738, leaving, of eleven children, only two living, viz., Dea. Richard and Rev. Samuel, pastor of the Old South.

Richard, who apparently erected the tomb here described, had a wife Sarah, but probably no children, as he left his property to his brother Samuel's children.

The arms, as above shown, are mentioned in Gore's Roll, (Vol. I., p. 119) and differ from the Chicele arms, which are gold, a chevron between three cinquefoils gules.

X.

* * * * lyes interred ye body of
Mary Tuthill relict of John Tuthill aged
67 years who departed this life
September yᵉ 19th 1705.
Here lyeth interr'd yᵉ body of
Deacon Thomas Hubbart who
departed this life yᵉ 17th day of
1717
November in yᵉ 64th year of his age.

Here lyes interred ye body of Mrs Mary
Hubbart **** òf Deacon Thomas Hubbard
*** departed this life Auguste ** **
anno domini 1720 in
** year of her ***
Here lyes interred ye **** of
Zechariah Tuthill
his *** *** *******
here ****************

This inscription, upon a large slab in the yard, has
suffered much from the effects of time. The reading is
restored from the copies made by Messrs. Bridgman and
Wyman at different times, and agrees with what we learn
from other sources. We do not know with certainty
that the first John Tuthill and his wife Mary were
the parents of those who follow, but the ages render it
extremely probable.

Zechariah Tuthill was the Lieutenant at Castle William,
and died 7 January, 1721, aged 52. His will mentions
sisters Sarah Gooch and Susanna Blish, and nephews
John and Zechariah Hubbart. These sisters were Sarah
Tuthill or Tuttle, who m. James Gooch, 12 Nov., 1702;
and Susanna Tuttle, who m. Abraham Blish, 8 May, 1707.
Another sister evidently was Mary, who m. Dea. Thomas
Hubbard. Her will, dated 29 Dec., 1718, mentions her
sisters and brothers, and her two sons.

Of these sons, Capt. John Hubbard, in his will of 6
March, 1732, mentions wife Elizabeth, and children,
James, Thomas, Tuthill, Joseph, John, Susanna, and Elizabeth. His inventory, (Suff. Wills, XXXIV., 316) dated
16 April, 1734, shows property amounting to £4,606.

XI.

17   42

THOMAS HUBBARD.

In the inventory of Capt. John Hubbard, just mentioned, there is one item, " 1 pr. sconces and coat-of-arms,
£15." From this fact we may be warranted in supposing
that this tomb belonged to Thomas, son of this John.

The arms resemble those of English families of the
name of Hubart, Hubert or Hubberd, except that the
field should be quarterly, and the lions in the coats cited
by Burke are in one case passant, in another rampant.

XII.

This tablet, probably erected during the present century,
is in the rear wall of the estate, No. 14 Beacon street.

The house was formerly occupied by William Payne,
Esq., and these are doubtless the arms used by him. We
have not been able to investigate the question of their
authenticity. The coat most nearly resembling it in
Burke's "Armory" is Argent, on a bend gules three
arrows, between a lion's head cabossed in chief, and in
base, an eagle's leg couped à-la-quise, holding a torteau,
proper.

The tablet is at present so placed in the wall that the
shield is entirely covered with earth, a state of affairs
almost equalled by the Jackson slab, page 140.

XIII.

This stone is placed at the entrance of the Bowdoin
tomb, and probably the arms were assumed on good
authority. The family here originated with Pierre Bau-
doin, a physician of La Rochelle, who fled to Ireland, in

1685, on the revocation of the Edict of Nantes. Thence he came to Casco and Boston, where his name was translated into Peter Bowdoin, and after a prosperous career as a merchant, he died here in September, 1706. He had two sons, William, who left an only daughter who married her cousin James Bowdoin, and James. This James Bowdoin was one of the wealthiest men in Boston, a member of the Council, &c., and died 8 September, 1747. By his three wives he had sons William and James, and three daughters.

Of these James, born 7 August, 1726, Harvard College, 1745, was a prominent leader in the political struggles of his time. He was a Representative from Boston in 1753–5, and in 1757 was elected a member of the Council, which office he filled for sixteen years. In 1774 he was elected President of the Provincial Congress at Watertown, and in 1779 was President of the State Convention. In 1785 and 1786 he was Governor of Massachusetts, and d. 6 November, 1790, aged 64. His wife was Elizabeth, daughter of John Erving, by whom he had James, and Elizabeth, wife of Sir John Temple, bart. James m. his cousin Sarah Bowdoin, but d. *s. p.* 11 October, 1811. The eldest dau. of Lady Temple m. Hon. Thomas L. Winthrop of Boston, and the name of Bowdoin has been adopted by one or more of that family.

John Bowdoin, son of the emigrant Pierre, removed to Virginia, and left descendants of the name, now living there. Another branch, bearing the bar sinister, is of very respectable standing in this state.

XIV.

SEARS OF CHATHAM.

Though we do not know the date of this inscribed slab, we presume it has been placed here during the present century. From information, now made public, we learn that the emigrant ancestor of the Sears family was Richard[6] Sears of Yarmouth, Mass., who died in 1676. He was born in Holland, and was the son of John[4] Bourchier Sears, by his wife Marie L., dau. of Philippe Van Egmonde of Amsterdam. John[5] Bourchier Sears, b. at Amsterdam, in 1561, was the son of John[4] Bourchier Sears and Elizabeth Hawkins, and grandson of Richard[3] Sayers, b. at Colchester in 1508, who m. Anne Bourchier, dau. of Edmund Knyvet of Ashwellthorpe, co. Norfolk. The Sayers had long been settled at Colchester, and John[1] Sayer, an alderman there, was buried in St. Peter's church in 1509. His eldest son John,[2] who d. in 1562, left two sons, Richard,[3] before mentioned, and George.[3]

Richard[3] was obliged to fly to Holland on account of his religious opinions, and his estates fell to his brother George.[3]

His son, the first John[3] Bourchier Sayers, seems to have made no attempt to recover his father's estate. He m. a daughter of Sir John Hawkins, and accompanied his father-in-law on several voyages.

Richard[5] Sears of Yarmouth had sons Knyvet,[7] Paul,[7] and Silas,[7] of whom Knyvet[7] died in England in 1686, at the residence of his relative Catherine, daughter of Sir John Knyvet. By wife Elizabeth Dimoke he had a son Daniel,[8] b. in 1682, who had three sons, Richard[9] and David,[9] both killed at Culloden, and Daniel,[9] b. in 1719. This Daniel,[9] by wife Fear Freeman, had sons Richard[10] and Daniel,[10] whose lines are extinct, and David,[10] b. in 1752, who was a great purchaser of lands in Maine, and married Ann Winthrop. His only son is Hon. David Sears of Boston, who married Miriam Clarke, dau. of Hon. Jona. Mason. Mr. Sears is too well known in Boston to render any sketch of his public services necessary. He has had ten children.

XV.

The tomb covered by this slab is recorded in the old record of the yard as belonging to Capt. Cyprian Southac and Francis Southac. Savage does not record these names, yet Cyprian S. was a noted man in his day. We find the name spelt Southwick once, and Southhack once, but usually it is rendered Southac.

Cyprian and Elizabeth Southac had, born at Boston, the following children: John, 15 July, 1692; Elizabeth, 2 May, 1695; Cyprian, 21 Feb., 1696-7; Hannah, 10 April, 1699; Francis, 9 Aug., 1700; Mary, 1 April, 1702; Mary, 7 June, 1704; William, 12 Jan., 1705-6; Hannah, 31 July, 1710, and John, 12 July, 1713.

It seems probable that Cyprian Southac made his will 9 May, 1743, in which he mentions son John, whose wife was named Elizabeth, and daughters Mary and Dorothy.

This will terms him Esquire, and we presume it was the father of the above family of ten or twelve children, though this would oblige us to consider eight of them had died before him, and that he lived to be at least 70 years old.

Our reason is, that Cyprian Southac and wife Elizabeth, he being termed first Captain, and then Esquire, sign deeds as late as 1720, and the last deed, in 1743, referred to in the will of Cyprian "Esquire," is of the same lands. Of course his son Cyprian, b. 1697, may have had a wife Elizabeth, but we find no other will or indication of a change of ownership in the property.

Assuming that there was but one of the name, we find that he was Captain of the Province Snow, of 14 Guns, in 1704; that he was a maker of charts, 1720-1725; lived in Tremont Street, owned land on Church Green and Valley Acre.

The arms are not recorded under this name in any English book which we have seen; and from the peculiarity of the Christian name we should be inclined to consider him of some other nationality, and Southac a corruption of some foreign name.

XVI.

JACKSON.

This tomb, situated next to the Quincy tomb in the easterly corner of the yard, is recorded as belonging to Thomas Jackson. The arms and motto seem to show that it was intended to be one of the coats recorded by Burke. These are all a fesse between three birds—in one case three shovellers; in another three shovellers, each charged with a trefoil slipped; in a third three magpies; in a fourth three shell-drakes; in a fifth three falcons, close. The motto is given to the family at Beach Hill, co. Surrey, baronets, who have three shovellers charged with a trefoil. The coats have undoubtedly a common origin, and the family seems to have been settled chiefly in Yorkshire.

ESSEX WILLS.

[From the Registry at Salem, Mass.]

THE following list comprises all the examples of armorial seals which I have been able to discover in a careful search of our probate files, from their commencement, until A. D. 1700. After that date examples are more numerous, and will be described in a subsequent article.

The seals are as follows:

1. Gold, a saltire ——, within a bordure engrailed ——. This is on the will of Robert Andrews of Rowley Village, dated 16 May, 1663, proved 2 July following. Witnesses, Robert Smith and James Hanscombe. In it Robert A. mentions sons Thomas, Robert, John and Joseph, daus. Mary, wife of Isaac Comins; Elizabeth, wife of Samuel Symonds; Hannah Peabody, Rebecca, Sarah and Ruth Andrews.

[Note. Instead of the field gold, it is very possible, from the arrangement of the dots, that the blazon should be " a saltire between four cross-crosslets."]

2. ——, a chevron between three roundles. On the will of Daniel Denison, dated 13 July, 1673. Proved, 16 April, 1683.

[These arms are the same as those on the tomb of John Denison, engraved in Vol. I., p. 91, except that there the chevron is engrailed.]

3. ——, a chevron, between three helmets, closed in profile, *probably*. The seal is quite imperfect, but the helmet visible is in the dexter chief. Crest, a demi-eagle, displayed. This seal is on the will of Zerobabel Endecott, dated 23 Nov., 1683, proved 27 March following. Wit-

nesses, Nathl. Felton, Senr. and Joane Read.   He was the son of Gov. John Endicott by his wife, Elizabeth Gibson.

4.   ——, a chevron between three fleurs-de-lys ——. On the will of Samuel Shattuck, Sr., dated 6 April, 1689, proved 26 November following.   Witnesses, Roger Derby, John Cromwell, and Richard Prytherch.

5.   ——, a chevron between three cronels or antique crowns.   This is on the will of Obadiah Wood, dated 26 October, 1694, proved December 3 following.   Witnesses, John Staniford, Jacob Foster, and John Sparke.   Also on the will of Rebecca Symonds, dated 15 July, 1695, proved 19 August following; witnesses, John Staniford, James Fuller, and Margaret Pynchon; and on the will of William Caldwell, dated 18 June, 1694, proved 30 March, 1696; witnesses, John Staniford, Samuel Bridges, and Margaret Staniford.   It will be noticed that John Staniford is a witness to all three wills, and they seem to be in his handwriting.   It is probable, therefore, that he was the owner of the seal, though the arms do not appear to belong to any one of the name.

6.   The seal on the will of John Arnold " of the City of London, in Thames St. dwelling," mariner, dated 12 Oct., 1680, proved 28 Jan., 1694–5 ; witnesses, Benj. Gerrish and Hilliard Veren, is quite imperfect.   It seems to be a bend dancettée, in chief three boar's heads couped, and in base are signs of other charges.   Crest, a demi-eagle, displayed.

7.   A seal,—three anchors,—is placed against the signatures of Mary, Nicholas and Daniel Noyes, on the settlement of the estate of John Noyes of Newbury, 30 July, 1695.   Witnesses, Edward Moers and Henry Short.

8. The will of Isaac Williams, Sr., dated Jan. 1, 1695, and codicil dated 23 Jan. following, proved 9 Nov., 1696, bears a seal in chief three boar's heads, and apparently a fesse embattled, thence issuing a pile to the base point. Crest, a demi-eagle displayed. Witnesses to will and codicil, Daniel Epes and Samuel Phillips; to the will alone, Daniel Grant, and to the codicil alone, "Alexander Mackmleion."

9. ——, two swords, crossed in saltire, hilts in base,— is the coat on the seal of Ebenezer Collins " of New England, now resident in Bilboa, Spain." It is dated 29 December, 1696, proved 21 June, 1697, and witnessed by Thomas Michell, John Beal, Grove Hirst, Timothy Lindall, Jr., and Joseph Pollard.

10. Hannah Endicott, on a bond dated 13 September, 1697, as guardian of Samuel, Ruth and Hannah E., uses a seal with the following arms: —— a chevron between three bugle-horns stringed,—on a chief three lions rampant. No crest. Witnesses, Samuel Phillips, John Croade; sureties, John and Nathaniel Felton.

11. Eleazer Gedney's acquittance to his mother, dated 28 Oct., 1690, in file of 9 Dec., 1699, bears apparently ermine, on a chevron several garbs, but the seal is very defective. Witnesses, Abraham Cole and Robert Gibbs.

12. Wm. Griggs, Sr., of Salem, will dated 10 Feb., 1693, proved 18 July, 1698; witnessed by Samuel Hardie, Sarah Hoare, and Samuel Hayward; used an armorial seal, but it has become impossible to decipher them.

A. C. G., JR.

THE COUNTY FAMILIES OF ENGLAND.

In our last number, p. 57–60, we reviewed Mr. Shirley's book, and gave a list of the families recorded by him. Our notice was based on the edition of 1859, but during the present year a new edition has appeared, which enables us to complete the record.

We will first correct one or two errors in our list as printed. On p. 57, *Butler* should be BULLER; and on p. 59, *Mainwaring*, *Manners*, *Markham* and *Massie* are twice given, instead of once; *Trelawney* should be spelled TRELAWNY, and *Vincint* should be VINCENT. RAWDON should be added.

In the new edition *Dukinfield* and *Popham* are omitted, for reasons not stated; *Cotton*, *Hanford* and *Hornyold* are also omitted, having become extinct.

On the other hand, the following are added: BASSETT, BERNEY, BERTIE, HUYSHE, LANGTON, LOVETT, MASSINGBERD, PATTEN, TEMPEST, and UPTON.

Longmans, Green & Co. have this year published a "Grammar of Heraldry," by John E. Cussans. The title-page further states it contains "the armorial bearings of all the landed gentry in England, prior to the sixteenth century." Our readers need not send to England in haste to procure this book, in hopes of a revised and authentic "Armory." It is in reality a little treatise on heraldry, quite an improvement in its plan on previous elementary works, but poorly printed, and with wretched illustrations. The "armorial bearings" are simply those mentioned in Mr. Shirley's book, and are of "all the landed gentry"— who have living representatives in the male line, now owning estates. This is evidently a very different thing from the promise on the title-page.

THE

HERALDIC JOURNAL;

RECORDING THE ARMORIAL BEARINGS AND GENEALOGIES
OF AMERICAN FAMILIES.

NO. XVI.   OCTOBER, 1866.

THE WASHINGTON FAMILY.

[PREFATORY NOTE.   In our April number, pp. 66–74, we published an abstract of what was known in regard to the Washington pedigree, feeling that this was a genealogy possessing a national importance.   We then copied the record of the family here as given by SPARKS, and such items as had been collected in England in reference to the presumed ancestors of the emigrants.   We called attention to the strong probability of a mistake in the supposed identification of the two emigrants to Virginia, and promised soon to lay before our readers, the result of very extensive searches in England then being made.

We are happy now to present the following essay, written by Col. Joseph L. Chester, which appears in the September number of the "Herald and Genealogist," and is here printed from advance sheets, by the kindness of the author.   It will be found most interesting, and is a fair example of the thoroughness with which our genealogist is pursuing a most important work.]

A PRELIMINARY INVESTIGATION OF THE ALLEGED
ANCESTRY OF GEORGE WASHINGTON; FIRST PRESI-
DENT OF THE UNITED STATES OF AMERICA; EXPOS-
ING A SERIOUS ERROR IN THE EXISTING PEDIGREE.

By Joseph Lemuel Chester,

Honorary Member of the New England Historic-Genealogical Society;
Author of the Life of John Rogers, the Marian Protomartyr, etc., etc.

In the year 1791 Sir Isaac Heard, then Garter King of
Arms, compiled a pedigree of the family of George
Washington, then the first President of the United States,
and transmitted a copy thereof to him, asking his opinion
as to its correctness, and requesting him to add to it any
other particulars within his knowledge. To this communication Washington responded on the 2nd of May,
1792, thanking Sir Isaac for his attention, and sending
certain information respecting the more modern history
of his family, but confessed that it was a subject to which
he had paid very little attention, and that he could not
fill up with much accuracy the sketch sent him. This
document, which was of considerable length, would now
be almost priceless as an autograph, but it has unfortunately disappeared. A volume containing the original
letter and other collections relating to the same subject,
passed subsequently, after Sir Isaac's death, into the possession of the late Mr. Pulman, Clarencieux. It was seen
and examined by Mr. Jared Sparks when collecting materials for his biography of Washington, but cannot now be
found.

Sir Isaac took as the basis of his pedigree the Heraldic
Visitations of Northamptonshire, in which the Washing-

ton family was included. Starting with the well-known fact that the first emigrants of the name to Virginia were two brothers named John and Lawrence Washington, who left England for that colony about the year 1657, he found recorded in the Visitation of 1618 the names of John and Lawrence, described as sons of Lawrence Washington of Sulgrave in that county who had died in the year 1616. The names being identical with those of the Virginia emigrants, and the period at which they lived not altogether inappropriate, Sir Isaac *assumed* their personal identity; and on this assumption constructed his pedigree, deducing the descent of the American President through this heraldic family of Northamptonshire from the still more ancient one of the name in Lancashire. It is but just to the memory of Sir Isaac to say that he himself only regarded the pedigree as a conjectural one, and that he took the precaution to leave on the margin of his own copy a note (which was seen and copied by Mr. Sparks) to the effect that he was not clearly satisfied that the connection of the President with the Sulgrave family was or could be substantiated.

Some years afterwards when Mr. Baker was preparing his History of Northamptonshire he pursued, in reference to his account of the Washington family, a precisely similar course. Either he acted independently, basing his pedigree on the same assumption, or, which is most probable, he had access to the collections of Sir Isaac Heard; and, presuming that Sir Isaac had thoroughly investigated the subject, adopted the pedigree which he had constructed. Sir Isaac's explanatory note, if seen, was ignored, and Baker confidently published the pedigree

with the statements that John Washington of the Sulgrave family was afterwards of South Cave, in the county
of York; that his brother Lawrence was a student at
Oxford in 1622; that both emigrated to America about
the year 1657; and that the former was the direct ancestor of the American President.

This pedigree has ever since been received as authoritative by all historians and biographers, everybody supposing that both Baker and Sir Isaac Heard had established
the connection and descents by unimpeachable evidence,
and no one dreaming for a moment of questioning the
accuracy of their statements.

The object of this paper is to prove that the conclusions of those eminent men, natural and reasonable as
they may have been (which is not denied), were nevertheless altogether wrong—in other words, that the John
and Lawrence Washington named in the Visitation of
1618 as the sons of Lawrence Washington of Sulgrave
were not the emigrants to Virginia in 1657, and consequently that the former was not the ancestor of the illustrious President.

Other articles concerning the Washington family may
follow this, but the present one aims only at the entire
demolition of the now universally received pedigree, so
far as the alleged American connection is concerned, and
is published at this time in the hope and belief that an
interest will be excited among genealogists which may
result in the discovery of the true ancestry of the great
and good man whose memory is equally honored on both
sides of the Atlantic.

The first doubt cast upon Sir Isaac Heard's pedigree

was, perhaps unconsciously, by President Washington himself, and it is not unreasonable to suppose that it may have induced the former to record the note already mentioned. The language used by Washington in one portion of the letter referred to is important and suggestive. He says: "I have often heard others of the family, older than myself, say that our ancestor who first settled in this country came from some one of the *northern* counties of England; but whether from Lancashire, Yorkshire, or one *still more northerly*, I do not precisely remember." Washington himself, when he wrote this, was about sixty years of age, and the memory of those older than himself, from whom he received the statement, must have reached back probably within half a century of the arrival of his first ancestor in Virginia. Traditions are valuable, or otherwise, as they are transmitted through the medium of ignorance or intelligence. In such a family as that of the Washingtons the original facts would be less likely to become perverted than if they had been successively communicated through persons of a less intelligent character. Taking the tradition, however, for what it may be worth, it is quite certain that Northamptonshire cannot be accounted "one of the northern counties of England." But Washington himself was perfectly clear upon this point, and, if his language means anything, it surely means that the county from which his first American ancestor emigrated, if not Lancashire, or Yorkshire, was one, as he says, "still more northerly." It must also be noted that he does not mention this locality as the ancient or original seat of the family, but says distinctly that his "ancestor who first settled" in Virginia emigrated from that county.

But, whatever may be the value of this testimony, the present object can be accomplished quite independently of it.

In order that all the references to the various persons hereafter mentioned may be perfectly comprehended, a copy of Baker's pedigree is herewith given, down to the generation including John and Lawrence Washington, the two brothers in question. By reference thereto (*vide post*. page 164), it will be seen that Lawrence Washington, of Sulgrave, by his wife Margaret Butler, had issue seven sons and seven daughters. This enumeration does not agree strictly with the Visitation of 1618, which gives another son named Robert (said to have died without issue), and omits Barbara, one of the daughters named by Baker (evidently in error, as she was doubtless the one of that name mentioned two generations before as one of the daughters of the first Lawrence Washington of Sulgrave). This accords, so far as the number of sons is concerned, with the inscription on his monument in Brington church, co. Northampt. which, however, states that he had nine daughters. Three of these probably died at an early age, unless we accept Barbara (named by Baker), and Lucy, who in 1633-4, was mentioned as headwoman (perhaps housekeeper) in the establishment of Lord Spencer at Althorp. The actual number of the children of Lawrence and Margaret Washington was seventeen, with the most of whom we shall have nothing further to do at present except to say that, as the marriage of their parents took place on the 3d of August, 1588, and their father died on the 13th of December, 1616, it is not difficult to determine at least the approximate dates of their respective births, which probably occurred, so far as the sons at least are concerned, in the order in which they appear in the Visitation, viz: 1. William; 2. John; 3. Robert; 4. Richard; 5. Lawrence; 6. Thomas; 7. Gregory; 8. George. Of these, George, the eighth and youngest son, was baptized at Wormleighton, in the county of Warwick, on the 3d of August, 1608. Gregory, the seventh son, was baptized at Brington, co. Northampt. on the 16th of January, 1606-7, and was buried there the following day. Thomas the sixth son, the writer has satisfactorily identified as the "Mr. Washington" (*vide* Howell's Familiar Letters) who was attached to the suite of Prince Charles on the occasion of his memorable matrimonial expedition to Spain. He died at Madrid in the year 1623, at the age of eighteen, which would establish his birth in about the year 1605. Richard, the fourth son, the writer has also discovered was apprenticed on the 7th of July, 1614, under the auspices of the Clothworkers' Company, to one Richard Brent, of London. If apprenticed for the usual time, seven years, he would then have been about fourteen years of age, and, consequently, born about the year 1600. Between him and Thomas last named came *Lawrence*, the fifth son (the precise date of whose birth we shall establish presently), and perhaps one or more of their sisters. The three elder brothers, William, *John*, and Robert, were of course, therefore, born between the years 1589 and 1599, as well, probably, as some of the nine daughters.

This recapitulation of dates is not unimportant, as it affords another strong presumptive proof against the correctness of Baker's pedigree. If the two brothers John and Lawrence above named were the Virginia emigrants, the former must have been about sixty, and the latter not far from fifty-five years of age, when they quitted England. It certainly was not usual for men so far advanced in life to seek new homes in the colonies, and as it is known that both of the real emigrants married again after they had been some time in Virginia, and both had issue there, the improbability that they were identical with the two brothers of Northamptonshire becomes greatly increased.

It is, of course, unnecessary to dwell long upon the history of William Washington, the eldest son, whose identity, if not otherwise sufficiently established, would be so by the will of his aunt Elizabeth, the widow of his uncle Robert Washington, dated on the 17th of March, 1622–3, in which, among other legacies to her nephews and nieces, she bequeaths him 100*l.*, and calls him "Sir William Washington." He was knighted at Theobalds on the 17th of January, 1621–2. He married Anne, the half-sister of George Villiers, Duke of Buckingham, who, after that event, appears to have taken the whole family under his protection, and continued to advance their fortunes (which, at that time, were at a very low ebb), in various ways, until down to the very time of his assassination. Sir William is described, in 1618, as of Packington, in the county of Leicester, but appears afterwards to have scarcely had a permanent home anywhere. Two of his children were baptized at Leckhampstead, in the county of Bucks, and two at St. Martin's-in-the-Fields, London, where he himself was buried on the 22d of June, 1643. Lady Washington was buried at Chelsea on the preceding 25th of May. According to the Visitation of 1618, his eldest son, Henry, was born in 1615, from which fact an approximate date of his own birth may be readily derived. His other children were George, Christopher, Catherine, Susanna, and Elizabeth. In his will, which is dated on the 6th of June, only sixteen days before his burial, he gives his residence as "Thistleworth" (Isleworth), in the county of Middlesex, and directs that his "manor of Wicke," and "Wicke farm," shall be sold.

This manor was in the parish of Isleworth, and had been purchased in the year 1638 by Sir William Washington from the coheirs of Sir Michael Stanhope, but he was compelled to mortgage it in 1640 to Sir Edward Spencer and Sir Richard Wynne, and it was in the possession of the latter at his death in 1649. By a singular coincidence, Sir William Washington's father, at his death, held of Lord Spencer a manor of the same name in Northamptonshire.

We now arrive at the great point of interest in the present discussion, and the main fact, destined to overthrow the assumptions of Sir Isaac Heard and Baker as to the origin of the American Washingtons, may as well be stated at once. JOHN WASHINGTON, the second son of Lawrence and Margaret, and brother of Sir William, was also knighted. He became *Sir* John, at Newmarket, on the 21st of February, 1622–3. His identity may be established in several ways.

In a series of old account-books preserved at Althorp, which have been carefully examined by the Rev. John Nassau Simpkinson, Rector of Brington (whose interest in the subject, and whose kind assistance the writer begs thus publicly to acknowledge), and to some extent by the writer himself, there is abundant evidence to show that the most friendly relations existed between the noble family at Althorp and their neighbors and tenants the Washingtons. Evidence to the same effect is also to be found in several of the wills of the family, of which, in some instances, Lord Spencer was appointed supervisor. The Washingtons were a gentle family, although greatly reduced in circumstances, having been compelled to part with the estate of Sulgrave, upon which they retired to Brington. The Lord Spencer of that day, however, did not forsake his friends in their adversity. They had hitherto been his frequent guests at Wormleighton, and, on their settlement at Brington, were as cordially welcomed to Althorp. It may also be mentioned that the two families were more or less nearly connected by intermarriage.

The old account-books referred to were the steward's usual household books, and also some that were kept by a person who had charge of the grain given out daily for the use of the horses of the establishment as well as those of Lord Spencer's guests. These books record the frequent presence, as guests at Althorp, of Mr. Robert Washington (who died on the 10th of March, 1622–3, and who is last mentioned shortly before his death); also of William, John, Lawrence, and Thomas Washington (evidently four of the sons of Lawrence and Margaret); Mistress Alice Washington (their sister); and also of the Curtises and Pills, with whom the Washingtons intermarried; but, which is more important, down to the 10th of November, 1621, William Washington is always mentioned as *Mr.* William, and on that date for the last time, reappearing on the 30th of March, 1622, as *Sir* William. He had been knighted on the preceding 17th of January. After the 30th of March, 1622, down to the 11th of January, 1622–3, the two brothers are mentioned as *Sir* William and *Mr.* John Washington. The latter is never so designated again, but, on the 22d of March following, the presence of *Sir* John Washington is recorded. He had been knighted between those two dates, on the 21st of February. Afterwards Thomas (who is last mentioned on the 12th of October, 1622) having died in Spain in 1623, the three brothers are always mentioned as *Sir* William, *Sir* John, and *Mr.* Lawrence Washington. There is abundant other evidence to show that these brothers were the sons of Lawrence and Margaret Washington, formerly of Sulgrave and afterwards of Brington.

The history of Sir John Washington was briefly as follows: and, to avoid numerous notes and references, the writer will simply remark that for every fact stated he has the evidences in his possession. He was first married, on the 14th of June, 1621, at St. Leonard's, Shoreditch, by virtue of a license, to Mary, one of the daughters of Philip Curtis, gentleman, by Catherine his wife, of Islip, Northants. The will of her mother, dated the 6th of December, 1622, mentions her as her daughter Mary Washington, and bequeaths a legacy of 50*l.* to her then only son Mordaunt Washington. She had two other sons, viz. John and Philip, and died on the 1st of January, 1624–5. She was buried in the church of Islip aforesaid, where her monument still exists, with the following inscription: "Here lieth the body of Dame Mary, wife unto Sr John

Washingtō knight, daughter of Phillipe Curtis, gent. who had issue by hur sayd husbande 3 sonns, Mordaunt, John, and Phillipe; deceased the 1 of Janu. 1624." The monumental inscription of her mother, Catharine Curtis, also in Islip church, states that by her husband Philip Curtis, gentleman, she had issue one son, Philip, and four daughters. This Philip Curtis married Amy Washington, one of the daughters of Lawrence and Margaret, at Brington, on the 8th of August, 1620. Of this connection there cannot be the slightest doubt, and as their wills are both otherwise important, as establishing the point at issue, full abstracts of them are here given.

That of Philip Curtis was nuncupative, and made on the 19th of May, 1636, in presence of Sir John Washington, knight and another. He bequeathed 1,000*l.* to his daughter Catharine, when of age or married, and to his nephews John Washington and Philip Washington each 50*l.* when of age. His nephew Mordaunt Washington he commended to the kindness of his wife, to whom he bequeathed the residue of his estate, and appointed as guardians of his daughter, the clergyman of the parish and "Sir John Washington of Thrapston, in the county of Northampton, knight." The will was proved on the 30th of May following by his relict Amy Curtis, and on the ensuing 27th of June, she made her own will. After directing to be buried in the chancel of Islip near her husband, she proceeds substantially as follows:—

Whereas there was given to my nephew Mordaunt Washington, the eldest son of Sir John Washington, knt. by the last will and testament of his grandmother Curtis, deceased, the sum of 50l., I now give to said Mordaunt 250l. more, to be employed for his benefit till he become of age or married. Whereas my husband, lately deceased, gave to John Washington, second son of Sir John Washington, 50l., I now give to said John, my nephew, 50l. more, to be employed to his use till he be of age, &c. Whereas my husband, lately deceased, gave by his last will to my nephew Philip Washington, third son of Sir John Washington, knt., 50l., I now give him 50l. more, &c. Whereas my husband Philip Curtis, by his last will, gave me and my heirs for ever all his lands, houses, &c., I now give the same to my only daughter Katherine Curtis and her heirs for ever, as well as the residue of all my estate, and appoint "my dear and loving mother, Margarett Washington, and my loving brother, Sir John Washington, knight," to be her guardians.

One of the witnesses to this will is William Washington, doubtless Sir William her brother. Administration thereon was granted, on the 19th of November following, to Sir John Washington, knight, who is described as the "lawful brother" of the testatrix, and who was to act during the minority of Katherine Curtis, daughter of the testatrix and the executrix named in the will.

There could not possibly be a more satisfactory document than this, as the testatrix not only gives the name of her mother, but also distinctly states her relationship to Sir John Washington, which is legally confirmed by the Court of Probate.

The subsequent personal history of Sir John Washington, except that he married a second wife, is almost entirely

unknown.   Among the Royalist Composition Papers at the
Public Record Office, in the case of the Earl of Northampton, there is an affidavit of a tenant who had paid
218*l.* to Thomas Farrer for the use of the said earl and
Sir John Washington.   Farrer responds, that what sums
of money he had received out of the estate of James Earl
of Northampton had been so received "as agent and on
behalf of Sir John Washington, by virtue of an Extent
which the said Sir John had on said estate in the county
of Bedford;" whereupon, on the 23d of February, 1653–4,
it was ordered, "that a letter be written to Sir John
Washington to pay in the money or show cause."

On the 14th of January, 1661–2, Lawrence Washington of Garsden, in the county of Wilts, esquire, made his
will, in which he left an annuity of 40*l.* per annum to his
"cousin John Washington, son of Sir John Washington
of Thrapston, in the county of Northampton, knight,"
the legal presumption from which is that both father and
son were then living, and the former at Thrapston.

The registers of Thrapston, although embracing the
period during which Sir John Washington is described as
of that place, and the time of his death, do not once
mention the name.   He died, however, before the 6th of
October, 1678, on which day Dorothy Washington made
her will, and described herself as "relict of Sir John
Washington, knight, deceased."   She directed to be
buried in the chancel of the church of Fordham, near her
grandchild, Mrs. Penelope Audley.   She bequeathed of
her "small estate," 5*l.* to her son, Mr. Thomas Kirkbey,
and 20*s.* to each of his sons and daughters, leaving the
residue of her goods to her daughter, Mrs Penelope

Thornton, whom she appointed her executrix. No children by Sir John Washington are mentioned. In the Probate Act she is described as of Fordham, in the county of Cambridge, and the record of her burial, in the parish register of that place, under the year 1678, is as follows:—"Dame Dorothy, relict of Sr John Wassington of Thrapston, in the county of Northampton, knight, was buryed the 15th day of October."

It is probable that Sir John had no issue by his second wife, and morally certain that none were living at her death, or she would scarcely have failed to notice them in some way in her will. Of the three sons by his first wife, John, we have seen, was still living in 1661–2. His eldest brother Mordaunt was visiting at Althorp on the 13th of February, 1640–1, but nothing further is known of him, nor of his youngest brother Philip, unless the latter was one of that name who was buried at St. Martin's-in-the-Fields on the 26th of September, 1643.

We proceed now to the history of LAWRENCE WASHINGTON, apparently the fifth son of Lawrence and Margaret, and certainly the younger brother of Sir William and Sir John Washington.

Baker was quite correct in stating that he was a student at Oxford in the year 1622. He was of Brasenose College, and matriculated on the 2d of November, 1621. The exact record in the Martriculation Register is as follows: "Laurent: Washington, Northamp: Gen. fil. an. nat. 19;" i. e. Lawrence Washington, of Northamptonshire whose father's rank was that of a gentleman, and whose own age was nineteen years at his last birthday.

It was not until little more than a year later that the officials commenced entering in the register the christian names and particular residences of the fathers of the students, but in the present instance the above record is almost as satisfactory as it would have been if the other particulars had been given. In the first place, the Washington family of Sulgrave, or Brington, was the only one of the name in Northamptonshire whose sons could be recognized and designated as the sons of gentlemen, unless, indeed, the Heralds of that time omitted others, which is not probable. Secondly, there was no other Lawrence Washington at Oxford for considerable periods before and after this date; unless, again, all the officials were guilty of omissions in all the Registers (for the writer has carefully examined them all), which is even more improbable. And, finally, the will of his aunt Elizabeth, widow of his uncle Robert Washington, dated on the 17th of March, 1622–3, among other legacies to his brothers and sisters, leaves him her husband's seal ring, and states that he was then at Oxford.

Lawrence Washington was born, therefore, about the year 1602. He appears to have entered at Brasenose College as early as 1619, but he did not sign the Subscription Book until the 2d of November, 1621, under which date his name also appears in the general matriculation register, in connection with thirty-five others—an extraordinary number, and indicating that from some cause this ceremony had hitherto been neglected. He took his B. A. degree in 1623, and became Fellow of Brasenose about 1624. He is recorded as serving the office of lector, then the principal educational office in the college, from 1627 to 1632 inclusive. On the 26th of August, 1631, he became one of the proctors of the university, filling a vacancy that had occurred by the deprivation of his predecessor by royal warrant. On the 14th of March, 1632–3, he was presented to the then very valuable living of Purleigh, in Essex, and resigned his fellowship. The records of a suit in Chancery, preserved at the Rolls Office, perfectly identify the rector of Purleigh with the fellow of Brasenose and the proctor of the university. He continued at Purleigh until the year 1643, when, according to Newcourt, he was "ejected by sequestration for his loyalty in the late rebellion of 1642," and had the honor of being pilloried in the infamous " Century." Walker states that he "was afterwards permitted to have and continue upon a Living in these parts: but it was such a poor and miserable one that it was always with difficulty that any one was persuaded to accept of it." The writer has been unable to ascertain the living mentioned; but it is to be hoped that some further trace of him may yet be discovered in the neighborhood of Purleigh, where, putting the usual construction upon Walker's language, he continued in his profession of a clergyman after the Restoration, and consequently some years after the date of his namesake's emigration to Virginia.

We are now prepared to test the question of identity first raised.

Referring again to the facts that the John and Lawrence Washington of the Northamptonshire pedigree were respectively at least sixty-two and fifty-five years of age in 1657, the date of the emigration, and that both of the real emigrants remarried and had issue in Virginia— facts, almost, if not quite, sufficient in themselves to settle the question without further dispute, especially as the evidences in the will of Lawrence of Virginia indicate that he was probably under thirty years of age at the time of his emigration—we may safely leave the issue to the effect of either of the following propositions,—

First. John Washington of Sulgrave and Brington was knighted, and became Sir John, while his brother Lawrence was a clergyman of the Established Church. If they were the Virginia emigrants the one must have abandoned his knighthood, and the other rejected his surplice and bands, for both were never known in Virginia except as "Esquires," or "Gentlemen," and by the latter appellation they described themselves in their wills. For either of these rejections there could have been no possible cause, as Virginia was then a loyal colony, and her established religion that of the mother country.

Secondly. Sir John Washington had at least two wives. The first, named Mary, was buried at Islip, in Northamptonshire, while the name of his widow was Dorothy, and she was buried at Fordham in Cambridgeshire. John Washington, gentleman, the Virginia emigrant, states distinctly in his will, dated the 27th of September, 1675, that he brought his first wife from England with him, that she died in Virginia, and was buried with two children on his own plantation, and that his second wife's name was Anne, whom he appointed his executrix.

It is clear, therefore, that if John Washington, son of Lawrence and Margaret of Sulgrave, was identical with Sir John Washington of Thrapston, knight, he could not have been the emigrant to Virginia in 1657; and, as there cannot be the slightest doubt upon that point, the assumption of Sir Isaac Heard and Mr. Baker unquestionably falls to the ground.

On a future occasion the writer proposes to review the Washington pedigree more at large, and to present other more reasonable theories as to the true ancestry of the American President. He has accumulated a large amount of information from almost every source accessible to him, and believes that it embraces the real history of the family; but he yet lacks the positive clue that would solve the mystery, and enable him to reduce the chaotic material to order. He will be very grateful for even the most apparently trifling note concerning the name which may be transmitted to him.*

* Any communications may be addressed to the care of W. H. Whitmore, Boston, or John Gough Nichols, Esq., London, Eng.

THE PEDIGREE OF WASHINGTON.

("From Baker's History of Northamptonshire," Vol. I., p. 513.)

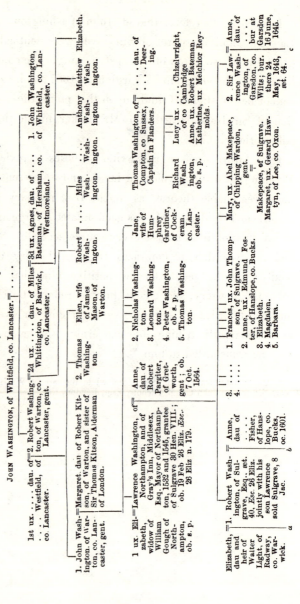

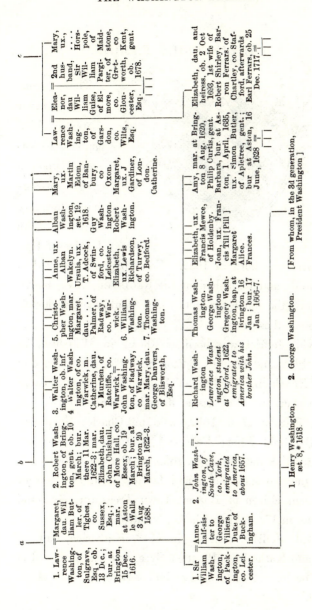

THE JEFFRIES FAMILY.

These arms, and three other coats of allied families, are engraved upon a silver candlestick formerly owned by John Jeffries of Boston, who was born in 1688. From papers preserved in the family and published in the REGISTER, XV., 14–17, we obtain the following facts which would seem to justify the use of these arms.

David[1] Jeffries was born at Rhoad, in Wiltshire, 18 Nov., 1658, and came to Boston in 1677. He married in 1686, Elizabeth, daughter of John and Elizabeth (Lidgett) Usher, and had issue, John,[2] b. 1688; David,[2] b. 1690; Elizabeth,[2] b. 1692, who m. Charles Shepreeve and Benjamin Eliot; Rebecca,[2] b. 1693, m. Ebenezer Wentworth; and Sarah,[2] b. 1695, m. George Jaffray.

Of the two sons, John[2] and David,[2] John[2] was a very prominent citizen of Boston, Town Treasurer, &c., and married, in 1713, Anne Clarke, but died s. p.

David[2] Jeffries, Jr., m. in 1713, Katherine, dau. of John and Katherine (Brattle) Eyre, and was drowned in 1716, on his return from London, leaving an only child, David.[3]

This David[3] Jeffries, third of the name, m. first his

cousin, Sarah Jaffrey, by whom he had eight children, but only one son, John,[4] survived. His second wife was Deborah, dau. of Byfield Lyde, by whom he had three children, but all died young, or unm.

Dr. John[4] Jeffries, b. 1745, H. C., 1763, studied medicine, and was, in 1771, appointed surgeon in the British Navy. He was, naturally, a Royalist, and went to Halifax during the Revolution. In England he obtained extensive practice, and was made famous by his excursion across the channel in a balloon, the first successful aerial voyage thus made. He returned to Boston in 1790, and died here in 1819. His representatives are all through his children by his second wife, Hannah Hunt; who were John,[5] Catherine,[5] wife of C. C. Haven, Julia Ann,[5] wife of Thos. E. Eckley, and George Jaffrey.[5]

Of these, John,[5] a distinguished physician of Boston, m. Anne-Geyer, dau. of Rufus-Greene and Ann (McLean) Amory, and has living—

John,[6] who m. Anne Lloyd Greene, and has issue; Catherine[6] A.; Anne[6] McL.; Sarah[6] Augusta, wife of Charles L. Andrews; Dr. B. Joy[6]; Edward[5] P.; and Henry[6] U.

———

The record from which the earliest dates were copied, was prepared by John Jeffries, son of the emigrant, and must be regarded as high authority. Although the name of the father of the first David is not given, the early use of the arms may aid us in identifying him; and from the intermarriages in the earlier generations, the family evidently ranked among the gentry here, at a date when social distinctions were maintained.

We have mentioned the four coats engraved upon the silver formerly owned by John² Jeffries. These arms are those of his father, David¹ Jeffries, his mother, Elizabeth Usher, his maternal grandmother, Elizabeth Lidgett, and his wife Anne Clarke. We will give a brief account of these three families.

USHER.

Elizabeth Usher, who m. David¹ Jeffries, Sr., was the daughter of John Usher of Boston, who was the son of Hezekiah Usher of Cambridge, Ms., and Boston. John Usher was a bookseller, and acquired a large fortune. Having married for his second wife, Elizabeth, dau. of Samuel Allen, he was interested in the proprietorship of New Hampshire, and was Lieutenant Governor there. He had been colonel of the Boston regiment, and Treasurer under Androsse, yet seems to have maintained the favor of his countrymen of more stubborn patriotism. He built a fine residence at Medford, where he d. in 1726.

Hezekiah Usher, Sr., was of Boston in 1651, and a very successful merchant. He was connected by marriage with John Harwood of Bednall Green, and Samuel Shrimpton of the same place. This may be a slight clue to the identification of this family. The arms were used by Gov. John Usher of N. H., and afterwards by his descendants, some of whom now reside in Rhode Island.

LIDGETT.

Elizabeth Lidgett, mother of Mrs. Elizabeth Jeffries, was the daughter of Peter Lidgett, a rich merchant of Boston, Mass., by his wife Elizabeth Scammon, and was born at Barbadoes, 4 Nov., 1651. Peter L. d. 1676, and his widow m. John Saffyn. His son, Charles Lidgett, died at London, 13 July, 1698, having married Mary, dau. of Wm. Hester of Southwark, sister of John H. of same place.

We do not find these arms recorded in Burke, yet they are used on the seal of Mrs. Saffyn, above mentioned, as will be seen in our present number. We must, therefore, regard them as claimed by Peter Lidgett or his wife.

CLARKE.

Anne Clarke, wife of John[2] Jeffries, was the daughter of Thomas Clarke of Boston, by his second wife, Rebecca, widow of Capt. Thomas Smith. This Thomas Clarke was the son of William and Anne Clarke, and was born at Salisbury, co. Wilts, 22 Dec., 1645. He was of Boston as early as 1678, when he had a wife Jane, the mother of Jane Clark, born in 1680, who married Rev. Benjamin Colman.

This Thomas Clarke died Dec. 16, 1732, and by his will and inventory was evidently possessed of a large property. There were at least two others of the same name contemporary with him, both very prominent citizens, but we have no reason to imagine any relationship.

To prevent any confusion arising from similarity of names, it may be well to speak of the Jaffrey family, intermarried with the Jeffries, yet of different origin. George[1] Jaffrey of New Hampshire, Speaker, &c., died in 1707; his son, George, Jr., m. Sarah, daughter of the first David Jeffries, in 1710. Their daughter, Sarah Jaffrey, married her cousin, David[3] Jeffries, whose grandson, George J. Jeffries, assumed the name of George Jaffrey in 1802, in accordance with the will of his grand-uncle, George Jaffrey, third and last of the name in that line. The family was one of great wealth and influence in New Hampshire in Colonial times, but we have no knowledge of any arms used by them, or of their original residence in England.

THE HUTCHINSON FAMILY.

In our April number, p. 83, we gave two examples of the arms used by the family of Gov. Thomas Hutchinson. At that time the only attempt to trace the English pedigree of this family was recorded in a little book published by P. O. Hutchinson, Esq., a descendant of the noted Governor. We have now the pleasure of laying before our readers a synopsis of the investigations made during the past eighteen months, by Joseph L. Chester, Esq., the results of which are published in the October number of the N. E. Historical and Genealogical Register. The search has been most thorough and persevering, and we regret exceedingly that our limits forbid the publication of the entire article, simultaneously with its appearance in the Register.

Somewhat to our surprise, Mr. Chester shows that not only was this family of Hutchinsons distinct from the family of the name in Yorkshire, entitled to arms, but that in 1634, one of the cousins of the emigrant presented his pedigree and claimed arms, but on the application was endorsed by the Heralds, "respited for proof." No proof seems to have been furnished, nor has any grant of arms been since made to any member of this family.

The emigrant hither was William[3]; son of Edward,[2] and grandson of John[1] Hutchinson. Here the pedigree stops, leaving us without any clue for further investigations. The father of this John[1] "lived before the period of parish registers, left no Will that can be discovered, and was evidently of a very humble rank in life." He was probably of the city of Lincoln, and had certainly four sons

and one daughter. These were Christopher,[1] a clergyman of South Leasingham, and of Scremby, co. Lincoln,
who died in 1556, *s. p.*; Thomas[1]; William[1], who was
Sheriff of the city of Lincoln in 1541, Alderman in 1545,
and Mayor in 1552, and died in 1557; JOHN[1]; and
Alice,[1] wife of James Remington of Branston, co. Linc.

Christopher[1] had three sons and three daughters, of
whom Margery m. John Neale of Horncastle, co. Linc.;
a grandaughter, Margery Hutchinson, m. Herbert Thorndike and was alive in 1611.

John[1] Hutchinson of the city of Lincoln was Sheriff in
1547, Alderman in 1556, and Mayor in 1556 and 1564,
holding the latter office at the time of his death, 24 May,
1565. He was possessed of considerable property, and
left houses and lands to his sons, all of whom he names in
his will. By his first wife, Margaret, he probably had
four sons and two daughters, viz., William,[2] Thomas,[2]
John,[2] Arthur,[2] Jane[2] and Alice.[2] By his second wife,
Anne, who was probably widow of —— Clink, he had
Edward[2] and Mary.[2]

Of these, William[2] m. Margaret Sisson, and died in
1584, leaving issue; Jane[2] m. Edmund Knight; and
Alice[2] m. Thomas Dynison.

The youngest son of John,[1] Mayor of Lincoln, was
Edward[2] Hutchinson, born about 1564. He was a mer-
cer of Lincoln, and of Alford, whither he removed. By
his wife Susan he had eleven children, viz., William[3];
Theophilus[3]; Samuel[3]; Esther,[3] wife of Rev. Thomas Rish-
worth; John[3]; Richard[3]; Susanna[3]; Susanna[3] again, who
m. Augustine Storre or Story; Anne[3] perhaps m. a
Leavitt; Mary[3] m. Rev. John Wheelwright; and Edward.[3]

Edward Hutchinson, Senr., was buried at Alford, 14 Feb. 1631-2; his widow was living in 1644.

Of the children, William[3] was the emigrant, and will be noticed hereafter; John[3] m. in 1626 Bridget, daughter of William Bury, (by Emme his wife, dau. of John Dryden, Esq.); and had ten children, of whom Samuel[4] was twice Mayor of Boston, co. Lincoln, and d. in 1696; Richard[3] was an Ironmonger, and citizen of London, and had children, Edward,[4] Samuel,[4] Jonathan,[4] Ezekiel,[4] William,[4] Eliakim,[4] and four daughters; from the youngest daughter the present Earl of Donoughmore is doubtless descended.

William[3] Hutchinson was baptized at Alford, 14 Aug., 1586, and evidently resided there till his emigration. By his wife Anne Marbury he had fourteen children, Edward,[4] Susanna,[4] Richard,[4] Faith,[4] Bridget,[4] Francis,[4] Elizabeth,[4] William,[4] Samuel,[4] Anne,[4] Mary,[4] Katherine,[4] William[4] and Susanna.[4]

From this period the history of the family belongs to New England, but before essaying an outline we will copy Mr. Chester's account of the pedigree of the famous Anne Hutchinson, wife of William,[3] the emigrant.

He has discovered conclusive evidence that her father was Francis Marbury of Alford, who late in life took orders, and was Rector of St. Martin Vintry, London, in 1605. He was the third son of William Marbury or Merbury, Esquire, of Grisby, in the parish of Burgh-upon-Bain, co. Lincoln; of a family whose arms were Argent, on a fesse engrailed gules, three garbs of the field. William Marbury m. Agnes, dau. of John Linton, Esquire, and his oldest son Edward was knighted in 1603, and died in 1605 while High Sheriff of the county, leaving a son George, also knighted in 1606. William had also three daughters, of whom Catherine m. Christopher Wentworth, 19 Aug. 1593.

William's third son, Francis, m. first, Elizabeth Moore, and secondly, Bridget, daughter of John Dryden, Esquire, of Canons Ashby. Her brother, Erasmus Dryden, was a baronet, and grandfather of John Dryden, the poet.

Francis and Bridget Marbury had eleven children baptized at Alford, and possibly others at London. He died late in 1610, or early in 1611. It thus appears that Anne Hutchinson was descended from heraldic families on both sides, but that her husband can claim no ancestor of higher rank than the Mayor of Lincoln.

It is indeed strange to notice the persistent employment of arms by the family. In our present number will be found an example from the seal on the will of Samuel Hutchinson of Boston, Mass., 1667. The branch descended from Richard H., and now represented by the Earl of Donoughmore, has used the coat for a century or more. It will be remembered that these arms are recorded in Gore's Roll, and though now shown to be invalid, this does not destroy our confidence in the general correctness of his list. It indeed appears that the arms were assumed long before Gore's time, and as he had no official authority, he could not discriminate between the rightful owners and pretenders.

———

We have said that there is a family of Hutchinsons entitled to bear this coat-of-arms. Very extensive examinations have been made in England, and a synopsis of the

results has been published in " Le Nobilaire Universal de
France, Receuil général des généalogies historiques des
maisons nobiles et titrées de la France. Publié sous la
direction de L. de Magny. Paris." In translating from
this account there is a chance to err in the spelling of
names, but we have corrected such as were recognized.

The first of the name yet ascertained was Barnard[1]
Hutchinson of Cowlam, co. York, who was living with
his wife, dau. of John Boyville, in 1282. From him was
descended Thomas[6] Hutchinson of Owlthorpe, second son
of Anthony[5] H. of Cowlam, who inherited Owlthorpe,
Colston-Basset and Cropwell-Bishop by marriage with
the heiress of —— Drake of Kynolton. The intervening
generations were John,[2] who m. Edith, dau. of William
Wouldbie; James,[3] who m. Ursula, dau. of —— Gregory
of Naffentone; and William,[4] who m. Anne, dau. of
William Bennet.

Thomas[6] Hutchinson had three sons, William,[7] ancestor
of Col. John Hutchinson, John[7] of Basseford, and Laurence[7] of Tollerton.

Laurence[7] Hutchinson died before 1577, when his
widow Isabel made her will. He left five children,
Thomas,[8] Robert,[8] Agnes,[8] Richard[8] and William.[8]

Of these, Thomas[8] Hutchinson of Arnold was buried
17 Aug. 1618; and his wife made her will 20 Jan. following. Their children were Robert,[9] RICHARD,[9] Thomas,[9]
Humphrey,[9] John,[9] Elizabeth[9] and Isabel.[9]

Richard[9] Hutchinson, born in 1602, married 7 Dec.
1627, Alice, dau. of Joseph Bosworth of Colgrave. He
had four children born in England, and he emigrated to
Salem, Mass., in 1634, A deposition on the Essex Court

files gives his age as 58 in 1660, and was the first point which served for identification. He received grants of land in 1636, 1637, 1654 and 1660, a part of which lands and the house erected by him, are still in the possession of his descendants. He died in 1682, leaving seven children, two sons, Joseph[10] and John,[10] and five daughters.

Of these, Joseph[10] Hutchinson of Salem was twice married and had a large family. His sons were Joseph,[11] John,[11] Benjamin,[11] Richard,[11] Samuel,[11] Ambrose[11] and Robert.[11]

Joseph[11] Hutchinson of Danvers had sons, Joseph,[12] Ebenezer,[12] Elisha[12] and Jasper,[12] and died in 1751.

Joseph[12] Hutchinson of Danvers, b. 1689, m. 19 Jan. 1720, widow Abigail (Elliot) Goodale, and, dying in 1731, left seven children.

Of these, Joseph[13] Hutchinson of Middleton m. in 1746, Hannah, dau. of David Richardson, and died in 1797. Of his five children, Joseph[14] Hutchinson of Middleton, b. 1757, m. 1780, Hannah, dau. of Archelaus Fuller.

Joseph[15] Hutchinson, son of this last named, and sixth of the same name, b. in 1782, m. Sarah, dau. of Samuel Curtis, and had a son Joseph,[16] who d. *s. p.*, as well as Hiram[16] and Elisha.[16] Hiram[16] Hutchinson, b. 1808, m. 1831, Mary, dau. of Abraham Lufberry of Burlington, N. J., and had eight children. He resided for several years in France.

His oldest son, Alcander[17] Hutchinson, m. in 1858, Emma-Aimée-Henriette Torrens, daughter and coheiress of Henri-Louis, Count de Loyauté. In 1859 he went to Singapore, where he was appointed U. S. Consul, and where he established plantations.

SUFFOLK WILLS.

(Continued from p. 91.)

We continue our examples of arms, from the Suffolk Registry, by mentioning some which have already been engraved, or are too well-known to require an illustration.

22. The seal of Sir Thomas Temple is engraved in our first volume, p. 92, copied from his will.

23. The Norton arms are engraved, II., p. 1, from a seal published in the "Winthrop Papers." This seal is also found on John Norton's will of 1663, on William Hudson's will of 1667, and on Thomas Gill's will of 1725.

24. Dean Winthrop's will, 1704, bears his arms.

25. The will of Leonard Vassall, 1737, bears the allusive arms which we have engraved, II., p. 15.

26. Andrew Faneuil, 1737, has on his seal the same arms which are on the family tomb, as engraved, II., p. 121.

27. Andrew Belcher's will, 1717, has an imperfect impression of the arms engraved by us, II., p. 62.

We will next describe various crests and devices which occur on wills, but do not afford means for identification.

28. William Hill, gentleman, 1710; crest, an arm embowed, holding a battle-axe.

29. On the wills of Joseph Belcher and Jonathan Mason, both in 1723, is a seal bearing a crest, a lion passant. This is probably the seal of Joseph Marion, a notary public.

30. The will of Joshua Henshaw has accompanying it an affidavit signed by Samuel Cranston, Governor of

Rhode Island, and the seal bears in chief three roses, or annulets.

31. George Raisin, 1728; shield, three lions' heads couped, within an orle of cross-crosslets. Crest, a lion's head, couped.

32. John Hale, 1701. On his seal is apparently a coronet, out of which issues a bird, flying. Motto, " Nunquam non paratus."

33. Edward Rawlins, 1715, uses a very peculiar seal. From a fesse issues a heart, and above it is the motto, " Fide et amore."

34. Thomas Hill, Governor of St. Kitt's, in 1693, uses a seal of a lion passant, between three garbs.

35. Thomas Gardner, 1659, has for a seal a heart, transfixed with two arrows, and surmounted with a crown. This seal is found on other wills.

36.

John Oxenbridge, on his will, dated 1674, uses this seal. It is probably the same as described in Burke, " Hampshire : visitation 1634. Gules, a lion rampant, argent, within a bordure vert, charged with eight escallops of the second. Crest, a demi-lion, tail forked, argent, langued and armed gules, holding in the dexter paw an escallop or." Rev. John Oxenbridge, says Savage, was son of Dr. Daniel O., was born in 1606, at Daventry, co. Northampton, was of Lincoln Coll., Oxford, in 1623, and a tutor at Magdalen Hall. He went, in 1634, to Bermuda, returned to England, was ejected in 1662, and went to Surinam and Barbadoes. In 1669 he came to Boston, and was made colleague with Rev.

James Allen, at the First Church. He had three wives; first, Jane Butler, who d. 1655; second, Frances, dau. of Rev. Hezekiah Woodward, Vicar of Bray, co. Berks; and third, Susanna ———. He died 28 Dec., 1674, leaving daughters Bathshua, wife of Richard Scott of Jamaica, and Theodora, who m. 21 Nov., 1677, Rev. Peter Thatcher of Milton.

37.

This seal is found on the will of John Nash, 1712, witnessed by Solomon Blake, Samuel Hunt and Sarah Knight. It is also on the will of Susanna Crawford, 1713, witnesses, Nicholas Bowes, Abraham Francis and Sarah Knight. It is probable, therefore, that it belonged to Sarah Knight, whom we presume to be the famous "Journalist," daughter of Thomas Kimball, or Kemble, and wife of Richard Knight.

38.

Francis Davenport, who m. Ann, dau. of Dr. William Snelling, uses on his will the well-known family arms. Nothing more appears to be known of him, and, from the difference in the crest, it seems probable that he belonged to a different branch from the Rev. John Davenport.

39.

John Bigg, whose seal is on his will of 1692, was possibly son of an early settler of the same name, who died before 1669. This will mentions wife, daughter of Simon Lynde, deceased, but gives no clue to his other relatives. By deeds we learn that his wife was named Hannah.

40.

Elizur Holyoke, whose seal is here given from his will, dated in 1711, was grandson of the emigrant. The original colonist, says Savage, was Edward Holyoke, or Holliocke, from Tamworth, co. Stafford, who came here by 1639, lived at Chelsea, and was often representative. He m. Prudence, daughter of Rev. John Stockton of Kinholt, 18 June, 1612, and, dying 4 May, 1660, left an only son, Elizur, and five daughters.

His son Elizur m. Mary, dau. of William Pynchon, was Captain and Representative, and died 6 Feb., 1676, leaving sons John, Samuel, Edward, and Elizur; as well as a widow, Editha, dau. of John Maynard. Of these sons all died unmarried, except Elizur, Jr., whose seal is here copied. He married Mary, daughter of Jacob Eliot, and was father of Rev. Edward Holyoke, for nearly thirty-two years President of Harvard College. President Holyoke was the father of Dr. Edward Augustus Holyoke of Salem, who was born Aug. 13, 1728, and died March 31, 1829, aged 100 years, 7 months, 19 days.

In the last volume of the Proceedings of the Massachusetts Historical Society, it is said (p. 440) that he was one of four, recorded as having completed the hundredth year of their lives. The others were Samson Salter Blowers, Dr. Ezra Green, and Hon. Timothy Farrar.

The will of George Dawson, baker, of Boston, 1692, mentions wife Elizabeth, and grandchildren George, Charles, and Elizabeth Crossweight. The seal is as represented in the margin ; the witnesses are William Paine, Richard Sherwin, and John Watson.

42.

This seal is on the will of Peter Oliver, 1712, but, from its position, was undoubtedly affixed by Isaac Addington, Jr. As the arms are not those of Addington, and as he indeed possessed and used his own seal, as we shall hereafter show, it is necessary to try to trace the owner. We find that Isaac Addington, who was Speaker, Assistant, Councillor, Secretary, and Chief Justice, and died in 1715, was the son of Isaac Addington, by his wife Ann, daughter of Thomas Leverett. Of his sisters, Ann m. Capt. Samuel Maudesley, Rebecca m. Eleazer Davenport, and Sarah m. Penn Townsend. These arms are identical with those of Moseley, and this was undoubedly the true name of Addington's brother-in-law. We may therefore assume that this seal had belonged to Samuel Moseley, who died in 1680, leaving Addington his administrator, as it is hardly possible that A. had accidentally obtained a seal thus coinciding with his relative's arms.

Capt. Samuel Moseley was the son of Henry M. of Dorchester, was a gallant soldier, and died January, 1680. His only son died young, but the name has been preserved by the descendants of John Mosely, also of Dorchester, who was probably a near relative. This family has been of Windsor, and of Newburyport.

43.

From the will of Rev. John Wilson, 1667. He was born at Windsor, in 1588, third son of Rev. William Wilson, who had a prebendal stall there. He was of Christ's College, Cambridge, and afterwards was minister at Sudbury, co. Suffolk. Mather says that his mother was a niece of Dr. Edmund Grindal, Archbishop of Canterbury. Mather says, also, that John Wilson married Elizabeth, daughter of Sir John Mansfield, sister of the wife of Robert Keayne of Boston, and of John Mansfield, a settler here, formerly of Exeter. Sir John is said to have been Master of the Minories.

Wilson came in the fleet with Winthrop, and was ordained minister of the First Church, then located at Charlestown. In 1630 the church removed to Boston, and in 1631 he went to England for his wife. He returned in 1632, and became the first pastor of the First Church in Boston, having Cotton and Norton for colleagues. His children were Edmund, a physician in London; Mary, wife of Rev. Samuel Danforth, and John, minister at Medfield. He died 7 August, 1667.

The arms here given are apparently those described by Burke as of "Wilson of Penrith, co. Cumberland, and Welborne, co. Linc., granted 24 March, 1586. Per pale, argent and azure, three lion's gambs erased, fessways, in pale, counterchanged. Crest, a lion's head argent, guttée de sang."

44.

The will of Samuel Hutchinson, 1667, bears the accompanying seal. He was a brother of William, the emigrant ancestor of so many of the name here, and dying a bachelor his will mentions many of his relatives, to whom he made bequests. We have elsewhere shown that these arms were probably assumed, without due warranty.

45.

These arms, as we have already said in the article about the Jeffries family, were undoubtedly used by the Lidgetts. This seal appears upon the will of Peter Lidgett, 1676, and again on the will of his widow Elizabeth, in 1693, who had remarried Hon. John Saffyn. We presume this name of Lidgett is a corruption of some other name, as nothing resembling it is to be found in the English books.

46.

From the will of Nathaniel Thayer, merchant of Boston, 1693. He probably died at Barbadoes, and his very brief will leaves his property to his wife Deborah, and their children. His friends, Capt. Thos. Horner and Joseph Groves, were appointed executors. The witnesses were Jonas Clay, Joseph Eldridge, and Thomas Brown. From the names it is probable that this Nathaniel Thayer was the son of Richard of Boston, recorded by Savage, ancestor of the late John Eliot Thayer, and of Nathaniel Thayer of Boston.

47.

The seal on the will of Joseph Dammer of Dorchester, 1721, is evidently that of one of the witnesses, William Avery. This is proved not only by the agreement of the arms with the name, but by the fact that the family possesses an old painting of this coat, which is mentioned in an inventory prior to 1750. The first of the family here was William of Dedham, a physician, whose sons, William and Robert, married two daughters of Job Lane.

48.

This seal is on the will of William Hawkins, 1693. In it he mentions wife Ann and two youngest daughters, Sarah and Martha, dau. Elizabeth, and grandson Edward Porter, son of William Porter. Savage does not seem to have noticed this man. The witnesses are Martha Savage, Constance Worcester, and Jona. Rawlings. The arms do not belong to Hawkins, but may have belonged to Martha Savage, who was no doubt the widow of Ebenezer S. and daughter of Bozoun Allen.

49.

Francis Wainwright of Boston, late of Ipswich, Mass., used this seal on his will of 8 April, 1692. It is evidently not the coat claimed by his family, as we have already shown (Vol. I., p. 89 and 110) by the examples dated in 1711 and 1728. The witnesses were John Higginson, Jr., William Hirst, and Simon

Willard. From this will, and Savage's account of the family, we find that Francis Wainwright was possibly from Chelmsford, in Essex, had wives Phillippa and Hannah, sons John, Simon, and Francis, and five daughters, all married, at the date of this will. He was a merchant, of large estate, and his descendants made good matches. His three sons each named a son John, and, according to the theory of the late Abner Morse, the probability would be that this was the name of the emigrant, also.

A. T. P.

THE TEMPLE FAMILY.

In our first volume, p. 92–5, we gave some account of the Temples, especially in the branches which have held the rank of baronet. Although this account was prepared from the only authorities then available, it was acknowledged to be imperfect. The death of Henry Temple, Lord Palmerston, gave rise to fresh investigations, and the most satisfactory attempts to construct the pedigree have been those made by John Gough Nichols, Esq. In the "Herald and Genealogist," Parts XVII. and XVIII., he has traced out the branches which successively held the title before it reverted to an American line represented by Sir John Temple of New York, eighth baronet.

Our pedigree needs correction, chiefly in the early generations, and should read thus:

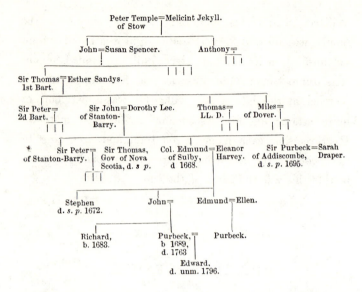

The most important corrections herein are in making Sir John of Stanton-Barry, (ancestor of the fifth, sixth, and seventh baronets,) the son of Sir Thomas the first baronet; and in showing a new branch, descended from this Sir John.

This branch was from Col. Edmund Temple of Sulby, in Northamptonshire. He was a Colonel in the Parliamentary service, and m. Eleanor, dau. of Sir Stephen Harvey, in 1647. His wife died 23 Nov., 1660, and he was buried 9 March, 1667–8, leaving three sons, Stephen, John, and Edmund, and four daughters.

Stephen died in 1672, doubtless unmarried; Edmund was of Leicester, and d. probably in 1672, leaving a widow Ellen, and a son Purbeck; John was of Sibbertoft, and died in February, 1701–2, leaving two sons, Richard and Purbeck, and four daughters.

Of these last we know nothing more of Richard, but Purbeck married, and died 16 May, 1763, leaving three daughters and one son, Edward, who died unmarried 15 September, 1796.

It is highly probable, says Mr. Nichols, that this last Edward was actually the Baronet, after the death of Sir Richard, in 1786, unless his uncle Richard left a son.

In tracing back the pedigree for the next heir, we come only to Purbeck, son of Edmund, and there closes the Stanton-Barry branch.

Our American line, now enjoying the baronetcy, must apparently come from Dr. Thomas Temple or his brother Miles, the two younger sons of the first baronet.

Of course the pedigree tracing them to Sir Purbeck is wrong. Of these two sons of Sir Thomas Temple, we at present know only that Thomas, LL. D., m. ——, dau. of —— Green, LL. D., and had issue ; and Miles, of Dover, had three wives, and two sons and one daughter by the first, the eldest son called Miles. (Hist. of Leicestershire, IV., 960.)

We may expect from Mr. Nichols, in succeeding articles, a full investigation of the descendants of these two brothers.

As at present advised the American branch can be traced only to Capt. Robert Temple, who was largely interested, in 1718, in bringing over the Scotch-Irish colonists to the Kennebec. We find incidental mention by him of the fact that his uncle was Nathaniel White of Plymouth, England. On our Boston Records, Robert Temple and Dorcas Courtney were published 14 Dec., 1715, but we do not know if this were our Captain. He certainly married 11 Aug., 1721, Mehitable Nelson, dau. of John and Elizabeth (Tailer) Nelson, and granddaughter of Robert Nelson, by his wife Mary, sister of Sir Thomas Temple of Nova Scotia.

By her Capt. Robert Temple had Margaret, bapt. 5 April, 1723; Thomas, bapt. 27 March, 1726; Elizabeth, bapt. 9 April, 1727; Robert, bapt. 10 March, 1728; Rebecca, bapt. 13 April, 1729; Mehitable, bapt. 20 Sept., 1730; JOHN, bapt. 16 April, 1732; Agnes, bapt. 28 July, 1734; and William, bapt. 14 Sept., 1735.

Capt. Robert Temple was buried 17 April, 1754, and his widow died 23 Dec., 1775, aged 84. Of his three sons, Robert m. Harriet, dau. of Gov. Shirley, and left three daughters. John was the eighth baronet, and William, who was probably a Councillor for New Hampshire, in 1761, left a son Robert, who died in 1833, leaving sons Robert Emmett, Charles, and William Grenville, all of New York.

Sir John Temple was, in December, 1761, appointed Surveyor General of the Customs in the Northern District of America, which he held till 1767, when he was appointed, with Henry Hulton, William Burch, Charles Paxton, and John Robinson, Commissioner of the Customs, salary £500 each. In 1774 he was superseded by Benjamin Hallowell. From 1768 to 1774, Temple was also Lieut.-Governor of New Hampshire, and probably held the appointment earlier. He was succeeded by Edward Foy. In 1786 he was Consul-General for Great Britain, in America, and held this post till his death in November, 1798.

In his Address at Bowdoin College, Hon. Robert C. Winthrop stated that Temple was, in December, 1771, "appointed Surveyor-General of the Customs in England, and that at his dismissal in 1774 he lost appointments worth upwards of £1000 per annum, and several very honorary appointments under the Crown." We do not find any record of this office, and it may be a mistake, for his appointment in December, 1761, to the office here.

In the chancel of St. Paul's Church, Broadway, New York, is a tablet, bearing the Temple arms, and the following inscription:

SACRED TO THE MEMORY OF
SIR JOHN TEMPLE, BAR^{T.}
CONSUL GENERAL
TO THE UNITED STATES OF AMERICA,
FROM HIS BRITANNIC MAJESTY,
THE FIRST APPOINTMENT TO THIS COUNTRY
AFTER ITS INDEPENDENCE.
DIED IN THE CITY OF NEW YORK,
NOVEMBER THE 17TH, 1798,
AGED 67.

We have not, as yet, seen any extended obituary of Sir John, published at the time, though such must have appeared.

Sir John married, 20 January, 1767, Elizabeth, dau. of Gov. James Bowdoin, and had sons, Grenville, born 16 October, 1768, and James Bowdoin, b. 7 June, 1776, and daughters Elizabeth Bowdoin, who m. Thomas Lindall Winthrop, Lieutenant-Governor of Massachusetts, and Augusta, wife of William L. Palmer.

Of these, Sir Grenville Temple, ninth baronet, married Elizabeth, daughter of Samuel and Elizabeth (Cheever) Hendley, widow of Thomas Russell. They were published at Boston, 21 February, 1797.   She was b. 6 September, 1744, m. Thomas Russell, 2 May, 1765.   By this wife Sir Grenville Temple had Grenville, b. 20 July, 1799; John, b. 1801; Elizabeth Augusta, m. Major-General Byam; Augusta Grenville, died young; and Matilda Margaret.

Sir Grenville Temple married, 2d, Maria Augusta, dau. of Frederick Manners, and widow of Sir Thomas Rumbold. He died in 1829.   His son was

Sir Grenville Temple Temple, tenth baronet, who m. 5 May, 1829, Mary, dau. of George Baring, Esq., who d. in 1847, by whom he had Grenville Leofric, b. 5 Feb. 1830; George Ernest A., b. 4 Jan., 1832, d. young; Algar Bowdoin, b. 25 May, 1833; Napoleon Grenville D'Evreux, b. 2 July, 1839; George Grenville; Blanche A.; Rosalie Milicent; and Eleanor.

He died, and was succeeded by his son, Sir Grenville Leofric Temple, eleventh baronet.

COAT ARMOR IN NEW YORK.

[By the kindness of Robert Bolton, Esq., the well-known historian of West Chester County, New York, we are enabled to present the following examples of coats-of-arms, used in that locality, before A. D. 1750.   We regret that the late date at which we have received this valuable communication compels us to assign it this position, but it has seemed best to place it in this volume as a commencement of the examination of a new and very important field.—ED.]

"After a close search I can only find the following coats-of-arms borne by West Chester families, prior to 1750, which can be well authenticated, viz., Allaire, De Lancey, Carpenter, Heathcote, Jay, Morris, Pell, Philipse, Van Cortlandt, and Wetmore.

1. ALLAIRE. ——, a bend between three estoilles in chief, and as many demi-spears in base, a crescent for difference. Crest, the coronet of a viscount of France. [Borne by Alexander Allaire, Esq., of New Rochelle, 1708, the son of Pierre Allaire of La Rochelle.]

2. DE LANCEY. D'or à un aigle de sable, ayant les ailes étendues et chargé sur l'estomac d'un écusson d'azur, à trois lances rangées en pale, les pointes en haut. [Borne by Etienne de Lancey of Caen, Normandy, 1681, descended of the ancient house of De Lanci.] Present arms, Azure, a lance in pale with a flag, its point in chief, debruised of a bar *or*. Crest, a sinister arm in armour, embowed, holding a standard with a flag. Motto, certum vote finem. [Borne by Hon. James de Lancey of Mamaroneck, 1744, eldest son of Etienne de Lancey.]

3. HEATHCOTE. Ermine, three pomeis, each charged with a cross *or*. Crest, a mural crown azure, a pomme as in the arms, between two wings displayed, ermine. Motto, Deus prosperat justos. [Borne by Hon. Caleb Heathcote, Lord of the Manor of Scarsdale, 1701, sixth son of Gilbert Heathcote, Esq., of Chesterfield in Scarsdale, Derbyshire, England.]

4. JAY. D'azur, au chevron d'or, en chief un demi-soliel splendant, entre deux de même en point, un roc propre surmonté par oiseaux. Crest, cœurs unis. [Borne by Augustus Jay of Rye, 1745, a native of La Rochelle, of

the house of Le Jay of Poictou.]   The present crest is a cross mounted on three grades or steps.   Motto, Deo Duce Perseverandum.

5.   MORRIS.   Quarterly, 1st and 4th.   Gules, a lion rampant reguardant or; 2nd and 3d, or, three ogresses or pellets barwise.   Crest, a castle in flames.   Motto, Tandem vincitur.   [Borne by Hon. Lewis Morris, Lord of the Manor of Morrisania, 1697.]

6.   PELL.   Ermine, on a canton dexter azure, a pelican or, vulned gules.   Crest, a chaplet vert.   [Borne by Hon. John Pell, Lord of the Manor of Pelham, 1687.]

7.   PHILIPSE.   Azure, a demi-lion, surmounted by a ducal coronet or, rising out of a ducal coronet.   Crest, a demi-lion, rising out of a viscount's coronet, argent, surmounted by a ducal coronet or.   Motto, Quod tibi vis fieri facias.   [Borne by Hon. Frederick Philipse, Lord of the Manor of Philipsburgh, 1693.]

8.   VAN CORTLANDT.   Argent, the wings or arms of a windmill, saltirewise sable, voided of the field, five estoilles gules.   Crest, an estoile gules, between two wings elevated argent.   Motto, Virtus sibi munus.   [Borne by Hon. Stephanus Van Cortlandt, Lord of the Manor of Cortlandt, 1697.]

9.   WETMORE.   Argent, on a chief azure, three martlets or.   Crest, a falcon proper.   Motto, virtus, libertas et patria.   [Borne by Rev. James Wetmore of Rye, 1726.]

R. B.

THE

HERALDIC JOURNAL;

RECORDING THE

𝔄rmorial 𝔅earings and 𝔊enealogies

OF

AMERICAN FAMILIES.

VOLUME III.

BOSTON:

WIGGIN & LUNT, PUBLISHERS,

221 WASHINGTON STREET.

1867.

PREFACE.

The third volume of the Heraldic Journal will, it is hoped, be found as valuable as either of the earlier ones, while the great variety of articles and range of subjects may perhaps make it even more interesting. The limits of New England have been more often crossed in search of information, and in New England the other states than Massachusetts have contributed a larger share than before. We earnestly call on antiquaries to send us faithful copies of arms and epitaphs from such grave-yards as are in their neighborhood, and we will thankfully receive any communications suited to the purposes of our work. It is the present intention of the publishing committee to continue the Journal for another year, during which we hope to make further inroads on the various files of original wills, contained in the County Probate Offices.

Among the articles in this volume, to which particular attention is called, and of which careful criticism is desired, are those on the Manors of New York, Herbert Pelham, and the Churches and Families of Virginia. We are desirous to obtain positive information concerning the Southern families, who are entitled to bear arms, but there seems to be almost nothing in print relating to them.

The Editor of the present volume begs the indulgence of the subscribers for any short-comings, which may have been noticed. Experience, of which he had had very little, in the duties of an editor is of great service, and he gladly resigns the charge of this work to the more able hands of the chairman of the committee, who will edit the volume for 1868.

GENERAL INDEX.

Arms, engraved :

Andrews, 160; Arnold, 167 ; Baily, 63; Barrett, 155; Baynton, 119;
Bell, 9; Brattle, 42 ; Brodhead, 1; Bromfield, 187; Brown, 14, 33 ;
Calvert, 21; Campbell, 151, 153; Chaloner, 66 ; Coffin, 54 ; Cranston,
59; Curwen, 33 ; Digby, 33 ; Dumaresq, 97 ; Ellery, 111; Fenner, 162 ;
Fiske, 124 ; Fitch, 31 ; Franklin, 67, 117; Freebody, 68 ; Gardner, 113 ;
Gibbs, 11, 165; Gidley, 6; Goulding, 10; Greene, 27 ; Harris, 158 ;
Hoar, 153; Hutchinson, 104; Lynde, 31 ; Merritt, 168 ; Milbourne, 93 ;
Moody, 92; Newdigate, 33; Oliver, 31; Paddy, 140; Paine, 189;
Parsons, 91; Pelham, 84 ; Penn, 140; Pownall, 56; Quincy, 179; San-
ford, 61; Schuyler, 145; Sears, 115; Sims, 118; Smith, 33 ; Tew, 161 ;
Thurston, 65 ; Tyler, 83 ; Wanton, 8, 64; Ward, 116; Wensley, 142.

Arms, engraved, but not identified : 89, 90, 91, 92, 174, 175.

Arms, described :

Apthorp, 23 ; Arnold, 18 ; Barrett, 45 ; Blackwell, 94 ; Blyth, 157 ;
Boylston, 23 ; Brenton, 174 ; Browne, 24 ; Charnock, 110 ; Cook, quarterings, 25, 26 ; Cortlandt, 71 ; Dumaresq, quarterings, 97, 98; Erving,
23 ; Foster, 22 ; Francis, 18 ; Godfrey, 177 ; Gorges, 176 ; Greenleaf,
22 ; Greenwood, 110 ; Gurdon, 176 ; Hall, 23 ; Harrison, 177 ; Heathcote, 73; Hooke, 177 ; Huger, 47 ; Hull, 46; Inglis, 17 ; Jeffries, 23;
Johnson, 45 ; Livingston, 78 ; Ludwell, 95; McCall, 17; Middleton, 96 ;
Morris, 72 ; Nanfan, 26 ; Paine, 178 ; Pell, 76 ; Philips, 23 ; Pinckney,
76; Proby, 46 ; Randolph, 48 ; Revere, 22 ; Roome, 47 ; Saltonstall, 22,
176 ; Sanger, 23 ; Southack, 47 ; Stevens, 110 ; Swan, 23 ; Swift, 18 ;
Symmes, 110 ; Thomas, 22 ; Tyler, 22 ; Wallace, 186 ; Wentworth,
172 ; Whalley, 177 ; White, 18 ; Williams, 47.

Antiquity of Heraldry, by W. S. Ellis, reviewed, 34.

Baronets, American, 182.

Book Plates, early American, 21.

Calvert, Baron Baltimore, 18.

Coote, Earl of Bellomont, 24.

Coat-Armour, early paintings of, 31.

Genealogies :

Archer, 71 ; Brenton, 173 ; Brodhead, 1 ; Bromfield, 187 ; Calvert, 18 ;
Campbell, 151 ; Charnock, 107 ; Coffin, 49 ; Cortlandt, 70, 150 ; Coote,
24 ; Cranston, 59 ; Dumaresq, 97 ; Fiske, 120 ; Gage, 148 ; Gardiner,

81 ; Gibbs, 12, 166 ; Greene, 27 ; Heathcote, 73 ; Johnson, 182 ; Livingston, 76 ; Lloyd, 82 ; Morris, 72 ; Paine, 189 ; Pelham, 84 : Pell, 75 ; Penn, 135 ; Philipse, 78 ; Pownall, 56 ; Quincy, 178 ; Sanford, 62 ; Schuyler, 145 ; Temple, 43 ; Tyler, 83 ; Wallace, 184 ; Wentworth, 170.
Grants of Arms :
    Coffin, 54 ; Fiske, 124.
Johnson, Isaac, 43.
Manors of New York, and their Lords, 69.
Monumental Inscriptions :
    Newport, R I., 6–15, 58–69, 111–117 ; Philadelphia, 118 ; Burlington, N. J., 119 ; Concord, Mass., 153–157 ; Providence, R. I., 157–169.
Notes and Queries :
    Barrell arms, 45 ; Carolina herald, 46 ; Hull arms, 46 ; Proby arms, 46 ; Southack arms, 47 ; grants to Americans, 47 ; Randolph family, 48 ; Brodhead arms, 94 ; Blackwell arms, 94 ; Ludwell arms, 95 ; Moody family, 95 ; Middleton family, 96 ; Heraldic terms, 143 ; Child arms, 190 ; Oldmixon family, 190 ; Hull arms, 191 ; Heraldic queries, 191 ; Chambers and Palmer tomb, 192.
Quincy, Josiah, Life of, Reviewed, 178.
Seals of the Governors of Massachusetts :
    Bernard, 4 ; Pownall, 56 ; Hutchinson, 104 ; Gage, 148.
Shippen Family Papers, 15.
Suffolk Wills, 84–94.
Titled Loyalists, 169.
Virginia, old Churches and Families, by Bishop Meade, 126.
Winthrop Papers, reviewed, 174.

INDEX OF NAMES.

Ambler, 127.
Andrews, 160.
Archer, 71, 128.
Armistead, 132.
Arnold, 167.

Bacon, 130.
Balch, 15.
Baring, 17.
Barradall, 128.
Barrell, 45.
Barrett, 155, 156.
Baylor, 134.
Bayly, 62, 63.
Baynton, 119, 144.
Bell, 9.
Bernard, 4.
Bingham, 17.
Brattle, 42.
Bray, 129.
Brenton, 60, 173.
Brinckman, 94.
Brodhead, 1, 94.
Browne, 14, 15, 32, 134.
Buckmaster, 67, 117.
Burwell, 130.

Callender, 23.
Calvert, 18.
Campbell, 151.
Carter, 131.
Cary, 131.
Chaloner, 66, 67.
Chambers, 192.
Charnock, 107.
Child, 190.
Coffin, 49.
Cole, 129.
Coote, 24.
Cortlandt, 70.
Cranston, 7, 59.
Cromp, 46.
Curwin, 33.

DeLancy, 150.
Digby, 33.

Diggs, 129.
Dumaresq, 97.

Ellery, 64, 111, 112.
Ellis, 34.
Everard, 130.

Fairfax, 131.
Fenner, 164.
Fisher, 89.
Fiske, 120.
Fowke, 134.
Foye, 151.
Francis, 16.
Franklin, 117.
Freebody, 68.

Gage, 148.
Gardiner, 81.
Gardner, 114.
Gibbs, 11, 166.
Gidley, 6, 7.
Godfrey, 177.
Gorges, 176.
Goulding, 9, 10.
Greene, 27.

Harris, 21, 158.
Harrison, 177.
Hayward, 90.
Heathcote, 73, 74
Hiller, 93.
Hoar, 153, 154.
Hooke, 177.
Howard, 92.
Huger, 47.
Hull, 46, 190.
Hunt, 92.
Hurd, 22, 23, 31.
Hutchinson, 105.

Inglis, 17.

Jacqueline, 127.
Jekyll, 16.
Johnson, 44, 182.

Johnston, 22, 31.
Joyliffe, 91.

Kemble, 150.
Kidder, 130.

Landon, 132.
Lawson, 92.
Lee, 132, 133.
Leete, 177.
Livingston, 76, 78.
Lloyd, 82.
Ludwell, 95, 128, 133.
Lynde, 33.

Marion, 93.
McCall, 16.
Meade, 126, 129.
Merritt, 169.
Middleton, 96.
Milborn, 93.
Moody, 89, 90, 92, 95.
Morland, 5.
Morris, 72.

Nanfan, 26.
Nelson, 129.
Newdigate, 32.

Oldmixon, 190

Paddy, 140.
Page, 127.
Paine, 178, 189.
Palmes, 192.
Park, 128.
Parker, 177.
Parsons, 91.
Pelham, 84, 89.
Pell, 75.
Penn, 135.
Perkins, 152.
Philipse, 79.
Pinckney, 76.
Pownall, 56.
Proby, 46.

Quincy, 178.

Randolph, 48, 127.
Rickson, 89.
Robinson, 130, 131.
Roome, 47.

Sanford, 61, 107.
Schuyler, 145.
Scott, 134.
Sears, 115.
Shippen, 15.
Sims, 118.
Skinner, 150.

Smith, 34.
Southack, 47.
Spotswood, 128.
Swift, 17.

Taylor, 131.
Temple, 43.
Tew, 162.
Thompson, 131.
Thurston, 65.
Tyler, 83.
Tyley, 93.

Vally, 89.

Vergoose, 92.

Wallace, 184.
Wanton, 8, 64.
Ward, 117.
Washington 134.
Watson, 43.
Wensley, 141, 142.
Wentworth, 170.
Williams, 47.
Willing, 17.
Winslow, 90, 91.

Young, 159, 160.

THE

HERALDIC JOURNAL;

RECORDING THE ARMORIAL BEARINGS AND GENEALOGIES OF AMERICAN FAMILIES.

NO. XVII. JANUARY, 1867.

FAMILY OF BRODHEAD.

A Sketch prepared in 1854 by JOHN M. BRODHEAD, of Washington, D. C.

The ancestor of the Brodhead family is said to have come from Germany to England, and to have settled at Royston, in Yorkshire, in the reign of Henry VIII. On the 28th Feb., 1610, King James I. granted the manor of Burton, or Monk Britton, in the West Riding of Yorkshire, to John Brodhead and George Wood, the principal freeholders of that place.

Daniel Brodhead, grand-nephew of John the above-named grantee, was the ancestor of those who bear the name in the United States. From family papers in the possession of Rev. Jacob Brodhead, D. D., it appears that he was born in Yorkshire, married Ann Tye, was an officer in the army of King Charles II., and accompanied the expedition of Col. Nicolls from England in 1664. He was appointed Commander-in-Chief of the military forces at Kingston the next year, 14 Sept. 1665, where he remained till his death. By his wife, Ann Tye, he had three sons, Daniel, who died unm. in 1705, Charles and Richard.

Richard Brodhead (son of Daniel) was born in Marbletown, N. Y., in 1666. His first wife was a Miss Jansen, his second Wyntie Paulding. He had an only son, Daniel.

Daniel Brodhead (son of Richard) was born at Marbletown, N. Y., in 1693, married Hester Wyngart, moved to Pennsylvania in 1737. He settled on the river, now called on the maps, Brodhead's Creek, near Stroudsburg, Monroe Co., where he was a large landholder, portions of his estate remaining in the possession of his descendants to this day. He died on a visit to Bethlehem, July 22, 1755. He was a man of great energy and intrepidity, and is mentioned in the History of Pennsylvania, as remaining with his sons and defending himself most stoutly from an attack of the Indians, when the whole of the surrounding country had been abandoned.

Daniel Brodhead left four sons —

1. Gen. Daniel Brodhead of the Revolutionary Army, who commanded at Fort Pitt in 1780–81. He married the widow of Governor Mifflin, and left several daughters, but no son. His correspondence with General Washington during the Revolution is on file in the United States Department of State, and is very interesting. Quite a number of letters from General Washington to him are in possession of the family.

2. Garrett Brodhead, also an officer of the Revolutionary Army.

3. Col. Luke Brodhead, who was commissioned on the same day with his brother, the General, served through the Revolutionary War, was the intimate friend of Lafayette, and was desperately wounded at the battle of Brandywine. He died at Stroudsburg.

4. Charles Brodhead, who married and moved to the State of New York. He was father of Hon. John C. Brodhead, M. C., and of Hon. Daniel Brodhead of New York.

The third son, Col. Luke Brodhead, married Elizabeth Harrison, and was father of Hon. John Brodhead of New Hampshire, who was born near Stroudsburg, Oct. 22, 1770, and died at Newmarket, N. H., April 7, 1838. He served in the Senate and other offices in New Hampshire, and was several years a member of Congress. He married Mary, daughter of Thomas Dodge, and granddaughter of William and Rebecca (Appleton) Dodge. She was born Aug. 27, 1783. Their children were —

1. Col. Daniel Dodge Brodhead, late Navy Agent, Boston, m. Almena Cutter.

2. John Montgomery Brodhead, Second Comptroller, Washington, graduated M. D. at Dartmouth College, August, 1825, married Mary Josephine, only daughter of Rev. Thomas Waterman, formerly of London.

3. Elizabeth Harrison Brodhead, married Rev. Samuel Norris, of Dorchester, N. H.

4. Anna Mudge Brodhead, married Alexander Ewins, of Salem, N. H.

5. Joseph Crawford Brodhead, Deputy Naval Officer, New York, married Sarah, daughter of Capt. John Wheeler, of Oxford, N. H.

6.   George Hamilton Brodhead, of New York, married Julia Phelps, of N. Y.

7.   Mehitable Smith Brodhead, married Wm. Weeks, of Greenland, N. H.

8.   Mary Rebecca Brodhead, married Rev. James Pike, of Salisbury, Mass.

9.   Hon. Thornton Fleming Brodhead, Postmaster at Detroit, Michigan.   He was an officer in the Mexican War, in most of the battles up to the capture of Mexico, was brevetted " for distinguished gallantry on the field of battle," and has been Senator in the Legislature of Michigan.   He married Archange, daughter of General William Macomb.

10.   Josiah Adams Brodhead, married Lizzie, daughter of Otis Tufts.

Some account of the English branch of the family may be read in the Peerage, under the Baronetcy of Brinckman.   The arms are not found in English works on Heraldry , perhaps the explanation of this consists in the German origin of the family.

OFFICIAL SEALS.

Francis Bernard, the next Governor of Massachusetts, was, says BURKE, the descendant of Godfrey Bernard of Wanford, co. York, living *temp*. Henry III.   Francis Bernard was in 1769 created a Baronet.   He married in 1741, Amelia, dau. of Stephen Offley, and had sons John, Thomas, Scrope, and William, who d. unm. in 1776, and daughters Jane, wife of Charles White, Amelia, wife of

Capt. Benjamin Baker, Frances Elizabeth, m. Rev. Richard King, and Julia, m. Rev. Joseph Smith.

Sir Francis died 16 June, 1779, and was succeeded in the title by his three sons successively,—Sir John dying unm. in 1809, and Sir Thomas, a graduate of Harvard in 1767, dying *s. p. m.* in 1818.

Sir Scrope Bernard, fourth baronet, m. 26 July, 1785, Harriet, only child of William Morland, and in 1811 assumed the additional name of Morland. He d. 18 April, 1830. His children were William, who d. unm., Francis, Thomas Tyringham, Richard Scrope, d. unm., Margaret, wife of Henry Pigott, and Mary Anne.

Thomas Tyringham Bernard m. Sophia Charlotte Williams, and had a son David Williams Bernard, the only son in that generation. The present (fifth) baronet is Sir Francis Bernard-Morland, the second son of Sir Scrope, mentioned above.

The arms of Bernard are, Argent, a bear rampant sable, muzzled and collared gold. They are borne quarterly with Morland, Azure, semée of leopards jessant-de-lys, a griffin segreant gold. Crests, a demi-bear, as in the arms, for Bernard; a griffin's head, wings endorsed azure, semée of crosses-crosslet and fleurs-de-lis, alternately, gold, for Morland. *Motto*, Bear and forbear.

[NOTE. The present family, owing to the change of name, place the Morland arms in the first and fourth quarters.]

MONUMENTAL INSCRIPTIONS.

NEWPORT, R. I.

The little grave-yard by the side of Trinity Church in Newport contains eight stones, on which are found Heraldic Insignia, giving the arms of only five families. One stone in the long-trodden path to the church-door bears the remains of a similar inscription, but the feet of many generations have left nothing legible, but a chevron in the shield and the name John.

I.

Here lieth Interred the Body
of Sarah the wife of John Gidley Junr.
& daughter of John Shackmaple Esqr.
oby! ye 12th of May Anno Domini
1727 Æ 23 Years.
A While She Shone A While My Sight She Cheerd
But soon the Short Liv'd Blessing Disappear'd.

II.

The same arms are carved above this and the next epitaph.

Beneath this lieth Mary who
was the Daughter of Colon^l. John
Cranston & wife of John Gidley
Aged 24 Years died Octob^r. ye 3 1737.

Great were her Ornaments Because Divine
And in all other Virtues she did shine
From hence she's gone untill the Judgment Day
And then her Blessed Soul will ioine her Clay
To be forever with the Glorious Three
And live with God to all Eternity.

III.

IN MEMORY
of John Gidley Esqr. who
departed this Life Septe ye 30
1744 aged 44 Years He having
receiv'd the Fatal Citation for Death
by a violent Explosion of Gun-Powder
eleven Days before He expired.

The following is read on another stone, which does not bear the arms of the family :—

John Gidley of Exon in
Devon Great Britain Fuller
who departed this life April
the 28, 1718 Ætatis suæ 44.

This name is not mentioned in Savage's Genealogical Dictionary, but from the Records of the Colony of Rhode

Island we know that John Gidley was admitted a Freeman in 1723, and in 1742 was appointed Judge of Admiralty during the absence in England of the regular
official. From Burke's General Armory we learn that
the arms of Gidley of Honiton, co. Devon, are, Or, a
castle sa. in a bordure of the second bezantée ; crest, a
griffin's head or, wings elevated sa. bezantée.

IV.

In Memory of
WILLIAM WANTON Esqr.
Son of the Honble Wm Wanton
Esqr. who departed this Life
the 18th day of July A. D. 1735
in the 39 Year of his Age.

On page 46 of Vol. II. may be seen another instance
of the use of these arms by a member of the same family.

V.

In Memory of Martha
the wife of M^r. William Bell
died Decem^r y^e 1st 1737 In y^e
36th Year of her age.

In Gore's roll are the arms of Bell of Boston, viz.,
Azure, a fess ermine between three bells or. Whether
the tincture of these be the same, and whether William
belonged to the same family, we cannot say.

———

VI.

IN MEMORY
of Mr George Goulding
who departed this life
the 24th of February
Anno Domini 1748
Ætatis Suæ 25.
Mortuus en Moneo.

VII.

These arms form part also of the foregoing inscription.

IN MEMORY OF
George Goulding Esqr. who died
Novem^r. y^e 24th A^o. D. 1742 In y^e
57th Year of his Age.

Religion that exalts the noble mind,
Makes Man Human, Generous, Just and kind,
Guided thro' Publick Life this Patriots way
To the blest Mansions of eternal Day.

George Goulding the elder seems to have been a person of some importance in the Colony; he was often Deputy for Newport in the Legislature. In Burke we find the arms of Golden, Gu. a chevron arg. between three bezants; those of Golding are, Gu. a chevron or between three bezants.

VIII.

This Monument is Erected by
GEORGE GIBBS Merchant
to the Memory of His Amiable Consort
SUSANNAH
Daughter of JOSEPH SCOTT Esq[r]
She departed this life June 24th 1767
in the 22[d] Year of her Age
After a long Sickness which She Sustained
with Patience Fortitude and Resignation
to the will of God.

Divine Persuasions with a heavenly Grace
Dwelt on her Lips and Pity on her Face :
Behold the Christian in the last great Strife
Recount her Actions, in the close of Life.

Here also lieth their Son George Gibbs
who died June 13th 1767 aged 11 Weeks.

This family is traced back to James Gibbs of Froome, in the county of Somerset, England. He had a wife Sarah, and the following children, but their place of birth does not appear in the record.

William, b. 24 May, 1691, d. 27 Dec. 1691.

Sarah, b. 14 March, 1693.

George, b. 13 August, 1695.

John, b. 24 Oct. 1699, was of Bristol, R. I.

Ann, b. 18 April, 1702, m. Simon Tilley of Bristol.

Jane, b. 24 Feb. 1708, m. James Fowler of Bristol.

James, b. 14 Nov. 1711, was of Bristol.

James Gibbs, the settler, seems to have lived first at Newport, whence he moved to Bristol in 1721, probably leaving his son George at the former place. James died 1 June, 1731. His will mentions his wife and the five children last born. He seems to have owned but little property, as five shillings is the principal legacy to each of his children. His widow d. 8 Oct. 1756, aged 82.

George Gibbs, the eldest surviving son, was of Newport. He married first Hannah dau. of Caleb Claggett of Bristol, by whom he had a dau. Hannah, who became wife of Jabez Champlin. His second wife was Ruth Hart, whom he married at Trinity Church, Newport, 19 Oct. 1733, and by whom he had the following children:—

George, b. 19 May, 1735.

James, b. 11 Sept. 1736, d. 23 July, 1737.

Sarah, b. 11 Jan. 1738, m. Oliver Champlin.

Ruth, b. 25 Oct. 1741, d. 25 Dec. 1741.

John, b. 11 April, 1743, d. 16 June, 1765.

Mary, b. 25 Nov. 1744, m. James Robinson.

Elizabeth, b. 21 Dec. 1746, m. Thomas Greene.

Ruth, b. 21 March, 1748, m. Samuel Whitehorne.

He d. 6 Aug. 1755.

George, the only surviving son, m. first Susannah, dau. of Joseph Scott, who with her only child is buried under the tomb bearing the inscription printed. He m. secondly, 9 Oct. 1768, Mary, dau. of John Channing, of Newport, who was mother of several children, as follows :—

Susannah, b. 15 April, 1770, d. 10 Sept. 1790.

Mary, b. 3 May, 1772, d. 27 May, 1772.

Mary, b. 23 Sept. 1773.

George, b. 7 Jan. 1776.

Ruth, b. 7 Nov. 1778.

{ John, b. 27 June, 1784.

{ Sarah, b. 27 June, 1784.

Elizabeth, b. 10 Dec. 1786.

William Channing, b. 10 Feb. 1789.

Susannah, b. 28 Nov. 1792, d. in 1825.

He died 11 Oct. 1803, and his widow in Dec. 1824.

The arms carved on the tomb were borne by a family of the name in Massachusetts, which claims to be descended from an ancient stock of knightly rank in the county of Warwick, England. Those of Newport show no connection with this family, and cannot be said to show a proved right to the shield. The arms with various tinctures are attributed to families of the name in several counties in England, but the crest here used, viz., An arm embowed in armor ppr. garnished or, holding in the gauntlet a poleaxe arg., belongs to those of Hertfordshire.

The next and last inscription is found on a mural monument in the church, just outside the chancel. Be-

tween the arms and the epitaph is a portrait bust of the
Rev. Marmaduke Browne.

———

IX.

SUIVEZ RAIZON.

To the Memory of the Reverend Marmaduke Browne,
formerly Rector of this Parish,
a Man eminent for Talents, Learning and Religion,
who departed this life on the 19th of March 1771,
and of Anne his Wife, a Lady of uncommon Piety, and
suavity of Manners,
who died the 6th of January 1767.
This Monument was erected by their Son
Arthur Browne Esqr.
now Senior Fellow of Trinity College Dublin in Ireland,
and Representative in Parliament for the same,
In token of his Gratitude and affection to the best and
tenderest of Parents,
and for a place where

He spent his earliest and his happiest Days.
Heu! Quanto minus est
Cum aliis versari,
Quam tui meminisse.
MDCCXCV.

Sabine includes the Rev. Marmaduke Browne among the American Loyalists; but there seems to be no good reason for placing him there. His father was an Irishman, and the Rector of Trinity is called also a native of Ireland. A biography of Arthur, who raised the monument, may be read in Peterson's History of Rhode Island.

REVIEW.

Letters and Papers relating chiefly to the Provincial History of Pennsylvania, with some Notices of the Writers. Privately printed. Philadelphia: 1855.

These two volumes contain what are known as the Shippen Family Papers, which were edited by Thomas Balch. As we find herein many interesting particulars about the prominent families of Pennsylvania and Maryland, we have prepared the following synopsis.

The Shippens are traced to Edward Shippen, born in 1639, who came to Boston in 1668, was a Quaker, and removed to Philadelphia, where he died. He was the son of William[1] Shippen, and brother of William S., Rector of St. Mary's, Stockport, in Cheshire. Edward was thus uncle of William Shippen, a noted member of Parliament.

Edward[2] Shippen, Sr., had sons Edward[3] and Joseph[3] ;
the latter had sons Edward,[4] Joseph[4] and William.[4]   This
Edward[4] was the father of Edward,[5] Chief Justice of
Pennsylvania, and of Col. Joseph.[5]   A son of this Joseph[5]
was Henry[6] Shippen, a Judge of the Sixth District of
Pennsylvania.

Of the other families mentioned in this book, we will
cite the following.   Margaret, a grand-daughter of the
first Edward Shippen, m. John Jekyll, Collector of the
Port of Boston.   He was a nephew of Sir Joseph Jekyll,
Master of the Rolls.   Chief Justice Edward Shippen m.
Margaret, daughter of Tench Francis, of Philadelphia.
The family is traced to Philip Francis, Mayor of Plymouth in 1644.   His son was John Francis, Dean of
Leighlin, father of John Francis, Dean of Lismore.   This
last m. a Miss Tench, and had sons Tench, Richard and
Philip ; this Philip was the father of Sir Philip Francis,
well known in connection with the "Junius" contro-
versy.   Tench Francis had nine children ; one of his
descendants was John Brown Francis, Governor of Rhode
Island ; and another was Philip Francis Thomas, Governor of Maryland.

Margaret Shippen, daughter of Edward Shippen and
Margaret Francis, m. the infamous Benedict Arnold.
Their descendants still survive in England.

Samuel McCall, of Glasgow, merchant, m. a daughter
of Robert Dundas of Arnistown, and had a son Robert,
who removed to Virginia, and was the father of George
McCall, who settled in Philadelphia about A. D. 1701.
George McCall had by his wife Ann Yeates, a daughter
Catherine, who married John Inglis, Collector of the Port

of Philadelphia, and has descendants in England. One son, John Inglis, was Rear Admiral in the British navy.

Connected with the McCalls were the Swifts, John and Joseph, sons of John Swift and Mary White, who came here about A. D. 1746. John m. Magdalen, widow of Joseph McCall, and left numerous descendants.

Eleanor McCall, daughter of the before mentioned George, m. Andrew Elliot, Lieutenant Governor of New York. Their only daughter m. Admiral Robert Digby.

To return to an earlier generation. Anne Shippen, daughter of Joseph,[3] married in 1731 Charles Willing of Philadelphia. He was the son of Thomas and Anne (Harrison) Willing of Bristol, and grandson of Joseph and Ann (Lowle) Willing of Bristol. Charles Willing was Mayor of Philadelphia in 1748, and died in 1754. His son, Thomas Willing, also Mayor, Representative, President of the U. S. Bank, &c., m. Ann McCall, and had a daughter Ann, born in 1764, who m. Hon. Wm. Bingham, U. S. Senator. From this marriage came Anne Louisa Bingham (who m. Alexander Baring, Lord Ashburton), and her sister, Maria Matilda Bingham, who m. Henry Baring, brother of Alexander.

It is said that all of these families used coats-of-arms. They are described in the notes as follows:—

McCall. Gules, a fesse chequy argent and of the field, surmounting two arrows in saltire argent, points upward, all between three buckles of the same, and within a bordure indented or. Crest, a boot, thereon a spur, all proper. Motto, Dulce periculum.

Inglis. Azure, a lion rampant argent, on a chief

argent three stars azure. Crest, a demi-lion argent, in his dexter paw a mullet or. Motto, Recte faciendo securus.

SWIFT. Or, a chevron barry nebulée argent and azure between three roebucks courant, proper.

WHITE. Gules, a bordure sable charged with eight estoiles or, on a canton ermines a lion rampant sable.

ARNOLD. Gules, three pheons argent, on a chief of the second, a bar nebulée azure. Crest, a demi-tiger sable bezantée, maned and tufted or, holding a broad arrow, its stick gules, feathers and pheon, argent. Motto, Nil desperandum.

FRANCIS. Per bend or and sable, a lion rampant counter-changed. Crest, an eagle displayed ermine, beaked and membered or.   W. H. W.

CALVERT, BARON BALTIMORE.

Burke's Genealogical History of the Extinct Peerages of the British Empire contains an account of this family, of which an abstract is here given. The first of the name appears to have been John Calvert, whose son, Leonard of Danbywiske, co. York, m. Alicia, daughter of John Crossland, and had a son George, b. in 1578.

This George, having served as secretary to Sir Robert Cecil, and afterwards as clerk to the Privy Council, received the honor of knighthood in 1617, and was appointed in the ensuing year secretary of state to the King, who employed him in the most important affairs, and in 1620 settled upon him a pension of £1000 a year, beyond his salary. Sir George resigned his post in 1624, on becoming Roman Catholic. The King continued him in the Privy Council, and having made him large grants of land in Ireland, elevated him to the peerage of that kingdom, 16 February, 1625, as Baron Baltimore, of Baltimore, co. Longford, Sir George being at the time representative in parliament for the university of Oxford. While secretary of state his lordship had obtained a grant of the province of Avalon in Newfoundland, with most extensive privileges, but after expending £25,000 in the settlement, he was obliged to abandon it in consequence of French encroachments. He thereupon received from King Charles a patent of Maryland, to him and his heirs forever, with the same title and royalties as in Avalon, to hold in common soccage as of the manor of Windsor, paying yearly to the crown two Indian arrows at Windsor Castle upon Easter Tuesday, and the fifth part of the gold and silver ore. His lordship did not live to see the grant pass the great seal, and his son Cecil, second Lord Baltimore, had it made out in his own name, bearing date 20 June, 1632. The province of Maryland was so named by the King, in honor of his Queen, Henrietta Maria. His lordship m. Anne, daughter of George Mynne of Hertingfordbury, co. Hertford, by whom he had

Cecil, his successor.

Leonard, appointed by his brother in 1633 first governor of Maryland, jointly with Jeremy Hawley and Thomas Cornwallis.

Anne, m. William Peaseley.

Grace, m. Sir Robert Talbot, of Carton, co. Kildare. The baron d. 15 April, 1632, and was succeeded by his eldest son,

Cecil, second baron, who m. Anne, third daughter of Thomas, Lord Arundel of Wardour, and was succeeded by his son,

John, third baron, who was present in King James' Irish Parliament in 1689, and dying soon after, left a son and successor,

Charles, fourth baron. This nobleman was outlawed for high treason in Ireland, although he had never been in that kingdom, but King William, upon his lordship's representation, caused the outlawry to be reversed, 25 January, 1691. He died 21 February, 1714, and was succeeded by his son,

Benedict Leonard, fifth baron, who had conformed to the established church in 1713, and was afterwards returned to parliament for Harwich. His lordship m. 2 June, 1698, Lady Charlotte Lee, eldest daughter of Edward Henry, first Earl of Lichfield, and had

Charles, his successor.

Benedict Leonard, M. P. for Harwich, and governor of Maryland, d. 1 June, 1732.

Edward Henry, commissary-general and president of the council of Maryland.

Cecil, b. 1702.

Charlotte, m. Thomas Breerwood, and d. in 1744.

Jane, m. —— Hyde, and d. in 1778.

His lordship d. 16 April, 1715, and was succeeded by his eldest son,

Charles, b. 29 September, 1699, sixth baron, who filled several high official employments between the years 1731 and 1745, and represented for some time the county of Surrey in parliament. His lordship m. 20 July, 1730,

Mary, youngest daughter of Sir Theodore Janssen, Bart., of Wimbledon, co. Surrey, and had issue,

Frederick, his heir.

Caroline, m. Sir Robert Eden, Bart., governor of Maryland, grandfather of the present baronet, Sir Wm. Eden.

Louisa, m. John Browning of Lincolnshire.

He d. 24 April, 1751, and was succeeded by his son,

Frederick, seventh baron, b. 6 February, 1732, who m. in 1753, Lady Diana Egerton, daughter of Scrope, Duke of Bridgwater, but died without issue at Naples, 4 September, 1771, when the title became *extinct*.

The arms borne by the family were as above, Paly of six, or and sable, a bend counter-changed. The accompanying wood-cut is copied from the shilling issued by Cecil, second Lord Baltimore, as the currency of his province of Maryland. Around it is the motto of the province, " Crescite et Multiplicamini."

BOOK-PLATES.

By the kindness of Edward D. Harris, Esq., of this city, we have had an opportunity to examine a collection of book-plates made by his father, Thaddeus William Harris, the late Librarian of Harvard, and his grandfather, Rev. William Thaddeus Harris.

Several of them are by Hurd, Johnston, and a later artist, Callender. We give the following description of them :—

1. Of Isaac Foster, engraved by Hurd. Argent, a chevron between three bugle-horns, stringed, sable. Crest, a dexter arm vambraced and embowed, the hand grasping a dart.

2. Of William Greenleaf, by Hurd. Argent, a chevron between three leaves erect, vert. Crest, a dove holding in its bill an olive branch.

3. Of Joseph Tyler, by T. Johnson. Gules, on a fesse gold, between three cats passant argent, a cross moline inclosed by two crescents of the field. Crest, a demi-cat rampant and erased gold, charged on the side with a cross-crosslet fitchée gules, springing from a crescent of the last. Motto, Fari quæ sentiat.

[NOTE. I think the field should have been sable, not gules, to conform with the coat described by Burke. Some account of the family is in Bridgman's King's Chapel Epitaphs.]

4. Of Paul Rivoire,—possibly by Hurd, though unsigned. Argent, three bars gules, over all a bend sinister (of the field?), charged with three fleurs-de-lys. Crest, an annulet. [The name is now spelt Revere.]

5. Of Walter Saltonstall. Argent, a bend gules, between two eagles displayed sable. Crest, out of a ducal coronet, a demi pelican vulning herself.

6. Of Isaiah Thomas,—doubtless by Johnston, though unsigned. Argent, on a cross sable five crescents of the field. Crest, a greyhound's head couped gold, collared and ringed ——. Motto, Nec elatus nec dejectus.

7. Of Dr. John Jeffries, by Callender. Sable, a lion rampant between three scaling-ladders argent. Crest, a castle, double towered.

8. Of James Swan, by Callender. Vert, three swans gold. Impaling, argent, on a bend gules between three roundles, as many swans gold, and on a canton sinister azure, a demi ram—debruised of a baton, two fleurs-de-lys in chief. Crest, out of a coronet, a dexter arm vambraced and embowed, the hand holding a helmet. Motto, Dum spiro, spero.

9. Of James Hall. Argent, a chevron between three talbot's heads erased sable. Crest, a talbot's head erased, bezantée.

10. Of William Hall. Quarterly, 1st and 4th. Sable, three talbot's heads erased argent, collared gules. 2nd and 3rd. Sable, three leopard's heads jessant-de-lys, gold. Crest, a talbot's head erased sable, collared —— ?

There are also in the volume several trickings of arms; among them the Phillips (argent, a lion rampant sable ducally gorged and chained gold); the Sanger (argent, on a pale between two demi-peacocks erased gules, three crescents of the field); and the Apthorp (per pale nebuly argent and azure, two mullets pierced in fesse, counter-changed.)

A book-plate of the Boylston Medical Library of Cambridge, by Callender, shows the Boylston arms. Gules, six cross-crosslets fitchée argent, on a chief gold three pellets, charged, the centre one with a fleur-de-lys, the others each with a lion passant gardant.

11. The arms of William Erving, by Callender. Argent, three holly branches each of as many leaves, proper,

banded gules, within a bordure chequy vert and of the
field.   Crest, a dexter arm vambraced and embowed, the
hand grasping a sword.   Motto, " Quo fata vocant," and
" Flourish in all weathers."   W. H. W.

[To these we may add a book-plate of Thos. Brown,
engraved by Hurd.   The arms are ——— on a chevron,
between three leopard's heads cabossed or, as many escallops ———.   Crest, an eagle's head erased or.   Motto,
" En esperance je vie."]

COOTE, EARL OF BELLOMONT.

In the first volume of the Heraldic Journal was printed
a pedigree of the family of Richard, Earl of Bellomont,
Governor of Massachusetts, 1695–1700.   It was copied
from an account full of errors and misprints, and consequently the coats quartered in his shield could not be
identified.   It is therefore thought desirable to prepare a
more correct pedigree, obtained from Burke's Extinct
Peerage, and from Harleian MS., 1177, in the British
Museum.   Some account of the ancestry of Lady Bellomont, the Nanfan family, may be read in Nash's History
of Worcestershire.

Sir John Coote, the first of the family, m. a dau. and
heiress of Lord Pois or Boys, and had a son,

Sir John of Devonshire, who m. a dau. of Sir John
Fortescue, and was father of

Sir William, whose wife was a dau. of Thomas Mansell.

His son, Sir William, m. a dau. and heiress of Wortesley or Worsley, and had a son,

Sir John, who m. a Sacheverel, and was father of Robert, whose wife was a Grantham, by whom he left Thomas, who m. a Darnell.

His son, Sir John, m. a Tyrwhit, and had two sons, John, his heir, and Robert, Abbot of St. Albans.

John, the elder son, m. a Fotherby, and left three sons, Robert, Richard and John, of whom

Richard, of Blewnorton, co. Norfolk, m. Margaret dau. and heiress of Sir William Calthrop, and had sons Robert and Christopher of Blewnorton.

The latter m. Elizabeth, dau. and coheiress of John Wichingham, and was father of Richard, Christopher and Francis.

Richard, the eldest son, m. Elizabeth, dau. and coheiress of Felton, by whom he left Nicholas and Christopher.

Sir Nicholas, his heir, m. Amy, dau. of Thomas Cooper of Thurgarton, and had several children, the eldest of whom,

Sir Charles, settled in Ireland, and was created a Baronet in 1621. He m. Dorothy, dau. and coheiress of Hugh Cuffe, by whom he left three sons and one dau.

The second son, Richard, was created Baron Coote in 1660, and was father of Richard, Governor of Massachusetts, advanced in 1689 to the Earldom of Bellomont. The marriage and descendants of the Earl are correctly stated in the former article.

The arms quartered by the Governor may be thus described :—

1. Argent, a chevron sable between three coots proper, for Coote.

2. Or, a fess between two cotises counter-indented vert, for Lord Pois.

3. Argent, a chief gules, for Wortesley.

4. Checky, or and azure, a fess ermine, for Calthrop.

5. Ermine, on a chief sable three crosses formées argent, for Wichingham.

6. Gules, two lions passant ermine, for Felton.

7. Argent, on a bend dancettée sable three fleurs-de-lis of the field, for Cuffe.

8. Coote, as in the first.

The arms borne on the escutcheon of pretense cannot at present be so perfectly explained. Lady Bellomont was dau. and heiress of Bridges Nanfan, of Birts-morton, co. Worcester, and she quartered the arms of Penpons, Coles-hill, Hastings, and perhaps more. The first quarter contains the arms of Nanfan, viz., Sable, a chevron ermine between three single wings arg. In the second are those of Hastings, Arg. a maunch sable, though according to the pedigree these should occupy the last place. The arms of Penpons are, Arg. three wolves courant in pale azure, and these are probably found in the engraving in the Historical Magazine, and described as three lions passant. The escutcheon of pretense should also contain two more coats, viz., Checky or and sable, a chief arg. guttée de sang, for Coleshill, and Arg. a lion rampant gules, a border sable bezantée. These we do not find in the engraving, and the substituted coats can not be satisfactorily identified.

ARMS AND PEDIGREE OF GARDINER GREENE, OF BOSTON.

Taken from the researches of Mr. H. G SOMERBY, and original documents in the possession of the family.

The arms are, azure, three stags tripping, gold. Crest, A stag's head, erased gold.

"The family of Greene, originally written de la Greene (says Mr. Somerby), derive their name from their ancient possessions in Northamptonshire, where they were seated so early as the time of Edward the First."

"In 1320, Thomas de Greene succeeded to the estates, and was Lord of the Manor of Boughton and Norton, afterwards Greenes Norton, where the family continued to flourish for several generations, sending off shoots into various counties."

"One of the branches, as verified by the similarity of arms recorded in the Heralds' College, was seated in Dorsetshire in the early part of the reign of Henry the Eighth, when Robert[1] Greene of Gillingham, from whom an unbroken line of descent is traced, was assessed to that king's subsidy, as appears by the Rolls of the Exchequer, bearing date 1545." He was the father of three sons and two daughters Peter,[2] Richard,[2] John,[2] Alice [2] and Anne.[2]

Peter[2] Greene having died *s. p.*, Richard,[2] the second son, became heir to the estate of Bowridge Hill in Gillingham, and died leaving two children, Richard[3] and Anne.[3]

Richard[3] Greene had by his wife Mary five sons, Peter,[4] Richard,[4] Robert,[4] John,[4] Thomas[4]; and four daughters, Rebecca,[4] Mary,[4] Rachel,[4] and Anne.[4]

John Greene,[4] fourth son of Richard[3] Greene of Bowridge Hill, resided some time at Salisbury in Wiltshire, where, November 4th, 1619, he married his first wife, Joan Tattershall.

In April, 1635, he with his wife and children, sailed in the ship James of London, from Southampton, and arrived in Boston on the third of June of the same year.

Mr. Greene and his family removed to Providence, R. I., and remained there until the year 1643, when with twelve others, he again moved to a settlement which had been purchased from the Narraganset Indians.

The government of Massachusetts attacked this plantation, and taking almost all of the settlers, subjected them to severe punishments. The wife of Mr. Greene, however, escaped to Conanicut, where she soon afterwards died.

The following year Mr. Greene went to England, and having succeeded in obtaining "a just assertion of his rights," he returned, bringing a second wife, Alice Danniels, who died soon after coming to America.

He m. a third wife Philippa, who survived him. On his return Mr. Greene resided at Warwick, the principal town of Narraganset, of which he was a magistrate, and clerk of the court. His will was proved January 7, 1660.

He was buried by the side of his first wife, by whom he had five sons and two daughters, all born in England.

His sons were, John,[5] Peter,[5] Richard,[5] James,[5] and Thomas[5]; his daughters were Joan[5] and Mary.[5]

Thomas[5] Greene, youngest son of John and Joan Greene was baptized at St. Thomas Church, Salisbury, June 4th, 1628, and m. June 30th, 1659, Elizabeth Burton, daughter of Rufus Burton, Esq., and had five sons and two daughters. The sons were Thomas,[6] Benjamin,[6] Richard,[6] Rufus,[6] and Nathaniel[6]; the daughters were named Wealthean[5] and Elizabeth.[6]

Nathaniel,[6] youngest son of Thomas[5] and Elizabeth[5] Greene, was born at Warwick, April 10th, 1679. He removed to Boston, where he married, February 27th, 1703–4, Anne, daughter of Thomas Gould, and d. August 8th, 1714. His children were, Thomas,[7] Rufus,[7] Nathaniel,[7] William,[7] and Benjamin.[7]

Benjamin,[7] youngest son of Nathaniel[6] and Anne[6] Greene, was born January 11th, 1712–13. He m. Mary Chandler, and had two sons and five daughters. His sons were Benjamin[8] and Gardiner[8]; his daughters were Hannah,[8] Mary,[8] Lucretia,[8] Sarah,[8] and Anne.[8]

Gardiner[8] Greene, second son of Benjamin and Mary Greene, was born at Boston, September 22d, 1753. He was thrice married. First, to Anne Redding, who died *s. p.* Secondly, he m. Elizabeth Hubbard, and had Mary-Anne[9]; Gardiner,[9] who died young; Benjamin-Daniel,[9] who m. Margaret, daughter of Hon. Josiah Quincy; and William-Parkinson,[9] who m. Augusta Borland. The second wife having died, Mr. Greene m. thirdly, in London, 1800, Elizabeth Clarke, daughter of John Singleton Copley, the celebrated painter, and oldest sister of John, Baron Lyndhurst, sometime Lord Chancellor of England. The children by this marriage were, Gardiner,[9] who died young; Rev. John[9] Singleton Copley, who m. first, Elizabeth Hubbard, secondly, Mary Anne Appleton, and thirdly, Isabel McCullah; Elizabeth[9] Hubbard m. to Henry Timmins of Broad Meddow, near Birmingham, England; Sarah[9]; Susannah,[9] m. to Samuel Hammond; Martha[9] Babcock, m. to Charles Amory; and Mary[9] Copley, m. to James Sullivan Amory.

As the Heralds' College recorded the arms of Robert Greene of Gillingham, 1545, as being the same as the arms of the Greenes of Greenes Norton, there can be but little doubt that they belonged to the same family. Mr. Somerby has reason to think that the Greenes of Gillingham and Boston, descend from Thomas Greene, third son of Sir Henry Greene, by his wife Matilda, daughter of Thomas Maudit. The pedigree of Sir Henry Greene is as follows:—

Sir Thomas[1] Greene, Lord of the Manor of Broughton, Northampton, m. Alice, daughter of Sir Thomas Boltsham, and had a son Thomas,[2] who was born 1292.

Thomas[2] Greene, born 1292, was twice m. His first wife was Lucy, daughter and heiress of Eudo, Lord Zouch, by whom he had a son Henry.[3]

Henry[3] Greene, afterwards Sir Henry Greene, Lord Chief Justice of England, 1353, m. Catherine, daughter of Sir John Drayton, and had four sons and two daughters. The sons were Sir Thomas,[4] Sir Henry,[4] who m. Matilda Maudit, Richard,[4] and Nicholas[4]; the daughters were Amabelia and Margaret.

The tomb of Lord Chief Justice Greene remains to this day perfect, and is ornamented with many shields,

showing the different houses with which he was connected; conspicuous among them is the coat of arms of
the family.

There are various instances of the use of the arms in
this country, both on tomb-stones and book-plates.

A. T. P.

EARLY PAINTINGS OF COAT-ARMOUR.

In our second volume, page 30, we mentioned that
there were extant two old paintings of arms, one by T.
Johnston, bearing date 1740; and the other being Oliver
quartering Fitch and impaling Lynde, and hence belonging to Andrew Oliver, who m. in 1752, Mary Lynde, and
which may be attributed to Nathaniel Hurd.

These having been engraved for the "Elements of
Heraldry," we are enabled to republish them, and our
readers will doubtless find them very convenient for reference and comparison with other works of the same artists.

The first is Oliver quartering Fitch and impaling Lynde. Lieut. Gov. Andrew Oliver m. Mary, dau. of Hon. Thomas Fitch. Their son, Judge Andrew Oliver, m. Mary, dau. of Hon. Benjamin Lynde, in 1752. These marriages explain the arms.

The second has an inscription upon it, which is nearly sufficient for explanation. These are not strictly quarterings, the marriages not being all with heiresses. Enoch Lynde m. Elizabeth Digby, and their son Simon m. Hannah Newdigate ; whose son Benjamin m. Mary Browne. Mary was dau. of William Browne and Hannah Curwin, and grand-dau. of William Browne and Sarah Smith.

The inscription on the back of the painting is as follows :—

"The arms on the other side belong to Benj. Lynde, jr. of Salem. 1740.

"The 3 upper ones belong to my father, the Hon. Benj. Lynde, Esq, whose father was Simon Lynde, Esq of Boston. The arms on ye Dexter chief are the original arms of Enoch Lynde of Lond°: my gr. grand father who died 1636. The field is *gules*, on a chief *or*, three mullets of the first. My grandfather Enoch Lynde Esq, died 22 Nov. 1687.

"The middle arms on the upper part of the escutcheon are the arms of my grandmother whose maiden name was Hañah Newdigate. She was the daughter of Mr. John Newdigate of Boston & Anne his wife. The field is *gules*, three bear's paws erased. Mr. Jno. Newdigate died 4 Sept 1665, æt 85 yrs, his wife Ann died 1679 aged 84 yrs.

"The other arms on the upper part of the escutcheon

are the arms of my gr. grandmother Eliz'th Lynde (wife of Mr Enoch Lynde) whose maiden name was Digby, and are the original arms of Sir John Digby (who lived temp Hen ^{ci} sept.) from whom she descended, and after whose family (as I have heard,) her son was named Simon Lynde. The field is azure, a fleur de luce argent, by ye name of Digby. My grandmother Father's name was Everard Digby, cosen to Simon Digby Esq of Rutland sh^r who was 2^d son of Sir John Digby, who was sherif of Warwick and Leicester 27th K H^{ry}. 7th. and was great uncle to Jno the famous Earl of Bristol.

"The first arms on y^e Dexter side of y^e lowest part of the Escutcheon are my mother's arms, whose maiden name was Mary Browne, y^e Daughter of the Honble William Browne, Esq. of Salem, whose Father was Hon^{le}. William Browne, Esq, who came from Engl^d. to Salem 1635, and died 20 Jany 1687–8.

"The midle arms on the lower part of the Escutcheon are the arms of my grandm°. Browne, whose maiden name was Hannah Curwen, daughter of Capt. Geo: Curwen of Salem, merch^t. who died 3 Jany. 1684. Her arms are

"The other arms on the lower part of the Escutcheon arms of my gr. grandm°. Browne, whose maiden name was Sarah Smith and was the daughter of the Rev. Saml. Smith of Enon now Wenham. The arms are the arms of Smith of Great Buckingham." W. H. W.

ANTIQUITY OF HERALDRY.

A Plea for the Antiquity of Heraldry, with an Attempt to expound its theory and elucidate its history. By William Smith Ellis, Esq., of the Middle Temple. London: 1853.

For the past twenty years there has been a growing tendency to discredit all forms of traditionary knowledge. In our histories we now expect to find the results of thorough research among the remaining relics of the past, and the pleasant fables which satisfied our ancestors are disdainfully discarded.

Most assuredly the science of heraldry is one that has been greatly benefited by the introduction of critical tests, and the present generation of heraldic authors in England is undoubtedly more learned than its predecessors for two centuries.

Yet though so much of the false has been wisely removed, it is possible that a portion of the true may have been confounded with it. Mr. Ellis has written a learned essay to show that in adopting too rigorous a code of criticism, due regard has not been given to certain probabilities. " Recent archæological research and discovery have done little, if anything, to elucidate the obscurity of the origin of modern family heraldry ; and as conjecture seems exhausted, the settled judgment of the day admits the science to have originated at no earlier period than when the amplest positive evidence commences." " These views are entertained by the most recent writers on the subject, by Lower, Planché, &c. But their argument is a negative one, and therefore inconclusive. The old writers on heraldry introduced so much that was fanciful and absurd in their speculations, that they brought discredit on the whole science, and on every statement that was not supported by positive sensible proof."

These propositions Mr. Ellis defends with spirit and learning. He boldly meets the objection that no example of the use of Coat Armour in England can be produced, bearing date prior to the middle of the twelfth century, by two arguments. On the one hand the state of the arts did not allow of the production of elaborate tombs or engraved seals, and on the other it is useless to attempt to decide what should have been the fashion in earlier days.

He points out many fashions which have risen and disappeared, and argues that we cannot assume that coats-of-arms were not used then, nor that the mode of use was the same as now. He writes, " We need not wonder at the omission of any allusion to armorial bearings in the Saxon literature, or indeed in that of any people. In our own time, coats-of-arms meet us every day, and at every

step, and every turn. They are painted on carriages;
they are to be seen in almost every church in stained
glass; they are in daily use on seals, and with crests, or
the latter alone are to be found on the note paper, the
knives and forks, and spoons, and on the buttons of the
livery servants of the whole gentry of the kingdom. Let
us imagine a few seals or crested spoons discovered by
some Australian antiquary a thousand years hence, and
let us imagine a few copies or even volumes of a newspaper, with a few hundred volumes of history, memoirs
and romances, rescued from the ' wreck of matter,' and
forming the sole remains of our literature. What curious
speculations would be made on the use of these strange
devices! Who would believe that they were in almost
universal use among us? Sceptics would triumphantly
refer to our newspapers and novels. Surely, they would
say, such household emblems would be constantly spoken
of in every journal, in every work in which manners and
customs were alluded to, if they were of such general
use. And yet the most lynx-eyed antiquary would not
probably find the blazonry of a single family ever mentioned in the *Times*, or in any book of general literature."

Though we are not disposed to attach too much force
to this argument, which does not admit of being carried
far, since it might soon become absurd, we find some very
interesting suggestions made by Mr. Ellis in its support.
For example, he says, — " There yet remains to be noticed the strongest proof, indirect though it be, of the
existence of armorial bearings at the Conquest; and it is
afforded by this undeniable fact, which does not appear
to have been noticed, viz., that in the middle of the

twelfth century, when, it is contended, arms were first introduced into England, the descendants of those Normans who came in with the Conqueror, are found to *possess the same bearings as their third and fourth cousins in Normandy and other provinces of France.* That is the case with the Courtenays, the D'Oyleys, the Stutevilles, and a host of others; and where it is not, it will be found that a change of arms has taken place by marriage with an heiress, or for some other good reason. How can this remarkable coincidence be explained, except by a reference in both cases to a remote common origin? Would the Anglo-Norman nobles go over to France and hunt out their obscure and distant relatives, to borrow from them, their own newly-assumed heraldic devices? The idea is preposterous. Yet it must have been so, or a most miraculous coincidence must have occurred, not in one or two solitary instances, but in thousands of cases, with families of the same name and lineage; *or else* the heralds of both countries must have hit upon such a vast scheme of invention, as human ingenuity never equalled for consistency and veri-similitude."

Of course this argument is one which rests entirely upon the number of examples produced; and the very possibility of such a result should lead to systematic researches to establish it. We are hardly prepared to go so far as Mr. Ellis, and to think that the simplest figures in heraldry, as the bend, the chevron, &c., were originally appropriated each by a single person and thence descended only to their issue. Still it seems probable that many families did preserve a common coat-of-arms with various modifications, and that a judicious use of this clue may often aid in tracing the origin of old English families.

Lastly Mᵣ. Ellis broaches a new theory on a very interesting point. It has often been remarked that certain charges prevail in particular counties; and the gentry will be found using arms having a certain family resemblance. Thus in Cheshire the garb or wheat-sheaf predominates, in Lincolnshire the cinquefoil, in Staffordshire the fret, and in Cornwall the rose. It has been commonly said that these *armigeri* derived their arms from their feudal superior, and that the tenant adopted or had conceded to him a portion of the arms of the baron from whom he held lands. In this case the similarity of arms was a proof simply of a common feudal allegiance. On this point Mr. Ellis writes, " Every topographer, genealogist, and herald, has entertained the feudal theory of the formation of derivative coats; no one has hitherto ventured to affirm or suspect that the feudal connection had nothing to do with the origination of a new coat-of-arms. Yet investigation repudiates this long and universally prevalent notion, as indeed might, at any time, *à priori* reasoning on the objects and extent of the feudal relationship. For every topographer well knows that a tenant *in capite* was frequently sub-tenant to one or more tenants *in capite;* that sub-tenants, who were not tenants *in capite,* held of different chiefs in different counties; that by marriage, sale, forfeiture, and exchange, fiefs both large and small, constantly changed hands, much more frequently than is generally thought. How then, could the tenant be said to have adopted his coat armour from his feudal lord? Whose, of two or more chiefs, was he to imitate ? Many arms are compounded, it is true, and therefore are derived from more than one source ; but the great majority of those of the early periods are simple and unchanged, in the chief line, for generations. Theoretically then, it will be seen, this mode of deriving armorial bearings could not have been carried out ; and the *actual practice* of the time, as ascertained by investigation, at once refutes this long cherished theory, and proves to be what theoretically would be pronounced to be the simplest and most explanatory, viz., a derivation by *family relationship*."

" The feudal connection was a coincidence, not the cause ; in the time of the Conqueror, as appears by Doomsday, a nearly invariable coincidence, a great baronial proprietor of course sub-infeudating his sons and sons-in-law in preference to strangers ; subsequently, in the time of Henry III., as appears by the Testa de Nevill, a rarer coincidence, from the changes that a century and a half had produced ; so that it will be found, in that monarch's time, few of the tenants of a barony were relatives of their chief, or bore similar coat-armour."

" *In every instance* where the alliances and their arms can be ascertained, investigation proves that family relationship *alone* (with few exceptions) was the source of each new coat-of-arms. And this fact is of immense importance in affording clues, and in leading to discoveries in topography, genealogy and heraldry. It proves, by the strongest presumptive evidence, that arms were borne at the Conquest, and it is a clue, *almost invariably to be relied upon*, in tracing the original connection of families, though of different names and countries."

Elsewhere Mr. Ellis says, " Hereditary ensigns would
in certain cases be relinquished in favour of those of a
wife's family of higher rank; on a younger son's succeeding
to an elder brother's inheritance, on obtaining the grant
of a forfeited feud. And the same processes would be
early introduced, that we know prevailed in the twelfth
and thirteenth centuries, viz., compounding coats of a
father's with a mother's, omitting something of each, and
of augmenting the charges in commemoration of some act
of valour."

" It is a common notion that the *differences* used by
younger sons were arbitrarily chosen, comprising as they
did the ordinaries as well as new charges. But investigation proves this practice, as many other heraldic ones, to
have been governed by strict rules, and that these differences were almost invariably taken from the maternal or
uxorial coat."

Of course all these remarks apply only to early coats-
of-arms, such as were adopted by the families before the
authority of the heralds was recognized. During the
sixteenth century and later, the demand for new coats-of-
arms undoubtedly led to a neglect of the system imag-
ined by Mr. Ellis, if previously in existence. The very
fact that recourse was had to the heralds, was a virtual
confession that the pedigree of the applicant was lost ;
and hence the heralds gave such arms as fancy or their
preconceived plans led them to adopt. We find various
indications that they did not venture to assign the arms
of existing families, even with a difference. to namesakes.
We see a striking example in the case cited by the " Herald and Genealogist." When the Shakspeare arms were

granted, it was the intention of the herald evidently to grant a quartering also of the Arden arms, that being the family name of the Poet's mother. The original draft shows that the herald first sketched these arms, but the gentle family of the name still flourished in that county, and he substituted the arms of the Ardernes of Cheshire, a totally different name.

We have given this sketch of Mr. Ellis's theories because they seem to be steps in the right direction. The science of Heraldry is now apparently in a transition period, and it requires all the critical ability attainable to establish the new and judicious basis for investigations.

It is probable that the best and easiest test of these ideas of Mr. Ellis would be the construction of such a Dictionary of Coat Armour as he has described ; viz., one in which each coat should be accompanied by the date of its earliest appearance and the authority therefor. In fact we see the great necessity of a double Dictionary, one describing the arms in each county with an abstract of known relationship between families now bearing different names; the other being an alphabetical list of arms and the authority for their use. We believe that the work has already been essayed for one county in England, and as its success can hardly be doubted, we may hope to see it soon followed by others. Whenever this desired result shall be attained, we shall see English heraldry placed upon a permanent foundation.

We have a strong interest in America in such a publication. One of our greatest difficulties in deciding the ownership of our early seals is the want of a sound authority. We hold to the belief that many coats-of-arms were rightfully used prior to A. D. 1600, which are not recorded in Berry or Burke. When we obtain a record more nearly complete, we may hope to make these witnesses of the past of more assistance to the genealogist trying to recover the link which connects the Englishman of this country with the parent stock.   w. h. w.

THE BRATTLE FAMILY.

Every Bostonian is familiar with the name of Brattle, which was borne by individuals prominent in the history of Boston and Cambridge. The first of the name here was Capt. Thomas Brattle, who m. Elizabeth, dau. of Capt William Tyng, about 1657, and had sons Thomas, William, and Edward, and daus. Elizabeth, wife of Nathaniel Oliver, Catharine, who m. John Eyre and Wait-Still Winthrop, Bethia, wife of Joseph Parsons, and Mary, wife of John Mico. He died 22 July, 1683, leaving an estate of nearly £8000, the largest probably in New England.

His son Thomas Brattle, an engraving of whose seal is here given, from the original in the possession of Edward D. Harris, Esq., was for twenty years Treasurer of Harvard College, and d. unm. 18 May, 1713. Rev. William Brattle, son of the first Thomas, was of Cambridge, and a Fellow of the Royal Society. He m. 3 Nov. 1697, Elizabeth, dau. of Nathaniel Hayman, and had an only child William, who was of the Council, a minister, a lawyer, and major-general of the militia. He m. first Katherine Saltonstall, and 2dly —— dau. of —— Fitch, and widow of James Allen.   w. h. w.

THE TEMPLE FAMILY.

In our last volume, page 189, we said that the wife of Sir Grenville Temple was Elizabeth Hendley. In this assertion we thought we were following an undoubted authority, but we are now assured that the lady was the widow of Thomas Russell, and daughter of George Watson. This is proved by the epitaph upon her tomb at Rome, for a copy of which we are indebted to the Hon. Robert C. Winthrop. It is as follows:—

QUIETI ÆTERNÆ

ELISÆ GEORGII WATSONI F. MASSACHUSETTENSIS

FEMINÆ SANCTISSIMÆ

FORMA VIRTUTEQUE INSIGNIS

AMORE IN MARITUM PIETATE IN LIBEROS

OFFICIO IN AMICOS IN OMNES BENEVOLENTIA

EXIMIÆ.

VIXIT AN XXXVIII. M. VIII. D. XIII

OBIIT PR. NON. NOV. AN. MDCCCVIII.

GRENVILLIUS TEMPLE EQUES BARONETTUS

UXORI DIGNISSIMÆ ET INCOMPARABILI

QUAM VIVAM UNICE AMAVIT, MORTUAM ACERBE

LUGET

H. M. CUM LACRYMIS P.

ANCESTRY OF ISAAC JOHNSON.

In the Collections of the Massachusetts Historical Society, (Fourth Series, Vol. VI.), are printed the will and two letters of Isaac Johnson, one of the signers of the

Agreement at Cambridge in 1629, who died on this side the water issueless in 1630. A later will is also found in Vol. VIII. of the third series of the same collections. He was certainly entitled to arms, though perhaps no instance is known of his use of them. The pedigree of the family is as follows:—

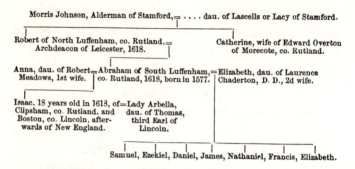

Morris Johnson, Alderman of Stamford,= . . . . dau. of Lascells or Lacy of Stamford.

Robert of North Luffenham, co. Rutland,=   Catherine, wife of Edward Overton
   Archdeacon of Leicester, 1618.   of Morecote, co. Rutland.

Anna, dau. of Robert=Abraham of South Luffenham,=Elizabeth, dau. of Laurence
Meadows, 1st wife. | co. Rutland, 1618, born in 1577. | Chaderton, D. D., 2d wife.

Isaac. 18 years old in 1613, of=Lady Arbella,
Clipsham, co. Rutland, and dau. of Thomas,
 Boston, co. Lincoln, after-   third Earl of
  wards of New England.   Lincoln.

Samuel, Ezekiel, Daniel, James, Nathaniel, Francis, Elizabeth.

In the chancel of the church of North Luffenham is a brass plate to the memory of Archdeacon Johnson, founder of the Oakham and Uppingham Grammar-schools, who died in 1625.

In the "Register" for 1854, may be read a curious document, purporting to be written in 1638, by Abraham Johnson, father of the emigrant. From it we learn that Archdeacon Johnson married first Susanna Davers, and secondly Maria Hird, by whom he had an only child, the writer. The paper is largely devoted to an attack on Isaac Johnson, who is said to have made an over high match, forbidden by his father, and afterwards by covetousness and ambition to have got possession of his grandfather's estate, esteemed at some £20,000, to the exclusion of his own father, and to have wasted a large part of it in the settlement of New England.

The arms of the family were, Arg. a chevron sable between three lion's heads couped gules, crowned or. Crest, a lion's head erased gules, ducally crowned or, between two ostrich feathers arg.

HERALDIC NOTES AND QUERIES.

(Continued from Vol. II., p. 96.)

XXXII.

We find this curious matter in the Letters of John Andrews, published in the Proceedings of the Massachusetts Historical Society. "Ruthy" was Mrs. or Miss Andrews, and "your uncle Joe" was Mr. Joseph Barrell, whose arms were of course those engraved. The arms of Barrell are, Ermine, on a chief azure three talbot's heads erased arg., or with different colors or one head. We shall be glad to know if this remarkable work is still in existence.

"1775, January 10th. Its about ten months since Ruthy began to cut a coat of arms, on vellum, for your uncle Joe: which hurt her eyes to such a degree as that she was oblig'd to lay it by. This fall she reassum'd it again, and completed it a few days since. Its about eight inches square, with his and his wife's arm quarter'd, supported at the lower corners by Jupiter and Minerva inimitably executed, and together with the embellishments of her fruitful fancy, forms the most extraordinary piece of workmanship of the kind, that I believe was ever perform'd."

XXXIII.

In Noble's "History of the College of Arms," we read thus :—

" York Herald—Laurence Cromp, Esq. Originally an herald-painter in Worcester, and an officer in the militia. His patron, Lord Windsor, recommended him to the deputy Earl Marshal. The lords proprietors of the province of Carolina gave him a patent, dated June 1, 1705, appointing him Carolina herald, with power to grant arms to the Casiques and Landgraves. He died June 11, 1715, and was buried in the cemetary of St. Bennet, Paul's Wharf, on the 14th"

Are any coats known to have been granted under the authority of this appointment?

XXXIV.

The arms on seal No. 20, engraved, Vol. II., page 90, have been identified as those of Hull of Surrey — Arg. on a chevron azure, between three demi-lions gules, as many bezants, on a chief sable two piles of the field. The seal probably belonged to Samuel Sewell, one of the witnesses, who married Hannah, only child of John Hull, the mint-master. This John Hull came from Market Harborough, co. Leicester, but must be presumed to have claimed to use the arms.

XXXV.

The seal No. 19, engraved, Vol. II., page 90, is found to show the arms of Proby of Huntingdonshire, granted 1586—Ermine, on a fess gules a lion passant or. Crest, An ostrich's head erased arg., ducally gorged or, in his mouth a key of the last.

XXXVI.

The extraordinary coat on the tomb-stone of Cyprian Southac, in the Granary burying-ground, engraved, Vol. II., page 138, has been found in the MS. Promptuarium Armorum of Wm. Smith, Rouge-Dragon, which was often quoted in our first volume. We find there the arms of "George Sowdeak, grocer," thus blazoned: Arg. a fess dancettée gules, in chief two spear-heads fess-wise, points opposed sable, and over them a dexter arm, habited of the second, issuing from the clouds, holding in the hand proper a human heart. Crest, a dexter arm, habited gules, cuffed proper, in the hand a human heart.

XXXVII.

The following grants are recorded in the Appendix to Edmondson's "Complete Body of Heraldry."

HUGER, Ar. a human heart emitting flames, betw. two laurel-branches fructed saltierwise in chief, and an anchor erect in base, all proper, betw. two flaunches az. each charged with a fleur-de-lis or. Crest, on a wreath ar. & gu. a sprig; thereon a Virginia nightingale, all proper. Motto, Ubi libertas, ibi patria. Granted to Daniel Huger, of South Carolina, 1771.

ROOME, Ar. a fesse pean; in chief a lion passant gu. Crest, a dexter arm embowed, habited az. charged with two bars ar. holding in the hand proper a caduceus of the last. Granted to —— Roome, of Newport, in America, July 21, 1772.

WILLIAMS, Or, a lion rampant gu. on a chief az. two doves rising ar. Crest, on a wreath an eagle with wings expanded proper, reposing his dexter foot on a mound or. Granted to John Williams, of Boston, in New England, 1767.

XXXVIII.

In Berry's "Pedigrees of Kentish Families," it is stated that Bernard Randolph of Biddenden, died 6 May, 1628, leaving five sons, William, Bernard, John, Herbert and Edmund; and that John, the third son, " went to Virginia, and was ancestor of the Randolphs of that country." Bernard Randolph bore for arms, Gules, on a cross argent five mullets pierced sable. This differs entirely from the account printed in Garland's Life of John Randolph, from which we will quote a paragraph:

" Richard Randolph of Curles was the fourth son of Col. W^m. Randolph of Warwickshire, England, who was the first of the name that emigrated to Virginia, and settled at Turkey Island. He died April 11th 1711. That he was of Warwickshire, we learn from a monument at Turkey Island; but the late John Randolph, who took great pride in searching into the genealogy of his family, says that he was of Yorkshire. Between the researches of the Hon. John, and the monument at Turkey Island, we leave the reader to judge."

It is evident that we have here another F. F. V., whose pedigree requires the most serious investigation.

THE

HERALDIC JOURNAL;

RECORDING THE ARMORIAL BEARINGS AND GENEALOGIES
OF AMERICAN FAMILIES.

NO. XVIII.   APRIL, 1867.

ARMS OF THE COFFIN FAMILY.

This family is one of those, which have always used
arms in this country, though unable to prove a right to
them, inherited from ancestors ranking among the gentry
of England.   In Prince's "Worthies of Devonshire" may
be read an account of the family of the name of Coffin,
which claims to have been seated at Portledge in the
parish of Alwington in the Northern part of that county,
since the time of the Norman conquest.   Burke states
their arms to be, Azure semée of crosses-crosslet or, three
bezants, and gives also under the name, Azure, four bezants within five crosses-crosslet or.   Smith's MS. Promptuarium Armorum contains a drawing of the arms borne
by "S.ʳ W.ᵐ Coffin of Portledge in Devon of yᵉ Privy Cha.
to K. H. 8,"—Vert, five cross-crosslets argent between
four plates.   It is possible however that the colors of the
drawing have been changed by time.

The family sent off branches into different parts of Devonshire, and it is highly probable that the Coffins of this
country are descended from some such branch, but the
connection has not yet been proved.   The emigrant to

New England was Tristram Coffin, who was born at Brixton near Plymouth in Devonshire, about the year 1605. He was son of Peter and Joan (Thumber) Coffin, and grandson of Nicholas Coffin. The family has not been traced farther back. Brixton is in the deanery of Plympton, and no wills of this deanery are known to exist of an earlier date than 1600, though the calendar runs back several years, and contains references to many more wills of members of the family of Coffin. The first volume of the register of the parish of Brixton is also lost to sight, if not to being.

Tristram Coffin married Dionis, daughter of Robert Stevens of Brixton, and came to New England in 1642, bringing his mother, his sisters Eunice and Mary, and several children. He lived for a time at Salisbury, Haverhill and Newbury, all in Massachusetts, and finally settled in the island of Nantucket, where he died in October, 1681. He had the following children: —

Peter, b. in England, 1631, who lived in Dover, N. H.

Tristram, b. in England, 1632, who lived in Newbury.

Elizabeth, b. in England, m. Stephen Greenleaf of Newbury.

James, b. in England, 1640, who lived in Nantucket.

John, b. in England, d. in Haverhill, 1642.

Mary, b. in Haverhill, 1645, m. Nathaniel Starbuck of Nantucket.

John, b. in Haverhill, 1647, lived in Nantucket.

Stephen, b. in Newbury, 1652, lived in Nantucket.

The five sons married, and left many children. Some account of the great increase of the family may be read in Joshua Coffin's History of Newbury. Extensive materials

for a genealogy of the family were collected by him, as
well as by Nathaniel W. Coffin, and it is to be hoped that
they may at some time be published.   We shall at present
confine ourselves to some account of the claims to heraldic
insignia, which have always been made in this country.

There is in the possession of the family at Newbury a
painting of the arms, which is said to have been brought
from England.   We have not lately been able to examine
it, but there is good reason for believing that in this case
report speaks correctly.   We are however owner of a
painting, which is sufficiently described by the inscription
under it, as follows : —

"He beareth 𝔅𝔞𝔯𝔬𝔫 and 𝔉𝔢𝔪𝔪𝔢 the first Vert five
Cross-Crosslets between four Bezants, By the Name
of COFFIN.   The Seconds is 𝔊𝔲𝔩𝔢𝔰 a Bend Lozengs
𝔈𝔯𝔪𝔦𝔫𝔢, By the Name of HALE."   The crest is a pigeon
ppr. between two roses (?) or, stalked and leaved vert.
Motto, "Post Tenebras Speramus Lumen de Lumine."
The drawing is very like that of the Oliver shield, engraved on p. 31, with leaves in place of the quills at the
base.   The work was done for Dr. Nathaniel Coffin of
Portland, Me., a gr.-grandson of Tristram, Jr.   He married Patience Hale of Newbury in 1739, and died in 1766.

This painting certainly represents the field of the Coffin
arms as *vert*, and an engraved book-plate agrees entirely
with this.   We have now to consider the document issued
from the College of Arms to Rear Admiral Sir Isaac
Coffin, a descendant of James, son of Tristram senior.
His father was Nathaniel, H. C. 1744, ,his grandfather
was William, and his gr.-grandfather was Nathaniel.
With several others of the family he adhered to the

British authority at the Revolution, and rose to high rank in the British navy and to a Baronetcy. In Playfair's British Baronetage may be read an account of the family and the career of Sir Isaac. He died without children, but descendants of his brother, General John Coffin, are living in England. All that follows is copied from the records of the College of Arms, London, and authenticated by Albert W. Woods, Lancaster Herald.

To the Most Noble Charles Duke of Norfolk Earl Marshal and Hereditary Marshal of England
The Memorial of Isaac Coffin Esquire
Rear Admiral of the White Squadron
of His Majesty's Fleet
Sheweth,
That the Family of your Memorialist long settled in New England is by tradition descended from the Family of Coffin of the West of England. But being now unable to ascertain his descent your Memorialist requests the favour of Your Graces Warrant to the Kings of Arms concerned for their granting confirming and exemplifying the Arms of Coffin with such distinctions as the Laws of Arms may require to be borne by your Memorialist and his descendants and by those of his late Father Nathaniel Coffin Esquire, deceased with their due and proper differences.

And your Grace's Memorialist &c.
ISAAC COFFIN
Rear Admiral.

Whereas Isaac Coffin Esquire, Rear Admiral of the

White Squadron of His Majesty's Fleet, hath represented unto me that his Family long settled in New England is by tradition descended from the Family of Coffin of the West of England but that being now unable to ascertain his Descent the Memorialist hath requested my Warrant for your granting confirming and exemplifying the Arms of Coffin with such distinctions as the Laws of Arms may require to be borne by the Memorialist and his descendants and by those of His late Father Nathaniel Coffin Esquire, deceased with their due and proper differences,

I Charles Duke of Norfolk Earl Marshal and Hereditary Marshal of England do hereby authorize and require you to grant confirm and exemplify to the said Isaac Coffin such Armorial Ensigns as may be proper to be borne by him and his descendants and by those of his late Father Nathaniel Coffin Esquire deceased, with due and proper differences according to the Laws of Arms. For which this shall be your Warrant. Given under my hand and Seal this fifteenth day of May 1804.

NORFOLK, E. M.

To Sir Isaac Heard Knight,
Garter Principal King of
Arms and George Harrison
Esquire Clarenceux King of Arms.

To all and Singular to whom these Presents shall come Sir Isaac Heard Knight Garter Principal King of Arms & George Harrison Esquire Clarenceux King of Arms of the South East and West Parts of England from the River Trent Southwards send Greeting;

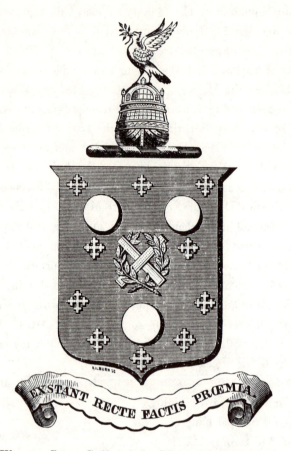

EXSTANT RECTE FACTIS PRŒMIA.

Whereas Isaac Coffin of the Magdelaine Islands in the Gulph of Saint Lawrence in British North America Esquire Rear Admiral of the White Squadron of His Majesty's Fleet hath represented unto the Most Noble Charles Duke of Norfolk Earl Marshal and hereditary Marshal of England that his Family long settled in New England is by tradition descended from the Family of Coffin of the West of England but that being now unable

to ascertain his descent He requested the favour of his
Grace's Warrant for Our granting confirming and exemplifying the Arms of Coffin with such distinctions as the
Laws of Arms may require to be borne by him and his
Descendants and by those of his late Father Nathaniel
Coffin Esquire deceased with their due and proper differences And forasmuch as the said Earl Marshal did by
Warrant under his Hand and Seal bearing date the fifteenth day of May Instant authorize and require Us to
grant confirm and exemplify such Armorial Ensigns accordingly Know Ye therefore that We the said Garter
and Clarenceux in pursuance of his Grace's Warrant and
by virtue of the Letters Patent of Our several Offices to
each of Us respectively granted have devised and do by
these Presents grant confirm and exemplify to the said
Isaac Coffin the Arms following that is to say Azure
semée of Cross Crosslets Or, in the centre two Batons in
Saltire entwined by a Wreath of Laurel of the second,
between three Plates two and one. And for the Crest,
On a Wreath of the Colours The Stern of a Man of War
Or thereon a hooded Dove wings elevated and in the bill
a Branch of Olive proper (a Mullet for difference) as the
same are in the Margin hereof more plainly depicted to be
borne and used for ever hereafter by him the said Isaac
Coffin and his Descendants and by those of his said late
Father Nathaniel Coffin deceased, with their due and
proper differences according to the Laws of Arms. In
Witness whereof We the said Garter and Clarenceux
Kings of Arms have to these Presents subscribed Our
names and affixed the Seals of Our several Offices this sixteenth day of May in the forty fourth Year of the Reign

of Our Sovereign Lord George the Third by the Grace of God of the United Kingdom of Great Britain and Ireland King Defender of the Faith &c. And in the year of Our Lord One thousand eight hundred and four.

OFFICIAL SEALS.

Thomas Pownall, who was the next Governor of Massachusetts, after Shirley, was descended from a family which claimed to represent the Pownalls or Paganels of Cheshire. An account of the family will be found in Burke's Landed Gentry; but the evidence there cited seems to carry the authenticated pedigree only to Thomas Pownall of Barnton, who was born in 1650, married Mary, daughter and heir of Richard Browne of Saltfleetby, co. Lincoln, and had a son William, who died in 1731. This William had two, John, b. 1720, (whose son Sir George Pownall was Secretary of Lower Canada, and d. unm. 1834) and Thomas, b. 1722, the Governor.

Hutchinson (Hist. Mass., III. 56) says of Gov. Pownall on his arrival here, Aug. 2, 1757: "This was his third passage to America. In 1754, when Sir Danvers Osborne came over to the government of New York, Mr. Pownall was in his family, and brought with him, or received soon after, a commission as lieutenant-governor of New Jersey, the Governor whereof, Mr. Belcher, was old and infirm."

In 1755 he went back to England, and returned to America with Lord Loudoun in 1756, but continued there a few months only. Upon his arrival again in England, he was appointed to succeed Mr. Shirley. He had acquired great knowledge of the geography, history and polity of the several American colonies, and came into office with many advantages."

"Governor Pownall's administration was short. In November, 1759, it was thought proper to nominate him to the government of South Carolina, in the room of Mr. Littleton, appointed governor of Jamaica. Mr. Bernard, governor of New Jersey, was appointed to succeed Mr. Pownall."

He sailed for England, June 3d, 1760. After his appointment to South Carolina he soon resigned his place and returned to England. He was appointed director-general or comptroller, with the rank of colonel in the army, in Germany in 1762, but resigned in 1763. He was a member of Parliament and made many speeches upon the American question, in which he maintained the decision of the colonists to refuse all taxation without representation.

Gov. Pownall m. Aug. 3, 1763, first, Harriet, daughter of Lt. Gen. Churchill, and widow of Sir Everard Faulkner. His wife died 6 Feb., 1777, aged 51, and a year or two afterwards he retired from public life. His second wife was Mrs. Askill of Everton-house, co. Bedford.

Gov. Pownall died at Bath, 25 Feb., 1805, and left no issue by either marriage. Besides the offices above noted he was Secretary to the Commissioners for Trade and

Plantations in 1745, and his brother John was Solicitor and Clerk of Exports to the Commissioners in 1761.

Pownall was quite a voluminous writer and a list of his works will be found in the Gentleman's Magazine for 1805.

The arms here given are copied from those on a portrait engraved by Earlom and published in London in 1777. They are Pownall quartering Browne, and impaling Churchill.

MONUMENTAL INSCRIPTIONS.

NEWPORT, R. I.

The large burial-ground near the northern end of Thames Street in Newport is probably the richest in this country, in material for the Heraldic Journal. It contains nearly twenty stones, on which Armorial Ensigns are cut. The larger part of these are engraved in this number; some of the other inscriptions are nearly illegible, but we hope to print them all during the year. All the stones lie flat on the surface of the ground, and of course have suffered every sort of injury, except wanton mutilation. The mantling and ornaments of the shields present but little variety, and are omitted in the wood-cuts. They are generally repetitions of the two designs shown in the yard of Trinity Church. We regret that we can give so little genealogical information about the families; and shall most gratefully receive more from our correspondents in Newport or elsewhere.

I.

Here lieth
The Body of JOHN CRANSTON
Esqr. Govr. of the Colony of Rhode
Island &c. He departed this Life March
the 12th 1680 In y^e 55th Year of
his Age.

Here lieth
The Body of SAMUEL
CRANSTON Esqr
Late Governour of This
Colony, Aged 68 Years &
Departed this Life April ye 26th
A. D. 1727, he was Son of John
Cranston Esqr Who also was
Governour here 1680. He was

descended from the Noble Scottish
Lord Cranston, And carried in his Veins
a Stream of the Antient Earls of
Crawford, Bothwell, & Traquair.
Having had for his Grandfather James
Cranston Clerk Chaplain to King Charles
The First, His Great Grandfather was
John Cranston of Pool Esq.ʳ This last
was Son to James Cranston Esq.ʳ Which
James was Son to William Lord Cranston.

Rest happy now Brave Patriot, without End,
Thy Country's Father, & thy Country's Friend.

We have not at present the means of either proving or
overthrowing the pedigree asserted in this epitaph.   Mr.
Savage, in his Genealogical Dictionary, calls it the claim
of fond tradition.   It certainly seems most improbable.
William, first Lord Cranston, was so created in 1609, and
died in 1627.   He had a son James, ancestor of the present Lord.   John Cranston, the Governor of Rhode Island,
was born about 1626, and it is barely in the bounds of
possibility that he should have been of the fourth generation from the first Lord.   The omission of John of Pool
in the printed accounts of the family is not of itself a fact
of much weight; but William the fifth Lord, who was of
the same generation with Governor John, through the
same gr.-grandfather James, lived till 1768, which throws
on the author of the inscription a burden of proof which
mere words do not bear out.

Sir Bernard Burke accepts this pedigree in his account
of the Baronetcy of Brenton, but omits two generations,

making James, the Royal Chaplain, to be son of William Lord Cranston. Sir L. C. L. Brenton, Bart., is descended from the Brentons, and Cranstons of Rhode Island.

II.

Here lyeth Interred the Body of
Mary the Wife of John Sanford, who
Dyed Decem^r y^e 15, 1721
In the 57 Year of her Age.

III.

The same arms precede the following epitaph : —

Here
Lyeth Interred the Body of
William Sanford M. A.
Aged nere 31 years and dyed
April the 24th 1721.

Here lyeth Dust that as we Trust
United is to Christ
Who will it Raise the Lord to praise
Join'd to a Soul now Blest,
With Holy Ones plac'd on Bright Thrones,
Crown'd with Eternal joyes,
In Heav'n to Sing to God our King,
There Thankful Songs Alwayes.

In the Genealogical Dictionary of N. E. may be read an account of John Sanford, who was driven from Boston to Rhode Island, where he established himself at Portsmouth. He had sons John, Samuel and Eliphal, of whom the first and second had families. John, whose wife we find buried here, was probably son of Samuel, and the same person as John Sanford of Newport, who was admitted freeman 1708. William seems to have been his son, and freeman 1718. He graduated at Harvard in 1711, and by the catalogue ranks first in his class. We do not find in Burke any arms exactly corresponding with this wood-cut, though there are several which hardly vary from it. The arms of Sandford of Northumberland are, Ermine on a chief gules two boar's heads couped or. Those on the stone are seen to be erased, and by the ignorant cutter are reversed.

IV.

The arms on the next page belong here also.

Here lieth Interred the Body
of Stephen Bayly who died
Octo^{br} y^e 17th 1724 in the
60th Year of his Age.

V.

Here lyeth Interred the Body
of Susanna y⁰ Wife of Stephen Bayly,
A Virtuous & Loving Wife to her
Husband & Loving & kind to her
Childred dyed April y⁰ 25ᵗʰ
Anno Dom. 1723 in y⁰ 51ˢᵗ Year
of her Age.

Concerning this gentleman and his arms we are able to give no information. There was a Richard Bailey at Newport 1670, and Stephen Baily of the same place was admitted freeman 1717. The arms are clearly heraldic, notwithstanding the peculiar shape of the shield. It is hard to say for what the design was intended ; nothing at all resembling it is found in Burke's "General Armory."

VI.

Here lieth entombed
The Body of Abigail
The Wife of M.ʳ George Wanton
Merchant of this Town
He being the eldest son of Col. W.ᵐ Wanton
She having been yᵉ Second Daugh.ʳ of Benj. Ellery Esq.
Both of Newport.
She changed this World for a better
On the 12ᵗʰ Day of May 1726
In the 28ᵗʰ Year of her Age
Having left Five Pledges of her Love.

Terras Astrea reliquit.

If Tears alas ! could speak a Husband's Woe,
My verse would streight in Plaintiff Numbers flow :
Or if so great a Loss deplor'd in vain
Could solace so my throbbing Heart from Pain,
Then would I, Oh sad Consolation ! chuse
To sooth my cureless Grief a Private Muse ;
But since thy Well-known Piety demands
A Publick Monument at thy GEORGE's hands
O ABIGAIL I dedicate this Tomb to The,
Thou Dearest Half of Poor Forsaken Me.

Twice before have we recorded these arms.   The family
was a prominent one in Rhode Island, and furnished a
goodly array of Governors to the Colony.

VII.

In Memory
of Mr Jonathan Thurston
Merch.^t who departed
this life April the 13th
A. D. 1749 in the 61st
year of his Age.

VIII.
The family arms are repeated with this epitaph:—
In Memory of
Jonathan Thurston
An honest, industrious, skilful Merchant
Whose Piety and Virtues

Procur'd Him the Love & universal Esteem
of His Acquaintance.
He departed this Life
August 24ᵗʰ A. D. 1757.
In the 33ᵈ Year of his Age.

This Stone also covers the Body of
Deborah his Daughter by Ruth his Wife
who dyed Septʳ 4ᵗʰ A. D. 1757
Aged 5 Months and 4 Days.

According to the printed genealogy of the family,
Edward Thurston, who was of Newport as early as 1647,
had a son Jonathan, born in 1659. The latter was probably father of the elder Jonathan, whose grave is seen.

IX.

In Memory
of Mʳ Ninyon Chaloner
who died August yᵉ 14, 1752
in yᵉ 65ᵗʰ year of his Age.

This name is not seen in Savage's Genealogical Dictionary, but we find a Ninyan Chaloner of Newport admitted
freeman of the Colony of Rhode Island 1736. A person
of the same name, undoubtedly a descendant, appears in
Sabine's American Loyalists. The stone seems to combine
the arms of Chaloner of Yorkshire,—Sable, a chevron
between three cherubim's heads or,—with the crest of
Challenor of Sussex,—A wolf statant reguardant argent,
pierced through the shoulder by a broken spear or, the
upper part in his mouth, the lower resting on the wreath.
The design and workmanship are of the rudest character.

x.

IN MEMORY
of Abiah the Wife of
Cap.ᵗ George Buckmaster
who departed this Life the
15ᵗʰ of October A. D. 1754
in the 29ᵗʰ Year of her Age.

This Stone a Monument which bears thy Name
Is all at Death the dearest Friends can claim
Vain is this World ! which at one Breath is o'er
Then opens for the Soul another Door.
May Angels guard thy Spirit as it goes
And waft it safe to Mansions of Repose.
Where Saints and Angels in still Concert sing
Loud Anthems to their Great and Heav'nly King.

———

XI.

SACRED TO THE MEMORY
of Cap.ᵗ JOHN FREEBODY, who
departed this Life the 3.ᵈ of Nov.ʳ
1759 aged about 80 Years. And
of SARAH his first Consort, who
died yᵉ 22.ᵈ of May 1736 aged
52 Years & 8 Mˢ

HE was a Merchant in this Town near
fifty Years & as he carried on an extensive
Commerce with the strictest Honor
and Probity, was a most useful and
beneficial Member of Society: And
for Integrity Temperance and other
Virtues, he was justly & highly distinguished.

SHE was a Woman of Honor & Virtue,
& exemplary for her steady Observance
of all Christian & relative Duties.

Neither the name of Buckmaster nor Freebody is mentioned in Mr. Savage's work, but John Freebody mariner was of Newport in 1720, and became a freeman in 1728. The arms are the same as those of Frebody of Sussex, Gules, a chevron argent between three human hearts or.

THE MANORS OF NEW YORK AND THEIR LORDS.

It is a fact probably known by our readers, that in the Province of New York there were a number of estates which were constituted Manors. We have not been able to procure a perfect list of these grants, but from various sources we obtain the following particulars. RENSSELAER-WYCK, the property of the Van Rensselaer family, was the earliest, CLAVERACK belonging to the same, LIVINGSTON Manor belonging to the Livingstons, CORTLANDT belonging to the Van Cortlandts, FORDHAM to the Archers originally, MORRISANIA to the Morrises, PELHAM to the Pells, PHILIPSBOROUGH to the Philipses, SCARSDALE to the Heathcotes, Lloyd's Neck to the Lloyds, GARDINER'S ISLAND to the Gardiners.

We propose to give some particulars in relation to the families who possessed these estates, and as many of them lived within the present county of Westchester, we shall rely mainly upon the authority of Mr. Bolton, whose admirable History is rich in genealogies.

The Manor of Cortlandt, containing 83,000 acres of land, was thus constituted by a Royal patent in 1697, in favor of Stephen[3] Van Cortlandt. The family is said to be descended from the Dukes of Courland in Russia, and is traced to Steven[1] Van Cortlandt, who was living in 1610 at Cortlandt in South Holland. His son Oloff[2] Stevens van Cortlandt came to New York about 1649 and left a large estate. Stephen,[3] son of Oloff, born 7 May, 1643, was Mayor of New York in 1677 and a member of the Governor's Council. He married Gertrude Schuyler and had a large family. At his death he left his estate, including the Manor of Cortlandt, to be divided among his heirs, but it was not finally partitioned until 1734. His oldest son John[4] left an only child Gertrude,[5] wife of Philip Verplank, and the representation passed to the heirs of the third son Philip,[4] who married in 1710 Catherine de Peyster. This Philip[4] had five sons, but only the oldest, Stephen,[5] and the youngest, Pierre,[5] left issue.

Pierre[5] van Cortlandt was on the side of the patriots during the Revolution, was elected Lieutenant-Governor and held the office for eighteen years successively. He died May 1st, 1814, aged 93, leaving issue by his wife Joanna Livingston, four sons and as many daughters. The oldest son Gen. Philip[6] Van Cortlandt died at the manor house at Croton, 21 Nov. 1831. He was the last heir in the entail, but the representation passed to his nephew Col. Pierre[7] Van C., son of his only married brother Major Gen. Pierre[6] Van C.

Col. Pierre[7] Van Cortlandt, third of these names, married Catherine, dau. of Theodric Romeyn Beck of Albany, and has issue.

The oldest son of Philip,[4] as before mentioned, was Stephen,[5] who m. Mary-Walton, dau. of Wm. Ricketts, and had issue, but these are all we believe in England.

The arms of the Cortlandt family, as evidenced by the seals of Oloff Stevensen Van Cortlandt, are, Argent, the wings of a windmill saltireways sable, voided of the field, between five estoilles gules. These arms were borne by the Dukes of Courland on an inescutcheon on their ducal shield.

The Manor of Fordham was constituted such by letters patent ·dated 13 Nov. 1671. The terms were that the "said parcel or tract of land and premises shall be forever hereafter held, claimed, reputed and be an entire and enfranchised township, manor, and place of itself." This Manor was the property of John Archer, who in 1676 mortgaged it to Cornelius Steinwyck, merchant of New York. In 1686 Steinwyck left it by will to the Nether Dutch Church in the city of New York, and this being confirmed also by a deed from John Archer, son and heir of the first lord of the Manor, the title was transferred to the Elders of the Church.

The pedigree of the Archers is traced by Bolton to Humphrey Archer, born in 1527. His son John Archer m. Eleanor Frewin and had a son John, who was father of John Archer, first lord of the Manor of Fordham.

This John or his son John, second lord of the Manor, m. in Fordham, 7 Oct. 1686, Sarah Odell and had sons Samuel, John and Richard. Samuel Archer seems to have owned land at Fordham, after the title passed from his family, and left issue there. Other branches of the family are recorded by Bolton, but it will be seen that they very soon lost any pretensions to be ranked among the great landed proprietors of the colony.

———

Far different from the preceding example was the connection of the Morris family with the manor of Morrisania. The land had first been known as Broncks land, from the original Dutch proprietor. It was purchased by Capt. Richard[2] Morris about 1670, who was the youngest son of William[1] Morris of Tintern, co. Monmouth. His two brothers were Col. Lewis[2] Morris, a distinguished officer under Cromwell, and William[2] Morris of Denham, co. Monmouth.

Richard[2] Morris married Sarah Pole, but died in 1672 leaving an only child. Col. Lewis[2] Morris, who had been living at Barbadoes, then came to New York and purchased a large tract of land in East Jersey. Dying in 1690–1, without issue, the Manor and other property devolved upon Lewis[3] Morris, his nephew, son of Richard[2] M.

Lewis,[3] the third proprietor of Morrisania, obtained a manorial patent in 1697, with very full rights and privileges. He was the first Governor of New Jersey, in 1738, and died in 1746 aged 73. By his wife Isabella, daughter of James Graham, he had two sons, Lewis[4] of Morrisania, and Robert-Hunter,[4] who inherited the New Jersey estates. Of these

Hon. Lewis[4] Morris, b. 23 Sept. 1698, was Judge of the Admiralty Court, and one of the Judges of Oyer and Terminer. He was twice married, first to Catherine Staats, by whom he had three sons, Lewis,[5] Staats-Long,[5] and

Richard[5]; secondly to Sarah Governeur, by whom he had one son Governeur.[5]

In the next generation, Lewis[5] the oldest son, b. 8 Apr. 1726, was a Brigadier General in the Continental army, a member of Congress and one of the Signers of the Declaration of Independence. His brother Richard[5] was a Judge of Admiralty, and his half-brother Governeur[5] was Minister to France and U. S. Senator.

Gen. Lewis[5] Morris married Mary Walton and had a large family, six sons and four daughers, of whom Col. Lewis[6] Morris, oldest son, married Anne Elliot and left issue ; and the other brothers having all married, the descendants in the sixth generation here are quite numerous. The Hon. Governeur[5] Morris m. Anne-Carey, daughter of Thomas Randolph of Roanoke, and had a son Governeur[6] Morris.

The arms of Morris as used by Lewis Morris, first of the name here, are Quarterly, 1st and 4th, Gules, a lion rampant regardant, gold ; 2nd and 3rd, Argent, three torteaux in fesse. Crest, a castle in flames. Motto, Tandem vincitur.

———

The extensive purchases of Col. Caleb Heathcote were erected into the lordship and manor of Scarsdale, 21 Mch. 1701. According to Bolton it seems that Caleb was brother of Sir Gilbert H., Lord Mayor of London, and was son of Gilbert Heathcote of Chesterfield in Scarsdale, co. Derby, by his wife Ann, dau. of Thomas Dickins.

Caleb[1] Heathcote came to America in 1692, and m. Martha, dau. of Col. Wm. Smith of Long Island, formerly

Governor of Tangier. Col. Heathcote was Mayor of New York in 1711, and in 1715 was appointed Surveyor-general of the province. He had a cousin George H. of Pennsylvania, and in his will mentions his brother William H. lately deceased in England. Although Col. Heathcote left at his death in 1719 several sons, they all died in infancy, and the Manor of Scarsdale with other possessions devolved upon his two daughters, Anne,[2] wife of Hon. James de Lancey, Lt. Gov. of the Province, and Martha,[2] who m. Dr. Lewis Johnston of Perth Amboy. Anne[2] de Lancey had two sons, James[3] and John-Peter[3]; the last of whom m. Elizabeth, dau. of Col. Richard Floyd, and became eventually the owner of Scarsdale.

At his death in 1823 this property was divided among his five children.

Martha[2] Johnston, the other coheiress of Caleb Heathcote, had daus. Anne,[3] wife of William Burnet, and Margaret,[3] wife of Gov. Bowes Read of New Jersey, and a son John L.[3] Johnston, who married Susanna Barbarie and left a large family.

Although the name of Heathcote was so soon extinct, it will be seen that the family long preserved the connection with the Manor.

The arms on the seal of Col. Caleb Heathcote are, Ermine, three pomeis each charged with a cross gold. Crest; on a mural crown azure, a pomeys as in the arms between two wings displayed ermine.

The Manor of Pelham, containing 9166 acres of land, was so constituted in 1666 in favor of Thomas Pell, gentleman.

He was the grandson of John[1] Pell, who married Margaret Overend, and had six sons and three daughters. The oldest son was Rev. John[2] Pell, Rector of Southwyck, co. Sussex, who died in 1616 leaving two sons, Thomas[3] of the Manor of Pelham, and Rev. Dr. John[3] Pell, Rector of Fobbing, co. Essex. This connection seems perfectly established by the documents printed by Mr. Bolton. One of these is a statement by John Allen, Secretary of Connecticut, that the Governor was fully satisfied that Mr. John[4] Pell, sewer in ordinary to his Majesty, and son of Dr. Pell of London, was the nephew of Mr. Thomas Pell[3] late of Fairfield, and the person made his heir in his last will. This was in 1670, and John Pell had undoubtedly just arrived here to inherit his uncle's estate.

In 1687 the estate at Pelham was more fully made into a Manor by Gov. Dongan in favor of this John Pell. After his settlement here John[4] Pell married Rachel Pinckney of East Chester, and dying about 1700 left issue two sons and several daughters.

Thomas Pell,[5] the oldest son, who died in 1739, left five sons, Joseph,[6] Thomas,[6] Joshua,[6] Philip[6] and Caleb.[6] As all of these sons married and left issue, the family must be quite numerous at the present time. The eldest branch, through Thomas,[5] Joseph[6] and Joseph,[7] was represented by Peter[8] Pell of East Chester.

Thomas[6] Pell had three sons and numerous descendants. The representatives of Joshua[6] are the Pells of New York and Robert L. Pell of Pelham, Ulster county.

Philip[6] Pell m. Hannah Mott 5 Mch. 1731, and his son Philip,[7] who m. Gloriana Tredwell, had sons Hon. Philip,[8] Major Samuel[8] and Col. David[8] Pell. Descendants of

Philip[8] and David[8] still own a portion of the original manor at Pelham. Major Samuel[8] Pell was distinguished at the battle of Saratoga, but died unm. 29 Dec. 1786, aged 31.

The seal of John[4] Pell gives the arms as Ermine, on a canton azure, a pelican gold, vulned gules. Besides this example we have seen a copy of a document found under the corner-stone of the old church at Pelham, signed by John Pell and his wife Rachel Pinckney. It contains a tricking of these arms and also those of the Pinckneys, viz: Gold, four fusils in fesse gules.

The Manor of Livingston, as established in favor of Robert Livingston by Gov. Dongan, in 1686, comprised over 120,000 acres, "commencing about five miles south of the city of Hudson, running twelve miles on the Hudson river, extending back to the line of Massachusetts, and widening as it receded from the river, so as to embrace not far from twenty miles on the boundary of the latter colony." The Livingston family here* is traced to Rev. Alexander[1] Livingston, minister of Monybrook in Stirlingshire, who married Barbara Livingston of Kilsyth and had a son Rev. William,[2] minister of Lanark in 1614. The son of this last was Rev. John[3] Livingston, who was born at Monybrook 21 June, 1603. He was settled at Ancram in Teviotdale, but died in Holland 9 Aug. 1672. By his

---

* Sir Bernard Burke says in his account of the extinct peerages of the Livingstones of Scotland, that "a flourishing branch of the family still remains, in high honor and distinction, in the United States of America," and again "the family of Livingstone of New York is unquestionably descended in the direct male line from the old Lords Livingstone."

wife Mary Fleming he had a son Robert,[4] b. 13 Dec. 1651, who came to New York in 1676, and apparently settled at Albany. He purchased of the Indians the lands afterwards constituting the Manor of Livingston, and by his will he also established or set off the Manor of Clermont, containing about 13,000 acres.

This Robert[4] Livingston was deeply involved in the political struggles of his time, and at one time his estate was declared confiscated. He soon after retrieved his position, was a member of the Assembly, and from 1718 to 1725 was Speaker thereof.

He married in 1683 Alida, daughter of Philip Pieterse van Schuyler, widow of Rev. Nicholas van Rensselaer of Albany, and died in 1728. His son Philip[5] Livingston inherited the estate of Livingston, m. Catherine Van Brugh, and had Robert,[6] who m. first Mary Tong and secondly Mrs. Gertrude Schuyler.

Robert[6] Livingston, who died 27 Nov. 1790, left by his first wife a son Peter[7] R. Livingston, who was b. 8 May, 1737, and m. 6 June, 1758, Margaret, dau. of James Livingston.

Their oldest son Robert-Tong[8] Livingston, b. Apr. 4, 1759, m. Margaret, dau. of John Livingston, who left only a daughter Mary,[9] wife of Alex. Crofts.

Many other branches of this family are recorded by HOLGATE, who has given the descendants also of Robert Livingston, a nephew of the first-named proprietor of the Manor.

The Livingstons have occupied a most important place in the history of New York, and we will only cite a few of the more important names. Philip, second lord of the

Manor, was at the capture of Port Royal. His son Philip, born at Albany in 1716, was one of the Signers of the Declaration of Independence. Brockholst Livingston was a Judge of the Supreme Court of the United States. Robert R. of Clermont was Chancellor of New York, and in 1801 was Minister to France. William Livingston, son of Philip, second proprietor of the Manor, having removed to New Jersey, was chosen Governor of that province in 1776, which office he held until his death in 1790.

According to BURKE'S Armory the arms of Livingston of Greenburgh, New York, Quarterly, 1st and 4th, Argent, three cinquefoils gules, within the royal tressure, flory counter flory vert; 2nd and 3rd, Sable, a bend between six billets gold. Crest, a demi Hercules wreathed about the head and middle, holding in the dexter hand a club erect, and in the sinister a serpent, all proper. Motto, Si je puis.

In Mapleson's Handbook of Heraldry the arms of the Livingstons of the Manor are given as above, except that three gillyflowers are put for the cinquefoils. The quartered arms are for Callendar.

In regard to the Philipse family many idle traditions have at times crept into print. The latest and best account is given by Hon. Henry C. Murphy, in a note to Dankers' "Journal of a Voyage to New York."

Frederick Flypsen was born in 1626 at Bolsward in Friesland. He came to New York as early as 1653 and was a carpenter. In Dec. 1662 he married Margaret (Hardenbrook) De Vries, widow of Peter Rodolphus De

Vries, a merchant of New York, who died leaving a considerable property. Frederick Philipse undoubtedly availed of the advantages arising from this marriage, and soon became the richest man in the colony. It is not certainly known when his first wife died, but she was alive in 1679 and was dead in 1692, when he married Catherine (van Cortlandt) widow of John Derval.

He was a member of the Council for many years. In 1693 he had his property on the Hudson erected into a Manor by the name of Philipsborough. The patent is printed in Bolton's West Chester, Vol. II, 418–428. In the same history, I. 322, will be found a tabular pedigree of the family, which, as we have said, is undoubtedly erroneous in the earlier generations. A coat of arms is there given, Azure, a demi-lion rampant issuing from a ducal coronet argent and crowned gold. Crest, a demilion crowned and issuing out of a coronet, as in the arms. We are not informed, however, from what source this example was taken.

Frederick[1] Philipse, the first, who d. 1702, had children by his first wife, Philip[2] b. 1664, Adolphus[2] 1665, Annetje[2] 1667, besides Rombout[2] b. 1670 who died young. He seems also to have adopted his wife's daughter Eva[2] De Vries, who m. Jacob van Cortlandt. Anne m. Philip French.

Of these sons, Adolphus[2] died unm. in 1749. The oldest son Philip[2] Philipse resided in Barbadoes, where he married Maria Sparkes, dau. of the Governor. He died in 1700, leaving an only child Frederick[3] Philipse b. 1698, who became the sole male representative of the family.

Frederick[3] Philipse m. in 1726 Joanna, dau. of Gov.

Anthony Brockholes of New York, and died of consumption in 1751. His children were Frederick,[4] Philip,[4] Susanna[4] who m. Col. Beverly Robinson, Mary[4] who m. Col. Roger Morris, and Margaret[4] d. *s. p.*

Col. Frederick[4] Philipse m. Elizabeth, dau. of Charles Williams and widow of —— Rutgers, by whom he had ten children. Though not an active partisan he became a refugee and in consequence his property, consisting of the Manor of Philipsbourgh, was confiscated. It was estimated to contain 150 square miles, and Col. Philipse received as compensation from the British Government the sum of £62,075. He died at Chester, Eng., in 1785. His sons were Frederick,[5] Philip,[5] Charles[5] and John,[5] all of whom distinguished themselves in the British service, but of whom only the oldest seems to have married.

Frederick[5] Philipse, the oldest son, m. Harriet, dau. of Thomas Griffiths, and left issue, a son Frederick-Charles[6] and a daughter Charlotte-Elizabeth.

Col. Frederick-Charles[6] Philipse of Rhual, co. Flint, m. a Miss Palliser and dying in 1851 left five sons, Frederick[7] being the oldest.

The junior branch of the family was descended from Philip[4] Philipse, who inherited part of the Highland Upper Patent, and m. Margaret Marston. He died in 1768 and his children being young their property was not disturbed. He had sons Adolphus[5] and Nathaniel,[5] who both died young, and Frederick,[5] who was in the British service.

Frederick[5] Philipse, who d. in 1829, m. first his cousin Mary, dau. of Nathaniel Marston, by whom he had an only child Mary.[6] He m. secondly Maria Kemble.

Mary[6] Philipse m. Samuel Gouverneur and had four children, of whom Frederick[7] Gouverneur was the proprietor of the entailed estate at Philipstown.

———

Gardiner's Island, which lies at the eastern extremity of Long Island and which contains about 3,300 acres, was bought by Lion Gardiner in 1639. He was an Englishman, who had been employed as an Engineer by the Prince of Orange, had married in Holland, and in 1635 came to Connecticut to instruct the colonists in building fortifications. He was commander of Saybrook fort, but finally removed to the island which bears his name and which was erected by Gov. Dongan into a Manor.

Lion[1] Gardiner, by his wife, Mary Williamson, had a son David,[2] b. 1636, and two daughters. He d. in 1663 and his widow in 1665.

David[2] Gardiner, second proprietor, m. 4 June, 1657, widow Mary Lerringham, at London, by whom he had John,[3] David,[3] Lyon[3] and Elizabeth.[3]

John[3] Gardiner, third owner, m. 1st, Mary King; 2d, widow Sarah Coit; 3d, widow Elizabeth Allen, and 4th, widow Elizabeth Osborn. He had children, David,[4] Samuel,[4] John,[4] Joseph[4] and Jonathan,[4] and died 25 June, 1738.

The oldest son, David[4] Gardiner, b. 1691, m. 1st, Rachel Schellinger, and 2d, Mehitable Burroughs. He died July 4, 1751, leaving issue, John,[5] Abraham,[5] Samuel,[5] David,[5] Mary,[5] Abigail[5] and Hannah.[5]

John[5] Gardiner, fifth owner, m. 1st, Elizabeth Mulford, and 2d, Deborah Avery. His children were David,[6]

Mary,[6] John,[6] Elizabeth,[6] Jerusha,[6] Hannah[6] and Septimus.[6] He died May 19, 1764, and his widow m. Gen. Israel Putnam.

David[6] Gardiner, b. 1738, m. Jerusha Buell, and dying 8 Sept. 1774, left issue, John-Lyon[7] and David.[7]

John-Lyon[7] Gardiner, b. 1770, m. Sarah Griswold, and died 22 Nov. 1816, leaving issue, David[8] J., Sarah[8] D., Mary[8] B., John[8] G. and Samuel[8] B. Of these, David-J., eighth proprietor, d. unm. 18 Dec. 1829, and his brother, John-Griswold[8] Gardiner, became the sole proprietor of the island. Samuel-Buell[8] Gardiner m. Mary G. Thompson and resided at Easthampton.

The descendants of Lion Gardiner are quite numerous, and a very good record is to be found in Thompson's History of Long Island, 2d edition, II., 378–381.

———

We have already given in the Heraldic Journal, II., 88, an account of the Lloyd family, the proprietors of Lloyd's Neck on Long Island. Thompson (Hist. Long Island, I., 491) says this Manor was established by grants from Gov. Nicoll and Gov. Andros.

———

We have thus traced some of the more prominent families who formerly possessed manorial rights in New York. We believe that there are other examples, but the references in the books to which we have had access do not allow us to decide. Perhaps some of the readers of this Journal will complete the list, or furnish a reference to any printed account of these estates.   W. H. W.

ARMS OF TYLER OF AMERICA.

Communicated by Rev. WILLIAM TYLER.

Armorial Ensigns, as here represented, were granted by the College of Arms, Nov. 21, 1774, to the descendants of Andrew Tyler of Boston in New England, Gent., and of William Tyler his brother:—Sable, on a fess Erminois, between three mountain-cats passant guardant Ermine, a cross formy on either side a crescent gules. Crest, A demi-mountain-cat issuant guardant Erminois.

This Coat Armor is emblazoned on the Chart containing the pedigree of Tyler of America, recorded at the College March 2, 1778, attested by Catherine, Lady Heard, a daughter of Andrew and Miriam (Pepperell) Tyler, and grand-daughter of Thomas Tyler from Budleigh in Devonshire, the immigrant ancestor of the family. A copy is in possession of Gen. John S. Tyler of Boston, a descendant of William Tyler, mentioned in the grant.

The late William Courthope, Esq., Somerset Herald, stated in a letter of Oct. 8, 1851, that "the family of Budleigh had no right to arms, and by the grant the said right is limited to the descendants of the two sons of Thomas of Budleigh." It follows that the Coat Armor adopted by Joseph, son of the afore-named William, for his book-plate (see p. 22), adopted also by Rev. Andrew, son of Andrew afore-named and brother of Lady Heard, was used without authority, probably before the grant in 1774.

HERBERT PELHAM, HIS ANCESTRY AND DESCENDANTS.

In the seventh volume of the Fourth Series of the Collections of the Mass. Historical Society we find Herbert Pelham using a seal with the arms of the Pelhams of Sussex, viz., Azure, three pelicans argent vulning themselves ppr. No satisfactory account of his ancestry and descendants can be read in any work, and we have undertaken to put together from various sources a more complete pedigree than has yet been printed.

The family is traced back to Walter de Pelham, who died in 1292, seized of the manors of Pelham in Hertfordshire, Cottenham in Kent and Twinsted in Essex, and left two sons, William and Walter.

Walter, the second son, was heir to his brother, who died without issue. He obtained lands in Sussex, and left a son and heir, Thomas, who was father of another Thomas who was living in 1346 and left a son John de Pelham.

This John was a person of great fame in the reign of Edward III., and was present at the battle of Poitiers in 1356. He afterwards received the honor of knighthood, and by his marriage with Joan, daughter of Vincent Herbert, alias Finch, left a son of his own name.

John de Pelham was no less famous than his father, being for a long time in the service of Henry Bolingbroke, afterwards Henry IV. In 1399 and afterwards he was in parliament for the county of Sussex, and was created a Knight of the Bath; in 1400 he was appointed Constable of the castle of Pevensey; and in 1401 he was Sheriff of Sussex. He died in 1429, full of honor, having been in the highest favor and the most honorable employments under two of the greatest Monarchs of this realm, who were famed for their courage and all manly virtues and raised the glory of the English nation to such a degree as never to be forgot; so that it must be owing to some uncommon instances of self-denial that he was not ranked amongst the Peers. He had married Joan, daughter of Sir John Escures, and left an only son John, and daughters, Agnes and Joan.

His son, Sir John Pelham, was also in the French wars of Henry V., and in 1415 was by his father appointed Constable of Pevensey castle; he was Chamberlain of the household to Queen Catherine, widow of Henry V. He married Joan de Courcy, by whom he had three sons, John, William and Thomas, and three daughters, Catharine, Cicely and Joan. He died in 1458, and was succeeded by his eldest son, but as both this John and his next brother, William, died without issue male, Thomas, the third son, became eventual heir, obtaining the manors of Laughton, Crowhurst, &c., in addition to Buxsted, where he had lived.

This Thomas Pelham died in 1516, having had by his wife Margaret four sons and two daughters. The sons were, John, who died childless before his father; Thomas, who died unmarried; William, ancestor of the Duke of Newcastle, the Earl of Chichester and the Earl of Yarborough; and Anthony. The daughters were Catharine and Joan.

Anthony, the fourth son, had a wife Margaret, and died in 1566, seized of lands in Sussex and Surrey. He left an only son Herbert, twenty years old.

Herbert, born about 1546, was of Michelsam in Sussex, and afterwards of Dorsetshire. He married Katherine, daughter of John Thacher of Preshull in Sussex, and had two sons, Herbert, of Swineshead in Lincolnshire, and Thomas, of Compton-Valence in Dorsetshire, and two daughters, Anne, wife of Edward Clarke of Dorchester, and Elizabeth, wife of John Humfrey of Chaldon. He took for his second wife, Elizabeth, daughter of Thomas, second Lord Delawar, a lady several years younger than himself, as she died in 1632, aged 59.

Herbert, the eldest son, married Penelope, daughter of Thomas, second Lord Delawar, sister of his step-mother, and lived at Swineshead in Lincolnshire. He seems to have been a knight,* and died in 1625, leaving a son

---

* King James I. knighted several persons of the name of Pelham, including an Anthony; but I find no Sir Herbert among them. The third Herbert is distinctly called son of a knight on his admission to College at Oxford, 12 November, 1619.—*Mass. Historical Collections, Third Series, VIII.*, 249.

Herbert, and two daughters, Penelope, wife of Richard Bellingham, and Elizabeth; perhaps he had also sons John and William.

Herbert, the eldest son, was born about 1601, and was educated at Magdalen Hall, Oxford. He married Elizabeth, daughter and coheiress of Thomas Waldgrave of Alphamston, Essex, with whom he obtained the manor of Ferrers in Bures Hamlet in that parish. Her mother was Elizabeth, daughter of Robert Gurdon of Assington, through whom Herbert Pelham was cousin to Richard Saltonstall; he was doubly, but distantly, connected with John Winthrop, through the Waldgraves and Cloptons, and through the Gurdons and Mildmays. By this wife he had—

Waldgrave, bapt. 26 September, 1627.

Penelope, born about 1630, married 1657 Josiah Winslow of Marshfield, Mass., died 7 December, 1703.

Nathaniel, bapt. 5 February, 1631, H. C. 1651, died 1657.

His wife being dead, he came to New England in 1638, and settled at Cambridge. He soon took a second wife, Elizabeth, daughter of Godfrey Bosseville of Gunthwayte in Yorkshire, widow of Roger Harlakenden, by whom he had—

Mary, born 12 November, 1640.

Frances, born 9 November, 1643.

Herbert, born 3 October, 1645, d. soon.

Edward.

Henry.

William, died probably before his father.

He had two other daughters, Katherine and Anne, but

by which wife does not appear. He was Treasurer of
Harvard College in 1643, and became a freeman of the
colony, and was chosen an Assistant in 1645. He returned to his wife's estate in England in 1647, and was a
member of Parliament in 1654. The date of his death
cannot be exactly stated, but it was before March, 1676,
when his will was admitted to probate. By it he left to
his son Waldgrave his lands in Sussex and the manor of
Swineshead in Lincolnshire; to his son Edward his lands
at Smeeth Hall and Chapel Hill in Lincolnshire and all
his lands in New England in the Massachusetts Bay in
America, situate, lying and being in Cambridge, Watertown, Sudbury or elsewhere within the said colony; to
his son Henry his lands in Ireland; he made provision also
for his sisters Penelope Bellingham and Elizabeth Pelham,
his daughters Penelope Winslow, Anne Pelham, Katherine
Clarke, the wife of Cuthlac Elliot, and his son Jeremiah
Stonnard. These two men probably married Mary and
Frances. Herbert Pelham's widow, Elizabeth, died 1
April, 1706, aged 88, and was buried at Marshfield, Mass.

Waldgrave Pelham, the eldest son, succeeded his father
at Ferrers. He married Abigail, daughter of Thomas
Glascock of Sible-Hedingham, Essex, and dying in 1699
left children, Waldgrave, Herbert, Jemima, Abigail, Penelope, Elizabeth, Margaret and Mary. His eldest son
Waldgrave succeeded him, but sold part of the estates in
Essex before his death in 1703. Herbert, the second son,
was living at Bures in 1738.

Edward Pelham, second surviving son of Herbert,
graduated at Harvard College in 1673, having passed
rather a disreputable youth, as appears from his father's

will. He married Godsgift, daughter of Benedict Arnold, Governor of Rhode Island, and lived at Newport. His children were Elizabeth, Edward and Thomas. He had a second wife, Freelove, perhaps sister of his first, and died 30 September, 1730.

SUFFOLK WILLS.

(Continued from Vol. II., p. 185.)

The seals which we shall now present have not been identified in most instances. Still, as examples of which use may hereafter be made they are placed in our collection :—

50.

This seal is on the will of Joseph Rixton or Rickston of London, "now residing in Boston," merchant. It is dated in 1707, and mentions his wife Rebecca and two children, and his wife's mother, " Madam Vally of Hampsteed near London." He makes bequests to Mr. Richard Procter and to Edward Weaver, scrivener. The witnesses are John Chipp, Ephraim Shrimpton and Richard Ellis.

51.

This seal is from the will of Anne Fisher, daughter of Joshua F. of Dedham, 1711. It is witnessed by Esther Fuller, John Dean and Eliezer Moody. The same seal occurs on the will of

Thomas Ward, 1711, witnessed by William Griggs, Hannah Griggs and Eliezer Moody, and on that of William Hughes, 1708. There can be no doubt, therefore, that it was the property of the notary, Moody, though not necessarily to be considered as containing his family arms. Concerning Moody, we find that he was of Boston in 1695, but his will, dated 13 April, 1720, proved 27 June, same year, calls him of Dedham, scrivener. He mentions his wife Eleanor, kinsman Edward Allen of Hartford in Connecticut, and his "wife's kindred Joseph Carew and Elizabeth Sanders now living with us," to whom £10 were to be given when they came of age.

52.

 This seal was undoubtedly the property of John Hayward, Sr., of Boston, scrivener, as it is found on the will of Mary Winslow, 1676, to which, with John Hands and Francis Hacket, he was a witness; and also on a deed signed by Joshua Scottow and Lydia, 1686, to which the witnesses were John Hayward, notary public, and Zechariah Shute, Sr. This deed, which is now in the possession of E. J. Foster, Esq., of Charlestown, has two fine impressions of the seal. As to Hayward, we find that he was of Boston, 1671, and postmaster in 1677. He died in 1687 or 1688, and left widow Elizabeth and sons Samuel and John. The arms seem to be those of Parler of Westminster, who bore as follows:—Gules, three lions passant in pale argent, over all on a bend sable three mullets or. Crest, a Cornish chough sable beaked and legged gules.

53.

This example is from the will of John Winslow of Boston, 1674. He was brother of Gov. Edward Winslow, and married, at Plymouth, Mary Chilton. As these arms belong to neither of these names, the seal may have belonged to one of the two witnesses, John Joyliffe or John Hayward. If to the latter, it would indicate that notaries may have owned and used armorial seals of other families.

54.

This coat of arms is an enlarged copy of a seal appended to the will of Timothy Prout, 1702, witnessed by Thomas Harwood, Thomas Hunt and Humphrey Parsons. It is evidently the property of the latter, being no doubt the arms ascribed by BURKE to Sir John Parsons, Lord Mayor of London in 1704, and to Humphrey Parsons, Lord Mayor in 1731, viz., Gules, two chevronels ermine between three eagles displayed gold. Crest, an eagle's leg erased at the thigh gold, standing on a leopard's head gules. The same arms with a different crest are used by a family long resident in Barbadoes, a branch of the Parsons family of Great Milton, co. Oxford. Of this Humphrey Parsons we only know that his name occurs as an inhabitant of Boston, in 1687, in the list of tax-payers. The family of the name descended from Jeffrey Parsons of Gloucester, 1657, has within a century used the same coat-of-arms, but we know of no early example of such use, nor of any connection with this Humphrey of Boston.

55.

This very curious seal is on the will of Susanna Vergoose, 1685, witnessed by Samuel Sewall, Daniel Quincy and Robert Howard. It seems to be an example of dimidiation of shields impaled, and is very probably of French or German origin. We cannot decide on the probable ownership of it, having mislaid our note of some other examples of its use on papers in the Probate Office.

56.

This seal is on the will of Ebbet Hunt, 1711, witnessed by Jonathan Gulliver, Peter Whyte and Eliezer Moody. It is also on that of Anne Shepperd, 1709, and Miriam Tyler, 1831. The arms must be intended for those of Moody, described on p. 96.

57.

From the will of Joseph Haward of Boston, 1722, witnessed by Francis Archbold, James Barber and Nicholas Cock.

58.

This seal is on the will of John Lawson, 1704, witnessed by Anthony Blount, John Bucannan, John Cronenshilt and Savill Simpson.

59.

This seal, of which several examples occur, as on the wills of Isaac Griffin, 1693, John Major, 1702, and William Davis, 1701, was clearly that of William Milborn, who appears as a witness on all of them. The arms are those described by BURKE as belonging to —— Milborne, alderman of London, 1535, viz., Sable, on a bend between two leopard's heads gold, three crosses pattée of the field; on a chief argent as many escallops of the field. Another Milborne, Lord Mayor in 1521, used the same arms, except that the crosses on the bend were formée. It is impossible in this seal to decide which variety was used. As to Milburn himself, nothing has been discovered, and his name does not appear on SAVAGE'S lists. He was evidently a lawyer, scrivener or notary public.

We have seen that there were several notaries here whose names occur repeatedly, and not improbably these seals which cannot be identified were the property of such scriveners. We have never seen any list of the notaries in Boston, but in Drake's History, p. 571, is a notice of a difficulty in regard to the office which was settled by the General Court in Dec. 1720. It appears that Joseph Hiller and Samuel Tyley, who were duly appointed notaries for the county of Suffolk, complained that Joseph Marion, scrivener, took upon him the character and office of a public notary under pretence of a commission from the Archbishop of Canterbury. Mr. Marion, who was the son of Dea. John Marion of Boston, did possess and produce his commission; but the House decided that no one had the right to grant such a license except this Government, and he was ordered not to practice.

A. T. P.

HERALDIC NOTES AND QUERIES.

(Continued from p. 48.)

XXXIX.

In our last number it was stated that the arms of Brodhead are not found in English works on Heraldry. We have since noticed that in the last edition of the Peerage and Baronetage, Sir Theodore Brinckman, Baronet, quarters with his own the arms of Brodhead, as engraved in the Heraldic Journal.

XL.

Mr. H. G. Somerby has communicated the description of a document in possession of a gentleman in London, indorsed "3ᵈ July 1688. Allotment between Joseph Dudley, William Stoughton, Robert Thompson, Daniel Cox and John Blackwell." The first was of Roxbury, the second of Dorchester, Mass., the third and fourth of London, and the last of Boston, Mass. Dudley uses the seal engraved in Vol. I., p. 185; Stoughton uses a seal with the arms as engraved in Vol. I., p. 10; and Blackwall's seal bore, Paly of six, on a chief a lion passant guardant, impaling three roses. Crest, a swan's head and neck erased, ducally gorged. The arms of Blackwell are found to be, Paly of six argent and azure, on a chief gules a lion pass. guard. or. John Blackwall seems to have been here as a speculator in lands, and is not thought to have left descendants here.

XLI.

An old copy of Longinus de Sublimitate contains the armorial book-plate of "Philip Ludwell of Green-Spring in Virginia Esqr." The arms are, Gules, on a bend argent between two towers or three eagles displayed sable. Motto, "I Pensieri Stretti ed il Viso Sciolto." On the opposite leaf is the autograph, "E: Lib: Philippi Ludwell, Coll: Gul: & Mar: Alum: Sept: 5°: die A. D. 1736." From Bishop Meade's work on the Old Churches and Families of Virginia, we learn, that Thomas Ludwell, a native of Bruton, in Somersetshire, England, was Secretary of the Colony of Virginia, and died in 1678. His nephew, Philip Ludwell, erected a monument to him at Williamsburg in 1727. I presume the owner of the book was this nephew, or a son of his. The arms are not found in English works on heraldry.

XLII.

Among the few titled persons who settled in New England was Deborah, Lady Moody. She was in 1640 of Lynn, but by religious persecution was soon driven away, and moved to Long Island, in the Dutch colony of New York. She and her son, Sir Henry Moody, Baronet, were of Gravesend, L. I., in 1645. We quote the following account of the family from Burke's Extinct and Dormant Baronetcies of England.

Henry Moody, Esq., of Garesdon in Wiltshire, who was created a Baronet in 1621–2, married Deborah, daughter of Walter Dunch, Esq., of Avebury in the same county, and dying about 1632 was succeeded by his son,—

Sir Henry Moody, who sold the estate of Garesdon, and settled in New England, where he is presumed to have died *s. p.* in 1662. If he did, the Baronetcy then became extinct.

Arms :—Vert, a fesse engr. arg. surmounted of another gu. between three harpies of the second crined or.

XLIII.

A family which obtained a title after leaving this country is that of Middleton of South Carolina. From Playfair's British Baronetage and Burke's Peerage and Baronetage we have prepared the following account, which is printed with a request for further information concerning the earlier generations and the sons who remained in America.

Arthur Middleton, Esq., was Governor of South Carolina in 1725, and dying in 1737 left three sons, William, Henry and Thomas. The second and third sons married and left issue in South Carolina. William, the eldest son, married Sarah, daughter of Morton Wilkinson of S. C., by whom he had William, Thomas, who died in S. C., John and Arthur. He lived at Crowfield Hall, Suffolk, England, and was succeeded by his eldest son, William, who was created a Baronet in 1804, which title devolved at his death in 1830, upon his only son, Sir William Fowle Middleton-Fowle, the second Baronet. He died without issue in 1860, when the Baronetcy became extinct and the representation of the family passed to the descendants, if any, of his uncle Thomas of S. C. The arms of the family are,—Argent, fretty sable; on a canton per chevron of the second and or, an unicorn's head likewise per chevron gules and gold, the horn of the last and sable. Crest, A garb or, banded vert, between two wings sable.

THE

HERALDIC JOURNAL;

RECORDING THE ARMORIAL BEARINGS AND GENEALOGIES
OF AMERICAN FAMILIES.

NO. XIX.   JULY, 1867.

ARMS AND PEDIGREE OF PHILIP DUMARESQ
OF BOSTON,

From the researches of J. Bertrand Payne, William Grant Dumaresq, H. G. Somerby, and documents from Colonel Malet de Carteret of Jersey, and papers in the possession of the Family.

Arms, Gules, three escallops or, in chief a mullet for difference; Supporters, two greyhounds rampant; Crest, a bull passant guardant; Motto, Dum vivo spero, for Dumaresq.

He quarters,—Sable, three dolphins embowed argent, for De Bagot; Argent, three trefoils sable, for Payne; Ermines, a cross-bow drawn charged with an arrow all argent, for Larbalistier; Gules, four fusils in fess argent, for De Carteret; Gules, a chevron between three towers or, for St. Ouen; Gules, four fusils conjoined in fess argent, for D'Albini; Sable, two shin-bones in saltire argent the dexter surmounted of the sinister, for Newton; Azure, three lions rampant or, a bordure sable, for De Caux; Argent, a saltire gules between four fleurs-de-lis azure, for Harleston; Gules, two bars ermine, in chief three martlets or, for Sarré; Gules, four fusils conjoined in fess, in base an annulet for a difference, for De Carteret junior;

Sable, three swords in pile argent points downwards hilts and pommels or, for Poulett; Argent, two wings conjoined ermine, for Raynez; Azure, six mascles argent three and three, for Credie; Party per fess gules and azure, three crescents argent, for Aumeral; Barry of eight argent and gules, over all a bend sable, for Bourton; Argent, a chevron gules between three garbs vert, for Bosco; Azure, on a chief argent a demi-lion couped gules, for Denebaud; Argent, three chevrons sable, for Archdeacon; Gules, a cross fleury or charged with seven roundles sable, for Latimer; Gules, a wyvern with wings erect argent, for Le Brent; Gules, three lions passant in pale argent, over all a label of three points sable, for Giffard; Argent, a fess between three cinquefoils gules, for Poutrell; Argent, a fess between three wolf's heads erased sable, for Seale; and Gules, three fleurs-de-lis one and two over all a bend or, for Ferry.

The family of Dumaresq, as its name indicates, is of Norman origin, but has been settled in the Island of Jersey for the last six hundred years, "holding from the earliest historic periods offices of trust and distinction in the public service."

They have also held as Seigneurs the fiefs of La Haute, Samares, Vincelles de Bas, Gorge, des Augrés, Du Morin, La Chené, des Columberes, Anneville, and St. Ouen, all in the Island.

Since the Dumaresqs have from time to time married with heiresses representing some of the most ancient English families, and have thereby become entitled to join to their own twenty-five other coats, this shield presents an unusually favorable opportunity for the student of heraldry to study the English system of quartering arms.

The earliest official record of the name occurs in the roll of the Exchequer, 21st of Edward the first, recording Assizes held at Jersey, 23 of November, 1291, where Jordan Dumaresq was a Judge of the Royal Court of the Island.

In the year 1327 William[2] Dumaresq, believed to be a son of Jordan,[1] was the Attorney General of Jersey. In the year 1390 William[3] Dumaresq, believed to be a son of William[2] Dumaresq the Attorney General, was the Royal Governor of the Island, a Judge of the King's Court, and Lord of the Seigneurie of La Haute. He made his will in 1407 and mentions his children, Thomas[4] Dumaresq, afterwards Lord of La Haute, a daughter the wife of John Payne, Seigneur of Samares, and another daughter the wife of the Seigneur Peras Nicholas of Gurnsey. From this William[3] descend all of the name in France, England, and in America.

Thomas[4] Dumaresq, second Seigneur of La Haute, married and left two sons, Jaquet,[5] afterwards Seigneur of La Haute, and Thomas.[5]

Thomas,[5] younger brother of Jaquet[5] Dumaresq, Seigneur of La Haute, married Jeannette, only daughter and heiress of John de Bagot, Seigneur of Gorge, and became Seigneur of Gorge in right of his wife, and brought the quartering of De Bagot into the family arms. He died leaving only one son John.[6]

John,[6] son of Thomas[5] and Jeannette Dumaresq, was Seigneur of Gorge, and married Mabel, only daughter and heiress of Philip Payne, Seigneur of Samares, and Vincelles de Bas, and became Seigneur of these fiefs in right of his wife, and also added the quartering of Payne to his arms.

He left two sons, the eldest, John[7] Dumaresq, Seigneur of Samares, and the second, Richard,[7] Seigneur of Vincelles de Bas, and of Gorge, and three daughters, Jane,[7] Catherine[7] and Colette.[7]

Richard,[7] second son of John[6] and Mabel Dumaresq, was Seigneur of Vincelles de Bas, and of Gorge, and married Colette, only daughter and heiress of Anthony Larbalistier, Seigneur des Augrés, and became Seigneur des Augrés in right of his wife, and added the arms of Larbalistier to his own. He had four sons, Edward,[8] John,[8] Hillier[8] and Clement,[8] and three daughters, Mabel,[8] Tomasse[8] and Elizabeth.[8]

Edward[8] having died unmarried, John,[8] second son of Richard[7] and Collette Dumaresq, became Seigneur des Augrés, Vincelles de Bas, and of Gorge. He was the Royal Governor of Jersey, and married for his second wife Collette, daughter of his kinsman Clement Dumaresq, Seigneur of Samares, and had by her four sons, Elias,[9] Abraham,[9] Daniel,[9] Joshua,[9] and five daughters, Elizabeth,[9] Sarah,[9] Judith,[9] Susan,[9] and Esther.[9]

Abraham,[9] second son of John[8] and Collette Dumaresq, was Seigneur des Augrés, and married Susan, daughter of Sir Philip De Carteret, Lord of St. Ouen, and the Royal Governor of Jersey. They had four sons, Elias,[10] Benjamin,[10] Gideon,[10] and John,[10] and three daughters, Frances,[10] Sarah,[10] and Anne.[10]

Elias,[10] eldest son of Abraham[9] and Susan Dumaresq, was Seigneur des Augrés, and also a Jurat of the Royal Council. He was a stanch Loyalist, and on account of his firm support of the King during the Commonwealth, he was visited at his Manor des Augrés by Charles 2d, who presented him with a grant of his fief, 1649, which had hitherto been held by Knight's Service. A copy of the grant is preserved in the Public Registry of the Island of Jersey, Book 14, folio 428, and also a curious receipt given to Elias Dumaresq, for performing the Knight's Service by which he held his fief, on the landing of the King in the Island.

"Charles R. Whereas our trusty and well beloved Elias Dumaresq holdeth our franc fee des Augrés by Knight's service, and is obliged at the comming of the King into that our Island, to attend him on horseback up to his saddle girts into the Sea, and in like manner at the King's departure,

We hereby acknowledge and declare to all whom it may concern that the said Elias Dumaresq, both at our arrival at that our Island, and likewise at our departure from it, did accordingly attend us on horseback, going with his horse into the sea up to his saddle girts, whereby we are fully satisfied.

Given at Constance the 13 day of February 1649, in the Second Year of Our Reign.

By his Majesties Command,
Rob Lant
PHILIP DE CARTERET, enregist."

Elias[10] Dumaresq married Jane, daughter of Thomas Payne, Rector of St. Lawrence, and had five sons, Elias,[11] Philip,[11] Edward,[11] John,[11] and Benjamin,[11] and four daughters, Anne,[11] Susan,[11] Jane,[11] and Elizabeth.[11]

Elias,[11] eldest son of Elias[10] and Jane Dumaresq, at the death of his father became Seigneur des Augrés, and was also a Jurat of the Royal Council. He married Frances, only daughter and heiress of Sir Francis de Carteret, Attorney General of Jersey, and added to the quarterings of his arms all those borne by his father-in-law, viz.: The arms of De Carteret, St. Ouen, D'Albini, Newton, De Caux, Harleston, Sarré, De Carteret junior, Poulett, Raynes, Credie, Aumeral, Bourton, Bosco, Denibaud, Archdeacon, Latimer, Le Brent, Giffard, Poutrell, and Seale. He had three sons, Elias,[12] afterwards Seigneur des Augrés, Philip,[12] the first of the family in Boston, John,[12] a Captain in the Royal Navy, and three daughters, Anne,[12] married Elias Le Maistre, Seigneur de Quiteval, Frances,[12] married to Edward Le Gros, and Magdalen,[12] married in Boston, 1722, to Thomas Wroe.

Philip[13] Dumaresq, second son of Elias[12] Dumaresq and Frances de Carteret, his wife, was first a Lieutenant in the Royal Navy.

At the death of his mother, having inherited a part of her fortune, he left the Navy, and bought a ship in which he made voyages between Havre, Jersey and Boston, and brought to this country many of the Huguenot families, the descendants of whom are still to be found here.

At the time of his death he was Captain and owner of "the Young Eagle Letter of Marque of 30 guns," as is shown by his commission from Governor Belcher of Massachusetts, and lately found among the papers of Thomas Hancock, with whom he seems to have been engaged in business.

He married in Boston, June 12, 1716, Susanah, only daughter and heiress of Henry Ferry, formerly of Havre de Grace, and added the quartering of Ferry to his arms.

In the records of the Probate Court of Boston, we find that Susanah Dumaresq, widow, was appointed 30 January, 1744, guardian of her "son Philip Dumaresq, a minor aged about seven years, son of Philip Dumaresq, late of Boston, mariner deceased, with full power to receive any part and portion of estate, accruing to him in right of his grandfather Elias Dumaresq, Lord des Augrés, late of the Island of Jersey deceased, and Madam Frances de Carteret his wife also deceased."

Philip[13] Dumaresq and Susannah Ferry, his wife, left two sons and five daughters; the sons were Edward,[14] m. Mary Bouteneau, and Philip,[14] m. Rebecca Gardiner; the daughters were Susan,[14] first wife of Mathew Saumerez, the father of Admiral Lord de Saumerez, Douce,[14] m. George Bandinel of Jersey, Elizabeth,[14] Anne,[14] m. Nicholas Mallet of Jersey, and Frances.[14]

Philip,[14] second son of Philip[13] Dumaresq and Susannah Ferry, his wife, was born in Boston, 1737. With his sisters he was sent to England to be educated. He returned to this country as an Aide-de-Camp to Lord Dunmore. He left the Army, and married at the King's Chapel, December 13, 1773, Rebecca, daughter of Dr. John Silvester Gardiner. He was a determined Loyalist, an addresser of Hutchinson, 1774, and of Gage, 1775, and two years later, says Sabine, was proscribed and banished. He retired to the Island of New Providence, and was appointed Collector of the King's Revenues at Nassau, where he died. He left three sons, James,[15] Philip[15] and Francis,[15] and six daughters, Anne,[15] Rebecca,[15] Susan,[15] Frances,[15] Hannah[15] and Abigail.[15]

James,[15] eldest son of Philip[14] and Rebecca Dumaresq,

was born in Boston, 1772. With his brother Philip,[15] afterwards a Commander in the Royal Navy, he was sent to England and educated under the care of his kinsman, Admiral Thomas Dumaresq.

Having inherited from his mother lands in Maine, he visited Vassalboro, where he married, Oct. 17, 1797, Sarah Farwell of that place. He settled at Swan Island, and lived in a house built by Dr. Gardiner, his grand-father, where he remained until his death, 1826. He left one son, Philip,[16] and two daughters, Jane Frances[16] Dumaresq, married to Thomas Handasyde Perkins, junior, and Louisa[16] Dumaresq, married to Hon. John Rice Blake.

Philip[16] Dumaresq, only son of James[15] and Sarah Dumaresq, was born at Swan Island, 1804, married June 9, 1836, Margaretta, daughter of Francis Deblois. They had four sons, Philip[17] Kerney, m. Sophia Hurlbut, James[17] Saumerez, Herbert[17] and Francis,[17] and three daughters, Margaretta,[17] Frances,[17] and Florence[17] Saumerez, m. George Wheatland.   A. T. P.

OFFICIAL SEALS.

We have placed here a fac-simile of the official seal of Thomas Hutchinson, who in 1769 succeeded Bernard as Governor of Massachusetts. In a previous article on the family history, (Vol. II., p. 171–176), we expressed the opinion that the arms used by that branch of the family to which the Governor belonged, had never been properly authenticated. Although this is probably true in a technical sense, by which we mean that no proof has been submitted to Heralds' College and there recorded, we are inclined to modify our expression. Two things seem to be proved by Mr. Chester's thorough examination of the pedigree of the family ; first, that William Hutchinson of Boston was the grandson of John H., Mayor of Lincoln in 1556, a man of considerable property. Second, that in 1634, Thomas Hutchinson (grandson of William Hutchinson who was Mayor of Lincoln in 1552, and was brother of John above mentioned), presented his pedigree to the Heralds who were then making their Visitation of Lincolnshire. He claimed the arms of the Hutchinsons of Yorkshire, but on his application were endorsed the words " Respited for proof." Mr. Chester adds that no proof has ever been furnished, nor is there any grant of arms to this family or branch on record.

As against this statement, however, the following arguments may be urged. It is evident that the family attained a respectable position during the sixteenth century, two brothers being Mayors of Lincoln, and either may have obtained a grant or confirmation of arms, which is now not on the records remaining at London. There was certainly every inducement for him to do so, and the early and continuous use of the arms would be an argument in favor of this supposition.

That the arms were early in use is shown by the seal of Samuel Hutchinson, a grandson of John, which was printed in our volume II., p. 183. The continued use is evinced by the tombstones at Boston, Mass., engraved in our volume II., p. 83; the silver plate mentioned in our volume I., p. 59; and by the statement in the funeral sermon on Hon. Thomas Hutchinson in 1740, that "The North Latin School House which wears the Atchievement of his Family in the Front of it, was his Gift to the Town." Lastly, we have the use by Gov. Thomas Hutchinson as shown by our wood-cut.

It is difficult to estimate the actual importance of the absence of a record of arms at Heralds' College. In theory, we believe, the record is deemed indispensable; in practice we are sure this rule is disregarded. Whether or not this case is one of such evident informality as to render it certain that the descendants of John Hutchinson ought not to use the arms, is a question for English antiquaries to decide.

In the article in our second volume, to which reference has been made, we traced this family to William[3] Hutchinson, who, with his famous wife Anne, came to New England and died c. 1642. His son Edward[4] of Boston, was twice married but left only one son, Elisha[5] Hutchinson, who was born 16 Nov., 1641.

Elisha[5] married 1st, Hannah Hawkins, and 2d, Elizabeth Clark. He died in 1717 leaving a son by each wife. Of these, the elder was Thomas[6] Hutchinson who m. in 1703, Sarah Foster and had a large family. His half-brother, Edward,[6] m. Lydia Foster, but though he had thirteen children, his only descendants are in the line of his daughter Elizabeth,[7] who m. Rev. Nathaniel Robbins.

Thomas,[6] had sons Thomas[7] and Foster,[7] but we believe no descendants of the latter remain.

Thomas[7] Hutchinson, the Governor, was born 9 Sept.,

1711, and died in 1780. He married Margaret Sanford and had sons Thomas and Elisha. His descendants are quite numerous in England.

It seems probable that the Governor's wife, who was of Newport, belonged to the family whose arms are engraved at p. 61 of the present volume. Her father, William Sanford, was son of Gov. Peleg Sanforth, and her mother was Griselda ———, who married secondly, ——— Cotton. Gov. Peleg S., whose wife was a Coddington, was grandson of John Sanforth and Bridget Hutchinson. SAVAGE has a different account of the Sanford pedigree, but we have followed the genealogical table prepared by Governor Hutchinson and published by P. O. Hutchinson, Esq.

W. H. W.

[The notice of Gov. Bernard was inadvertently printed before that of Gov. Pownall, but the order should be exactly reversed.—ED.]

CHARNOCK FAMILY.

Communicated by ISAAC J. GREENWOOD.

Capt. John Charnock, merchant of Boston, was admitted to the Old North, Nov. 5, 1710, his wife Mary having previously become a member of the same church, Dec. 5, 1708. After her death he married about 1721, Hannah, dau. of Elizur Holyoke of Boston, and sister of the Rev. Edward Holyoke, afterwards President of Harvard College; this lady, born Feb. 15, 1686, was adm. to O. N., Dec. 12, 1726. Capt. Charnock, by his will of Oct. 5, 1723, left legacies to his sisters, Mary Belcham and Elizabeth

Piper, to be remitted to them in Great Britain soon after his death ; also legacies to his kinswoman Jane King; to the poor widows of the O.N.; to Dr. Cotton Mather ; and to the charity-school, to be expended in books for poor children. To his wife Hannah one fifth of his personal estate, together with all such estate, real cr personal, as she had brought to him upon marriage; all the rents of house and land then occupied by Ephm. Mower, during her life; and the use of his dwelling-house, &c., during the time she remained his widow. A certain proportion of his two brigantines, " William and Mary" and "John and Elizabeth," was bequeathed to his son John, and the remainder of his estate was to be equally divided between his four children, John, Elizabeth, Mary and William; his wife, son John, and Mr. John Ruck to be executors. Mrs. Hannah Charnock married, secondly, Theophilus Burril of Lynn, but had no issue by him, and was living as his widow in Boston, 1756.

I. John, b. Dec. 1701, bap. 22 Mar. 1702; shipwright and merchant of Boston; married Emma, dau. of Rev. Thomas Blowers of Beverly, and g. dau. of Pyam and Eliz. (Belcher) Blowers of Cambridge. The widow, as administratrix, presented, 14 July, 1747, an inventory of his estate, which was rendered insolvent in 1749; one of the creditors was his sister Widow Mary Greenwood, who is then reported to have had in her possession many articles, which, as she said, her brother had given her. Mrs. Emma Charnock died Oct. 6, 1786, Æ. 83, and was buried at Beverly.

 1. John, bap. June 12, 1726, d. yng. 2. Thomas, bap. Nov. 12, 1727, d. yng. 3. Emma, liv. unm. in Boston, 1756.

II.   William, b. March; bap. April 2, 1704; d. yng.

III.   Richard, bap. Nov. 4, 1705; d. yng.

IV.   Elizabeth, bap. Sept. 14, 1707; she chose as guardian, Nov. 25, 1723, Capt. Jeffery Bedgood of Boston; married Thomas Lee, prob. as 2d w., and died before 1753, leaving only dau. Elizabeth, living unm. in Boston, 1756.

V.   Mary, b. 9 March, bap. 12 March, 1710; she chose as guardian, Feb. 25, 172¾, Elder John Baker; married, 1 Dec. 1726, as 2d wife, to Capt. Samuel Greenwood of Boston, merchant and shipbuilder, eldest son of Samuel and Elizabeth (Bronsdon) Greenwood of Boston. Capt. Greenwood died Feb. 22, 174½, Æ. 52, leaving issue, two daughters, Mary, who d. unm. at Marblehead in 18 * *, aged over 70 years, and Hannah, who in 1763 married Ebenezer Symms; also several sons by either marriage. Widow Mary Greenwood, as one of the coheirs of her step-brother, William Charnock, repeatedly disposed of lands at Rutland, Worc. co., but 1757 sold out her entire interest to Capt. Joseph Prince of Boston, whose 2d wife, it would appear, she soon after became. Mr. Prince died in 1758, and the "widow Prince," in Feb. 1762, became the 3d wife of Capt. Humphrey Devereux of Marblehead, who died 21 Jan. 1777, aged 75; his widow died at Marblehead, July 22, 1794, aged 85, leaving no issue by her two later marriages. Her eldest son, John Greenwood, died at Margate, Kent, Sept. 15, 1792, Æ. 65, having long been a resident of London; his widow Frances (Stevens) Greenwood died at Turnham-Green, Middlesex, March 31, 1808, aged 63, leaving children, of whom John Greenwood, jr., married in 1802 an American

lady, Mary Ann Symmes, and is supposed to have removed
to India. This latter gentleman bore the following arms:
quarterly, first and fourth, sable, a chevron ermine betw.
three saltronels argent, for Greenwood;* second, argent, on
a bend sable three cross-crosslets of the first, for Charnock; third, per chevron azure and argent, in chief two
falcons rising or, for Stevens; impaling, ermine, three
increscents gules, for Symmes.

VI.   Stephen, bap. Sep. 7, 1712; d. yng.

VII. Richard, bap. Feb. 7, 171¾; d. yng.

VIII. Stephen, bap. April 17, 1715; d. yng.

IX.   Joanna, bap. May 12, 1717: d. yng.

X.   George, bap. Jan. 11, 1718–9; d. yng.

XI.   William, bap. Feb. 17, 172⅜. After his father's
death, his mother was appointed as his guardian, Jan. 30,
172¾. He graduated at Harv. Coll. 1743, but died the
next year, leaving an estate of £1041:7s, consisting of
a house on Bennet Street, appraised at £900 (exclusive of
furniture,) a costly wardrobe, and a library of Latin,
Greek, and Theological Books. His inventory was presented Jan. 17, 1745, by "Madam Hannah Burrill his
mother," who was discharged July 6, 1753, from all
further responsibility as guardian and administratrix.

* These are the arms of Greenwood of Greenwood-Lee, co. York; more
correctly he should have borne the arms of Greenwood of Norwich, Eng.,
H. J., II., 78.

MONUMENTAL INSCRIPTIONS.

(Continued from p. 69.)

XII.

IN MEMORY of
the Honble BENJAMIN ELLERY Esqr
who
was for many Years
A Deputy of the Town of Newport
A Judge of the County Court
&
An Assistant of the Colony.
Having served his Generation
according to the will of God
he died in Faith
the 26th of July A. D. 1746 Æt: 76

XIII.

The same arms accompany this and the next epitaph :—
IN MEMORY
of Mrs Abigail Ellery
the virtuous Consort
of Benjamin Ellery Esqr
who departed this Life
Decemb^r the 15th A. D. 1742,
Æt^s Suæ 65.

———

XIV.

M. S.
GULIELMI ELLERY Armigeri
Qui
COLLEGII HARVARDINI NOV. ANG.
Optimarum Artium Studia olim excoluit,
Deinde per multos Annos
variis Mercaturæ Negotiis
Opes non magis Sibi honeste quæsivit
quam Patriæ inserviit,
Et Civium Suffragiis
Ad præcipuos hujusce Coloniæ Honores
evectus
Judicis Officio, Senatoris
et demum
VICE-GUBERNATORIS
functus est,
Semper Veri Rectiq. tenax,
Christianus

Fide et Charitate verè Apostolica,
Libertatis religiosæ et civilis
Decus et Præsidium floruit;
Hospitii Muneribus gaudens
probos et honestos licet infortunatos
Liberalitate et Benevolentia
prosecutus est,
donec
Vita utili et honesta jucunde peracta
ad Sedes Animorum æternas
transivit
Idibus Martiis Anno Salutis MDCCLXIV
Ætatis suæ LXIII.

An account of this family was printed in the Heraldic
Journal, I., 177. We have to notice the fact that these
arms are quite different from those engraved with the
former article.

XV.

To the Memory of
The Honble John Gardner Esq.
Late Lieu^t Governor of this Colony
This Tomb is dedicated.
He changed this Life for one more glorious
on the 29th Day of January A. D. 1764,
in the 69th Year of his Age.
His Death was to the Community the Loss of
a useful and worthy Member: To his Discon-
solate Wife and numerous Offspring a Loss
irreparable.   He was a loving & indulgent Husband,
as well as a tender and affectionate Parent: and
remarkable for his affable and courteous
Deportment to all Men.
While young he devoted himself to the service
of his Country in which he was advanced to
many Posts of the greatest Trust which he
discharged with Honour and Fidelity.
He was early received into the Baptist Church
in the Communion of which he remained a worthy
Member till his Death.   His Life was Exemplary
and few men had a more extensive Charity for
Christians of every Denomination.
In his last hour he bore his Sickness with becoming
Patience and Resignation, a glorious Presage of his
futur Happiness: And we trust he is now at rest
in the Mansions of Bliss with his Redeemer
and the Spirits of just Men made perfect.

These seem to be the same arms as borne by Rev.
Richard Gardiner, Canon of Christ Church, Oxford, who

died in 1670, viz., Sable, a chevron ermine between two griffin's heads erased in chief and a cross formée in base or. We are unable to give any account of the family.

XVI.

Here lyeth ye body of
THOMAS SEARES,
son of Lieut. Sylas Sears,
of Yarmouth P. C.
and Grandson of Richard
the Pilgrim
Born in 1664, and died
Aug. 16, 1707,
Aged 43 years.

Beneath this stone the empty Casket lies,
The polished jewel brightens in the skies.

This stone was not erected in 1707, but has been recently put in its place, though there is no evidence of the time. A short account of the family was printed in the Journal, II., 137.

XVII.

THIS MONUMENT
is erected to the Memory
Of the Hon. RICHARD WARD, Esqʳ
Late Governor of this Colony.
He was early in Life
Employed in the Publick Service,
And for many Years sustained
Some of the most important Offices
In the Colony,
With great Ability and Reputation.
He was a Member
Of the Sabbatarian Church in this Town ;
And adorned the Doctrines of his Savior,
By a sincere and steady Practice
Of the various Duties of Life.

He died on the 21st Day of August 1763,
In the 75th Year of his Age.

And also MARY his Wife
Who was a Member of the same Church
Fifty five Years,
And in every Station of a long Life,
Truly exemplary in her Conduct.
She died the 19th of October 1767
In the 78th Year of her Age.

In Savage's Genealogical Dictionary may be traced the line of Richard Ward, who was son of Thomas, and grandson of John of Newport. There is a tradition concerning supposed service of one of these in Cromwell's army. Peterson's History of Rhode Island contains a Memoir of Governor Ward. The arms of Ward, of various counties of England, are, Azure, a cross flory or ; the crest is frequently a wolf's head.

———

[NOTE.—A careful examination, under more favorable circumstances, shows that the bend in the shield on the grave-stone of Abiah Buckmaster, p. 67, is charged with a dolphin embowed between two martlets, instead of the three martlets given in the cut. These are the arms of Franklin, engraved in Vol. II., 97. We know that James Franklin, brother of Benjamin, moved to Newport, and among his children was Abiah, who married Capt. Buckmaster. The stone therefore bears the arms of the lady, and not those of her husband.]

PHILADELPHIA, PENN.

In the outside wall of the east end of St. Peter's Church is a large stone with the following inscription, occupying only part of the surface.

Near this Stone are deposited the Remains of
ELIZABETH SIMS, who departed this Life
    December 8th 1773, Aged 28 Years,
ESTHER WYNKOOP, who departed this Life
    November 20th 1774, Aged 3 Years,
JOSEPH SIMS, who departed this Life
    June 21st 1779, Aged 66 Years.
BENJAMIN WYNKOOP, who departed this Life
    September 10th 1789, Aged 11 Years,
WOODDROP SIMS, who departed this Life
    August 29th 1793, Aged 35 Years.

Ann Sims, who departed this Life
    August 30ᵗʰ 1802, Aged 79 Years.
Ann Wooddrop Gilpin, who departed this Life
    January 8ᵗʰ 1803, Aged 40 Years.
The arms are those of Sims, described in this number,
p. 110.

BURLINGTON, N. J.

In the graveyard is a flat tombstone, lying even with
the ground, bearing the following inscription:

In Memory of
PETER BAYNTON Esq.
Of this City Merchᵗ who departed
This Life the 22 Day of Febʸ A. D. 1743–4.

The Bayntons were a distinguished family in England,
long settled in Wiltshire. A notice of them will be found
in Burke's Extinct Baronetcies, under the name of Rolt.
The arms are there described as sable, a bend lozengy
argent, which is palpably a wrong description, and should
no doubt be, sable four lozenges conjoined in bend, argent.
Our engraving is rightly a bend lozengy, but of course of
two tinctures.   W. H. W.

PEDIGREE OF FISKE.

The oft-quoted manuscript, believed to be the work of Matthias Candler, and numbered 6071 of the Harleian collection in the British Museum, mentions several persons of the name of Fiske, who emigrated from the county of Suffolk to New England. Extensive researches concerning this family have been made by Mr. H. G. Somerby, and the present account is prepared from his collections, with the help furnished by various other sources of information. The earliest recorded ancestor is

Simon Fiske, who was of Stadhaugh in the parish of Laxfield, Suffolk, in the times of Henry IV., V. and VI. He had two wives, Susan Smith and Katherine, and died 1463–4. He left by his first wife four sons, William,[2] Jeffrey,[2] John[2] and Edmund,[2] and a daughter Margaret[2] Dowsing.

William[2] Fiske, the eldest son, married Joan Lynne, and lived till the reign of Henry VII. He left six sons, Thomas,[3] William,[3] Augustine,[3] Simon,[3] Robert[3] and John,[3] and two daughters, Margery,[3] and Margaret.[3]

Simon[3] Fiske was of Laxfield, and had four sons, Simon,[4] William,[4] Robert[4] and John.[4]

Simon,[4] the eldest son, died in 1538, leaving eight sons, Robert,[5] John,[5] George,[5] Nicholas,[5] Jeffrey,[5] Jeremy,[5] William,[5] and Richard,[5] and three daughters, Joan,[5] Gelyne[5] and Agnes.[5]

Robert[5] Fiske, the eldest son, fled for religion's sake in the days of Queen Mary, but was afterwards of St. James', South Elmham. He married Sybil, daughter of

—— Gold, and widow of —— Barber, and died in 1602, leaving four sons, William,[6] Jeffrey,[6] Thomas[6] and Eleazer,[6] and a daughter Elizabeth[6] Bernard.

William[6] Fiske, the eldest son, fled with his father, but was afterwards of St. James', South Elmham, and of Ditchingham, Norfolk, where he died in 1623. He left a widow Alice, but his children were by his first wife, Anne, daughter of Wm. Austye of Tibbenham Long Row, Norfolk. They were three sons, John,[7] Nathaniel[7] and Eleazer,[7] and three daughters, Hester[7] wife of John Chalke, Hannah[7] wife of Wm. Candler, and mother of Matthias, author of the volume of pedigrees, and Eunice.[7]

Jeffrey,[6] the second son of Robert,[5] was of Metfield, married Sarah Cooke, and left three sons, Samuel,[7] Nathan[7] and David,[7] and two daughters, Mary[7] and Lydia.[7]

Thomas,[6] the third son of Robert,[5] was of Fressingfield, and died in 1611, leaving wife Margery, three sons, Thomas,[7] James[7] and Phineas,[7] and two daughters, Elizabeth[7] and Mary.[7]

John[7] Fiske, eldest son of William,[6] married Anne, daughter of Robert Lanterce, and had three sons, John,[8] Nathan[8] and William,[8] and two daughters, Ann[8] Chickering, and Martha[8] Thompson. He was of St. James', South Elmham, and died in 1633.

Nathaniel[7] Fiske, second son of William,[6] was of Weybred; he married Alice, daughter of —— Henel and widow of —— Leman, by whom he left a son, Nathaniel,[8] and a daughter Sarah[8] Rogers.

Nathaniel[8] Fiske, only son of Nathaniel,[7] married

Dorothy, daughter of John Simonds of Wendham, and had two sons, John[9] and Nathaniel,[9] and a daughter, Esther.[9]

Several of this family, all apparently cousins, moved to New England, and settled in Massachusetts.

John[8] and William,[8] sons of John,[7] their sisters Ann Chickering and Martha Thompson, John,[9] son of Nathaniel,[8] Samuel[7] and David,[7] sons of Jeffrey,[6] and the children of their brother Nathan,[7] certainly emigrated to this country, and probably James[7] and Phineas,[7] sons of Thomas,[6] did so also.

John[8] Fiske married Ann Gipps of Norfolk, and emigrated in 1637. He was first at Cambridge, then at Salem, was afterwards settled as minister at Wenham, but removed again to Chelmsford, where he died in 1677. He had several children, but only one son lived to maturity. This was Rev. Moses[9] Fiske, who was born in 1642, graduated at Harvard College in 1662, and was settled at Braintree, where he died in 1708.

William[8] Fiske married Bridget Muskett, and probably came to New England with his brother. He was first of Salem, afterwards of Wenham, and had several children, but of his descendants there is no account. He died in 1654.

John[9] Fiske emigrated about the year 1648, having, according to tradition, lost his father on the passage from England. He was of Watertown, where he took the oath of fidelity 1652, and died in 1684. He married in 1651 Sarah, daughter of Nicholas Wyeth of Cambridge, by whom he had a number of children. The descendants of his sons, John[10] and William,[10] may be found in Bond's

Genealogies and History of Watertown. Of the fifth generation from William[10] is Francis S. Fiske of Boston, Brevet Brigadier General of U. S. Volunteers, to whom we are indebted for access to the collections of Mr. Somerby.

Samuel[7] Fiske, in the Candler manuscript, is said to be "now of New England," while of his brother Nathan it is said that his "children went into New England." It would seem that these remarks may have been misplaced, as we do not find an early Samuel on this side of the water, while there was a Nathan at Watertown, who is quite as likely to have been brother of David[7] as his nephew. This Nathan was of Watertown in 1643, in which year he became Freeman. He died in 1676, leaving several children; an account of his numerous descendants may be read in Bond's History.

David[7] Fiske married Sarah Smith, and was in New England, in Watertown, as early as 1637. He had one daughter, and one son David,[8] and died in 1661. David[8] was a prominent man in Cambridge Farms, now Lexington; only one son, David,[9] left descendants.

James[7] Fiske, though not mentioned by Candler as leaving England, was undoubtedly the man whom we find at Salem in 1641, and afterwards at Haverhill. He became Freeman in 1642, and had children.

Phineas[7] Fiske was at Salem with his brother James, but moved thence to Wenham. He was Freeman in 1642, and left three sons.

The Fiskes have always claimed to bear coat-armor, and in 1633 a charter of confirmation was issued from Heralds' College. We have thought it worthy of reproduction, as a specimen of the style of such documents, one hundred and seventy years before that of Coffin, printed in our last number. It acknowledges the use of the arms by an ancestor of all the emigrants :—

To all and singular Persons to whom these Presents shall come, William Seger, Knight, Garter Principall King of Armes of English men, Sendeth his due commendations & greeting in our Lord God everlasting. Knowe yee that aunciently from the beginning it hath been a custome in all countries and comon wealthes well governed, that the bearing of certaine signes in Shields (commonlie called Armes) hath bene and are the onely marks and demonstrations either of prowes, vertue, & valour in times of war or peace, & of good life & conversation for learning, magistracy, & civill government in times of peace, diversly distributed according to the qualities & deserts of the persons demeriting the same, which order, as it was most prudentlie devised in the beginning to stirr & kindle the harts of men to the imitation of virtue & nobleness, even so hath the same been & yet is continually observed to the end that such as have done commendable service to their Prince & country either in warr or peace may receave due hono[r] in their lives, and also devise after their deathes successively to their posterity, amongst the w[ch] number I find Nicholas Fiske of Studhaw, in the parish of Laxfield in the countie of Suffolk, Professor in Phisick, son of Mathew Fiske of the same, son of William, son of

Thomas, son of William Fiske, of Studhaw aforesaid that
lived in the raignes of King Henry the sixt, Edward the
iiij, Richard the third, and King Henry the 7th, who
beared for their coats armo^r, as followeth vizt. checkey
arg^t. & gules, uppon a pale sable, three mullets or,
pearced, and wanting further for an ornament unto his
saide coate of Armes, as diverse auntient coates are found
to want, a convenient Creaste or Cognizance fitt for him
the saide Nicholas to beare, who hath requested me the
saide Garter to assigne him such a one as he may lawfullie
use without wrong doing a prejudice to any person or
persons whatsoever, wch according to his due request I
have accomplished and granted in maner & forme following, (that is to say), on a Healme a Torse argent and
gules, a Triangle, argent, above the upper angle an
Estoile, or, mantelled gules, doubled argent, as more
plainly appeareth depicted in the margent hereof. All
which Armes and Creaste, I the said Garter King of
Armes by power & authoritie of my office, under the
Great Seal of England, doe appoint, give, graunt, ratifie
& confirme unto the said Nicholas Fiske, & to his
posteritie forever, & that it shall be lawfull for him &
them to use & shew forth the same in Signet, Shield,
ensigne, coate armo^r or otherwise at his or their pleasure,
at all times & in all places according to the antient lawes
of armes & laudable custome of England, without let
or mollestation. In witnes whereof I the saide Garter
have hereunto set my hand and seale of office, the 16th
day of November A^o 1633, & in the 9th yeare of the
raigne of o^r Soveraigne Lord Charles by the Grace of
God King of England, Scotland, France & Ireland,
defender of the Faith, &c.

REVIEW.

OLD CHURCHES, MINISTERS AND FAMILIES OF VIR-
GINIA. By Bishop Meade. In two volumes. Philadelphia: J. B. Lippincott & Co. 1857.

These volumes, by the late Episcopalian Bishop of
Virginia, form a very truthful representation of the state
as it was prior to the Rebellion. Undoubtedly the fore-
most of the Slave-holding colonies,—applying the name
distinctively,—she had fallen far behind the younger
southern states in material prosperity. Unquestionably
possessing a larger proportion of gentlemen in the
heraldic sense, than any other colony except New
England, her claims to the distinction are obscured if not
extinguished by a neglect of all authoritative records.
Proud of her "First Families" to a degree that "F. F.
V." has passed into a proverb, she has established no
criterion for the decision of thousands of spurious claims.
The Colony dedicated by law to the perpetual main-
tainance of the Church of England, she has allowed her
churches to be desecrated and destroyed, her churchyards
to be effaced, and her church property to be confiscated
or stolen.

Such are the melancholy facts related by Bishop
Meade, and verified by his personal examination of most
of the parishes in his diocese. Since this date, indeed,
the struggles of contending armies in Virginia have
doubtless contributed to the destruction of monuments,
and possibly of records. The depredations of marauders

from both armies have destroyed valuable evidences preserved in families, and the exigencies of the times have led to the sale and dispersion of family plate and jewels. Unless therefore some zealous antiquary, or energetic society, take in charge the task of gathering up the remaining fragments, we may doubt if much will ever be proved concerning the pedigrees of the Virginian planters.

We propose to collect in this article such items as can be extracted from Bishop Meade's volume, which throw any light upon the ancestry of any family. His book indeed may be regarded in the light of a Visitation of Virginia, chiefly clerical in its aim, often genealogical, seldom, unfortunately, heraldic.

As he has pursued no definite plan in his relation, we will follow the book, chapter by chapter.

Vol. I., p. 101. Edward Jacqueline, of Huguenot descent, came from Kent, in England, in 1697, to Virginia. P. 104. "Edward Jacqueline was the son of John Jacqueline and Elizabeth Craddock of the county of Kent."

P. 103. The Amblers are said to be from Leeds in Yorkshire, their ancestor being Richard Ambler, who is thought to have been the son of John Ambler of the city of York, and sheriff of the county in 1721.

P. 138–9. The Randolphs are traced to William Randolph of Turkey Island, who was the nephew of Thomas Randolph, the poet.

P. 147 and 195. The Page family is descended from Col. John Page, Knt., a merchant of London, one of the Council in Virginia, who died 23 Jan. 1691–2, aged 65. It is added that from their coat-of-arms and many circumstances the family was supposed to be nearly allied to Sir Gregory Page, a very wealthy merchant.

P. 165–6.   The Spotswoods are descended from Governor Alexander Spotswood, who was son or grand-son of Sir Robert S., Lord-President of the Court of Sessions, Scotland, who was son of Arch-bishop Spottis-wood.

P. 180.   Daniel Parke of Bruton parish, 1676, was from Surrey, Eng.

P. 195.   Thomas Ludwell, Esq., Secretary of Vir-ginia, was born at Bruton, co. Somerset, and d. in 1678.

P. 198.   An epitaph is given which we transcribe in full:

"Here lies ye body of MICHAEL ARCHER, Gentleman, who was born the 29th of September, 1681, near Rippon in Yorkshire, and died ye 10th of February, 1726, in the 46th year of his age. Also, Joanna Archer, wife of Michael Archer, who departed this life Octo. 1st, 1732."

P. 199.   Another epitaph reads:

"EDWARDUS BARRADALL, armiger, qui in legum studiis feliciter versatus, Attornati-Generalis et admiral-itatis judicis amplissimas partes merito obtinuit fideliter. Collegium Gulielmi et Mariæ cum Gubernator tum in Conventio Generali, Senator, propugnavit. SARAM Viri Honorabilis GULIELMI FITZHUGH serenissimæ Reginæ Annæ in Virginiæ Conciliis, filiam natu maximam, Tam mortis quam vitæ sociam, uxorem habuit. Obierunt—ille 13th Cal. Julii; illa the 3d. of the Non. Oct. Anno Domini, 1743."*

---

* There are evidently some mistakes in this epitaph. We cannot say if the fault be that of Bishop Meade, or of his printer. Perhaps the last sentence should read "illa die 3d. ante Non. Oct.," &c.—ED.

P. 199.   An inscription to David Bray, Armiger, who died Oct. 1731, aged 32.

P. 205.   Thomas Nelson was from Penriff, near the border of Scotland.   His sons, Thomas and William, were respectively Secretary and President of the Council of the Colony.   The following inscription is printed on p. 213 :

"Hic jacet, spe certa resurgendi in Christo, Thomas Nelson, Generosus; Filius Hugonis et Sariæ Nelson, de Penrith, in comitate Cumbriæ.   Natus 20mo die Februarii, Anno Domini 1677.   Vitæ bene gestæ finem implevit 7mo die Octobris, 1745, ætatis suæ 68."

P. 244.   " To the memory of Edward Digges Esquire, sonne of Sir Dudley Digges, of Chilham, in Kent, Knight and Baronett,* Master of the Rolls in the reign of King Charles the 1st.   He departed the life the 15th of March, 1675, in the 55th year of his age, one of his Majesty's Councill for this his Colony of Va.   A gentleman of most commendable parts and ingenuity and the only introducer and promoter of the silk-manufacture in this Colonie, and in every thing else a pattern worthy of all pious imitation. He had issue six sonnes and seven daughters by the body of Elizabeth his wife, who of her conjugal affection hath dedicated to him this memorial."

There is also an inscription to his son Dudley Digges, " Armiger," who died in 1710, and to Dudley's wife Susan, daughter of William Cole, " Armiger."

At p. 291 there is a rather confused account of the Meade family, to which the Bishop belonged.   The

---

* This title of Baronet is probably wrongly given to Sir Dudley.   His grandson Sir Thomas was made a Baronet in 1666, but died *s. p.*

ancestor was Andrew Meade, who was born in the county of Kerry, and who settled in Nansemond county, Va. His son David married Susanna,* dau. of Sir Richard Everard, bart., Gov. of North Carolina, by his wife Susanna, dau. of Dr. Richard Kidder, bishop of Bath and Wells.

On p. 353 we find the following inscriptions:

"To the lasting memory of Major Lewis Burwell, of the county of Gloucester, in Virginia, gentleman, who descended from the ancient family of the Burwells, of the counties of Bedford and Northampton, in England, who nothing more worthy in his birth than virtuous in his life, exchanged this life for a better, on the 19th day of November, in the 33d year of his age, A. D., 1658."

"To the sacred memory of Abigail, the loving and beloved wife of Major Lewis Burwell, of the county of Gloucester, gent., who was descended of the illustrious family of the Bacons and heiress of the Hon. Nathaniel Bacon, Esq., President of Virginia, who not being more honourable in her birth than virtuous in her life, departed this world the 12th day of November, 1672, aged 36 years, having blessed her husband with four sons and six daughters."

P. 378. "The first of the Robinson family of whom we have any account was John Robinson of Cleasby, Yorkshire, England, who married Elizabeth Potter of Cleasby, daughter of Christopher Potter." "The fourth son of John Robinson was Dr. John Robinson, Bishop of

---

* It must be said that BURKE (Extinct Baronetcies) says this Susanna m. a Mr. White in Virginia, and does not mention the Meade alliance. The New England family of Kidders claim a common origin with the Bishop's family.

Bristol." "He afterwards became Bishop of London, in which office he continued until his death in 1723. He was twice married, but left no issue. He devised his real estate to the eldest son of his brother Christopher, who had migrated to what was Rappahannock, on the Rappahannock River." "His older son, who inherited the Bishop of London's estate, was John Robinson, who was born in 1683, and became President of the Council of Virginia."

P. 455. "Miles Cary, the son of John Cary of Bristol, England, came to Virginia in 1640, and settled in the county of Warwick, which in 1659 he represented in the House of Burgesses. In 1667 he died, leaving four sons."

Vol. II., p. 78. The Rev. John Thompson was a Master of Arts at Edinburgh, and received Priests' Orders in 1739 at London. He came to Virginia, and in 1742 married the widow of Gov. Spottswood.

P. 98. The Taylors trace their ancestry back to James Taylor of Carlisle, England.

On p. 106–8 is some account of the Fairfaxes, but we have already printed what is known of the pedigree.

P. 121. On p. 121 is a long Latin epitaph upon Robert Carter:

H. S. E.

" Vir honorabilis Robertus Carter, Armiger, qui genus honestum dotibus eximiis et moribus antiquis illustravit Collegium Gulielmi et Mariæ temporibus difficillimis propugnavit, Gubernator.

"Senatus Rogator et Quæstor sub serenissimis Principibus Gulielmo, Anna Georgio Primo et Secundo.

" A publicis concilliis concillii per sexennium præses; plus anno Coloniæ Præfectus, cum regiam dignitatem et publicam libertatem æquali jure asseruit.

" Opibus amplissimis bene partis instructus, ædem hanc sacram, in Deum pietatis grande monumentum propriis sumptibus extruit.   Locupletavit.

" In omnes quos humaniter excipit nec prodigus nec parcus hospes.   Liberalitatem insignem   testantur debita munifice remissa.

" Primo Juditham, Johannis Armistead, Armigeri, filiam; deinde Betty, generosa Landonorum stirpe oriundam, sibi connubio junctas habuit; e quibus prolem numerosam suscepit, in qua erudienda pecuniæ vim maximam insumpsit.

" Tandem honorum et dierum satur, cum omnia vitæ munera egregiæ præstitisset, obiit Pri. Non. Aug. An. Dom. 1732, æt. 69.

" Miseri solamen, viduæ præsiduum, orbi patrem, ademptum lugent."

On p. 122 there is an inscription to his second wife, Betty, " youngest daughter of Thomas Landon, Esq., and Mary his wife, of Grednal, in the county of Hereford, the ancient seat of the family and place of her nativity." She died 3d July, 1710, aged 35.

P. 136. " Richard Lee of good family in Shropshire, and whose picture, I am told, is now at Cotton, near Bridgenorth, the seat of Lancelot Lee, Esq., some time in the reign of Charles I. went over to the Colony of Virginia, as Secretary and one of the King's Privy Council." " This Richard Lee had several children; the two eldest, John and Richard, were educated at Oxford." By his will he ordered an estate he had in England (I think near Stratford-by-Bow in Middlesex) at that time worth eight hundred or nine hundred pounds per annum, to be sold."

P. 138. "The Ludwells, though the name is now extinct, are an old and honorable family of Somersetshire, England, the original of them many ages since coming from Germany. Philip Ludwell and John Ludwell, being brothers, and sons of a Miss Cottington, who was heiress of James Cottington, the next brother and heir to the famous Lord Francis Cottington, of whom a pretty full account may be seen in Lord Clarendon's History of the Rebellion, were in court favor after the restoration of Charles II."

P. 144. "The will of the first Richard Lee, dated 1663, may be seen in Mr. Charles Campbell's History of Virginia, p. 157. From it I extract the following: I, Colonel Richard Lee of Virginia, and lately of Stratford-Langton in the county of Essex, Esquire, &c. &c."

P. 152. A tombstone in Cople parish, Westmoreland county, has the following inscription:—

"Hic conditur corpus Richardi Lee, Armigeri, nati in Virginia, filii Richardi Lee, generosi, et antiqua familia, in Merton Regis, in comitatu Salopiensi, oriundi.

In magistratum obeundo boni publici studiosissimi, in literis Græcis et Latinis et aliis humanioris literaturæ disciplinis versatissimi.

Deo, quem summa observantia semper coluit, animam tranquillus reddidit xii mo. die Martii, anno MDCCXIV, ætat LXVIII."

At p. 166 we find a mention of the Washingtons and

notice is taken of the two brothers, John and Lawrence, who settled in this country. In a previous number of this Journal, we have fully discussed the present position of this pedigree, and we have only to express our strong desire that the wills of these two pioneers should be published in full. From Bishop Meade's abstracts it would seem probable that these documents contain information which would enable us to ascertain the locality in England from which the Washingtons emigrated.

P. 197. " Here lies the body of Rev. Alexander Scott, A. M. and presbyter of the Church of England, who lived near twenty-eight years minister of Overwharton parish, and died in the fifty-third year of his age,— he being born the 20th day of July A. D. 1686, and departed this life the 1st day of April, 1738." " Gaudia Nuncio Magna."

" This is written upon his coat of arms, which is engraved upon his tomb."

P. 199. " Here lyeth the body of Frances, the wife of Dr. Gustavus Brown, of Charles county, Maryland. By her he had twelve children, of whom one son and seven daughters survived her. She was a daughter of Mr. Gerard Fowke, late of Maryland, and descended from the Fowkes of Gunster Hall, in Staffordshire, England. She was born February the 2d, 1691, and died, much lamented, on the 8th of November, 1744, in the fifty-fourth year of her age."

P. 464. " John Baylor the elder, and first of the name who came to the New World, was born at Tiverton, in England, where, from old Sellers, we learn that he was related to the Freres, Courtenays, Tuckers, Hedjers,

Nortons and others. His son John was born in 1650, and emigrating to Virginia, was followed by his father, a very old man. He settled in Gloucester county, and was married to Lucy Tod O'Brien, of New Kent, in 1698. Large grants of land had been made to father and son in various parts of the Colony, and the latter being of an enterprising character, embarked extensively in mercantile schemes by which a large fortune for that day was amassed,—the inventory of his personal effects amounting to £6500."

We here close our extracts from Bishop Meade's book, having copied every item which seems to be of value to the genealogist. Of course other facts of a general nature are therein printed, as lists of early settlers, vestrymen &c., but we have tried to omit nothing which possessed a sufficient degree of particularity of description. w. h. w.

PENN OF PENNSYLVANIA.

"Granville John Penn, Esq., formerly of Stoke Park, Bucks, who died on the 29th ult., was the lineal representative of Sir William Penn, Admiral of the Fleet, *temp.* King Charles II., and of the Admiral's only and illustrious son, William Penn, the founder of Pennsylvania, and was the eldest son of Granville Penn, Esq., of Stoke Park, by his wife, Isabella, eldest daughter of General Gordon Forbes, Colonel 29th Foot, and grandson of His Excellency Governor Thomas Penn, and his wife, Lady Juliana Fermor, daughter of Thomas, first Earl of Pomfret. Mr. Granville John Penn was a Deputy Lieutenant

and magistrate for Bucks, with which county he and his
ancient and distinguished family had been so long associated.   He died unmarried, and is succeeded by his only
surviving brother, the Rev. Thomas Penn, M. A., of
Christ Church, Oxon. * * *   The Penns have left their
memory lastingly connected with their former seat, Stoke
Park, and its neighbourhood.   Stoke Park, since their
time the residence of Lord Taunton, and now in the possession of Mr. Coleman, has close to it the time-honoured
and beautiful churchyard of Gray's elegy, where Gray
himself reposes, with little as yet to notify the fact; and
where his grave might be passed by unheeded but for the
magnificent cenotaph erected not far from the churchyard
to the poet's memory by the worthy John Penn, Governor of Portland, in the county of Dorset, and last
hereditary Governor of Pennsylvania, grandson of the
founder, William Penn, and grandfather of the Mr. Penn
just deceased.   To the poet the Penns thus did honour,
whilst, pursuant to the stringency of Quaker custom,
their own great William Penn lies in an unmarked humble grave, in the Quakers' burial-ground of Jordans, a
few miles from Stoke.   Yet, as stated, the whole district
is replete with recollections of the Penns, few visitors failing to see Jordans, and to associate the Penn name
with Stoke Park and village, and the monument of
Gray."

This extract, taken from the Illustrated London News
of April 27th, 1867, will serve as the text for an account
of the family of Penn of Pennsylvania.   For the following
facts we are principally indebted to Sir Bernard Burke's
Dictionary of the Landed Gentry of Great Britain and
Ireland.

The family is traced back to William[1] Penn, of Minety, in Gloucestershire, and of Penn's Lodge in Wiltshire, who died in 1591, and was buried at Minety. His son William[2] married a Miss Rastall, and died before his father, leaving two sons, William,[3] whose line is extinct, and Giles.[3]

Giles[3] Penn was a Captain in the Royal Navy, and for some time English consul in the Mediterranean. He married a Miss Gilbert, and had two sons, George,[4] envoy to Spain, who died unmarried, and William,[4] afterwards Sir William.

William[4] Penn was born at Bristol in 1621, and followed the profession of his father, entering the Navy, in which he highly distinguished himself. Before he reached the age of thirty-two, he had gained the rank of captain, rear-admiral of Ireland, vice-admiral of England, and commander-in-chief, under the Duke of York, in the victory over the Dutch in 1665, for which he received the honor of knighthood. He was afterwards member of Parliament for Weymouth, was a commissioner of the admiralty and navy, governor of Kinsale, vice-admiral of Munster, and a member of that provincial council. He retired from active service a few years before his death, which took place in 1670, at Wanstead, Essex. The duties of his profession enabled him to pass through the great civil war, without taking an active part on either side, and at various times he occupied himself with writing and issuing pamphlets on matters connected with the improvement of the navy.

Sir William Penn married Margaret, daughter of John Jasper of Rotterdam, by whom he had a son William,[5] and a daughter Margaret,[5] who became wife of Anthony Lowther of Mask, Yorkshire. He died, as has been said, in 1670, and his widow, (who died in 1681–2), erected to his memory a marble monument, which is now one of the sights of the Church of St. Mary Redcliffe, Bristol. The inscription contains some account of the life and services of the Admiral.

William[5] Penn, only son of Sir William, was born in London, 14 October, 1644. In 1681 King Charles II., in consideration of the services of Admiral Sir William Penn, and of several debts due to him from the crown, granted to William Penn and his heirs, the province lying on the West side of the river Delaware, in North America, which received the name of Pennsylvania, and comprised the state now called by the same name. It was soon settled through the exertions of Penn and a company, which was organized under the name of "The Free Society of Traders in Pennsylvania." Penn himself and many of his followers were Quakers, and the principles of this body were strictly followed in all dealings with the native Indians, who were treated with kindness in place of cruelty. Penn stood high in favor at the English court under the Stuarts, but was of course greatly benefited by the revolution of 1688. By this the position of the Quakers was bettered, and Penn afterwards revisited America. After residing a few years in Pennsylvania, he returned to England, to conclude certain arrangements concerning the commerce of the colony, which he never again visited.

William Penn married Gulielma Maria, daughter of Sir William Springett, by whom he had a son William,[6] of Ireland, who died at Liege in Germany, 23 June, 1720. He married secondly Hannah, daughter of Thomas Callowhill of Bristol, by whom he left three sons, John,[6] Thomas[6] and Richard.[6] He died in 1718, at Ruscomb, Berkshire, and was buried at Jordans, as above stated.

John[6] Penn died unmarried in 1746, and bequeathed his moiety of the province of Pennsylvania to his brother Thomas.

Thomas[6] Penn purchased in 1760, of the executors of Anne Viscountess Cobham, the manor of Stoke Park in Stoke Poges, Buckinghamshire. He married in 1751 Lady Juliana Fermor, fourth daughter of Thomas, first Earl of Pomfret, by whom he had two sons, John[7] and Granville,[7] and two daughters, Sophia Margaret[7] and Louisa.[7] He died in 1775, and was succeeded by his eldest son.

John Penn[7] of Stoke Park was born 22 February, 1760. He was a justice of the peace for Buckingham-shire, and Governor of Portland Castle, Dorset. He was the last proprietary governor of Pennsylvania, and dying unmarried, 21 June, 1834, was succeeded by his next brother Granville,[7] father of the gentleman lately deceased.

Richard[6] Penn, the youngest son of William, founder of Pennsylvania, married Hannah, daughter of Richard Lardner, M. D., and left two sons, John,[7] who died without issue, and Richard.[7]

Richard[7] Penn married Mary Masters of Philadelphia, and had two sons, William[8] and Richard,[8] and two daughters, Hannah[8] and Mary,[8] wife of Samuel Paynter of Richmond, Sarrey. All descendants of William Penn in this country must derive their origin from Richard.[7]

The arms of the family are, Argent, on a fess sable three plates.　Our cut is copied from a fac-simile of the seal used by William Penn.

THE PADDY AND WENSLEY FAMILIES.

These Arms appertain to the Name and Family of

Paddy.

William Paddy of Plymouth came here in 1635. He was termed a skinner, late of London, from which Mr. Savage concludes that he was one of the guild of skinners there. He m. first Alice Freeman, and secondly Mary (Greenough) widow of Bezaleel Payton. He had a large family, a portion being born at Boston. He died Aug. 24, 1658, and his tombstone in the King's Chapel Yard, though often quoted, has not, we believe, been correctly printed before.

The head stone is inscribed

Hear lyeth
the body of Mr
William Paddy. aged
58 Years. departed
this life Avgust the * *
1658

On the reverse

HEAR SLEEPS THAT
BLESSED ONE WHOES LIEF
GOD HELP VS ALL TO LIVE
THAT SO WHEN TIEM SHALL BE
THAT WE THIS WORLD MUST LEIFE
WE EVER MAY BE HAPPY
WITH BLESSED WILLIAM PADDY.

The footstone is inscribed

O: my Father, my father
The Chariots of Israel
The Horsemen thereof
1658

And on its reverse

Erected | in the year | Anno | 1672.

William Paddy had by his first wife a daughter Elizabeth, b. 12 Nov. 1641, who m. John Wensley of Boston, about 1662. Their children were Richard, Elizabeth, Mercy and Sarah. Sarah m. 1700, Isaac Winslow, and Mercy undoubtedly married Joseph Bridgham of Boston; and afterwards Thomas Cushing.

These Arms appertain to the Name and Family of Wensley,
and is the Coat of Mr. John Wensley, Merchant.

We have no means of deciding the amount of credit to be given to these arms. It would seem from the style of the shield that they were painted after 1730. The inscriptions are also of a very suspicious form, and point to some herald-painter as the sole authority. John Wensley was a prominent and wealthy merchant, but it is not improbable that some descendant in the Winslow branch may have had these memorials prepared many years after the male line of the Paddys and Wensleys was extinct. As specimens of the work of our early artists these engravings are interesting.   W. H. W.

ON CERTAIN TERMS IN HERALDRY.

It is rarely that we have attempted any discussion of the technicalities of heraldry in these pages, inasmuch as it is presumable that the English books would contain all the requisite information. In some few cases however, there are differing authorities, and it is then necessary to attempt to find the most probable solution of the question. One such problem is the proper form in which to represent a shield as barry nebuly. Our readers are aware that the line *nebuly* is curved in a series of figures resembling an inverted cup or flask, and differing therein slightly from the line *wavy*. When a fesse is represented as nebuly these curves are made in such a mode that the widest portions of each are opposed, instead of being two parallel lines, with curves corresponding each to the other. An example will be seen at p. 92 of this volume, seal No. 58, although the engraving should have had the lower line a little more to the right. Now in representing for example, argent, two bars nebuly sable, it would be only necessary to repeat this fesse, but it will then be evident that the four division lines would not be parallel but alternate. This is an essential variation from other forms of *barry*, inasmuch as there the difference between barry of six (being six divisions of the field) and two bars, (i. e. five divisions) is simply the addition of one line.

As we have said, the English books on heraldry have failed to mark this distinction, and while some represent barry nebuly by a series of parallel curves, others use the alternate curves which seem to leave no mode of expressing two or more bars nebuly.

The same difficulty occurs with the lines *engrailed* and *invected*. We are not sure that we have seen an example of barry engrailed, but to draw it must require a different form from the fesse engrailed, or the fesse invected.

Another case of a difference in nomenclature was suggested by the Baynton arms in the present number. It is described for example, as argent, a bend lozengy gules and azure. Burke on the other hand gives the lozenges without the distinctive lines on the sides which constitute a bend, and thus would make what we should term "argent four lozenges conjoined in bend azure." This is intelligible; but his blazon is "argent, a bend lozengy azure."

We submit therefore that his blazon must be wrong; as a bend or chief or other ordinary cannot be lozengy of one tincture, and that unless the distinctive lines of a bend are represented, the figure is not a bend, but so many lozenges or fusils conjoined in bend.   W. H. W.

FILŸP PIETERSEN SCHVŸLER
COMMISSARIS
1658.

THE

HERALDIC JOURNAL;

RECORDING THE ARMORIAL BEARINGS AND GENEALOGIES
OF AMERICAN FAMILIES.

NO. XX. OCTOBER, 1867.

THE SCHUYLER FAMILY.

Philip[1] Pieterson Von Schuyler, the ancestor of this
very distinguished family, came from Amsterdam to New
York in 1650. From the fact that silver plate, bearing
the family arms and the year marks of his time, are still
preserved by his descendants, it is fair to infer that he
was of good position at home. He married Margaret
Van Slechtenhorst, 12 Dec., 1650, at Rensselaerwyck,
and had by her ten children, viz:—

Guysbert.[2]

Gertrude,[2] m. Stephen Van Cortlandt.

Alida,[2] m. { 1. Rev. Nicholas Van Rensselaer.
{ 2. Robert Livingston.

Peter.[2]

Brant,[2] m. Cornelia Van Cortlandt.

Arent,[2] settled in New Jersey, and had issue.

Sybilla.[2]

Philip.[2]

John.[2]

Margaret.[2]

He died 9 March, 1684, and was buried at Albany.

Of these children, Peter[2] and John[2] were especially noted.   Peter[2] Schuyler was the first Mayor of Albany, acting as such from 1686 till 1694.   He was also a Major in the militia, and obtained a controlling influence over the Mohawks and other Indian tribes.   He was President of the Council, and for a short time acting Governor.   For many years he was Commissioner for Indian affairs, and went to England in 1710, with four of their chiefs.   He had at least two sons, Peter[3] and Col. Philip,[3] of the Flats, now Watervliet, though we have not been able to trace this branch farther.

Capt. John[2] Schuyler was a very prominent man, and as LOSSING (Life of Philip Schuyler,* I., 25) says, "his name appears frequently in the Colonial records of the period between 1701 and 1730 as one of the most active of the servants of the government in keeping the Iroquois in alliance with the English."   He was a member of the Assembly from 1705 to 1713.   He married Elizabeth Staats, widow of John Wendell, in April, 1695.   His wife died in 1737, and he died in 1747.

Of his children we find mention of,

John,[3] bapt. 31 Oct., 1697.

Philip[3] of Saratoga, killed by the French and Indians, in 1745.

Peter,[3] Col. and Indian Commissioner.

Maria.[3]

John[3] Schuyler, eldest son, married his cousin Cornelia, daughter of Stephen and Gertrude (Schuyler) Van

---

* We are indebted to this book, of which only the first volume, printed by Mason Brothers in 1862, has appeared, for most of our facts.   It is to be regretted that the author has not finished the work so well begun.

Cortlandt, making the third intermarriage between the families. He died in 1741, six years before his father, leaving five small children, four sons and one daughter.

Of these,

Philip,[4] born 22 Nov., 1733, became the most distinguished of all the inheritors of the name. He was carefully educated, and on the 17 Sept., 1755, he married Catherine, daughter of Col. John Van Rensselaer, of Claverack, by whom he had fourteen children. By law and custom he inherited all his father's real estate, but this he generously shared with his brothers. He also inherited the estates at Saratoga, of his uncle Philip Schuyler.

In 1755 he was appointed Captain in the troops to be raised for the French war, and served under Johnson. Soon after he took service under Bradstreet, but quitted the army in disgust.

In 1758 he served under Lord Howe as deputy commissary, with the rank of Major, and in 1761 he visited England.

From 1763 to 1767 he remained in private life, and in 1768 Col. Schuyler, as he was then entitled, was elected to the Assembly from Albany. Here he soon became conspicuous on the side of the colonists, and was re-elected the following year. In 1774 he was appointed a delegate to the Congress at Philadelphia, but a continued sickness prevented his acceptance. In 1775 he was a member of the Provincial Congress, and was recommended as the most suitable person for Major-General, Richard Montgomery being nominated as Brigadier-General. He was accordingly so appointed by the General Congress and assigned to the Northern department. His health prevented his taking command of the expedition, which under Montgomery captured Montreal and attacked Quebec. He however rendered efficient service in forwarding supplies, and in directing and harmonizing transactions in his department. He exerted himself in 1777 to prevent the advance of Burgoyne, but owing to the unreasonable clamor against him after the evacuation of Ticonderoga, he was superseded by Gates.

After the adoption of the Constitution he was appointed Senator from New York, and again in 1797, in the place of Aaron Burr.

He died in Albany, Nov. 18, 1804.

[NOTE. The arms here engraved are those which were on a window in the old Dutch church at Albany. The glass is preserved by the family. Our readers will remember the similar instances of the Van Rensselaer and Wendell windows.]   W. H. W.

OFFICIAL SEALS.

In 1774 Gov. Hutchinson decided to go to England, and as the Lieutenant-Governor Oliver had just died, it was necessary to appoint a successor. The English government accordingly decided to place in that office the commander of the royal troops, and on May 2, Gen. Thomas Gage was nominated in council here.

He was the second son of Sir Thomas Gage, eighth Baronet and first Viscount Gage. The family can be traced for several generations prior to Sir John Gage, K. G., who was a distinguished statesman and commander in the reign of Henry VIII. From him was descended

Sir John Gage, who was made a baronet in 1622, whose second son was also created a baronet in 1662, and was the ancestor of another line.

Gen. Thomas Gage entered the army in early life, and rose rapidly in the service. He was lieutenant-colonel in Braddock's expedition, and was severely wounded then. After the conquest of Canada in 1760, he was made Governor of Montreal, and in 1763 succeeded Amherst as Commander-in-chief. In 1774 he succeeded Hutchinson, and was thus the last Royal Governor of Massachusetts. In May, 1775, the Provincial Congress declared him disqualified to act as Governor, and in October he sailed for England. His successor in the command of the troops was Sir William Howe.

Gov. Gage married in 1758 Margaret, daughter of Peter Kemble, Esq., of New Jersey, and had issue one son and two daughters. He died 2 April, 1788, and his widow in 1824.

A portrait of Gov. Gage is in Sumner's History of East Boston. The arms borne by this family are, Quarterly, 1st and 4th—Per saltire azure and argent, a saltire gules; 2d and 3d—Azure, the sun in splendor or. Crest, a ram passant argent, armed and unguled or. Motto, Courage sans peur. Supporters, two greyhounds tenée, each gorged with a coronet composed of fleurs-de-lys or.

Henry Gage, only son of the Governor, succeeded his uncle in 1791 as third Viscount Gage of Ireland, and second Baron Gage of England. He married in 1782 Susanna Maria, daughter of Col. William Skinner of New Jersey, and had issue, Henry Hall Gage, fourth and present Viscount Gage. Descendants of Henry, the third Viscount, are numerous, as any "Peerage" will show.

[NOTE. Col. William Skinner was the son of Rev. William Skinner, rector of St. Peter's Church in Perth-Amboy. It is said that this clergyman was a Mac-Gregor, was wounded at Preston Pans, and obliged to change his name. His second wife, the mother of all his children, was Elizabeth, daughter of Stephen Van Cortlandt. His oldest son, Cortlandt Skinner, was Attorney General of New Jersey, but was a royalist, and was afterwards a Brigadier-General. Stephen Skinner, second son, was Treasurer of the Province, and a refugee. William above mentioned was in the French wars, and died in England in 1778.

The intermarriages in the family are so strange, that we give the following brief tabular pedigree:

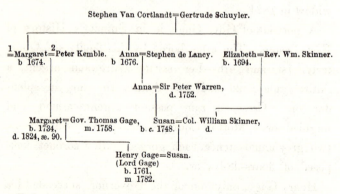

Stephen Van Cortlandt=Gertrude Schuyler.

1
=Margaret 2=Peter Kemble.   Anna=Stephen de Lancy.   Elizabeth=Rev. Wm. Skinner.
b 1674.   b 1676.   b. 1694.

Anna=Sir Peter Warren,
d. 1752.

Margaret=Gov. Thomas Gage,   Susan=Col. William Skinner,
b. 1734,   m. 1758.   b. c. 1748.   d.
d. 1824, æ. 90.

Henry Gage=Susan.
(Lord Gage)
b. 1761,
m 1782.

It is not surprising that the son of Elizabeth Skinner, should marry the grand-daughter of Anna de Lancy, as there was a difference of eighteen years in the ages of these sisters. It *is* strange that the grandson of a still

older sister, Margaret Kemble, should marry her great-
grand-niece. The authorities all agree as to the facts,
and as will be noticed, Margaret, wife of Gov. Gage, was
born when her mother was sixty years old. Surely there
must be some mistake as to the persons above mentioned.

An engraving of the arms of Philip Kemble, viz.,
"Sable on a bend ermine, three leopard's faces of the
first; Crest, a wolf's head trunked and embrued or," will
be found in Bridgman's Pilgrims of Boston, p. 92.]

W. H. W.

CAMPBELL FAMILY.

The seal here engraved was undoubtedly the property of John Campbell of
Boston, as we shall show by tracing its
ownership.

John Campbell, who was of Boston
as early as 1695, was Postmaster for
many years, but is better known as the proprietor of the
Boston Newsletter, the first newspaper published in the
Colonies. The first number appeared April 24, 1704,
and Campbell continued to issue it until 1722. He
died March 4, 1728, aged 75, and his will mentions
wife Mary, daughters Sarah Bowdoin, deceased, and
Elizabeth Foye, sons-in-law James Bowdoin and William Foye.

William Foye was a very prominent citizen of Boston,
for many years Treasurer of the Province. He died 21
March, 1759, aged 78, as appears by a mourning ring in
the possession of his descendants. His daughter Mary,

b. 8 Sept. 1721, m. Rev. William Cooper, who d. 13 Dec., 1743, and had an only daughter Mary.

Mary Cooper married, 22 May, 1766, Dr. Samuel Gardner of Milton, and had six children, of whom Sarah, b. 11 Sept., 1772, married John Amory of Boston.

John Amory (see REGISTER, X., 64) was born in 1773, and died in 1834. His children were John G., Nathaniel, George T., Mrs. William Perkins, Mrs. Amory Davis, and two other daughters. This Campbell seal is now in the possession of this branch of John Campbell's descendants.

———

As a proof that William Foye claimed arms, we give the following copy of a letter from him, preserved with the seal :

" The Seal which I send you is an half spread Eagle and a Naked Arm with a Drawn Sword upon a green field, a dove for the Crest, and the Motto is Audaces Fortuna Juvat, which in English is, Fortune favours the Bold : it is the Arms of the Family of Foye who came into England with William the Conqueror, it being a Norman Family, & I took it legally out of the Heralds' Office. I forgot to mention I wrote Ld Hallifax & Mrs. Cosby and some other people of rank by a Vessell which sail'd for London last week, which has us'd all my Gilt paper, and beg you 'ld send me a quire or two."

And on a mourning ring for his funeral is the following inscription, which terms him " Armiger : "

" Hon. W. Foye, Arm. ob. Mar. 21, 1759. Æ. 78."

This engraving is from the seal of Duncan Campbell of Boston, as found on a bond for Nathaniel Pickman's guardianship, dated 15 March, 1695–6, and now on file in Essex County. He was a bookseller of Boston, and by wife Susanna had four sons and two daughters. He was also Postmaster under a commission from England. His relationship to John has not been ascertained, though SAVAGE thinks they were probably brothers. W. H. W.

MONUMENTAL INSCRIPTIONS.

CONCORD.

The hill burying-ground in Concord, Mass., contains three erect stones, on which are carved heraldic insignia. They are of rather late date, and show the arms of only two families; the work is very careful and elaborate.

I.

M. S.
Lieu! Daniel Hoar

1773
Ob.^t Feb.^r y^e 8th Æt^t 93.

By Honest Industery & Prudent
Œconomy he acquired a hand-
som Fortune for a man in Privet
Carrecter He Injoy'd a long Life
& uninterrupted state of health
Blessings that Ever attend Excer-
sies & Temperance.

S. V.

Here's the last end of mortall story
He's Dead!

The family of Hoar has been at times a prominent one
in the annals of Massachusetts. It is traced to a widow
Joanna, who died at Braintree in 1661. The report that
her husband was a "wealthy banker from London, and
died soon after his arrival in Boston," is by Hon. James
Savage called an "absurd tradition." Mrs. Joanna Hoar
had six children. The sons were, Daniel,[2] who returned
to England; Leonard,[2] who graduated at Harvard College,
1650, and was President of the College, 1672–75; Hezekiah,[2] who was of Scituate and Taunton; and John.[2]
This last lived first in Scituate, but moved to Concord
about 1660. He died in 1704, leaving by his wife, Alice,
two daughters and one son, Daniel.[3] Daniel[3] Hoar was
born about 1650, married in 1677 Mary Stratton, and
secondly, in 1717, Mary Lee. By the first wife he had
eleven children, of whom Lieut. Daniel[4] was second.
Daniel[4] was born about 1680, married in 1705 Sarah
Jones, and died in 1773, as the grave-stone says, having
had four sons and three daughters. Jonathan,[5] H. C.

1740, rose to the rank of lieutenant colonel in the provincial service, and after 1763 was appointed Governor of Newfoundland, but died on the passage thither. John,[5] born in 1707, was married twice, and died in Lincoln, 1786, having had four sons and seven daughters. The second son was Hon. Samuel[6] of Lincoln, father of Hon. Samuel[7] of Concord, H. C. 1802, LL. D. 1838, and grandfather of Hon. Ebenezer Rockwood,[8] H. C. 1835, LL. D. 1861, Justice of the Supreme Court of Massachusetts.

The arms of Hoare are, Argent, an eagle displayed with two heads sable, and, Sable, an eagle displayed with two heads argent. The date of this stone is not early enough to be of much authority; the arms may have been previously used in this country, but we are not aware of the fact.

II.

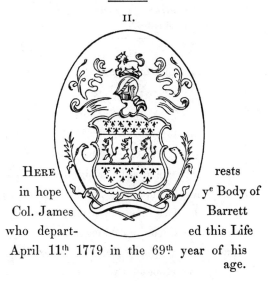

Here
in hope
Col. James
who depart-
rests
y[e] Body of
Barrett
ed this Life
April 11th 1779 in the 69th year of his
age.

Sudden the summons came, & quick the flight !
We trust to be with Christ in realms of light.

In public & privet life, he was courteous, benevo-

lent & charitable. His fidelity, uprightness and
ability in various offices & employments justly
procured him esteem. For many years he represented this Town in General Court. He early stept
forward in ye contest with Britan, & distinguished
himself in ye cause of America. His warm attachment to, & careful practice of ye religion of Christ
compleated his worthy character, & with his
other virtues will preserve his memory & rank
it with that of the just which is blessed.

> *O reader, from this pale monument learn*
> *Wisdom for Eternity, wisdom for*
> *Thyself, and be reminded of thy fate,*
> *Which hastens on the swiftest wings of time !*
> *Death steals upon you like a midnight thief !*
> *His step is secret, but yet sure, and may*
> *Be near and unexpected !*

III.

The same arms belong here also.

In Memory of
Col. Nathan Barrett
who died Feb^ry ye 22^d AD. 1791 ;
In the 56th year of his age.
His amiable Disposition
endeared him to his family and acquaintance ;
his Usefulness in society
gained him Esteem,
and his attention to Religion inspired
the Hope of the Gospel.

> *Relentless death nor tears nor pray'rs regards ;*
> *Nor worth nor usefulness his hand retards !*

Humphrey Barrett, the first of this family, was born about 1592, and settled in Concord about 1640. He died in 1662, and Mary, his widow, in 1663. They had three sons, Thomas,[2] who died before them in 1660, Humphrey[2] of Concord, and John.[2] Humphrey[2] was a deacon, and died in 1716, leaving two sons, Joseph[3] and Benjamin,[3] both of whom left descendants. Benjamin[3] was born about 1681, married in 1705 Lydia Minot, and died in 1728, leaving eight children, of whom Col. James[4] was third. James[4] was born in 1710, and married Rebecca Hubbard, by whom he had eight children. He was a prominent citizen of Concord, and in 1775 was appointed colonel of a regiment of militia, and was in command on the memorable 19th of April. Of his children Col. Nathan[5] was second.

The arms are not seen under the name of Barrett in any heraldic work, but in Smith's MS. Promptuarium Armorum, often quoted in the Journal, we find this coat, Ermine, on a fess gules three lions rampant or, with crest a lion sejant gules, ascribed first to Barret of London, but with the correction, "This is Blyth, as in fol. 113." On this leaf and in heraldic dictionaries we find the coat as Blithe of London, 1575.

PROVIDENCE, R. I.

The Old North Burial Ground in this city contains a number of stones ornamented with shields; in many cases, however, the same coat of arms is repeated. With one exception these bearings are all new to the Heraldic

Journal, and this exception (Gibbs) belongs to a different family from that previously noticed.

I.

Here lyeth y^e Body
of Sarah y^e Daughter
of William Harris Esqr
and of Abigail his
Wife died Octo^r
y^e 4th 1723 Aged
21^{ll} Years & 3 Months.

II.

The same arms are found with this epitaph :—

In Memory of
Mrs Dorcas Smith, ye Wife
of Mr Daniel Smith, Dec^d
ye 19th Day of November
Anno : Dom : 1745
Aged 41 Years & 6
Months.

Two brothers, Thomas and William Harris, were among the early settlers of Providence. Thomas died in 1686, leaving Thomas,[2] Richard,[2] Nicholas,[2] William,[2] Henry,[2] Elethan,[2] Joab,[2] Amity[2] and Mary.[2] I presume William[2] was the father of Sarah, who is here buried. His name occurs among the representatives in General Assembly, 1714, 17, 18, 20. I suppose Dorcas, the wife of Daniel Smith, was a daughter of William Harris. The coat of three birds is not found under the name of Harris or Smith, and we are not able to give any explanation of it. The stones are small perpendicular ones.

III.

Here lies Interred yᵉ Body
of Gidion Young, yᵉ Son of
Mʳ. Archibald Young & Alice
his Wife. Deceased July yᵉ
8th Anno Dom. 1738, Aged
4 Years & 1 Day.

IV.

The last coat accompanies this and the next epitaph.

Here lies Interred yᵉ Body
of Archibald Young, yᵉ Son of

M.ʳ Archibald & M.ʳˢ Alice Young.
Deceased July yᵉ 20th Anno Dom.
1738 Aged 5 Years 10 Months &
5 Days.

v.

In Memory of
M.ʳˢ ALICE YOUNG
The Daughter of Col.ˡ Joseph
Whipple, Wife to M.ʳ Archibald
Young. She Departed this Life
the sixth Day of April AD 1749
in the 53.ᵈ Year of her Age.

Among the arms attributed to the name of Young we find Argent, three roses gules, and Or, three roses gules. We can give no information about the family, except that Archibald Young was admitted freeman 1740, and Gidion Young, Jr., 1759. The three inscriptions are on the top of large brick tombs.

VI.

Hear   Lieth
The   Bodey
of   Abigail
Wife To   IOHN
ANDREWS   Esq.ʳ daugt.ʳ
of Cap.ᵗ John Whipplle & Abigail

his Wife Who depart^d this life April y^e
19th A D 1751 Aged 25 years
2 Months & 6 days.

We find the name of John Andrew or Andrews occasionally occurring in the Colonial Records;—as Deputy for Providence, 1750, and as Colonel of the militia of Providence County, 1757. According to Burke's General Armory, the arms of Andrews of Winwick and Charwelton, Northamptonshire, are, Gules, a saltire or, surmounted of another vert.

VII.

In Memory of LYDIA
Wife of Mr PAUL TEW
who Departed
this Life Augt the 30th
ANNO Dom. 1751
Aged *EIGHTEEN* Years

Eight months & six days.
Psa. XXXIX. v. yᵉ 5ᵗʰ
1 Cor. Chap. XV. 54, 55, 56
& 57ᵗʰ Verses.

In the Genealogical Dictionary of New England we find Richard Tew, who was of Newport, 1654, was a Representative and Assistant, and a grantee in the Royal Charter, 1663. According to Mr. Savage, he left only daughters. The family was continued here, and the name occurs often in the Colonial Records of Rhode Island. Before 1750 there were George, Edward, James, Richard and Thomas Tew. The Hon. Col. Henry Tew was Deputy Governor, 1714. Of Paul we only find that he was freeman, 1736, and Sheriff of Providence County, 1762, &c.

The union of different types in this inscription gives a most curious effect. We do not find the arms.

VIII.

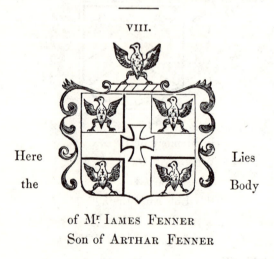

Here   Lies

the   Body

of Mͬ Iames Fenner
Son of Arthar Fenner

Esqr & Mary his Wife
Who Departed this life
Octob.^r the 25th 1751
Aged 21 Year
8 Months
& 27 Days.

IX.

The arms belong also in the other inscriptions of the family here given.

Here   Lies
The   Body
of IOSEPH FENNER
the Son of Arthur Fenner
Esqr & Mary his Wife
Who Departed This Life
November the 17th
1751 Aged 17 Year &
9 Months.

X.

In Memory of
Mrs SARAH FENNER,
Daughter of Arthur Fenner
Esqr and Mrs Mary his Wife,
Dec.^d January the 3.^d 1756
Aged 14 Years 8 Months
and 8 Days.

XI.

In Memory of
Mrs MARY FENNER,
late Wife of
Arthur Fenner Esqr Dec^d
the 18th Day of March
1756, Aged 54 Years
5 Months and 18 Days.

These four inscriptions, as well as those of Andrews
and Tew, are on small perpendicular stones. All the six
are of very similar workmanship. Concerning this family
we find an Arthur Fenner among the freemen in 1655,
who was a Captain in King Philip's war, and afterwards
was commonly distinguished by that title. He was an
Assistant, 1679, and a Justice of the Inferior Court of
Common Pleas, 1688. Another Arthur, probably his son,
was Deputy for Providence, 1700, 1707, &c., and Assistant,
1718, 1721. Arthur Fenner, Jr., with Edward and John,
was made freeman, 1723, and again Arthur Fenner, Jr.,
1746, so that the name seems to have been regularly
handed down from father to son. Among the arms
attributed to this name we find, Azure, on a cross
argent, between four eagles displayed or, a cross formée
sable, and, Vert, on a cross between four eagles displayed argent, a cross formée gules. Crest, an eagle
displayed argent, membered or.

————

The next two inscriptions are on the top of large brick
tombs, like those of Young.

XII.

Here Lieth Interred the Body of
AMEY, Wife of, ROBERT GIBBS
Esq[r] and Daughter, of Colon[l].
JOSEPH WHIPPLE, who died
Decem[r] 23[d] A. D. 1757, in the
58th Year, of her Age.

XIII.

The same arms are placed here.

Here Lieth Interred, the Body of,
ROBERT GIBBS Esq[r] who was
Born in Boston, and was Descended,
from the Antient and Honorable
Family of Sir HENRY GIBBS of
Dorsetshire in England, who died
June 29th A. D. 1769, in the 73[d]
Year of his Age.

The family of Gibbs, to which this Robert belonged, is
descended from Robert[4] Gibbs, a prominent merchant of

Boston.   He was the fourth son of Sir Henry[3] Gibbs, who was son of Sir Ralph[2] Gibbs, and grandson of Robert[1] Gibbs of Honington, co. Warwick, A. D. 1528–1584.

Robert[4] Gibbs of Boston, by wife Elizabeth Sheaffe,* had sons, Robert,[5] Henry[5] and Jacob,[5] the latter of whom died unm.

Henry[5] Gibbs was a minister at Watertown, and died leaving a son Henry,[6] who left descendants.   (See Register, XIX., 208.)

Robert[5] Gibbs married Mary Shrimpton, and had sons, Jacob,[6] Henry,[6] Robert[6] and Samuel,[6] and died in 1702. Of these children, Rev. Henry[6] was of Newton, and in his will leaves to his nephew, Robert Gibbs, Jr., of Providence, only son of his brother Robert, "my silver box which was my grandfather Sir Henry Gibbs', with his arms on it."   We may conclude that the other brothers, Jacob[6] and Samuel,[6] had died unm.

Robert[6] Gibbs, b. 29 Nov., 1696, moved to Providence, R. I., and m. 26 June, 1722, Mrs. Amy Crawford, by whom he had:—

Amy,[7] b. 4 July, 1725, m. John Mawney, 29 Oct., 1745.

Elizabeth, b. 10 Nov., 1728; d. unm.

Robert, b. 20 June, 1730.

Mary, b. 20 Feb., 1731–2; m. —— Young.

Hannah, b. 19 April, 1735; m. David Tillinghast, 14 Dec., 1752.

We are not aware of the existence of any descendants of this Robert Gibbs, in the line of his son Robert, Jr., but David and Hannah Tillinghast had a large family.

---

* She m. 2dly., Jonathan Corwin, and in her will gives "to my son Henry Gibbs, aforesaid, my great silver tankard which his grandfather, Sir Henry Gibbs sent me as a present."

In the January number of this Journal will be found a notice of a different family of the name.

XIV.

In Memory of
OLIVER   ARNOLD,   Esq.
Attorney General of this Coloney
A Gentleman descended from an antient and
honourable Family; but his principal Renown was
the Fruits of his Genius and indefatigable Industry.
His Abilities and Accomplishments were
equal to every Station and Character
in Life which he sustained.   Living
he justly acquired the Love of
his Country ;   and dying
She dropt an unavailing
Tear. He dy'd Octo.^r
9, 1770 in the
35.th Year of
his Age.

We have not at present the means of giving a satisfactory account of this family, but shall try to do so as soon as possible. The arms are, Gules, a chevron ermine between three pheons or. The whole inscription is cut on a large lozenge of white marble, inserted in the side of a brick tomb several feet high.

The little yard by the side of St. John's Church, Providence, contains two large tombs, on which is the same coat of arms, with these inscriptions :—

I.

Here lieth the Body of
JOHN MERRETT Esq ;
of LONDON, *Merchant*, who
came to Boston in the Year
1728, retired from Business
to a Farm near this Town, in
1748, and died on the 28th

of June, Anno 1770, in humble
Hope of a joyful Resurrection
to eternal Life ; aged 70
Years.

II.

Here lieth the Body of
MARGARET MERRETT,
the beloved Consort of
John Merrett Esquire. She
was born in LONDON, and
died on the 10th Day of
March ADom. 1769, in
humble Hope of a joyful
Resurrection to eternal
Life ; aged 66 Years.

We find the arms of Meritt of Wiltshire to be, Barry
of six or and sable, a bend ermine.

TITLED LOYALISTS.

In the first volume of the Heraldic Journal some
account was given of three families, members of which
became Baronets in the colonial times of Massachusetts.
After the separation from Great Britain, a few of those,
who adhered to the Royal Government, attained the
same rank. We have already noticed one of these, Sir
Isaac Coffin, and will now treat of two others, Sir John

Wentworth and Sir Jahleel Brenton.   Much of our information will be derived from the pages of Sabine's American Loyalists, Playfair's Baronetage, and of course Savage's Genealogical Dictionary.

The Wentworths of this country are descended from Elder William Wentworth of Dover, N. H., where he finally settled in 1650, after trying Exeter and Wells. He had a wife Elizabeth, and children, Samuel,[2] John,[2] Gershom,[2] Ezekiel,[2] Timothy,[2] Paul,[2] Sylvanus,[2] Ephraim,[2] Benjamin[2] and Elizabeth.[2]   He died 16 March, 1698. Eight of his sons seem to have left a numerous posterity.

Samuel,[2] born about 1640, the eldest son of Elder William, freeman 1676, had a wife Mary, who bore him Samuel,[3] Daniel,[3] John,[3] Mary,[3] Ebenezer,[3] Dorothy[3] and Benning.[3]   He died 25 March, 1690.

John,[3] the third son of Samuel, was born 16 June, 1672, and married Sarah, daughter of Mark Hunking. They had sixteen children, or, according to one account, eighteen, among whom were Benning,[4] John,[4] Samuel[4] and Mark Hunking.[4]   John[3] was Lieutenant-Governor of New Hampshire, 1717–29, and died at Portsmouth, 12 December, 1730.

Benning,[4] the eldest son of John,[3] was born 24 July, 1696, graduated at Harvard College, 1715, was Governor of New Hampshire, 1741–66, and died 14 October, 1770. He was twice married, but left no children.   His widow, who is said to have been one of his servants, Martha Hilton, married secondly Col. Michael Wentworth of Wooley, Yorkshire, England, and by this second husband left an only daughter Martha, who married John[6] Wentworth, as will appear farther on.

Mark Hunking,[4] sixth son of John,[3] was born 1 March, 1709, and married Elizabeth, daughter of John Rindge, by whom he had John,[5] Thomas[5] and Ann.[5] He was one of the council of New Hampshire, and died in 1785.

Thomas,[5] second son of Mark Hunking, graduated at Harvard College, 1758, married Anne, daughter of John Tasker, and died 1768. He left Mark,[6] an officer in the Royal Navy, John,[6] of the Inner Temple, barrister, who married Martha Wentworth, as above; Elizabeth,[6] wife of Edward Minchin, Annabella,[6] wife of Francis Gore, and Ann,[6] wife of William Sheafe.

John,[5] the eldest son of Mark Hunking, was born in 1736, graduated at Harvard College, 1755, and married his cousin Frances Deering, daughter of Samuel Wentworth, and widow of Theodore Atkinson, by whom he had one son, Charles Mary.[6] He was Governor of New Hampshire, 1767–75, and surveyor of the King's woods in America. At the Revolution he took part with the supporters of the royal government, was proscribed by the New Hampshire Act of 1778, and went to England. In 1792 he was appointed Lieutenant-Governor of Nova Scotia, which office he held till 1808. He received the degree of Doctor of Laws from the Universities of Oxford, Dartmouth and Aberdeen, and in 1795 was created a Baronet of Great Britain, as of Parlut, in the county of Lincoln. Sabine says of him;—"No royal Governor of his time in the thirteen Colonies was so highly respected by the Whigs as Wentworth; and not one of the official dignitaries, who clung to the royal cause, will go down to posterity with a more enviable fame. Had Bernard and Hutchinson been like him, the Revolution might have been delayed." Lady Wentworth died in England, in 1813, and Sir John at Halifax, Nova Scotia, 8 April, 1820.

Charles Mary,[6] only son of Sir John, was born in Portsmouth, 18 Jan., 1775. He was appointed a member of the Council of Nova Scotia, 1801, and succeeded to the Baronetcy at the death of his father in 1820. He was never married, and died in England, 10 April, 1844, when the title became extinct.

The arms of Wentworth, as borne by the Baronets, are, Sable, on a chevron engrailed or, between three leopard's faces argent, two antique keys, chevronways azure, bows to the centre, wards upwards. Crest, on a mount vert a griffin passant, per pale or and sable, charged with two antique keys erect in fess counterchanged. The keys in the shield and crest were given as an augmentation to the first Baronet, for his fidelity to the Royal cause. Motto, En Dieu est tout.

Sabine mentions a Benning Wentworth, who was proscribed in New Hampshire in 1778, moved to Nova Scotia, where he held various positions, and died in 1808. "His son, Lieutenant Benning William Bentwick Wentworth, of the Royal Navy, and heir to the titles and honors of the Earldom of Strafford, died in England, in 1810, at the age of twenty-one years." Who he was, it is not safe even to guess.

The Brentons spring from William Brenton, who was of Boston in 1633, but soon moved to Rhode Island, where he held high positions, and was Governor for several years. He owned large estates in Rhode Island and New Hampshire. He died at Newport in 1674, leaving by his wife Martha, daughter of Thomas Burton, three sons, Jahleel,[2]

William[2] and Ebenezer,[2] and probably six daughters, Mehitable,[2] Elizabeth,[2] Sarah,[2] Abigail,[2] Martha[2] and Mary.[2] All of these daughters were married.

Jahleel,[2] was collector of the customs at Newport, and died in 1732, without children.

William,[2] was collector of Boston, 1691, and by his wife Hannah, had William,[3] Samuel[3] and Jahleel.[3]

Jahleel,[3] was born 15 August, 1691, was twice married, and had twenty-two children, of whom Jahleel[4] was the eighth, and among whom may have been Benjamin, William, James and Edward, all of whom find a place among the American Loyalists. He died in 1767.

Jahleel,[4] was born 22 October, 1729, married in 1765, Henrietta, daughter of Joseph Cowley, by whom he had three sons, Jahleel,[5] Edward Pelham[5] and James Wallace,[5] and five daughters, Elizabeth,[5] Mary,[5] Martha,[5] Henrietta[5] and Frances.[5] He rose to the rank of Rear-Admiral in the British Navy, and died in 1802.

Jahleel[5] was born at Newport, 22 August, 1770, married in 1802 Isabella, daughter of Anthony Stewart of Maryland, and by her, who died in 1817, had Launcelot Charles Lee[6] and Frances Isabella.[6] He married secondly in 1822 his cousin Harriet, daughter of Hon. James Brenton, Judge of the Supreme Court, Halifax, and had by her a daughter Harriet Mary.[6] He rose to the rank of Vice-Admiral in the Navy, received the decorations of K. C. B. and G. C. S. F. and M., and was created a Baronet in 1812. Sir Jahleel[5] died 22 April, 1844, and was succeeded by his only son.

Sir Launcelot C. L. was born 15 February, 1807, and married in 1839 Anna Maria, daughter of Major-General

Chester. She died without children in 1849. He died 13 June, 1862, when the Baronetcy became extinct.

The arms borne by the Baronet are, Gules, a lion rampant double queued between three martlets argent, on a canton Or the stern of a ship of the line proper. Crest, out of a naval crown Or, the circle inscribed " SPARTAN," a swan argent, guttée de sang. Motto, Go through.

REVIEWS.

THE WINTHROP PAPERS.

Our readers are doubtless aware of the most valuable contribution to our early history, furnished by the last two volumes of the Collections of the Massachusetts Historical Society. Consisting of letters addressed to Gov. John Winthrop by the most distinguished of the colonists, they are of prime importance to all who desire to be acquainted with our early history. These volumes are also interesting to the student of heraldry, since they contain numerous examples of the use of armorial seals by the first generation of settlers here.

The first volume (4th Series, Volume VI.) contains the following interesting seals :—

1. That of John Humfrey, of which an engraving will be found in H. J., I., 192.

2. Emmanuel Downing uses, besides the seals of a griffin segreant, and a crest seal, both published in our first volume, p. 164, the seal here engraved; but the authority for its use is not apparent.

3. Hugh Peter uses the seal figured in our first volume, p. 190, and there authenticated.

4. John Endicott uses a seal not armorial, shown in our first volume, p. 68.

5. Edward Winslow uses a seal, probably a crest or badge, of a pelican " in her piety," i. e. in a nest with her young, and wounding her breast.

6. Roger Williams uses the seal here figured, but it does not appear in BURKE as appertaining to any family of this name. PAPWORTH assigns it to the Roope or Rope family.

7. Edward Hopkins, Governor of Connecticut, writing from Hartford, uses this seal, charged with an impalement. On other occasions he uses the crest seal.

8. Gov. John Haynes, whose true coat of arms is shown in our first volume, p. 50, also uses at times the crest here engraved.

9. Sir George Downing uses the impaled seal which we engraved for our first volume, p. 165. It seems very possible that the impalement is meant for Winthrop, as the chevronels of the latter coat might not appear on a poor impression of the seal.

10. Abraham Shurt uses the seal here presented, but we believe other examples of its use by other persons will be found among the unpublished letters.

11. Nathaniel Ward writing from Stondon uses the

following seal: Quarterly, 1st and 4th, three quatrefoils; 2d and 2d, three water-bougets: on the fesse point a crescent for difference. This is figured in the second volume of the Winthrop Papers, (4th Series, Vol. VII.) as are the following:

12. Thomas Mayhew uses his family arms. On a chevron between three birds, five lozenges; in chief a mullet for difference.

13. Herbert Pelham uses his family arms, and an engraving of the seal is in the current volume, p. 84. He also uses as a seal, the well-known badge of a buckle, which was assumed by his ancestor.

14. Richard Saltonstall, (concerning whom see H. J., I., 161,) uses a seal of the Saltonstall arms, impaling a coat of three leopard's faces, jessant-de-lys. These are the arms of the Gurdons, to which family his wife belonged.

15. John Norton uses his family arms engraved in our second volume, p. 1.

16. Samuel Mavericke uses two armorial seals, one being three battle-axes, the other a cross couped compony, between four mullets, and bearing one on the fesse point.

17. Thomas Gorges uses the arms of his family; lozengy argent and azure, a chevron gules. Sir Ferdinando Gorges used, Quarterly, 1st, Gorges as above; 2d, ———, on a chief three roses or mullets; 3d, a lion rampant; 4th, a chevron between three fleurs-de-lys. Burke terms these arms those assigned to the family in the time of Edward III., though more recently they have assumed their ancient and allusive coat of Argent, a

gurges or whirlpool azure. In the pedigree of Gorges, published by S. G. Drake, Esq., we find no marriages to explain these quarterings, but the pedigree is evidently defective in many respects.

18. Edward Godfrey, a prominent man among the early settlers at Acomenticus, under the Gorges patent, uses his family arms, described by BURKE as belonging to a family at Bolleyne, viz., a cross potence between four crosslets; and impaling a coat apparently, paly of ten.

19. Rev. Thomas Harrison of New England, 1648, who married a daughter of Samuel Symonds, uses on his seal the arms used by many families of the name, viz., three demi-lions rampant, a crescent for difference.

20. Rev. James Parker of Dorchester uses a very peculiar shield of a chevron between three Bowen Knots, apparently.

21. Rev. John Davenport used his arms as figured in our first volume, p. 37.

22. William Leete uses the very curious arms of his family, and a fac-simile of his seal is in our second volume, p. 47.

23. Rev. William Hooke of New Haven, who married a sister of Whalley, the Regicide, uses an impaled seal which evidently refers to this match. The seal is hard to decipher, but seems to be, 1st, Hooke; a cross between four escallops; impaling three boar's heads erased. A Whaley bore this coat, yet BURKE says the Regicide's family used three whale's heads. Nearly all of the family use allusive arms of whale's heads.

Hooke also uses a seal bearing a coat of three birds.

24. William Paine uses on his seal the following arms: on a fesse between three birds, as many mascles; all within a bordure. These are evidently the family arms, as appears by the seal of John Paine engraved in the present number.

It will be noticed that most of these seals belonged to the persons using them, and in the other cases they may have been heirlooms, acquired by marriage in former generations.   W. H. W.

LIFE OF JOSIAH QUINCY OF MASSACHUSETTS. By his son Edmund Quincy. Boston: Ticknor & Fields, 1867. Pp. 560.

No citizen of Boston will pass by this life of the most famous Mayor of the city, since his name is identified with all the transitional measures which raised the town to its present position. Many, however, will be surprised to see how great was his services, and how extended his influence, on broader and national fields of action.

Josiah Quincy was born in Boston, on the 4th of February, 1772, and was the son of Josiah Quincy, by his wife Abigail, daughter of Hon. William Phillips. We shall take this opportunity to give a short account of the family, especially as we are reminded by the title-page of this Memoir, that the use of coat-armor by the Quincys, dates back to the second generation in this country, and to one who was born in England.

The first of the name here was Edmund[2] Quincy, who was baptized May 30th, 1602, at Wigsthorpe, co. Northampton, and was the son of Edmund[1] Quincy and Ann

Palmer, his wife, of that place. Edmund[2] lived at Achurch, near Wigsthorpe, and m. July 14, 1623, Judith Pares, who accompanied him to this country in 1633. As his descendant writes, "that he was a man of substance may be inferred from his bringing six servants with him; and that he was a man of weight among the founders of the new commonwealth, appears from his election as a representative of the town of Boston, in the first General Court ever held in Massachusetts Bay." It may be added that on our records he has the honorary prefix of "Mr."

Another interesting proof is the fact that the arms figured in the margin are found on the seal to an unexecuted will of his son Edmund[3] Quincy, as well as on a silver cup bequeathed by the same gentleman to the church in Braintree. Undoubtedly the seal came from England with the first settler.

Edmund[2] Quincy died in 1637, the same year in which he had purchased a tract of land at Mount Wollaston, now Quincy, leaving one son Edmund,[3] and a daughter Judith,[3] wife of John Hull.*

Edmund[3] Quincy, Lt. Colonel, &c., died in 1698, leaving two sons, one by each wife, viz., Daniel[4] and Edmund.[4] Of these, Daniel[4] Quincy had a son John,[5] a distinguished politician, who was Speaker of the House, and Member of the Council; but as John[5] left descendants only in

---

* Our readers will find in Vol. II., p. 90, a seal of the Hull arms. As was shown (Vol. III., p. 46,) it was used by Daniel Quincy, but undoubtedly belonged then to one of the witnesses, Samuel Sewall, who married Daniel's first cousin, Hannah, only child of John Hull, above noted.

the female line, this branch of the name is extinct. Elizabetn[6] Quincy, (dau. of John[5]), married Rev. William Smith, and her daughter, Abigail[7] Smith, married John Adams, President of the United States. Their son, John[8] Quincy Adams, was thus quite remotely related to Josiah Quincy, yet owing to their friendship the connection was often erroneously supposed to be closer. In one instance, indeed, mentioned in the Memoir, Adams was termed the uncle of Josiah Quincy.

To revert to the male line:

Col. Edmund[4] Quincy was Judge of the Supreme Court, and Agent of the colony to England. He died in London, in 1738, aged 57, leaving two sons, Edmund[5] and Josiah.[5] Of these,

Edmund[5] Quincy, Judge C. C. P., had many descendants. His daughter Dorothy m. Gov. John Hancock.

Josiah[5] Quincy, b. 1709, was a merchant, and Colonel of the Suffolk Regiment. He removed however to Braintree, where he died in 1784. He had three sons, Edmund,[6] Samuel[6] and Josiah,[6] of whom Samuel[6] was Solicitor-General, but, being a Royalist, went to England and never returned. His descendants of the name reside in Boston.

Josiah[6] Quincy, a lawyer, was at the age of twenty-six so prominent, that he was selected with John Adams to defend Capt. Preston after the Boston Massacre. He was, however, an ardent patriot, and in 1774 he visited England as the confidential agent of his party. His health failed rapidly, but from a consciousness of the importance of the duty intrusted to him, he persisted in endeavoring to return to America. He died off Gloucester, 26th April, 1775.

His only child, Josiah[7] Quincy, whose life forms the subject of this article, was educated at Phillips Academy, at Andover. After studying the law for some time, he became more attached to public life, and early embraced the doctrines of the Federalists. He married June 6, 1797, Eliza-Susan, daughter of John Morton, Esq. On the 4th July, 1798, he delivered the oration at the town celebration. In 1800, he was the candidate for Congress, but was defeated by the Democratic candidate, Gov. Wm. Eustis. In 1804, he was elected to the State Senate, and in the same year to Congress. Though his party was in the minority, the talents of Mr. Quincy, who became its practical leader, gave him a prominent position in public affairs. After serving eight years he retired from his post in Congress, and in 1813 was elected to the State Senate. For the next ten years he was comparatively at leisure, though he was a part of the time in the General Court, and was elected Speaker. He next accepted office as Judge, delivering his famous decision on the law of libel, in 1822. Elected Mayor of Boston in 1823, he carried through the important reform in the fire department, and built the great Market, known to all Bostonians by his name. In 1829 he was elected President of Harvard University, holding that office until 1845.

From that time till his death, in July, 1864, he was removed from public life, but his opinions were always received by his fellow-citizens as the most valuable instructions. His death is too recent to render any detail necessary of the patriotic and humane sentiments he avowed. His sons are Josiah[8] and Edmund.[8]

Josiah[8] Quincy, well known as an efficient Mayor of

the city is still in public life. By his wife Mary-Anne,
daughter of Samuel R. Miller, he has sons, Josiah[9] P.,
and Gen. Samuel[9] M. Quincy.

Josiah P. Quincy m. Helen F., daughter of Hon.
Charles P. Huntington, and had a son Josiah[10] H. Quincy,
born in 1859.   w. h. w.

SIR WILLIAM JOHNSON, BARONET.

William[2] Johnson, whose name is so prominent in the
history of New York, was the eldest son of Christopher[1]
Johnson, Esq., of Warrentown, co. Down, Ireland, by
his wife Anna Warren, sister of Sir Peter Warren.
William Johnson was born in 1715, and came to New
York in 1738, where he settled on the estate of his uncle,
in the Mohawk country. He acquired a great influence
over the Mohawks, and was made a chief by the tribe in
1746. In 1755 he was placed in command of the New
York troops in the expedition against Crown Point, and
was victorious in the battle of Lake George, over
Dieskau. For this success he was created Baronet, by
patent bearing date of 27 Nov., 1755, and received a
grant of £5000 from Parliament. In 1759 he commanded at the capture of Niagara. He died at Johnson's Hall on the Mohawk river, July 11th, 1774, and as
he had been strongly in favor of the Royalists, his death
was undoubtedly a gain to the Colonists. His life has
been written by William L. Stone, who has published two
large volumes upon the subject.

Sir William[2] Johnson married a German girl named
Catherine Wisenberg, who died about 1745. By her he

had a son John,[3] and two daughters, Nancy,[3] wife of Daniel Claus, (m. July, 1762), and Mary,[3] who m. her cousin, Guy Johnson.

His will mentions brothers John and Warren Johnson, and sisters Dease, Sterling, Plunkett and Fitzsimons.

Sir John[3] Johnson, second baronet, was born in 1742. He was made a Major-General in the New York militia in 1774, but became a prominent Royalist and fled to Canada. He was a Colonel of Loyalists, and defeated Gen. Herkimer in 1777. After the war he was made Superintendent of Indian Affairs in Canada, and a Member of Council.

By his wife Mary, daughter of Hon. John Watts of New York, he had:—

William,[4] Lt. Col., m. Susan De Lancy, d. 1811.

Warren,[4] Major, d. 1802.

Adam-Gordon.[4]

John,[4] b. 1782, Col.

James-Stephen.[4] Killed in Barbadoes.

Robert-Thomas,[4] Capt., d. 1811.

Charles-Christopher.[4]

Archibald-Kennedy,[4] b. 1792.

Anne,[4] m. Col. Edward M. Donnell.

Catherine-Maria,[4] m. Major-General Bowes.

Sir John died at Montreal, 1830, and was succeeded by his son, Sir Adam-Gordon[4] Johnson, third baronet, who died in 1843, and was succeeded by his nephew, Sir William-George[5] Johnson, fourth baronet, who is the son of Col. John[4] Johnson, by Mary-Diana, dau. of Richard Dillon, Esq., of Montreal, and who was born in 1830.

W. H. W.

WALLACE OF PENNSYLVANIA.

We extract from Burke's Visitation of Seals and Arms, the following account of the Wallace family.

The pedigree is traced back to Rev. John Wallace, who was born in 1674, and died 3 June, 1733, at Drummelier, on the Tweed, of which parish he had charge from 1705. He married 5 March, 1705, Christian, daughter of William Murray of Cardon, son of Adam Murray, Laird of Cardon, a cadet of Murray of Philiphaugh, whose descent can be traced from Robert Bruce, and the Plantagenets. Rev. John Wallace had :—

> Christian,[2] born in 1707, married Alexander Stevenson of Smithfield.
>
> William,[2] born in 1708, successor to his father in the parish of Drummelier, died unm. 11 July, 1786.
>
> Helen,[2] born in 1710, died unmarried.
>
> Archibald,[2] born in 1712, died unmarried.
>
> Agnes,[2] born in 1713, died in 1784.
>
> John,[2] born in 1718, of whom as follows:—

John Wallace, the youngest son, sailed for the British Plantations in America, 20 February, 1742. He first went to Newport, R. I., but in 1748 is found in Philadelphia, as one of the managers of the first City Assembly. He was one of the founders of St Andrew's Society in 1749, and a member of the Common Council of Philadelphia, 1755–76. Near the beginning of the American Revolution he retired to his estate, Hope Farm, Somerset Co., New Jersey, which was at one time the headquarters of Gen Washington, and where Mr. Wallace died, 26 Sept., 1783. He married Mary, only daughter of Joshua Maddox, a prominent citizen of Philadelphia, and by her, who died 21 January, 1784, he left three children—

Joshua Maddox,[3] born at Philadelphia, 4 October, 1752.

William,[3] born in 1763, who lived at Hope Farm on the Raritan, and died 26 September, 1796.

Agnes.[3]

The elder son, Joshua Maddox Wallace of Ellerslie, Somerset Co., New Jersey, graduated at the University of Pennsylvania, 1767. In 1787 he was a member of the convention which ratified, in behalf of the State of New Jersey, the Constitution of the United States of America. He married 4 August, 1773, Tace, daughter of Colonel William Bradford, died 17 May, 1819, and is buried at Burlington, N. J.. His widow died 29 February, 1829. They had these children—

Joshua Maddox,[4] born 4 September, 1776.

John Bradford,[4] born at Ellerslie, 17 August, 1778.

Mary Maddox,[4] died unmarried 19 October, 1843.

Rachel Budd,[4] died unmarried 10 March, 1848.

Elizabeth.[4]

Susan Bradford.[4]

Joshua Maddox Wallace,[4] the elder son, married in 1805, Rebecca, daughter of William McIlvaine of Burlington, N. J., and died January, 1821, leaving,

Mary Coxe,[5] born 5 May, 1807, died unmarried 11 February, 1826.

Elizabeth.[5]

Joshua Maddox,[5] born 13 January, 1815, m. 7 June, 1847, Alice Lee, daughter of William Shippen,

and died 10 November, 1851. His eldest child,
William McIlvaine Wallace,[6] born 28 August,
1848, is the present representative of the family.

William Bradford,[5] born 4 May, 1817, died unmarried 9 November, 1841.

Ellerslie,[5] born 15 June, 1819, married 13 April,
1847, Susan, daughter of Bartholomew Wistar of
Philadelphia, and has issue.

John Bradford Wallace,[4] the second son, of Philadelphia and Burlington, an eminent lawyer, married 2 April,
1805, Susan, daughter of Barnabas Binney, and died in
Philadelphia, 7 January, 1837. His widow died 8 July,
1849. Their children were,

Susan Bradford,[5] married 16 June, 1841, Charles
Macalaster, and died 18 April, 1842.

William Bradford,[5] born 29 October, 1809, died 28
April, 1812.

Mary Binney,[5] married 21 November, 1837, John
S: Riddle, and died 13 May, 1852.

Marshall,[5] born 16 September, 1812, died 30 September, 1813.

John William,[5] born 17 February, 1815.

Horace Binney,[5] born 27 February, 1817, died 16
December, 1852. He was a distinguished lawyer
of Philadelphia.

Elizabeth,[5] died 23 August, 1824.

The arms borne by this family are, Gules, a lion
rampant argent, within a bordure gobonated of the last
and azure. Crest, a demi-lion rampant. Motto, Pro
Patriâ.

THE BROMFIELD FAMILY.

The seal here represented is copied from the original on a warrant dated 10th Jan., 1699, issued by Edward Bromfield, Justice of the Peace.

Concerning the ancestry of this gentleman, who was one of the later immigrants, we find a very complete record in the obituary published in a Boston newspaper of June 10th, 1734. We quote as follows:

"Thursday last were here entombed the remains of Hon. Edward[3] Bromfield, late one of his Majesty Council for this Province, &c., who deceased here at his house, in the eighty-sixth year of his age. He was the third son of Henry[2] Bromfield, Esq., the son of Arthur[1] Bromfield, Esq., and was born at Haywood house, the seat of the family, near New Forest in Hampshire, in England, on January 10, 1648, and was baptized at the neighboring church at Chancroft, on January 16, following. He came to this country in 1675, and soon became a member of the South Church in this town, and has been therein a distinguished ornament, giving a very bright example of strict piety, of unspotted justice, of extensive charity, of a public spirit, and of steady zeal against every vice, and for good order, and for the advancement of religion for above fifty years."

He was twice married, and by his second wife Mary, daughter of Rev. Samuel Danforth, he had twelve children, most of whom died young. Of these,

Edward[4] Bromfield, born Nov. 5, 1695, was also a distinguished citizen, as appears from the following extract from the Boston Gazette of April 19, 1756:

"Died, on the 10th inst., Mr. Edward Bromfield, an eminent merchant in this place. . . . . The town of Boston, his native place, observed his accomplishments, and called him to fill some of their most important places of trust; all which he discharged with great honor to himself and advantage to the public. In the House of Representatives he appeared the firm uncorrupted patriot; careful to assert the just prerogative of the crown, and to defend the invaluable liberties of the people."

He married 21st Feb., 1722, Abigail Coney, and had eight children. Of these, Edward,[5] the oldest son, was the subject of a warm eulogy at his decease, Aug. 18th, 1746, from the pen of Rev. Thomas Prince. He speaks of him as having a great fondness for mechanics, and especially as having constructed an organ better than any that had been imported from England. He had also constructed microscopes, and given much attention to the results of observations made with them. His brother,

John[5] Bromfield, born in 1734, m. May 3d, 1770, Ann, daughter of Robert Roberts of Newburyport. He was afterwards a merchant in Boston, and subsequently resided in Billerica. He had sons, Edward[5] and John.[6]

The latter, John[6] Bromfield, died unm. in Boston, Dec. 9, 1849, and will be remembered as one of the most liberal donors to our charitable societies, bequeathing $110,000 for such objects.   W. H. W.

PAINE FAMILY.

 We are indebted to Dr. E. B. O'Callaghan of Albany, for the accompanying seal of John Paine of Rhode Island. By a reference to Arnold's History, (I., 362–3), we find that John Paine was a merchant of Boston, who removed to Rhode Island, and in 1672, was the owner of Prudence Island. Very imprudently he accepted a patent for it, from Gov. Lovelace of New York, constituting it a free manor to be called Sophy Manor, and of which he was to be Governor.

This question of the bounds of the Colony was immediately met by Rhode Island, and Mr. Paine was imprisoned. He was soon released, and the matter was allowed to die out.

As we find no mention of him in SAVAGE, we are unable to say if he was married or left descendants.

. Mr. O'Callaghan adds that these arms agree with those ascribed by BURKE to the Paines of Market Bosworth, co. Leicester, viz., Argent, on a fesse engrailed gules between three martlets sable, as many mascles *or*, all within a bordure of the second, bezantée. Crest, a wolf's head erased azure, charged with five bezants saltireways.   W. H. W.

HERALDIC NOTES AND QUERIES.

(Continued from p. 96.)

XLIV.

Dr. John Appleton of Boston has a volume containing the book-plate of Thomas Child, engraved by Nathaniel Hurd. The arms are,—a chevron engrailed ermine between three birds, and are probably intended to be, Gules a chevron engrailed ermine between three eagles close argent. This Thomas Child may not improbably have been the one born in 1703, son of Benjamin, and grandson of Benjamin, both of Roxbury.

XLV.

Mr. J. G Nichols of London, England, has sent us the following extract from the Gentleman's Magazine for 1818, to which he has prefixed the query "Do you know any Oldmixons in America?"

"In 1818 died in the United States of America Sir John Oldmixon, once known in fashionable life, (of the same family as Pope's Oldmixon, the Whig historian.) He married Miss George, a celebrated vocal performer. They unhappily disagreed during their residence in America, and were divorced according to the laws of the U. S. His children are singularly and indeed unhappily situated; one half being born in, are citizens of the United States, while the other half (Englishmen) are actually Lieutenants in the British Navy.

XLVI.

On p. 46 we identified a certain seal as bearing the arms of Hull of Surrey, and as probably derived from John Hull of Boston. Mr. Jeremiah Colburn has a document, by which John Hull of Boston, in 1669, leased to John Evans of Muddy River, land at that place. John Hull used a seal with the arms engraved in the Journal, II., 90, and the piles are plainly shown to be such.

XLVII.

We have received from a correspondent the following queries, which may be of some interest to others of our readers, and we accordingly print them.

1. Is it proper or necessary for each member of a family to bear a mark of cadency on his arms?

2. In former times was any mark of cadency, except the label, used by the eldest son?

3. How do the descendants of the younger sons use their marks of cadency after the extinction of the older branch? Do they still retain the original mark or assume those of the older branch?

4. Is there any meaning attached to the tassels which on old trickings of arms terminate the mantlings?

5. Is a widow entitled to use the crest and motto of her husband, or a daughter those of her father?

6. Does a wife use the same arms as her husband; for example, on a seal with the crest, &c.?

[NOTE. We reply to the Queries:

1, 2 and 3. The most recent authorities, as Boutell and Planché, agree, that the present mode of marking the younger branches by a mark of cadency, as a mullet, label, &c., in the first generation, and in the second by repeating these distinctions, as by a crescent on a martlet, &c., is merely theoretical, and cannot be used in practice. If these differences are to be used to indicate that a person belongs to a certain branch of a family, they should be of a size to be at once recognizable. The impossibility of continuing to superimpose one upon another, condemns this mode.

It is also evident that the mode of distinguishing different branches has varied greatly at different times, and therefore we answer the second query in the affirmative.

To the fourth we reply that the details of the mantlings of a shield are left to the taste of the artist.

To the fifth and sixth we reply, on the authority of Boutell, (Third Edition, p. 139), "the arms of the husband and wife are borne together by the husband and wife and by the survivor of them." This we understand to mean that they use the same shield, not that the wife uses the arms on a lozenge; but we do not find the rule clearly laid down.

A widow bears the arms of her late husband, but in a lozenge and without a crest; an unmarried daughter bears her father's arms in the same way.

XLVIII.

We have lately identified, by means of the motto, the coat of arms in the Charlestown burying-ground, Vol. I., 57. It is on the tomb of Hon. Charles Chambers, but the motto, "Justus ut Palma," shows that the arms are intended for those of Palmes, I., 159. On the stone the chief is countercompony instead of vaire. At the Suffolk Registry of Deeds we learn that, in 1696, Edward and Sarah Palmes of New London deeded to Charles Chambers, land in Boston formerly belonging to William Davis, whose widow had become wife of Edward Palmes. It is evident that the tomb at Charlestown underwent the same change of owners. This discovery is most satisfactory, as the arms on the tomb bore no resemblance to those of Chambers; our list of puzzling coats is thus reduced by one.

THE

HERALDIC JOURNAL;

RECORDING THE

𝔄𝔯𝔪𝔬𝔯𝔦𝔞𝔩 𝔅𝔢𝔞𝔯𝔦𝔫𝔤𝔰 𝔞𝔫𝔡 𝔊𝔢𝔫𝔢𝔞𝔩𝔬𝔤𝔦𝔢𝔰

OF

AMERICAN FAMILIES.

VOLUME IV.

BOSTON:

WIGGIN & LUNT, PUBLISHERS,

221 WASHINGTON STREET.

1868.

Committee of Publication:

W. H. WHITMORE,
A. C. GOODELL, Jr.,
A. T. PERKINS,
W. S. APPLETON.

———

W. H. WHITMORE,
Editor of the present Volume.

PREFACE.

THE publication of the Heraldic Journal ceases with the completion of its fourth volume. This determination however does not proceed from any decrease in the public interest in the topics herein discussed, but has been forced upon the Committee by the inability of its members to devote the necessary time to a regular publication. For four years the burden has been cheerfully borne, but now they consider it fair to ask to be relieved from the task.

It is believed that these four volumes have been a material contribution to American genealogy, and that in a division of the subject hitherto almost totally disregarded. The diligence of friends has brought many new facts to light, and our pages have been honored with several of the most interesting and valuable genealogical memoirs that have appeared in print during that time. In this respect the present volume may claim precedence, enriched as it is with the first authentic pedigrees yet published of the ancestry of John Cotton and John Eliot.

We hope that the work of the Committee has also been of service in awakening the attention of genealogists to the actual and comparative values of coats-of-arms.

It has been our object to point out errors in proofs
no less than to substantiate rightful claims. It can
hardly be our fault if our readers cling to the use of
shields painted by Cole or his successors, after our
repeated warnings of their lack of authority. We
have discountenanced as far as was in our power
these absurd mistakes, and have tried to keep our
pages free from errors.

We have now only to reaffirm our belief in the
genuineness of the older evidences of seals and
inscriptions. The accumulation of examples seems
clearly to show that for the first century after the
colonization of New England, there was no fashion
of adopting arms, but that the seals and rings of their
ancestors were preserved as heir-looms by the settlers
here. Though considerable has been done in bringing
to light the instances of such use, more remains to
be done, and undoubtedly will be done year by year.

Although the publication of a distinct magazine
has now ended, the New England Historic-Genealogical Society still retains its Standing Committee on
Heraldry, and a place will be reserved in the Register
for such essays and notes as have formed the Heraldic
Journal. We close therefore with an urgent request
that our readers will not consider the field abandoned,
but will forward to us such information as they may
acquire concerning the early use of Coat Armor in
New England.

GENERAL INDEX.

Arms, engraved:
Alleyne, 110; Armstrong, 23; Barton, 130; Bethune, 172; Burges, 8; Brown, 145; Chase, 153; Cotton, 49; Green, 112; Higginson, 168; Holton, 5; Jordaine, 5; Moody, 169; Munning, 80; Neville, 32; Norton, 31; Phippen, 9; Pierce, 4; Pye, 7; Russell, 32; Sheaffe, 81; Sturgis, 133; Thatcher, 75; Tothill, 142; Usher, 34; Worthington, 70.

Arms, engraved, but not identified: 29, 30, 34, 109, 110, 111, 139, 167, 169, 170, 171, 172.

Arms, described:
Atkinson, 119; Brown, 26; Bulkeley, 30; Chase, 166; Clinton, 96; Colden, 45; De Lancy, 95; Ellery, 42; Fletcher, 95; Gardiner, 97; Gedney, 170; Hayward, 91; Henshaw, 124; Hicks, 44; Houghton, 124; Hunter, 95; Linzee, 39; Monckton, 95; Moore, 95; Murray, 95; Russell, 107; Saffin, 42; Sheaffe, 89; Spooner, 45; Tryon, 96; Whittingham, 43; Wilson, 140; Wray, 140.

Earldom of Stirling, claimants of, 59.

Essex Wills, seals on early, 167.

Genealogies:
Atkinson, 119; Barton, 130; Bethune, 173; Bigelow, 27; Boylston, 28; Brown, 26, 148; Chase, 153; Chester, 28; Coolidge, 27; Copley, 175; Cotton, 49; Cushing, 57; Fairfax, 150; Gardiner, 97; Green, 112; Hawkridge, 57; Henshaw, 121; Jordaine, 5; Lawrence, 27, 35; Lechmere, 44; Linzee, 38; Pelham, 175; Phippin, 1; Pye, 7; Russell, 32, 102; Schuyler, 20; Sheaffe, 81; Spotswood, 114; Sturgis, 133; Thatcher, 75; Van Cortlandt, 20; Wentworth, 125; Worthington, 69.

Governors of New York, 94.

Governors of Nova Scotia, 24.

Grant of Arms, example of, 146.

Herald-Painters, 192.

Heraldic Notes and Queries:
Use of arms, 41; Saffin arms, 42; Ellery arms, 42; Whittingham, 43; Lechmere family, 43; Mourning flag, 44; Spooner arms, 45; Change of arms, 46; Faxon arms, 47; Holyoke family, 90; Heyford arms, 91; Trecothick arms, 91; Governors of New York, 94; Katherine wheel, 136; De Carteret family, 139; Virginian families, 139; Harrison's estate, 141; Tuttle arms, 142; American coat-armor, 143.

Middlesex Wills, seals on, 29.

Official seals: Gov. Armstrong of Nova Scotia, 23.

Reviews: Bond's Watertown, 25; Spotswood Genealogy, 114; Fairfax genealogy, 149.

Suffolk Wills: Armorial Seals, 109.

Ta xon Armorial Bearings, 47, 142.

Titled Americans: Sir Charles Hobby, 116; Benjamin Thompson, Count Rumford, 117; Sir Roger Hale Sheaffe, 88.

INDEX OF NAMES.

Alexander, 59.
Allen, 110.
Amory, 39.
Atkinson, 119.
Austin, 93.

Barton, 130.
Belcher, 25.
Bethune, 172.
Bigelow, 27.
Bland, 140.
Blyth, 192.
Bond, 25.
Boylston, 28.
Breslaw, 192.
Bright, 26.
Brown, 26, 44, 145.
Burges, 8.

Campbell, 25.
Chambers, 105.
Chase, 153.
Chester, 28, 32, 125.
Clinton, 96.
Colden, 45.
Congalton, 175.
Coolidge, 26, 93.
Copley, 175.
Cornwallis, 25.
Cotton, 49.
Courland, 21.
Cunningham, 39.
Cushing, 57.

Dandridge, 115.
Deblois, 41.
De Carteret, 139.
Doucett, 24.
Dutton, 106.

Ellery, 42.
Elliot, 109, 182.

Fairfax, 149.
Farrar, 30.
Fowler, 69.
Fox, 30.
Francklin, 25.

Garden, 192.
Gardiner, 97.
Greene, 40, 112.
Gulliver, 77.

Harrison, 141.
Hawkridge, 57.
Henshaw, 122.
Heyford, 91.
Hicks, 44.
Higginson, 168.
Hobby, 77, 116.
Holyoke, 90.
Hopps, 192.
Hopson, 25.
Horton, 41.
Houghton, 124.
Hurd, 45, 192.

Ivers, 92.

Jordaine, 5.

Kent, 78.
King, 121.

Lake, 75.
Lawrence, 27, 35.
Lechmere, 33, 43.
Legg, 25.

Linzee, 38.
Long, 31.
Lowell, 33, 106.

Mascarene, 24.
Mather, 55.
Mayo, 140.
Mitchell, 111, 192.
Munning, 80.

Nanfan, 96.
Nash, 109.
Neville, 33.
Nicholson, 24.
Norton, 31.

Pelham, 175.
Penn, 110.
Perkins, 101.
Phippen, 1.
Phipps, 29.
Prescott, 38.
Pye, 7.

Russell, 32, 102.

Saffin, 42.
Saltonstall, 27.
Sargent, 43.
Schuyler, 20.
Searle, 192.
Sharp, 34.
Sheaffe, 81, 109.
Smith, 74.
Sohier, 40.
Solley, 44.
Somerby, 2, 49, 102, 182.
Spooner, 45.
Spotswood, 114.

Staggers, 46.
Stearns, 26.
Story, 54.
Sturgis, 133.

Thatcher, 75.
Thompson, 117.
Tilden, 39.
Torrey, 41.
Trecothick, 91.
Trumbull, 42, 44.
Tryon, 96.

Tuthill, 142.

Usher, 34.

Van Cortlandt, 20.
Van de Weyer, 135.
Vassall, 105.
Vetch, 24.

Warren, 40.
Washington, 115.
Wentworth, 125.

White, 110.
Whitmore, 44, 190.
Whittemore, 30.
Whittingham, 43.
Willett, 42.
Wilmot, 25.
Wilson, 140.
Winchester, 41.
Winthrop, 44.
Worthington, 69.
Wray, 140.

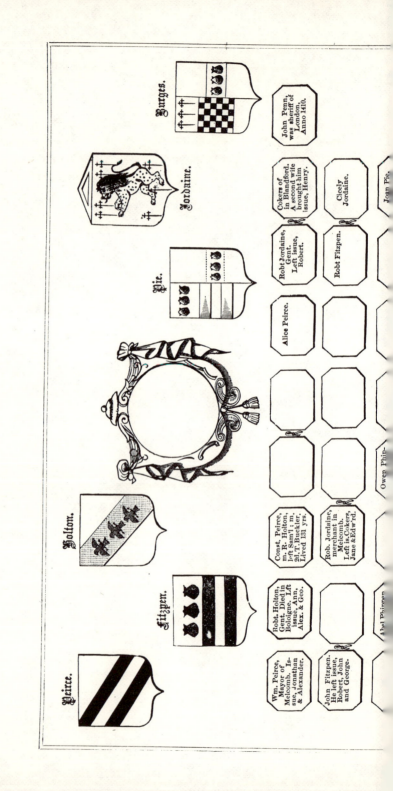

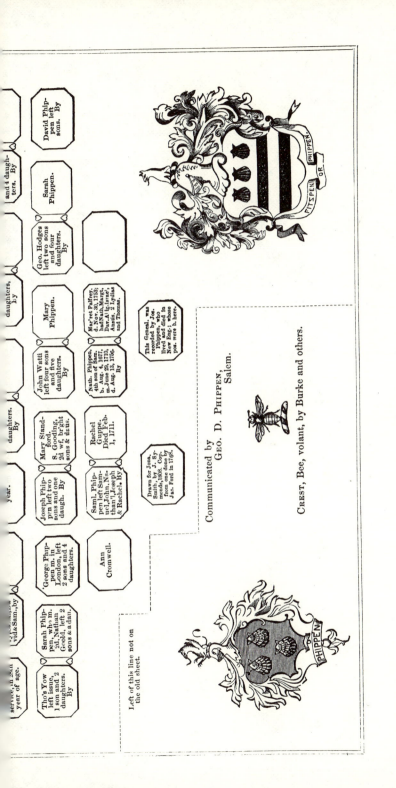

service, in 26th year of age.

…vid & Sam., by

and 4 daughters. By

David Phippen sons. By

Sarah Phippen.

Geo. Hodges left two sons and four daughters. By

Mary Phippen.

John Watti left four sons and five daughters. By

Mary Standford. S. Gooding, 2d wf, bright sons & daurs. By

Joseph Phippen left two sons and one daugh. By

Rachel Guppe. Died Feb. 1, 1711.

Saml. Phippen left Samuel, John, Nathan, Joseph & Rachel. By

Nath. Phippen, 4th son of Sam. b. Aug. 4, 1677, m. June 29, 1710, d. Aug. 13, 1756. By

Mar'ret Palfrey, d. Nov. 30, 1753; had Nath, Mary, Dav, Al'lg, Irene, Annis, 2 Lydias and Thomas.

This Geneal. was recorded by Jos. Phippen, who lived and died in New Eng.; whose pos. were b. here.

Drawn for Jona, Smith, by J. Symonds, 1808. Copied from one done by Jas. Ford in 1768.

George Phippen m. in London, left 2 sons and 4 daughters.

Ann Cromwell.

Sarah Phippen, who m. 2d, Nathan Gεold, left 2 sons & a dan. By

Tho's Yow left issue, 1 son and 2 daughters. By

Left of this line not on the old sheet.

FITZPEN OR PHIPPEN

PHIPPEN

Communicated by
GEO. D. PHIPPEN,
Salem.

CREST, Bee, volant, by Burke and others.

THE

HERALDIC JOURNAL;

RECORDING THE ARMORIAL BEARINGS AND GENEALOGIES
OF AMERICAN FAMILIES.

NO. XXI.   JANUARY, 1868.

FITZPEN OR PHIPPEN, AND ALLIED FAMILIES.

[By GEORGE D. PHIPPEN, of Salem.]

The foregoing emblazoned sheet has been preserved in
the American family, under sundry mutations, for upwards
of two centuries. As stated upon one of the tablets or
enclosures, it "was recorded by Joseph Phippen, who
lived and died in New England: whose posterity were
born here." He was the eldest son of David Phippen, of
Weymouth, or Melcomb-Regis, united boroughs, in Dorsetshire, England, (eight miles from Dorchester, that
nursery of Massachusetts,) who, with his family, consisting, as is believed, of his wife Sarah, four sons, and two
daughters, came to this country and settled at Hingham,
Massachusetts Colony, with the Rev. Peter Hobart, in
1635; who, with the first thirty settlers, drew for their
house lots Sept. 18 of that year, and where he subsequently had many other grants of land.

Joseph was made a freeman in 1644, about which time
he removed to Boston, afterward to Falmouth, now Portland, where he resided fifteen years, till 1665, when he

removed to Salem, Mass., where many of his descendants
have lived to the present day.

In the inventory of the effects of David Phippen, who
d. Feb. 15th, 1782, aged 67, a gr.-gr.-grandson of the primitive David, we find this item: " One large frame, containing
the Genealogy of the Phippen family." This was a copy
of the original, and was elegantly drawn, in 1768, by James
Ford, a Scotchman, at that time a school teacher in Salem.

This copy suffered an accident during the Revolutionary
War, whereby the circular caption and other important
tablets were defaced, or rendered illegible. The extant
copy, being the third in order, was drawn from this
defaced one many years afterward, in 1808, by John
Symonds of Salem, with additional tablets to later times.
What became of the defaced copy, or of the original, all
efforts thus far have failed to discover.

From the Symonds copy, which is drawn upon a sheet
4 ft. by 20 in., enclosed in a frame composed of three
plates of glass, the foregoing engraving is made, exclusive, however, of some of the recent additions made by
him.

All the tablets above the middle line relate to the family
and its connections in England; those below that line relate
to this country. Other copies have recently been multiplied by the writer; one of which exists, with other plates
and emblazonry, in a copious manuscript of the Phippen
family by the same hand.

Through the successful research of H. G. Somerby, Esq.,
among English archives, we are able also to present a copy
of the Fitzpen or Phippen Arms and Pedigree, as furnished
and certified to before the Clarenceux King of Arms at the

Herald's Visitation of Cornwall, in 1620, by the Rev. Geo. Phippen of Truro, in said county. He was brother of the primitive David of New England, and was at that time master of the grammar school there,* and subsequently rector of St. Mary's Church of the same place.

VISITATION OF CORNWALL, A. D. 1620.

Harleian MSS., Book 1162.

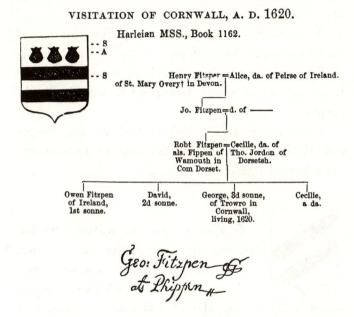

```
-- S
-- A

-- S        Henry Fitzpen ═ Alice, da. of Peirse of Ireland.
        of St. Mary Overy† in Devon.

                Jo. Fitzpen ═ d. of ——

            Robt Fitzpen ═ Cecilie, da. of
            als. Fippen of │ Tho. Jordon of
            Wamouth in  │  Dorsetsh.
            Com Dorset.  │

Owen Fitzpen    David,      George, 3d sonne,    Cecilie,
of Ireland,     2d sonne.   of Trowro in          a da.
1st sonne.                  Cornwall,
                            living, 1620.
```

Geo: Fitzpen ☞
at Phippen ⚓

This original document, with his sign-manual attached, a fac-simile of which is above given, may be seen among the Harleian Manuscripts, Book No. 1162, in the British Museum, London.

---

* Polwhele says of this long-standing institution, "It may be well classed with the first seminaries of England, and its masters and scholars have frequently been formidable rivals to those of the royal foundations, in genius, taste and learning. Its masters have been almost uniformly men of great respectability.

† "St. Mary Overy" may possibly be correct; there is, however, a parish in Devon, called "Ottery St. Mary," about nine miles from Exeter.

This book "consists of original returns of the Cornish
Gentry, subscribed by the hands of those gentlemen
who, in 1620, gave the information touching their several descents, and is written chiefly by Henry St. George
Richmond, Herald, and Mr. Sampson Leonard Blewmantle,
Marshalls and Deputies to William Camden Clarenceux,"
or second King of Arms.

The discovery of the above document furnishes perfect
corroboration, as far as it goes, of the ancient heraldic-
genealogical record of our thoughtful ancestor, and from
it several of the empty tablets could undoubtedly be
supplied.

Of the arms of Peirce, Holton, Jordaine, Pie, Burges
and Fitzpen, allied English families, we communicate
the following items:

PEIRCE.

Two bends sable. From BURKE we find
this ordinary in use, under various forms,
by the family of Pearse. The old record
in its complete state undoubtedly repre-
sented William Peirce, Mayor* of Melcomb, as the ancestor
of Constance Peirce, who married, 1st, Robert Holton, and
2d, Thomas Buckler,† and that she lived to the great age
of 131 years; also that Alice Peirce of the same family
married Henry Fitzpen of St. Mary Overy in Devonshire,

---

* If so, he must have been mayor before 1516, as the list from that time
is before us.

† Ed. Buckler was minister of Melcomb in 1650. Richard Buckler was
member of common council of Weymouth and Melcomb-Regis at the time
of their united charter, June 1, 1571. A street of that place was named
after this family, who are said by Ellis, in History of Weymouth and Melcomb, to have emigrated to America.

who must have been born about the time of the discovery
of America, and from whom the present family of Phippen,
in an unbroken line, trace their descent.

HOLTON.

On a bend *or*, three eagles displayed.
These arms are described by BURKE,—
"Azure, on a bend *or*, three eagles dis-
played gules; for a crest a map proper."

The second and third tablets of the record state that
"Robt Holton, Gent., died at Boloigne, leaving issue, Ann,
George and Alexander." Robert Holton, probably a son,
married Constance Peirce, as before stated, and left a son
Samuel. This completes our knowledge of this family.

JORDAINE.

A lion rampant between nine* crosses
crosslet fitchée. Jordaine or Jordan of
Dorsetshire, arms described by Burke and
others are, "Azure semée de crosses crosslet, a lion rampant or," which arms are
said to have been used as early as Edward I.

Hutchins, in History of Dorset, says: "The Jordans
were an ancient family in Dorsetshire, and occur very
early in Coker-Frome, at Frome-Whitfield, where they
had some interest about 1400. Their arms, similar
to those here engraved, are quartered with Trenchard,
——, and Mohun, upon the painted glass windows of
the ancient manor house of Wolveton, long since in ruins,
but for the time when it was built one of the grandest in

---

* Two Crosses are here accidentally omitted in the engraving. ED.

England. These windows are its noblest remaining ornament, and contain almost a complete pedigree of the family.

Wolveton or Wolverton Manor lies about eight miles from Weymouth. John Jurdaine, its ancient owner, was escheator of the county, the 5th of Henry IV., and his name also occurs, in a list of Gent., 12th Henry VI. He bought this place of John Mohun and Alice his daughter, heir to Henry Trenchard of Hampshire.

John, son of this John of Wolveton, married Christie, one of the heiresses of John Chantmarle, by whom the manors of East Stoke, Beltwale, and Stoke Hyde, near Blandford, or part of them, accrued to the Jordaines.

This John granted John Wells, clerk, land in Weymouth and other places.

By our records, "Robt Fitzpen, or Fippen, of W^a-mouth," son of John and grandson of Henry of Devon, m. Cecilie Jordan, dau. of Thomas Jordan, 18 Sept., 1580, and had a dau. Cecilie, who was baptized March 10, 1593. This Thomas Jordan was probably son of "Robt, Merchant of Melcomb," brother of Henry and grandson of Robert Jordaine, who married Cokers ———— of Blandford.

Blandford lies twenty-four miles from Melcomb. John Coker, who d. 1635, wrote a history or survey of Dorset. The parish records of Melcomb-Regis state that Robert Jordan was buried there October 12, 1589.

Other members of the Dorset family are mentioned by Hutchins, as John Jordan, who held land at Weymouth in 1440, John Jurdeyne, member of Parliament, 1553, Richard Jordan, Mayor of Melcomb, 1596, William, who in 1575 made the gift of a musket to the grand fleet then fitting out from England. Another William, or perhaps the same, of West Truro, in 1611 published a work on the Creation and the Deluge ; also, in 1611, he wrote a manuscript of Interludes in the Cornish language. A hill in Weymouth is called, after this family, "Jordan's hill."

Without doubt it was this connection with the Jordan family that induced Joseph Phippen to settle at Falmouth (Portland) with the Rev. Robert Jordan, the Episcopalian, who was so conspicuous in the early settlement of that place, and whose pedigree, in all probability, we have to a considerable extent above given. He m. Sarah, the only child of John Winter, the first settler at Casco Bay, and became thereby the chief proprietor of land on the south side of Casco River. One of his first conveyances of land was to Joseph Phippen, who with his sons carried on farming and fishing at Purpooduck and House Island. Most of the Jordans of this country have descended from this man. LOWER, in Hist. Surnames, says the name is known to have been borrowed from the famous river of that name in Palestine.

PIE, OR PYE.

The charge shown in this empalement are three escallop shells, which, until the sheet was defaced, were without doubt upon a fesse, here indicated by dotted lines.

According to Burke, the arms of Pye of St. Stephens in Cornwall are, "Argent on a fesse azure, three escallop shells of the field." Pie of London have the same, with additions granted March 2, 1634.

George Fitzpen, A. M., called also George Phippen, who in 1620 responded to the Herald Visitation, married Joan Pie, dau. of Constance Pie.

The above arms by empalement with Fitzpen signalize that marriage, Fitzpen on dexter and Pie on sinister side of shield as husband and wife. Gilbert's Cornwall, Vol. III., 449, says that this family with the Spreys, during the interregnum of Cromwell, turned decimators and sequestrators upon the lands and revenues of the royal laity and clergy of Cornwall, to that degree of hurt and damage that it occasioned the making of that short litany not yet forgotten in Cornwall,—

> "From the Pyes and the Spreys,
> Good Lord, deliver us."

The name of Pye is said to be a corruption of the Welsh Ap Hugh, *u* sounding as *y*. The name is still common in Cornwall. Rev. Charles Pye was a successor of George Phippen, as rector of St. Mary's Church at Truro, in 1761.

BURGES.

A fesse chequey argent and gules, in chief cross-crosslets fitchée.

Described by Burke as "Chequey argent and gules, on a chief *or*, three crosses botoniée azure. Crest, a lion rampant gules, holding in the dexter paw an annulet enclosing a fleur-de-lis argent." From the empaling of the above shield with Pye, Burgess is the husband and Pye the wife.

This surname of Burgess is often mentioned at cotemporary dates, by Hutchins, in History of Dorset.

William Burgess officiated at the church at Radipole, two miles from Weymouth, in 1650.

FITZPEN, OR PHIPPEN.

These arms are represented on the old record in three forms, and another form found in the family is also added on the left of the engraved plate.

The colors in these are not uniform, perhaps the result of fading, or otherwise of the caprice of the copyists. In one shield the bars are vert. In the one empaling Pie they are azure. In the mantled one they are correctly colored sable.

Burke describes Fitzpen, or Phippen, of Dorset and Cornwall,—"Argent two bars sable, in chief three escallops of the second. Crest, a bee volant in pale or, winged vert."

This shield is also described by the letters S. A. S., sable, argent, sable, in the Herald's Visitation of 1620.

The above crest, and that on page 10, are two forms of a griffin, and differ from the bee crest of Burke,

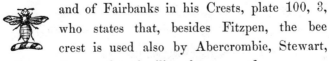

and of Fairbanks in his Crests, plate 100, 3, who states that, besides Fitzpen, the bee crest is used also by Abercrombie, Stewart, and some dozen other families there named.

The history of the separated shield in the left hand corner of the engraved plate we are unable to give. It is about ten inches square, framed in diamond form, and appears very ancient. Possibly it is cotemporaneous with the old sheet, as they were found together in the same branch of the family; or it may have been drawn at a later day. Its charge is the same, three escallop shells, though differently arranged, i. e., Azure three escallops or.

The principal charge upon the Fitzpen arms—the three escallop shells, imply their antiquity, as they were without doubt conferred or assumed at the time of the Crusades, or, if later, in commemoration of a part taken by some leading spirit in those strange wars for the rescue of the Holy Land from the avowed enemies of the Cross.

THE NAME PHIPPEN is patronymic, and is a corruption of Fitz-pen or Fils-pen, (Fitz or Fils from the Latin Filius, meaning Son) being a Norman prefix to an old British name. Camden says Pen, in British, signifies the head or top of any thing, whence the Pennine Alps and the Apennines, and some mountains among us, as Pennon's Hill in Devonshire, &c.

There is an old couplet still common in Cornwall,—

"By Tre, Ros, Pol, Lan, Caer and Pen
You may know the most of Cornish men."

Polwhele says those families of Cornwall who held lands before the Conquest have been distinguished by the appellations Tre, Pol and Pen, and he bears witness that of Tre and Pol, if not of Pen, there existed in his day families who have preserved from all antiquity, and still retain, unalienated, the very estates whence they derived their names.

The name Pen, or Penne, is of frequent occurrence in early English Records, such as the Hundred Rolls, Patent Rolls, Fine Rolls, &c., extending back from the Crusades even to the time of the Conquest, and is found in the Roll of Battel Abbey.

The first tablet on the right reads, " John Pen, Sheriff of London, 1410," which fact is corroborated by Baker's Chronicle, p. 168. John Penne, perhaps the same person, was member of Parliament, returned from Weymouth, 1413, '20 and '22, " which place, since its union with Melcomb, has the extraordinary privilege of sending four members to Parliament, a right enjoyed by no other place in the kingdom except London."

If this man be indeed a progenitor of the family, there are wanting three or four generations to unite him with Henry Fitzpen of Devonshire. As all the other parts of the old record have been remarkably corroborated by the public archives, we infer that John Pen was not placed at the head of the list without authority.

The first transition from Fitzpen to Phippen with which we meet, occurs with the great-grandchildren of Henry, as George of Truro, who styles himself George Fitzpen, called Phippen. His nephews in New England signed documents still extant with an alias, sometimes "Fitz-pen, als. Phippen," at others "Phippen, als. Fitzpen." Their children used only the name Phippen, as now written, and as still in use, though rare, in Devon and Somerset, England. Fitzpen being now obsolete in both countries.

In the early records of this country we meet frequent cases where it is recorded Phippeny, but it was always a perversion and not so written by the family, as their signatures abundantly show.

A branch of the family, that of James Phippen, of the fourth generation in New England, whose children removed from Boston to Stratford, Conn., about 1680, and their descendants, have adopted the form of Phipany.

The name Phippeny, or Phippany, appears to be also a natural sequence from Fitz-Pain, or Fitzpaine, the name of an ancient knightly family who held lands in Dorset-shire and other counties of England, and in which the Christian name of Robert figures largely, as it also does in the foregoing line of Fitzpen.

Robert Fitz Payne was Sheriff of Dorset and Somerset in 1150, and was Lord of the Manor of Oaksey, in Wilts. In Parliamentary writs we find Robert Fitz Payne in 1277, Robti Phippayne in 1509, and so on. The chief seat of this family was called Fipany Okeford as late as 1600. If future investigation should unite these families, the line could be extended to a very remote period. The circular caption on the old sheet was sufficiently large, being three and a half inches in diameter, to have settled by its once legible contents, any such speculations.

Descendants OF Henry Fitzpen OF Debon.

GENEALOGY, IN PART.

Without further attempt to trace descent from John Pen of London, 1410, or from the more ancient family of Robert Fitzpaine of Dorset, in the time of Henry I., we are content to commence with that which has been proved to be authentic and reliable, but shall not in this article carry down many branches to the present time.

1 Gen. Henry Fitzpen of St. Mary Overy in Devon, who m. Alice Peirse and had a son John.

2 Gen. John Fitzpen, son of Henry, m. ———, had children Robert, John and George.

3 Gen. Robert Fitzpen, son of John of Weymouth in Dorset, m. Sept. 18, 1580, Cecilie, dau. of Thomas Jordan of Dorset, and had Owen, David, George and a dau. Cecilie, who was bapt. at Melcomb, March 10, 1593, and m. ——— Reynolds.

4 Gen. Owen Fitzpen, or Phippen, son of Robert and Cecilie, born at Melcomb, 1582, m. Annie Coinie, 3 July, 1603, died at Lamorran, five miles from Truro, Cornwall, in 1636.

The old record says, "Owen Phippen who most valiently freed himself from the Turkes." This relates to his rescuing himself and companions with great bravery after a seven years' bondage on board an Algerine corsair ; the history of which exploit is engraved upon a monument or tablet erected to his memory by his brother George, in St.

Mary's Church, while he was settled over it.   This church
is a handsome Gothic structure built during the reign of
Henry VIII., on the north side of the chancel of which is
a monument with the following inscription; a copy of
which is given in Lysson's Magna Britannia, Vol. III.,
Cornwall, p. 312, in Hitchin's Cornwall, Vol. II., 648,
and in Orchard's Epitaphs.

" Δοξα εν Ζειςοις Θεῶ.*

" To the pious and well-deserved memory of Owen Fitz-
Pen, alias Phippen, who travelled over many parts of the
world, and on the 24 Mar., 1620, was taken by the Turkes
and made captive in Argier.   He projected sundry plots
for his libertie and on yᵉ 17 of June 1627 with ten other
Christian captives, Dutch and French [perswaded by his
counsel and courage] he began a cruel fight with sixty-five
Turkes in their owne ship, which lasted three howers; in
which five of his company were slaine, yet God made him
conquer, and so he brought the ship into Cartagene, being
of 400 tons and 22 ord.

" The King sent for him to Madrid to see him; he was
proffered a captaines place and the Kings favor if he would
turne Papiste, which he refused.   He sold all for 6.000£ returned into England, and died at Lamorran 17 March 1636.

Melcombe in Dorset, was his place of birth,
Age 54, and here lies earth to earth.

George Fitz-Pen alias Phippen ipsius frater et hujus eccel-
esiæ rector H M P." †

---

* " Glory to God in the highest."
† H. M. P.   Hoc monumentum posuit.   This monument erected by
George Fitz-Pen, or Phippen, his brother, and rector of this church.

4 Gen. David Fitzpen, or Phippen, second son of Robert and Cecilie, m. Sarah ——, came to New England with his family, settled at Hingham, Mass., 1635, removed to Boston, 1641, where he died; will proved, 31 of 8mo., 1650; his widow m. Geo. Hull of Fairfield, Ct.; he had Robert,(?) Joseph, Thomas, Rebecca, who m. Geo. Vickary, Benjamin, Gamaliel, Sarah, who m. 1st, Thos. Yeo,* 2d, Nathan Goold, George, John and John.

4 Gen. George Fitzpen, or Phippen, A. M., son of Robert and Cecilie, Rector of St. Mary's Church at Truro, Cornwall, for twenty-six years, from 1625 till his death, m. 1st, Joan Pie, dau. of Constance Pie, m. 2d, Mary ——, who survived him; by will dated July 20, 1650, proved March 1, 1651, he made bequests, among others, to the sons of his brother David in New England, also to the poor of Lamorran. In it he complains of imprisonment and the loss of his goods for adhesion to Parliament,—probably during the usurpation by Cromwell.

Other members of this immediate family in England, which our scanty investigation forbids us to assign their place with precision, are—

Abel Phippen, who m. Jane Francis and had dau. Elizabeth, who d. Aug. 2, 1636; his widow Jane had a legacy from her brother-in-law, Rev. George, in 1651.

Roger of Pennycomquick, Eng.,—perhaps a son of Owen.

Thomas Phippen of Clemence, and William, who d. going to Portland, Nov. 24, 1596; also Eleanor, who m. Francis George, and her sister, wife of Hugh Boscawen. These,

---

* This name was common in Dorset; as late as 1785 the Yeos had a seat at Forsten, twelve miles from Weymouth.

mentioned as kinsmen in the will of Rev. George, may have been children of John and George, sons of the first John.

Hugh Boscawen was Recorder of Truro in 1620 ; another of the same name held that office sixty-four years afterward.

The island and town of Portland, above mentioned, noted for its famous building stone, lies about three miles off the harbor of Weymouth.

The above four generations, derived from the old record, Herald Visitation, will of Rev. George, and the parish records of Melcomb-Regis, complete our knowledge of the English family.

5 Gen.   Joseph Phippen, who commenced the old record, settled at Hingham, Mass., with his father David ; had grants of land there in 1637, was afterward of Boston, then of Falmouth, or Portland, where he purchased one hundred acres of land in 1650 and improved many years,* and lastly at Salem, Mass., where he died, " being stricken in years," in 1687.   He m. Dorcas Wood and had, viz.: ch^l born 1642, Joseph, Mary, Sarah, David, Samuel and Elizabeth.

*It is certain that both of the names by which the city of Portland, in this country, has been known, originated from the local attachment of its early settlers to places bearing their names in the land of their birth.   This, we think, has been made manifest by the account here given of the families of Jordan and Phippen in the old country, before their association at Casco Bay.   The name Falmouth was applied, in 1658, after an ancient sea-port which lies at the *mouth* of the river *Fal* in Cornwall, not far from Truro.   Portland, the name it now bears, was from the settlement of Cape Elizabeth applied to Bangs' Island, off its coast, and to this day the promontory opposite is called Portland Head ; this island, no doubt, strongly reminded such men as Joseph Phippen of the island of Portland, which lies just without the harbor of Weymouth, in England, the home of their youth.

5 Gen. Benjamin Phippen of Boston, son of David and
Sarah, m. Wilmeth Youer, had David, Benjamin,
Benjamin, Benjamin, Sarah, James, Rebecca, Mary,
Thomas, John and Joseph. Perhaps descendants
are only from James, whose family removed to
Connecticut, and now write their name Phipany.

5 Gen. Gamaliel Phippen of Boston, son of David and
Sarah, m. Sarah Purchase, had Sarah, Gamaliel,
Hannah, Rebecca, Elizabeth, Gamaliel, Ann and
Mehitable. The father Gamaliel d. 1671, probably
had no grandchildren of the name.

5 Gen. George Phippen, son of David and Sarah, m.
Elizabeth —— in London, lived in Boston, Falmouth
and Hull, Mass., had James, Elizabeth, Mary, Ruth,
son, daughter. His son James had a family.

6 Gen. Joseph Phippen, son of Joseph and Dorcas,
lived at Purpooduck—Falmouth, many years, until
driven by the Indian war to Salem in 1676; had
three wives, 1st, Mary Sandford, had son Joseph; m.
2d, Seaborn Gooding (perhaps Sibborn Goodwin), had
Joseph, Daniel, Samuel, Sarah, Dorcas, John, Israel,
Anne and Rachel; m. 3d, Damaris Searl, had Elizabeth, Susanna and Benjamin. Of these sons, Joseph,
Daniel, Samuel, Israel and Benjamin had families and
descendants; but it is supposed none of the name
now remain.

6 Gen. David Phippen, son of Joseph and Dorcas, bap. 4
of 2 mo., 1647, m. Anne Ager, June 26, 1672, formerly
Anne Cromwell, dau. of Thomas Cromwell and gr.-
dau. of Giles of Newbury; had David, Thomas, Ann,
Cromwell, Joseph, Jane, Abigail and Elizabeth. He

lived at Salem and Falmouth; he owned an extensive tract, running six miles inland, on N. E. Presumpscot River, mill, &c., at Casco Bay. He was treacherously killed in the Indian war, about Aug. 10, 1703, when accompanying a flag of truce outside the fort at Falmouth, after which the family removed to Salem. His son Thomas had two sons, probably also two daughters; can trace no farther.

6 Gen. Samuel Phippen of Salem, bap. 6 of 3 mo., 1649, son of Joseph and Dorcas, m. Rachel Guppy, 1 of 12 mo., 1676, had Samuel, John, Stephen, Rachel, John, Nathaniel, Rachel, Sarah and Joseph. Sons Samuel, John, Nathaniel and Joseph had families.

7 Gen. Samuel Phippen, son of Samuel and Rachel, b. 1677, m. 1st, Mary Beadle, had Samuel, Joseph and Mary, m. 2d, Rebecca Beadle, had Ruth, Rebecca, Jonathan, Atwater, Atwater and Mehitable. His son Samuel removed to Westminster, Vermont, and has descendants in that State; son Atwater married, had no children.

7 Gen. John Phippen, son of Samuel and Rachel, b. 1685, m. Elizabeth Hathorne, had Elizabeth, Rachel, Hannah, John, Benjamin, Ebenezer, James and Susanna; son John had a family, but no grandchildren of the name.

7 Gen. Nathaniel Phippen, son of Samuel and Rachel, b. Aug. 6, 1687, m. Margaret Palfrey, June 29, 1710, had Nathaniel, Margaret, David, Abigail, Israel, Austis, Lydia and Thomas. The father died about 1755. These sons had families and have descendants of the name. His son Thomas m. Margaret Driver, whose

first son Thomas m. Rebecca Wellman, who had son Thomas, m. Sarah Lufkin, who had son George, who has family in Boston. The second son of Thomas and Margaret had son William, m. Lois Hitchings, who had son George, Baptist clergyman, who has children and grandchildren in Connecticut and New York.

8 Gen. Nathaniel Phippen, eldest son of Nathaniel and Margaret, b. July 5, 1711, m. Seeth Hardy, Oct. 14, 1734, dau. of Joseph and Sarah Hardy, had Joshua, Hardy, Joseph and Seeth. The children had families; Hardy only two daughters.

9 Gen. Joshua Phippen, son of Nathaniel and Seeth, b. Jan. 27, 1742, m. 1st, Hannah Sibley, Oct. 3, 1764, had Nathaniel, Joshua, Samuel, Hannah, Mary, Sarah, Joshua, Eunice, Margaret, Hardy, Eunice and Joseph, m. 2d, Ursula Knapp, widow of Jonathan Symonds, 25 October, 1801. Sons Nathaniel, Joshua, Hardy and Joseph had families and descendants.

10 Gen. Hardy Phippen, son of Joshua and Hannah, b. July 6, 1778, m. Ursula K. Symonds, March 18, 1804, dau. of the above Jonathan Symonds, and fifth in descent from the primitive John Symonds of the Salem church, 1637 ; had four children, Joseph Hardy, Ursula S., (who m. Isaac N. Chapman and has a family,) Joshua and George Dean.

11 Gen. Joseph Hardy Phippen, son of Hardy and Hannah, m. March 26, 1840, Susan Harris, dau. of David and Lucy (Harris) Lord.

11 Gen. Joshua Phippen, son of Hardy and Hannah, m. April 22, 1841, 1st, Betsey Barr, dau. of Jonathan

and Betsey (Barr) Holman, and had Mary Elizabeth,
m. 2d, Eunice, dau. of David and Eunice Safford
Daniels, and has Joshua, Edward A. and Hardy.

12 Gen. George D. Phippen m. April 13, 1840, Margaret, dau. of John and Mary (Webb) Barton, had four
sons, George B., Samuel W., d., Arthur H. and
Charles E.

Descendants of the fourteenth generation from Henry
Fitzpen of Devonshire are living in Salem, Mass.

THE VAN CORTLANDT AND SCHUYLER FAMILIES.

In our last volume, p. 70, we gave an account of the
noted Van Cortlandt family of New York, which contained certain statements which have been criticised by a
learned correspondent. The points thus examined are in
regard to the supposed descent of Steven van Kortland
from the Dukes of Courland, and the assumed use of the
same coat of arms by these two families. We think that
our correspondent proves that neither the pedigree nor the
arms relate to the ducal family. We must premise, however, that the error, if such, belongs rather to the historian
than the family, and that at the time the statements were
first printed our writers were less exact in verifying traditions than at present.

The true pedigree of the Dukes of Courland is given in
many works, but our informant quotes specially the following work : "De Doorlughtige Weereld ; bevattendo een
zeer nette Historische en Politische Beschryringh der

voornaemste en bekendste Regeeringen, Staten en Republiquen van Europa, bysonderlyk van Italien en de Vereenighe Nederlanden ; als oock die van Asia en Africa. Nevens een eygentlyck berigt der Voornaemste Ridder-Ordens in Europa ; Afbuldingen en Verklaringen der gewoone Zee-Vlaggen aller Natien, &c. Vertaeld door S. de Vries. Men vindse te Koop 'T 'Amsterdam by Johannes van Oosterwyck, Boeckverkooper besyden 't Stadhuys, in Cicero, 1700,"—or, in English, "The Illustrious World ; containing a very neat and compact Historical and Political Account of the chief and best-known Governments, States and Republics of Europe, particularly of Italy and the United Netherlands ; also of Asia and Africa. Besides a correct account of the principal Orders of Knighthood in Europe ; Illustrations and Explanations of the usual Maritime Flags of all Nations, &c. Translated by S. de Vries. For sale in Amsterdam at Johannes van Oosterwyck, Bookseller, alongside of the City Hall, in Cicero, 1700." 3 vols., small 8vo., illustrated.

It seems that the founder of the house of Courland was Gothard Kettler, of the Duchy of Bergen, who died about the end of the fifteenth century. His grandson Gothard was Grand Master of the Order of Duneberg in Livonia in 1559 ; and having placed himself under the protection of Sigismund Augustus, King of Poland, was by him created, in 1562, first Duke of Courland and Semigallen. He died 17 May, 1587, and was succeeded by his oldest son, Frederic, who lost his capital city Mittauw, in 1622, but had it restored at the truce of 1629. He died without issue, and was succeeded by his nephew Jacob, who, after various vicissitudes, was restored to his duchy in 1670.

As Steven, the father of Oloff van Kortland, was living at Kortland, a little village in South Holland, in 1610, it is highly improbable that he had any connection with the Kettlers, then reigning dukes of Courland.

As to the idea that the ducal house bore the same arms, we find that the arms of the Dukes of Courland were,— Quarterly, 1 and 4, Argent, a lion rampant gules, queue fourché, crowned *or*, the lion of the first quarter being contourné; 2 and 3, azure, a demi-hart, trippant argent, crowned *or*, issuing from the dexter and sinister sides of the shield. These two coats were respectively for the Duchy of Courland and the Principality of Semigallen.

Over all, on the quartered shield was placed the escutcheon bearing the family arms of the Kettlers, viz., " Party per pale gules and *or*, in the dexter fesse-point a Kettle-hook argent crowned of the second (for Kettler), and on the sinister fesse-point the letters S A, inter-wreathed, sable." This latter monogram was in honor of Sigismund Augustus, who erected the possessions of the Kettlers into a duchy. These arms are very different from those of the New York family, which are the wings of a windmill sal-tirewise, between five estoilles. This coat, indeed, has a very close resemblance to the arms of the city of New York.

We conclude, then, that the coincidence of the arms and the probability of the pedigree are both disproven; but we may add that we have no reason to think the family has ever made any serious claim of their correctness.

———

As to the Schuyler pedigree, our corespondent writes that John Schuyler, grandfather of the General, had only two sons, Philip and John, the latter being the younger son. He also thinks that the Saratoga estates belonged to the grand-uncle, and not the uncle, of Gen. Philip. He adds that the father of the emigrant was a merchant at Amsterdam, having his country seat at the small village of Schuyler; and that letters remain from prominent merchants of Amsterdam, styling the Schuylers "cousins," a proof of the rank of the family at home. There were Davids, Samuels and others of the Schuyler name in the Colony at an early date, whose connection with the more opulent branch is not known; very possibly descendants of these remain in New York.

OFFICIAL SEALS.

We here place the seal of Lawrence Armstrong, "Lieutenant Governor and Commander-in-chief of His Majesty's Province of Nova Scotia, and Lieut. Colonel to his Excellency Colonel Richard Philipps' Regiment of foot, &c., &c." It is affixed to a grant of Robinson's Island to William Clarke of Boston, dated 24th August, 1726.

Though we have not learned anything concerning Gov. Armstrong's family, this seal is evidently a family one, and used in the same way as the private seals of our Massachusetts governors. From a letter of Gov. Mascarene, printed in Mass. Hist. Soc. Collections, 1st S., Vol. VI., p. 124, it seems that Col. Armstrong obtained a commission as Lieutenant Governor in 1725, and Haliburton (Hist. Nova Scotia, I., 316) adds that he committed suicide, Dec. 8, 1739, in a fit of despondency. Burke's "Commoners" contains an account of several families of Armstrong, many members of which were in the English army at this time, but their coat of arms is different. This shield seems to belong to the Armstrongs of Lincolnshire and Nottinghamshire alone, and hence our Governor is to be sought there.

The government of Nova Scotia was quite peculiar and is well explained in Mascarene's letter, and the list in Haliburton coincides in the main. We will state the facts and dates :

1710. Oct.   Col. Vetch was Governor.

1714. Francis Nicholson.

1719. Col. Richard Phillips.

1722. In Philipps' absence, Capt. John Doucett succeeded as senior Councillor, being thus placed over his Lt. Col.

1725. Lt. Col. Lawrence Armstrong made Lt. Gov. and held office till his death, Dec. 8, 1739.

1740. A similar dispute occurs, the senior Councillor being Capt. Paul Mascarene, thus placed over his Major, Alexander Cosby, now become Lt. Col. It was repeatedly rumored that Cosby was appointed Lt. Gov., and both seemed to have claimed the place.

Cosby died 27 Dec., 1742, and Mascarene obtained both posts, civil and military.

1749. July 14, a new government was established by the Hon. Edward Cornwallis, Governor.

1752. Aug. 3. Peregrine Thomas Hopson.

1754. Oct. 21. Charles Lawrence, Lt. Governor.

1756. July 23. do. Governor.

1760. Oct. 19. Jonathan Belcher, in place of Lawrence, deceased.

1761. Nov. 21. do. Lt. Governor.

1763. Sept. 26. Montague Wilmot, Lt. Gov.

1764. May 31. do. Governor.

1766. Lord William Campbell, Governor.

Michael Francklin, Lt. Governor.

1773. Francis Legge, Governor.

Michael Francklin, Lt. Governor.

There were a few months when these officers were absent, but this represents the usual and established government.

REVIEW OF BOND'S GENEALOGIES OF THE SETTLERS OF WATERTOWN, MASS.

It would be superfluous for us to praise the general execution of Dr. Bond's well-known work, since it is confessedly the greatest of all our numerous town histories. In tracing back, as he has done, the pedigree of many of the Watertown settlers to an English origin, he has in a few instances discovered some families entitled to coat armor. Our interest at present lies mainly in these, and we will extract from his pages the necessary facts:

The BRIGHT pedigree has already been traced in our first volume, p. 82–3.

The BROWNES, descended from Abraham, Richard, and John Browne, are traced first to Thomas Browne of Swan Hall in the parish of Hawkendon, co. Suffolk, father of the first two, and grandfather of John. He died in 1591, and was descended through three generations of Christophers, from John Browne of Stamford, who died about 1470. The family is traced three generations farther back to John Browne, Alderman of Stamford, 1376. From the oldest son of the first Christopher were descended the Brownes of Tolethorpe, co. Rutland, a family which was merged in that of Trollope about 1767. It was to this branch that Robert Brown, the founder of the Brownists, or Independents, belonged.

In the Hawkendon branch we find, that of the emigrants only Abraham Brown left descendants of the name. The arms are sable, three mullets argent: Crest, a stork's head couped, nowed, ppr. between two wings expanded argent. Motto, "Apprendre à mourir."

At page 450 of Vol. I. there is an engraving of the STEARNS arms, a copy of a painting preserved in the family. No authority attaches to this, of course, and it is a matter of conjecture only that Isaac Stearns, the emigrant, was from Nayland, co. Suffolk.

We find a pedigree of the COOLIDGES on p. 186, and on pp. 744–5 an additional pedigree, showing the descent of Simeon Coolidge of Cottenham from Thomas Colynge of

Arrington, A. D. 1495. Among the grandchildren of this Simeon was John, bapt. 16th September, 1604, whose age corresponds with that of the settler here, John of Watertown, who died 7 May, 1691, aged 88. As the name is a peculiar one, this coincidence is a strong evidence, but it is the only proof, we believe, of the connection. We can hardly consider this pedigree as fully proved.

Concerning the SALTONSTALLS much is given, but we have already quoted the history of that family in this journal.

As to the LAWRENCES, there seems to be no question that John Lawrence of Watertown was bapt. at Wisset, co. Suffolk, 8 Oct., 1609, since his brother, Robert L., 20 July, 1639, makes a deposition referring to him as being then in New England. We have every confidence in the seven preceding steps in the pedigree here given, which show that the Lawrences were a substantial family, living at Rumburgh and Wisset in Suffolk, and traced by wills to Thomas Lawrence of Rumburgh, who died between July 17 and Nov. 6, 1471, leaving sons John and Richard. According to this pedigree, this Thomas may be identified with a son of John and grandson of Nicholas Lawrence of Ayercroft, and thus the family may be connected with the Lawrences of Ashton Hall, co. Lancaster.

Another family is the BIGELOW, whose English ancestry has been ascertained. The name was formerly spelt Baguley, and John, the emigrant, was the son of Randle Baguley of Wrentham in Suffolk, descended from an ancient family in Cheshire. The latter part of the pedigree in one branch will be found in the Genealogical Register, Vol. 10, p. 297.

The BOYLSTONS are descended from Thomas of Fenchurch Street, London, who came here at the age of twenty. He was the son of Thomas of London and grandson of Henry B. of Lichfield, which last was of the family of Boylston of Boylston, co. Derby, England. We have already published in our third volume, p. 23, a tricking of the Boylston arms, and from the position held by the family they are doubtless authentic.

Thomas Boylston, son of the emigrant, left numerous descendants, among them Rev. Zabdiel Boylston Adams, John Adams and his family, Dr. Zabdiel Boylston, Nicholas Boylston, Ward Nicholas Boylston (who was a Hallowell), and Sir Benjamin Hallowell. The name has been endeared to the State by the liberality of some of its bearers.

The arms of CHESTER have been engraved in our second volume, p. 44. In this History of Watertown the English pedigree of the emigrant Leonard Chester is given, and we here repeat it, though undoubtedly it could be much enlarged by our learned correspondent, Col. Joseph L. Chester. William Chester of London and of Barnet, co. Hertford, had a son Leonard C. of Blaby who had three sons. Of these, the oldest was John, who married Dorothy Hoker and had Leonard, b. 1610, who settled in Watertown.

There are several other families in Bond's History who are traced to their birthplace in England, but we believe we have omitted none who are proved to be entitled to coat armor. We confidently expect, however, that in examining the probate records for Middlesex we shall be able to add to the list, and in closing our review we have to express our deep regret that this enterprise had not been commenced during Dr. Bond's lifetime. His perseverance and skill would have been of incalculable service, and the fruit of his search for armorial distinctions in the families of the settlers of Watertown would have added to the value even of his immense collections.

MIDDLESEX WILLS.

Under this title we commence a series of descriptions of the armorial seals affixed to Wills in the Registry for Middlesex County at East Cambridge, Mass. We regret to state that the facilities for examining the documents here are less than in other counties, since an alphabetical arrangement of the papers has been adopted. As all the documents from the earliest date to A. D. 1800 are thus huddled together, we cannot separate the wills prior to 1750, and the task of searching the files is made extremely laborious. We begin our list, however, with such as have met our view in casual examinations.

1.

This seal is one that occurs on many of the documents, and was undoubtedly the property of one of the Registers of Probate, Samuel Phipps. A good example is seen on the administration bond, in 1701, of Mary (Danforth) Phipps, widow of Solomon P. of Cambridge. It is used there by the widow and by Solomon Phipps of Muddy River and Samuel P.

of Cambridge. The witnesses are Samuel Phipps, the Register, and Pelatiah Whittemore.

The arms are recorded in Papworth's "Ordinary of British Armorials" as belonging to the family of Bradway of Potsclip, co. Gloucester. Possibly they may have come to the Phipps family through an intermarriage.

This family of Phipps is not to be confounded with that of Gov. Sir William Phips, but was one of good standing in this county. Solomon Phipps of Charlestown, 1641, carpenter, had Samuel, H. C. 1671, who m. Mary Phillips, and Solomon. Samuel was Representative, Register, and Clerk of the County, and died August, 1725, aged 79. His brother Solomon m. Mary, daughter of Thomas Danforth, and left issue.

2.

On the will of Thomas Fox, 1657, is a seal of a chevron between three bulls' heads cabossed; but this was evidently the property of one of the witnesses, Edward Bulkeley of Concord, whose arms have been given in a preceding volume.

3.

We copy this seal from the administration bond on the estate of John Farrar of Marlborough, 1707. It is used by the three signers, Elizabeth (Merriam) Farrar, George Farrow of Concord, and Nathaniel Oake. The witnesses were Thomas Berry and Margaret Hubbard. John and George Farrar, or Farrow, both spellings being used by the family, were sons of Jacob F. of Lancaster. He is said (Register, VI., ?21)

to have been born in England, and married Hannah, daughter of George Hayward of Concord. This Jacob was son of Jacob Farrar, one of the original proprietors of Lancaster, who was living there with his brother John in 1653.

There were several early colonists of the name, but we find no trace of the origin of any of them. The arms here given cannot be traced to the name of any of the signers of the document.

4.

 We copy this coat of arms from the seal of Capt. Francis Norton of Charlestown, on his will dated 18th June, 1667. He was sent out to New Hampshire in 1631, says Savage, by Mason and the other patentees, as their steward; but settled as early as 1637 at Charlestown, and was Representative for many years. He died 11 July, 1667, and in his will mentions his wife Mary, daughters Abigail Long, and Deborah, Elizabeth and Sarah, unmarried, gr.-children John, Mary, Robert and Norton Long, children of Abigail. He probably had no son. His social position is shown by the names of his overseers, viz., " Worshipfull Mr. Francis Willoughby, Capt. Thomas Park, Capt. Thomas Lake, and Mr. John Richards."

The arms here figured are mentioned by Burke, and the tinctures there are as follows: " Argent, a chevron between three barrels sable hooped *or*, standing on their bottoms." We presume they might rather be styled "tuns," with some reference to the name Norton, according to the fancy of early heralds.

5.

This seal, bearing the arms of Russell impaling another coat, is copied from a warrant of appraisement, dated 2 Sept., 1700, on the estate of John Eaton, signed by James Russell, Judge of Probate. The seal is evidently that of the judge, and occupies the usual place at the upper corner of the left side.

The ancestor of this noted family of Russell was Richard,[1] who came, with newly married wife Maud, from Hereford, where he was born in 1611, son of Paul Russell, as is commonly said, but was apprenticed 4 Oct., 1628, at Bristol, says Savage. He was a man highly esteemed in the community, a Representative, Speaker, Treasurer of the Colony for twenty years, and an Assistant. His second wife was Mary, widow of Leonard Chester. He died 14 May, 1676, in his 65th year, leaving two daughters and two sons, Daniel[2] and James.[2]

Rev. Daniel[2] Russell m. Mehitable, daughter of Samuel Willis of Hartford, and died 4 Jan., 1679–80, leaving an only daughter.

James[2] Russell, the judge, married 1st, Mabel, dau. of Gov. John Haynes, by whom he had sons James,[3] b. 1668, and John,[3] b. 1673; he married 2d, Mary, dau. of Henry Wolcott, and had Daniel,[3] b. 1685; his third wife was Abigail (Corwin), widow of Eleazer Hathorne. He was Representative, Treasurer of the Colony and Assistant, Councillor named in the new charter, Judge of Probate, and Treasurer of the Province. He died 28 April, 1709.

Daniel³ Russell* m. 1st, Rebecca, daughter of Charles Chambers, and had Chambers,⁴ b. 1713, d. *s. p.* in London, 23 Nov., 1766, and James,⁴ b. 5 Aug., 1715, who married, in 1738, Katherine, daughter of Thomas Graves, and had many children. From a very good account of the family in Burke's "Landed Gentry," we learn that of these children of James⁴ Russell five died unm. or *s. p.*, Rebecca⁵ m. Hon. John Lowell, and Margaret⁵ m. Hon. John Codman, 15 July, 1781, the father of the late Rev. Dr. John Codman.

James⁵ Russell, the only son of James⁴ who has left descendants, was in England during the Revolution, and is classed by Sabine among the Royalists. He m. at Bristol, 22 Sept., 1780, Mary, dau. of Richard Lechmere, formerly of Boston, and had Lechmere Coore Graves,⁶ b. 25 Dec., 1786, Charles James⁶ (R. N.), Mary Anne,⁶ Elizabeth Penelope,⁶ Katherine Sarah,⁶ and Lucy Margaret.⁶

Major Gen. Lechmere Coore Graves Russell⁶ of Ashford Hall, co. Salop, m. 14 June, 1814, Harriet Elizabeth, dau. of Olyett Woodhouse, and had Edward Lechmere,⁷ Frederick Thomas Lechmere,⁷ Lechmere,⁷ and four daughters. He died some twenty years since, and Drake (Hist. Boston, p. 355) terms this branch the only male representatives of Richard¹ Russell. Reference is made by Burke to a seal ring, evidently the same as the one used by Judge James Russell; he adds the empalement is the arms of the Nevilles of Rostell, Gules, on a saltire argent a martlet of the field. Mary, second wife of Richard¹ Russell was a Nevill, and hence the use of this coat.

---

* His epitaph is given in our first volume, p 57.

6.

We are indebted to Edward D. Harris, Esq., for a drawing of this seal, which is on the will of Elizabeth Sharp, who died 9 March, 1699. Her tombstone remains at Cambridge, and the inscription is given by Harris, p. 27. She was the widow of John Sharp, merchant, who died Aug. 30, 1693. In his widow's account of administration is a charge for making a " brick grave" and tombstone, " and engraving his name and coat of arms thereon." Though these inscriptions have disappeared, no doubt his tomb is one of the several remaining in the Cambridge yard which evidently bore armorial tablets formerly.

We find nothing in Savage in reference to this John Sharp beyond the above account, and we have not been able to trace these arms to any family of the name of Sharp. Possibly the seal belonged to his wife, or to some maternal ancestor of the emigrant.

SEAL OF JOHN USHER.

We have already given (Vol. II., p. 168,) an engraving of the Usher arms, but we here reproduce the seal of John Usher, Lt. Governor of New Hampshire. The persistent use of the arms in several generations makes the presumptive evidence very strong in favor of their correctness, and it is to be hoped that some good account of the family of the famous Archbishop Usher may yet be printed.

THE LAWRENCE FAMILY OF ENGLAND AND NEW YORK.

It has been claimed by Holgate and other writers that one or more families of the name of Lawrence settled in New York, and of a different stock from those resident in New England, were descended from the Lawrences of St. Ives, co. Huntington, England.

Much curiosity has lately been evinced in England in regard to the pedigrees of various Lawrence families there, and it seems very certain that some remarkable corrections are to be made in the existing rolls. In the "Miscellanea Genealogica et Heraldica," for July and October, 1867, will be found certain extracts from the Visitations. In the "Herald and Genealogist," Part XXIV. (October, 1867), is a very learned article, exposing these mistakes of the Heralds.

There seems to be no question that there was a Sir Robert[1] Lawrence of Ashton Hall, Lancashire, about 1450, who had sons Robert[2] and Thomas,[2] and possibly others. Robert[2] died in 1450, leaving Sir James[3] and Robert.[3] Sir James[3] had a son John[4] killed at Flodden Field, and a part of his property went to his cousins, the four daughters of Robert[3] Lawrence. An attempt has been made to fasten on here a third brother of Sir James,[3] viz., a Nicholas Lawrence of Agercroft. But if he had been a real person, he would have inherited those estates of Sir James[3] Lawrence, which in fact passed at his son's death to the nearest heir-male, viz., Launcelot Lawrence of Yeland Hall, who was the grandson of Thomas,[2] who had married the heiress of Yeland Redmain. This

seems conclusive against the existence of Nicholas of
Agercroft.

The other absurdities of Faulkner's account are treated
in detail by the critic, who adds that Faulkner calls
Nicholas the father of a well-known and famous Sir Oliver
Lawrence.

This Sir Oliver was a very noted man in his day, and
married Anne Wriothesley, sister of Thomas, Earl of
Southampton.   He is thought to have belonged to the
Yeland Hall branch.

There were numerous other families of the name, some
of very considerable importance, but it is clearly one of
the class of surnames derived from Christian names, and
hence there may have been scores of distinct families.

The article in the "Herald and Genealogist" further
adds that all this invention of Nicholas Lawrence of Agercroft, and his progeny, was due to Isaac Lawrence of a
substantial family of the yeomanry of Gloucestershire, who
was living about the time of Charles II.   His claim was
that his great-grandfather, William Lawrence of Withington, was the nephew of Sir James,[3] and that Robert[3]
had three sons.   He added on the Nicholas as a still
younger branch, but it seems entirely fictitious.

One family of Lawrence was settled at Chelsea and at
Iver, co. Buck.   Of these, Thomas, a goldsmith of London, who died in 1593, was son of Thomas of Chilmarth,
near Bridgenorth, co. Salop, and grandson of Thomas of
the same place.   Sir John L., son of the goldsmith, was
made a baronet, and his son, Sir Thomas Lawrence, bart.,
was Secretary of Maryland.   At the death of this latter,
in 1712, the title became extinct.

Another family was that of St. Ives, co. Huntington, to which belonged Henry Lawrence, President of the Council under Cromwell. He was descended from William[1] Lawrence, who was grandnephew of John Lawrence, Abbot of Ramsey, 1508–1539, and the family was one of note in the successive generations. In the "Gentleman's Magazine" for 1815 there is an account of this family by Sir James Lawrence, a descendant. He says that William[1] had sons Henry,[2] William[2] and Robert,[2] and died 1572. Henry[2] had Sir John,[3] who had Henry[4] and John.[4]

Henry[4] Lawrence, the President, had seven sons, Henry,[5] Edward,[5] John,[5] William[5] and three others. John[5] settled in Barbadoes and died in 1690, leaving John,[6] who had six sons.

At this point the American genealogists place the connection of certain families.

In the "Herald and Genealogist," Part XXIII., p. 465, it is stated that Thomas Lawrence, born at St. Albans in 1666, came to New England and left issue now of Philadelphia. His son Lawrence Lawrence m. a granddaughter of John[5] Lawrence of Barbadoes.

Holgate however claims that there were three brothers, John, William and Thomas, who were descendants of John Lawrence, nephew of the Abbot of Ramsey. The St. Ives branch used the Lawrence arms, a cross raguly, with the addition of a lion on a chief. Holgate says these arms are on the seals appended to the wills of William Lawrence, 1680, and Richard Lawrence, 1711, on record at New York.

We know from Bond's Watertown, and other sound authorities, that one of these three, viz., John Lawrence, aged 17, William Lawrence, a. 12, Maria Lawrence, a. 6, with their stepfather, John Tuttell, and their mother, Joan Tuttell, aged 42, came from Great St. Albans, co. Hertford, to Boston, in 1635. These two brothers are considered to be the settlers at Flushing.

There is no doubt that there were various offshoots of the St. Ives family; since the genealogist of the family mentions branches at Selscomb, co. Sussex, Chichester, Aldingbourn and Brokedish, co. Norfolk. There is, therefore, a good chance to trace these St. Albans Lawrences to the St. Ives stock, though it must be said that the "Herald and Genealogist," as already cited, while mentioning the marriage of Lawrence Lawrence with the President's granddaughter, gives no intimation of any connection in the paternal line.

We must regard this New York affiliation, therefore, as one not sufficiently proved, but still very promising in its present state, and worthy of careful investigation in England.

THE LINZEE FAMILY.

It will be remembered by many of our readers that in the library of the late William H. Prescott there were formerly two swords hanging, crossing each other, which had been respectively the property of his grandfather, Col. William Prescott, and of his wife's grandfather, Capt. John Linzee, R. N.

As the descendants of Capt. John Linzee, who commanded the British sloop-of-war "Falcon" at the battle

of Bunker's Hill, are quite numerous, we have obtained
the following account of the family :

It is thought that this is a branch of the well known
Scottish family of Lindsay, as its members have always
used the same arms as those of the Lindsays of Kirkfor-
thar, co. Fife, viz., Gules, a fesse checky arg. and az.
between three stars in chief and a hunting horn in base,
argent. Crest, an ostrich with a key in its bill.

The father of Capt. John[2] Linzee was John[1] Linzee,
whose brother, Edward[1] Linzee of Portsmouth, was father
of Susanna,[2] wife of Samuel, Viscount Hood, the famous
Admiral. She was created Baroness Hood of Cathering-
ton in 1795.

Capt. John[2] Linzee married at Boston, 1 Sept., 1772,
Susanna Inman, who died in 1792, aged 39.

Their children were,—

   i. Samuel Hood,[3] b. 1773, died 1820. He was an
      Admiral, R. N., and left two sons and three
      daughters.

  ii. Hannah Rowe,[3] b. 1775 ; m. Thomas C. Amory.

 iii. Susannah Inman,[3] b. 1779 ; m. Joseph Tilden.

 iv. John Inman,[3] b. 1781.

  v. Rose,[3] b. 1783 ; m. John Fitch, and had a daughter
      Maria, now living.

 vi. Ralph Inman,[3] b. 1785 ; d. 1834. He m. 1st, Anna
      Cutler Dummeler, and 2d, Mary Ingersol. He
      left three daughters.

 vii. Sarah Inman,[3] b. 1787 ; m. J. L. Cunningham.

viii. Mary Inman,[3] b. 1789 ; d. 1793.

 ix. George Inman,[3] b. 1792 ; d. 1793.

He died at Milton, Mass., 1798, aged 56.

John Inman[3] Linzee, second son of Capt. John[2] Linzee, married Elizabeth, daughter of Joseph Tilden of Boston, and had,—

    i.   Thomas C. A.,[4] b. 1819; m. Sarah, daughter of John Torrey, and has,—

                John T.,[5]
                Elizabeth,[5]
                Marion.[5]

    ii. John William,[4] b. 1821; American Consul General at Calcutta. He has been twice married, and has two sons and two daughters.

   iii. Elizabeth Tilden,[4] m. 1st, S. Eliot Green, 2d, J. Sullivan Warren.

   iv. Susan Inman.[4]

He died at Boston in 1859.

Hannah Rowe[3] Linzee m. Thomas C. Amory in 1795 and died, December, 1846. Their children were, Col. Thomas C.[4] Amory; Samuel Linzee[4] Amory (who died in 1829); William,[4] who m. Anna, dau. of Hon. David Sears and has issue; Charles,[4] who m. Martha, dau. of Gardiner Greene and has issue; Mrs. Thomas A. Dexter,[4] Mrs. William H. Prescott,[4] Mrs. George M. Dexter[4] and Mrs. Edward D. Sohier.[4]

Susan Inman[3] Linzee m. Joseph Tilden* and had sons, George,[4] d. unm.; Charles,[4] m. Sarah Horton, and had

---

* We may here note that the Tildens are said by Berry to be a branch of the Tyldens of Kent and Sussex, a Visitation family. We have seen that of the children of Joseph Tilden of Boston a son and a daughter intermarried with the Linzees. Another son, William, m. an Inman and was the father of William Tilden of Calcutta, Mrs. G. M. Barnard, Mrs. J. Templeman Coolidge, Mrs. G. Burroughs and Mrs. A. S. Chase.

four children, Mrs. Edward Codman,[5] Joseph,[5] C. Linzee,[5] and George[5]; and Mrs. John Torrey,[4] who has issue.

Sarah Inman[3] Linzee m. Joseph L. Cunningham of Boston, and had,—

I. Lewis,[4] died at sea.
II. Edward Linzee,[4] m. 1st, Adeline Elizabeth, dau. of Rufus G. Amory, who d. *s. p.*; 2d, Mrs. Deblois.
III. Sarah Linzee.[4] .

Joseph L. Cunningham[3] married 2d, Mary Ann Inman, by whom he had one son, George Inman Cunningham, who m. Mary, dau. of Col. William P. Winchester, and died leaving one daughter; he m. 3d, Catherine Greene Amory, sister of his son's wife.

We hope in our next number to give some account of other families allied to the Linzees. A. T. P.

HERALDIC NOTES AND QUERIES.
(Continued from Vol. III., p. 192.)

XLIX.

USE OF ARMS.—In an "Essay on the True Rise of Nobility, Political and Civil," &c., (London, C. Rivington, 1718,) we find, on pp. 173, 4, the following statement:

"At a Chapter holden by the Officers of Arms at the Imbroiderers' Hall in London, 4 *Eliz.* it was order'd, *viz.*

"That no Inheretrix, whether Maid or Wife, should bear, or cause to be borne, any Crest or Cognizance of her Ancestors, otherwise than followeth.

"If she be a Maid, then to bear in her Ring, the Crest, Cognizance or first Coat of her Ancestors, in a Lozenge.

"If a Widow, to impale the first Coat of her Husband with the first Coat of her Ancestors, upon a Lozenge.

"If she marry one that is no Gentleman, then to be clearly exempt from the former Conclusions."

L.

SAFFIN ARMS.—Hon. J. Hammond Trumbull has communicated a description of the seal used by John Saffin of Boston on letters to Connecticut, 1676, 7, now preserved in the archives of that State. The arms are those of Saffin, or Chaffin, of Somersetshire, viz., Azure, three crescents argent, jessant as many estoiles or. Crest, on a mural coronet an estoile of sixteen rays or. In another coat the crescents of the shield are or. The same arms are found on an old piece of silver plate now owned by Leverett Saltonstall, Esq., to whom it came from the Cooke family. Both on the seal and plate a coat is empaled, which contains a lion passant on a fess. The first wife of John Saffin, living in 1676, was Martha, dau. of Capt. Thomas Willett of Plymouth, but we do not find the empaled arms as belonging to that name; so that seal and plate probably commemorate an earlier marriage, and were therefore brought from England. John Saffin lived at Scituate, Boston and Bristol, and held several offices of honor and trust; he died in 1710, leaving no descendants whatever.

W. S. A.

LI.

ELLERY ARMS.—In our first volume we gave an account of the Ellery family and arms. We have lately been shown a piece of embroidery marked "Nathaniel and Mary Ellery,

Anno Dom. 1745," consisting of an empaled shield, as follows :—Argent, a chevron between three dolphins embowed sable ; empaling, sable on a chevron between three leaves argent, as many cross-crosslets of the field. Crest, an arm erect, the hand grasping a serpent.

This is supposed to have been the work of Mary Ellery, the daughter of Nathaniel Ellery by his first wife, Abigail Norwood, and yet the arms seem to refer to his second wife, Anne, daughter of William and Ann (Duncan) Sargent.

LII.

WHITTINGHAM ARMS.—On page 121 of Vol. I. of the Journal we gave a description of the Whittingham arms, as empaled by Saltonstall in a drawing in Gore's Roll of Arms. We have lately met with the Whittingham coat in a form quite different from any thing yet mentioned by us. It is made of narrow rolls of colored papers, pasted on a flat surface. The design is plainly visible, when the surface is viewed at the proper angle. The arms are, Argent, a fess vert, over all a lion rampant gules. Crest, a lion's head erased gules, langued azure. Beneath is an inscription, " The Armes of the Antient Family of Whittingham." We are unable to say if the family is still found in this country. The work has been in the possession of descendants of the Brattle family, to whom it may have come from the Saltonstalls. w. s. a.

LIII.

LECHMERE FAMILY.—As we have had occasion in the present number to refer to the Lechmeres, we will here repeat the substance of a note in the Register, XIII., 302. The Lechmeres trace their descent from Adam de Lechmere, co. Worcester, through Richard Lechmere, who married Joan, daughter of John Whitmore of Hanly, 21 *Hen.* VII., to Sir Nicholas Lechmere, who m. Penelope, dau. of Sir Edwin Sandys, and had sons Edmund and Sandys. The latter left descendants, represented at the beginning of this century by John S. and Thomas A. Lechmere, who m. respectively Catherine and Jane, daughters of John Whitmore of the Haywood, co. Hereford.

Edmund, oldest son of Sir Nicholas Lechmere, m. Lucy, dau. of Sir Anthony Hungerford, and had Anthony, Nicholas and Thomas. Of these, Nicholas was a famous lawyer and was created Lord Lechmere of Evesham; at his death, *s. p.*, in 1727, the title became extinct, and his estates went to the son of Anthony, now represented by Edmund Patteshall Burnham.

Thomas Lechmere, brother of Lord Lechmere, was Surveyor General of the Customs for the Northern District of America for many years. He m. 17 Nov., 1709, Anne, dau. of Wait Still Winthrop, and died 4 June, 1765. He left sons, Nicholas, b. 29 July, 1722, and Richard; and two daughters, Lucy, b. 5 March, 1710–11, m. Samuel Solley of Portsmouth, 5 Feb., 1756, and Margaret, b. 4 March, 1719–20, m. Jonathan Simpson, 1 Feb., 1754.

LIV.

MOURNING FLAG, Vol. I., p. 88.—We have before mentioned an armorial flag probably used at the funeral of some distinguished citizen in colonial times. We are indebted to J. Hammond Trumbull, Esq., for the information that the arms on the dexter half of the shield, viz., Gules, a fesse wavy between three fleurs-de-lys *or*, belong to the family of Hickes, baronets.

We feel quite confident that this flag was used at the funeral of Hon. Benjamin Browne of Salem, who d. in 1708, or of his wife. He married Mary, dau. of Rev. John Hicks, and left no sons; his niece Mary Browne m. Benjamin Lynde, whose descendants own this flag, with other armorial insignia. Of this Mary Hicks we only know what is reported by Dunton, that she came here in 1686 and made a very advantageous marriage, which gives him a pretext for some raillery.

LV.

SPOONER ARMS.—We are indebted to a correspondent for a book plate, engraved by N. Hurd, of the Spooner arms, viz., Vert, a boar's head in bend, couped. Crest, a boar's head couped, pierced through the neck with an arrow. These arms are evidently intended to be the same as those of Sponer or Spooner of Wickwantford, co. Worcester, 1589, mentioned by Burke. The engraving was in a book belonging formerly to Alden Spooner, a noted printer, born 22 Aug., 1757, d. 1 May, 1827. He was the son of Thomas Spooner, who went from Newport to New London in 1753.

LVI.

In the Historical Magazine for January, 1865, will be found a portrait of Cadwallader Coldenand a tricking of his coat of arms. This is Gules, a chevron argent between three stag's heads erased *or*. No crest is given, but Alden says, " The motto which he inherited from his ancestors and has transmitted to his posterity" was, " Fais bien ne crains rien."

Colden was the son of the Rev. Alexander Colden, minister of Dunse in the Merse, Scotland; but was born in

Ireland during a visit of his mother there, 7 Feb., 1687. He was educated at the University of Edinburgh, and came to Pennsylvania about 1710, where he practised physic for some five years. He went to Scotland and was married to Alice Christy at Kelso, 11 Nov., 1715; but he soon returned to this country. He settled in New York, and about 1720 obtained a patent for a grant of land to be termed Coldingham. He filled many high offices in the Province, being President of the Council and Lieutenant Governor. He was also noted as a scholar and philosopher, maintaining a frequent correspondence with distinguished scientific men in Europe.

He died 20 Sept., 1776, having had five sons and five daughters, of whom a quite extended account is given by Alden, Vol. V., 271–4. We will only note that among his descendants are families of Hoffman, DeLancy, Izard, Barclay, Willett, and other well known names. His grandson Cadwallader D. Colden was a distinguished lawyer, a member of Congress, &c.

LVII.

It is so seldom that a change of surname is reported, that we give space for the following extract from the New York Tribune:

"The Kingston (S. C.) Star publishes the following heart-rending card:

"'To the Respectable White Citizens of the State:— Drs. J. W. Staggers and J. G. Staggers have concluded to change their names to that of Standard, of Grand Maternal descent on paternal side—of Virginia fame in years gone by—from the fact that the larger number of their former slaves have assumed their names; and as it is likely it

will be Africanized in time to come, they are determined not to be on an equality with them socially, since their original position from slaves to freemen has been changed by no agency of theirs, but by the demagogues of this country—and from the fact that in the scale of creation their rank is inferior, even descending to the beast—as per Ariel, of which we are convinced.   J. W. STAGGERS,
                                J. G. STAGGERS."'

LVIII.

The question of assumed arms has called forth some very good suggestions from Mr. Boutell, in his latest book, entitled "English Heraldry." He urges that the public interest in Heraldry in England calls for some action on the part of the officers of Heralds' College, and that some simple plan should be adopted for the registration of all arms that are borne by right. He adds it would be almost equally desirable to register all those that are borne *without* right. He recognizes the fact that it would be nearly impossible to revert to the former system of Visitations, but through the agency of the tax collector the registration can be made very nearly complete. He proposes to establish a moderate sum for the recording arms held by inheritance and a small annual tax for their use, but a much larger sum for the grant of new arms and for their use without registration. It would then be the interest of each tax-payer to attend to the registry of his own coat of arms, inasmuch as he would thereby reduce his annual tax, even if he felt but little interest in preserving the genealogical record.

Any such plan, if faithfully executed for a few years, would prove of incalculable value to the genealogist.

With such a list of all the families in England now claiming coat armor, the antiquarian would be encouraged to trace out those families whose representation has ceased or fallen into neglect. The line of separation would be plain, and a new value would attach to such heraldic evidences as could be found in other countries to which Englishmen had emigrated.

Mr. Boutell also advocates the granting of family badges, as distinct from coats of arms, though we must confess our inability to see their utility. It will however be felt, by all interested in American heraldry, that a great step has been gained in the commencement of a discussion of any improvement of the existing College. Our English friends have the reputation of being averse to change, and of being willing to suffer inconveniences if of long duration, but they also are apt to do in earnest what they commence.

The subject of Heraldry has been brought before Congress by a proposal to tax armorial bearings, and as it was formally referred to the Committee on Ways and Means we may yet see such a section in the revised Act for collecting the Internal Revenue. The consideration of the subject will be somewhat embarrassing to our worthy legislators unless they know more of heraldry than their constituents, and we presume they will decline to be led into such abstruse discussions. We might regard it as a practical joke, on the part of the member from New York who proposed it, were it not for the fact that heraldry has been in a certain measure recognized officially by the use of national seals and flags.

THE

HERALDIC JOURNAL;

RECORDING THE ARMORIAL BEARINGS AND GENEALOGIES OF AMERICAN FAMILIES.

NO. XXII. APRIL, 1868.

THE COTTON FAMILY.

[From investigations made by H. G. SOMERBY, Esq.]

A great interest attaches to the personal history of the Rev. John Cotton, one of the most noted of the ministers of the Massachusetts Colony, and it is with much pleasure that we now lay before our readers a well authenticated

ARMS OF COTTON.*

account of his ancestry. This pedigree was prepared by a most competent antiquary, H. G. Somerby, Esq., for the Hon. Caleb Cushing; and it is to the kindness of the latter-named gentleman that we are indebted for this opportunity to publish all the essential portion of the record.

The family of Cotton has been one of importance in the county of Cambridge for many generations, several generations being of

---

* Sable, a chevron between three griffin's heads erased, argent, quartering Fleming, Hastings and Doggett. In Drake's History of Boston, knightly rank, and the senior line was, in 1641, raised to the dignity of Baronet, a title extinguished in 1863.

In Cole's MSS., in the British Museum, Vol. XI., p. 237–345, is an account of the family, prepared in 1763, which has served as a basis for the present pedigree. It is held to be most probable that the family derived its name from Cotton in Kent, but was settled in Cambridgeshire in 1374, when Sir Henry[1] Cotton was living there, who married Anne, dau. and heir of Sir Henry le Fleming.

His son and heir was Thomas[2] Cotton, who was father of Humphrey[3] Cotton, who m. Anne, dau. of Sir Thomas Holbrooke.

The son of this marriage was Sir Thomas[4] Cotton, who m. Alice, dau. and heir of Sir John de Hastings of Landwade, co. Camb., which manor became the chief seat of the Cottons.

John[5] Cotton of Cotton Hall and Landwade, oldest son and heir, married Bridget, dau. of Richard Grace of Norfolk, and d. in 1393, leaving sons, Thomas[6] and Walter,[6] of whom Thomas[6] died unm. Walter[6] Cotton succeeded his brother in 1434, and married Joan, dau. of Sir Robert Reade of Oxfordshire. He built a church at Landwade, and dying 14 May, 1445, was buried

---

p. 157, is an engraving of the arms of the totally distinct family of Cotton of Ridware, to which family the author wrongly supposed that John Cotton belonged. This family, however, had exchanged these arms for the coat of the Ridwares, Azure, an eagle displayed argent, and the pedigree is given by Burke (Extinct Baronetcies) under Cotton of Connington. The first Baronet was Sir Robert Cotton, who died May 6th, 1631, and who immortalized his name as the collector of the Cottonian Library. The sixth Baronet died *s. p. m.* in 1752, when the baronetcy became extinct. There were several other families of the name but they are in no way connected with the subject of which we treat.

there. His children were William,[7] Walter,[7] Thomas,[7] Edmund[7] and one daughter.

At this point the family was divided into two branches. William,[7] the eldest son, inherited Landwade, and his descendants continue to possess it. The successive generations were William,[7] Vice-Chamberlain to King Henry VI., Thomas,[8] (d. 30 July, 1499), Sir Robert,[9] Sir John,[10] (Sheriff of Camb. and Hunt., d. 21 April, 1593), Sir John,[11] (M. P. for Camb., d. in 1620), Sir John,[12] and Sir John[13] created Baronet 14 July, 1641, whose descendants are easily traced.

This first Baronet, born in 1615, was distinguished for his loyalty, and was obliged to live abroad for some years. He obtained the manor of Maddingley, co. Camb., with his wife Jane, only daughter of Edward Hinde. He died about 1690, and was succeeded by his son Sir John[14] Cotton, M. P. for Camb., who m. Elizabeth Sheldon, and left one son and nine daughters. Sir John-Hinde[15] Cotton succeeded his father, was M. P. and held several high offices. He died 4 Feb., 1752, and was succeeded by his only son, Sir John-Hinde[16] Cotton. This last named d. 23 Jan., 1795, and by his wife Anne Parsons had six sons and three daughters, yet the baronetcy expired in 1863, on the death of his grandson. His second son, Admiral Sir Charles[17] Cotton, inherited the title and dying 24 Feb., 1812, was succeeded by his son, Sir S[t] Vincent[18] Cotton, who died in 1863.

The representation of the senior line must therefore be carried back first to the descendants of Sir Robert[11] Cotton of Wood Ditton, co. Camb., grand-uncle of the first Baronet, or to the Cottons of Clavering, co. Essex, and

Redgrave, co. Suff., descended from William[8] and Edmund[8] Cotton, younger sons of William[7] Cotton of Landwade.

———

The second son of Walter[6] Cotton was Walter[7] of Cotton Hall and Trumpington, who by wife Blanch had Clement[8] Cotton, who received Cotton Hall by gift of his grandfather. By his wife Madwen, dau. of —— Doggett, he had children, Clement,[9] John,[9] (who left issue), Gregory[9] and Blanche.[9]

Clement[9] Cotton m. Constance, dau. of Nicholas Leverthorpe of Hatfield in Essex, and had Roger,[10] Thomas,[10] d. s. p., George[10] and Jane.[10] Of these, Roger[10] Cotton left numerous descendants.

George[10] Cotton, grandfather of the Rev. John, resided in London, in the parish of St. Giles-without-Cripplegate, where he made his will Oct 14, 1558, proved, Prerogative Court, 21 March, 1559–60. He mentions wife's brother Thomas Whittacre, sons Roland and Thomas and daughter *Tymothy*. His wife Margaret was buried at South Ockenden, co. Essex, 20 Sept., 1557, and his son Thomas d. s. p. about the end of the year 1557, his will being dated 2 Dec., 1577, and proved 27 Jan. following.

Roland[11] Cotton, only surviving son of George, was instructed in the law under the charge of his relative John Cotton, and removed to Derby, where he married 16 Aug., 1582, Mary Hurlbert; and dying in 1604 was buried in the church-yard of St Alkmund's.

His children's baptisms recorded in that church are as follows,—

Mary,[12] bapt. 1 Sept., 1583; m. 3 Aug., 1608, Robert Bamford.

John,[12] bapt. 15 Dec., 1584.

Roland,[12] bapt. 17 March, 1587–8.

Thomas,[12] bapt. 19 May, 1594.

His will, dated 29 Jan., 1603–4, mentions these four children and his wife. Nothing more is known of these younger sons; though Mr. Somerby thinks from the similarity of the arms, that one was the Thomas Cotton of Boston, whose will was proved 15 May, 1646, and mentions wife Mary, and kinswoman Bridget Gill. Thomas Cotton m. Mary Gill at Boston, 1 May, 1624, but probably left no issue.

John[12] Cotton, born in Dec., 1584, was placed at Trinity College, Cambridge, where he took his degree of A. B., in January, 1602–3, and of A. M. in 1606. From Trinity he removed to Emmanuel College, where he took his degree of Bachelor of Divinity. In 1612 he was inducted Vicar of the church of St. Botolph, in Boston, co. Linc., and on the 3d July, 1613, he married at Balsham, co. Camb., Elizabeth Horrocks.

By this wife Cotton had no children, and she dying about 1631, he married at Boston, 25 April, 1632, Sarah, daughter of Anthony Hawkridge, and widow of William Story. The marriage is recorded as of John Cotton and Sarah Story, but we shall hereafter show that she was doubtless a widow, as in fact Cotton Mather terms her.

In the Magnalia, Mather adds the following touches:

" Our John Cotton, besides the advantage of his Christian profession, had a descent from honorable progenitors to render him doubly honorable. His immediate progenitors being by some injustice deprived of great revenues, his father, Mr. Rowland Cotton, had the education of a lawyer bestowed by his friends upon him, in hopes of his being the better capacitated thereby to recover the estate, whereof his family had been wronged ; and so the profession of a lawer was that unto which this gentleman applied himself all his days." " Settled now at Boston, his dear friend, holy Mr. Bayns, recommended unto him a pious gentlewoman, one Mrs. Elizabeth Horrocks, the wife of Mr. James Horrocks, a famous minister in Lancashire, to become his consort in a married estate." " Nevertheless by the same sickness, he then lost his excellent wife, who having lived with him childless for eighteen years, went from him now to be forever with the Lord ; whereupon he travelled further a field, unto London and some other places, whereby the recovery of his lost health was further perfected. About a year after this, he practically appeared in opposition to Tertullianism by proceeding unto a second marriage ; wherein one Mrs. Sarah Story, a virtuous widow very dear to his former wife, became his consort ; and by her he had both sons and daughters."

Cotton had gradually become attached to the reforming portion of the Church of England, and at last letters missive was issued against him from the High Commission Court. His friends were unable to protect him, and by their advice he decided to seek shelter in New England. He arrived at Boston, Sept. 3, 1633, in company with Rev. Thomas Hooker and Rev. Samuel Stone, and about two hundred passengers, " men of good estates." On the 10th of October he was ordained Teacher of the First Church, John Wilson being the Pastor thereof; and this office he held till his death, Dec. 23d, 1654.

During this long period of nearly twenty years, Cotton was one of the most important actors in our history. His advice was always sought, and his counsels often prevailed. In the two exciting controversies with Roger Williams and Mrs. Anne Hutchinson he was conspicuous, and has naturally incurred blame as well as praise for his action. One custom of his indeed became universal here, as Mather writes: " The Sabbath he began the evening before: for which keeping of the Sabbath from evening to evening, he wrote arguments before his coming to New England: and I suppose that 'twas from his reason and practice that the Christians of New England have generally done so too."

His published books are numerous, and several of them have been reprinted for their historical interest.

AMERICAN GENEALOGY.

1. John[12] Cotton had children by his second wife, Sarah, only, and these were the following:
2. Seaborn,[13] b. 1633.
    Sarah,[13] b. 12 Sept., 1635; d. 20 Jan., 1650.
    Elizabeth,[13] b. 9 Dec., 1637; m. Jeremiah Egginton.
3. John,[13] b. 15 March, 1640.
    Maria,[13] b. 16 Feb., 1642; m. Rev. Increase Mather.
    Rowland,[13] b. Dec., 1643; d. 29 Feb., 1650.

He died 15 or 23 Dec., 1652. His widow m. 26 Aug., 1656, Richard Mather, and died 27 May, 1676.

2. Rev. Seaborn[13] Cotton m. 1st, Dorothy Bradstreet, and had, with several daughters, a son, Rev. John[14] of

Hampton, father of Rev. Thomas[15] of Brookline. He married 2nd, Prudence Wade, and had a son Rowland,[14] who settled in England.

3. Rev. John[14] Cotton, younger son of the first minister, was of Wethersfield, Guilford, and finally of Charleston, S. C., where he died 18 Sept., 1699. He married Joanna Rossiter, and had sons, John,[15] Rowland,[15] Josiah,[15] and Theophilus.[15]

Of these, Rev. John[15] was of Yarmouth, and left six daughters; and Rev. Theophilus[15] was of Hampton Falls, was married, but left no children. Rowland[15] and Josiah[15] both left large families, and the number of their descendants must be very large. A tabular pedigree is given in the first volume of the Register, and another in the folio edition of Drake's History of Boston. We have room, however, only for one branch, that of the gentleman to whose liberality we are indebted for these thorough researches in England.

Elizabeth[15] Cotton married 1st, Rev. James Alling, and 2nd, Rev. Caleb Cushing of Salisbury, Mass. She was undoubtedly a grand-daughter of Rev. John C., of Boston, though accounts differ as to whether she was the daughter of Seaborn or John. SAVAGE is inclined to consider her the daughter of Seaborn and Dorothy (Bradstreet) Cotton. By her first husband she had three daughters, all of whom were married.

She married 14 March, 1697–8, Rev. Caleb Cushing of Salisbury, son of the first John Cushing, of a family recorded in our second volume, p. 123–4. Their children were,

Caleb,[16] b. 10 Oct., 1703.

James,[16] b. 25 Nov., 1705; min. of Plaistow, d. 13 May, 1764.

John,[16] b. 10 April, 1709; min. of Boxford, d. 25 Jan., 1772, leaving issue.

Joanna.[16]

Mary.[16]

Elizabeth.[16]

He died 24 Feb., 1752, aged 80.

Hon. Caleb[16] Cushing of Salisbury was Col. of the Essex Regiment, of the Council, and C. J. Court of Common Pleas. He married Mary, dau. of Rev. John Newmarch of Kittery, Me., and had, with four daughters,

Benjamin,[17] bapt. 20 Jan., 1739.

Caleb,[17] bapt. 23 Sept., 1750, d. unm.

Benjamin[17] Cushing of Salisbury m. Dec. 17, 1767, Hannah Hazeltine, and had—

Hannah,[18] b. 30 March, 1769.

Caleb,[18] b. 21 May, 1770.

Mary,[18] b. 11 May, 1772.

Benjamin,[18] b. 21 June, 1776.

John Newmarch,[18] b. 18 May, 1779; d. 5 Jan., 1849, father of Hon. Caleb Cushing.

Nathaniel,[18] b. 29 July, 1782.

Mary, b. 22 March, 1789.

HAWKRIDGE FAMILY.

In relation of the second wife of Rev. John Cotton, "the widow Story," Mr. Somerby has discovered the following facts:

She was undoubtedly the Sarah Hawkrit who married William Storey at Boston, Eng., 1 May, 1619; and her first husband was buried there 16 March, 1627–8. Her marriage to John Cotton was 25 April, 1632. By her first marriage she had a daughter, Elizabeth Story, bapt. 11 June, 1622, who doubtless married a person named Day, and had at least one daughter named Elizabeth Day, who m. a Symonds. This is rendered positive, as John Cotton mentions dau. Elizabeth, and grand-daughter Betty Day; Rev. Richard Mather mentions his wife's grand-daughter, Elizabeth Day, and Sarah (Cotton) Mather, mentions her grand-daughter, Elizabeth Symonds, and mentions also a Sarah Symonds. SAVAGE believes that this grand-daughter was the wife of Harlakenden Symonds.

As to the parentage of Sarah Hawkrit, Hawkridge or Hawkredd, as the name is variously spelt, it seems clear that she was the daughter of Anthony H., of Boston. Rev. John Cotton in his will mentions "my brother Coney," and his wife Mary.

The will of Anthony Hawkredd, dated Aug. 12, 1626, mentions sons Anthony, John, and Samuel, Mary, wife of Thomas Coney, and Elizabeth, wife of John Coney. Though Sarah is not mentioned, she is evidently another daughter. It seems that Hawkredd had been twice married. His second wife was a widow Ascough, and his first was a Tuckney, aunt of Anthony Tuckney, who succeeded John Cotton at Boston. Tuckney was thus first cousin to Cotton's wife, Sarah Hawkridge.

THE EARLDOM OF STIRLING.

The claims to the probably extinct title of Earl of Stirling have a considerable interest to Americans, since the province of Nova Scotia was at one time owned by Lord Stirling.

Sir William Alexander, Secretary of State to James I., obtained in 1621 a charter granting him the territory of Nova Scotia, and 2 Feb., 1628, he received a grant of the province of Canada. Sept. 4th, 1630, he was made Viscount Stirling, and June 14, 1633, was farther advanced to the title of Earl of Stirling and Viscount Canada by patent to him and his *heirs male.* He died in February, 1640, having had seven sons and two daughters.

The title probably became extinct in 1639, on the death of Henry, fifth Earl of Stirling. William, eldest son of the first Earl, died in the life time of his father, and his son, the second Earl, d. *s. p.* Henry, the third son of the first Earl, then succeeded, as third Earl, and his son and grandson, both named Henry, were the fourth and fifth Earls of Stirling.

It was always supposed that the second, fourth, and all younger sons of the first Earl, died without male issue, and accordingly the first claimant of the dormant honors was the heir male of the uncle of the first peer. This claimant was William Alexander, commonly called Lord Stirling, a Major General of the American forces during the Revolution. He was born in New York in 1726, and was the son of James Alexander, an officer of engineers in the service of the Pretender, who had been obliged to seek refuge here in 1716.

James Alexander was appointed Surveyor-General of New York and New Jersey, and also a member of Gov. Burnet's Council. He was distinguished as a lawyer, a politician, and a man of science, and died in 1756, leaving one son and four married daughters.

William Alexander, who married Sarah, daughter of Philip Livingston, laid claim to the title, and seems to have proved his right to the representation of the family as heir of John Alexander, uncle of the first Earl, since in 1759 a "jury of service" specially found this verdict. (Life of Lord Stirling, 24.) He proposed to claim the American possessions of his family, and made arrangements with the grandsons of the last Earl, who as descendants in the female line could not inherit the title.

It is believed that no decision was ever made by the House of Lords as to his claim, the point being that though by the Scotch law William Alexander was heir to the title as "heir male," yet he was not by the English law. It was urged that after the union of the two countries the English rule prevailed, and though it has been said that his claim was rejected by the Lords, March 10th, 1762, this was probably only the vote that he should not use the title till the claim was allowed; and the last proceeding recorded on their Journal is that "the further consideration was postponed until the next session of Parliament." (Life of Stirling, 62.)

As the American Earl of Stirling had no son, leaving only two daughters, Mrs. Watts and Mrs. Duer, the title would have again fallen into abeyance; and the facts we have presented seem sufficient to remove any stigma of false assumption from his use of it. He was for years recognized as Earl of Stirling by the English authorities, and not improbably might have been confirmed by the House of Lords, had not his political sins been unpardonable. He died at Albany, January 15th, 1783.

The next claimant was Alexander Humphreys, whose trial for forgery of documents put forth in favor of his claim, was the scene of some of the most curious revelations that ever occurred in a court-room. He was acquitted of being a party to the forgery, though the falsity of the documents was established at the trial in 1839, and a few months afterwards his claim was rejected by the Court of Sessions. He died in 1859, but his son was in 1864 joined in the suit, and in February of this year (1868) the case has come up on appeal to the House of Lords to reverse the former decision. The motion is opposed on technical grounds, and also on the score that the case was rightfully decided before. As this revival of the claim brings the matter anew for discussion, we propose to give a synopsis of the former trial in 1839, as reviewed in Blackwood's Magazine for April and May, 1851. The articles from which our account is constructed were based on the "Report of the Trial of Alexander Humphreys or Alexander, claiming the title of Earl of Stirling," by Archibald Swinton.

Alexander Humphreys was born in 1784, and was the son of William Humphreys, a respectable merchant of Birmingham, by his wife Hannah, youngest child of the Rev. John Alexander, a Presbyterian minister at Dublin. His paternal pedigree is immaterial, as the claimant depended of course on his position as heir of his grandfather, John Alexander.

As the claimant pursued his course with success for

some years, it may be well to note the dates.   In 1815 or
'16 he seems to have entertained the idea of claiming the
peerage ; and in 1824, by the advice of Mr. Thomas C.
Banks, the well known writer on peerages, he obtained a
royal license to assume his mother's family name, and became known as Alexander Humphrey Alexander.   In
1825, he attended and voted at the election of a representative Peer for Scotland, and having obtained various
documents he procured himself to be declared in 1830
nearest lawful heir, as great-great-great-grandson of William, first Earl of Stirling.   By a peculiarity of Scotch law,
a case of this kind to establish a pedigree, is tried *ex parte ;*
and if there be no opponent claiming in precisely the same
character, the claimant alone is heard.   Moreover, if the
proceedings continue unchallenged for twenty years, it
would not be possible to set aside or annul the decision.

He was also declared heir to the Nova Scotian and Can-
adian possessions of the first earl, created several baronets,
offered to sell lands, claimed the rank of hereditary-lieu-
tenant of Nova Scotia, and in every way made his
pretensions as notorious as possible.

In 1833 the Crown officers commenced proceedings
to have these acts annulled ; and in December, 1836,
judgment was rendered that the evidence was utterly
insufficient to sustain the previous verdicts, and consequently the claimant was defeated,

We will see what evidence had already been produced
at this point.   It was *claimed* that John Alexander, fourth
son of the first Earl, called " John of Gartmore," did not
die without male heirs, but had a son, John Alexander
of Antrim, who was father of Rev. John Alexander, the
claimant's grandfather.

To prove this pedigree the claimant produced two old women who professed to have heard that the Rev. John Alexander was son of John of Antrim and grandson of John of Gartmore; a scrap of paper containing what was said to be the inscription on John of Gartmore's tomb, though the stone had disappeared; and a professed abstract of a charter said to have been granted to the first Earl, under date of 7 Dec., 1639, *altering the line of succession.*

As we have said, the first point decided was that the pedigree had not been made out, it having been shown that John of Gartmore had by his known wife, Agnes Graham, a daughter only; and there was no evidence of a second marriage, except this production of an alleged son.

The second point, not then argued, was more peculiar. The known charters limited the descent of the titles to William, Earl of Stirling, and his *heirs male*, and as we have seen, our American Lord Stirling claimed as heir male. Humphreys, however, claimed that the first Earl, only two months before his death, surrendered his honors and took out a fresh grant to himself and heirs-male; and failing them, to the eldest heirs female without division of the last of such heirs-male, and to the heirs-male of such females.

This charter was never found, but Humphreys asserted that an abstract was made in 1723 for his grandfather, and he desired to put this in evidence.

This new line of succession was just shaped to suit the claimant's position, but it seems hard to understand why the Earl should have devised such a plan to perpetuate his honors. There were heirs to the representation through females, but this case was that the heir female only of the latest Earl was to succeed, or rather of the titular Earl only. The Rev. John Alexander lived four years after the death of the fifth Earl, yet he never claimed the title though it would so greatly have aided his daughter in her alleged rights. But, as we shall see, the charter was pronounced to be a forgery, though not at the first trial.

Soon after the crushing decision of December, 1836, the claimant obtained fresh proofs to establish the two dubious points in his pedigree, and in Nov., 1837, he put these documents into the case. A year later he was examined as to how he obtained these remarkable documents, and the reply not being satisfactory, he was finally brought to trial in April, 1839, on the charge of having forged them, or used them knowing them to be forged.

We hasten to add that the jury found unanimously that the charter was forged, as well as certain other documents; but *not proven* that the claimant forged them or uttered them, knowing them to be forged; also *not proven* that certain less essential documents were forged. The prisoner was accordingly dismissed, but his claim to the peerage seemed extinguished, since even if his pedigree were correct he was not the heir-male.

We will therefore examine the proofs adduced, first, of his right to the title; and secondly, of his descent from the first Earl. His right depended entirely upon a presumed new grant and limitation of the honors, but the original charter was confessedly not forthcoming. It was indeed suggested that the American claimant stole and destroyed the original; and in the place of it the proposition was made to admit an abridged copy said to have been made in 1723, for the Rev. John Alexander, and which was found by Mr. T. C. Banks in Ireland. This copy was written on several leaves of paper stitched together, and at the beginning were the abbreviations " REG. MAG. SIG., LIB. LVII.," *i. e.* " *Registrum Magni Sigilli, Liber* LVII." At the conclusion it was witnessed by the Chancellor, John, Archbishop of St. Andrews, and others, Dec. 7th, 1639. — " [Gratis]." " Per Signetum." All of these four endorsements were used to prove the falsity of the copy produced, as follows :

First, there were four separate records in which the charter must have been mentioned, the Signature Record, the Comptroller of the Exchequer's Record, the Privy Seal Record, and the Great Seal Record, but it was on neither. Secondly, the reference to the Great Seal Record, Vol. 57, was indeed to a volume in which twelve pages were missing, but two ancient indexes remained and showed that this volume contained charters subsequent to 1639. The endorsed reference to Lib. LVII. was contemporaneous with the presumed copy of 1723, but it was proved that this mode of reference and even the numbering was invented in 1806, for the witness was there who then re-bound the volumes.

Thirdly, James Spottiswode, Archbishop, not only was not Chancellor, Dec. 7, 1639, when he signed the charter (having resigned 13th Nov., 1638,) but he actually died Nov. 26th, 1639, eleven days previous, and his signature was necessarily forged.

Fourthly, it was shown that the words " Gratis," and " Per signetum," could never have both been on the same document, but this was a mere technical proof. Still, after all these preceding facts were shown, we cannot wonder that the jury unanimously called the abstract of a charter a forgery.

To prove the pedigree, and also to substantiate the charter, the claimant presented a French map of Nova Scotia, dated in 1703, on the back of which were several inscriptions of the utmost importance. This map was received from an anonymous source by a certain Madamoiselle Le Normand, of Paris, a noted fortune-teller, who was the friend of the claimant's wife. The map was that of Canada, *dated* in 1703, and engraved by Guillaume Delisle. The inscriptions were, 1st, one by a M. Mallet, dated 1706, stating that during his residence in Nova Scotia, he had seen the original charter of the new grant to the Earl of Stirling, and had obtained a copy. He recites also the limitations, and gives the reason for copying it, that if the province ever reverted to the English the family would possess this immense territory. 2nd, A certain C. St. Estienne wrote in 1707, that his friend Mallet had just died. 3d, Esprit Flechier, Bishop of Nismes, testifies that he has read the copy of the charter, and that M. Mallet has translated it very correctly. 4th, A letter is pasted on the map, dated Antrim, 1707, from John Alexander, alleged father of Rev. John A., to the Marchioness de Lambert, in which he says that his father John was fourth son of the first Earl, and had two wives, that his mother was a Maxwell, that his wife was a Hamilton, and that his son is named John, and is to be a minister of the Church of Scotland. 5th, A memorandum written by the great Fenelon, Archbishop of Cambray, authenticating the above letter, which he says the friends of M. Mallet will read with interest. 6th, A copy of the inscription on the tablet to the memory of John Alexander, of Antrim, copied in 1723, by W. C. Gordon, Jr., and pasted on the map. 7th, A statement that this inscription was given by the Marchioness de Lambert, who, since the death of John of Antrim, had been a friend to his son, who was well known as a clergyman at Stratford. 8th, A note in the handwriting of Louis XV. ordering the copy of the charter to be sent to him.

This wonderful document was indeed evidence both to the pedigree and the charter, and yet the jury unanimously pronounced it a forgery. The reason was plain. These documents were several of them dated in 1707, and as Bishop Flechier died in 1711, and Fenelon died in 1715, these dates were in accord. It was conclusively proved, however, that the map was not printed before the 24th August, 1718, and therefore these signatures were all forgeries.

The proof was this. Although the map was dated in 1703, it was marked thus: "Par Guillaume De l' Isle de l' Academie Royal des Sciences *et Premier Geographe du Roy*, A Paris, chez l' Auteur sur le Quai de l' Horloge à l' Aigle d' Or, avec Privilege de sa Maj^{te} pour 20 Ans 1703." The words in italic referred to an appointment as "premier Géographe du Roi," which De l'Isle received August 24th, 1718. His copyright was for twenty years from the first publication in 1703, but after he was thus honored he interpolated the title on the inscription, and used the same plate. The fact was proved by abundant evidence that he altered many maps in this way, but of

course he could not do it until after the date of his appointment. The inscription confirmed it, this line having
evidently been squeezed in between two others, and not
having the proper space between them.

This evidence was indeed crushing, though the signatures seem to have been skilfully imitated, and down went
one more section of the claimant's proofs.

A second bundle of papers was received in 1837 by
Messrs. De Porquet & Co. of London, directed to the
Earl of Stirling. An unknown lady, a Mrs. Smith, wrote
that these papers were stolen from William Humphreys,
the father of the claimant, but the thief had never dared
to open the packet. As the thief had just died, his family had decided to return the papers, but must remain
unknown. In the package was a genealogical tree
purporting to be drawn up by one Thomas Campbell
in 1759, and of course giving the three generations of
Johns, a letter from Benjamin Alexander to his brother
John, both uncles of the claimant who died young, and
containing genealogical information.

It was clearly proved, and this seems to be the only
grain of comfort in the whole case for the prisoner, that
this De Porquet bundle was in a package marked " some
of my wife's family papers " in the hand-writing of the
claimant's father, and that some papers had been lost at
the time of some change of habitation. Still neither party
seems to have made much account of this matter, as the
pedigree without the charter was hardly worth proving,
and the jury pronounced the charge of forgery as to this
bundle of documents *not proven*.

It would be impossible probably for any one to avoid
the belief that all these papers had a common origin, so

remarkably did these various genealogies and letters coincide. To us here, indeed, it will seem strange that such
immense possessions and lofty honors could ever have
been seriously considered dependent upon such trifling
proofs. We see none of the evidences so common here, no
town record of births or marriages, no attempt apparently to trace the true parentage of Rev. John Alexander.
Although a clergyman would have an exceptional prominence here, we doubt if any ordinary man of the name
could have lived in New England a century ago, and have
been as difficult to trace, as was this " Presbyterian minister of good position."

We do not anticipate any decision by the House of
Lords which will restore the Humphreys to their coveted
position; but at all events it is satisfactory to remember
that Long Island and Pemaquid were sold by the Earl of
Stirling to the Duke of York, and the titles of the present
occupants will hardly be controverted. A study of the
whole proceedings in this case will fill the minds of our
American " fortune-hunters " with envy and admiration.

NOTES ON THE FAMILY OF WORTHINGTON.

[By W. Worthington Fowler.]

> For Wetharynton my harte is woe
> That ever hee slayne shulde bee,
> For when hys leggs were hewne intoe,
> He knyled and fought on hys kne.
> BALLAD OF CHEVY CHASE.

The surname *Worthington*, like many other family
names, is derived from the locality where the first known

progenitor of the family resided. As to its etymology, it is generally agreed to be from three Saxon words, viz: — Wearth-in-ton, i. e. Farm in Town. About twenty miles northeast of Liverpool, in the Hundred of Leyland and Parish of Standish is the township of Worthington. Here, or on the adjacent manors, resided, for many centuries, the family of *Worthington*, "established," says Burke, "in high repute from the time of the Plantagenets." "Hereabouts (we quote from Camden's description of Lancashire) are little towns which gave name to considerable families, and are to-day possessed by persons of their own name, as Aston, of Aston; Atherton, of Atherton; Tillesley, of Tillesley; Standish, of Standish; Bold, of Bold; Hesket, of Hesket; Worthington, of Worthington; . . . . . These, and such like families in these North Counties owe their rise to their valor, and their progress to their frugality, content with their own estates," etc., etc. The family of Worthington appear to have been distinguished rather by "plain living and heroical acting," rather than by the arts of courtiers. The main stock can be traced in the public archives as far back as Worthington de Worthington (20th of Henry III., 1236–7), the progenitor of all the Lancashire Worthingtons. The old Hall at Worthington, where the family resided for seven hundred years, was pulled down not many years since. The

present representative of the direct line is Edward
Worthington of the Bryn, co. Chester. By intermarriage
(about the time of Henry VII.) of William Worthington
with Jane, daughter of William Norreys, of Speke, the
family trace their descent to the Norrises, ancestors of the
Earls of Abingdon, the Molyneux of Sefton, the Villiers,
senior branch of the Ducal stem of Buckingham and the
Baronial House of Harrington. About the time of Edward IVth, three branches shot off from the main stock,
viz.: the Worthingtons of Crosshawe, of Blainsco and of
Shevington, who, by marriage, became allied with many
of the leading gentry of Lancashire, the Andersons,
Levers, Orrells, Radcliffes, Lawrences, the Ashtons, By-
rons and Standishes, ancestors of stout Myles Standish,
the Captain of the Pilgrim Band.

The descendants of these progenitors were very numerous in the county of Lancaster in the time of Charles I.

All those who now bear the name of Worthington in
this country, so far as known, derive their origin from
two sources, viz.: 1st, from an emigrant ancestor, who
settled in Maryland, from whom, among others, descended
the late Governor Worthington of Ohio, and L. Worthington, M. D., of Cincinnati, Ohio. 2d, from Nicholas
Worthington, who came to New England in 1650, and
who was the only early emigrant of that name who settled
in that section of the country.

We learn, from a relative of the late Governor Worthington, that his branch of the family claimed descent from
the Worthingtons of Lancashire, and were accustomed to
bear the same arms as those given at the head of these
notes. What evidence they have of their connection with

the English stock I cannot say. No attempt has been made to connect the New England branch with the parent stem in England by documentary proof. But circumstantial evidence of such connection is not wanting. According to family tradition, Nicholas Worthington, the emigrant, was a considerable landholder near Liverpool, in the county of Lancaster, and fought and was wounded in the Cromwellian wars, in which conflicts his estates were confiscated. This tradition, transmitted to Rev. William Worthington, of Saybrook, (grandson of Nicholas) was by him transmitted through his daughter Elizabeth (Worthington) Chauncy to her son Worthington Gallop Chauncey, of Durham, Conn., an accurate preserver of historical facts and traditions, and by him, prior to his death in 1858, communicated to the present writer.

The rather uncommon name of *Nicholas* was borne by two of the Shevington Worthingtons, viz.: by Nicholas W., of Shevington, time of Henry VIII., and by Nicholas W., his grandson, time of Elizabeth and James I.

There is now in possession of William Chauncey Fowler, of Durham, Conn., an ancient silver tankard or pitcher which has descended in the family as an heirloom, for at least four generations. Its massive mould and antique shape would indicate an age coeval with the settlement of the country.* Deeply though rudely engraven on the front, are the ancient armor of Worthington, a copy of which is given at the head of these notes,—described in

---

* I observe on reference to certain ancient engravings in the Astor Library, that tankards of exactly this fashion and shape were in common use in the reign of Henry VIII.

heraldic terms as follows, viz.: Argent, three dung forks
sable ; crest, a goat statant (or passant) argent holding
in the mouth an oak branch vert fructed or ; motto, *virtute Dignus avorum.*   These arms are still borne by the
Worthingtons of Lancashire and Cheshire.

Nicholas Worthington, the emigrant ancestor, was first
of Saybrook, then of Hartford, Conn. He afterwards
removed to Hatfield, Mass., where he died, 1683. He
married as his first wife, in 1668, Sarah, widow of Jno.
White and daughter of Thomas Bunce, of Hartford.* By
her he had a son William, and two daughters, Elizabeth
and Mary.

His second wife was Susanna, by whom he had Jonathan and John. From these sons and daughters descended
a numerous family, now scattered over the country.
Among these were the Worthingtons, who settled in Colchester, Conn., Rev. William Worthington, of Saybrook,
Conn., the Worthingtons of Springfield, Worthington and
Dorchester, Mass., Anthony Worthington of Brooklyn,
and Henry R. Worthington, of Irvington, N. Y. The
descendants of the daughters of the first and second generations are equally numerous.

A tabular statement of many of the descendants of
Nicholas Worthington may be found in Goodwin's Genealogical Notes.

William, eldest and only son of Nicholas Worthington,
by his first wife, married Mehitable, daughter of Isaac
Graves, of Hatfield.† By her he had, among other chil-

---

* *Thomas Bunce* was, perhaps, from Kent, where the family of Bunce was
numerous.   Some of this family were seated at Padbury, co. Bucks.
† A family of Graves, Greaves or Grevis, were ancient and numerous in
Lancashire ; a family of that name were also of co. Kent, time of Elizabeth.

dren, William Worthington, born December 5, 1695 ; graduated at Yale College, 1716 ; settled as pastor of that part of Saybrook afterwards known as Westbrook ; died, 1756. He is said to have been a gentleman of fine person, and bland, elegant manners. By his first wife Elizabeth (daughter of Major Samuel Mason, and great grand-daughter of Captain John Mason) he had, among other children, Mary, who married Hon. Aaron Eliot. By his second wife, Temperance Gallop, he had I., Elizabeth (who married first, Col. Samuel Gale, of Saybrook, and had by him two children, Benjamin and Asa ; second, Rev. Elnathan Chauncey, of Durham, Ct., and had, by him, I., Nathaniel William, who died unmarried ; II., Catharine, who married Reuben Rose Fowler ; III., Worthington Gallop, who died unmarried). II., Temperance, who, by Rev. Cotton Mather Smith, her second husband, was mother (among other children) of Gov. John Cotton Smith. Temperance 2d, wife of Rev. William Worthington, of Saybrook, was daughter of William Gallop and Sarah, (daughter of Samuel Chesebrough) his wife.* William Gallop was third son of John Gallop, Jr., of Stonington, Conn., and Hannah (Lake) Gallop his wife.

John Gallop, Jr., was a noted Indian fighter, and was one of the six Captains killed at the great Narragansett swamp fight. He was the eldest son of John Gallop, the emigrant ancestor, and Christobel, his wife. John Gallop senior was also distinguished by his prowess against the Indians, as his punishment of the murderers of John Oldham will bear witness. Vide Colonial Histories of Connecticut. He was educated at a military school in

---

* The Chesebroughs were from Boston, co. Lincoln.

Holland, where he became accquainted with Captain John
Mason, afterwards of Connecticut, between whom and
himself a warm friendship afterwards grew up. He is
supposed to have been a younger son of Thomas Gallop
(or Gollop) of Strode, co. Dorset, and Frances (Paulet)
Gallop, his wife.

Hannah Lake, wife of John Gallop, 2d, was the daughter
of *Mrs.* Margaret Lake, daughter of Col. Edmund Read,
of Wickford, co. Essex, and elder sister of Elizabeth,
second wife of John Winthrop, junior. John Lake, husband of Mrs. Margaret Lake, was descended from the
Lakes of Normanton, Yorkshire, who claimed descent
through the Cailleys from the Albinis, Earls of Arundel and
Sussex, from the Counts of Louvaine, (the right line of
Charlemagne) and from William the Conquerer.

THE THATCHER FAMILY.

The family of Thatcher has been one of
considerable note from the first generation
of settlers here, and though we have not
tried to trace their English pedigree, the
annexed cut shows that they had at an early date made a claim to rank among the gentry.

We learn from the MAGNALIA, that the Rev. Thomas[2]
Thatcher was born at Salisbury, Eng., 1 May, 1620,
and was the son of the Rev. Peter[1] Thatcher, who was
Rector of St. Edmund's in that place. His religious scru-
ples prevented his having a university education; but he

decided to come to Boston, where he arrived 4 June, 1635. He studied with the Rev. Charles Chauncy, married 11 May, 1643, Elizabeth, daughter of the Rev. Ralph Partridge, of Duxbury, and was ordained at Weymouth, 2 Jan., 1644. By her he had Thomas,[3] Ralph,[3] Peter,[3] Patience[3] and Elizabeth.[3] He married secondly Margaret, dau. of Henry Webb, and widow of Jacob Sheaffe, was called to the Old South Church in Boston, and died 15 Oct., 1678.

An uncle of Thomas[2] was Anthony[1] Thatcher, minister at Marblehead, who in 1636 lost all his family but his wife, by shipwreck off Cape Ann. He had, after this, sons John[2] and Judah,[2] both of Yarmouth. Descendants of this branch are numerous, since as SAVAGE writes of John Thatcher, "fourteen of his twenty children married for the blessing of the Cape."

To return to the main line. Of the sons of the Rev. Thomas[2] Thatcher, Thomas[3] was a merchant of Boston and had three sons, of whom Peter[4] was bapt. 26 Aug., 1677, H. C. 1696, was settled at the New North Church in Boston, and died 26 Feb., 1739. Ralph[3] was of Duxbury and Martha's Vineyard and left issue.

The Rev. Peter[3] Thatcher, son of the emigrant, was the minister at Milton, Mass. He m. 21 Nov., 1677, Theodora, dau. of the Rev. John Oxenbridge, whose family is noticed in our second volume, p. 178. By her he had—

Theodora,[4] b. ———.

Bathsheba,[4] b. ———.

Oxenbridge,[4] b. 17 May, 1681.

Elizabeth,[4] b. 7 March, 1682–3; m. Rev. Samuel Niles, the historian.

Mary,[4] b. ———.

Peter,[4] b. 6 Oct., 1688, H. C. 1706, minister at Middleborough.

John,[4] b. ———; d. young.

Thomas,[4] b. 1693; d. 1722.

John.[4]

His wife died 18 Nov., 1697, and he m. 2d, Susanna, widow of the Rev. John Bailey. After her death, 4 Sept., 1724, he m. thirdly, Elizabeth, widow of Joshua Gee, and died 17 Dec., 1727.

Of these children we will mention first, Thomas,[4] who died in 1722, as our engraving is taken from the seal on his will in the Suffolk registry. He mentions mother Susanna, brother Oxenbridge Thatcher, brother Peter T., and his son Peter, sister Gulliver, nephew Nathaniel Niles, niece Elizabeth Niles. The arms are undoubtedly those mentioned by Burke, Gules, a cross moline argent, on a chief three grasshoppers proper.*

Oxenbridge[4] Thatcher was first a minister at Punkapoag, now Stoughton, but settled at Milton, and was for several years a representative thence, as he had previously been from Boston. He married Elizabeth Lillie, sister of Sir Charles Hobbie, according to a pedigree in possession of the family. Among his children were Oxenbridge,[5] who died July 8, 1765, aged 45, a distinguished lawyer on the

---

* These arms are on the seal of a letter written Oct. 16, 1676, by the first Thomas Thatcher at Boston to his son Peter in London, printed in the H. and G. Register, VIII., 177–8. In this letter he mentions that he had heard from his brother Paul Thatcher, who lived in Salisbury, that his brother John died three years before. He also mentions his " mother-in-law's sister, Mrs. Elizabeth Coombs, widow to Mr. Coombs, the great Anabaptist," who was also at Salisbury. This fact carries back the use of the arms to the English family. I am informed also that a seal bearing the same arms is in the possession of the Boston branch of the family, being an heirloom.

side of the Colony in the discussions which preceded the Revolution, and who married Sarah Kent.*

Among the children of Oxenbridge[5] Thatcher, Jr., were,

Thomas,[6] H. C. 1775, minister at Dedham, d. Oct. 1812, aged 56.

Nathaniel,[6] and

Peter.[6]

The Rev. Peter[6] Thatcher was born 21 March, 1752, H. C. 1769, and was settled at Malden, 19 Sept., 1770. He was a warm supporter of the claims of the Colonists. In 1785 he was called to Brattle Street Church in Boston, was made Doctor of Divinity by the University of Edinburgh, and died 16 Dec., 1802.

He married 8 Oct., 1770, Elizabeth Pool, and had—

Thomas Cushing,[7] b. 11 Oct., 1771; H. C. 1790.

Peter,[7] b. 1 Dec., 1772; d. 6 Sept., 1775.

Sarah,[7] b. 7 March, 1774; d. 7 Sept., 1775.

Joseph Warren,[7] b. 4 July, 1775; d. 19 March, 1809.

Peter Oxenbridge,[7] b. 22 Dec., 1776.

Charles,[7] b. 12 Sept., 1779; d. 13 Nov., 1779.

Sarah,[7] b. 5 Oct., 1781; d. 13 Jan., 1802.

Mary Harvey,[7] b. 17 March, 1783; d. 24 June 1849.

Samuel Cooper,[7] b. 14 Dec., 1785.

Charles,[7] b. 15 June, 1787.

His wife died 26 Jan., 1816, aged 71.

Of these children, Charles[7] was a merchant in Boston,

---

* From a record in the family Bible we find that John Kent, born 29 Sept., 1694, married Bathsheba Doggett (b. 18 June, 1695) 13 Sept., 1719, and had John, b. 5 June, 1720, d. 18 Sept., 1720; Bathsheba, b. May 14, 1721, d. 14 July, 1729; John, b. 15 June, 1723, d. Dec. 12, 1723; Sarah, b. 25 Dec., 1729; John, b. 25 Jan., 1729, d. 31 Oct., 1737.

married Caroline Hutchins, and died 18 May, 1833, leaving a son, Dr. Charles Thatcher.

Peter Oxenbridge[7] Thatcher m. 7 April, 1808, Charlotte-Ignatius McDonough, and had George-McDonough,[8] b. 5 March, 1809 ; Theodore-Oxenbridge, b. 18 June, 1810 ; Joseph S. B., b. 11 May, 1812 ; Peter O., b. 31 Dec., 1813, d. 1818 ; Samuel C., b. 22 July, 1816, d. 6 May, 1861 ; Peter O., b. 18 Feb., 1823. The father, who was Judge of the Municipal Court in Boston, died 22 Feb., 1843.

The Rev. Samuel Cooper[7] Thatcher was ordained minister of the New South Church in Boston, but was obliged to resign, owing to ill health, and died at Moulins, 1 Jan., 1818.

In this branch therefore there were four ministers connected with Boston churches, Thomas,[2] the emigrant, Peter,[4] Jr., his grandson, Dr. Peter of Brattle Street, and Samuel C.

From an article in the New England Magazine for 1834, upon the Thatcher family, we take some particulars concerning Anthony's descendants. His son John[2] was a member of the Council, and died 8 May, 1713, aged 75. He married first Rebecca Winslow, and secondly Lydia Gorham, and by them he had seventeen children. Of his sons, Peter,[3] b. 26 April, 1665, was chief justice C. C. P. for Barnstable, and died in 1735 ; John,[3] b. 28 Jan., 1674, was a colonel, register of deeds and judge C. C. P., and died in 1764, aged 90 ; and Joseph[3] was also colonel, and served in the expedition against Cape Breton in 1745.

Peter[4] Thatcher, son of Peter,[3] b. 24 Aug., 1712, married Anna Lewis, and had eleven children. Of these, George,[5] b. 12 April, 1754, was a distinguished lawyer, member of Congress, and judge of the Supreme Court of Massachusetts. He died 6 April, 1824, leaving issue. In several other branches of this family have been other bearers of the name who have held prominent positions.

SEAL OF MAHALALEEL MUNNINGE.

The seal, of which we annex an enlarged representation, is used by Mahalaleel Munninge, on a charter-party made October 22, 1659, between John Jackson of Boston, master of the Ketch called the Rebecca, and the said Munninge, in behalf of John Allen, merchant, of Barbadoes. The proposed voyage, for this little vessel of sixty tons, was from Boston to Piscataqua, thence to Madeira, Barbadoes and the Leeward Islands, returning to Boston. The document is witnessed by Robert Howard, notary-public at Boston. Another witness to certain endorsements signs his name William Howard, and Gov. Bellingham calls him in the acknowledgement, William *Hayward*, a good proof that the names were interchangeable.

Of Mahalaleel we find in SAVAGE, that he was the son of Edward Munnings or Monnings of Dorchester, who is thought to have belonged in Malden, co. Essex. The son came here in 1635, aged 3 years, went home, came again in 1656 in the Speedwell, married Hannah Wiswall in 1657, and died in 1660, leaving an only daughter, Hannah, who married Josiah Willis.

We know of no authority for attributing these arms to him, but as he wrote a good hand and was a man of some position, it is not unreasonable to suppose that the seal belonged to him rather than to any of the witnesses.

THE SHEAFFE FAMILY.

The seal which we here present was used by Jacob Sheaffe in 1713 as a witness to James Osborn's will, and also on the will of Mathias Smith in 1715, both in the Suffolk Registry. We have, however, a better proof that these arms were claimed by the Sheaffes. In the Bentley collection of papers in the possession of the American Antiquarian Society there is a tricking of the arms of Curwin impaling Sheaffe, made by George Curwin, 1698. He describes the arms thus: " The second is ermyn, on a chevron gules charged three garbs *or*, between three pelletts. By the name of Sheaf." As his mother was Elizabeth Sheaffe, the proof is strong.

There were three early emigrants of the name: Edmund, whose line has continued to the present time ; Jacob, undoubtedly a cousin, whose daughter married Edmund's son, so that his descendants bear the family name ; and William of Charlestown whose connection with the others is unknown. The tombstone of Jacob, still remaining in Boston, states that he was of Cranbrook in Kent, and in the N. E. Historical and Genealogical Register, IV., 310–315, are numerous entries copied from the parish records.

It seems quite certain that Jacob Sheaffe was the son of Edmund S. of Cranbrook, and was bapt. there Aug. 4, 1616. His sister Mary, bapt. Sept. 26, 1620, was the wife of Robert Merriam of Concord, Mass., and another sister, Joan, m. William Chittenden, as is shown in the REGISTER, XXII., 160–1.

Though the family can thus be shown to have lived for two or three generations, and probably longer, at Cranbrook, we believe no attempt has been made to look up the wills in England, and thus to perfect the pedigree or verify the claim to use coat-armor. These arms are not recorded by BURKE, who registers the arms of Sir Roger-Hale Sheaffe, Bart., who was an American, and who obtained undoubtedly a grant for himself of a new and different coat.

The bearers of the name are now but few, and the family has been chiefly connected with Portsmouth, N. H. Still there are very many descendants through females, and a very good pedigree of the family is preserved in manuscript, by Francis E. Parker, Esq., of Boston, from which we have prepared the following genealogy of those descended from Sampson Sheaffe of Boston :

GENEALOGY.

1. Edmund[1] Sheaffe of Boston married Elizabeth, daughter of Sampson Cotton of London, and had Rebecca,[2] Elizabeth,[2] and Sampson.[2]

2. Jacob Sheaffe[1] of Boston, 1643, married Margaret, only daughter of Henry Webb, and had several children. He was very wealthy, and at his death, 22 March, 1659, aged 42, his property went to his two surviving children—

>Elizabeth,[2] b. 1 Oct., 1644, m. 1, Robert Gibbs, 7 Sept., 1660; 2, Jona. Corwen, 20 March, 1675.

>Mehitable,[2] b. 28 May, 1658, m. her relative, Sampson Sheaffe. His widow m. 2dly, Rev. Thomas Thatcher, and died 23 Feb., 1694.

3. Sampson[2] Sheaffe, b. 1650, was of London and Boston, and married his cousin, Mehitable Sheaffe. He was of New Hampshire, Collector of the Customs, Councillor, Secretary, and Judge of the Superior Court. He died in Boston in 1724. His children were—

>Mehitable,[3] b. Dec. 1, 1677; d. Dec. 4, 1677.

>Mehitable,[3] b. Nov. 27, 1678.

(4) Jacob,[3] b. Feb. 18, 1680.

(5) Sampson,[3] b. Aug. 14, 1681.

>Mathew,[3] b. Jan. 1, 1685.

4. Jacob[3] Sheaffe is said to have had the following children, though our information does not include the name of his wife, or other particulars—

>Margaret,[4] b. 1709; d. 1710.

>Mehitable,[4] b. 4 Sept., 1711.

>Mary,[4] b. 1713; d. 1714.

>Abigail,[4] b. 1715.

>Margaret,[4] b. 1717; d. 1717.

>Margaret,[4] b. 1718; d. 1718.

>Eliza,[4] b. 1720; d. 1720.

>Lydia,[4] b. 1722.

Jacob,[4] b. 1727.

Sarah,[4] b. 1729; d. 1730.

5. Sampson[3] Sheaffe, Jr., m. Sarah Walton, Nov., 1711,
and had—

Sampson.[4]

(6) Jacob,[4] b. 21 Oct., 1715.

Mehitable,[4] ——— ; m. —— Burleigh of Newmarket.

Mary,[4] ——— ; m. —— Bell of Newcastle.

Sarah,[4] ——— ; m. Capt. John Simpson.

Elizabeth,[4] ———; m. —— Branscom of Newcastle.

6. Jacob[4] Sheaffe m. 24 July, 1740, Hannah Seavy,
who died in 1773, and 2d, Mrs. Abigail (Halyburton)
Hamilton. By his first wife he had—

Matthew,[5] b. Aug., 1741; d. unm.

Abigail,[5] b. 26 April, 1744; m. Hon. John Pickering.

(7) Jacob,[5] b. 6 Sept., 1745.

Sarah,[5] b. 1 Aug., 1748; m. John Marsh.

Hannah,[5] b. 26 April, 1750; m. 1st, Hugh Hender-
son; 2d, William Hart.

(8) Thomas,[5] b. 16 April, 1752.

Mary,[5] b. 22 Nov., 1753; m. Jos. Willard.

(9) James,[5] b. 17 Nov., 1755.

(10) William,[5] b. 11 Sept., 1758.

Mehitable,[5] b. 12 April, 1760.

(11) John,[5] b. 3 July, 1762.

Jacob[4] Sheaffe died 26 June, 1791.

7. Jacob[5] Sheaffe married Mary Quincy and had three
sons who married, viz., Henry,[6] Jacob,[6] and Edmund,[6] besides several daughters. Of his sons, Henry[6] Sheaffe m.

Lucy Cushing, and had a son Charles[7]; Jacob[6] m. Mary Haven and had a son Charles[7]; and Edmund[6] married his cousin Susan Sheaffe.

8. Thomas[5] Sheaffe m. 1st, Abigail Bell, and 2d, Mary Hale. He died 4 Sept., 1831, but though he had numerous children, two only seem to have married, Mehitable,[6] who m. Charles Coffin, and John-Hale,[6] who m. a cousin, Maria Sheaffe.

9. James[5] Sheaffe m. 1st, Sarah Meserve, and 2d, Sarah Fisher. He died 5 Dec., 1829, having had six children, but we believe none of the name remain in this branch.

10. William[5] Sheaffe m. Mary Wentworth, and died March 2, 1839. He had, besides other issue, two sons, Mark W.[6] and Augustus,[6] both married.

11. John[5] Sheaffe m. Betsey Bunbury, and died 24 Jan., 1812. He had but one son, Gustavus,[6] who d. unm.

THE CHARLESTOWN FAMILY OF SHEAFFE.

There was also a family of the name at Charlestown, descended from William Sheaffe, and we are enabled, by the kindness of Mr. Thomas B. Wyman, to give some notes concerning it.

1. William[1] S., mariner, who was aged 36 in 1685, m. 1st, Ruth Wood, 15 Aug., 1672; secondly, Mary ——, before 1679, and third, Elizabeth (Rand) Penny (widow of John) 2 March, 1703-4. His children were—

 Margaret,[2] b. 12 May, 1673; m. Richard Stratton.
 William,[2] b. ——; d. 1677-8.
 Rebecca,[2] b. 17 Nov., 1679; d. 1680.
(2) Edward,[2] b. 10 April, 1682.

(3) William,[2] b. 3 Feb., 1683–4.

Mary,[2] b. 14 Jan., 1685–6; d. 19 Jan., 1702–3.
He had a brother, John S. of Boston, who m. Sarah, dau.
of Lawrence Waters, before 1699.

2. Edward[2] Sheaffe of Charlestown, m. 29 Aug., 1704,
Mary Cater, and had—

Mary,[3] b. 28 March, 1706.

Elizabeth,[3] b. 21 March, 1706–7; m. Nathaniel
Webber.

Margaret,[3] b. 30 Sept., 1709; d. 21 Oct., 1709.

Edward,[3] b. 1 Oct., 1711; m. Abigail Pierce, and
had 11 children.

Margaret,[3] b. 20 June, 1713; m. Nathaniel Rand.

Rebecca,[3] b. 6 Aug., 1715.
His wife died 1 Nov., 1740.

3. William[2] Sheaffe, Jr., of Charlestown, m. Mary
(Davis) Longfellow, a widow, 13 Jan., 1704–5, and had—

(4) William,[3] b. 13 Jan., 1705–6.

Nathaniel,[3] bapt. 7 March, 1717–8.

Mary,[3] b. 13 May, 1710; m. Gershom Griffith.

Benjamin,[3] b. 3 Feb., 1711–2.

James,[3] b. 5 Jan., 1713–4.

Anne,[3] b. 19 Feb., 1715–6; d. 1720.

Ebenezer,[3] b. 2 Feb., 1717–8; d. 1718.
He died 14 Oct., 1718, and his widow d. 11 Jan., 1720,
aged 41.

4. William[3] Sheaffe was at College in 1722, when his
father's estate was settled, and he is mentioned as being
of Boston and deceased, in his brother Nathaniel's will
of 1772, which mentions also William's son Nathaniel.
There can be no doubt then that he was of H. C. 1723,

and was the William Sheaffe of Boston, who for forty years was connected with the Custom House there. The only discrepancy in the account is that the newspaper at his death, in 1771, says he was in his 69th year, three years more than his real age, but this cannot controvert the evidence in favor of this identification.

William Sheaffe of Boston married Susanna Child, 1 Oct., 1752, and had a large family, one of whom was Sir Roger-Hale Sheaffe, Bart., of the British Army. SABINE, in the second edition of his American Loyalists, has given a full account of the family from which we propose to make some extracts.

William Sheaffe, from his long connection with the office, often acted as Collector, as in 1759 when Sir Henry Frankland had been removed. He then issued the famous " Writs of Assistance " to search for smuggled goods. In 1762 he became deputy under Roger Hale, and continued under Joseph Harrison, the last Royal Collector. He died suddenly, 29 Nov., 1771, of apoplexy, leaving his family in poverty. His wife was the sister of Thomas Child, an officer of the Customs at Falmouth, Me. She died about 1811. Of their children, SABINE notices—

    I. Susanna m. Capt. Ponsonby Molesworth, of the British Army, nephew of Lord Ponsonby. It was a runaway match, the lady being but fifteen years old, but proved a very happy marriage. She died in 1834, leaving descendants.

    II. Margaret m. 20 July, 1779, John R. Livingston of Boston, (see Holgate's American Genealogy, p. 182) and d. s. p. in 1785.

III. Helen, m. James Lovell, and had Mary, m. Henry Loring, and Ann, m. Rev. Mr. Carr. Her grandson is Gen. Mansfield Lovell of the late Rebel Army.

IV. Anne, m. John Erving, Jr., 24 Sept., 1786.

V. Sarah.

VI. Mary.

VII. Nathaniel, named in his uncle's will. He went to Jamaica, and dying, 25th Jan., 1777, on his passage to Hispaniola, was buried at Morant's Bay.

VIII. Thomas Child, was of New York, and also went to the West Indies. He died before 1793.

IX. William, went to England and probably remained there. His son William was heir to his uncle, Sir Roger H.

X. Roger-Hale Sheaffe, born in 1763, was by far the most distinguished of the family. While the British troops occupied Boston, Lord Percy, afterwards the Duke of Northumberland, was quartered in the house of the widow of William Sheaffe. He took a great interest in Roger, and in 1776 sent him to England to be educated. In 1779, Lord Percy gave him a commission in his own regiment, the Fifth; and long continued his favor and assistance. In 1791, Lieutenant Sheaffe was in Detroit, and in 1801, in the attack on Copenhagen under Nelson. In 1813 he had reached the rank of Major-General, and commanded the British troops at the capture of Toronto. The late Gen. Winfield Scott, who was captured at this time, met Gen. Sheaffe, and learned from him many particulars of his life. Gen. Sheaffe said that the war found him stationed in Canada, and being reluctant to serve against his countrymen, he had solicited to be employed elsewhere, but his request had not been granted.

Soon after this he was created a Baronet. He married Margaret, daughter of John Coffin, and cousin of Admiral Sir Isaac Coffin, R. N. She was the mother of four children, who all died before 1835, and in 1834, Sir Roger writes that his nephew and name-sake, the son of his brother William, had also died.

Sir Roger-Hale Sheaffe died in Edinburgh in 1851, when the title became extinct. His heir was his nephew, William Sheaffe.

We find in Burke the following arms recorded as borne by the baronet, and we presume granted to him : " Azure, three garbs *or*, between two barrulets argent ; in chief two lion's heads erased erminois, in base a mullet of the third. *Crest*, issuant out of a mural crown argent, a cubit arm vested gules cuffed vert, the hand grasping a sword in bend sinister proper pommel and hilt *or*, between a branch of laurel and another of oak, also proper."

We feel convinced that Sir Roger could trace no relationship with the Sheaffes of Portsmouth, who had so long used a coat-of-arms, or he would have used it on his promotion to a dignity where coat-armor was indispensable.

[NOTE. We may add that Edward[3] Sheaffe, cousin of William[3] S., the father of the baronet, was for several years a Representative from Charlestown, and was at the time of his death, 26th May, 1771, Commissary General.]

W. H. W.

HERALDIC NOTES AND QUERIES.

(Continued from p. 48.)

LIX.

HOLYOKE FAMILY.—In our second volume, p. 180, we gave the arms of the Holyoke family, and mentioned the fact that one of the name, Dr. Edward Augustus Holyoke, lived to be more than one hundred years old. Inasmuch as great interest is attached in England to the subject of centennarianism, some persons indeed holding that no well authenticated example has been produced, we have obtained from the Town Clerk of Marblehead, Mass., the record of President Holyoke's family. It is as follows:—

June 22, 1718. Elizabeth Holyoke, of Edward and Elizabeth Holyoke.

May 31, 1719.   Elizabeth Holyoke, of Edward and Elizabeth Holyoke.

Sept. 22, 1726. Margaret Holyoke, of Edward and Margaret Holyoke.

Aug. 1, 1728. EDWARD A. Holyoke, of Edward and Margaret Holyoke.

Aug. 30, 1730. Mary Holyoke, of Edward and Margaret Holyoke.

Aug. 25, 1732. Elizabeth Holyoke, of Edward and Margaret Holyoke.

Feb. 18, 1734. John Holyoke, of Edward and Margaret Holyoke.

Rev. Edward Holyoke, aged 80 years, died at M., June 1, 1769. His first wife was Elizabeth Brown; his second was Margaret, dau. of Col. John Appleton, and his third was the widow of Major Epes. It will be seen that he had children by his first two wives, and from the close order in which the births occur, there is no room for another and younger Edward to be inserted.

LX.

HEYFORD ARMS.—The arms engraved on page 30 of this volume bear a resemblance to those of Heyford, Argent, a chevron sable between three bucks springing Gules, attired Or. The mother of John Farrer, in connection with whose estate the seal was used, is stated to have been daughter of George Hayward of Concord. The arms of Hayward are quite different, but the similarity of sound suggests a query, whether the names and arms were not sometimes confused, and whether the Haywards of Concord may not have been Heyfords. We are not as yet able to go farther than this. W. S. A.

LXI.

TRECOTHICK ARMS.—We find recorded in Burke the arms of " TRECOTHICK, (Lord Mayor of London, 1770) Or, a chevron between three round buckles, sable." These were the arms of BARLOW TRECOTHICK, a distinguished citizen of London, who has sometimes been claimed as an American by birth. We are informed that this is a mistake, and that he was born in London ; yet his mother lived here for a time, and his nearest relatives were of this town.

We find in our Suffolk Registry that Mark Trecothick, mariner of Boston, in his will of 2 Aug., 1745, mentions his wife Sarah, his mother, widow Hannah T., his brother Edward T., and sister Hannah Trecothick. These were the brothers and sister of Barlow T. Their mother, Hannah Trecothick, was widow doubtless of Mark Trecothick, who died in 1734.

Barlow Trecothick was presumed to be friendly to the Colony, as in 1769, copies of the Appeal of the Town of Boston were ordered to be sent to him, as well as to Isaac Barré, Gov. Pownall, Franklin, William Bollan, and Denys De Berdt. He died 2 June, 1775, and his property passed to his nephew James Ivers, who was born in Boston, and who died in London in Sept., 1843, aged nearly ninety years. He assumed the name of James Trecothick, and we presume it was his son Barlow T. who m. Oct. 14, 1814, Eliza, dau. of Rev. Dr. Strachey, Archdeacon of Suffolk.

Other relatives remain in Boston. Hannah, sister of Barlow Trecothick of London, married James Ivers and had numerous descendants. We are indebted to correspondents for the following sketch of the family :—

1.   William[1] Ivers of Boston, b. March 6, 1690, m. 23 April, 1724, Jane Barber, and had—

> William,[2] b. Feb., 1726 ; m. —— Flagg.

(2)   James,[2] b. April 28, 1727 ; m. Hannah Trecothick.
>   John,[2] b. Nov. 7, 1728 ; d. young.

(3)   Thomas,[2] b. Jan. 26, 1729 ; m. 1, Jane Jones ; 2, Mary Cutler.
>   Charles,[2] b. April 20, 1732 ; d. 1749.

He died 22 May, 1745, and his widow d. 25 March, 1789, æ. 89.

2.   James[2] Ivers m. 23 Sept., 1755, Hannah, dau. of Mark Trecothick, and had—

(4)   James,[3] b. ——— ; name changed to James Trecothick.

(5)   Hannah,[3] b. ——— ; m. Jonathan L. Austin.

(6)   Jane,[3] b. ——— ; m. Benjamin Austin.

Barlow,[3] b. ———; d. young.

He d. 1815; his wife (b. 1729) d. 1807.

3. Thomas[2] Ivers m. Jane Jones, and had—

William,[3] b. ———.

Thomas,[3] b. ———.

Elizabeth,[3] b. ———; m. William Cleland of Greenwich, Eng.

Anna,[3] b. ———; m. Oliver Brewster.

5. Jonathan Loring Austin* m. Hannah[3] Ivers, 4 April, 1782, and had—

James Trecothick,[4] b. ———; m. Catherine, dau. of Elbridge Gerry.

Loring,[4] b. ———; m. Sarah Orne.

Hannah,[4] b. ———

6. Benjamin Austin, Jr., m. July 26, 1785, Jane[3] Ivers, and had—

Benjamin,[4] b. Aug. 27, 1786; d. 8 Dec., 1792.

Charles,[4] b. Feb. 6, 1788; shot in State Street, 4 Aug., 1806.

(7) Eliza,[4] b. Nov. 21, 1789; m. Charles Dawes Coolidge.

Jane,[4] b. June 2, 1791; d. Jan. 8, 1792.

(8) Benjamin,[4] b. April 9, 1793; m. Anna B. Cleland.

Hannah-Trecothick,[4] b. June 26, 1795.

He d. May 4, 1820, aged 68.

7. Charles Dawes Coolidge m. Eliza[4] Austin and had—

Jane Eliza,[5] m. Dummer Rogers Chapman, and had Jane Eliza and Emily D., still surviving.

---

* These were the sons of Benjamin Austin of Boston, by his wife Elizabeth Waldo. Their sister Rebecca was the wife of John Kneeland.

Charles Austin,[5] m. Anna Rice, and d. in 1848,
leaving three children.

James-Ivers-Trecothick,[5] m. Mary R. C. Rogers,
and has three children.

Hannah-Trecothick-Austin,[5] m. Reuben J. Todd.

8. Benjamin[4] Austin, m. Anna Brewster, dau. of Wm.
Cleland, and had—

William C.,[5] b. 18 Sept., 1822; d. 15 June, 1823.

Anna J.,[5] b. 25 Dec., 1823; d. 6 Oct., 1825.

Benjamin,[5] b. 26 Aug., 1825; m. Harriet E. Pen-
nock, and left one son, William C. Austin, b. 1851.

Jane-Ivers,[5] b. 1828; d. 1829.

Hannah-Elizabeth.[5]

Mary-Louisa,[5] m. 1, William R. Barton; 2, Daniel
C. Hood, and has issue.

Frederick-Henry.[5]

LXII.

THE ROYAL GOVERNORS OF NEW YORK.—Inasmuch
as Dr. O'Callaghan has published a sheet of the seals of
nine of the Colonial Governors of New York, we propose
to give a list of the English officers, before noting the arms
copied by him. These were, including the acting Governors, and not noting re-appointments :

1664. Richard Nicholls.

1667. Col. Francis Lovelace.

1674. Sir Edmund Andros.

1682. Anthony Brockholst.

1688. Col. Thomas Dongan.

1688. Francis Nicholson.

1689. Jacob Leister.

1689. Col. Henry Sloughter.

1691. Maj. Rich. Ingoldsby.

1692. Col. Benj. Fletcher. 1.

1698. Richard Coote, E. of
Bellomont.

1701. John Nanfan.

1702. Edward Hyde, Vis't
Cornbury.

1708. John, Lord Lovelace.

1710. Gerard Beeckman.

1710. Robert Huuter. 2.

1719. Peter Schuyler.

1720. William Burnet.

1728. John Montgomerie.

1731. Rip Van Dam.

1732. William Crosby.

1736. George Clarke.

1743. Admiral Geo. Clinton.

1753. Sir Danvers Osborn, Bart.

1753. James De Lancey. 3.

1755. Sir Cha's Hardy, Knt.

1759. Cadwallader Colden. 4.

1761. Gen. Rbt. Monckton. 5.

1765. Sir Hen'y Moore, Bt. 6.

1770. John Murray, Earl of Dunmore. 7.

1771. William Tryon. 8.

1780. James Robertson.

1783. Andrew Elliot.

The last two being military governors only.— (Hough's N. Y. Civil List, Albany, 1855.)

1777. Geo. Clinton, State. 9.

Of these thirty-four Governors, there were a number whose arms are well known. We have numbered those published by Dr. O'Callaghan, and will proceed to describe them:

1. Col. Benjamin Fletcher used Quarterly, 1st and 4th, Sable, a cross flory between four escallops argent; 2nd and 3rd, a chevron between three crosses (?) Impaling a chevron between three martlets.

2. Robert Hunter used Sable a bugle horn stringed argent. Crest, a greyhound's head erased.

3. James De Lancey.—The arms given in our second volume, p. 191, as the ancient arms of the family.

4. Cadwallader Colden, arms as in this volume, p. 45.

5. Gen. Rob't Monckton, Gules, on a chevron *or* between three martlets argent as many mullets of the third.

6. Sir Henry Moore, Bart., Ermine, three greyhounds courant gules. Crest, a moor-cock, sable.

7. John Murray, Earl of Dunmore, Quarterly, 1st and 4th, azure three mullets argent within a double

tressure flory-counter-flory *or*. 2nd and 3rd, a quartered coat of—Or a fesse chequy argent and azure—and Paly of six azure and argent. On an escutcheon of pretence, the arms of the Isle of Man. Coronet, supporters and motto, but no crests.

8. William Tryon, Azure a fesse embattled *or*, between six estoilles in orle, argent. On an escutcheon of pretence, Argent two bars gules, in chief three annulets. Crest a bear's head erased argent powdered with estoilles sable.

9. George Clinton, the State Governor, bore Argent six cross crosslets fitcheé three, two, and one, sable, on a chief azure two martlets *or* pierced sable, a crescent for difference. He was the son of Charles C. of Ulster county, N. Y., who was born in co. Longford, Ireland, in 1690. Charles was son of James and Elizabeth (Smith) Clinton, and grandson of William C., who being an adherent of Charles I., took refuge in Ireland. This Gov. George was named after Admiral George Clinton, who was Gov. in 1743, and who was a friend of the father, Charles C. Admiral George C. was son of the Earl of Lincoln, and father of the English General Sir Henry Clinton. It is worth noticing that the New York family use the arms of the Earls of Lincoln, with only the mark of cadency.

We may add that others of the Governors had arms—as Sir Edmund Andros, the Earl of Bellomont, Lord Cornbury, Lord Lovelace, Sir Danvers Osborn, and undoubtedly Sir Charles Hardy. John Nanfan was a relative of Lady Bellomont's, who inherited arms, and Burnet and Montgomerie are we believe well known.

THE
HERALDIC JOURNAL;

RECORDING THE ARMORIAL BEARINGS AND GENEALOGIES OF AMERICAN FAMILIES.

NO. XXIII. JULY, 1868.

THE GARDINER FAMILY.

THE family of Gardiner is one of those which have a prescriptive right to coat-armor, by use from the early Colonial times. We find repeated instances of members of the New England family using the arms of GARDINER, of Wigan, co. Lanc., and of London, viz.: On a chevron gules between three griffin's heads erased, two lions counter-passant of the field. Crest, a Saracen's head, couped at the shoulders, proper; on the head a cap *or* wreathed gules and azure.

Joseph[1] Gardiner, one of the first settlers of Narraganset, was the American ancestor of the family. His son was

Benoni[2] Gardiner, who married ———— and had a son,

William[3] Gardiner, b. 1671, who married Abigail Remington. He was a man of handsome property and good position. At his death, in 1732, he left four sons and three daughters, viz.: John,[4] William,[4] Thomas,[4] Sylvester,[4] Abigail,[4] (who m. 1st, Caleb Hazard, and 2d, Gov. William Robinson,) Hannah,[4] (wife of Rev. James McSparran, D. D.), and Lydia,[4] who married Josiah Arnold.

Of these children we propose to notice chiefly the fourth son.

Sylvester[4] Gardiner was born, says Updike, "at the family mansion in South Kingston, in 1717." His father determined to educate him as a physician and surgeon, and to that end sent him abroad, where he studied in England and France during eight years, under the most distinguished teachers. Returning to Boston he became at once famous as a physician and surgeon, and also as a lecturer on the theory and practice of medicine.

Besides this he engaged largely in mercantile ventures, and acquired, for those times, what was called an "immense estate." His real property alone, confiscated during the Revolution, amounted to one hundred thousand acres of land, chiefly in Maine, on which he had already built one Episcopal church, seventeen dwelling houses, with their out-buildings, besides mills, smithies, &c., &c. His house in Boston was the resort of all the most noted people of the time, for he mentions as his frequent visitors, Governor Hutchinson, Dr. Cooper, Sir William Pepperell, John Hancock, Earl Percy, Major Pitcairn, Samuel Adams, Admiral Graves, Mr., afterwards Colonel Hitchburn of the Continental Army, General Gage, Captain Philip Dumaresq, his son-in-law, (Aid de Camp to Lord Dunmore), Mr. John Singleton Copley, and another son-in-law, Colonel Arthur Browne.

He was indefatigable in his endeavors to promote the importance of the Province of Maine, and had succeeded in founding a colony there, when the Revolution broke out. Being a determined Loyalist he left Boston with the English troops. After the peace he returned to Newport,

R. I., where he died 1786. He was thrice married; first to Anna Gibbons, by whom he had eight children, viz.:

    I. William,[5] bapt. Jan. 27, 1736, died unm.

    II. John,[5] bapt. Dec. 11, 1737.

    III. James,[5] bapt. Sept. 9, 1739, died young.

    IV. Annie,[5] bapt. May 3, 1741, m. Colonel, the Right Honorable Arthur Browne, second son of the Earl of Altamont.

    V. Hannah,[5] bapt. July 27, 1743, m. Robert Hallowell, and had, among other children, a son who took the name of Robert Hallowell[6] Gardiner, and who married Emma I. Tudor, from whom descend the Gardiners of Gardiner, Maine.

    VI. Rebecca,[5] bapt. April 17, 1745, m. Dec. 15, 1762, Philip Dumaresq, grandson of Elias Dumaresq, Seigneur des Augres in the Island of Jersey.

    VII. Thomas,[5] bapt. April 18, 1747, died young.

    VIII. Abigail,[5] bapt. August 1, 1750, m. Oliver Whipple.

The second wife of Dr. Gardiner was Abigail Epps of Virginia. The third wife was Catherine Goldthwait, who survived him, and afterwards m. Mr. William Powell.

John[5] Gardiner, second son of Dr. Sylvester Gardiner, was educated as a lawyer. He was sent to London in 1748, and studied his profession in the Inner Temple, under Sir Charles Pratt, better known as Lord Chancellor Camden, and afterwards practised extensively in the courts at Westminster. An ardent Republican, he was the friend of Churchill the poet, and of John Wilkes; and by a brilliant defence of the latter, in 1763, attracted the attention of Lord Mansfield, before whom the case was tried. There is in the possession of his grandson, William Howard Gardiner, a piece of plate bearing his coat-of-arms, which was presented to him by his friends, in admiration of the courage and eloquence which he displayed in this celebrated trial. He was appointed Attorney General of the British West Indian Islands, in 1768, and he remained in this position for many years.

During the American Revolution, owing to his strong Whig principles, his position at St. Christophers became so distasteful to him that he resigned and returned to Boston in 1783, where he endeavored, with some success, to recover a portion of his father's confiscated estates. In a letter to Dr. Gardiner, on this subject, he says, "I had an interview yesterday with your friend Hancock . . . . . Samuel Adams, Dr. Cooper, &c. received me with the greatest cordiality, and General Washington, in consequence of the letters of the French ministry, overwhelmed me with civilities during the four days I stayed with him." On this visit to General Washington, Mr. Gardiner was accompanied by his son, afterwards the Rev. John-Sylvester-John Gardiner, at that time about eighteen years of age.

In religion Mr. Gardiner was a Unitarian, and was the principal mover in transforming the King's Chapel in Boston into a Unitarian Society. He also succeeded in abolishing the laws of primogeniture in Massachusetts, and commenced an attack which finally ended in ousting special pleading from the courts of this Commonwealth.

He had, says Updike, an astonishing memory, was an admirable *belles lettres* scholar, learned in his profession, and particularly distinguished for his wit and eloquence.

He married in Wales, Margaret Harries, a lady of excellent family. He was lost at sea, in 1793, on a voyage from Maine, whence he was coming as a representative to the General Court of Massachusetts. His children were:

    I. Rev. John-Sylvester-John[6] Gardiner, D. D.

    II. William,[6] who married Sarah Allen, and had Margaret,[7] m. Thomas Nelson; George,[7] m. Caroline Tallman; and Marianne,[7] m. Isaac Elder, who left one daughter, Marianne-Osgood[8] Elder.

    III. Anne,[6] married James M. Lithgow.

The Rev. John-Sylvester-John[6] Gardiner was born in 1765, was sent to England with his brother William,[6] and placed under the instruction of the celebrated Dr. Parr, who superintended his education until his eighteenth year. He was Rector of Trinity Church, Boston, from 1805 until the time of his death, in 1830. He was conspicuous as a divine, for his virtues and eloquence; as a classical scholar, preëminent. He wrote the English language with great purity and elegance, "and was not without a happy talent for poetry." He married Mary, daughter of Colonel William Howard of Hallowell, and had four children, viz.:

    I. William-Howard.[7]

    II. Charles,[7] d. young.

    III. Louisa,[7] m. John Perkins Cushing of Belmont, Mass.

    IV. Elizabeth,[7] d. unmarried.

William-Howard[7] Gardiner graduated first in his class at Cambridge, 1816, m. Caroline, daughter of Thomas Handasyde Perkins, and has been for many years one of the most prominent members of the Suffolk bar. He has had six children, viz.:

I. William-Prescott.[8]

II. Edward[8] m. Sophia Harrison Mifflin of Philadelphia, who has William Howard,[9] Eugenia,[9]
Edward G.,[9] Elizabeth,[9] and Maud.[9]

III. Mary-Cary[8] m. William Nye Davis.

IV. John-Sylvester.[8]

V. Caroline-Louisa.[8]

VI. Charles-Perkins[8] m. Emma, daughter of William
T. Glidden, has one daughter, Mary-Caroline[9]
Gardiner.

A. T. P.

THE RUSSELL FAMILY.

In our present volume, pp. 32, 33, we gave an account
of Richard Russell of Charlestown, and an engraving of
the arms used by his son, Judge James Russell, A. D. 1700.
Although we followed the statements of BURKE, we find
that we were led into error in accepting this seal as proof.
By the kindness of the representatives of the family, we
have been allowed to examine the true pedigree, as ascertained by H. G. Somerby, Esq., and we now correct and
perfect our account.

Richard Russell of Charlestown, in his will, mentions
his sisters, Mrs. Elizabeth Corbett and Mrs. Sarah Russell, both living at Bristol.* On the records at Bristol it
appears that Richard, the son of Paul Russell of the City

* He mentions also his sister-in-law, Mrs. Mary Newall. The Charles-
town Records mention the death, 26 September, 1684, aged 77, of Mrs.
Mary, daughter of William Pitt, Sheriff of the City of Bristol, widow of
Andrew Newell. Probably Russell's first wife was another daughter of
William Pitt.

of Hereford, was bound apprentice to Robert Elliott, 4 Oct. 1628. Following this clue Mr. Somerby was enabled to trace the family for several generations previous to this Paul.

It is sufficient to say of the early history of this family, that it derives its name from Rozel in Normandy, and that this branch is traced to Robert[1] de Russell of Kingston Russell, co. Dorset, who had Odo[2] (ancestor of the Duke of Bedford) and seven other sons.

Thomas[2] de Russell, fourth son of Robert,[1] held lands at Strensham, co. Worcester, about A. D. 1150–1180, and left a son Thomas,[3] who was father of Robert.[4] James[5] Russell, son of the last named, was lord of Strensham, and presented to the living in 1300. His son Nicholas[6] Russell married Alice, daughter of John Gryndon, and had sons Robert,[7] John[7] and Thomas[7]; of whom Robert[7] Russell, living in 1361, married Catherine, daughter of Sir John Vampage. Their son

Sir John[8] Russell was Master of the Horse to King Richard II., and died in 1405, leaving, by wife Agnes Planches, sons William,[9] and John[9] (Sergeant at Law) and two daughters.

William[9] Russell married Joan, daughter and co-heir of Thomas Hodington of Somery, and had Robert[10] Russell, who by wife Elizabeth, daughter of John Throgmorton, had sons Robert,[11] John[11] and Nicholas.[11]

Robert[11] Russell of Strensham m. Joan, daughter of Sir Kynard Delabere, Knt., and had, besides two daughters, sons Robert,[12] Kynard,[12] and John,[12] who died at Rhodes.

Robert[12] Russell of Strensham, oldest son, was the ancestor of Sir William Russell, created Baronet in 1627.

The title became extinct on the death of the last heir, Sir Francis Russell, in 1705. (See Burke's Extinct Baronetcies, p. 458, 9.)

Kynard[12] Russell, second son as above, married Elizabeth, daughter and heir of Humphrey Connesby, lord of Mordington, Woolhone and Townhope, and had three sons, Sir Anthony,[13] Knight of Rhodes; William,[13] and John,[13] of Witley, whose son John[14] was incumbent of Strensham in 1574.

William[13] Russell, second son of Kynard,[12] was of Herefordshire, and married Elizabeth, daughter and co-heir of John Blaney of Kinsham, co. Hereford. Their children were Richard,[14] who settled in Gloucestershire, James,[14] John,[14] Thomas,[14] William[14] and Elizabeth.[14] Of these

James[14] Russell was Mayor of the City of Hereford, and died in 1612, in which year his will was proved. His children were Paul,[15] Edward,[15] (vicar of Stoke-Bliss, co. Worcester, 1619) and Henry.[15]

Paul[15] Russell, of the City of Hereford, by wife Katherine, had James,[16] who was admitted at Gray's Inn in 1639, Richard,[16] the emigrant, and one or more daughters.

AMERICAN FAMILIES.

James[2] Russell* (son of Richard[1] the emigrant) was married four times. His second wife was Mary, daughter of Capt. Eliezur Holyoke of Springfield, whom he married 5 Feb., 1677, and by whom he had Eliezur, b. Jan., 1678: both the mother and child died soon after. His third wife (married Jan. 3, 1679) was Mary Wolcott, who died 5 Aug., 1683, leaving an only daughter; his fourth wife

---

* We correct Savage's account from the Pedigree before mentioned. ED.

(married 28 Aug., 1684) was Abigail (Curwin) Hathorne. She died 4 May, 1709, and was the mother of Daniel[3] Russell.

The surviving issue of James[2] Russell, therefore, were:—

By wife Mabel Haynes,

    i. Mabel,[3] b. 21 Jan., 1670, m. David Jenner.

    ii. Maud,[3] bapt. 25 Jan., 1676, m. Daniel Lawrence, d. *s. p.*

By wife Mary Wolcott,

    iii. Mary,[3] b. 6 Oct., 1680, m. Capt. J. Miller.

By wife Abigail Curwin,

    iv. Daniel,[3] b. 30 Nov., 1685.

Daniel[3] Russell of Charlestown m. 1st, Jan. 9, 1711, Rebecca, only daughter of Hon. Charles Chambers, and had issue, as recorded in our previous article, p. 33. By this wife he had also a son Richard,[4] born 21 Feb., 1723, d. May, 1761, who married Mary, daughter of Samuel Cary, and had several children: among the grandchildren were James,[6] and Charles[6] Russell of Boston. Daniel[3] Russell, after the death of his first wife, 26 March, 1729, married widow Faith Savage, who died 6 June, 1775, aged 84, and by whom he had no issue.

James[4] Russell (son of Daniel[3]) had by wife Katherine Graves,*

    i. Charles,[5] b. 7 Jan., 1739, m. Elizabeth Vassall, and d. at Antigua, 27 May, 1780, leaving four daughters.

    ii. Thomas,[5] b. 18 April, 1740; by 1st wife, Elizabeth Henley, he had four sons, who all d. unm., and one daughter, Elizabeth,[6] m. John L. Sullivan;

---

* We omit some branches, which are not represented now.

by 2d wife, Sarah Sever, he had Sarah,[6] m.
Richard Sullivan. By 3d wife, Elizabeth
Watson, no issue.

III. Katherine,[5] b. 9 Sept., 1741, m. Samuel Henley.

IV. Rebecca,[5] b. 27 Feb., 1747, m. 1st, James Tyng ;
2d, John Lowell.

V. James,[5] b. 22 Feb., 1749; vide ante, p. 33.

VI. Sarah,[5] b. Dec., 1750, d. unm., Oct., 1819, leaving
property to her grand nephew, James R. Dutton,
on condition that he took the name of Russell.

VII. Margaret,[5] b. Dec., 1757, m. Hon. John Codman,
and had sons, John,[6] b. 3 Aug., 1782, and
Charles R.,[6] b. 19 Dec., 1784.

The name of Russell was thus again revived by the
change made by James Russell Dutton in 1819, and we
will therefore trace this branch of the family.

Judge John Lowell, (b. 17 June, 1743, d. 6 May, 1802)
son of Rev. John L. of Newburyport, was thrice married.
By his first wife, Sarah Higginson, he had John Lowell,
father of John Amory Lowell. By his second wife, Susan,
daughter of Francis Cabot, he had Francis-Cabot Lowell,
founder of the City of Lowell, whose sons were John,
Francis C., and Edward J. By his third wife, Rebecca
Russell (widow of James Tyng) he had

I. Rebecca-Russell, m. Samuel P. Gardiner.

II. Charles, the clergyman, who had four sons.

III. Elizabeth-Cutts, m. Warren Dutton, 3 June, 1806.

Warren Dutton had sons, John, James Russell, and
Francis-Lowell, of whom (the name being changed as
before mentioned)

James Dutton Russell married Sarah Ellen, daughter of
William Hooper, and died 10 June, 1861, leaving two
daughters,

I. Ellen-Hooper Russell, m. George M. Barnard, Jr.

II. Elizabeth-Lowell-Dutton Russell, m. Henry R.
Dalton.

He had also two sons, who have since died, so that the
name is again extinct.

Notes on the Russell Pedigree.

1. The arms of the Russells of Strensham were argent,
a chevron between three cross-crosslets fitchée, sable.
(Burke does not mention the fact that the crosslets were
fitchée, but this probably arose from some error on his
part.) The seal which we have engraved, on p. 32, has
these arms within a bordure bezantée.

It seems, however, that in 1820, James[5] Russell of Clifton,
co. Gloucester, Eng., father of Gen. Lechmere Russell,
applied for a confirmation of arms on the ground of traditionary descent from the Russells of Worcestershire and
the alleged use of a seal bearing these arms* on the will of
the emigrant Richard Russell. In consequence of this
application arms were then granted to the said James
Russell, and to James and Charles Russell of Boston,
grandsons of his uncle Richard Russell, as follows—
Argent, on a chevron between three cross-crosslets sable,
an eagle's head erased *or*, a bordure engrailed gules
charged with eight plates. Crest, a demi-lion rampant
argent, charged on the shoulder with a saltire couped

---

* "A chevron between three cross-crosslets fitchée, a bordure engrailed
bezantée."

azure, between the paws a cross-crosslet fitchée erect, sable. These were in effect the same arms, with the slight difference of an eagle's head erased on the chevron.

It seems however that the seal on the will of Richard Russell the emigrant was only a merchant's mark, and not armorial. The seal which we have before given is found on the will of his son Daniel Russell in 1678, and was afterwards used by another son, Judge James Russell. As the impalement is said to be the Neville arms, and as Richard Russell's second wife, the widow Mary Chester, was of that family, we presume Richard had the seal engraved. Certainly his sons would have no reason to have a seal made impaling their step-mother's arms. Thus the representation was true in spirit that Richard had a seal bearing such arms, though not using it on his will.

Of course all the American families entitled to impale or quarter the Russell arms will use the original coat inherited, and not the new one granted in 1820. The heirs of Charles and James of Boston, however, could use both.

2. Chambers Russell, who died s. p., in 1766, mentions in his will some interesting relics. To his niece, Mary Russell Atkins, he left all his plate marked with the arms or crest of the Dudley family. To John Winthrop the portrait of his late wife's father, Francis Wainwright. The portrait of his grandmother was given to his brother James Russell; and to his friend John Cotton the portrait of his wife's grandmother Addington.

Chambers Russell m. Mary, daughter of Francis Wainwright, by his wife Mary, daughter of Gov. Joseph

Dudley. Mary Dudley married, secondly, Joseph Atkins, and had a son Dudley Atkins, half-brother to Mrs. Russell. The niece was the daughter of this Dudley Atkins; she married George Searle. Her sister, Catherine Atkins, married Samuel Elliot of Boston, and her brother, Dudley Atkins, added the name of Tyng, and was father of Rev. Stephen H. Tyng, D. D. (Adlard's Sutton-Dudleys, p. 118.)

SUFFOLK WILLS.

(Continued from Vol. III., p. 94.) *

60.

The Thatcher arms, as used on the will of Thomas Thatcher of Boston, are given by us on p. 75 of the present volume.

61.

The engraving of the Sheaffe arms given on p. 81 of the present volume is copied from a seal which occurs on several wills in the Suffolk office, being those to which Jacob Sheaffe was a witness.

62.

We here engrave No. 37 again, being the seal on John Nash's will of 1712, as the former drawing was imperfect. We are still unable to assign the name.

---

* The Parsons seal, No. 54 (Vol. III., p. 91), seems to have a mullet for difference on the chief point.

63.

This seal is on the will of Katherine Penn, widow of James Penn, dated 25th October, 1679. The witnesses are Humphrey Davis and John Fayerweather. In it she mentions only her kinsmen James Allen and his sons James, John and Jeremiah Allen.

There seems no reason to doubt that these arms were those of Allen or Alleyne, as the same are given by Burke. The Rev. James Allen mentioned in the will was the son of a minister in Hampshire, and a fellow of New College, Oxford. He was thrice married, as Savage records, and by his second wife, Elizabeth, daughter of Jeremy Houchin, had sons James, John and Jeremiah. The latter, Jeremiah Allen, was Treasurer of the Province in 1715.

I presume that Henry Alline of Boston, notary public in 1782, was of this family. At all events, he used the same arms, as is shown by a copy of his seal furnished me by J. Hammond Trumbull, Esq.

The same arms are borne by the present baronet, Sir Reynold Abel Alleyne, whose ancestor, John Gay Alleyne of Barbadoes, received the title in 1769. The family had been settled in that island for four generations, and was before that resident at Grantham in Lincolnshire.

64.

This seal is on the will of Thomas White of Weymouth, one of the early settlers, but the arms do not belong to any family of the name. The witnesses are William Chase and Thomas Dun, the latter using a mark; but here also we are at fault for an owner of the seal. Similar arms, the field guttée, and two chevrons, were borne by the Moores and St. Maures; Ermine, two chevrons, by the Bagots, Sumners, Houghtons, and perhaps others.

65.

From the will of Benjamin Allen of Boston, merchant, 9 May, 1679. He mentions brothers Daniel Allen and Eleazer Allen, and his friend, Mrs. Mary Scottow. Savage does not seem to record this family, though he says that Eleazer Allen embarked 27 May, 1679, in the Prudence and Mary, to come to Boston, of whom nothing farther is known. The witnesses were Sarah Pepper and Nathaniel Barnes; but the arms are not yet identified.

66.

Robert Mitchell of Dartmouth, Eng., mariner, uses this seal on his power of attorney in 1702 to his friend Abigail Wilkinson of Malden in New England. The witnesses are James Read, Jonathan Allen and Edward Weaver, but the arms are found in none of these names.

67.

We give an enlarged representation of the seal on the will of John Green of Stow, 1688, as it is a very elaborate one. It also occurs on the will of Penelope Turner, 1678, to which Bartholomew Green was a witness. The arms are mentioned by Burke as belonging to the Greenes

of Hertfordshire, Nottinghamshire, and Awkley Hall, co. York.

The first of this branch here was John[1] Greene of Charlestown, 1632, who came with his wife Perseverance, daughter of Rev. Francis Johnson of Amsterdam, and three children, John,[2] Jacob[2] and Abigail.[2] He married 2d, Joanna, widow of John Shatswell, and died 22 April, 1658, aged 65. His son John[2] had been servant of William Willoughby of Portsmouth, Eng., and seems to have died *s. p.;* but Jacob[2] was of Charlestown, and had sons Jacob,[3] John,[3] Bartholomew[3] and Joseph.[3] Two of these grandsons of the settler were the persons who used the above seal. Jacob[3] had a son Bartholomew.[4]

There seems to be some reason for believing that John[1] Green was related to other settlers of the name. The name of Bartholomew occurs in two generations of his descendants, and at Cambridge, Mass., one of the settlers in 1633 was Bartholomew Green, father of the famous printer, Samuel Green. If these two colonists were near relatives, perhaps also was Percival Green of Cambridge, 1635, who brought over his wife Ellen and two servants. We are told that the name Percival is quite unusual, and may be a clue to identify the family.   A. T. P.

[NOTE. As we shall here conclude our examination of the Suffolk Probate Office, it is proper to state that we have by no means exhausted the field there opened to the antiquary. Owing to the miserable accommodations afforded to the custodian of these valuable papers, it has been impossible to make a thorough examination of the files of original papers. We have had every facility extended to us by the Register and his clerks, but the papers are crammed into pigeon-holes without arrangement or system, and we have consequently been obliged to take whatever was accessible. The series of contributions to this Journal from our associate, Mr. Perkins, has sufficiently shown that the Suffolk wills prior to 1750 contain numerous interesting specimens of armorial seals. It is to be added that though many seals which might be presumed to be there were not found, and their non-existence was demonstrated, still we have no reason to doubt that the future examiner will find much of interest which has escaped us.

It will hereafter be hardly believed that the wealthy county of Suffolk for many years neglected to provide decent apartments in which to preserve the records of all the property owned within its borders. At present the space given to the papers recorded prior to 1750 would not suffice to properly accommodate one half of the number, and each year renders the condition of the office worse.

It is with pleasure that we add that there is some prospect of a reform in the existing establishment. It is understood that the City Government has under consideration the matter of more suitable apartments, and necessarily of a new arrangement of the existing records. The necessity of prompt action will be so evident to every investigator that any examination will enforce reform. We hope, therefore, that our successors will be soon able to complete the task which we have commenced, and to furnish genealogists with a correct and perfect list of all our early armorial seals.—ED.]

REVIEW.

GENEALOGY OF THE SPOTSWOOD FAMILY IN SCOT-
LAND AND VIRGINIA. By Charles Campbell. Albany:
Joel Munsell, 1868. 8vo., pp. 44.

In our third volume (p. 128), in noticing the old families of Virginia, we briefly mentioned the Spotswoods,
descended from the royal Governor of the colony; but at
that time we had only Bishop Meade's imperfect notes
as a guide. The book above cited gives a much larger
account of the family, though it is unfortunately meagre
in genealogical dates.

Alexander Spotswood, governor of Virginia from 1710
to 1723, was born at Tangier in 1676. His father was
Robert S., physician, who by wife Catherine Elliott, had
this only son; and was the brother of Sir Alexander
Spottiswood. The family was one of distinction in Scotland, being traced to Robert de Spottiswoode, of that ilk,
living in the reign of Alexander III. The line is traced
to John Spottiswoode, born in 1565, Archbishop of St.
Andrews, Lord High Chancellor, who died in 1639, having
had by his wife Rachel Lindsay two sons, John and Robert. The male line of John terminated in 1650, when the
representation devolved on the junior branch. Sir Robert
Spottiswoode, second son, born in 1596, was one of the
Privy Council, and in 1636 Secretary for Scotland to
Charles I. He married Bethiah Morrison and had three
sons, the youngest being Dr. James S., father of the
governor.

Alexander Spotswood "was bred in the army from his
childhood." He served with distinction under the Duke

of Marlborough, and was wounded at the battle of Blenheim in 1704.

He was an energetic and capable governor of the colony, doing much to aid in developing the extent and value of its territory. He married Ann Butler and had two sons, John[2] and Robert,[2] and two daughters, Anne Catherine,[2] who married Bernard Moore, and Dorothea,[2] who married Capt. Nathaniel West Dandridge, R. N. Gov. Alexander Spotswood died 7 June, 1740, and as his youngest son Robert died unm. in 1756 the name has been continued only in the line of the older son, John.

John[2] Spotswood married in 1745 Mary, daughter of Capt. William Dandridge, R. N., by his wife Unity West,* by whom he had

Gen Alexander[3] Spotswood, of the Revolutionary army, who m. Elizabeth, daughter of Gen. William Augustus Washington, and niece of George Washington. He has eight children, three sons and five daughters. Of these, Captain John[4] Spotswood m. Sally Rowsie and had eleven children, of whom several were sons. We presume, therefore, that the name is not extinct in Virginia; and of course there are many descendants in the female lines, many of whom are recorded by Mr. Campbell.

The arms of Spotswood are Argent, a chevron gules, between three oak-trees, eradicated vert. Crest, an eagle displayed gules, looking to the sun in splendor. Supporters, two satyrs proper.

---

* The Dandridges, of whom apparently a brother and sister married into the Spotswood family, were of Worcestershire, Eng. It is said that John Dandridge of the same family was the ancestor of Mrs. Martha Washington. Their arms are Azure, a lion's head erased *or*, between three mascles argent. ♱

TITLED AMERICANS.

I.

Sir Charles Hobby, Knt., was the son of William Hobby of Boston, and was brought up in this country even if not born here. Of him Hutchinson writes, " Sir Charles Hobby (who had been knighted as some said for fortitude and resolution at the time of the earthquake in Jamaica, others for the further consideration of £800 sterling)" was prevailed upon by the enemies of Dudley to go to England in 1705 to solicit the appointment as Governor. " He was recommended to Sir H. Ashurst, who at first gave encouragement of success. Hobby was a gay man, a free liver, and of very different behavior from what one would have expected should have recommended him to the clergy of New England; and yet, such is the force of party prejudice, that it prevails over religion itself, and some of the most pious ministers strongly urged in their letters that he might be appointed their governor instead of Dudley; for which Ashurst himself, after his acquaintance with Hobby, reproves and censures them." (Hist. Mass., II., 153.)

He returned from England in 1710, and had command of one of the Massachusetts regiments at the taking of Port Royal. He was of the Artillery Company 1702, and died in London in 1714. His wife survived him, dying in November, 1716, and the estate was declared insolvent in 1716. He seems to have had no children.

The genealogical record of the family is as follows:

William Hobby of Boston, by wife Ann, had

John,[2] b.   , 1661.

Charles,[2]   , (knighted in 1692, d. *s. p.* 1714.)

William,[2] b. 9 Feb., 1669.

Ann,[2] b. 9 Sept., 1670.

Mercy,[2] b. 4 Oct., 1672.

Judith,[2] b. 8 May, 1674; m. John Colman, 19 July, 1694.

Elizabeth,[2] b. 18 Oct., 1676; m. 1st, Thomas Lillie, 2 June, 1698, and 2d, Oxenbridge Thatcher. (See H. J., IV., 77.)

John[2] Hobby of Boston had, 1st, wife Hannah, who died 26 June, 1690, aged 27. By second wife, Ann, he had

Charles,[3] bapt. 9 April, 1699.

Wensley,[3] " 30 Sept., 1706; H. C. 1723; m. Rachel Cookson, 13 July, 1732.

William,[3] " 17 Aug., 1707; H. C. 1725; minister at Reading.

Edward,[3] " 16 Jan., 1709.

He died 7 Sept., 1711, aged 50, and Mrs. Anne Hobbie (no doubt the widow) married Thomas Archer, 10 April, 1712. An Elizabeth Hobby married James Gooch, 30 Sept., 1715, at Boston; but we cannot trace her paternity.

II.

Sir Benjamin Thompson, Knt. in England and Count of Rumford in Bavaria, was born in Woburn, Mass., 26 March, 1753. The recent history of the town, by the late Rev. Samuel Sewall, contains a very interesting account of him, which we abridge:

Benjamin Thompson was a descendant in the fifth generation from James Thompson of Charlestown, one of the first settlers at Woburn in 1640. The family has always enjoyed a respectable position and numerous branches are to be traced throughout New England. Benjamin was the only son of Benjamin and Ruth (Symonds) Thompson, his father dying 7 Nov., 1754, when the boy was about twenty months old. His mother married in March, 1756, Josiah Peirce, Jr. Benjamin received the usual common school education, but, though soon set to work as a clerk, he managed to pursue one or two favorite branches of study, and acted as schoolmaster for several terms. In 1770 he taught school at Rumford (now Concord), N. H., and there made the acquaintance of Mrs. Sarah Rolfe, widow of Col. Benjamin R., and daughter of Rev. Timothy Walker. This lady he married in 1772, and thus came into the possession of a large property.

When the Revolution commenced, Thompson was accused wrongly by his enemies of traitorous correspondence with the British commander, and notwithstanding his innocence he was fairly driven away by insult and persecution. He was at Boston at the evacuation by Gen. Howe, and was by that officer sent to England with dispatches. This trust recommended him to the Colonial Secretary, Lord George Germaine, and he was offered employment in that department. This he accepted, and within four years rose to be Under Secretary of State.

Towards the end of the war he came to New York, where he commanded a regiment called the King's American Dragoons; but he was in no battle and never actually served against his native country. Returning to England, he was knighted, and, his regiment being disbanded, was put on half pay.

In 1784 he was induced to take employment in the service of the Duke of Bavaria, and becoming the favorite minister of that Prince, he was enabled to introduce many important reforms in the administration of the government. At the death of the Emperor Joseph and before the coronation of his successor Leopold, the Elector of Bavaria became the Vicar of the Empire, and in virtue of his position created Sir Benjamin a Count of the Holy Roman Empire. Thompson selected as his title that of Count Rumford. In 1799 the Elector of Bavaria died, and his successor was not inclined to favor the Count, who accordingly left Munich and finally settled in France. Here he married the widow of Lavoisier, the celebrated chemist, in 1804; and here he devoted himself to philosophical inquiries and studies. He died August 21, 1814, at his villa at Auteuil.

Count Rumford left but one child, Sarah, Countess of Rumford. She was never married, and resided during many years in Europe with her father. She finally returned to Concord, N. H., where she died in 1852, aged seventy years.

THE ATKINSON FAMILY.

The Hon. F. E. Parker of this city has a small volume of old law-reports, which contains the book-plate of William King Atkinson, engraved by Callender. The arms are, Vert, a cross voided between four lions rampant *or*, Crest, a dove with expanded wings. Motto, Nil pacimus non sponte Dei.

The Atkinson family, which has been of some prominence in New England, is descended from Theodore,[1] a felt-maker from Bury, in Lancashire, who joined the Church of Boston, in 1635, and became freeman in 1642. He had sons, John[2] of Newbury, Theodore,[2] Nathaniel,[2] born in 1645, H. C. 1667, Thomas,[2] and daughter Abigail.[2] He died in August, 1701, aged 89.

Theodore[2] Atkinson, second son of the settler, was born 19 April, 1644, and married Elizabeth, daughter of Edward Mitchelson, by whom he had Elizabeth,[3] Theodore,[3] Edward,[3] Abigail.[3] He was killed by the Indians 19 December, 1675, at Narraganset, and his widow married Henry Deering.

The third Theodore[3] was a Councillor of New Hampshire and died in 1719, leaving widow Mary. His son Theodore[4] was born at Newcastle in 1697, H. C. 1718, and settled at Portsmouth, N. H. He was one of the most prominent men of the colony, being Councillor, Judge, Secretary, Collector and Naval Officer. He was also for many years colonel of the first regiment, and being a man of very considerable property, his establishment was one of the handsomest in the province. In 1746 he bought one-fifth of the proprietary rights in New Hampshire from John Tufton Mason; the town of Atkinson received its name from him, and Frances Town and Deering were named in honor of his son's wife.

Theodore[4] Atkinson married Hannah Wentworth, sister of Gov. Benning W., by whom he had an only child, Theodore,[5] born in 1736, H. C. 1757. This fifth Theodore married 13 May, 1762, his cousin Frances Deering Wentworth, daughter of Samuel W., and died 28th Oct.,

1769, leaving no issue ; his widow married on the 11th of the following month Gov. John Wentworth.

Theodore[4] Atkinson died in 1779, and having no issue he left his property by will to "his relation George King of Portsmouth" and his eldest heir male forever on condition that they took the name of Atkinson. Failing this line, to William King, brother of said George, and his heir, on the same terms. The former complied with the terms, and was known as George King Atkinson. He married Susanna Sparhawk, but died *s. p.*, and his brother, William King Atkinson, who married Abigail Pickering, became the heir.

We have not succeeded in tracing the connection of the Kings and Atkinsons, but presume it was not through the Wentworths, as Theodore[4] A. mentions several of his wife's relatives as such. W. S. A.

THE HENSHAW FAMILY.

The Henshaw family in New England has been the subject of an article in the N. E. Historical and Genealogical Register for April, 1868, and as therein a claim to use coat-armor seems to be substantiated, we propose to give a recapitulation of the principal facts :

Joshua and Daniel Henshaw were born in Lancashire, Eng., and were brought to this country when the older brother was less than ten years of age. It is said that they were sent here by parties interested in keeping them out of England, as they were heirs to considerable property; and this tradition is to a certain degree corroborated by documents remaining.

Joshua Henshaw was married in Dorchester in 1670, and in 1688 he went to England with the purpose of claiming certain lands which had belonged to his father and were then in the possession of the heirs of his steward, one Peter Ambrose. On his arrival in England, Mr. Henshaw filed a bill in chancery against Joshua Ambrose, son of Peter, who was then in possession of the land. The bill was dismissed on technical grounds in 1690, but on the necessary proofs being produced, in 1692, the case was restored to the docket. The suit seems to have been dropped at the time of Joshua Henshaw's decease in England, in 1719, but the extracts from the records which we have seen seem to concede the fact of his father's former ownership of certain lands.

In 1701, and for the purposes of this suit, Mr. Henshaw had a brief account of his immediate ancestry prepared by Robert Dale, Richmond Herald, and this pedigree is now remaining at Herald's College, London.

From this we learn that Thomas[1] Henshaw was of Derby, co. Lanc., and died at Toxteth Park, near Liverpool, about 1630. By his wife ——, daughter of —— Kendrick of Kendrick's Cross in the parish of Prescot, co. Lanc., he had

    I. William.[2]

    II. John,[2] went to Ireland and died, leaving a son, deceased before 1701.

    III. —— (a son), d. unm.

    IV. Ellen,[2] m. —— Harrison of Toxteth Park, d. 1699.

William[2] Henshaw of Toxteth Park married Katherine,

daughter and heir of Evan Houghton of Wartre Hall, parish of Childo, co. Lanc., and was killed at the taking of Liverpool in 1644. He had

    I. Joshua,[3] b. 1643.

    II. Daniel,[3] b. 1644, went to New England and had an only child

        Daniel,[4] who d. unm.

Joshua[3] Henshaw of Dorchester m. Elizabeth, daughter of William Sumner (son of William Somner of Burcester, co. Oxford), and had

        William,[4] b. 1670.

        Joshua,[4] b. 1672.

        John,[4] b. 1680.

        Elizabeth,[4] b. 1684.

        Katherine,[4] b. 1687.

Of his descendants we may especially note his grandson Joshua[6] Henshaw, born at Boston, 2 Aug., 1703, son of Joshua[5] and Mary (Webster) Henshaw. He was a Representative and a warm advocate of the revolutionary party in the State, an associate of Otis, Hancock, and Adams, but died 5 Aug., 1777, before his hopes of his country's independence could be realized. His son Andrew[7] Henshaw was clerk of the House of Representatives; and another son, Joshua,[7] was Register of Deeds for Suffolk from 1776 to 1786; both died *s. p.* Sarah[7] Henshaw, the only daughter, married her cousin Joseph[7] Henshaw in 1758, and her husband was associated with his father-in-law in his patriotic duties.

Daniel[6] Henshaw, another son of Joshua[5] and Mary (Webster) Henshaw, b. 3 Dec., 1701, m. Elizabeth Bass, and had a son David[7] Henshaw of Leicester and Boston, who m. Mary Sargent. A daughter Sarah[8] of this last named married her cousin Andrew Henshaw Ward, well known to many of our readers as an accomplished genealogist.

The arms of the family are described as being—Argent, a chevron between three moor-hens proper ; quartering Houghton,—Sable, three bars argent. Crest, a falcon proper, billed *or*, beaked and numbered sable, preying upon the wing of a bird, argent.

The pedigree states that Katherine Houghton (wife of William[2] Henshaw) was the daughter of Evan[3] H. He was the son of Richard[2] Houghton of Wartre Hall and Penketh (who died in Haighton parish near Knowsley), and married Ellen, daughter of —— Parker of Kridgehall, co. Lanc. Richard[2] Houghton married Margaret, daughter of Henry Stanley of Bickerstagh, co. Lanc., in 1585, and was the son of Evan[1] Houghton of Great Carleton, near Poulton, co. Lanc., by his wife ——, daughter and coheir of —— Carleton. This Evan[1] Houghton died at Knowsley, 20 Jan., 1608.

In the "Miscellanea Genealogica et Heraldica" for July, 1867, p. 182, there is a short pedigree of Henshaw.

Thomas Henshaw of Milnehouse, co. Chester, m. Joanna Lockwood, and had a son John Henshaw, who by wife Joan Moreton had a son Thomas. This Thomas Henshaw m. Elizabeth Hollinshead, and had John H., father of Thomas Henshaw, living in 1618.

It is possible that this last Thomas was the one who died in 1630 at Toxteth Park, or that he was of the same family as the grandfather of the emigrant.

THE WENTWORTH FAMILY.

IN the April number of the Register, Mr. Joseph L. Chester has published an account of the English ancestry of the Wentworths, for so many generations prominent in the political affairs of New Hampshire. Although this sketch is to be extended and republished, we are desirous to enrich our pages with the results of Mr. Chester's investigations, as the Wentworths are thereby placed among the limited number of American families entitled to use coat-armor.

The original founder of the family was Reginald[1] de Wynterwade, living at the time of the Conquest, the owner of the lordship of Wentworth in the wapentake of Strafford, west riding of Yorkshire. From him the line is traced through Henry,[2] Richard,[3] Michael,[4] Henry,[5] Hugh,[6] and William,[7] to Robert[8] Wentworth, who was living about 1275, and married Emma, daughter and heir of William Woodhouse. His son William[9] of Wentworth-Woodhouse had sons Richard[10] (Bishop of London, 1338, and Lord High Chancellor) and William.[10]

William[10] Wentworth had sons Sir William[11] and John[11]; the latter of whom married Alice, daughter and heir of John Bissell of North Elmsall, co. York, and left this estate to his nephew and namesake.

Sir William[11] Wentworth had two sons. William[12] and John,[12] and from William,[12] after ten generations, was descended Sir William Wentworth, bart., father of the Earl of Strafford, the unfortunate Prime Minister of Charles I. This branch is extinct in the male line, but the different generations are duly recorded in the Peerages.

The second son, John[12] Wentworth, inherited from his uncle the estate of North Elmsall, which long remained in the family. His son John[13] had, besides an oldest son John,[14] three other sons, of whom Roger[14] was the ancestor of the Barons Wentworth of Nettlested, co. Suffolk, and the Earls of Cleveland, as well as other branches, now extinct; and Richard[14] was the ancestor of the Wentworths of Bretton, co. York, among whom was a line of baronets, which ceased in 1792.

The main line, at North Elmsall, was continued through John,[14] John,[15] and Thomas[16] Wentworth, the last named dying about 1522. In the senior line from this Thomas[16] was descended Sir John Wentworth of Brodsworth and North Elmsall, created baronet in 1692, whose only son, Sir Butler Wentworth, died *s. p.* in 1741, when the title ceased.

Oliver[17] Wentworth, a younger son of Thomas[16] of North Elmsall, was the ancestor of the American branch, and as this is the point at which Mr. Chester commences on entirely new ground, our account will be more expanded than heretofore.

Oliver[17] Wentworth settled at Goxhill, co. Lincoln, and died about January, 1559, leaving sons William[18] and Francis[18]; the latter was of Saltfletby, co. Lincoln, and died at Waltham, in 1611, leaving issue, but they have not been traced.

William[18] Wentworth was of Waltham, and died 22 May, 1574, evidently in early life. He married, first, Ellen, daughter of John Gilby, and had three sons,

Oliver[19] and Thomas,[19] who both d. *s. p.*, and Christopher.[19] The last named,

Christopher[19] Wentworth, was probably born about 1556, and m. 19 August, 1583, in the city of Lincoln, to Katherine, youngest daughter of William Marbury. She was the sister of the Rev. Francis Marbury, and therefore aunt of the famous Mrs. Anne (Marbury) Hutchinson. (See Heraldic Journal, II., 174.)*

This Christopher seems to have been of a roving disposition, having been found at Waltham, Lincoln, Grimsby, Irby, Coninsholm, Ravendale, Barrow, and Alford. He had eight children, and died about May, 1633, when his will was proved. His oldest son was William[20] Wentworth, baptized at the church of St. Peter at Gowts, in the city of Lincoln, 8th June, 1584. There can be no doubt that this William, who was living in 1628, when his father's will was made, was the William Wentworth who married the widow Susanna (Carter) Fleming, 28th Nov., 1614, at Alford; who had there sons William, baptized 1616, Edward, 1618, and Christopher, 1620, and who then removed to the neighboring parish of Rigsby, where Christopher was buried in 1621.

We say the proof is as ample as the case requires, because, while the pedigree is brought down to Christopher,[19] who had a son William living in 1628, Mr. Chester could find no other person of the name than this William of Alford, and it would be absurd to reject

---

* We published, in an article on the Hutchinsons, the fact of this marriage, which had just been discovered by Mr. Chester. The clue which was thus given to the Wentworths' pedigree has since been followed up, through the liberality of Hon. John Wentworth of Chicago, a gentleman much interested in genealogy.—ED.

the natural conclusion that Christopher's son William
was the William who lived in the same village with
him, viz., Alford. Carefully as we scrutinize all attempts
to prove the connection between English and American
families, we confess ourselves satisfied with the evidence
here given.

This William[20] Wentworth appears to be the man mentioned in 1636 as having owned a messuage at Bilsby,
another parish adjoining Alford, but this is the last we
hear of him.

His son William[21] Wentworth was baptized at Alford,
15th March, 1615–16, and is believed to have been the
emigrant to New Hampshire; another son, Edward,[21] was
a surgeon at Boston, co. Lincoln, but this branch soon
became extinct in the male line.

Having proved the pedigree thus far, the only remaining
point of interest is that of the identity of William[21] Wentworth and the emigrant. The evidence must be circumstantial, since there is no mention by the emigrant of his
relatives in England; and no record has been found in any
will, of any Wentworth being in America from which
relationship could be traced.

We find, however, that a William Wentworth appears
at Exeter, in New Hampshire, and that he was one of a
party composed of the Wheelwrights, Hutchinsons, and
others who were relatives. What doubt can there be
that he was also one of the family connection, the grandson of Christopher Wentworth and Catherine Marbury?
Especially is this conjecture strengthened by the fact that
two other grandsons of Christopher Wentworth, viz.,
Christopher Helme and Christopher Lawson were repre-

sented by namesakes at Exeter in 1639, unless we adopt the natural explanation all three were the veritable colonists.

Accepting this William[21] Wentworth, therefore, as a part of the pedigree, we find that he was of Exeter in 1639, and died at Dover, N. H., 15 March, 1696–7, aged 81 years, In our third volume, p. 169–172, we have given a sketch of the more prominent of the descendants of Elder William Wentworth, and will now add only that a full genealogy is being printed for Hon. John Wentworth of Chicago. We there quoted from Sabine a remark that Benning William Bentwick Wentworth, who died in 1810, was heir to the title of Earl of Strafford. If he were descended from William the emigrant, as seems probable, the claim is undoubtedly unfounded. It must be said that Burke and other writers have acknowledged a connection between the Yorkshire Wentworths and the family here. We believe that during the colonial times some interchange of professions of relationship passed between the Governors Wentworth and their titled namesakes; but we regard these as being but empty compliments. Mr. Chester has undoubtedly shown how these different branches came from a common stock, but so obscure were the fortunes of the immediate ancestors of the emigrant, that their existence was probably unknown to their titled contemporaries.

We would say, in conclusion, that the American family seems fully entitled to the family coat-of-arms, and possibly to the honor of the male representation of this ancient family.

THE BARTONS OF SALEM.

THE arms at the head of this article are copied from the official seal of Robert Barton[2] of London, supposed to have been a brother of Doctor John Barton[2] of Salem, from whom the family there is descended. The same arms are to be seen upon an ancient hatchment, long preserved in the family, and claimed, by very positive and direct tradition, to have been brought by the founder from England.

Dr. John Barton,[2] son of John[1] of Huntingdon, fellmonger, came to New England in the year 1672, leaving behind him at least three brothers,—Robert,[2] Thomas,[2] and Furley.[2] He was originally an apothecary, but afterwards practised as a physician, in which capacity he was employed as an expert in examining the persons accused of witchcraft in the memorable year, 1692. He was married at Marblehead by the Rev. Samuel Cheever, 7 June, 1675, to Lydia, the daughter of Thomas Roberts of Boston, whose widow, Eunice, on the 22d Oct., 1656, became the wife of Moses Maverick of Marblehead, at whose house Barton's marriage was solemnized. He died at the island of Barbadoes, in Dec., 1694,—tradition says "of the yellow fever," and that he was then on a voyage to

England to secure property left by his father, tidings of whose death he had previously received.

John[2] and Lydia had six children: the eldest two, named John,[3] died in infancy, Thomas[3] was born 17 July, 1680, Zaccheus[3] was born three years later, and died *s. p.*, Samuel[3] was born 30 Aug., 1688, and Elizabeth[3] was married to Samuel King, and left descendants. One of Samuel's[3] descendants possesses the hatchment before described, and Thomas's descendants have preserved the notarial seal.

Thomas,[3] twelve years after his father's death, proceeded to England by way of Barbadoes, provided with affidavits duly certified under the hand of Gov. Dudley and the seal of the Province, showing his relationship to John[1] of Huntingdon, the fellmonger, and evidently intended to be used in substantiating his claim to estates in England. These affidavits, singularly corroborating the rather romantic traditions of the family, are preserved in a book of notaries' records in the office of the Clerk of the Courts, in Salem, where they were discovered a few years since; and from them the foregoing facts have been chiefly gathered. Although no other evidence thereof is now remembered, the comparative opulence of John's[2] children and grandchildren, and the fact that they appear to have enriched others, connected with them by marriage, seem to warrant the inference that property of considerable value fell to this family, and was, probably, recovered by Thomas.[3]

Thomas[3] returned to Salem, established himself as a merchant and apothecary, and was otherwise distinguished. He married Mary, daughter of Nehemiah Willoughby of Salem, and they had children: John, born 5 Dec., 1711, who d. unmarried, 21 Dec.,1774, and Mary, born 5 Oct., 1715, who was married to Doctor Bezaleel [not *Barzillai*, as Derby has it, from Salem town records] Toppan or Tappan, son of Rev. Christopher T. of Newbury. Their descendant, Mary Toppan,[7] wife of Dr. Geo. B. Loring, is the possessor of the notarial seal referred to.—*See Heraldic Journal, Vol.* II., p. 28.

Samuel[3] married, 1st, Dec. 26, 1723, Mary Butler, and 2d, Sept. 29, 1737, Elizabeth Marston of Salem, and he died 13 March, 1772, in the 84th year of his age. His only child, Samuel,[4] was born 9 Sept., 1738, married, 11 Dec., 1764, Margaret, daughter of Jonathan and Elizabeth Gardner of Salem, and died 9 Nov., 1773, of the small pox. Samuel,[4] Jr., was selectman of Salem, and sometime Captain of a military company. Of his seven children, John,[5] who was born 22 June, 1774, married Mary Webb of Salem, 21st Oct., 1802, and they had nine children. He was apprenticed to an apothecary, but afterwards sailed many sea voyages, chiefly to the East Indies, as shipmaster and supercargo, and was one of the pioneers in the pepper trade. He died 24 Feb., 1818. His daughter, Margaret,[6] born (twin to her brother Gardner) 23d July, 1815, was married April 13, 1840, to George Dean Phippen, esquire, of Salem, the possessor of the hatchment.   A. C. G., JR.

NOTE.—Around the arms upon the seal is inscribed the following: SIGIL: TABEL: MEI: RO: BARTON: NOT: PVB: LOND: ADIVR: 17 SEPT: 1670.

THE STURGIS FAMILY.

THE arms here engraved are those belonging to the Sturgis family of New England. From a printed pedigree we transcribe the following account:

The original form of the family name was probably de Turgis, derived from a village of that name in the county of Northampton. The authenticated pedigree begins with Roger[1] Sturgis of Clipston, in Northamptonshire, whose will is dated 10 Nov., 1530. He had a wife Alice, and children Richard,[2] Robert,[2] Francis,[2] Ellen,[2] and Agnes.[2] Of these

Robert[2] Sturgis of Clipston had Roger,[3] John,[3] and Thomas.[3]

Roger[3] Sturgis, whose will is dated 4 Sept., 1579, by wife Agnes, had sons John,[4] and Robert[4]; the latter was of Faston, co. Northampton, where he was buried 2d January, 1611.

The son of Robert,[4] was Phillip[5] Sturgis of Honnington, co. Northampton, who was buried there 18th June, 1618. He was twice married; and by the first wife had Edward,[6] Robert,[6] and Elizabeth.[6] His second wife was Anne Lewes, by whom he had Alice,[6] Anne,[6] and William[5]; the second marriage, and baptisms of the children by it, are recorded at Honnington.

Edward[6] Sturgis, eldest son, removed to New England, was of Charlestown, 1634, and Yarmouth. By wife Alice he had Alice,[7] bapt. 23 Dec., 1619, Mary,[7] bapt. 2 Oct.,

1621, Edward,[7] bapt. 10 April, 1624, and Rebecca,[7] bapt. 17 Feb., 1726–7.

Edward[7] Sturgis came to Yarmouth with his father, with whom he seems confounded in Savage's account of the family. The authority which we follow says that this Edward,[7] Jr., by first wife, Elizabeth, who d. 14 Feb., 1691–2, had Elizabeth,[8] b. 20 April, 1647, Joseph,[8] b. 6 April, 1650, Edward,[8] (who m. a daughter of Capt. John Gorham, and d. 1678), Samuel,[8] (who died 1674) and Thomas.[8] Edward,[7] m. for second wife, Mary, widow of Zachariah Rider.

Thomas[8] Sturgis of Yarmouth, m. Abigail ———, and had sons Edward,[9] b. 10 Dec., 1684, Thomas,[9] b. 4 April, 1686, John,[9] b. 2 Dec., 1690, Jacob,[9] b. 14 Jan., 1700, besides several daughters.

Thomas[9] Sturgis* of Barnstable, m. 26 Dec., 1717, Martha, daughter of Rev. John Russell. She d. 17 June, 1774. Their children were Martha,[10] b. 1718, Elizabeth,[10] b. 1721, Thomas,[10] b. 22 July, 1722, Elizabeth,[10] b. 1725, Rebecca,[10] b. 1727, Jonathan,[10] b. 17 June, 1730, Abigail,[10] b. 1732, Hannah,[10] b. 1735.

Thomas[10] Sturgis of Barnstable, m. ——— and had

    I. Martha.[11]

    II. William,[11] b. 19 Dec., 1748, m. Hannah, dau. of Rev. Jonathan Mills, and had only one son, William,[12] b. 25 Feb., 1782, an eminent merchant of Boston. The last named m., 1810, Elizabeth M. Davis, and had one son and five daughters. He d. 21 Oct., 1863.

---

* Freeman, Hist. Cape Cod, II., 216, gives this wife and children to Edward[9] instead of Thomas.[9]

III. Russell,[11] b. 23 Aug., 1750.

IV. Abigail.[11]

v. Thomas,[11] b. 15 April, 1755, father of Russell[12] and William[12] of New York.

VI. John.[11]

VII. Elizabeth.[11]

VIII. Samuel,[11] b. 20 Sept., 1762, m. —— Jennings, and had, with other children, Lucretia Augusta,[12] who m. Joshua Bates, Esq., of London, and had an only daughter, Elizabeth Anne,[13] wife of M. Van de Weyer, Belgian minister to the Court of St. James.

Russell[11] Sturgis of Boston m. Elizabeth Perkins, and had, with other children,* Nathaniel Russell[12] Sturgis of Boston, who m. Susanna Parkman, sister of Mrs. Robert G. Shaw. Their children were

I. Russell[13] of London.

II. Henry-Parkman.[13]

III. Samuel-Parkman.[13]

IV. Sarah,[13] m. Francis G. Shaw.

v. Susan,[13] m. John Parkman.

VI. Elizabeth,[13] m. Henry Grew.

VII. George,[13] m. Josephine Boras, and had Joseph B.,[14] Susan P.,[14] Josephine B.,[14] Robert S.,[14] James P.[14]

VIII. Harriet T.,[13] m. William A. White.

IX. James,[13] m. Catherine Townsend, and had Susan,[14] Charles,[14] and Frank S.[14]

x. Robert S.,[13] m. Susan, dau. of Charles Inches, and had Robert,[14] Charles,[14] and Roger.[14]

* One daughter, Hannah,[12] m. Frederic W. Paine of Worcester, and had a daughter Elizabeth, who m. her cousin, H. P. Sturgis.

Russell[13] Sturgis of London, m. 1st, Lucy Lyman Paine, who d. *s. p.*, and 2d, Mary Green Hubbard, by whom he had

    I. Russell,[14] who m. Susan, dau. of Benj. Wells, and had Russell,[15] Susan,[15] Richard C.,[15] William C.[15]

    II. Lucy L.,[14] m. Charles Codman.

    III. John H.,[14] m. Frances Codman, and had Julia O.,[15] John H.,[15] Gertrude G.,[15] Frances C.[15]

He m. 3d, Julia Overing Boit, and had

    IV. Henry P.[14]

    V. Julia O.[14]

    VI. Mary G.[14]

    VII. Howard.[14]

Henry Parkman[13] Sturgis, of Boston, m. 1st, Mary Georgiana Howard, and 2d, Elizabeth Orne Paine. By his first wife he has three children living.

    I. Henry H.,[14] m. Caroline A. Manson.

    II. Frederick R.[14]

    III. Mary Howard.[14]

HERALDIC NOTES AND QUERIES.

[Continued from p. 96.]

LXIII.

THE KATHERINE WHEEL.—The Martyrdom of St. Katherine, painted by Gaudenzio Ferrare, early in the 15th century, now in the Breras Gallery at Milan, represents the Katherine wheel with five (5) spokes.

Gwillim, in his "Display of Heraldry," invariably represents the Katherine wheel with five (5) spokes.

The ancient arms of Baliol College, Oxford (dedicated to St. Katherine) was a Katherine wheel of five (5) spokes.

The Hasted Papers, in the British Museum, has the arms of Scott of Scott's Hall,—three Katherine wheels, five (5) spokes in each wheel, while a display of arms in possession of a branch of the same family in Rhode Island has six (6) spokes in the Katherine wheel.

There are monuments in the Churches of Ashford, Brabourne, Smeeth and Monks-Horton, Kent, bearing Katherine wheels with five (5) spokes, and in the Isle of Thanet in the same county is a monument of the same family with six (6) spokes in the wheel.

Clark's "History of Knighthood" represents the Katherine wheel, in the badge of the Knights of St. Katherine of Mount Sinai, with six (6) spokes—and in the order of St. Catherine of Russia, with eight (8) spokes.

Whitmore, in his "Elements of Heraldry," represents the Katherine wheel with eight (8) spokes.

According to the laws of Heraldry, what is the correct number of spokes in the Katherine wheel? Or are they like "the details of the mantlings of a shield, left to the taste of the artist?"   M. B. S.

Cleveland, Ohio, June 3, 1868.

[NOTE.—In reply to the query we would say that the Oxford Glossary of Heraldry, p. 325, says, "Wheel, or Cart-Wheel, usually of eight spokes. Katherine-Wheel, the instrument of the martyrdom of St. Katherine." The cut (of which a fac-simile is given in the "Elements of Heraldry") has eight spokes. Planché's edition of Clark's Heraldry (Bell & Daldy, 1866) Plate VII., No. 17, has a Catherine Wheel of *eight* spokes. Gwillim, 4th edition, p. 286-7, has but five spokes to the wheel. It would seem that no definite rule is laid down, and therefore the number would be at the discretion of the artist.—ED.]

LXIV.

COTTON FAMILY.—We are indebted to W. G. Brooks, Esq., for the following note on the parentage of Elizabeth Cotton, wife of Rev. Caleb Cushing, (*ante*, p. 56.) It makes it certain that she was the daughter of Rev. John :

"My eldest sister was first married to the Rev. Mr. James Alling, minister of Salisbury, a gentleman well accomplished, and of a sweet disposition, who died March 3, 1695–6, and left three daughters, the eldest of whom, named Joanna, married Mr. Elias Pike of Salisbury. The second, named Mary, married Mr. John Appleton of Ipswich, 1716. The third, named Elizabeth, married Mr. Joshua Moody, preacher at the Isle of Shoals. On all which God has bestowed the fruit of the womb.

" The successor to Mr. Alling, in the work of the ministry at Salisbury, was ye Rev. Mr. Caleb Cushing, a gentleman of considerable knowledge and prudence, and son to John Cushing, Esq. of Scituate, deceased, (with whom my sister Cushing was happily married) and by whom she had three sons. My sister is now above 63 years of age, which is a greater age than any of our family have attained to since our grand parents. And as she has spent her time in duties proper to her, and still continues very active and diligent in business, so God grant she may finish well.

"In September, 1742–3, my only sister, Mrs. Elizabeth Cushing of Salisbury died, aged 80 years and about a month, and now I am the only survivor of my father's family."

(From the "Cotton Annals," or Journal of Josiah Cotton, son of Rev. John of Plymouth.)

LXV.

The annexed cut was used on the title-page of a book published some years ago by James Munroe & Co. of this city. Can any of our readers supply the title, or name the family to which the arms belong?

LXVI.

De Carteret Family.—In the Suffolk Registry we find Letters of Administration granted 9th August, 1745, to Philip de Carteret of Charlestown, on the estate of Edward de Carteret, formerly of the parish of St. Johns, in the Island of Jersey. We learn from Mr. T. B. Wyman, that Philip de Carteret was of Charlestown, taxed there as late as 1766. He m. 16 November, 1727, Elizabeth Dunster, and had Philip, and Abigail, wife of William Whittemore. He died 15th April, 1767.

Philip de Carteret, Jr., married Rebecca Stone in Boston, 5 March, 1740, and had John, bapt. in Charlestown, 26 May, 1745, Richard, born there, 28 February, 1746–7, and Hannah, born 16 March, 1748–9, bapt. at Christ Church, Boston, three days later. Eliza Cartaret, 30th June, 1772, freed a negro slave.

Mr. Wyman adds, that the name is often spelt Cartwright on the records, thus suggesting a new derivation for a name which appears to be entirely English, and which is quite often encountered in this vicinity.

LXVII.

Virginian Families.—We are indebted to a correspondent for an account of the arms of the Mayo and

Bland families. As quartered by Joseph Mayo of Richmond they are, 1st and 4th, Mayo, Azure, a chevron vairré gules and argent, between three coronets *or*. Second and third, Bland, Argent, on a bend sable, three pheons of the first. Crest, a lion's head ppr. erased, on a coronet *or*.

"Both of these families were settled in Virginia at an early period. In the Byrd MSS., lately published by Munsell, Col. Byrd mentions one of the family as the surveyor engaged with him in running the boundary line between Virginia and North Carolina. The family seal of some of his descendants has been till very recently at Powhatan, near Richmond, notable in our history as the place "one mile below the falls," at which Capt. John Smith first saw the King of that name. In the family burial ground, near the residence, are the tombs of two of the family, (one of them that of Joseph Mayo, gentleman, born in the Island of Bermuda, who died 1731) both of them having the Mayo arms above the inscriptions. The wife of Gen. Winfield Scott was of this family.

The Blands have figured conspicuously in the councils of the state; the Bland Papers, published many years since, by Charles Campbell of Virginia, giving many interesting details of their history."   T. H. W.

We add to this the memorandum of the arms engraved on two tombstones at Hampton, Va. They were copied by W. T. Spiller. The first bears a heart, transfixed with arrows, between four cherubim's heads, and was on the tomb of Capt. Wilder Wilson, who died 19 Dec., 1701.

The other, on the tomb of Capt. George Wray, who died 19th April, 1758, aged 61 years, bears ——, on a chief three martlets. Crest, a bird. Motto, "Et juste et vray."

LXVIII.

THE HARRISON ESTATE.—"It will be gratifying if the large estate in England, which is advertising for heirs, should find its proper owners in the Harrisons who have been since the Revolution so well known in New York, Philadelphia and Brooklyn, in various developments of art and genius. About the year 1783, William Harrison, son of William Harrison of England, came over to this country by invitation of the officers of the United States Bank, to engrave its notes. He brought with him his wife and several children, to whom others were added after his arrival. One of those was Charles .P. Harrison, who was a distinguished artist and bank note engraver in New York, a contemporary of Peter Maverick, so skilful in the same department, and well-known by him. He was the father of a large family in New York, which includes Gabriel Harrison, the first lessee of the Park Theatre in Brooklyn, an able artist, and Lafayette Harrison, of New York, well known as a concert manager.

It has for some years been well understood that William, the great grandfather of this family, left an estate to Benjamin, his son, (a grand uncle of this family, and brother to the William who came over here,) who largely increased it by East Indian investments, and dying left it to his brother William and his heirs. Of the immediate heirs of William there is but one living, a son, a very aged and highly respected gentleman in Philadelphia. The other heirs are the later descendants of the William who came over, grandchildren and great grandchildren. They are well known and easily traceable, and are people of fine character and qualities, meriting all that comes to

them from their ancestors."—*New York Evening Post,*
May 25, 1868.

LXIX.

A correspondent sends the following query :—"I have in my possession an ante-nuptial agreement executed by my ancestor, John Tuthill of Southold, L. I., New York, with Sarah Youngs, bearing date the 5th day of May, 1690.
The seal (wax) appended to his name is somewhat broken, but I can plainly make out *a bend* on the shield and three (perhaps carbuncles) on the bend. If there ever was a crest it is missing. I would like to know to whom said arms belonged. The names on the instrument are the parties, John Tuthill and widow Sarah Youngs, and, as witnesses, George Wolcott and Samuel Arnold. As none of my works on heraldry describe such arms I will be greatly obliged to you for your opinion of the owner's name."   W. H. T.

LXX.

AMERICAN COATS OF ARMS.—Some of our readers may have seen a pamphlet written by the editor of this journal, advocating a system of taxing all use of coat-armor in this country. At the risk of seeming unduly fond of his own scheme, it has seemed proper to give in this magazine the outline of the plan, since this journal is devoted to the discussion of matters of interest to those who appreciate heraldry.

The reason for proposing a regular system, was the action of Congress in ordering the Committee on Ways and Means to report a bill for such taxation, and it seemed to the writer that any tax imposed by the General Government, would necessarily give a certain recognition and authority to such coats-of-arms. There was, therefore, an opportunity given to institute a new and national system of heraldry, and if it should seem unwise to do this, it would be best for Congress to avoid the subject entirely.

The chief features of our plan were the recording in the United States Court of the District in which a man resided, such arms as he desired to bear; and the necessity of making use always on such coat-of-arms of the date when the arms were assumed. These two provisions would suffice probably to give a family device to all those desiring one, and at the same time would point out distinctly to all familiar with heraldry, the true origin of the arms.

Thus far the criticisms of the press have been mainly directed to the folly or impropriety of any use of coat-armor in this country; but whether true or wrong, this objection fails to meet the fact of an existing and increasing illegitimate use, or the fact that taxation is authorization.

Our readers will probably agree with us that our present custom is absurd and ought to be effectually stopped. They probably, also, will not sympathize with those who regard heraldic insignia as unfit for our use as republicans, nor with those who prefer to let error continue rather than to take the pains to devise and perfect the proper mode to explain the truth. We hope that Congress, since the subject has been once introduced, will either forbid the use of coat-armor, or perceiving its value will regulate and legalize it.

We annex the memorandum of the plan which has been suggested as feasible for Congress to adopt:

1.—The use of coat-armor shall be prohibited to all but those who pay an annual tax.

2.—The description of the arms shall be filed in the District Court, and a fee of at least fifty dollars paid therefor; the record being always open for inspection. Officers now or formerly in the military or naval service of the United States to be allowed to record their arms without paying such fee; and in the case of an officer deceased, his children should be allowed the privilege of entering arms in their father's name.

3.—The date of entry at the Court is in all cases to decide the ownership, if two persons have entered the same arms, unless one party prove inheritance, in which case he shall have the exclusive right. In all cases the person dispossessed may amend his first description, and thus obtain a new coat-of-arms without further charge.

4.—The date of the year when the arms were assumed, to be a necessary part of them, except that the date of an inherited shield may be used instead; or by an officer of the United States, the name of any battle, &c.

5.—These provisions to apply only to personal use, and not to refer to existing monuments or records.

6.—After the record at the Court, the right shall remain although no use is made. The tax is to be only for such years as personal use is intended.

7.—In all cases where persons have paintings of arms, or engraved plate or seals, they must take out a license annually, though they need not file a description nor alter the existing shields by adding the date.

THE

HERALDIC JOURNAL;

RECORDING THE ARMORIAL BEARINGS AND GENEALOGIES OF AMERICAN FAMILIES.

NO. XXIV.   OCTOBER, 1868.

THE BROWN FAMILY.

In our present volume, p. 26, we mentioned a family of Browns, resident chiefly at Watertown, Mass., which was entitled to coat-armor, as being an off-shoot from a family of gentry settled at Swan Hall, co. Suffolk. By the kindness of one of the family we are enabled to present

the annexed engraving of the arms, and also a transcript
of the original grant, as recorded in 1640. This copy is
taken from the second volume of Grants, p. 627, in the
Heralds' College, and was made in 1860 by Albert W.
Woods, Lancaster Herald. It is as follows:

A tous présens et advenir qui ces presentes l'res verront
ou orront, John More, autrement dit Norrey Roy d'Armes
des parties du North de cestuy Royaume d'Anglet're
salut et dilection avec humble recom'endation. Equite
veult et raison ordo'ne que les hom'es vertueux et de
noble courage soient par leurs merites par reno'mee
remunerez et non pas seullement leurs p'sones en ceste
vie mortelle tant briefue et transitoire, maiz apres eulx
ceulz qui de leurs corps ystront et seront procriez soient
en toutes places de grant honneur perpetuellement devant
autres reluisans p' certaines ensaignes et demonstrances
de honneur et gentillesse, cestassavoir de blazon, heaulme
et tymbre; affin que a leur example aultres plus sefforcent
de perserveraument user leurs jours en fais d'armes et
oeuvres vertueuses pour acquerir la renomne d'auncienne
gentillesse en leur lignie et posterite. Et pour ce, Je.
Norrey Roy d'Armes, dessusd' qui non pas seullement
par com' une reno'mee maiz aussy par le rapport et
tesmoignage dautres nobles hom'es dignes de foy,
suy pour vray adverty et enforme que CRISTOFER
BROWNE de la Conte de Lincoll., Gentilhom'e lequel
la longement poursuy le fait d'armes et tant en ce qu'en
aultres ses affaires sest porte vaillaument et honourable'nt
gouverne lettement qui la bien de servy, et est digne que
dorefsenavant perpetuallement luy et sa posterite soient
en toutes places honorables admiz, reno'meez, complez

nombrez et receuz en nombre et en la compaigne des aultres anciens gentilz et nobles ho'mes : Et pour ce moy voyant toutes cestes choses ainsy noblement feites, Il me convient accomplir sa requeste en cestuy cas co'me droit et raison le veult, pour la remembrance dycelle sa gentillesse par la vertue de l'auctorite et povoir annexez et attribuez a mon d'office de Roy d'Armes, J'ay devise ordonne et assigne audit CRISTOFER BROWNE pour luy et sa posterite le Blazon, Heaulme et Timbre en la maniere qui sensuit—Cest assavoir *d'Argent en Sable parte en bende trois Mascles entrechanges ;* en son Heaulme, *la moitie d'une Grue, desploiant ses elles la queue nouee, tenant ung escrit en son bee "pour aprendre a mourir."* Sycome la picture en la marge cy devant le demonstre, a avoir et tenir pour luz et sa posterite et eulx en revestir a tousjoursmaiz. Entesmoing de cc, Je, Norrey Roy d'Armes dessus nom'ee, ay signe de ma main et celle de mon seel ces presentes. Fait et donne a Nothinghm le vingtesme jour de Jullet l'an de grace, mil cccc quatre vingt.

Norrey Roy d'Armes.

·This is a true copie of the originall Patent now remayning in the custodie of Christofer Browne of Tolthorpe in the Countie of Rutland, gent., being examined therewith the 12th of May, 1640, by us,

Wm. Le Neve,   Clarencieux.

Wm. Dugdale,   Rouge Croix.

Ro. Browne,   Blanch Lyon.

Geo. Browne.

GENEALOGY.

As Bond's History of Watertown is so easily accessible

we will merely say that this family is traced to John Browne, Alderman of Stamford, co. Lincoln, A. D., 1376. The family seems to have divided into three branches, settled respectively at Stamford, Tolethorp, co. Rutland, and Swan Hall, co. Suff. The latter branch is descended from the Christopher Browne, to whom the foregoing grant of arms was made, and the descendants are therefore entitled to use this coat. It is highly probable, however, that there was an earlier coat, viz., Sable, three mallets argent, to which they would also be entitled as a junior branch, with the customary difference.

The Swan-Hall branch is traced through Christopher,[2] who d. 1531, (son of the grantee), Christopher,[3] (d. 1574), and Thomas,[4] who died in 1590. Of his three sons, Richard[5] and Abraham[5]* settled in New England, as did also John,[6] son of his eldest son John.[5]

Of these only Abraham[5] Browne, who settled at Watertown, Mass., has left descendants here of the name. He left sons Jonathan[6] and Abraham,[6] of whom Jonathan[6] Browne m. Mary Shattuck, and had Abraham,[7] Benjamin,[7] and William,[7] all of whom left descendants.

William[7] Browne, b. 1684, d. 1756, was of Waltham, and was twice married. He had a large family, of whom we will mention two sons, Isaac[8] and Josiah.[8]

Isaac[8] Brown m. Mary Balch, and died in 1771. His son Moses[9] Brown (H. C., 1768) was a captain in our Revolution, and afterwards a merchant at Beverly, with his brother-in-law, Israel Thorndike. His son was

Charles[9] Brown (H. C., 1812) of Boston, who m. Eliza-

* It is, however, possible that Abraham, the emigrant, was a grandson instead of a son of Thomas[4] Browne. Edmund Browne of Boston, an early settler, is also believed to be a grandson.

beth Isabella Tilden, and had sons Francis P., and Edward
I. (H. C., 1855), now of Boston.

Josiah[8] Brown was the father of William[9] Brown of
Boston, a State Senator, &c., who d. in 1816, and whose
daughter Zebiah[10] m. Bryant Parrott Tilden, by whom
she had Elizabeth Isabella, who m. her second cousin,
Charles Brown.

REVIEW.

THE FAIRFAXES OF ENGLAND AND AMERICA IN THE
SEVENTEENTH AND EIGHTEENTH CENTURIES, includ-
ing Letters from and to Hon. William Fairfax, Presi-
dent of Council of Virginia, and his sons Col. George
William Fairfax, and Rev. Bryan, eighth Lord Fairfax,
the neighbors and friends of George Washington.
By Edward D. Neill, author of "Terra Mariœ," &c.
Albany, N. Y., Joel Munsell, 1868. 8vo., pp. 234.

As is well known to our readers, the title of Baron
Fairfax of Cameron, in the peerage of Scotland, has been
for several generations held by a family which has pre-
ferred to remain American. As recently as 1800 the title
was recognized by parliament as belonging to a citizen of
this country, and we presume the head of the family
would have no difficulty in obtaining a renewed acknowledgement of his rights.

In the book above cited we find a number of letters
belonging to different members of the family of Fairfax,
and a certain amount of genealogical information. We
regret to add that on the latter subject but little new

light is given, in addition to what we obtain from English
" Peerages." However, for all these sources we will
endeavor to give an account of the pedigree of the Fairfax
family.

Sir Thomas[1] Fairfax of Denton, co. York, was in 1627
created Baron Fairfax of Cameron. His oldest son,
Ferdinando,[2] the famous Parliamentary general, succeeded
as second Lord Fairfax, and his son Thomas[3] was the
third lord, and died s. p. in 1671.

He was succeeded by his first cousin, Henry,[3] fourth
baron, who had sons, Thomas,[4] fifth baron, and Henry[4]
Fairfax.

Thomas,[5] the sixth baron, and Robert,[5] the seventh
baron, were the sons of the fifth Lord Fairfax, but both
dying without issue the title went to the representative of
Henry[4] Fairfax above named.

This Henry[4] Fairfax of Toleston, co. York, left but one
son, who married, viz., William[5] Fairfax, who came to
New England as Collector of the Customs at Salem, about
1725. By his first wife, Sarah, daughter of Major
Walker, he had

George William,[6] b. 1724, m. Sarah Cary, d. s. p.
3 April, 1787.

Thomas,[6] d. unm. 26 June, 1746.

Anne,[6] m. 1, Lawrence Washington; 2, George Lee.

Sarah,[6] m. ——— Carlyle of Alexandria, Va.

By a second wife, Deborah Clarke of Salem, he had

Bryan.[6]

William Henry,[6] d. s. p. 1759. Killed at Quebec.

Hannah,[6] m. Warner Washington.

He died 3 September, 1757, aged 65.

Thomas[5] Fairfax, the sixth baron, inherited a very large fortune, a portion of which consisted of immense estates in Virginia. About the year 1739 he came to this country and took up his residence on these estates, where for forty years he exercised an unbounded influence in the colony. His name occurs conspicuously in the history of Virginia, and his patronage of George Washington is not his slightest claim on our regard. He died in 1782, and for the next nine years the title was enjoyed by his brother Robert,[5] who was twice married, but died *s. p.*

As we have seen, in 1793, the sole male heir of Henry[4] Fairfax, and in fact very probably of the first baron, was Rev. Bryan[6] Fairfax, who had been a soldier, and who had remained neutral during the Revolution. In 1789 he became an Episcopal minister, and for some time after his accession to the title, he refused to take any steps to secure his rights. At last, in 1798, he visited England to make his claim, and in 1800 it was allowed by Parliament.

Rev. Bryan[6] Fairfax, eighth baron, m. a Miss Cary, sister of the wife of his half-brother, George William, by whom he had

Thomas,[7] b. 1762.

Ferdinando.[7]

Elizabeth,[7] m. David Griffith.

And by a second wife ——— he had

Anne,[7] m. Charles Catlett.

He died in 1802, at Mount Eagle, near Alexandria, Va.

Thomas[7] Fairfax, ninth titular baron, was three times married. 1st to Mary Aylett, 2d to Louisa Washington, 3d to Margaret Herbert, and died 21 April, 1846. He left a large family, all by the last wife, viz.:

Albert,[8] of whom hereafter.

Henry,[8] m. Caroline Herbert.

Orlando,[8] m. Mary R. Cary.

Raymond,[8] d. 1813.

Eugenia,[8] m. 1st, Edgar Mason; 2d, Charles K. Hyde.

Ethelbert,[8] d. 1827.

Aurelia,[8] m. James W. Irwin.

Lavinia,[8] d. 1822.

Monimia,[8] m. Archibald Cary.

Reginald,[8] d. 1862.

Ferdinando[7] Fairfax, brother of the last, married Elizabeth Cary, and had

George William,[8] m. Isabella M. Neill.

Wilson-Miles-Cary,[8] m. Lucy Griffith.

Ferdinando,[8] m. 1st, Mary Jett; 2d, —— Jett.

Farinda,[8] m. Perrin Washington.

William-Henry,[8] d.

Mary-Munro,[8] d.

Archibald,[8] m. Sarah Herbert; Eliza Norris.

Edwin,[8] d.

Christine,[8] m. Thomas Rayland.

Louisa,[8] m. —— Tapscott.

Octavius,[8] d.

Floretta.[8]

Herbert,[8] d.

Washington,[8] d.

Albert[8] Fairfax, oldest son, m. Caroline Snowden, and d. *vita patris*, leaving two sons,

Charles Snowden.[9]

John,[9] a physician of Woodburne, Maryland.

Charles-Snowden[9] Fairfax, tenth baron, married 10 January, 1855, Ada, daughter of Joseph S. Benham of Cincinnati. The Peerage states that he resides at San Francisco, but does not mention his having any children.

THE CHASE FAMILY.

From investigations made by H. G. SOMERBY, Esq., and the papers of the late THEODORE CHASE, Esq.

AN old story, and one often, though never wholly told, is that which at one time called " Lord Townley's Estate," at another the " Chase Inheritance," ran through our New England press about twenty years since, setting forth with much apparent precision the conditions under which vast landed estates with centuries of accumulated rental awaited the decision of the English Chancery Courts in favor of the lawful heirs of Aquila and Thomas Chase, brothers, who settled in New England soon after the landing of the Pilgrims.

Into the history of this delusion we have not the space, nor is the place to enter, although on some accounts desirable, as there are many respectable people in Massachusetts, shrewd and cautious otherwise in all their dealings, who still declare that there is " something in it," and who,—while unable to tell even the names of their grandfathers,—are, or till quite recently were, ready to subscribe money to test the claims of ancestors from whom they cannot and never have undertaken to prove descent.

The late Mr. Theodore Chase, of Boston, as the possessor by inheritance of some of the family papers of Aquila Chase, who was one of the first settlers and grantees of Hampton, in 1639 or 1640, was often applied to by persons of the name when the periodic excitement relative to these fancied claims arose. Yet, while he possessed and carefully preserved many records and papers relating to each generation of his family in this country, proving his descent from Aquila of Hampton, he had never himself instituted any search for traces of his family in England, and was unable to give any information beyond the simple but essential fact,—which, wearied at last by the calls for information that were made upon him, he caused Messrs. Baring Brothers & Co. to obtain from their legal advisers, —that there were no estates awaiting heirs of the names of Chase or Townley in Chancery at all.

A short time after his death in 1859, the story was revived and inquiries were made of Mr. George B. Chase, by several respectable people of Essex County, who had agreed to raise funds for a new investigation in England;— a scheme, however, which fell at once to the ground on their learning from him that their first course, even if they believed in the existence of the Estates in Chancery, was to find out the names and dates of birth of their grandfathers, of which, all but one of their number were ignorant.

In 1861, Mr. Theodore Chase's voluminous Collection

of papers were submitted to Mr. Somerby for classification, and to enable him to take full notes for investigations to be pursued by him on his return to England in the spring of that year. Mr. Somerby's investigations, which were very diligent and thorough, and which led him among the records of every county in England, continued at intervals for some years, until he had noted the names and dates of birth of all of the name of Chase during the latter half of the sixteenth and early part of the seventeenth centuries. From them we extract the following pedigrees, and the facts relating to them.

In the Herald's visitation of Buckinghamshire in 1634, the Coat engraved at the head of this article is found, with the note, "This coate is testified by a letter from Mr. Robert Calvert, dated at Whitehall, July 18, 1634," together with a pedigree entered by Matthew Chase, which we copy, as follows :—

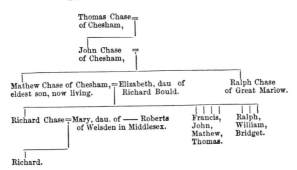

As Aquila Chase was supposed to have come from Cornwall, no importance had ever been attached to this pedigree by the American Genealogists, and Mr. Somerby, influenced by the traditions that Aquila and Thomas Chase were mariners, had searched in vain for some months the records of Cornwall, Hampshire, Kent, and other sea-coast Counties, for traces or indications of the emigrant's family. Cornwall, especially, had been most diligently searched, as Mr. Coffin, in his "History of Newbury" had stated that Aquila Chase was from that County. Although Mr. Coffin had, upon inquiry, stated to Mr. Somerby, as he had also done to the writer, that this statement rested merely upon tradition, it led at the outset to the most thorough investigation of that County's registers.

Turning at last to the interior, and recurring to the above pedigree, Mr. Somerby visited Chesham to examine its parish register, which from the time of 1538 he found complete to the present day, with the exception of baptisms in the reign of Queen Mary. From the larger pedigree made by him from this register we give the following extract, which shows the births of two brothers, Aquila and Thomas Chase, towards the end of the sixteenth century.

Thomas[1] Chase, of Hundrich, in the Parish of Chesham.
> John[2] Chase, of Hundrich, bap. Nov. 30, 1540.
> Richard[2] Chase, of Chesham, bap. Aug. 3, 1542.
> Agnes,[2] bap. Jan. 9, 1551.
> William,[2] born in reign of Queen Mary.
> Christian,[2]   "   "   "   "

Richard[2] Chase of Chesham m. Joan Bishop, April 16, 1564. Their children were

> Robert,[3] bap. Sept. 2, 1565.
> Henry,[3]   "   Aug. 10, 1567.
> Lydia,[3]   "   Oct. 4, 1573.

Ezekiel,[3] bap. April 23, 1576.

Dorcas,[3]   "   March 2, 1578.

AQUILA,[3] "   Aug. 14, 1580.

Jason,[3]   "   Jan. 13, 1583.

THOMAS,[3] "   July 18, 1585.

Abigail,[3]   "   Jan. 12, 1588.

Mordecai,[3] " July 31, 1591.

The discovery of the unique name of *Aquila*, found no where else in England, before or since, in any records of families bearing the name of Chase, was deemed conclusive proof by Mr. Somerby, as it has been since by other distinguished antiquarians, of the identity of the American with the English families. The date of birth coincided with another tradition lingering in some branches of the American family, that Aquila Chase, of Newbury, had called his first son, but the fifth child that was born to him, after his father's name as well as his own, "that Aquila the first was Aquila the second, too." The register at Chesham contains no other mention of Aquila, Thomas and Mordecai than the record of their births. Of the seven remaining children of Richard Chase, their marriages or deaths, in some cases both, are recorded. This shows that the three younger sons left Chesham, and lived and died elsewhere.

Aquila[3] Chase married ——,* and had

Thomas.[4]

Aquila,[4] b. 1618.

---

* Tradition has handed down the name of Sarah —— as the wife of Aquila[3] Chase of Chesham, and it here conforms to the rule of baptism, curiously general, if not in the great majority of cases absolute, which prevailed among the early colonists, of naming the first-born son after the paternal grandfather, the first-born daughter after the paternal grandmother, the second son after the mother's father, and so on.

It is probable that Thomas[4] and Aquila[4] acquired a knowledge of navigation in the employ of Thomas Chase, who in 1626 was part owner of the "John & Francis," and is named in a warrant of letter of marque issued in that year for that vessel, according to the Records of the State Paper Office.

We now come to New England, and give herewith the

AMERICAN GENEALOGY.

Thomas[4] Chase, one of the original settlers of Hampton, was in New England as early as 1636. In 1639 he was, together with his brother Aquila,[4] afterwards of Newbury, one of the original settlers of Hampton, where he died in 1653. He married Elizabeth, daughter of Thomas Philbrick. His children were

    I. Thomas,[5] born 1643. In 1670 he had a grant of land of 100 acres in Hampton, and was chosen selectman in 1695. He died October 23, 1714, unmarried.

    II. Joseph,[5] born in 1645, was also of Hampton. He was taken prisoner at Dover, in the assault on Major Waldron's house, 27th of June, 1689. He married, Dec. 31, 1671, Rachel, daughter of William Partridge, of Salisbury. He died January 12, 1718.

    III. Isaac,[5] born in 1647. He was sometime of Hampton, but removed to Edgartown, where he died May 9, 1727. He married Mary, daughter of Isaac Perkins, of Hampton.

    IV. James,[5] born in 1649. He married September 2, 1675, Elizabeth Greene.

    V. Abraham,[5] born August 6, 1652. He "was slaine

in ye warres" in 1676, and his estate was divided among his brothers.

Aquila[4] Chase, of Newbury, was one of the first settlers or grantees of Hampton, 1639 or 40. He married Anne, daughter of John Wheeler. About the year 1646 he removed to Newbury, and received several grants of land there. He made frequent voyages from Newbury as master. He made his will on the 19th of September, 1670, and died on the 27th of December following. His children were

   i. Sarah.[5]

   ii. Anne,[5] b. July 6, 1647.

   iii. Priscilla,[5] b. March 14, 1649.

   iv. Mary,[5] b. February 3, 1651.

   v. Aquila,[5] b. September 6, 1652.

   vi. Thomas,[5] b. July 25, 1654.

   vii. John,[5] b. November 2, 1655.

   viii. Elizabeth,[5] b. September 13, 1657.

   ix. Ruth,[5] b. March 18, 1660.

   x. Daniel,[5] b. December 9, 1661.

   xi. Moses,[5] b. December 24, 1663.

Of these children we propose to notice Aquila,[5] Thomas[5] and Moses,[5] and some of their descendants.

Aquila[5] Chase, of Newbury, a Sergeant in the Essex Regiment, was born September 26, 1652, and died July 29, 1720. He married Esther, daughter of John Bond of Newbury. His children were

   Esther,[6] b. January 15, 1674.

   Joseph,[6] b. March 25, 1677.

   Priscilla,[6] b. October 15, 1681.

   Jemima.[6]

   Rebecca.[6]

Anne.[6]

Hannah.[6]

Abigail.[6]

Benjamin.[6]

Joseph[6] Chase, of Newbury, was born March 25, 1677. About the year 1726, he sold his extensive estates in Newbury, and removed to Littleton, Mass. He is usually styled Planter. He married November 8, 1699, Abigail Thurston. His children were

Nathan,[7] b. August 2, 1701.

George,[7] b. February 17, 1703.

Stephen,[7] b. October 26, 1705.

Anne,[7] b. February 11, 1707.

Abigail,[7] b. March 27, 1709.

Hannah,[7] b. February 25, 1711.

Rebecca,[7] b. November 16, 1714.

Benjamin,[7] b. June 21, 1717.

Joseph,[7] b. December 8, 1719.

His son, the Reverend Stephen[7] Chase, was graduated at Harvard College in 1728, and was ordained at Lynn, now Lynnfield, November 24, 1731. He was resettled over the Parish at Newcastle, December 5, 1750, where he died January, 1778. He was distinguished for great scholastic attainments, and enjoyed the repute of a profound theologian. He married in 1732, Jane, daughter of Colonel Joshua Wingate, of Hampton, who, as Captain Wingate, commanded a company at the siege of Louisburg, and died at Hampton in 1769, having filled many offices of trust in the County and Province. The children of Reverend Stephen Chase were

I. Abraham,[8] b. March 25, 1734, d. same day.

II. Stephen,[8] b. Feb. 22, 1735; d. Dec. 1, 1739.

III. Joshua,[8] b. March, 1738.

IV. Jane,[8] b. January 7, 1740.

V. Stephen,[8] b. June 22, 1742.

VI. Mary,[8] b. October 19, 1744.

VII. John Wingate,[8] b. August 14, 1749.

Stephen[8] Chase, Merchant, of Portsmouth, was graduated at Harvard College in 1764. In 1778 he removed from Newcastle to Portsmouth, where he died in 1805. He was a gentleman of much literary culture, and was one of the founders of the Portsmouth Athenæum, for which he drew up the Constitution and By-Laws. He married Mary, daughter of Joseph Frost, Esquire, of Newcastle, and grand-daughter of the Honorable John Frost, who was born at Kittery, March 1, 1683, and who in early life, as an officer in the Royal Navy, commanded a British ship of war, and was of the Governor's Council in 1727. He married Mary, daughter of William, and sister of the first Sir William Pepperell, Baronet. The mother of Mary (Frost) Chase was Margaret, daughter of Samuel Colton of Springfield.

The children of Stephen[8] Chase, of Portsmouth, were

I. Joseph,[9] b. April 22, 1772, m. Margaret Chesley, of Durham.

II. William,[9] b. Feb. 10, 1774, a merchant of Portsmouth, m. Sarah Blunt, of Portsmouth; died, s. p., Aug. 30, 1834.

III. Mary,[9] b. Nov. 15, 1776, m. Edmund Toppan, Esq., of Portsmouth.

IV. Harriet,[9] b. Aug. 14, 1778, m. Oliver Crosby, Esq., of Dover, N. H.

v. Sarah,[9] b. Oct. 23, 1780, m. J. H. Woodman, Esq., of Rochester, N. H.

vi. Theodore,[9] b. March 16, 1786, was fitted for Harvard College at Exeter Academy, under Dr. Abbott, from 1796 to 1800, but did not enter as candidate, as the condition of his father's health necessitated his return to Portsmouth. He became a large ship-owner, and in 1831 removed to Boston, where he died March 13, 1859. He married April 26, 1831, Clarissa Andrews, daughter of Tyler Bigelow, Esq., of Watertown. Their children were

i. Theodore,[10] born February 4, 1832, a graduate of Harvard College in 1853 ; married, November 17, 1868, Alice Bowdoin, daughter of James Bowdoin Bradlee, Esq., of Boston.

ii. George[10] Bigelow, born October 1, 1835.

iii. Charles[10] Henry, b. March 5, 1841, d. February 27, 1849.

George[10] Bigelow Chase, of Boston, a graduate of Harvard College in 1856, married January 10, 1860, Anne, daughter of Rawlins and Gertrude (Livingston) Lowndes, of South Carolina. Their children are

i. Stephen,[11] born January 30, 1863.

ii. Gertrude[11] Lowndes, born October 23, 1868.

———

Thomas[5] Chase, of Newbury, married Rebecca, daughter of Thomas Follansby, and had Thomas[6] Chase, of Newbury, born September 15, 1680, who married Sarah ——. Their children were Thomas,[7] Abel,[7] Jonathan,[7] Roger,[7] Sarah,[7] Ezekiel,[7] Josiah,[7] Abigail,[7] Martha.[7] His son

Josiah[7] Chase was born November 30, 1713, graduated at Harvard College in 1738, and ordained as the first minister over Spruce Creek Parish, Kittery, September 19, 1750. He was drowned in the night by falling into Spruce Creek, not far from his own house, on his return from a wedding during a violent snow storm.

To return to the youngest child of Aquila[4] Chase and Anne Wheeler,—Moses[5] Chase, of Newbury, an Ensign in the Essex Regiment, married Anne, daughter of Thomas Follansby. His children were

Moses[6] and Daniel,[6] twins, born Sept. 20, 1685.

Moses,[6] b. with Daniel, b. Sept. 20, 1685, d. young.

Daniel,[6] b. with Moses, " " " "

Moses,[6] b. January 20, 1688.

Samuel,[6] b. May 13, 1690.

Elizabeth,[6] b. September 25, 1693.

Stephen,[6] b. August 29, 1696.

Hannah,[6] b. September 13, 1699.

Joseph,[6] b. September 9, 1703.

Benoni,[6] b. April 5, 1708.

Daniel[6] Chase removed to Littleton, once a part of Groton, in 1725, together with his family. Soon after he again removed to Sutton, where he died April, 1768. He married January 6, 1706, Sarah March, and had

Samuel,[7] b. September 28, 1707.

Daniel,[7] b. September 18, 1709.

Anne,[7] Joshua,[7] Judith,[7] Nehemiah,[7]

Sarah,[7] Caleb,[7] Moody,[7] Moses.[7]

Samuel[7] Chase married Mary Dudley, and removed with his family to Cornish, N. H., on the Connecticut River, of which place he was one of the founders. He died August 12, 1800. His children were

Samuel,[8] Jonathan,[8] Dudley,[8] b. 1730, March,[8]

Sarah,[8] Elizabeth,[8] Solomon,[8] Anne,[8] and Mary.[8]

Dudley[8] Chase married August 23, 1753, Alice Corbet, of Mendon, and died April 13, 1814. He was the father of a distinguished family of sons :

   I. Salmon[9] Chase, born July 14, 1761, at Sutton, an eminent lawyer of Portland.

   II. Ithamar,[9] b. 1763, at Sutton.

   III. Baruch,[9] b. March 27, 1764, at Cornish.

   IV. Heber,[9] b. September 2, 1770.

   V. Dudley,[9] b. December 30, 1771.

   VI. Philander,[9] b. December 14, 1775.

The Hon. Ithamar[9] Chase, a distinguished citizen of Vermont, married Janet Ralston, of Keene, and among others had

Alexander[10] Ralston, b. December 22, 1794, and

Salmon[10] Portland, b. at Cornish, January 13, 1808.

The Hon. Dudley[9] Chase, a graduate with honors of Dartmouth College, 1791, was for many years a leader of the Vermont Bar. He was a Senator of the United States, from 1813 to 1817, and Chief Justice of Vermont from 1817 to 1821.

The Rev. Philander[9] Chase, one of the most remarkable men of his time, and whose Reminiscences and Autobiography constitutes one of the most interesting and valuable books illustrative of the early history of the West, was graduated at Dartmouth College, 1796. He was ordained a Deacon of the Episcopal Church in 1798, and after some years' service as a Missionary Preacher, became Rector of Christ's Church, Poughkeepsie, which office he resigned to become Rector of Christ's Church, New

Orleans, in 1805. He became Bishop of Ohio in 1818, which office he resigned in 1831. He was the founder and first President of Kenyon College. In 1835 he was chosen Bishop of Illinois, and continued his active exertions in behalf of the Protestant Episcopal Church, founding Jubilee College in 1838, till his death in 1852.

The Hon. Salmon Portland[10] Chase, now Chief Justice of the United States, was graduated at Dartmouth College in 1826, with high honors. He was a Senator of the United States, from 1849 to 1855 ; Governor of Ohio, from 1855 to 1859; again a United States Senator in 1861; Secretary of the Treasury, from 1861 to 1864; and was appointed Chief Justice of the United States in 1865. He married, 1st, Catherine Jane Garniss, March 4, 1834; 2d, Eliza Ann Smith, September 26, 1839; 3d, Sarah Bella Dunlop Ludlow, November 6, 1846, and has several children, one of whom is the wife of the Hon. William Sprague, United States Senator from Rhode Island.

The name in this country has, from the earliest times, been usually spelled Chase—sometimes Chace. In the English records it is found variously spelled Chase—Chaace—Chaase. But in the early records, previous to the first half of the sixteenth century, it is always spelled Chase, as at the present day. The printed books of Arms and Crests, as is usually the case with such works, are all wrong in their description of the Chase arms, which correctly read thus ; Gules, 4 crosses patonce Argent, on a canton Azure, a lion passant or. Burke gives Chase *vel* Chansey; he should have given Chasey—the name of a modern family, who have assumed the arms of Chase.

He is wrong again in his description of the arms of the Chesham family, inasmuch as he calls the crosses flory, whereas they should be patonce. It is not improbable that the different variety of arms are in fact the same, as the persons who copied shields of arms from monument were often not careful to read correctly. Fairbairn, in his book on Crests, a later work, gives the arms as in Burke, and the Crest as in Berry's Hertfordshire Genealogies, where the engraving represents crosses patonce, while the author describes them as crosses flory, but Edmonson, in his work on Heraldry gives the arms and crest of Chase, no place named, as follows:

Arms, Gules, 4 crosses pat. argent 2 and 2, on a canton azure a lion passant Or. Crest, a lion rampant, Or, holding between his feet a cross patonce—Gules.

In this case the arms are precisely those of Chase, of Chesham, the only difference being in the color of the cross in the crest.

In a visit to Chesham, in 1864, the writer learned with much pleasure that it was the intention of Mr. William Lowndes,* the present Lord of the Manor, and a gentleman of much antiquarian feeling, to repair and refit for the use of his tenants in that neighborhood, a small chapel,—large enough perhaps, to give sittings for thirty people,—which stands in the rear of the old house of Hundrich, and is the only building left upon the estate as it existed when in possession of the Chase family, during

---

* This gentleman is a descendant of William Lowndes, a Secretary of the Treasury under Queen Anne, and author of the funding system—familiarly known as "Ways and Means" Lowndes in English history—and himself a descendant of the ancient family of Lowndes of Leigh Hall, a branch of which settled in South Carolina, in the early part of the last century, and from whom all of the name in this country trace their descent.

the sixteenth and seventeenth centuries. Soon after they disappeared from the Parish, their estate passed into the hands of the Lord of the Manor of Chesham, whose estates adjoined, and by whose family it has since been leased as a farm,—the little chapel having for some years past served as. a brewhouse.

The notes and investigations, a portion of which have afforded us the materials and pedigrees for this paper, developed the fact that the families of Chase are as small, indeed the name is as rarely found—at the present day in the Mother Country—as it is numerous and wide spread throughout the United States.

ESSEX WILLS.

In our second volume, pp. 141-143, we gave an account of such seals as had been found on documents in the Essex Probate files, bearing date prior to 1700. Since the publication of that article a thorough search has been made of all the papers in the files prior to 1750, and we are enabled therefore to furnish a complete record of all the armorial seals remaining there. For the sake of convenience we will continue the enumeration commenced in our former article.

13. —— three greyhound's heads erased ——, collared ——. This seal occurs on a bond of Judith Davis of Newbury, sealed at Salem, Oct. 5, 1692, with John March and William Nisbitt as sureties; John Gyles and

John Dodge, witnesses. The same seal is used by Thomas Nelson and Henry Brown, as sureties on a bond of T. Nelson of Rowley, Nov. 16, 1692, witnessed by William Longfellow and Margaret Sewall.

14. The Browne arms, already cited, are to be found on the seal on the will of John Browne, April 7, 1719, and that of William Browne, Sept. 11, 1753.

15. The Wainwright arms given in Vol. I., p. 89, occur, as we have mentioned (I., 110), on a deed of Stephen Minot, in 1728, and also on a discharge signed 23 Jan., 1722–3, by Thomas and Lydia Bancroft, heirs of Dr. Philei̲on Dane of Ipswich, the witnesses being Thomas Manning, James Pearson, Samuel and Mary Howard. This case seems peculiarly instructive, since, though the arms are perfectly identified, the name of Wainwright does not occur in the document. Had we not other evidence of the existence of a family using this as its coat-of-arms, this seal, like so many others, would have proved but an enigma.

16. This seal on the will of John Lander, 25 Nov., 1698, witnessed by John Higginson, Jr., John Westgate and Samuel Beadle, Jr., clearly gives us the Higginson arms. Burke gives a coat of Higginson of Ireland as Or, on a fesse sable, a tower of the first. The crest is different, but another family of the name, of the county of Hereford, difference the shield slightly but have a tower for the crest. Not improbably this American example preserves the original form of shield and crest. It is hardly necessary to say much about this well-known family. The Rev. Francis Higginson of Salem was the father of Rev.

John of Salem, whose son John, Jr., (m. Sarah Savage in 1672, and died in 1720,) was doubtless the above witness and owner of the seal.

17. A letter on file to Robert Pike of Salisbury, in regard to the estate of Benjamin Collins, May 29, 1684, has on its seal, ——, a chevron between three pelicans vulning themselves.

18. The seal on a bond of Sarah Atwood, Richard Kimball and James Hood, and also on the will of Philip Atwood of Bradford, April 4, 1722, witnesses, Timothy White, John West and Zecheriah Hardy, is plainly the one engraved as No. 56 of the Suffolk seals, (Vol. III., p. 92,) and represents the Moody arms. It is highly probable that Eliezer Moody, who was a scrivener and notary at Boston, was employed to prepare these documents, as his seal has been found on three other wills; here, however, the fesse is, clearly, " *vert.*"

19. The seal bearing two dolphins in pale, naiant, is on the will of Joseph Dorety, 23 April, 1743, witnessed by Benjamin Prescott, Joseph Twiss and Benjamin *Nurse* (?).

The date is so late that it would be useless to search the pedigrees of these signers in the hope of identifying the original owner of this seal.

20. The will of Rebecca Bartlett, *alias* Bayley, wife of Isaac Bayley of Newbury, is dated 18 April, 1723, and witnessed by Joseph Worth, Elias Whitton and Timothy *Putnam* (?).

This will bears a seal of a fesse between three grey-hound's heads erased. The same arms, although probably on a different seal, were used by Samuel Bartlett on his will of 9 Aug., 1720, witnessed by John Swett, John Titcomb, Jr., Samuel Short and William Titcomb. Thirdly, it appears on a bond of division signed by Edmund Worth, 12 April, 1723, witnessed by Nathaniel Noyes and Daniel Sawyer before Henry Somerby, J. P. It was thus twice associated with the Bartletts and twice with the Worths, but neither family used these arms.

 21. The seal of a griffin segreant is found on the will of John Giddings of Ipswich, 12 Nov., 1742, witnessed by William Giddings, Thomas Andrews, Robert Rust and Thomas Andrews, Jr., It is also on the will of Jonathan Raymond, 17 May, 1743, witnessed by William Giddings, Peter Woodbury and John Balch. It seems probable, therefore, that this seal was the property of William Giddings, though the coat does not belong to any family of the name. It is worthy of notice, however, that two families bearing this charge have been resident in Essex county, viz., the Downings and the Collins or Collings. From either, Giddings might have inherited or otherwise acquired this seal.

22. The Gedney arms, three eagles displayed, are on the seal used 6 Jan., 1698-9, by Deliverance Parkman and his wife Susanna, who was the daughter of John Gedney. They are also on a receipt of the heirs of Bartholomew Gedney, Dec. 10, 1698.

23. This seal ——, guttée a chief ——, a crescent for difference, Crest an animal's head couped, occurs three times on our files. First, on a bond of guardianship of Samuel Wainwright, 21 Sept., 1708, signed and sealed by Elizabeth Wainwright, John Staniford and Mathew Perkins. Second, on a warrant of appraisement of the estate of John Wainwright, appraisers John Staniford, Capt. Daniel Ringe and Capt. Matthew Perkins. Third, on bond for the same date, 21 Sept., 1708. The coincidences would be equally divided between the Wainwrights, Stanifords and Perkins, if these instruments were not, evidently, in the handwriting of Staniford.

24. The will of Elizabeth Newton, dated 15 Jan., 1733, proved 14 Feb., 1742-3, bears the seal which we have already given in our second volume, p. 10. It is the quartered shield there shown, which was used by Thomas Newton of Boston, and this Elizabeth is, doubtless, the daughter of that name mentioned in his will.

25. The will of Israel Porter, of 7 Nov., 1706, witnessed by Daniel Rea, John Preston, Thomas Preston and Stephen Sewall, bears an armorial seal, viz., three arrows erect and feathered, points in base. A similar seal occurs often on the Suffolk wills, but the only New England family who could claim this coat perhaps is that of Hale or Hales. In fact we have seen a book-plate of Robert Hale, Esq., of Beverly, who died in 1767, which bears these arms. We are not aware of any earlier claim by this family, nor have we traced the seal itself, as used on Porter's will, to any one related to the Hales.

26. —— a lion rampant, is the seal on the will of Moses Eams of Boxford, 27 Feb., 1754, witnessed by Robert Gray and John Cushing.

27. This seal of two stag's heads couped in chief, and a fleur-de-lys, probably, in base, is on the will of Elizabeth Bartlett of Newbury, 31 July, 1753. The witnesses are Nathan Chase, John Chase and Israel Bartlett, but the arms of Chase as already given in this number of the Journal are entirely different.

28. The division of the estate of Norden Pedrick of Marblehead, 3 March, 1723–4, bears two seals. The signatures are those of Mary and Ann Pedrick, Lattimore Waters, George Bethune and others. The arms on one seal, and the crest on the other, clearly identify them as the property of George Bethune.

The arms of Bethune of Balfour, co. Fife, are described by Burke as, Quarterly, first and fourth, argent a fesse between three mascles or; second and third, argent a chevron sable charged with an otter's head erased, of the first. Crest, an otter's head erased proper. Motto, Debonnaire.

This list completes all the shields of arms which a thorough search has discovered on the Essex files, although many others have doubtless perished or become illegible. There are a few which bear heraldic crests and we will briefly note them.

29. A horse's head couped, bridled, is on a paper relating to John Shillaber of Salem, 4 Jan., 1758, and

a similar seal on one relating to Benjamin Smith, 24 Feb., 1740.

30. A griffin's head erased is on the seal of a document signed 2 June, 1737, by Benjamin Bradstreet, Jedediah Davis and Abraham Davis; and also 22 June, 1737, on a matter relative to Hannah Davis, witnessed by Daniel Davis and Daniel Appleton.

31. A seal showing the helmet and crest—a crown out of which issues a spear erect—occurs on three documents, but the shield is not distinguishable. The instances are bonds of Mary Pilsbury, 9 Feb., 1703–4, Hannah Ayres, 4 Aug., 1706, and Francis Greenleaf, 8 Dec., 1760.

There are a few other instances of seals possibly heraldic though not necessarily so, as a lion rampant without the wreath, or shield; a pelican *in her piety*, or less technically, feeding her young; and a coronet surmounting a rose. Such devices seemed to have been used, however, as emblems or fanciful decorations.

A. C. G., JR.

THE BETHUNE FAMILY.

On the preceding page we have an example of the use of an armorial seal by George Bethune, in 1724. This gentleman was undoubtedly the American ancestor of the Boston family of Bethune, whose genealogy is already in print.* It appears that he was the heir male of the old Scottish family of Bethune of Balfour, conspicuous on

---

* See " Records, Genealogical Charts and Traditions of the Families of Bethune and Faneuil." Collected from authentic documents. Dedicated to the Descendants of the Family, by J. L. Weisse. New York: 1866.

many occasions in the history of Scotland. It is stated that this family was long settled in Picardy, in France, and was of great distinction there. The accounts vary as to the date, when a branch of the family settled in Scotland, and there married with the heiress of Balfour. NISBET (Heraldry, 1722) seems to regard the family as of Scotch origin, stating that he finds the name of Robert de Bethune in King William's reign, David de Bethune, about A. D., 1296, and Alexander de Bethune, in 1314. Among the noted members of the family were James Bethune, Chancellor of Scotland, 1518, and his nephew, Cardinal David Bethune, Chancellor, 1522–1549.

By the above noted marriage the family became known as the Bethunes of Balfour, and have been styled Barons of Balfour; by which title we understand, not a peerage but a territorial designation. After several descents the representation seems to have been in Robert[1] Bethune, who married Margaret Wardlaw, and had five sons, the eldest named John[2] and the second, Robert.[2] The eldest, John[2] Bethune, m. Katherine Haliburton and had six sons, but they seem to have died without male issue, since in 1719, on the death of James[5] Bethune of Balfour, (son of David,[4] grandson of James[3] and gr. grandson of John[2] and Katherine (Haliburton) Bethune,) the representation passed to the heirs of Robert.[2]

This Robert[2] married Marion Inglis, and had David[3] and William.[3] David[3] m. Anna Wardlaw, and had David[4] (who m. his cousin Anna Bethune, sister and heiress of the last James[5] of Balfour,) and Henry.[4] David[4] left no son, and his brother Henry[4] succeeded to the representation. He married Isabel Maxwell, and had an only daughter. The next line was that of William,[3] uncle of these two brothers. He was the father of George[4] Bethune, the person whose seal we have found, who came to New England, and m. Miss Carey. Their son was George[5] Bethune, who m. at Boston, 13 October, 1754, Mary Faneuil, and had three sons and five daughters. The sons were Nathaniel,[6] (who d. 1814, leaving only a daughter), Henry,[6] (Major in the English army, d. unm.) and George,[6] who m. Mary Amory, and had sons, Dr. George Amory[7] Bethune, and John McLean[7] Bethune, both of Boston.

The representative of the family is, therefore, Dr. George A. Bethune. It seems that Henry[4] of Balfour broke the entail and settled his estate upon his daughter, who m. a Mr. *Collerton*, as our book terms him. We find, however, that Burke says that the representation is in the Drinkwater family. This he explains (Commoners III., 420,) by the marriage, in 1799, of John Drinkwater with Eleanor, dau. of Charles Congalton, and sister of Gilbert (Congalton) Bethune of Balfour. The name *Collerton* seems an error for Congalton or Congilton.

THE COPLEYS AND PELHAMS OF NEW ENGLAND.

In our third volume, pp. 84–89, our associate, Mr. Appleton, gave an account of Herbert Pelham and his family, which rendered it almost certain that none of the name, of this family, remain in this country. There are however many descendants remaining of Peter Pelham, an eminent artist and engraver, the founder indeed of these arts in New England. Our attention has been called to this pedigree by a curious statement in the last edition of Burke's Commoners or Landed Gentry. Peter Pelham was step-father of John Singleton Copley, having married Mary Singleton, widow of Richard Copley.

Burke says (p. 1379) of the Singletons, "This family is one of importance and station in the county Clare, descended from the Singletons of Lancashire. John Singleton, Esq., a scion of the Lancashire house, m. Jane Bruffe, and had, with an only son John, two daughters, viz., Anne, wife of Samuel Cooper, Esq., of Cooper Hill, co. Limerick, and SARAH, who m. 1st, Richard Copley, then of the co. Limerick, but afterwards of Boston in America, and was mother by him of John Singleton Copley, R. A., father of Lord Lyndhurst; she m. 2d, Henry Pelham, Esq., by whom she had Henry and Edward Pelham; the former m. Miss Butler, daughter of William Butler, Esq., of Castle Crine, and had issue, Peter and William Pelham, twin brothers, who d. *unm.*"

There are errors in this account. Mary (not *Sarah*) Singleton's second husband was Peter Pelham, and by him she had a son Henry. We find no record of a child named Edward, and in fact Burke does not give any particulars of him. Henry Pelham, who married Miss Butler, was an artist, was born at Boston, 14 February, 1748–9, and was drowned in 1806, in the river Kenmare in Ireland. He was the agent of the Marquis of Lansdowne.

1. John Singleton² Copley, son of Mary Singleton and Richard¹ Copley, was born in Boston, 3 July, 1737. His fame as an artist renders any memoir of him unnecessary.

He married, November 16, 1769, Susan, daughter of Richard Clark, and had

 2. John Singleton,[3] b. 21 May, 1772.

 3. Elizabeth,[3] m. Gardiner Greene.

 4. Mary, d. unm., 1867.

He died in London, 9 September, 1815. His widow died 11 January, 1836.

 2. John Singleton[3] Copley, Jr., b. at Boston, 21 May, 1772, was created Baron Lyndhurst in 1827. He m. 13 March, 1819, Sarah Garay, dau. of Charles Brunsdell, and widow of Lt. Col. Charles Thomas, by whom he had

  I. Sarah,[4] born and died, 1820.

  II. Sarah Elizabeth,[4] b. 16 March, 1821, m. 8 January, 1850, Henry John Selwin.

  III. Susan Penelope,[4] b. 23 July, 1822; d. unmarried, 9 May, 1837.

  IV. John Singleton,[4] b. 3 Aug., 1824, d. Sept., 1825.

  V. Sophia Clarence,[4] b. 15 April, 1828, m. 14 Dec., 1854, Hamilton Beckett.

His wife d. 15 Jan., 1834, and he m. 2d, 5 August, 1837, Georgiana, dau. of Lewis Goldsmith, by whom he had

  VI. Georgiana Susan,[4] b. 5 May, 1838, m. Charles Du Cane, Esq., M. P. for North Essex.

He died October 12, 1863.

Gardiner Greene married for his third wife, Elizabeth Copley (3), and had

  I. Gardiner, died young.

  II. Eliza, m. Henry Timmins, and had George, m. Nina Menunzio; Maryanne, m. Martin Brimmer; Susan, m. Augustus T. Perkins.

III. Sarah, died unmarried.

IV. Susan, m. Samuel Hammond, and had Gardiner
G., m. Elizabeth C. Mifflin; Samuel, m. Mary C.
Warren.

v. Martha, m. Charles Amory, and had Charles, m.
Mary Louisa Dexter; Susan, m. F. Gordon Dexter; Copley, m. Catherine Chase ; and Linzee.

VI. John Singleton Copley, m. 1st, Elizabeth Hubbard,
who d. *s. p.*

2d, Mary Ann, dau. of William Appleton, and
had John S. C., m. Mary Meyer; Elizabeth,
m. Caspar Crowninshield.

3d, Isabel McCulloh, had Margaret and Mary.

VII. Mary, m. James Sullivan Amory, and had

James, d. unmarried.

Arthur, m. Mary Ingersoll.

Robert, m. Mary Lawrence.

Frederick.

Augustine H.

Harcourt.

Gardiner Greene died in 1832 ; his widow died 1 February, 1866.

––––––––

We will here turn to the family of Pelhams, connected
with Mary Singleton, by her second marriage, though not
descended from her.

PELHAM GENEALOGY.

1. —— Pelham, Esq., living in 1748, died before 1763.
He lived to be over eighty. His children were

2. Helen, living, aged, in 1763.

[2.] 3. Peter.

2. Peter Pelham, an artist, engraver, &c., was of London, and by wife Martha ———— had

> [3.] 4. Peter, bapt. at St. Paul's, Covent Garden, London, 17 December, 1721.
> [4.] 5. Charles, bapt. at St. Paul's, Covent Garden, London, 9 December, 1722.

He came to Boston prior to 1727, and here had

> [5.] 6. William, born 22 February, 1729.

He m. 2dly, Mary (Singleton) widow of Richard Copley, 22 May, 1748, and had

> [6.] 7. Henry, born 14 February, 1748–9.

He was buried at Trinity Church, Boston, 14 December, 1751, and in the Boston Gazette, No. 1692, for August 18, 1752, will be found the following advertisement: "All persons indebted to the estate of Mr. Peter Pelham, late of Boston, deceased, are hereby requested to pay the same to Mary Pelham, widow, administratrix to said estate; and those to whom the Estate is indebted are desired to apply to the same administratrix in order for a settlement." His widow, Mary (Singleton) Pelham, died 29 April, 1789.

THIRD GENERATION.

[3.] Peter Pelham, Jr., m. 25 June, 1746, Ann Creese, and had

> [7.] 8. Peter, born 1 May, 1747.
> [8.] 9. Charles, born 22 July, 1748.

He then moved to Virginia, and there had

> 10. Thomas, born 2 September, 1750, at Hampton.
> 11. Ann, born 15 November, 1752, at Hampton, died 6 July, 1756.
> 12. Sarah, born 4 October, 1754, at Suffolk.

13. Lucy, born 30 January, 1757, at Williamsburg, died 10 August, 1758.

14. Ann, born 31 July, 1758, at Williamsburg, died 26 August, 1758.

[9.] 15. William, b. 10 August, 1759, at Williamsburg.

16. Lucy, born 13 July, 1761, at Williamsburg, d. 25 April, 1764.

17. John, born 19 April, 1763, at Williamsburg.

18. Elizabeth, born 23 March, 1767, at Williamsburg, died 1767.

19. Henry, born 6 July, 1768.

20. Parthenia, born 19 October, 1772.

His wife died 10 September, 1778.

[4.] Charles Pelham of Medford, m. Mary Tyler, 6 December, 1766, and had

21. Helen, born 2 April, 1767–8, m. Thomas Curtis, 9 January, 1791, and d. 16 February, 1812, leaving children.

22. Charles, born 10 May, 1769, died unmarried.

23. Peter, born 27 June, 1771, died unmarried.

His wife died 1 December, 1776, and he married 1778, Mehitable Gerrish, and had

24. Henry, born 23 March, 1779.

25. Harriet, born 22 February, 1781, m. Abraham Carter, 20 July, 1802.

He died 16 October, 1793.

Of William [5] nothing more is known, but it is almost certain that he was buried at Trinity Church, Boston, 28 January, 1760–1.

[6.]   Henry went to England and was drowned, 1806. Burke says that he married a Miss Butler, and had sons Peter and William, who died unmarried.

NOTE.—A Maria Pelham was buried at Trinity Church, Boston, 25 May, 1751. No doubt this was a daughter of Peter.

FOURTH GENERATION.

[7.]   Peter Pelham, m. Parthenia Browne, at Hampton, 3 October, 1772, and had

26.   Peter, b. 3 August, 1773, at Brunswick City, Va., and d. 16 December, 1774.

27.   Charles, b. 23 April, 1775, at Brunswick City, d. *s. p.*, 14 November, 1796.

[10.] 28.   Thomas, b. 15 Feb., 1777, at Brunswick City, Va., d. 9 April, 1803, leaving one son.

29.   Elizabeth, b. 28 February, 1779, at Brunswick City, Va., m. —— Blagrove.

30.   Ann, b. 17 January, 1781, at Brunswick City, Va., d. 9 April, 1809.

31.   Samuel, b. 26 April, 1783, at Greenville City, d. 3 July, 1824, leaving son, William.

32.   Sarah Creese, b. 4 June, 1785, at Greenville City, m. —— Dromgoole.

33.   Jesse Brown, b. 24 July, 1788, at Greenville City, d. 17 February, 1823, leaving three sons.

34.   Mary, b. 8 Dec., 1790, at Greenville City, d. unm.

35.   Peter Aston, b. 4 January, 1793, at Greenville City, d. 27 December, 1813.

36.   Caroline, b. 28 November, 1795, at Greenville City, m. —— Davis.

The family moved to Xenia, Ohio.

[8.] Charles Pelham of Maysville, Ky., m. Isabella Atkinson, and had

>Peter, d. in Xenia, leaving by wife, Martha Coffin,
>>Mary Ann, m. Thomas Mott of Philadelphia.
>Charles, lived in Arkansas, and d. at Little Rock.
>Atkinson, a physician in Alabama, has several sons.
>William, (Surveyor-Gen. of Arkansas), has two sons.
>John.
>
>Richard Henry
>>and several daughters.

[9.] William Pelham, d. at Harmony, Ind., and had a son, William, who has three sons and one daughter.

FOURTH GENERATION.

[10.] Thomas Pelham (son of Peter 3d), had a son, John Burwell, who m. —— and had

>I. John Burwell.
>II. ——, a son, killed at Buena Vista.
>III. ——, a son.

WILL OF BENNETT ELLIOTT, OF NASEING,
CO. ESSEX,
THE FATHER OF JOHN ELIOT THE APOSTLE TO THE INDIANS.

(Communicated by H. G. SOMERBY, Esq., of London.)

In the name of God, Amen. The fifth day of November, 1621, I Bennett Elliott of Nasinge in the County of Essex, Yeoman, beinge crasy and weake in body yet blessed be god of p'fect memory beinge willinge to render

my soule into the hands of my god that gave it and my
body to the earth from whence it came to be buried in
decent and xtian manner hopeinge of my eternall salva-
con by the death and merritts of Jesus Christ my alone
Savio[r] and redeemer doe in the feare of god make this my
last will and Testam[t]. in manner and forme followeinge.
And first I give and bequeath all the rents and profitts of
all my coppy and customary lands and Tenements w[th]
theire and every of theire appertenncs lyeinge and beinge
in the sevall p'ishes of Ware, Widford, Hunsdon and
Estweeke in the County of Hartford unto my Trusty and
welbeloved freinds William Curtis my sonne in lawe,
Nicolas Camp the younger and John Keyes all of the
sayde parishe of Nasinge for the space of eight yeares
from the time of my decease quarterly to pay unto my
sonne John Elliott the some of eight pounds a yeare of
lawfull money of England for and towards the maintenance the maintenance in the univ'sity of Cambridge
where he is a Scholler and the residue of the rents and
profitts I give and bequeath for and towards the bringing
up of my youngest children That is to say Francis Jacob
Mary and Lydia. And the Inheritance of all my sayde
lands lyinge in the sayde parishes I give and bequeth as
followeth. And first I give and bequeath unto Francis
my youngest sonne and to his heires forever one parcell
of land called crottwell croft conteyninge twoe acres more
or less and one oth p'cell of land called Coles Croft conteyninge one acre more or lesse and one parcell of land
called Dameter in great Hyfeild one oth' parcell of land
lyeinge in little westney by estimacon one acre and a halfe
more or lesse and one parcell of land lyeinge in Souters

Comon meade conteyninge halfe an acre wth all the rents
and profitts after the end of the sayde eight yeares expired
and I give and bequeath unto my sonne Jacob and to his
heires forev all that my messuage or Tenement in the
sayde parishe of Widford wth all the lands thereunto
belonginge lyeinge in the sayde sev'all parishes of Wid-
ford, Ware, Hunsden and Estwick wth all oth^r the appurtennes oth^r than those lands before given to my sonne
Francis wth all the rents and profitts of the same from and
after the sayd eight yeares. Itm I give and bequeath
unto my Daughter Lydia the some of fifty pounds of lawfull money to be payde unto her at the age of eighteene
yeares or day of marriage wch shall first happen. Itm I
give unto my Daughter Mary the some of twenty pounds
of like lawfull money to be payde unto her in like manner
and I give unto my goddaughter Mary Curtis the some of
three pounds of like money payable to her and to the
oth^r and my will and mind is that if eith of my saide twoe
daughters dye before theire sayde age or marreage, that
then the Survivo^r to have her part or legacy as is aforesayde and that if they both happen to dye before the
sayde time that then the some of forty pounds thereof be
payde to my sonne John and the residue to and amongst
my younger children. Itm my will and mind is that soe
soone as may be after my decease my Executo^{rs} make sale
of all my Stock of Cattle corne and all oth^r goods and
chattles that be abroade out of my house and of soe much
of my moveable goodes wthin the house as in theire dis-
cretions cannot well be kept in theire own property till my
sayde children be of age to use the same to such psons as
will give most money for the same and the money riseinge

thereof to imploy for the use behoofe and maintenance of
my sayde children to the best advantage they lawfully
may or can and further, my will and mind is that my
daughter Mary and my daughter Lidia shall have the
right in the yellowe chamber and all that is in the same
over and above theire parts in the rest of my goodes and
my will and mind is that my sonne Phillip shall have soe
much of my houshold implem^{ts} as cannott well be
removed wth out losse for his part of my sayde goods if it
rise to soe much if his part come not to the value then
that he may have them at a reasonable price if he will,
before any other, and I give unto my sonne Francis foure
silver spoones wch were given him at his Christning over
and above his part of my goodes and my will is that my
daughter Mary Curtis have the keepinge of them till he
be of age and for that my sayde daughter Mary Curtis
hath heretofore had a good and competent part of my
goodes for her portion and preferment in marriage
whereby she is already provided for I give unto her onely
the some of five shillings to make her a small ringe to
were in remembrance of my love to her and because my
estate in goodes and chattles will hardly be sufficient for
the education of my younge children, Francis, Jacob,
Mary and Lydia. Therefore I more give unto my sayde
Friends William Curtis Nicolas Camp and John Keyes
whom I trust for theire bringinge up the some of tenn
pounds a yeare yearely for the space of eighteene yeare
after my decease out of my messuage and customary lands
in the parishe of Nasinge or out of any part thereof for
the better maintenance of my s^d children, and the inheritance of my sayde messuage lands & Tenements wth theire.

appurtennes wth all the rents and profitts thereof oth^r then the sayde tenn pounds a yeare out of the same for the time aforesayde I give and bequeath unto my sonne Phillip Elliott and to his heires forever and my will and mind is that my sayde Friends pay all such fine or fines as shall be due to the Lord or Lords for theire sayde lands when they shalbe thereunto admitted and the rest of my estate in goodes rents money debts or chattles wth the profitts thereof, if any be to deliver to my sayde children by even and equall porcons and the end and expiracon of the sayde eighteene yeares, and for that cause I doe hereby ordeine and appoint my sayde beloved friends William Curtis Nicolas Camp the younger and John Keyes my full and sole Executo^rs of this my last will hopeinge they will pforme the same accordinge to the trust wch I doe repose in them and I give to eith^r of them for theire paines herein taken forty shillings a peece and my earnest request is that Mr. John Dey of the sayde parishe of Nasinge Esquier would be aydinge and helpinge to my sayde Executo^rs by his good councell and advice for the better execution thereof and my will and mind is that if any question or doubt doe arise betweene my s^d Executo^rs concerninge this my sayde will that they submitt themselves to be ordered and ruled by him w^thout any further trouble or contencon. In witnes whereof I have hereunto putt my hand and seale the day and yeare first above written in the p'sence of Robert Wounam, Parnell Borum, John Dey, John Camp, William Curtis.

BENNETT ELLIOT.

Proved March 28, 1628.

Notes on the foregoing Will.

It is with the greatest pleasure that we publish the will of Bennett Eliot, the father of the famous John Eliot and others of the early settlers here. The original will was lately found by Mr. Somerby and all genealogists will join us in thanking him for sending this copy to Boston so promptly.

It had been a matter of surmise that John Eliot was born at Nasing in Essex, but this supposition rested on uncertain grounds. In W. S. Porter's Genealogy of the Eliots (New Haven, 1854), some extracts from the Nasing records are given, but John Eliot's birth was not among the number.

We now know that his father was Bennett or Benit Eliot of Nasing, whose will dated 5 Nov., 1621, was not proved till March 28, 1628. He no doubt died soon after his will was made, and was the "Benit Elyot" buried at Nasing, Nov. 21st, 1621. Of the children, Philip was probably the oldest son, as he seems to have had three children in England, prior to his coming here. John was A. B., at Jesus College, Cambridge, in 1623, and is called by Savage younger than Jacob. Francis was the youngest son. There seems to be an error in calling the wife of William Curtis, *Mary*, as it is in the will. The Nasing records say that William Curtis and *Sarah* Eliot were married 6 Aug., 1618. We do not think it probable that Benit Eliot had two daughters of the name of Mary, and therefore shall venture to style this a clerical error in the will.

We should, therefore, construct the family record thus:
Benit Eliot had

    I. Philip, m. about 1621, Elizabeth ——; came to
       N. E.

    II. Sarah, m. 6 Aug., 1618, William Curtis and
       came to Roxbury.

    III. Jacob, prob. m. Margaret, before coming hither.

    IV. John, betrothed in England, to Ann Mountfort,
       and m. here.

    V. Lydia, bapt. at Nasing, 1 July, 1610.

    VI. Francis, bapt. at Nasing 10 April, 1615, came
       hither.

    VII. Mary, bapt. at Nasing, 11 March, 1620, prob.
       came here.

    VIII. John, (probably), bapt. at Nasing, 6 Feb., 1602–
       3, and buried on the 18th, same month; Benit
       Eliot, buried 21 Nov., 1621.

In this record we differ from Mr. Savage, in assigning
the birth of Mary to the daughter of Benit, rather than
his grand-daughter, the child of Philip. This we do
because the record of the age of Philip's daughter is 13
years in 1635, and as the ages of two others, Elizabeth
and Sarah, are given correctly, as 8 years and 6 years in
1635, we presume that the first was also right. Still
this is but surmise.

    Of the children,

    1. Philip Eliot, says Savage, probably came here in
1635, with his family, though his name is not on the list.
He brought over wife Elizabeth, aged 30 years, and
children,

    Mary, b. 1622, prob. m. John Smith of Dedham.

Elizabeth, bapt. at Nazing, 8 April 1627, m. Richard
   Withington.

Sarah, bapt. at Nazing, 25 Jan., 1629, m. John Aldis.

Philip, b. 1633, d. before his father.

He died 22 Oct., 1657. We think it evident that his
daughter Mary married John Smith, and died before her
father. Savage could not take this view, and had to
imagine a fourth daughter to be the wife of Smith,
because he found that Mary Eliot m. Edward Payson,
1 Jan., 1642, and lived long after Philip. He could not
explain, therefore, why Smith was called a son-in-law, and
Mary (Eliot) Payson was omitted. The will of Benit
Eliot seems to make it clear. Mary, the sister of Philip
and John, was probably born in 1620, and was thus but
two years older than her niece, Philip's daughter Mary.
Mary, the sister of Philip, m. Payson, and lived until
1697, having a large family; Mary the daughter no doubt
married Smith, and died before her father, perhaps childless.

There is one other curious point to consider. We have
followed Savage in adding Philip, aged 2 years, as a son
of the emigrant, and as coming over with the family.
The original list, as published by Mr. Savage and Mr.
Drake, do not give families as such. Thus we find
among the passengers by the Hopewell, Marie Elliot
aged 13, then three other names, then Sara Elliott aged
6, then four names, then Elizabeth Elliot aged 8, then
eight names, and then Eliz. Elliott, aged 30, Lyddia
Elliott, aged 4, Phelip Elliot, aged 2, lastly four other
names. Now Savage ignores Lydia, but why should not

she have been considered to be another daughter of Philip's?

Our theory would be rather that there was a mistake on the original list, and that the last two items should be Lydia, aged 24, and Philip, aged 32. In other words that Philip came with his wife and sister, and had no son. This seems as probable as the supposition which gives him a son, who is never elsewhere heard of.

2.   Sarah Eliot, m. William Curtis. They are doubtless the settlers at Roxbury, who came over in 1631, in the Lion, and who have, probably, many descendants of the name.

3.   Jacob Eliot, who died in 1651, left a widow, Margaret, and children,

Jacob, who m. and left issue.

Hannah, who m. Thomas Wyberne.

Susanna, who m. 1st, Peter Hobart, and 2d, Thomas Downes.

Asaph, who m. and had issue.

The record of these is given in full by Savage.

4.   John Eliot, the minister, m. and left issue as recorded in the Eliot Genealogy before cited. A tabular pedigree is likewise to be found in Drake's History of Boston, folio edition.

5.   Lydia Eliot we presume came here, and research hereafter *may* prove that she married here.

6.   Francis Eliot, m. Mary Saunders, and had

Mary, who m. Caleb Hobart.

Rachel, who m. 1st, John Poulter, and 2d, John Whitmore.

John, who d. young.

Hannah, who m. Stephen Willis.

Abigail, who d. unm. (?)

Mary.   Of this name we find two daughters. Savage says that the first was b. 1641, and d. young; and the second was born in 1653. Yet Mary m. Caleb Hobart in 1662. We suggest that the last name should be Mercy, and that the oldest daughter was Hobart's wife, since the youngest was only nine years old in 1662.

7.   Mary Eliot m. Edward Payson of Roxbury, and left numerous descendants, of whom were Rev. Edward (H. C. 1677), father of Samuel (H. C. 1716), ancestor of Rev. Phillips (H. C. 1754), Seth (H. C. 1777), and Edward (H. C. 1803).

We have thus given, to the best of our knowledge, the marriages and families of the children of Benit Eliot. It must be remembered, however, that there were several other early settlers of this surname, not connected with this family. One branch, which has been long resident at Boston, is descended from Andrew Elliott of Beverly; among these are to be named Andrew and Samuel, the booksellers; three generations of ministers by the name of Andrew Elliott; the Rev. John Elliott, author of the Biographical Dictionary; Samuel, a prominent merchant, and Samuel A., formerly Mayor of Boston. Of late years the mode of spelling the surname has been changed to Eliot.

HERALD PAINTERS.

In our first volume we mentioned as Herald painters, Thomas Johnson, Nathaniel Hurd and the two John Coles; and in our second volume, James Turner. We have now to record that we have seen a painting signed "George Searle *pinx'*, Newb^y Port, 1773" which represented the Kinsman coat-of-arms. This artist is therefore to be added to the list of herald painters in New England.

From the records of the Committee on Heraldry, it appears that armorial paintings have been shown to them, bearing the names of the following artists, "S. Blyth" (probably before 1800); "Benjamin Hurd, Jr.," (about 1750); "Hopps and Breslaw, Heraldry Painters, 75 Union St., Boston," probably not earlier than 1820; "John Stott, seal engraver, herald painter &c., 9 State St., Boston, 1846;" and by the well-known engraver, Mitchell of Boston.

We may here add as a probable maker of some of our earlier paintings, the person named in the following advertisement in the Boston Evening Post, for March 4th, 1745:

"Francis Garden, Engraver from London, engraves in the newest Manner and at the cheapest Rates, Coats of Arms, Crests or Cyphers on Gold, Silver, Pewter or Copper. To be heard of at Mr. Caverley's, Distiller, at the South End of Boston. *N. B.* He will wait on any Person in Town or Country, to do their Work at their own Houses, if desired; also Copper-plate printing perform'd by him."

The publication of the Heraldic Journal, ceases with the present number, completing the fourth volume.